INSTITUTE OF ECONOMICS
AND STATISTICS
OXFORD
WITHDRAWN
QA276.SAR
KU-511-317

Applied Statistics (Continued)

HANSEN, HURWITZ, and MADOW · Sample Survey Methods and Theory, Volume I
HOEL · Elementary Statistics
KEMPTHORNE · An Introduction to Genetic Statistics
MEYER · Symposium on Monte Carlo Methods
MUDGETT · Index Numbers
RICE · Control Charts
ROMIG · 50–100 Binomial Tables
SARHAN and GREENBERG · Contributions to Order Statistics
TIPPETT · Technological Applications of Statistics
WILLIAMS · Regression Analysis
WOLD and JURÉEN · Demand Analysis
YOUDEN · Statistical Methods for Chemists

Books of Related Interest

ALLEN and ELY · International Trade Statistics
ARLEY and BUCH · Introduction to the Theory of Probability and Statistics
CHERNOFF and MOSES · Elementary Decision Theory
HAUSER and LEONARD · Government Statistics for Business Use, *Second Edition*
STEPHAN and McCARTHY · Sampling Opinions—An Analysis of Survey Procedures

Contributions to Order Statistics

A WILEY PUBLICATION IN APPLIED STATISTICS

Contributions to Order Statistics

Edited by AHMED E. SARHAN

Professor of Statistics, Alexandria University, Egypt (UAR)
(and Visiting Research Professor of Biostatistics, School of Public Health, University of North Carolina)

and

BERNARD G. GREENBERG

Professor and Chairman, Department of Biostatistics, School of Public Health, University of North Carolina, Chapel Hill

ECONOMICS
LIBRARY
AND STATISTICS
WITHDRAWN

John Wiley & Sons, Inc.

New York · London

1962

INSTITUTE OF ECONOMICS
AND STATISTICS
OXFORD.
WITHDRAWN

44,689

COPYRIGHT © 1962
BY
JOHN WILEY & SONS, INC.

All Rights Reserved

This book or any part thereof must not be reproduced in any form without the written permission of the publisher.

LIBRARY OF CONGRESS CATALOG CARD NUMBER: 62-10932

PRINTED IN THE UNITED STATES OF AMERICA

Contributors

	CHAPTER
Gunnar Blom, Assistant Professor, Department of Mathematical Statistics, Lund University, Lund, Sweden	4B
H. A. David, Professor of Statistics, Virginia Polytechnic Institute, Blacksburg, Va.	1, 7A, 9
Wilfrid J. Dixon, Professor of Preventive Medicine and Public Health (Biostatistics), University of California Medical School, Los Angeles 24, California	10H
B. Epstein, Consultant, Palo Alto, California	11C
B. G. Greenberg, Professor of Biostatistics, University of North Carolina, Chapel Hill, North Carolina	10C, D, 11A, B 12A, B
E. J. Gumbel, Adjunct Professor, Department of Industrial and Management Engineering, Columbia University, N.Y.	6, 12C.3
S. S. Gupta, Member of Technical Staff, Bell Telephone Research Laboratories, Allentown, Pa.	12D
H. O. Hartley, Professor of Statistics, Iowa State University, Ames, Iowa.	Foreword
Jan Jung, Assistant Professor, Department of Mathematical Statistics, University of Stockholm, Sweden	4A
Julius Lieblein, Mathematician, David Taylor Model Basin (Code 820), U.S. Navy Department, Washington 7, D.C.	7B, 12C.1, 2
E. H. Lloyd, Assistant Director, Mathematics Department, Imperial College of Science and Technology, London, England	3, 12E

Junjiro Ogawa, Professor of Mathematical Statistics, Department of Mathematics, Nihon University, Tokyo, Japan	2, 5, 10E, F, G 11D, E
H. Ruben, Head, Department of Statistics, The University, Sheffield, England	10A
A. E. Sarhan, Professor of Statistics, Alexandria University, Alexandria, Egypt, U.A.R.	10C, D, 11A, B 12A, B
Daniel Teichroew, Associate Professor of Management, Graduate School of Business, Stanford University, Stanford, California	10B
John E. Walsh, Senior Statistician (Biomedical Project) and Senior Operations Research Scientist, System Development Corporation, Santa Monica, California	8

Foreword

Modern statistical methodology is predominantly concerned with the study of small samples $x_1, x_2, \ldots, x_n$ drawn from a population about whose parameters information is sought. Sometimes it has been found expedient to arrange the sampled values in ascending order of magnitude so that $x_{(1)}$ is the algebraically smallest value and $x_{(n)}$ the largest. When the subscript (i) of $x_{(i)}$ denotes this ascending order, $x_{(i)}$ is known as "the ith order statistic in a sample of size n."

As long as the full information contained in the *complete* sample is utilized for purposes of estimation or for setting up decision criteria, this full information is in no way altered by the process of ordering the values in the sample. For varying reasons, however, it is often relevant to single out the information contained in *particular* order statistics for the computation of estimates or for use in decision procedures. The reasons for employing information, so restricted, are manifold, and we confine ourselves here to mentioning the following.

1. It is clear that any statements concerning the *relative ranking* of order statistics of two or more samples (from the same population) are invariant to monotonic scale transformations. Such statements are therefore reducible to the corresponding statements on relative rankings of order statistics in samples from the uniform distribution. This has given rise to a great wealth of distribution-free test criteria based on the relative rankings of order statistics (e.g., the Wilcoxon test). It has become customary to regard this area as part of the theory of "nonparametric tests"; therefore this subject area is not extensively treated in this book on order statistics, which deals primarily with the "distribution-dependent" techniques involving the actual scale values of the order statistics.

2. There are numerous occasions when only *some* order statistics are available for the computation of estimates and/or test criteria. Such situations arise notably in the important area of "censorship and multiple censorship" and have important applications to problems of "life testing."

The present treatise offers a wealth of formulas and numerical tables of the distribution (and moment constants) of order statistics for a great variety of (parental) life distributions. It is well known that in the area of censored life testing estimators and decision criteria may vitally depend on the assumed life table. Therefore this comprehensive study of a great variety of life distributions is of great help in the judicious use of these methods, if only because it reveals the sensitive dependence of many of these methods on the form of the basic life table and thereby emphasizes the experience with life tables based on extensive empirical data.

3. In certain statistical problems the appropriate estimator and/or test criterion is a quantity computed from selected order statistics. For example, the range of a uniform distribution is appropriately estimated from the sample range. Again, techniques of rejecting "rogue observations" or "outliers" are commonly based on the first and *n*th order statistic. Safeguards against the "selection" of an insignificant extreme treatment effect are intrinsically linked with the distribution of such statistics as the "extreme deviate from the sample mean," the "extreme variance ratio," or the "sample range." The criteria required in the techniques of multiple decisions and multiple comparisons should also be included in this category. The present treatise may be regarded as the first comprehensive summary of recent results to be published; until now these results have had to be looked up in scattered journal articles and reports.

4. Finally, a great deal of space is devoted to what have become known as "short-cut procedures" or "quick and dirty methods" of analysis. The justification of these methods, admittedly of lower statistical efficiency than their "optimum" counterparts, lies in the reduction of the computational labor of analysis and must therefore depend on the relative "cost" of data processing as compared with the expense and effort of obtaining the data. Best known under this category are the "range-based" estimates of the population standard deviation so well established in the area of quality control charts of mass-produced articles. This book gives a very comprehensive discussion of these short-cut statistics, including the modern extensions to analysis of variance. Of particular interest here are the results on optimum spacing and grouping of data in terms of order statistics, particularly the reduction in computational labor when processing large samples.

This book is arranged in two parts, one giving the mathematical theory and theoretical foundations and the other the applications.

On examining the theory and methods offered in this volume, we cannot help wondering why procedures so simple in use were not employed more extensively in the early development of statistical methodology. There is no doubt, however, that the modern trend of applied statistics (notably in industry) is witnessing a growing use of methods based on ordered samples. The publication of this first comprehensive treatise on the subject is therefore welcome and timely.

H. O. HARTLEY

Preface

In recent literature the field of order statistics has been occupying an important and increasing role in statistical theory as well as in methods of application. This claim needs no further verification than that readily obtained by glancing through *Biometrika Tables for Statisticians*, volume 1. In that outstanding compilation of statistical tables, more than one-fifth are devoted to this subject. Rarely does an issue of a statistical journal appear in which there is not at least one article that includes an application of order statistics.

Many of the research workers who have been concerned with order statistics have felt a pressing need for a monograph that would include both theory and application. Such a monograph would help to assemble in one place much of the work done at varying times and published in different journals throughout the world.

This feeling was strengthened during our informal meeting with several of the contributors during 1955. After that original expression of need and interest, a tentative outline of the articles in this monograph was planned by us with the cooperation of Dr. Julius Lieblein (who was with the National Bureau of Standards at the time) and was circulated among potential authors in 1956. The original plan has been modified only slightly to take into account current developments.

The first aim of this monograph has been to assemble scattered materials to help applied research workers learn how to use the tools of order statistics. A secondary aim is to provide materials and references that will facilitate further research in methodology. In several instances, gaps in theory and knowledge have been pointed out to stimulate further research.

The subjects covered are divided into two parts. Chapters 2 to 9 cover the theory of order statistics as a general survey. Chapters 10 to 12 contain specific applications of the foregoing theory.

We have tried to interrelate the sections of the monograph as much as possible and to maintain standard notations throughout. The latter has not always been possible because of different conventions in usage.

The original objective was to prepare the monograph in simple language. Because of the number of contributors and the desire to keep editorial changes to a minimum, we felt that carrying out this objective might lead to interference with the ideas of the various contributors. Thus, simplicity has sometimes been sacrificed in favor of retaining the original thoughts of the authors.

The contributors are to be thanked for the fine spirit of cooperation and the prompt handling of correspondence. We are also indebted to the editors of *Annals of Mathematical Statistics*, *Biometrics*, *Biometrika*, *Journal of the American Statistical Association*, *Journal of the Royal Statistical Society*, *Osaka Mathematical Journal*, *Sankhya*, and *Technometrics*, and to McGraw-Hill Book Company, the National Bureau of Standards, the Office of Naval Research, and the U.S. Army Research Office (Durham) for permission to reproduce the tables and graphs included herein.

We wish to acknowledge the support provided by the Office of Ordnance Research, now called the U.S. Army Research Office (Durham).

A. E. SARHAN
B. G. GREENBERG

Chapel Hill, North Carolina
June 1962

Contents

PART II SPECIFIC APPLICATIONS

List of Tables

H. A. DAVID[1]

CHAPTER I

ECONOMICS
LIBRARY
AND STATISTICS

Introduction

1.1 The Scope of This Book

If the elements $x_1, x_2, \ldots, x_n$ of a sample drawn from a continuous population $f(x)$ are rearranged in ascending order of magnitude and then denoted by $x_{(1)}, x_{(2)}, \ldots, x_{(n)}$, we call $x_{(i)}$ the *ith-order statistic* in the sample of n. The subject of *order statistics* deals with the properties as well as applications of these ordered random variables and of functions involving them. Examples are provided by the *extreme values* $x_{(1)}$ and $x_{(n)}$, the range $x_{(n)} - x_{(1)}$, and the *studentized range* $(x_{(n)} - x_{(1)})/s$, where s is a root-mean-square estimate of the population standard deviation σ calculated from an independent sample. Usually, but not necessarily, the x_i are assumed to be statistically independent.

Order statistics enter in a basic fashion in selection procedures where interest centers on assessing the degree of superiority of the top individuals in a sample. Statistical aspects of floods and droughts, longevity, and breaking strength can all be studied by the theory of extreme values. The range is widely used, particularly in statistical quality control, as an estimate of σ. Many short-cut tests have been based on the range and other order statistics. In dealing with small samples the studentized range is useful in a variety of ways. Apart from supplying the basis of many quick tests, it plays a key role in procedures for ranking "treatment" means in the analysis of variance situation. The studentized range is one of many order statistics important in methods for the rejection of outlying (and therefore possibly spurious) observations.

By applying the Gauss-Markoff theorem of least squares, it is possible

[1] Work supported by the U.S. Army Research Office (Durham).

to use linear functions of order statistics rather systematically for estimation in distributions depending only on one or two parameters. This application is very useful particularly when some of the observations in the sample have been "censored," since in that case standard methods of estimation tend to become laborious or otherwise unsatisfactory. Life tests provide an ideal illustration of the advantages of order statistics in censored data. Since such an experiment may take a long time to complete, it is often advantageous to stop after failure of the first r out of n similar items under test. The observations are times to failure and arrive ordered by the nature of the experiment; that is, we have $x_{(1)}, x_{(2)}, \ldots, x_{(r)}$ from which to estimate the true mean life and possibly a second parameter.

We have highlighted some of the chief applications of order statistics which will be considered in this book. The underlying theory is also often discussed, or references are given. It should be stressed that the practical value of order statistics is largely dependent on the availability of suitable tables. Many such tables are therefore given throughout the book.

The sampling distributions of order statistics are dependent on the form of the parent population $f(x)$. Nevertheless, it is sometimes possible to use order statistics for the construction of confidence intervals and tolerance regions without assuming more than that $f(x)$ is continuous. For example, the population median lies between $x_{(r)}$ and $x_{(s)}$ $(r < s)$ with a probability depending only on r, s, and the sample size n. These methods are treated in this book, but other distribution-free procedures not explicitly involving order statistics are omitted, even though the evaluation of the power of such procedures is often an exercise in order statistics. In particular, tests using the *rank* i $(i = 1, 2, \ldots, n)$ in place of the ith order statistic $x_{(i)}$ are not discussed. Statistics based on ranks have been termed *rank-order statistics* to distinguish them from order statistics. This distinction has not always been made. Thus Wilks's fine summary article entitled "Order Statistics" (*Bull. Amer. Math. Soc.*, Vol. 54, 1948) is in fact of wider scope than this book. However, the increased interest in the subject of order statistics, in our narrower sense, is well indicated by the fact that the major portion of the subject matter treated here has been developed since 1948.

We proceed now to a more detailed description of contents.

1.2 Outline of Contents

The book is divided into two parts. In Part I the general theory of order statistics is presented together with an over-all survey of the subject. Part II is concerned primarily with applications of the theory to a number of specific parent populations, with special emphasis on the normal distribution. There are consequently close interrelations between the two parts which will be pointed out in the course of the following summary. Apart from a few exceptions, the treatment is not at an advanced level. The use of the many tables is frequently illustrated by examples, and it is hoped that this will prove a most useful aspect of the book.

In Chapter 2 a fundamental formula giving the joint distribution of any k out of the n order statistics $x_{(1)}, x_{(2)}, \ldots, x_{(n)}$ is derived. Expressions for the moments and product moments of these order statistics can then be written down as integrals. Of particular importance are the means, variances, and covariances, partly because these allow the determination of mean and variance of order statistics which are linear functions of the $x_{(i)}$, and partly for another reason which will become apparent shortly. For some parent populations $f(x)$ these moments are readily found, for example, for the exponential and rectangular distributions (Sections 11A, 12A). In other parent populations numerical integration is necessary (normal, extreme-value, and gamma distributions—Section 10B, 12C, and 12D). Modern high-speed computing methods have made practicable the very accurate tabulation of the first two moments of normal order statistics for sample size $n \leq 20$. Even when $f(x)$ is standardized to have zero mean and unit variance, there can be considerable variation from parent to parent in the value of these moments. It is possible, however, to set bounds for the mean, variance, and coefficient of variation of $x_{(i)}$ which hold for any standardized parent distribution, discrete as well as continuous.

Other basic results given in Chapter 2 concern the asymptotic distributions of the $x_{(i)}$. Here two main situations may be distinguished: as $n \to \infty$ either $i/n \to 0$ or 1, or $i/n \to \lambda$ with $0 < \lambda < 1$. The former situation corresponds to the extremes $x_{(1)}, x_{(n)}$ and more generally to the mth extremes $x_{(m)}, x_{(n-m+1)}$, with m fixed. When the extremes, after suitable standardization, have a limiting distribution, this turns out to be one of only three possible types, whatever the parent distribution. For an important class of parent populations, which includes the normal, the limiting distribution is the doubly exponential extreme-value distribution. Similar results hold for the mth extremes. The main developments of the statistical theory of extremes, mth extremes, and functions thereof are treated in Chapter 6. In particular, the estimation of the parameters of the three types of limiting distributions is discussed, with special emphasis on the use of suitable probability paper. The extreme-value distribution is further treated in Section 12C where the parameter estimates are based on order statistics. On the other hand if $i/n \to \lambda$, the λ-quantile of the sample[2] is asymptotically *normally* distributed about x_λ, the λ-quantile of the

[2] The λ-quantile of the sample is the order statistic $x_{(r)}$ where r is the largest integer less than $n\lambda + 1$.

population (i.e., the $100\lambda\%$ point). Similarly, the asymptotic joint distribution of k sample quantiles is the k-variate normal.

Much of the book is based on the following idea introduced in Chapter 3. Suppose that the parent distribution $f(x)$ is or can be cast into a form in which it depends on two parameters only, one of location μ and one of scale σ. These need not be mean and standard deviation. Many important distributions belong to this class, including all those treated in Part II. If the means α_i and the variances and covariances v_{ij} of the ordered standardized variates $(x_{(i)} - \mu)/\sigma$ can be obtained by the methods just described, the corresponding moments of the $x_{(i)}$ will be linear functions of μ and σ, with known coefficients. Hence the Gauss-Markoff theorem of least squares can be applied to yield unbiased estimates μ^*, σ^* of μ and σ which are linear in the $x_{(i)}$ and have minimum variance in the class of linear unbiased estimates. An extremely useful aspect of this procedure is that it can be applied equally well to censored data. For any form of censoring it is therefore possible to tabulate the coefficients by which the observed values of the $x_{(i)}$ must be multiplied to give μ^* and σ^*. This is done in Section 10C for all cases of double censoring (above and below) in samples of 20 or less from a normal parent. The variances and covariance of μ^* and σ^* as well as the efficiencies of these estimates relative to the corresponding estimates in uncensored samples are also tabulated. Corresponding results for exponential, rectangular, and extreme-value parent distributions are discussed in Section 11B and Subsections 12A.2, and 12C.2.2, respectively. Tables for $n \leq 5$ are given in Subsection 12B.2 for symmetrical two-parameter distributions of the following forms: U-shaped, rectangular, parabolic, triangular, normal, and doubly exponential.

In practice there are, however, some difficulties in the generalized least-squares approach. For a complete sample of size n the α_i and v_{ij} must all be known and the $n \times n$ matrix (v_{ij}) has to be inverted to give the coefficients of the $x_{(i)}$ in μ^* and σ^*. If r observations have been censored, only the relevant α_i and v_{ij} enter, so that the covariance matrix is of order $(n - r) \times (n - r)$. It is, of course, generally much more difficult to determine the v_{ij} than the α_i. A convenient *ad hoc* device is to replace the matrix (v_{ij}) by the unit matrix but to leave the α_i intact. This results in simple solutions for the coefficients and gives linear estimates which are still unbiased although no longer best. In Subsection 10C.3 this procedure is applied to a normal parent and found to be surprisingly satisfactory. A more fundamental approach is described in Section 4B. Here also the exact α_i are used but the v_{ij} are replaced by their asymptotic values. Only a 2×2 matrix has to be inverted, and the resulting estimates may be called "unbiased nearly best linear estimates." More drastic and less satisfactory methods have to be adopted if the α_i themselves are not known exactly. Replacing them as well as the v_{ij} by asymptotic values gives estimates which are only approximately unbiased or "nearly unbiased, nearly best linear estimates." In complete samples the estimates treated in Subsection 10C.3, like the best linear estimates, are generally jointly asymptotically efficient. Another asymptotically efficient procedure which is best restricted in its use to large samples is described in Section 4A.

Chapter 5 deals with the large-sample estimation of location and scale parameters by a selected set of $k < n$ sample quantiles. The choice or "spacing" of these quantiles may be specified by k probability levels λ_t where $0 < \lambda_1 < \lambda_2 < \ldots < \lambda_k < 1$. Estimation of the parameters is possible from the joint distribution of sample quantiles obtained in Chapter 2. It is shown that for any prescribed spacing linear estimates of μ and σ can be found which are asymptotically as efficient as the best possible estimates *for the same spacing*. The question then arises how the spacing should be chosen. This problem of optimal spacing is tackled in Section 10E. Explicit expressions for the best linear unbiased estimates of the mean with optimum spacing are given for $k \leq 10$ in the case of a normal distribution with *known* variance and also for σ with known μ. (Optimal spacing for the estimation of μ is, of course, not optimal for the estimation of σ.) The efficiencies are also listed. Some tests of significance using sample quantiles are given in Subsection 10G.1 for a normal parent. Similar results for a one-parameter exponential parent distribution are obtained in Sections 11D and 11E.

Although the use of sample quantiles is designed to facilitate estimation in *large* samples, order statistics are well adapted for quick, yet fairly efficient, small-sample estimation and testing procedures. In particular, the range $w = x_{(n)} - x_{(1)}$ has many such applications. Its expectation in random samples from a normal population with $\sigma = 1$ is commonly denoted by d_n (sometimes by d_2 in quality control circles). Thus w/d_n is, for a normal parent, an unbiased estimate of σ which is very simply computed with the help of tables of $1/d_n$ (Section 7A). In small normal samples ($n \leq 12$, say) the efficiency of the range is quite satisfactory for many purposes; in somewhat larger samples ($n \leq 20$) it is advantageous to use the sum of the range and suitably selected quasi-ranges

$$x_{(n-i+1)} - x_{(i)}, \qquad i = 2, 3, \ldots, 6.$$

The efficiencies of these statistics are tabulated in Section 10D, as are the efficiencies of median, midrange $\frac{1}{2}(x_{(1)} + x_{(n)})$, and similar estimators of the mean. Arguments for the use of range are strengthened in Section 7A where it is pointed out that, in small samples, the range is no more susceptible to departures from normality in the parent distribution than is the sample standard deviation. This is important in control charts both for the mean μ and for the standard deviation σ. The latter charts are based on the percentage points of w in normal samples (Table 10H.7). In Section 7A a variety of short-cut tests are described and the necessary tables provided. It is shown that many standard tests on the means and variances of normal populations have computationally simpler counterparts in which sample standard deviations are replaced by ranges or mean ranges. Quick tests applicable to censored data are also considered.

Chapter 8 is the only one in the book dealing with distribution-free methods. It is a classical result (i.e., pre-1940) that order statistics can be used to set confidence intervals for any percentage point θ_p of a continuous population, the probability with which the stochastic interval $(x_{(r)}, x_{(s)})$ covers θ_p being expressible as the difference of two incomplete beta functions. A related property of the interval $(x_{(r)}, x_{(s)})$ is that it contains at least a specified proportion γ of the population, with a probability depending only on r, s, n, and γ. Consequently $(x_{(r)}, x_{(s)})$ is also a distribution-free tolerance interval. For a continuous multivariate population it is similarly possible to obtain distribution-free multivariate tolerance regions.

Order statistics enter into many procedures involving multiple decisions and multiple comparisons, as is pointed out in Chapter 9. Most familiar in this connection is the use of the studentized range q of "treatment" means in the analysis of variance. With the help of q in various guises (and the usual assumptions) it is possible to rank the treatments, or to make multiple confidence statements about the differences of the true treatment means; such statements include simple tests for equality of two treatments *after* inspection of the results. Similar techniques can be employed on a group of sample variances by means of the maximum variance ratio $s^2_{\max}/s^2_{\min}$. The other main topics discussed are (*a*) methods for the selection of the best treatment or a group of superior treatments in the presence of a control group; (b) slippage tests, which are concerned with the detection of a change in *one* of the population parameters from the value common to the group; (c) methods of approximation to upper percentage points of statistics expressible as maxima.

Closely related to slippage tests are procedures for the rejection of observations; if the problem is one of testing for a single outlying observation, the two are indeed the same. Often, having rejected one outlier by the use of a certain test criterion, we repeat the test on the reduced sample until no more outliers are found. This is clearly a multiple-decision procedure. A systematic discussion of the use and logic of the large number of test criteria which have been proposed, generally on the grounds of intuitive plausibility, is given in Section 10H. Usually the null hypothesis is that the n observations available are a random sample from a $N(\mu, \sigma^2)$ population. Even without considering what the most appropriate alternative hypothesis may be in any given situation, we see that different tests are needed depending on whether μ and σ are known or not. The alternative may specify that one observation or a certain proportion of the observations comes from a different population, and may be one-sided or two-sided. Guidance is provided for which test to use, and the "performance" of several competing tests are compared under certain assumptions, mostly by experimental sampling. Many tables of percentage points are given which make it easy to carry out the tests. The frequent practice of making three determinations of a given quantity and then discarding the most discrepant one is discussed separately in Section 7B.

Two major sections remain to be mentioned, Section 10A on the moments of the order statistics and of the range in samples from normal populations, and Subsection 12C.3 on an application of extreme-value theory. These topics happen to be, respectively, the most theoretical and the most applied subjects treated in this book. It is shown in Section 10A that the moments of order statistics in normal samples are expressible as linear functions of the contents of certain hyperspherical simplices. This geometrical interpretation not only throws light on the interconnection between the moments but also points the way to practical methods of computing them. The first ten moments of the extreme up to sample size 50 are tabulated. Although applications of the theory of order statistics are given in many places throughout the book, Subsection 12C.3 is the only section that deals at length with a particular case. An attempt is made to arrive, by means of extreme-value theory, at a statistical procedure for the estimation of the endurance limit in fatigue tests.

1.3 Some General Comments

It is hoped that this book covers all major areas of work in order statistics. References are given in the sections to which they are appropriate. For convenience they have also been collected into a single list at the end of the book. Completeness has not been an aim of this list and has certainly not been achieved. Particularly in connection with extreme-value theory the reader is referred to the compilation of references in Gumbel's *Statistics of Extremes.*

PART I

General Theory (Over-all Survey of General Nature)

JUNJIRO OGAWA

CHAPTER 2

Distribution and Moments of Order Statistics

2.1 Exact Distribution and Moments of Order Statistics

We assume, for the sake of simplicity, that the population under consideration has the distribution function $F(x)$, with density function $f(x)$ which is continuous almost everywhere.[1] Consider the elements of the random sample $X_1, X_2, \ldots, X_n$, drawn from the population, that is, mutually independent random variables. Rearranging them in the order of their magnitude, we write

$$X_{(1)} \leq X_{(2)} \leq \ldots \leq X_{(n)}$$

and call them the *order statistics* drawn from the population. $X_{(1)}$ and $X_{(n)}$ are called the *minimum* (*the smallest value*) and *maximum* (*the largest value*) of the sample, repectively. $X_{(i)}$ is called the *ith order statistic*. The difference

$$R = X_{(n)} - X_{(1)} \tag{2.1.1}$$

is called the *range* of the sample.

In our case, where the distribution $F(x)$ is of the continuous type, it is clear that

$$P(X_i = X_j) = 0, \qquad \text{for all } i \neq j\,; \tag{2.1.2}$$

hence we can consider the order statistics

$$X_{(1)} < X_{(2)} < \ldots < X_{(n)} \tag{2.1.3}$$

with probability one.

[1] For discrete distributions, readers are referred to the works of Abdel-Aty, Burr, Rider, and Siotani as given in additional bibliography 1, 2, 18, 19, and 22 at the end of Section 7A.

If we select $k(1 \leq k \leq n)$ integers such that

$$1 \leq n_1 < n_2 < \ldots < n_k \leq n,$$

the probability element of the joint distribution of the k order statistics $X_{(n_1)}, X_{(n_2)}, \ldots, X_{(n_k)}$ is given by [8]

$$\Psi_k(x_{(n_1)} \ldots x_{(n_k)})\, dx_{(n_1)} \ldots dx_{(n_k)}$$

$$\begin{cases} = \dfrac{n!}{\prod_{i=1}^{k+1} (n_i - n_{i-1} - 1)!} \prod_{i=1}^{k+1} [F(x_{(n_i)}) - F(x_{(n_{i-1})})]^{n_i - n_{i-1} - 1} \\ \quad \cdot \prod_{i=1}^{k} f(x_{(n_i)})\, dx_{(n_i)}, \qquad \text{for the domain } x_{(n_1)} < x_{(n_2)} < \ldots < x_{(n_k)} \\ = 0, \qquad \text{elsewhere} \end{cases} \tag{2.1.4}$$

where

$$n_0 = 0, \quad n_{k+1} = n + 1 \qquad \text{and} \qquad x_{(n_0)} = -\infty, \quad x_{(n_{k+1})} = +\infty.$$

As a special case of (2.1.4) the probability element of the joint distribution of $X_{(1)}, X_{(2)}, \ldots, X_{(n)}$ is given by

$$\Psi_n(x_{(1)}, \ldots, x_{(n)})\, dx_{(1)} \ldots dx_{(n)} = n!\, f(x_{(1)}) \ldots f(x_{(n)})\, dx_{(1)} \ldots dx_{(n)}, \quad \text{for the domain } x_{(1)} < x_{(2)} < \ldots < x_{(n)}. \tag{2.1.5}$$

The joint distribution of the ith and the jth order statistics for $i < j$ is

$$\Psi_2(x_{(i)}, x_{(j)})\, dx_{(i)}\, dx_{(j)} \begin{cases} = \dfrac{n!}{(i-1)!\,(j-i-1)!\,(n-j)!} [F(x_{(i)})]^{i-1} \\ \quad \cdot [F(x_{(j)}) - F(x_{(i)})]^{j-i-1}[1 - F(x_{(j)})]^{n-j} \\ \quad \cdot f(x_{(i)}) f(x_{(j)})\, dx_{(i)}\, dx_{(j)}, \qquad \text{for } x_{(i)} < x_{(j)}, \\ = 0, \qquad \text{elsewhere.} \end{cases} \tag{2.1.6}$$

In particular, for $i = 1$ and $j = n$, we obtain

$$\Psi_2(x_{(1)}, x_{(n)})\, dx_{(1)}\, dx_{(n)} \begin{cases} = n(n-1)[F(x_{(n)}) - F(x_{(1)})]^{n-2} f(x_{(n)}) f(x_{(1)})\, dx_{(1)}\, dx_{(n)}, \\ \qquad \text{for } x_{(1)} < x_{(n)} \\ = 0, \qquad \text{elsewhere,} \end{cases} \tag{2.1.7}$$

which gives the distribution of the range.

The distribution of the ith order statistics is given by

$$\Psi_1(x_{(i)})\, dx_{(i)} = \frac{n!}{(i-1)!\,(n-i)!} F^{i-1}(x_{(i)})[1 - F(x_{(i)})]^{n-i} f(x_{(i)})\, dx_{(i)}. \tag{2.1.8}$$

The product moments of the order statistics are defined as follows:

$$E(X_{(n_1)}^{a_1} X_{(n_2)}^{a_2} \cdots X_{(n_k)}^{a_k})$$

$$= \int_{-\infty}^{\infty} \cdots \int_{-\infty}^{\infty} x_{(n_1)}^{a_1} x_{(n_2)}^{a_2} \cdots x_{(n_k)}^{a_k} \cdot \Psi_k(x_{(n_1)}, \ldots, x_{(n_k)})\, dx_{(n_1)} \cdots dx_{(n_k)}$$

$$= \frac{n!}{\prod_{i=1}^{k+1} (n_i - n_{i-1} - 1)!} \int \cdots \int_{-\infty > x_{(n_1)} < \cdots < x_{(n_k)} < +\infty} \prod_{i=1}^{k} x_{(n_i)}^{a_i}$$

$$\cdot \prod_{i=1}^{k} [F(x_{(n_i)}) - F(x_{(n_{i-1})})]^{n_i - n_{i-1} - 1} \prod_{i=1}^{k} f(x_{(n_i)}) \prod_{i=1}^{k} dx_{(n_i)}. \tag{2.1.9}$$

This can be calculated by specifying the population.

The mean value of the ith order statistic $X_{(i)}$ is

$$E(X_{(i)}) = \frac{n!}{(i-1)!\,(n-i)!} \int_{-\infty}^{\infty} \xi F^{i-1}(\xi)[1 - F(\xi)]^{n-i}\, dF(\xi)$$

or

$$= \frac{n!}{(i-1)!\,(n-i)!} \int_{-\infty}^{\infty} \xi F^{i-1}(\xi)[1 - F(\xi)]^{n-i} f(\xi)\, d\xi, \tag{2.1.9a}$$

and the variance of the ith order statistic $X_{(i)}$ is

$$V(X_{(i)}) = E(X_{(i)}^2) - E^2(X_{(i)})$$

$$= \frac{n!}{(i-1)!\,(n-i)!} \left(\int_{-\infty}^{\infty} \xi^2 F^{i-1}(\xi)[1 - F(\xi)]^{n-i}\, dF(\xi) \right.$$

$$\left. - \left\{ \int_{-\infty}^{\infty} \xi F^{i-1}(\xi)[1 - F(\xi)]^{n-i}\, dF(\xi) \right\}^2 \right). \tag{2.1.9b}$$

Furthermore, the covariance of the ith and jth $(i < j)$ order statistics is

$$\operatorname{Cov}(X_{(i)}, X_{(j)}) = E(X_{(i)} X_{(j)}) - E(X_{(i)}) \cdot E(X_{(j)})$$

$$= \frac{n!}{(i-1)!\,(j-i-1)!\,(n-j)!} \int_{-\infty}^{\infty} \int_{-\infty}^{\eta} \xi\eta F^{i-1}(\xi)[F(\eta) - F(\xi)]^{j-i-1}$$

$$\cdot [1 - F(\eta)]^{n-j}\, dF(\xi)\, dF(\eta) - \frac{(n!)^2}{(i-1)!\,(j-1)!\,(n-i)!\,(n-j)!}$$

$$\cdot \int_{-\infty}^{\infty} \xi F^{i-1}(\xi)[1 - F(\xi)]^{n-i}\, dF(\xi)$$

$$\cdot \int_{-\infty}^{\infty} \eta F^{i-1}(\eta)[1 - F(\eta)]^{n-j}\, dF(\eta). \tag{2.1.9c}$$

In the case of the rectangular population [2], we have

$$E\left(\prod_{i=1}^{k} X_{(n_i)}^{a_i}\right) = \frac{n!}{\left(n + \sum_{1}^{k} a_i\right)!} \prod_{j=1}^{k} \frac{\left(n_j + \sum_{i=1}^{j} a_i - 1\right)!}{\left(n_j + \sum_{i=1}^{j-1} a_i - 1\right)!}. \tag{2.1.10}$$

Now, if we let

$$F(Z_r) = \frac{r}{n+1}, \qquad r = 1, 2, \ldots, n, \tag{2.1.11}$$

then, under certain mathematical conditions on the distribution function, it follows that

$$X_{(r)} = Z_r + Z'_r\, h(X_{(r)}) + \tfrac{1}{2} Z''_r\, [h(X_{(r)})]^2 + \ldots \tag{2.1.12}$$

in probability as $n \to \infty$, where

$$h(X_{(r)}) \equiv F(X_{(r)}) - \frac{r}{n+1} \tag{2.1.13}$$

and

$$Z'_r = \left.\frac{dZ}{dF}\right|_{Z=Z_r}, \qquad Z''_r = \left.\frac{d^2Z}{dF^2}\right|_{Z=Z_r}, \qquad \ldots, \tag{2.1.14}$$

provided $X_{(r)}$ is not near the extremes. By using the relation (2.1.12), asymptotic values of moments of order statistics can be calculated. Readers should consult references 2 and 9.

Moriguti [6] obtained more general results. Denote by $\mathscr{F}$ the class of distribution functions for which the variance is constant σ^2, that is,

$$\mathscr{F} = \{F;\ \sigma(F) = \sigma\}$$

then for this class of populations we have

$$\sigma^{-1}[E_F(X_{(n)}) - \mu] \leq \frac{n-1}{\sqrt{2n-1}}, \qquad \text{for all } F \in \mathscr{F} \tag{2.1.15}$$

and

$$\sigma^{-1}[E_F(X_{(n)}) - E_F(X_{(1)})] \leq \frac{\sqrt{2}\,.\,n}{\sqrt{2n-1}}\left(1 - \frac{1}{\binom{2n-2}{n-1}}\right)^{1/2},$$

$$\text{for all } F \in \mathscr{F}. \tag{2.1.16}$$

If we restrict ourselves to a subclass $\mathscr{F}_0$ of $\mathscr{F}$, which consists of symmetric distribution functions, that is,

$$\mathscr{F}_0 = \{F;\ \sigma(F) = \sigma\},$$

where F is symmetric, then we have

$$\frac{\sqrt{V_F X_{(n)}}}{E_F(X_{(n)})} \geq \sqrt{(1/M_n) - 1}, \qquad \text{for all } F \in \mathscr{F}_0, \tag{2.1.17}$$

where

$$M_n = \frac{n}{2^n} \int_0^{+1} \frac{[(1+t)^{n-1} - (1-t)^{n-1}]^2}{(1+t)^{n-1} + (1-t)^{n-1}}\, dt. \tag{2.1.18}$$

The values of M_n for small values of n are as follows:

$$M_2 = 0.33333, \qquad M_3 = 0.64381, \qquad M_4 = 0.81677,$$
$$M_5 = 0.90695, \qquad M_6 = 0.95300,$$

and for large n

$$M_n = 1 - \frac{\pi}{2^n}\left[1 + 0\left(\frac{1}{n}\right)\right]. \tag{2.1.19}$$

The results were further revised by Hartley and David [4]. Their result is

$$\frac{|E(X_{(m)}) - \mu|}{\sigma} \leq \left\{\frac{B(2m-1, 2n-2m+1)}{[B(m, n-m+1)]^2} - 1\right\}^{1/2} \tag{2.1.20}$$

for $1 \leq m \leq n$. In addition, they have a table for the lower bound of $E(X_{(n)} - X_{(1)})/\sigma$, given that $-X \leq x \leq X$, where X denotes a fixed bound.

A theorem of a general nature was given by Hoeffding [5]: In order to determine the least upper (or greatest lower) bound of the expected value $E[K(X_1, \ldots, X_n)]$ of a given function K of n random variables $X_1, \ldots, X_n$ under the assumption that $X_1, \ldots, X_n$ are independent and each X_j has a given range and satisfies k conditions of the form

$$E[g_i^{(j)}(X_j)] = C_{ij}, \qquad \text{for } i = 1, \ldots, k,$$

then under general conditions we need consider only discrete random variables which take on at most $k + 1$ values.

2.2 Asymptotic Distribution of Order Statistics[2]

First we consider the following theorem due to Gnedenko [3], which gives the possible types of the limiting distribution function of the maximum $X_{(n)}$ as n tends to infinity.

[2] Readers are referred to a recent book by E. J. Gumbel, *Statistics of Extremes*, Columbia University Press, New York, 1958, Chapter 5.

Theorem 1. The distribution function of the maximum of the random sample of size n is $F^n(x)$. If there exist sequences of constants $\{a_n\}$, $a_n > 0$, and $\{b_n\}$, such that $F^n(a_n x + b_n)$ converges to a certain distribution function $\Phi(x)$ in all its points of continuity as n tends to infinity, the possible type of $\Phi(x)$ must be either

$$\Phi_\alpha(x) = \begin{cases} 0 & \text{if } x \le 0 \\ e^{-x^{-\alpha}} & \text{if } x > 0 \end{cases} \tag{2.2.1}$$

or

$$\Psi_\alpha(x) = \begin{cases} e^{-(-x)^\alpha} & \text{if } x \le 0 \\ 1 & \text{if } x > 0 \end{cases} \tag{2.2.2}$$

or

$$\Lambda(x) = e^{-e^{-x}}. \tag{2.2.3}$$

We say that the distribution function $F(x)$ belongs to the *domain of attraction* of $\Phi(x)$ if there exist sequences of constants $\{a_n\}$, $a_n > 0$, and $\{b_n\}$ such that as $n \to \infty$

$$F^n(a_n x + b_n) \to \Phi(x), \qquad \text{in all points of continuity of } \Phi(x).$$

Gnedenko [3] also gave the necessary and sufficient conditions for a distribution function $F(x)$ to belong to the domain of attraction of each type of the limiting distribution.

If we make the following transformations,

$$X = nF(X_{(1)}), \qquad Y = n[1 - F(X_{(n)})], \tag{2.2.4}$$

the limiting joint distribution of X and Y as n tends to infinity is given by

$$e^{-x-y}\, dx\, dy \tag{2.2.5}$$

which shows that the maximum $X_{(n)}$ and the minimum $X_{(1)}$ of the sample are *mutually independent in the limit* as n tends to infinity [1].

Now, let the frequency function of the population be $g(x)$,[3] and for any given number λ, which is $0 < \lambda < 1$, we define the *λ-quantile* or $100\lambda\%$ *point* of the population as the value $x = x_\lambda$ such that

$$\int_{-\infty}^{x_\lambda} g(t)\, dt = \lambda. \tag{2.2.6}$$

For example, when $\lambda = 0.5$, the value $x_{0.5}$ is called the *median* of the population; for $\lambda = 0.25$ and 0.75, the values $x_{0.25}$ and $x_{0.75}$ are called the *quartiles* of the population, and the difference $x_{0.75} - x_{0.25}$ is the *inter-quartile range* of the population.

We define the *λ-quantile* of the sample as follows:

$$Z_\lambda = \begin{cases} X_{(n\lambda)} & \text{if } n\lambda \text{ is an integer} \\ X_{([n\lambda]+1)} & \text{if } n\lambda \text{ is not an integer} \end{cases} \tag{2.2.7}$$

[3] The symbol $f(x)$ is reserved for a normalized frequency function.

where $[n\lambda]$ denotes the largest integer not exceeding $n\lambda$, that is $[n\lambda]$ is the Gauss symbol.

Now we have the following theorem.

Theorem 2. If $g(x)$ is differentiable in the neighborhood of $x = x_\lambda$ and $g(x_\lambda) \equiv g_\lambda \neq 0$, the distribution of the variate

$$\sqrt{n/\lambda(1-\lambda)}\,g_\lambda(Z_\lambda - x_\lambda) \tag{2.2.8}$$

tends to $N(0, 1)$ as n tends to infinity. Hence the frequency function of the distribution of Z_λ is asymptotically equal to

$$\sqrt{n/2\pi\lambda(1-\lambda)}\,g_\lambda \exp\left[-\frac{n{g_\lambda}^2}{2\lambda(1-\lambda)}(Z_\lambda - x_\lambda)^2\right] \tag{2.2.9}$$

for sufficiently large values of n [1].

The limiting joint distribution of two sample quantiles is also given [1], but we consider only the limiting joint distribution of k sample quantiles due to Mosteller [7].

Theorem 3. For k given real numbers for which

$$0 < \lambda_1 < \lambda_2 < \ldots < \lambda_k < 1,$$

let the λ_i-quantile of the population be x_i, that is,

$$\int_{-\infty}^{x_i} g(t)\,dt = \lambda_i, \qquad i = 1, 2, \ldots, k. \tag{2.2.10}$$

Assume that the frequency function $g(x)$ of the population is differentiable in the neighborhoods of $x = x_i$, $i = 1, 2, \ldots, k$, and

$$g_i \equiv g(x_i) \neq 0, \qquad \text{for } i = 1, 2, \ldots, k.$$

Then the joint distribution of the k sample quantiles $X_{(n_1)}, X_{(n_2)}, \ldots, X_{(n_k)}$, where

$$n_i = [n\lambda_i] + 1, \qquad i = 1, 2, \ldots, k$$

tends to a k-dimensional normal distribution with means $x_1, x_2, \ldots, x_k$ and with covariance matrix

$$\frac{1}{n}\Lambda = \frac{1}{n}\begin{bmatrix} \dfrac{\lambda_1(1-\lambda_1)}{{g_1}^2} & \dfrac{\lambda_1(1-\lambda_2)}{g_1g_2} & \cdots & \dfrac{\lambda_1(1-\lambda_k)}{g_1g_k} \\ \dfrac{\lambda_1(1-\lambda_2)}{g_1g_2} & \dfrac{\lambda_2(1-\lambda_2)}{{g_2}^2} & \cdots & \dfrac{\lambda_2(1-\lambda_k)}{g_2g_k} \\ \cdot & \cdot & \cdot & \cdot \\ \dfrac{\lambda_1(1-\lambda_k)}{g_1g_k} & \dfrac{\lambda_2(1-\lambda_k)}{g_2g_k} & \cdots & \dfrac{\lambda_k(1-\lambda_k)}{{g_k}^2} \end{bmatrix} \tag{2.2.11}$$

as n tends to infinity. Hence the frequency function of the limiting distribution becomes

$$h(x_{(n_1)}, x_{(n_2)}, \ldots, x_{(n_k)}) = (2\pi)^{-k/2}\Lambda^{-1/2} \exp\left[-\frac{n}{2}(\mathbf{x}_{(\ )} - \mathbf{x})'\mathbf{\Lambda}^{-1}(\mathbf{x}_{(\ )} - \mathbf{x})\right]$$

$$= (2\pi)^{-k/2} g_1 g_2 \ldots g_k [\lambda_1(\lambda_2 - \lambda_1) \ldots (\lambda_k - \lambda_{k-1})(1 - \lambda_k)]^{-1/2} n^{k/2}$$

$$\times \exp\left\{-\frac{n}{2}\left[\sum_{i=1}^{k} \frac{\lambda_{i+1} - \lambda_{i-1}}{(\lambda_{i+1} - \lambda_i)(\lambda_i - \lambda_{i-1})} g_i^2 (x_{(n_i)} - x_i)^2\right.\right.$$

$$\left.\left. - 2 \sum_{i=2}^{k} \frac{g_i g_{i-1}}{\lambda_i - \lambda_{i-1}} (x_{(n_i)} - x_i)(x_{(n_{i-1})} - x_{i-1})\right]\right\} \qquad (2.2.12)$$

where

$$\mathbf{x}_{(\ )} = \begin{bmatrix} x_{(n_1)} \\ x_{(n_2)} \\ \cdot \\ \cdot \\ \cdot \\ x_{(n_k)} \end{bmatrix}, \qquad \mathbf{x} = \begin{bmatrix} x_1 \\ x_2 \\ \cdot \\ \cdot \\ \cdot \\ x_k \end{bmatrix}$$

and where we have put $\lambda_0 = 0$, $\lambda_{k+1} = 1$.

From this theorem we can obtain the limiting distribution of the sample quantiles when the population frequency function depends only on a location parameter μ and a scale parameter σ, that is, $g(x)$ is of the form

$$g(x) = \frac{1}{\sigma} f\left(\frac{x - \mu}{\sigma}\right). \qquad (2.2.13)$$

Let the λ_i-quantile of the standardized population be u_i, that is

$$\int_{-\infty}^{u_i} f(t)\, dt = \lambda_i.$$

Then it follows that

$$\lambda_i = \int_{-\infty}^{(x_i - \mu)/\sigma} f(t)\, dt = \int_{-\infty}^{u_i} f(t)\, dt$$

so we obtain under quite general conditions on $f(x)$

$$x_i = \mu + \sigma u_i. \qquad (2.2.14)$$

Thus, as a corollary to Theorem 3, we obtain the following theorem [8].

Theorem 4. Under the same conditions as those of Theorem 3, if the frequency function $g(x)$ depends only on a location parameter μ and a scale parameter σ, that is, if $g(x)$ is of the form

$$g(x) = \frac{1}{\sigma} f\left(\frac{x - \mu}{\sigma}\right),$$

the frequency function of the limiting distribution of the k sample quantiles $X_{(n_1)}, X_{(n_2)}, \ldots, X_{(n_k)}$ is [8]

$$h(x_{(n_1)}, \ldots, x_{(n_k)}) = \left(\frac{n}{2\pi\sigma^2}\right)^{k/2} \Gamma^{-1/2} \times \exp\left[-\frac{n}{2\sigma^2}(\mathbf{x}_{(\,)} - \mu\mathbf{1} - \sigma\mathbf{u})'\mathbf{\Gamma}^{-1}(\mathbf{x}_{(\,)} - \mu\mathbf{1} - \sigma\mathbf{u})\right]$$

$$= (2\pi\sigma^2)^{-k/2} f_1 \ldots f_k[\lambda_1(\lambda_2 - \lambda_1) \ldots (\lambda_k - \lambda_{k-1})(1 - \lambda_k)]^{-1/2} n^{k/2}$$

$$\times \exp\left\{-\frac{n}{2\sigma^2}\left[\sum_{i=1}^{k} \frac{\lambda_{i+1} - \lambda_{i-1}}{(\lambda_{i+1} - \lambda_i)(\lambda_i - \lambda_{i-1})} f_i^2(x_{(n_i)} - \mu - \sigma u_i)^2 - 2\sum_{i=2}^{k} \frac{f_i - f_{i-1}}{\lambda_i - \lambda_{i-1}}(x_{(n_i)} - \mu - \sigma u_i)(x_{(n_{i-1})} - \mu - \sigma u_{i-1})\right]\right\} \tag{2.2.15}$$

where

$$\mathbf{\Gamma} = \begin{bmatrix} \frac{\lambda_1(1-\lambda_1)}{f_1^2} & \frac{\lambda_1(1-\lambda_2)}{f_1 f_2} & \cdots & \frac{\lambda_1(1-\lambda_k)}{f_1 f_k} \\ \frac{\lambda_1(1-\lambda_2)}{f_1 f_2} & \frac{\lambda_2(1-\lambda_2)}{f_2^2} & \cdots & \frac{\lambda_2(1-\lambda_k)}{f_2 f_k} \\ \cdot & \cdot & \cdot & \cdot \\ \frac{\lambda_1(1-\lambda_k)}{f_1 f_k} & \frac{\lambda_2(1-\lambda_k)}{f_2 f_k} & \cdots & \frac{\lambda_k(1-\lambda_k)}{f_k^2} \end{bmatrix}$$

and

$$\Gamma = \det \mathbf{\Gamma}$$

$$f_i = f(u_i), \qquad i = 1, 2, \ldots, k.$$

REFERENCES

1. H. Cramér, *Mathematical Methods of Statistics*, Princeton, 1946.
2. F. N. David and N. L. Johnson, "Statistical treatment of censored data, Part 1, Fundamental formulae," *Biometrika*, Vol. 41 (1954), pp. 228–240.
3. B. Gnedenko, "Sur la distribution limite du terme maximum d'une serie aléatoire," *Ann. Math.*, Vol. 44 (1943), pp. 423–453.
4. H. O. Hartley and H. A. David, "Universal bounds for mean range and extreme observations," *Ann. Math. Statist.*, Vol. 25 (1954), pp. 85–99.
5. W. Hoeffding, "The extreme of the expected value of a function of independent random variables," *Ann. Math. Statist.*, Vol. 26 (1955), pp. 268–275.
6. S. Moriguti, "A modification of Schwarz's inequality with application to distributions," *Ann. Math. Statist.*, Vol. 24 (1953), pp. 107–113.
7. F. Mosteller, "On some useful inefficient statistics," *Ann. Math. Statist.*, Vol. 17 (1946), pp. 377–407.
8. J. Ogawa, "Contributions to the theory of systematic statistics, I," *Osaka. Math. J.*, Vol. 3 (1951), pp. 175–213.
9. R. L. Plackett, "Linear estimation from censored data," *Ann. Math. Statist.*, Vol. 29 (1958), pp. 131–142.
10. S. S. Wilks, *Mathematical Statistics*, Princeton University Press, Princeton, N.J., 1950.

E. H. LLOYD

CHAPTER 3

Generalized Least-Squares Theorem

3.1 Introduction

When we are concerned with a continuous variate X whose distribution function has the form $F(ax + b)$, the method of generalized least squares may be applied to ordered observations on X to yield highly accurate linear estimates of the parameters a and b. This is a fairly wide class of distribution functions containing, as it does, all the distributions which, like the normal, can be specified by a locator and a measure of spread, and also the special distributions, such as the negative exponential with known origin, in which only one parameter appears.

From the point of view of least-squares estimation theory all systems of nonsingular linear transforms of a given set of parameters are equivalent. This means that it is a matter of indifference whether we estimate the parameters a and b or any pair of independent linear combinations of them. Usually the most natural specification will be in terms of a location parameter μ and a dispersion parameter σ, and we accordingly develop the theory in terms of those. In various applications μ may denote the expectation, the median, the mode, an extremity of the range, the $p\%$ point of the distribution, and so on; σ may denote the standard deviation, the range, the interquartile distance, and so on.

Where the natural parameters are not of the μ and σ type, they can be expressed as linear compounds of μ and σ, and their least-squares estimates are then the same linear compounds of the estimates of μ and σ. Thus the theory in terms of μ and σ can be made to cover all cases, although of course it is sometimes more convenient to work directly in terms of the natural or desired parameters, making suitable modifications to the μ, σ theory.

3.2 Least-Squares Estimates of Location and Dispersion Parameters

Suppose then that we have n independent observations $X_1, X_2, \ldots, X_n$ on the continuous variate X whose distribution function is $F[(x - \mu)/\sigma]$. It is emphasized that μ is not necessarily the expectation, nor need σ be the standard deviation. We now arrange the observations in order of (increasing) magnitude and denote them when so arranged by

$$X_{(1)}, X_{(2)}, \ldots, X_{(n)}.$$

The standardized variate $U = (X - \mu)/\sigma$ will have a parameter-free (and hence completely known) distribution, and the standardized ordered observations $U_{(r)} = (X_{(r)} - \mu)/\sigma$ can be regarded as ordered observations on U. The expectations, variances, and covariances of the $U_{(r)}$ may then be calculated by the methods explained in Chapter 2. Denote these by

$$\begin{gathered} E(X_{(r)}) = \alpha_r, \qquad V(X_{(r)}) = v_{rr}, \\ \text{Cov}\,(X_{(r)}, X_{(s)}) = v_{rs}. \end{gathered} \tag{3.2.1}$$

These, together with the data, are the basic quantities on which the computation of the estimates depends.

The expectations, variances, and covariances of the actual ordered observations $X_{(r)}$ are

$$\begin{aligned} E(X_{(r)}) &= \mu + \sigma\alpha_r \\ V(X_{(r)}) &= \sigma^2 v_{rr} \\ \text{Cov}\,(X_{(r)}, X_{(s)}) &= \sigma^2 v_{rs}. \end{aligned} \tag{3.2.2}$$

The expectations depend linearly, with known coefficients, on the unknown parameters, and the variances and covariances are known up to a scalar factor. All the conditions therefore exist for the application of the generalized least-squares theorem and the consequent extraction of unbiased linear estimates of minimal variance.

The relevant part of this theorem may be stated as follows [1]: If $\mathbf{x}$ is a vector of observations whose expectations

$$E(\mathbf{x}) = A\boldsymbol{\theta} \tag{3.2.3}$$

depend linearly, with known coefficient matrix A, on a vector $\boldsymbol{\theta}$ of unknown parameters, and whose variance matrix

$$V(\mathbf{x}) = V\omega^2 \tag{3.2.4}$$

is known up to a scalar factor ω^2, the least-squares estimate of $\boldsymbol{\theta}$ is the vector $\boldsymbol{\theta}^*$ which minimizes the quadratic form

$$(\mathbf{x} - A\boldsymbol{\theta})' V^{-1} (\mathbf{x} - A\boldsymbol{\theta}). \tag{3.2.5}$$

It is thus the vector of solutions of the "normal equations"

$$A'V^{-1}A\boldsymbol{\theta}^* = A'V^{-1}\mathbf{x}. \tag{3.2.6}$$

This solution is, explicitly,

$$\boldsymbol{\theta}^* = (A'V^{-1}A)^{-1}A'V^{-1}\mathbf{x} \tag{3.2.7}$$

and its variance matrix is

$$V(\boldsymbol{\theta}^*) = (A'V^{-1}A)^{-1}\omega^2. \tag{3.2.8}$$

The estimates θ^*_r are unbiased and, in the class of unbiased linear statistics, have minimal variance.

The complete theorem goes on to give a method (not necessarily optimal in any sense) of estimating the unknown factor ω^2 from the "residuals," but in the present application this is not required.

The theorem is, of course, commonly used only when the observations are uncorrelated, so that the variance matrix V is diagonal, if not indeed scalar. In practical situations where V is not known to have this form, its elements are usually too inaccurately known for the theorem to be applied. For ordered observations from known distributions, however, this is no longer true, and full use may be made of the theorem [4].

We rewrite (3.2.2) in matrix form as follows:

$$E(\mathbf{x}_{(0)}) = (\mathbf{1} \vdots \boldsymbol{\alpha})\begin{pmatrix}\mu \\ \sigma\end{pmatrix}, \qquad V(\mathbf{x}_{(0)}) = V\sigma^2, \tag{3.2.9}$$

where $\mathbf{1}$ denotes a column of ones, and $\mathbf{x}_{(0)}$ denotes the vector of ordered observations. Comparing these with the general formulas of the previous paragraph, we find the normal equations

$$\begin{aligned}(\mathbf{1}'\Omega\mathbf{1})\mu^* + (\mathbf{1}'\Omega\boldsymbol{\alpha})\sigma^* &= \mathbf{1}'\Omega\mathbf{x}_{(0)} \\ (\mathbf{1}'\Omega\boldsymbol{\alpha})\mu^* + (\boldsymbol{\alpha}'\Omega\boldsymbol{\alpha})\sigma^* &= \boldsymbol{\alpha}'\Omega\mathbf{x}_{(0)}\end{aligned} \tag{3.2.10}$$

where $\Omega = V^{-1}$. Solving, we obtain the estimates as

$$\mu^* = -\boldsymbol{\alpha}'\Gamma\mathbf{x}_{(0)}, \qquad \sigma^* = \mathbf{1}'\Gamma\mathbf{x}_{(0)} \tag{3.2.11}$$

where

$$\Gamma = \Omega(\mathbf{1}\boldsymbol{\alpha}' - \boldsymbol{\alpha}\mathbf{1}')\Omega/\Delta \tag{3.2.12}$$

and

$$\Delta = (\mathbf{1}'\Omega\mathbf{1})(\boldsymbol{\alpha}'\Omega\boldsymbol{\alpha}) - (\mathbf{1}'\Omega\boldsymbol{\alpha})^2.$$

By inverting the matrix of coefficients of the normal equations (3.2.10), the variances and covariances of these estimates are found to be

$$\begin{gathered}V(\mu^*) = (\boldsymbol{\alpha}'\Omega\boldsymbol{\alpha})\sigma^2/\Delta, \qquad V(\sigma^*) = (\mathbf{1}'\Omega\mathbf{1})\sigma^2/\Delta, \\ \operatorname{Cov}(\mu^*, \sigma^*) = -(\mathbf{1}'\Omega\boldsymbol{\alpha})\sigma^2/\Delta.\end{gathered} \tag{3.2.13}$$

It will be seen that the practicability of the method turns on having available the vector $\boldsymbol{\alpha}$ of ordered expectations and the inverse Ω of the variance matrix of the standardized ordered observations. We would like these to be available for all reasonable sample sizes, for selected distributions, as they already are for the normal and certain other cases. Ideally we would want tables of the vectors $\boldsymbol{\alpha}'\Gamma$ and $\mathbf{1}'\Gamma$ [the elements of these being the coefficients which when applied to the ordered observations yield the required estimates (3.2.11) and the various scalar combinations required for the variances and covariances (3.2.12)]. If $\boldsymbol{\alpha}$ and Ω only are available, it is probably simplest to work directly from the normal equations (3.2.10). If V is available, but not its inverse Ω, inversion by means of triangular resolution is recommended [3].

It is convenient at this point to record one or two simple properties of α and V that will be required later. First,

$$\sum U_{(r)} = \sum U_r \tag{3.2.14}$$

whence, taking expectations,

$$\mathbf{1}'\boldsymbol{\alpha} = nE(U). \tag{3.2.15}$$

If μ denotes the expectation of X, $E(U) = 0$, so that in this case

$$\mathbf{1}'\boldsymbol{\alpha} = 0. \tag{3.2.16}$$

Similarly, by taking variances instead of expectations,

$$\mathbf{1}'V\mathbf{1} = n. \tag{3.2.17}$$

3.3 Symmetrical Distributions

These formulas for the estimates and their variance matrix simplify considerably when the original variate X has a symmetrical distribution [4]. Then it is natural to take μ to be the center of the distribution and σ a symmetrical measure of dispersion. The standardized variate $U = (X - \mu)/\sigma$ then has a symmetrical distribution centered at the origin, and this distribution coincides with that of $-U$. Now the ordered obervations $U_{(r)}$ satisfy

$$U_{(1)} \leq U_{(2)} \leq \cdots \leq U_{(n)} \tag{3.3.1}$$

and hence also

$$-U_{(n)} \leq -U_{(n-1)} \leq \cdots \leq -U_{(1)}. \tag{3.3.2}$$

Since the latter set may be regarded as increasingly ordered observations on the variate $-U$, which by symmetry has the same distribution as U, it follows that the joint distributions of

$$(U_{(1)}, U_{(2)}, \ldots, U_{(n)})$$

and

$$(-U_{(n)}, -U_{(n-1)}, \ldots, -U_{(1)})$$

coincide. This may be expressed formally as

$$\text{distr}\,(\boldsymbol{u}_{(0)}) = \text{distr}\,(-J\boldsymbol{u}_{(0)}) \tag{3.3.3}$$

where **J** represents the permutation matrix

$$J = \begin{bmatrix} & & & & & 1 \\ & & & & 1 & \\ & 0 & & 1 & & \\ & & \cdot & & & \\ & & \cdot & & & \\ & \cdot & & 0 & & \\ \cdot & & & & & \\ 1 & & & & & \end{bmatrix}. \tag{3.3.4}$$

In particular, taking expectations and variances, we find

$$\boldsymbol{\alpha} = -J\boldsymbol{\alpha}, \qquad V = JVJ \tag{3.3.5}$$

and hence

$$\Omega = J\Omega J. \tag{3.3.6}$$

The immediate effect of this on the estimation procedure is to render the normal equations diagonal and the estimates uncorrelated. The off-diagonal coefficient in (3.2.10) is

$$\begin{aligned} \mathbf{1}'\Omega\boldsymbol{\alpha} &= \mathbf{1}'(J\Omega J)(-J\boldsymbol{\alpha}) = -\mathbf{1}'J\Omega J^2\boldsymbol{\alpha} \\ &= -\mathbf{1}'\Omega\boldsymbol{\alpha} \end{aligned} \tag{3.3.7}$$

since $\mathbf{1}'J = \mathbf{1}'$ and $J^2 = I$, the unit matrix. It follows that $\mathbf{1}'\Omega\boldsymbol{\alpha} = 0$. The formulas for the estimates then take the very simple forms

$$\mu^* = \mathbf{1}'\Omega\boldsymbol{\alpha}_{(0)}/\mathbf{1}'\Omega\mathbf{1}, \qquad \sigma^* = \boldsymbol{\alpha}'\Omega\mathbf{x}_{(0)}/\boldsymbol{\alpha}'\Omega\boldsymbol{\alpha} \tag{3.3.8}$$

with

$$\begin{gathered} V(\mu^*) = \sigma^2/\mathbf{1}'\Omega\mathbf{1}, \qquad V(\sigma^*) = \sigma^2/\boldsymbol{\alpha}^2\Omega\boldsymbol{\alpha}, \\ \text{Cov}\,(\mu^*, \sigma^*) = 0. \end{gathered} \tag{3.3.9}$$

3.4 One-Parameter Distributions

The estimating equations may also be expected to simplify when there is only a single parameter to be estimated. Let us consider distributions of the form $F(x/\sigma)$. We then have

$$E(\mathbf{x}_{(0)}) = \boldsymbol{\alpha}\sigma, \qquad V(\mathbf{x}_{(0)}) = V\sigma^2 \tag{3.4.1}$$

and the normal equations reduce to

$$(\boldsymbol{\alpha}'\Omega\boldsymbol{\alpha})\sigma^* = \boldsymbol{\alpha}'\Omega\mathbf{x}_{(0)} \tag{3.4.2}$$

so that

$$\sigma^* = \boldsymbol{\alpha}'\Omega\mathbf{x}_{(0)}/\boldsymbol{\alpha}'\Omega\boldsymbol{\alpha} \quad \text{and} \quad V(\sigma^*) = \sigma^2/\boldsymbol{\alpha}'\Omega\boldsymbol{\alpha}. \tag{3.4.3}$$

For distributions of this type the expectation is obviously a multiple of σ.

By similar arguments, distributions of the form $F(x - \mu)$ reduce to

$$\mu^* = \mathbf{1}'\Omega\mathbf{x}_{(0)}/\mathbf{1}'\Omega\mathbf{1}, \qquad V(\mu^*) = \sigma^2/\mathbf{1}'\Omega\mathbf{1}. \tag{3.4.4}$$

3.5 Relative Efficiencies of Sample Mean and μ^* as Estimates of Expectation

It will be shown (Chapter 12A) that the least-squares estimate of the center of a rectangular distribution, namely, the midrange, has smaller variance than the sample mean. A simple condition can be found to determine whether an analogous effect occurs in general.

Since our estimate is by construction a linear compound of the observations with minimal variance, its variance cannot exceed that of the particular linear compound which is the sample mean. Hence

$$V(\mu^*) \leq \sigma^2/n \tag{3.5.1}$$

where σ^2 now represents the population variance. What we wish to establish is a set of conditions which determines when this becomes an equation and when a strict inequality.

We first note two useful cases of the Cauchy-Schwartz inequality: for vectors $\mathbf{a}$, $\mathbf{b}$ and positive-definite symmetric matrix M,

$$(\mathbf{a}'M\mathbf{a})(\mathbf{b}'M\mathbf{b}) \geq (\mathbf{a}'M\mathbf{b})^2, \tag{3.5.2}$$

the equality sign holding if and only if $\mathbf{a} = \lambda\mathbf{b}$ for some scalar λ, and

$$(\mathbf{a}'M\mathbf{a})(\mathbf{b}'M^{-1}\mathbf{b}) \geq (\mathbf{a}'\mathbf{b})^2, \tag{3.5.3}$$

equality obtaining if and only if

$$M\mathbf{a} = \lambda\mathbf{b}. \tag{3.5.4}$$

These are easily obtained from the usual form of the inequality by writing $M = LL'$ and taking $L'\mathbf{a}$ and $L\mathbf{b}$, or $L'\mathbf{a}$ and $L^{-1}\mathbf{b}$, as the fundamental vectors.

Symmetrical Distributions. We first consider symmetrical distributions, for which

$$V(\mu^*) = \sigma^2/1'\Omega\mathbf{1}, \tag{3.5.5}$$

where $\Omega = V^{-1}$. By (3.5.3) we have

$$(\mathbf{1}'\Omega\mathbf{1})(\mathbf{1}'V\mathbf{1}) \geq (\mathbf{1}'\mathbf{1})^2 \tag{3.5.6}$$

or

$$(\mathbf{1}'\Omega\mathbf{1}) \geq n$$

since $\mathbf{1}'\mathbf{1} = n$ and, by (3.2.17), $\mathbf{1}'V\mathbf{1} = n$. Hence

$$V(\mu^*) \leq \sigma^2/n. \tag{3.5.7}$$

This, of course, we knew already. This derivation [4], however, allows us to see that there can be equality if and only if $\Omega\mathbf{1} = \lambda\mathbf{1}$, in which case λ clearly must be 1.

Thus for symmetrical distributions the least-squares estimate μ^* has variance strictly smaller than has the sample mean, unless the variance matrix satisfies the condition

$$\Omega\mathbf{1} = \mathbf{1} \qquad \text{or equivalently} \quad V\mathbf{1} = \mathbf{1}, \tag{3.5.8}$$

that is, the row sums of V are all unity.

It is easily seen that when this condition holds the estimate μ^* reduces to the sample mean.

A general conclusion which follows is that if, in a symmetric distribution of the "location-and-dispersion parameters" class, the sample mean is an efficient statistic, for that distribution condition (3.5.8) holds. This is, for example, true of the normal distribution.

One-Parameter Distributions. For one-parameter distributions of the type $F(x/\theta)$, as remarked earlier, the expectation μ is proportional to θ, and by suitable choice of the scale of θ they may therefore be made equal. Assuming the scale to be so chosen, it follows that we always have $V(\theta^*) \leq \sigma^2/n$. We have seen that $V(\theta^*) = \sigma^2/\boldsymbol{\alpha}'\Omega\boldsymbol{\alpha}$ in this case. Now

$$(\boldsymbol{\alpha}'\Omega\boldsymbol{\alpha})(\mathbf{1}'V\mathbf{1}) \geq (\boldsymbol{\alpha}'\mathbf{1})^2 \tag{3.5.9}$$

where

$$\boldsymbol{\alpha}'\mathbf{1} = E\left(\sum U_{(r)}\right) = E\left(\sum U_r\right) = nE(U) = n$$

and

$$\mathbf{1}'\Omega\mathbf{1} = n,$$

since in this case

$$E(U_r) = E(X_r/\theta) = 1. \tag{3.5.10}$$

We then have

$$V(\theta^*) \leq \sigma^2/n \tag{3.5.11}$$

with equality if and only if

$$V\mathbf{1} = \lambda\boldsymbol{\alpha}, \tag{3.5.12}$$

where, since

$$\mathbf{1}'V\mathbf{1} = n = \mathbf{1}'\boldsymbol{\alpha} = \lambda n,$$

we have

$$\lambda = 1. \tag{3.5.13}$$

Thus the condition for equality is

$$V\mathbf{1} = \boldsymbol{\alpha}, \tag{3.5.14}$$

that is, the row sums of V are equal to the elements of $\boldsymbol{\alpha}$.

As an example we may consider the case of the exponential distribution for which $F(x) = 1 - \exp(-x/\sigma)$, where $\sigma = E(X)$. For this distribution it is known from general theory that $\bar{x}$ has absolutely minimal variance as an estimate of σ. It follows that the condition must hold for this distribution.

General Case. In the general case of two parameters and absence of symmetry we have

$$\frac{\sigma^2}{V(\mu^*)} = \frac{(\mathbf{1}'\Omega\mathbf{1})(\boldsymbol{\alpha}'\Omega\boldsymbol{\alpha}) - (\boldsymbol{\alpha}'\Omega\mathbf{1})^2}{(\boldsymbol{\alpha}'\Omega\boldsymbol{\alpha})}. \tag{3.5.15}$$

Consider the following case [2] of the Cauchy-Schwartz inequality

$$[(\Omega\mathbf{1} - \mathbf{1})'V(\Omega\mathbf{1} - \mathbf{1})](\boldsymbol{\alpha}'\Omega\boldsymbol{\alpha}) \geq [(\Omega\mathbf{1} - \mathbf{1})'\boldsymbol{\alpha}]^2. \tag{3.5.16}$$

On simplification, by using the facts that $\mathbf{1}'\boldsymbol{\alpha} = 0$, $\mathbf{1}'\mathbf{1} = n$, and $\mathbf{1}'V\mathbf{1} = n$, this becomes

$$(\mathbf{1}'\Omega\mathbf{1} - n)(\boldsymbol{\alpha}'\Omega\boldsymbol{\alpha})^2 \geq (\mathbf{1}'\Omega\boldsymbol{\alpha})^2 \tag{3.5.17}$$

whence

$$V(\mu^*) \leq \sigma^2/n, \tag{3.5.18}$$

equality holding if and only if

$$V(\Omega\mathbf{1} - \mathbf{1}) = \lambda\boldsymbol{\alpha} \quad \text{or} \quad V\mathbf{1} = \mathbf{1} + \lambda\boldsymbol{\alpha}. \tag{3.5.19}$$

It is easily verified that, if this condition does hold, the estimate of μ reduces to the sample mean, a result due to Downton [2].

REFERENCES

1. A. C. Aitken, "On least squares and linear combinations of observations," *Proc. Roy. Soc. Edin.*, Vol. 55 (1935), pp. 42–48.
2. F. Downton, "A note on ordered least squares estimation," *Biometrika*, Vol. 40 (1953), pp. 457–458.
3. L. Fox and J. G. Hayes, "More practical methods for the inversion of matrices," *J. R. Statist. Soc., B*, Vol. 13 (1951), pp. 83–91.
4. E. H. Lloyd, "Least-squares estimation of location and scale parameters using order statistics," *Biometrika*, Vol. 39 (1952), pp. 88–95.

CHAPTER 4

Approximation to the Best Linear Estimates

JAN JUNG

4A APPROXIMATION OF LEAST-SQUARES ESTIMATES OF LOCATION AND SCALE PARAMETERS

4A.1 Introduction

Let X be a random variable with cdf $F\left(\frac{x-\theta_1}{\theta_2}\right)$ and pdf $\frac{1}{\theta_2}f\left(\frac{x-\theta_1}{\theta_2}\right)$ where θ_1 and θ_2 are parameters and where $F(y)$ and $f(y) = F'(y)$ are such that $f(y)$ and $yf(y)$ tend to zero when y approaches the finite or infinite end points of the distribution. Furthermore, we assume that the second moment of X is finite.

By rearranging n independent observations of X in order of magnitude, we obtain the order statistics

$$x_{(1)} \leq x_{(2)} \leq \cdots \leq x_{(\nu)} \leq \cdots \leq x_{(n)}.$$

A random variable $Z = \sum_{\nu=1}^{n} h_\nu^{(n)} x_{(\nu)}$ is called a linear systematic statistic. For fixed n, it is possible to choose the constants $h_\nu^{(n)}$ so that Z is an unbiased estimate of θ_1 or θ_2, with minimum variance among all unbiased linear estimates [4].

The computation of the best constants $h_\nu^{(n)}$ is difficult, and we would like to approximate $h_\nu^{(n)}$ with a function of ν and n, depending on $F(y)$ only. For several reasons a natural approach is

$$h_\nu^{(n)} \sim \frac{1}{n} h\left(\frac{\nu}{n+1}\right)$$

where $h(u)$ is a given function.

4A.2 Linear Estimates Defined by a Continuous Weight Function

Let $h(u)$ be a continuous differentiable function defined in the interval (0, 1). We are interested in linear estimates of the type

$$Z(h) = \frac{1}{n} \sum_{\nu=1}^{n} h\left(\frac{\nu}{n+1}\right) x_{(\nu)}.$$

If $h(u)$ and its first four derivatives exist and are bounded in the interval (0, 1), it is possible to prove the following by using Taylor expansions [3]:

$$EZ(h) = M(h) + O(n^{-1}) \tag{4A.2.1}$$

$$M(h) = \int_{-\infty}^{\infty} (\theta_1 + \theta_2 x) h[F(x)] f(x)\, dx \tag{4A.2.2}$$

$$D^2 Z(h) = \frac{\theta_2^{\,2}}{n} V(h) + O(n^{-2}) \tag{4A.2.3}$$

$$V(h) = \int_{-\infty}^{\infty} \int_{-\infty}^{\infty} K(x, y) h[F(x)] h[F(y)]\, dy\, dx \tag{4A.2.4}$$

where

$$K(x, y) = \begin{cases} F(x)[1 - F(y)] & \text{when } x < y \\ [1 - F(x)]F(y) & \text{when } x > y \end{cases} \tag{4A.2.5}$$

and where the remainder terms $O(n^{-1})$ and $O(n^{-2})$ depend on the upper bounds of the derivatives of $h(u)$.

4A.3 Asymptotically Best Linear Estimates

We want to choose the function $h(u)$ in a way that gives an estimate $\theta^* = Z(h)$ of the parameter $\theta = \alpha_1\theta_1 + \alpha_2\theta_2$, where α_1 and α_2 are arbitrary constants. Among all linear estimates $Z(h)$ satisfying $M(h) = \theta$ we consider that the estimate $\theta^* = Z(h_0)$ is asymptotically best, for which $V(h)$ is a minimum.

In equations (4A.2.2) and (4A.2.4) let $H(x) = h[F(x)]$; then we want

$$V(h) = \int_{-\infty}^{\infty} \int_{-\infty}^{\infty} K(x, y) H(x) H(y)\, dy\, dx$$

to be minimum with respect to $H(x)$, subject to the conditions

$$\int_{-\infty}^{\infty} H(x) f(x)\, dx = \alpha_1, \tag{4A.3.1}$$

$$\int_{-\infty}^{\infty} H(x) x f(x)\, dx = \alpha_2. \tag{4A.3.2}$$

By calculus of variation we obtain the solution

$$H_0(x) = a_1 H_1(x) + a_2 H_2(x)$$

where $H_1(x)$ and $H_2(x)$ are the unique solutions of the integral equations

$$\int_{-\infty}^{\infty} K(x, y) H_1(y)\, dy = f(x) \tag{4A.3.3}$$

$$\int_{-\infty}^{\infty} K(x, y) H_2(y)\, dy = x f(x) \tag{4A.3.4}$$

and where a_1 and a_2 are determined from (4A.3.1) and (4A.3.2).

From the special form of $K(x, y)$ the solutions $H_1(x)$ and $H_2(x)$ may be obtained by differentiating the equations (4A.3.3) and (4A.3.4).

Statement of the Result. Put

$$\gamma_1(x) = -\frac{f'(x)}{f(x)}, \qquad \gamma_2(x) = -x\frac{f'(x)}{f(x)} - 1$$

$$d_{\mu\nu} = \int_{-\infty}^{\infty} \gamma_\mu(x)\gamma_\nu(x) f(x)\, dx, \qquad \mu, \nu = 1, 2$$

and use the matrix notations

$$\mathbf{a} = \begin{bmatrix} a_1 \\ a_2 \end{bmatrix}, \qquad \boldsymbol{\alpha} = \begin{bmatrix} \alpha_1 \\ \alpha_2 \end{bmatrix}, \qquad \mathbf{D} = \begin{bmatrix} d_{11} & d_{12} \\ d_{21} & d_{22} \end{bmatrix}.$$

Then the asymptotically best estimate $\theta^* = Z(h_0)$ of $\theta = \alpha_1\theta_1 + \alpha_2\theta_2$ is the statistic

$$\theta^* = Z(h_0) = \frac{1}{n}\sum_{\nu=1}^{n} h_0\left(\frac{\nu}{n+1}\right) x_{(\nu)}$$

with

$$h_0[F(x)] \equiv H_0(x) = -a_1\gamma'_1(x) - a_2\gamma'_2(x) \tag{4A.3.5}$$

where

$$\mathbf{a} = \mathbf{D}^{-1}\boldsymbol{\alpha}.$$

The resulting variance is

$$D^2(\theta^*) = \frac{\theta_2^{\,2}}{n}\boldsymbol{\alpha}'\mathbf{D}^{-1}\boldsymbol{\alpha} + 0(n^{-2}).$$

The Asymptotic Efficiency of θ^*. If we denote the pdf $\dfrac{1}{\theta_2} f\left(\dfrac{x - \theta_1}{\theta_2}\right)$ by $g(x;\ \theta_1\theta_2)$, it is easily proved that

$$d_{\mu\nu} = E\left(\frac{\partial \log g}{\partial\theta_\mu}\frac{\partial \log g}{\partial\theta_\nu}\right),$$

and thus it follows that the estimates θ^*_1 and θ^*_2 are asymptotically jointly efficient, and that each of them is efficient when the other is regarded as a nuisance parameter, with efficiency measured according to Cramér [2]. If one of them is known, an easy simplification of these arguments gives us asymptotically efficient estimates.

4A.4 Application (Student Distribution)

For the Student distribution with m degrees of freedom ($m \geq 3$) we have

$$F(x) = S_m(x)$$

and

$$f(x) = s_m(x) = \frac{1}{\sqrt{m\pi}} \frac{\Gamma\left(\frac{m+1}{2}\right)}{\Gamma\left(\frac{m}{2}\right)} \left(1 + \frac{x^2}{m}\right)^{-(m+1)/2}. \tag{4A.4.1}$$

Thus we obtain

$$\gamma_1(x) = \frac{m+1}{m} \frac{x}{1 + (x^2/m)}, \qquad \gamma_2(x) = \frac{m+1}{m} \frac{x^2}{1 + (x^2/m)} - 1,$$

$$H_1(x) \equiv h_1[S_m(x)] = \frac{m+1}{m} \frac{1 - (x^2/m)}{[1 + (x^2/m)]^2},$$

and

$$H_2(x) \equiv h_2[S_m(x)] = \frac{m+1}{m} \frac{2x}{[1 + (x^2/m)]^2}. \tag{4A.4.2}$$

Putting $1 + x^2/m = 1/\xi$, we may easily compute

$$d_{11} = \frac{m+1}{m+3}, \qquad d_{12} = d_{21} = 0, \qquad \text{and} \quad d_{22} = \frac{2m}{m+3}. \tag{4A.4.3}$$

For the location parameter θ_1 we thus obtain ($\alpha_1 = 1$, $\alpha_2 = 0$)

$$\mathbf{a} = \begin{bmatrix} \frac{m+1}{m+3} & 0 \\ 0 & \frac{2m}{m+3} \end{bmatrix}^{-1} \begin{bmatrix} 1 \\ 0 \end{bmatrix}, \qquad a_1 = \frac{m+3}{m+1}, \qquad a_2 = 0,$$

$$\theta^*_1 = Z(h_0),$$

where

$$h_0[S_m(x)] = \frac{m+3}{m} \frac{[1 - (x^2/m)]}{[1 + (x^2/m)]^2}$$

and also

$$D^2(\theta^*_1) = \frac{\theta_2^{\,2}}{n} \frac{m+3}{m+1} + O(n^{-2}). \tag{4A.4.4}$$

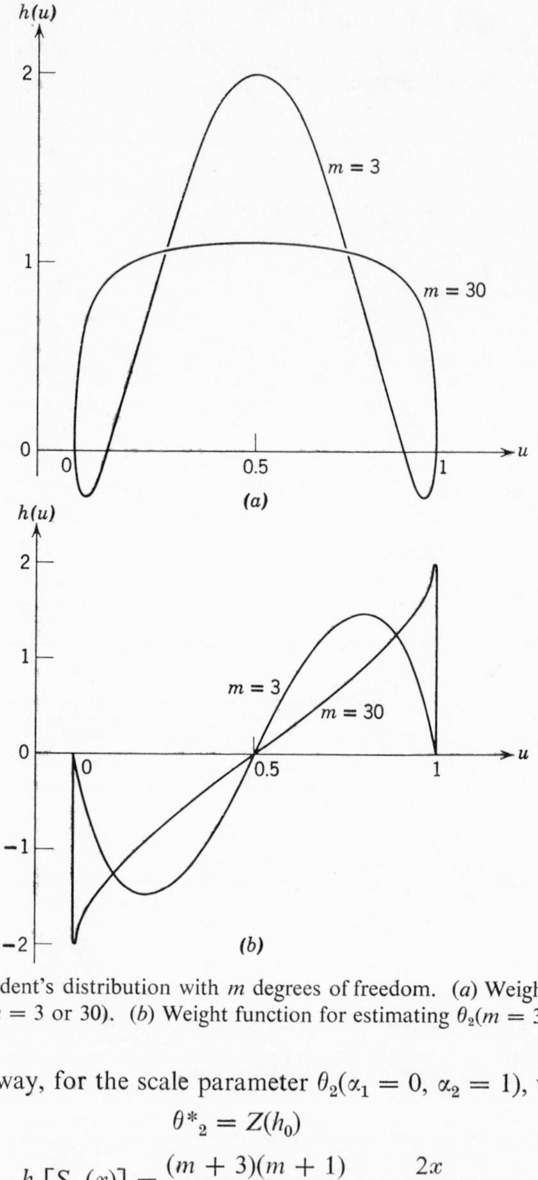

Fig. 4A.1 Student's distribution with m degrees of freedom. (*a*) Weight function for estimating $\theta_1(m = 3 \text{ or } 30)$. (*b*) Weight function for estimating $\theta_2(m = 3 \text{ or } 30)$.

In the same way, for the scale parameter $\theta_2(\alpha_1 = 0, \alpha_2 = 1)$, we obtain

$$\theta^*{}_2 = Z(h_0)$$

where
$$h_0[S_m(x)] = \frac{(m+3)(m+1)}{m^2} \frac{2x}{[1 + (x^2/m)]^2}$$

and also

$$D^2(\theta^*{}_2) = \frac{\theta_2{}^2}{n} \frac{m+3}{2m} + O(n^{-2}). \tag{4A.4.5}$$

The functions $h_0(u)$ for $m = 3$ and 30 are shown in Fig. 4A.1.

4A.5 Remarks

When $m \to \infty$, $S_m(x)$ tends to the normal distribution function $\phi(x)$, and the weight function for θ^*_1 tends to 1. On the other hand, the weight function for θ^*_2 tends to $\phi^{-1}(u)$, which is not bounded in (0, 1), and thus we may not apply the equations (4A.2.2) and (4A.2.4). However, it may be shown by other methods that the estimate θ^*_2 with $h_0(u) = \phi^{-1}(u)$, where $\phi(x)$ is the normal cdf, has the asymptotic mean θ_2 and variance $\theta_2^2/2n$ given by these expressions [1].

The case for $m = 1$ is interesting since we obtain the Cauchy distribution, where the mean does not exist. Except for the four extreme observations, the order statistics $x_{(3)}, \ldots, x_{(n-2)}$ have finite means and covariances. Thus there is no function $h(u)$ independent of n that will use all the observations $x_{(3)}, \ldots, x_{(n-2)}$ and still give reasonable estimates of the parameter. Correspondingly, for $m = 2$ we cannot use the observations $x_{(1)}$ and $x_{(n)}$ since their variances are infinite.

4A.6 Application for Small n

Many statisticians have a tendency to use asymptotical results for $n \geq 2$. With the estimates just given, this method is not advisable. From the tables of means and cross products for order statistics from a normal population given in Teichroew [5] and reproduced in Table 10B.2, the estimate σ^* of σ in a normal population has the mean

$$E\sigma^* \sim 0.7\sigma \qquad \text{for } n = 9$$

and

$$E\sigma^* \sim 0.8\sigma \qquad \text{for } n = 19.$$

REFERENCES

1. C. A. Bennett, "Asymptotic properties of ideal linear estimators," unpublished dissertation, University of Michigan, Ann Arbor, 1952.
2. H. Cramér, "A contribution to the theory of statistical estimation," *Skand. Aktuartidskr.*, Vol. 29 (1946), pp. 85–94.
3. J. Jung, "On linear estimates defined by a continuous weight function," *Ark. Mat.*, Band 3, Nr. 15 (1955), pp. 199–209.
4. E. H. Lloyd, "Least-squares estimation of location and scale parameters using order statistics, "*Biometrika*, Vol. 39 (1952), pp. 88–95.
5. D. Teichroew, "Tables of expected values of order statistics and products of order statistics for samples of size twenty and less from the normal distribution, "*Ann. Math. Statist.*, Vol. 27 (1956), pp. 410–426.

GUNNAR BLOM

4B NEARLY BEST LINEAR ESTIMATES OF LOCATION AND SCALE PARAMETERS

4B.1 Introduction

This is an expository article on a general method of constructing estimates of location and scale parameters of continuous distributions. The method was briefly described in reference 1 and in more detail in Chapters 10 through 13 of reference 2.

Let z be a random variable with the continuous cdf $F[(z - \mu)/\sigma]$, where F is known and μ and σ are unknown parameters. An ordered random sample $z_{(1)} < z_{(2)} < \ldots < z_{(n)}$ is available. It is required to estimate μ and σ by means of suitable linear combinations of the order statistics $z_{(i)}$. Infinitely many such estimates can be found. In order to select an estimate with useful properties, we may use different principles. Two alternatives will be considered.

1. The estimate should be unbiased and of minimum variance.
2. The estimate should have minimum mean square deviation (MSD).

The main part of this section concerns the first alternative. In the last part of Section 4B.7, the second alternative is dealt with briefly.

4B.2 Best Linear Estimates

If we are prepared to perform all necessary calculations, it is possible to find an exact solution to the problem of selecting a minimum variance estimate from the class of all unbiased estimates. We then have a problem in least squares, which can be solved by the method described by Lloyd [7] and shown in Chapter 3. The resulting estimate will be called the *best linear estimate.* In order to find numerical values of the coefficients in this estimate, it is necessary to

1. Calculate the means $E(x_{(i)})$ of the $x_{(i)}$.
2. Calculate the variances and covariances of the $x_{(i)}$.
3. Invert the $n \times n$ variance-covariance matrix.

Here $x_{(1)} < x_{(2)} < \ldots < x_{(n)}$ denotes an ordered random sample from the cdf $f(x)$.

Even when n is small, say less than 10, the calculations are time-consuming and mostly involve numerical integrations. For moderate or large n the work is so great that an exact approach becomes impracticable (except in some very special situations where the solution happens to be quite simple). Sarhan and Greenberg [10] have facilitated these calculations for the normal distribution by tabulating the appropriate coefficients for sample sizes up to 20; these are shown in Table 10C.1.

4B.3 Unbiased Nearly Best Linear Estimates

In practice, it is not often necessary to use the best estimate; a "nearly" best estimate, that is, an estimate with nearly minimum variance, might do very well. We now demonstrate how such an approximation to the best linear estimate can be found. The condition of unbiasedness will be retained in this section (later we relax it): that is, we wish to find an unbiased estimate of μ or σ which has a small, but not necessarily the least possible, variance of all unbiased estimates. To derive the approximation, we proceed as follows, leaving out certain mathematical details.

Let λ_i be defined by

$$F(\lambda_i) = p_i = \frac{i}{n+1}, \qquad (4B.3.1)$$

that is, λ_i is a fractile of the reduced variable x with the cdf $F(x)$. The covariance of any two order statistics $x_{(i)}$ and $x_{(j)}$ (including the variance) may be written (cf. references 4, p. 369, and 2, p. 55)

$$\text{Cov}\,(x_{(i)}, x_{(j)}) = \frac{p_i(1-p_j)}{(n+2)f(\lambda_i)f(\lambda_j)} + R_{ij}, \qquad i \le j$$

where $f(x)$ is the frequency function of x. Under general conditions, which will not be specified here, the error term tends to zero when $n \to \infty$ and $i/(n+1) \to c_1$, $j/(n+1) \to c_2$ $(0 < c_1 \le c_2 < 1)$.

Set

$$\theta_i = f(\lambda_i), \qquad i = 1, 2, \ldots, n. \qquad (4B.3.2)$$

Then, if the sample size is large, we have approximately

$$\text{Cov}\,(\theta_i x_{(i)}, \theta_j x_{(j)}) \sim \frac{p_i(1-p_j)}{n+2}.$$

Setting

$$y_{(i)} = \theta_{i+1}x_{(i+1)} - \theta_i x_{(i)}, \qquad i = 0, 1, \ldots, n; \quad \theta_0 = \theta_{n+1} = 0$$

we find

$$\begin{aligned} V(y_{(i)}) &\sim n(n+1)^{-2}(n+2)^{-1}, \\ \text{Cov}\,(y_{(i)}, y_{(j)}) &\sim -(n+1)^{-2}(n+2)^{-1}. \end{aligned} \qquad (4B.3.3)$$

The importance of these expressions lies in the fact that they are independent of $F(x)$.

Now consider a general unknown parameter $\alpha = k_1\mu + k_2\sigma$, where k_1 and k_2 are given quantities. Any linear estimate $\alpha^{*\prime}$ of α can be written

$$\alpha^{*\prime} = \sum_{i=1}^{n} g_i z_{(i)} = \sum_{i=1}^{n} g_i(\mu + \sigma x_{(i)}).$$

We introduce the $y_{(i)}$ instead of the $x_{(i)}$ in this expression. It is then convenient also to replace the g_i by new coefficients $h_0, h_1, \ldots, h_n$ defined, apart from an additive constant, by

$$g_i = \theta_i(h_i - h_{i-1}), \qquad i = 1, 2, \ldots, n.$$

After an obvious rearrangement we obtain

$$\alpha^{*\prime} = \sum_{i=0}^{n} h_i[\mu(\theta_i - \theta_{i+1}) - \sigma y_{(i)}].$$

Let us write, for $i = 0, 1, \ldots, n$,

$$\begin{aligned} C_{1i} &= \theta_i - \theta_{i+1} \\ C_{2i} &= \theta_i E(x_{(i)}) - \theta_{i+1} E(x_{(i+1)}). \end{aligned} \tag{4B.3.4}$$

Then the mean of $\alpha^{*\prime}$ can be written in the form

$$E(\alpha^{*\prime}) = \mu \sum_{i=0}^{n} C_{1i} h_i + \sigma \sum_{i=0}^{n} C_{2i} h_i. \tag{4B.3.5}$$

Furthermore,

$$V(\alpha^{*\prime}) = \sigma^2 \left[\sum_{i=0}^{n} h_i^2 V(y_{(i)}) + \sum_{i \neq j}^{n} h_i h_j \operatorname{Cov}(y_{(i)}, y_{(j)}) \right].$$

Using the approximate expressions (4B.3.3), we find after a slight rearrangement

$$V(\alpha^{*\prime}) \sim \frac{\sigma^2}{(n+1)(n+2)} \sum_{i=0}^{n} (h_i - \bar{h})^2 \tag{4B.3.6}$$

where $\bar{h} = \dfrac{1}{(n+1)} \sum_{i=0}^{n} h_i$. Thus, the original least-squares problem has been transformed to one that is easier to deal with. On the other hand, since all error terms are discarded, the demand for an exact solution has to be given up. This may not be so serious as it appears at first sight. It might be expected that the surface generated by $z = V(\alpha^{*\prime})$ in the $(n+1)$-dimensional space with z and the h_i as coordinates is rather flat in the neighborhood of the minimum. Hence we may hope that the situation turns out to be of the kind sketched in Fig. 4B.1.

After this admittedly weak defense of formula (4B.3.6), we can solve the resulting least-squares problem. By (4B.3.5), $\alpha^{*\prime}$ is an unbiased estimate of α provided

$$\sum_{i=0}^{n} C_{ri} h_i = k_r, \qquad r = 1, 2.$$

We now seek the minimum of (4B.3.6) subject to the given side conditions. The calculations are straightforward, and we only state the result, namely

$$h_i = \bar{h} + a_1 C_{1i} + a_2 C_{2i}.$$

Here a_1 and a_2 are two Lagrange multipliers given by

$$a_1 = d^{11}k_1 + d^{12}k_2,$$

$$a_2 = d^{21}k_1 + d^{22}k_2.$$

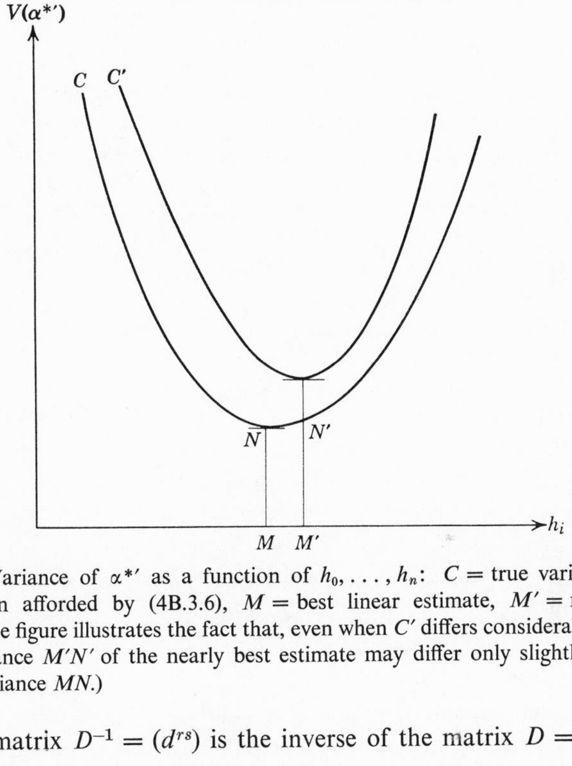

Fig. 4B.1 Variance of $\alpha^{*\prime}$ as a function of $h_0, \ldots, h_n$: C = true variance, C' = approximation afforded by (4B.3.6), M = best linear estimate, M' = nearly best estimate. (The figure illustrates the fact that, even when C' differs considerably from C, the true variance $M'N'$ of the nearly best estimate may differ only slightly from the minimum variance MN.)

where the matrix $D^{-1} = (d^{rs})$ is the inverse of the matrix $D = (d_{rs})$ and

$$d_{rs} = \sum_{i=0}^{n} C_{ri} C_{si}, \qquad r, s = 1, 2. \tag{4B.3.7}$$

The resulting estimate $\alpha^{*\prime}$ is called an *unbiased nearly best linear estimate* of $\alpha = k_1\mu + k_2\sigma$. If, in particular, $k_1 = 1$, $k_2 = 0$ or $k_1 = 0$, $k_2 = 1$, we obtain the following unbiased nearly best estimates of μ and σ:

$$\mu^{*\prime} = \sum_{i=1}^{n} g_{1i} z_{(i)},$$

$$\sigma^{*\prime} = \sum_{i=1}^{n} g_{2i} z_{(i)}.$$

where

$$g_{ri} = \theta_i[d^{r1}(C_{1i} - C_{1\,i-1}) + d^{r2}(C_{2i} - C_{2\,i-1})], \qquad r = 1, 2. \quad (4B.3.8)$$

The variances are given approximately by

$$\begin{aligned} V(\mu^{*\prime}) &\sim \sigma^2 d^{11}(n+1)^{-1}(n+2)^{-1} \\ V(\sigma^{*\prime}) &\sim \sigma^2 d^{22}(n+1)^{-1}(n+2)^{-1} \end{aligned} \quad (4B.3.9)$$

and the covariance by

$$\text{Cov}\,(\mu^{*\prime}, \sigma^{*\prime}) \sim \sigma^2 d^{12}(n+1)^{-1}(n+2)^{-1}. \quad (4B.3.10)$$

These three approximations may be crude, even though the method works excellently in other respects (cf. Fig. 4B.1).

Let us compare the approximate solution from a numerical point of view with the exact solution outlined in Section 4B.2. Of the three main steps mentioned there, only the first one remains unchanged. The remaining two steps disappear; instead, the following more convenient steps should be taken.

1. Compute θ_i in (4B.3.2).
2. Compute $\theta_i E(x_{(i)})$.
3. Compute C_{1i} and C_{2i} in (4B.3.4).
4. Compute the elements d_{rs} of D defined by (4B.3.7) and the elements of the inverse D^{-1}.
5. Insert the resulting numerical values in (4B.3.8).

A numerical example illustrating this scheme of calculations will be given in the next section.

It should be remarked that the method can be used both when the frequency function is continuous and when it is discontinuous. For example, it can be applied to rectangular or exponential distributions, which have discontinuities at the end of the range of variation. It is not known whether the method yields satisfactory results when the discontinuity points are located in the interior of the range, but there is nothing fundamental which precludes applications to such special cases.

Naturally, nearly best linear estimates can be constructed even when only one parameter μ or σ is unknown. Suppose, first, that μ is unknown. Then calculate

$$g_i = \frac{\theta_i(C_{1i} - C_{1\,i-1})}{d_{11}}.$$

Also compute d_{12}. The unbiased nearly best estimate is given by

$$\mu^{*\prime} = \sum_{i=1}^{n} g_i z_{(i)} - \frac{\sigma d_{12}}{d_{11}}.$$

The expression becomes particularly simple when d_{12} is zero, which happens, for example, when the distribution is symmetrical.

By analogy, if σ is unknown, take

$$g_i = \frac{\theta_i(C_{2i} - C_{2i-1})}{d_{22}}$$

and

$$\sigma^{*\prime} = \sum_{i=1}^{n} g_i z_{(i)} - \frac{\mu d_{12}}{d_{22}}.$$

4B.4 A Numerical Example

We shall show by an example how the method works when applied to a particular distribution. Let z be distributed according to the cdf

$$\exp\,(-e^{-(z-\mu)/\sigma+\gamma})$$

where μ and σ are unknown and γ is Euler's constant. This means that the reduced variable $x = (z - \mu)/\sigma$ follows the extreme-value distribution with cdf

$$\exp\,(-e^{-x+\gamma}).$$

The mean and variance of x are 0 and $\pi^2/6$, respectively. Thus μ is the mean of z, and $\pi\sigma/\sqrt{6}$ is the standard deviation. Let us demonstrate how μ and σ can be estimated when a sample of five values is available.

The successive steps in the calculations have been reproduced in Table 4B.1. The values of θ_i and $E(x_{(i)})$ have been taken from references 8 and 6, respectively. We shall compare the resulting nearly best linear estimates to the best linear estimates determined in reference 6. By using accurate values of the variances and covariances of the $x_{(i)}$ (which were also published in reference 6), it is found that $V(\mu^{*\prime}) = 0.330\sigma^2$ and $V(\sigma^{*\prime}) = 0.173\sigma^2$, and the best linear estimates have the variances $0.325\sigma^2$ and $0.167\sigma^2$, respectively. In view of the small sample size, the approximation to the best estimate must be considered to be very good. Further examples are given in reference 2, Section 10.8.

4B.5 Censored Samples

It is a notable feature of the method described that it can easily be adapted to censored samples. Suppose that the r_1 smallest and r_2 largest observations are missing (which covers the most common situations).

We may then proceed as in Section 4B.3, with the following modifications. C_{1i} and C_{2i} defined in (4B.3.4) should be replaced by

$$C^*_{1i} = \begin{cases} -\theta_{r_1+1}/(r_1 + 1) & \text{for } 0 \leq i \leq r_1 \\ C_{1i} & \text{for } r_1 + 1 \leq i \leq n - r_2 - 1 \\ \theta_{n-r_2}/(r_2 + 1) & \text{for } n - r_2 \leq i \leq n \end{cases}$$

$$C^*_{2i} = \begin{cases} -\theta_{r_1+1}E(x_{(r_1+1)})/(r_1 + 1) & \text{for } 0 \leq i \leq r_1 \\ C_{2i} & \text{for } r_1 + 1 \leq i \leq n - r_2 - 1 \\ \theta_{n-r_2}E(x_{(n-r_2)})/(r_2 + 1) & \text{for } n - r_2 \leq i \leq n. \end{cases}$$

In all other respects the procedure is the same as before.

4B.6 The Efficiency of Nearly Best Linear Estimates

The following discussion concerns the case in which complete samples are available, but has wider application.

Efficiency in the Linear Sense. We define efficiency (in the linear sense) of a nearly best estimate as the quotient of the variance of the best linear estimate and that of the nearly best estimate. Comparatively little is as yet known about the behavior of nearly best estimates from this point of view, but the few available results are very promising. In Section 10.8 of reference 2 calculations were made for samples of five from seven distributions of different shape. The lowest value of the efficiency (for both μ and σ) was about 94%, and in several cases the efficiency was above 98%. Since such a small loss of information is insignificant from a practical point of view, we conclude that there exist nearly best linear estimates which may serve as excellent approximations to best linear estimates. It would be valuable to know more about the nature of this approximation; it is hoped that more comparisons will be performed so that our knowledge of the performance of nearly best estimates is increased. In particular, it would be important to know what characterizes a distribution which yields nearly best estimates of high (or low) efficiency.

Asymptotic Efficiency. In Chapter 13 of reference 2 it is demonstrated that, under rather general conditions, nearly best linear estimates of location and scale parameters are asymptotically joint efficient.

The concept of asymptotic joint efficiency was introduced by R. A. Fisher and was studied in detail by Cramér and Rao in the 1940's in connection with the derivation of the Cramér-Rao inequality. These authors for the most part discussed what was termed by Cramér "regular" estimation problems, which include many important situations but not all possible ones. Since nearly best estimates may be used both in regular and nonregular cases, the latter including, for example, rectangular and exponential distributions, it proved necessary to introduce in reference 2 a more general concept of efficiency. It is outside the scope of this work to describe this theory, and hence we shall not demonstrate that nearly best estimates are asymptotically efficient in the general sense. The reader is referred to Part I of reference 2, where the theory is briefly discussed, and to Chapter 13 where it is applied to nearly best estimates.

Instead of furnishing a general proof, we explain, partly in a heuristic way, why asymptotic efficiency is obtained when the distribution satisfies the regularity conditions used by Cramér and Rao.

Let V be the variance-covariance matrix of any two estimates $\mu^{*\prime}$ and $\sigma^{*\prime}$ of μ and σ in the cdf $F[(z-\mu)/\sigma]$. Denote the corresponding frequency function $f[(z-\mu)/\sigma]/\sigma$ by $f_1(z)$. Further, let E be the 2×2 matrix with the elements

$$e_{11} = E\left(\frac{\partial \log f_1}{\partial \mu}\right)^2, \qquad e_{12} = e_{21} = E\left(\frac{\partial \log f_1}{\partial \mu}\frac{\partial \log f_1}{\partial \sigma}\right), \qquad (4B.6.1)$$

$$e_{22} = E\left(\frac{\partial \log f_1}{\partial \sigma}\right)^2.$$

We shall suppose that the inverse E^{-1} of E exists. Cramér [5] and Rao [9] have proved a result which is essentially equivalent to stating that the matrix

$$V - \frac{1}{n}E^{-1}$$

is positive definite or semidefinite for any n. This means, among other things, that the generalized variance $|V|$ can never fall below the limit

$$\frac{1}{n^2}|E^{-1}| = \frac{1}{n^2(e_{11}e_{22} - e_{12}{}^2)}. \qquad (4B.6.2)$$

If the generalized variance of two estimates is asymptotically equivalent to this limit, the estimates are said to be asymptotically joint efficient (in the restricted sense used by Cramér and Rao).

Now let us investigate the behavior of the unbiased nearly best estimates $\mu^{*\prime}$ and $\sigma^{*\prime}$ from this point of view. To see what happens to their variances, we use (4B.3.9) and have then to determine the asymptotic behavior of the elements d_{rs} of D. We have, for example, from (4B.3.7) and (4B.3.4)

$$d_{11} = \sum_{i=0}^{n}(\theta_i - \theta_{i+1})^2 = \sum_{i=0}^{n}(f(\lambda_i) - f(\lambda_{i+1}))^2$$

where λ_i is defined by (4B.3.1). If $f(x)$ tends to zero at the ends of the range of variation of x and can be differentiated for any x, we have approximately

$$f(\lambda_i) - f(\lambda_{i+1}) \sim -\frac{1}{n}\frac{f'(\lambda_i)}{f(\lambda_i)}.$$

Consequently, d_{11} can be approximated by

$$d_{11} \sim \frac{1}{n}\int_0^1 \left[\frac{f'(x)}{f(x)}\right]^2 du$$

where $u = F(x)$, or by a change of variable

$$d_{11} \sim \frac{1}{n}\int_{-\infty}^{\infty} \left(\frac{\partial \log f}{\partial x}\right)^2 f(x)\, dx.$$

By similar approximations it can be shown that, if $xf(x)$ also tends to zero at the ends, then

$$d_{12} \sim \frac{1}{n}\int_{-\infty}^{\infty} \frac{\partial \log f}{\partial x}\left(1 + x\frac{\partial \log f}{\partial x}\right) f(x)\, dx$$

$$d_{22} \sim \frac{1}{n}\int_{-\infty}^{\infty} \left(1 + x\frac{\partial \log f}{\partial x}\right)^2 f(x)\, dx.$$

All these expressions are given in terms of the frequency function $f(x)$ of the reduced variable. Now we change over to the frequency function $f_1(z)$ of the original variable z. By calculation it is verified that we may then write

$$d_{rs} \sim \frac{\sigma^2}{n} e_{rs}, \qquad r, s = 1, 2 \tag{4B.6.3}$$

where the e_{rs} are defined by (4B.6.1).

We use this result in order to determine an approximate expression of the generalized variance of the nearly best estimates. Omitting the error terms in (4B.3.9) and (4B.3.10), we find

$$|V| = V(\mu^{*\prime})V(\sigma^{*\prime}) - [\mathrm{Cov}\,(\mu^{*\prime}, \sigma^{*\prime})]^2$$

$$\sim \frac{\sigma^4}{n^4}\frac{1}{d_{11}d_{22} - d_{12}^{\;2}}$$

or by (4B.6.3)

$$|V| \sim \frac{1}{n^2(e_{11}e_{22} - e_{12}^{\;2})}. \tag{4B.6.4}$$

In other words, the limit (4B.6.2) is attained. Note that (4B.6.4) implies that the quotient of the right and left members tends to unity when n tends to infinity.

Hence we conclude that the nearly best linear estimates are asymptotically joint efficient. It must, however, be emphasized that we have skipped one very important point. The result holds only if we can prove that the error terms in (4B.3.9) tend to zero faster than the leading terms. In addition, the error term in (4B.3.10) should behave properly. It would be too involved to state conditions that ensure that the error terms converge in an appropriate way, and the reader is referred to Chapter 13 of reference 2 for more details. Suffice it to say here that all the common distributions behave well in this respect.

4B.7 Some Extensions and Modifications of the Method

We shall briefly mention three variations of the method described in the previous sections.

Nearly Unbiased, Nearly Best Estimates. This estimate is obtained by using the approximation

$$E(x_{(i)}) \sim F^{-1}\left(\frac{i-\alpha}{n-\alpha-\beta+1}\right)$$

where α, β are appropriately chosen constants. In this way the first of the three steps mentioned in Section 4B.2 is simplified. The bias introduced by this approximation is often very small, and the resulting estimates may be equivalent, for all practical purposes, to unbiased nearly best estimates. For example, if F is the normal cdf, an approximation of reasonable accuracy is obtained for $\alpha = \beta = \frac{3}{8}$. Further details are given in Chapter 6 and in Section 10.7 of reference 2.

Modified Nearly Best Estimates. These estimates can be obtained by replacing the second-order differences of the sequences $\{\theta_i\}$ and $\{\theta_i E(x_{(i)})\}$ by derivatives. Here we must impose certain restrictions on $f(x)$ and $xf(x)$. For example, we must require that $f(x)$ and $xf(x)$ tend to zero at the ends of the range of variation.

The general form of coefficients of these estimates is given in Section 12.2 in reference 2. It might be added that when F is the normal cdf, the modified nearly best estimate of σ is closely related to the graphical estimate obtained from a normal probability paper. For further details see Section 12.6 in reference 2; compare also reference 3.

Linear Estimates of σ with Nearly Minimum MSD. The estimate which has the least-possible mean square deviation $E(\sigma^{*\prime} - \sigma)^2$ about σ of all linear estimates of σ in $F\left(\frac{z-\mu}{\sigma}\right)$ so that their means are proportional to σ is called a minimum MSD estimate. Like the best linear estimate, it is often difficult to determine for numerical reasons. An approximation is afforded by the linear estimate ${\sigma^*}'_1$ with nearly minimum MSD.

The nearly minimum MSD estimate may be derived from the approximate formula (4B.3.6) by calculations which are very similar to those reproduced in Section 4B.3. We state only the final result, namely

$$ {\sigma^*}'_1 = \left[1 + \frac{d_{11}}{(n+1)(n+2)\,|D|}\right]^{-1} \sigma^{*\prime}, $$

where $\sigma^{*\prime}$ is the unbiased nearly best estimate, and d_{11} and D are defined in Section 4B.3.

Thus, if unbiasedness is not essential, we may improve $\sigma^{*\prime}$ by multiplying with a suitable factor. From a practical point of view, however, the difference between the two estimates is rather unimportant unless the sample size is very small, and therefore the topic discussed in this subsection has mainly theoretical interest.

4B.8 Some Remarks

When assessing the value which the new method of estimation may possess, the following three points seem to be of some importance.

1. Nearly best linear estimates are generally asymptotically efficient, and hence nonlinear methods of estimation are not necessary when asymptotic efficiency is aimed at.

This fact does not seem to have been recognized earlier; at least, it has not been proved before that there exist linear estimates of a comparatively simple structure which possess this property.

2. It seems that, for the first time, an alternative to the maximum-likelihood method has been proposed, one that has the same good properties as this method and, in addition, is rather convenient to handle.

It must of course be remembered, however, that the classical maximum-likelihood method has a much wider scope than the present method which concerns only estimation of parameters of location and scale.

3. In the field of applied statistics, the new method may open up new roads for handling nonnormal distributions.

Up to now, location and scale parameters of nonnormal distributions have often, for lack of a better method, been estimated by the mean and the standard deviation, although the efficiency may then be rather poor. It may be hoped that the proposed method will fill the need for a more efficient but still reasonably simple procedure. However, tables of coefficients of nearly best linear estimates must then be prepared for the benefit of workers in different areas.

TABLE 4B.1

Extreme-Value Distribution. Calculation of Unbiased Nearly Best Estimates $\mu^{*\prime}$ and $\sigma^{*\prime}$. Sample Size $n = 5$

i	θ_i	$\theta_i E(x_{(i)})$	C_{1i}	C_{2i}	$\theta_i(C_{1i} - C_{1\ i-1})$	$\theta_i(C_{2i} - C_{2\ i-1})$	g_{1i}	g_{2i}
0	0	0	−0.2986	0.3785				
1	0.2986	−0.3785	−0.0676	−0.1280	0.06900	−0.15124	0.1925	−0.4329
2	0.3662	−0.2505	0.0196	−0.1980	0.03193	−0.02563	0.2248	−0.0114
3	0.3466	−0.0526	0.0763	−0.1860	0.01963	0.00414	0.1991	0.0776
4	0.2703	0.1335	0.1184	−0.1111	0.01138	0.02026	0.1700	0.1211
5	0.1519	0.2445	0.1519	0.2445	0.00510	0.05403	0.2137	0.2457

$$D = \begin{bmatrix} \sum C_{1i}^2 & \sum C_{1i}C_{2i} \\ \sum C_{1i}C_{2i} & \sum C_{2i}^2 \end{bmatrix} = \begin{bmatrix} 0.1370 & -0.0984 \\ -0.0984 & 0.3056 \end{bmatrix}, \qquad D^{-1} = \begin{bmatrix} 9.494 & 3.059 \\ 3.059 & 4.258 \end{bmatrix}$$

Calculation of last two columns: $g_{11} = 9.494 \cdot 0.06900 + 3.059 \cdot (-0.15124)$, etc.

$g_{21} = 3.059 \cdot 0.06900 + 4.258 \cdot (-0.15124)$, etc.

Note. The entries on the original work sheet have been rounded off to the number of decimals given above.

REFERENCES

1. G. Blom, "On linear estimates with nearly minimum variance," *Ark. Mat.*, Band 3, Nr. 31 (1956), pp. 365–369.
2. G. Blom, *Statistical Estimates and Transformed Beta-Variables*, Almqvist and Wiksell, Uppsala, Sweden, 1958; John Wiley and Sons, New York, 1958.
3. H. Chernoff and G. J. Lieberman, "Use of normal probability paper," *J. Amer. Statist. Ass.*, Vol. 49 (1954), pp. 778–785.
4. H. Cramér, *Mathematical Methods of Statistics*, Princeton, 1946.
5. H. Cramér, "A contribution to the theory of statistical estimation," *Skand. Aktuartidskr.*, Vol. 29 (1946), pp. 85–94.
6. J. Lieblein, "A new method of analyzing extreme-value data," NACA, Tech. Note 3053, 1954.
7. E. H. Lloyd, "Least-squares estimation of location and scale parameters using order statistics," *Biometrika*, Vol. 39 (1952), pp. 88–95.
8. National Bureau of Standards, "Probability tables for the analysis of extreme-value data," Appl. Math. Ser. 22, U.S. Dept. Commerce, Washington, D.C., 1953.
9. C. R. Rao, "Minimum variance and the estimation of several parameters," *Proc. Camb. Phil. Soc.*, Vol. 43 (1947), pp. 280–288.
10. A. E. Sarhan and B. G. Greenberg, "Estimation of location and scale parameters by order statistics from singly and doubly censored samples, Parts I, II, III," *Ann. Math. Statist.*, Vol. 27 (1956), pp. 427–451; Vol. 29 (1958), pp. 79–105; and Tech. Rep. 4, OOR Project 1597, 1958.

JUNJIRO OGAWA

CHAPTER 5

Estimation of the Location and Scale Parameters by Sample Quantiles (for Large Samples)

5.1 Introduction

Our main interest in the theory of statistical estimation has been in "efficient estimators." But from the point of view of economy, and from the practical point of view, it is reasonable to inquire whether the output of information is comparable in value to the input measured in money, manhours, or other measures. Alternatively we may inquire whether it would have been possible to obtain comparable results by smaller expenditure.

Mosteller [3] proposed the use of order statistics for such purposes, basing his proposal on the fact that, however large the sample size is, all individual values of the sample can easily (that is, quickly with low costs) be ordered in magnitudes by punched-card equipment.

He considered the problem of estimating the mean and the standard deviation of an univariate normal distribution as well as estimating the correlation coefficient of a bivariate normal distribution (which will be explained in Section 10F). Later, Ogawa [4] considered the problem of estimating the location and scale parameters more systematically. He was able to obtain the optimum solutions in some cases. Higuchi [2] contributed a great deal in the mathematical development of a mechanism for the determination of optimum spacing in the normal distribution.

5.2 Relative Efficiencies

For the purpose of estimating the location and scale parameters, we must start with the limiting frequency function $h(x_{(n_1)}, x_{(n_2)}, \ldots, x_{(n_k)})$, given by (2.2.15).

First, we define the *relative efficiency* of the systematic statistics [3] (which are functions of order statistics) by the ratio of the amount of information in Fisher's sense derived from (2.2.15) to that derived from the original whole sample.

The following three cases are considered separately.

Case 1. *The scale parameter σ is known.* Put for the sake of convenience

$$S = \sum_{i=1}^{k} \frac{\lambda_{i+1} - \lambda_{i-1}}{(\lambda_{i+1} - \lambda_i)(\lambda_i - \lambda_{i-1})} f_i^2(x_{(n_i)} - \mu - u_i\sigma)^2$$
$$- 2\sum_{i=2}^{k} \frac{f_i f_{i-1}}{\lambda_i - \lambda_{i-1}} (x_{(n_i)} - \mu - u_i\sigma)(x_{(n_{i-1})} - \mu - u_{i-1}\sigma) \quad (5.2.1)$$

where the right-hand side is the exponent in (2.2.15); then we have

$$\log h = -\frac{n}{2\sigma^2} S + \text{term independent of } \mu.$$

Therefore

$$-\frac{\partial^2 \log h}{\partial \mu^2} = \frac{n}{2\sigma^2}\frac{\partial^2 S}{\partial \mu^2} = \frac{n}{\sigma^2} K_1 \quad (5.2.2)$$

where

$$K_1 = \sum_{i=1}^{k+1} \frac{(f_i - f_{i-1})^2}{\lambda_i - \lambda_{i-1}}; \quad (5.2.3)$$

here we have put

$$\lambda_0 = 0, \qquad \lambda_{k+1} \equiv 1 \quad \text{as before,} \qquad \text{and} \quad f_0 = f_{k+1} = 0. \quad (5.2.4)$$

Hence the amount of information $I_s(\mu)$ of systematic statistics with respect to the location parameter μ is

$$I_s(\mu) = E\left(\frac{\partial \log h}{\partial \mu}\right)^2 = -E\left(\frac{\partial^2 \log h}{\partial \mu^2}\right) = \frac{n}{\sigma^2} K_1. \quad (5.2.5)$$

The likelihood function of the original whole sample is

$$L = \frac{1}{\sigma^n}\prod_{i=1}^{n} f\left(\frac{X_i - \mu}{\sigma}\right). \quad (5.2.6)$$

Hence we have

$$\log L = \sum_{i=1}^{n} \log f\left(\frac{X_i - \mu}{\sigma}\right) - n \log \sigma$$

and therefore

$$\frac{\partial \log L}{\partial \mu} = -\frac{1}{\sigma}\sum_{i=1}^{n}\frac{f'\left(\frac{X_i-\mu}{\sigma}\right)}{f\left(\frac{X_i-\mu}{\sigma}\right)}; \tag{5.2.7}$$

consequently the amount of information of the original sample with respect to the location parameter μ [that is, $I_0(\mu)$] is

$$I_0(\mu) = E\left(\frac{\partial \log L}{\partial \mu}\right)^2 = \frac{1}{\sigma^2}E\left[\sum_{i=1}^{n}\frac{f'\left(\frac{X_i-\mu}{\sigma}\right)}{f\left(\frac{X_i-\mu}{\sigma}\right)}\right]^2$$

$$= \frac{n}{\sigma^2}E\left[\frac{f'\left(\frac{X-\mu}{\sigma}\right)}{f\left(\frac{X-\mu}{\sigma}\right)}\right]^2 = \frac{n}{\sigma^2}E\left[\frac{f'(U)}{f(U)}\right]^2. \tag{5.2.8}$$

For example, if $g(x) = (2\pi\sigma^2)^{-\frac{1}{2}} \exp[-(x-\mu)^2/2\sigma^2]$, we obtain

$$\frac{f'(U)}{f(U)} = -U;$$

hence

$$I_0(\mu) = \frac{n}{\sigma^2}E(U^2) = \frac{n}{\sigma^2}. \tag{5.2.9}$$

Thus the relative efficiency of the systematic statistics with respect to the location parameter μ is

$$\eta(\mu) = \frac{I_s(\mu)}{I_0(\mu)} = \frac{K_1}{E(f'/f)^2}. \tag{5.2.10}$$

In particular, for the normal distribution, we have from (5.2.9)

$$\eta(\mu) = K_1. \tag{5.2.11}$$

Case 2. *The location parameter μ is known.* In this case

$$\log h = -k\log\sigma - \frac{n}{2\sigma^2}S + \text{term independent of } \sigma.$$

Since we have

$$\frac{\partial^2 S}{\partial\sigma^2} = 2K_2$$

where

$$K_2 = \sum_{i=1}^{k+1}\frac{(f_i u_i - f_{i-1}u_{i-1})^2}{\lambda_i - \lambda_{i-1}}, \tag{5.2.12}$$

we obtain

$$I_s(\sigma) = E\left(\frac{\partial \log h}{\partial \sigma}\right)^2 = -E\left(\frac{\partial^2 \log h}{\partial \sigma^2}\right) = \frac{2k}{\sigma^2} + \frac{n}{\sigma^2} K_2. \quad (5.2.13)$$

On the other hand we have

$$\frac{\partial \log L}{\partial \sigma} = -\frac{n}{\sigma} - \frac{1}{\sigma^2}\sum_{i=1}^{n} \frac{(X_i - \mu) f'\left(\frac{X_i - \mu}{\sigma}\right)}{f\left(\frac{X_i - \mu}{\sigma}\right)}. \quad (5.2.14)$$

Hence by using the relation

$$E\left[\frac{Uf'(U)}{f(U)}\right] = -1 \quad (5.2.15)$$

where

$$U = \frac{X - \mu}{\sigma},$$

we obtain

$$I_0(\sigma) = E\left(\frac{\partial \log L}{\partial \sigma}\right)^2 = E\left\{\frac{1}{\sigma^2}\left[n + \sum_{i=1}^{n} \frac{U_i f'(U_i)}{f(U_i)}\right]^2\right\}$$

$$= \frac{n}{\sigma^2}\left\{E\left[\frac{Uf'(U)}{f(U)}\right]^2 - 1\right\}. \quad (5.2.16)$$

For example, in the case of the normal distribution

$$E\left[\frac{Uf'(U)}{f(U)}\right]^2 = E(U^4) = 3,$$

and thus we have

$$I_0(\sigma) = \frac{2n}{\sigma^2}. \quad (5.2.17)$$

Thus we obtain the relative efficiency of systematic statistics with respect to the scale parameter σ, as

$$\eta(\sigma) = \frac{2k/n + K_2}{E[Uf'(U)/f(U)]^2 - 1} \approx \frac{K_2}{E[Uf'(U)/f(U)]^2 - 1}. \quad (5.2.18)$$

In particular, for the normal distribution we have

$$\eta(\sigma) = \tfrac{1}{2}K_2. \quad (5.2.19)$$

Case 3. *Both the location and scale parameters are unknown.* In this case we have

$$\log h = -k \log \sigma - \frac{n}{2\sigma^2} S + \text{term independent of } \mu \text{ and } \sigma;$$

thus we have

$$\frac{\partial^2 \log h}{\partial\mu\,\partial\sigma} = \frac{n}{\sigma^3}\frac{\partial S}{\partial\mu} - \frac{n}{2\sigma^2}\frac{\partial^2 S}{\partial\mu\,\partial\sigma}$$

and therefore

$$E\left(\frac{\partial^2 \log h}{\partial\mu\,\partial\sigma}\right) = -\frac{n}{2\sigma^2}E\left(\frac{\partial^2 S}{\partial\mu\,\partial\sigma}\right) = -\frac{n}{\sigma^2}K_3 \tag{5.2.20}$$

where

$$K_3 = \sum_{i=1}^{k+1}\frac{(f_i - f_{i-1})(f_i u_i - f_{i-1}u_{i-1})}{\lambda_i - \lambda_{i-1}}. \tag{5.2.21}$$

Hence the greatest lower bound of the areas of ellipses of concentration of the joint estimators of μ and σ is proportional to the following:

$$E\left(\frac{\partial^2 \log h}{\partial\mu^2}\right)E\left(\frac{\partial^2 \log h}{\partial\sigma^2}\right) - \left[E\left(\frac{\partial^2 \log h}{\partial\mu\,\partial\sigma}\right)\right]^2 = \frac{n^2}{\sigma^4}(K_1K_2 - K_3^2) + \frac{2nk}{\sigma^4}K_1. \tag{5.2.22}$$

On the other hand, the area of the ellipse of concentration of the maximum-likelihood estimators is asymptotically proportional to [1]:

$$E\left(\frac{\partial \log L}{\partial\mu}\right)^2 E\left(\frac{\partial \log L}{\partial\sigma}\right)^2 - \left[E\left(\frac{\partial \log L}{\partial\mu}\cdot\frac{\partial \log L}{\partial\sigma}\right)\right]^2. \tag{5.2.23}$$

Since

$$\frac{\partial^2 \log L}{\partial\mu\,\partial\sigma} = \frac{1}{\sigma^2}\sum_{i=1}^{n}\frac{f'\left(\frac{X_i-\mu}{\sigma}\right)}{f\left(\frac{X_i-\mu}{\sigma}\right)} + \frac{1}{\sigma^3}\sum_{i=1}^{n}\frac{(X_i-\mu)f''\left(\frac{X_i-\mu}{\sigma}\right)}{f\left(\frac{X_i-\mu}{\sigma}\right)} - \frac{1}{\sigma^3}\sum_{i=1}^{n}\frac{(X_i-\mu)f'^2\left(\frac{X_i-\mu}{\sigma}\right)}{f^2\left(\frac{X_i-\mu}{\sigma}\right)}$$

$$= \frac{1}{\sigma^2}\sum_{i=1}^{n}\frac{f'(U_i)}{f(U_i)} + \frac{1}{\sigma^2}\sum_{i=1}^{n}\frac{U_i f''(U_i)}{f(U_i)} - \frac{1}{\sigma^2}\sum_{i=1}^{n}U_i\left[\frac{f'(U_i)}{f(U_i)}\right]^2$$

and

$$E\left[\frac{f'(U)}{f(U)}\right] = 0,$$

we have

$$E\left(\frac{\partial^2 \log L}{\partial\mu\,\partial\sigma}\right) = \frac{n}{\sigma^2}\left\{E\left[\frac{Uf''(U)}{f(U)}\right] - E\left[u\frac{f'^2(U)}{f^2(U)}\right]\right\}. \tag{5.2.24}$$

Thus we have

$$E\left(\frac{\partial \log L}{\partial \mu}\right)^2 E\left(\frac{\partial \log L}{\partial \sigma}\right)^2 - \left[E\left(\frac{\partial \log L}{\partial \mu} \cdot \frac{\partial \log L}{\partial \sigma}\right)\right]^2$$

$$= E\left(\frac{\partial^2 \log L}{\partial \mu^2}\right) E\left(\frac{\partial^2 \log L}{\partial \sigma^2}\right) - \left[E\left(\frac{\partial^2 \log L}{\partial \mu\, \partial \sigma}\right)\right]^2$$

$$= \frac{n^2}{\sigma^4}\left\{E\left(\frac{f'}{f}\right)^2\left[E\left(\frac{Uf'}{f}\right)^2 - 1\right] - \left[E\left(\frac{Uf''}{f}\right) - E\left(U\frac{f'^2}{f^2}\right)\right]\right\}^2, \quad (5.2.25)$$

but under some general condition we obtain

$$E\left(U\frac{f''}{f}\right) = \int_{-\infty}^{+\infty} uf''(u)\, du = [uf'(u)]_{-\infty}^{+\infty} - \int_{-\infty}^{\infty} f'(u)\, du$$

$$= [uf'(u)]_{-\infty}^{+\infty}. \quad (5.2.26)$$

If the frequency function has the property

$$\lim_{u \to \infty} uf'(u) = \lim_{u \to -\infty} uf'(u) = 0 \quad (5.2.27)$$

as in the normal distribution, then we have

$$E\left(U\frac{f''}{f}\right) = 0. \quad (5.2.28)$$

Consequently we obtain the relative efficiency of the estimators based on the systematic statistics as follows:

$$\eta(\mu, \sigma) = \frac{K_1K_2 - K_3^2 + \dfrac{2k}{n}K_1}{E\left(\dfrac{f'}{f}\right)^2\left[E\left(U\dfrac{f'}{f}\right)^2 - 1\right] - E^2\left(U\dfrac{f'^2}{f^2}\right)}$$

$$\approx \frac{K_1K_2 - K_3^2}{E\left(\dfrac{f'}{f}\right)^2\left[E\left(U\dfrac{f'}{f}\right)^2 - 1\right] - E^2\left(U\dfrac{f'^2}{f^2}\right)}. \quad (5.2.29)$$

For the normal distribution it is easily seen that

$$\eta(\mu, \sigma) \approx \tfrac{1}{2}(K_1K_2 - K_3^2). \quad (5.2.30)$$

5.3 The Best Linear Unbiased Estimators

Under the present circumstance the distribution of the sample quantiles is given by (2.2.15), and the unknown parameters are μ and σ. Thus to find the best linear unbiased estimators of the parameters, case by case, we apply the Gauss-Markoff theorem of least squares.

Case 1. *σ is known.* In this case we can find the best linear unbiased estimator μ^*_0 of the location parameter μ:

$$\left(\frac{\partial S}{\partial \mu}\right)_{\mu=\mu^*_0} = 0, \tag{5.3.1}$$

that is,

$$\left[\sum_{i=1}^{k} \frac{\lambda_{i+1} - \lambda_{i-1}}{(\lambda_{i+1} - \lambda_i)(\lambda_i - \lambda_{i-1})} f_i^2 - 2\sum_{i=2}^{k} \frac{f_i f_{i-1}}{\lambda_i - \lambda_{i-1}}\right]\mu^*_0$$

$$= -\sum_{i=1}^{k}\left(\frac{f_{i+1} - f_i}{\lambda_{i+1} - \lambda_i} - \frac{f_i - f_{i-1}}{\lambda_i - \lambda_{i-1}}\right) f_i(x_{(n_i)} - u_i\sigma)$$

to obtain

$$K_i\mu^*_0 = X - \sigma K_3 \tag{5.3.2}$$

where

$$X = \sum_{i=1}^{k+1} \frac{(f_i - f_{i-1})(f_i x_{(n_i)} - f_{i-1} x_{(n_{i-1})})}{\lambda_i - \lambda_{i-1}}. \tag{5.3.3}$$

Hence we have the best linear unbiased estimator μ^*_0:

$$\mu^*_0 = \frac{1}{K_1} X - \sigma \frac{K_3}{K_1}. \tag{5.3.4}$$

It can easily be seen that

$$V(\mu^*_0) = \frac{\sigma^2}{n} \frac{1}{K_1}. \tag{5.3.5}$$

From this we can see that the best linear unbiased estimator μ^*_0 is an "efficient estimator" from the point of view of relative efficiency.

If the frequency function $f(t)$ is symmetric with respect to the origin, and the spacing of the sample quantiles $x_{(n_1)}, x_{(n_2)}, \ldots, x_{(n_k)}$ is symmetric, that is,

$$n_i + n_{k-i+1} = n, \qquad i = 1, 2, \ldots, k \tag{5.3.6}$$

or in terms of λ_i

$$\lambda_i + \lambda_{k-i+1} = 1, \qquad i = 1, 2, \ldots, k, \tag{5.3.7}$$

then we have

$$u_i + u_{k-i+1} = 0, \qquad i = 1, 2, \ldots, k \tag{5.3.8}$$

and

$$f_i = f_{k-i+1}, \qquad i = 1, 2, \ldots, k. \tag{5.3.9}$$

In such a case it follows that

$$K_3 = 0. \tag{5.3.10}$$

Hence we have

$$\mu^*_0 = \frac{1}{K_1} X \tag{5.3.11}$$

and variance of μ^*_0 is the same as before.

Case 2. *μ is known.* In a similar way we can find the best linear unbiased estimator σ^*_0 of the scale parameter σ by solving the following equation:

$$\left(\frac{\partial S}{\partial \sigma}\right)_{\sigma=\sigma^*_0} = 0. \tag{5.3.12}$$

This turns out to be

$$K_2\sigma^*_0 = Y - \mu K_3 \tag{5.3.13}$$

where

$$Y = \sum_{i=1}^{k+1} \frac{(f_i u_i - f_{i-1}u_{i-1})(f_i x_{(n_i)} - f_{i-1}x_{(n_{i-1})})}{\lambda_i - \lambda_{i-1}}. \tag{5.3.14}$$

Hence we obtain

$$\sigma^*_0 = \frac{1}{K_2} Y - \mu \frac{K_3}{K_2}. \tag{5.3.15}$$

If the frequency function $f(t)$ is symmetric with respect to the origin and the spacing is symmetric, we have

$$\sigma^*_0 = \frac{1}{K_2} Y. \tag{5.3.16}$$

In any case, it can easily be shown that

$$V(\sigma^*_0) = \frac{\sigma^2}{n} \frac{1}{K_2}. \tag{5.3.17}$$

Thus we can see that σ^*_0 is the "efficient estimator" from the point of view of relative efficiency.

Case 3. *Both μ and σ are unknown.* In this case the best linear unbiased estimators μ^*, σ^*, of μ, σ are obtained from the following simultaneous equations:

$$\left(\frac{\partial S}{\partial \mu}\right)_{\substack{\mu=\mu^* \\ \sigma=\sigma^*}} = 0, \qquad \left(\frac{\partial S}{\partial \sigma}\right)_{\substack{\mu=\mu^* \\ \sigma=\sigma^*}} = 0. \tag{5.3.18}$$

This can be reduced in the following:

$$\begin{aligned} K_1 \cdot \mu^* + K_3 \cdot \sigma^* &= X \\ K_3 \cdot \mu^* + K_2 \cdot \sigma^* &= Y. \end{aligned} \tag{5.3.19}$$

Hence we have

$$\begin{aligned} \mu^* &= \frac{1}{\Delta}(K_2 X - K_3 Y) \\ \sigma^* &= \frac{1}{\Delta}(-K_3 X + K_1 Y) \end{aligned} \tag{5.3.20}$$

where

$$\Delta = K_1 K_2 - K_3^2. \tag{5.3.21}$$

It can be shown that

$$V(\mu^*) = \frac{\sigma^2}{n}\frac{K_2}{\Delta}, \qquad V(\sigma^*) = \frac{\sigma^2}{n}\frac{K_1}{\Delta}, \qquad \text{Cov}\,(\mu^*, \sigma^*) = -\frac{\sigma^2}{n}\frac{K_3}{\Delta}. \tag{5.3.22}$$

If $f(t)$ is symmetric and the spacing is also symmetric, then since $K_3 = 0$ by (5.2.21), we can see that μ^* and σ^* are asymptotically independent and they reduce to μ^*_0 and σ^*_0, respectively.

REFERENCES

1. H. Cramér, *Mathematical Methods of Statistics*, Princeton, 1946, pp. 497–506.
2. I. Higuchi, "On the solutions of certain simultaneous equations," *Ann. Inst. Statist. Math., Tokyo*, Vol. 5, No. 2 (1956), pp. 77–90.
3. F. Mosteller, "On some useful 'inefficient' statistics," *Ann. Math. Statist.*, Vol. 17 (1946), pp. 377–407.
4. J. Ogawa, "Contributions to the theory of systematic statistics, I," *Osaka Math. J.*, Vol. 3 (1951), pp. 175–213.

E. J. GUMBEL[1]

CHAPTER 6

Statistical Theory of Extreme Values (Main Results)

6.1 Introduction

The aim of the statistical theory of extreme values is to derive the distributions of certain order statistics and different combinations obtained therefrom, either for a given initial distribution and small sample sizes or asymptotically for certain types of initial distributions. The solution of the first problem leads to a decision whether a certain outlier should be rejected, the solution of the second one to a test for the regularity of a series of extremes and to their forecast. Lack of space forbids the inclusion of proofs. They may be found in the articles quoted or in reference 27.

We consider only continuous variables and start, in 6.2, by introducing certain statistical notions which are necessary for the analysis. The next section deals with the exact distribution of extremes, Sections 6.4 and 6.5 with the asymptotic distributions of extremes. The methods are generalized in Section 6.6 for extreme order statistics and in Section 6.7 to extremal functions. Finally, we briefly consider bivariate extremal distributions, although the solutions to this problem are still too general to allow for practical applications.

This chapter encompasses what has developed since reference 27 was finished, but no attempt has been made to cover questions arising from the estimation of the parameters.

[1] Work done in part under a grant from the National Science Foundation.

6.2 Definitions

A distribution is called *symmetrical* with respect to median zero if

$$F(-x) = 1 - F(x), \qquad f(-x) = f(x). \tag{6.2.1}$$

A natural generalization is the notion of *mutual symmetry* between two distributions identified by the indices 1 and 2. This holds if

$$F_1(-x) = 1 - F_2(x), \qquad f_1(-x) = f_2(x). \tag{6.2.1a}$$

If a moment generating function $G_1(t)$ for the first distribution exists, the moment generating function $G_2(t)$ for the second one is

$$G_2(t) = G_1(-t). \tag{6.2.1b}$$

It follows that the convolution (addition) of two variables which are mutually symmetrical creates a symmetrical distribution, but the subtraction of these two variables may create an asymmetrical distribution. The even central moments in these two new distributions are equal.

The expected value will be written $\bar{x}$, the median $\check{x}$, the mode $\tilde{x}$.

If we arrange n independent observations in increasing magnitude, these values are called order statistics $x_{(m)}$ where $m = 1, 2, \ldots, n-1$, n is counted from the bottom. The first $x_{(1)}$ is the *smallest* value, the last $x_{(n)}$ the *largest* one. If we speak of both at the same time, they are called *extremes.* A related notion is the *absolute extreme*, namely, $x_{(n)}$ or $-x_{(1)}$, whichever is larger. This notion is of interest if the distribution is symmetrical.

The number n is the sample size from which the extreme values of the initial distribution have been taken. If this operation is repeated N times, we obtain a sample of N extremes whose properties should conform to the theory of the extreme values to be derived in the following sections.

The difference w_n and the "midsum" v_n of the extremes [23]

$$w_n = x_{(n)} - x_{(1)}, \qquad v_n = x_{(n)} + x_{(1)} \tag{6.2.2}$$

are of specific interest if the initial distribution is symmetrical. The first is called the *range.* One-half of the midsum is called the center (and sometimes the midrange) [51].

For symmetrical initial distributions we may define the *extremal quotient* q_n by

$$q_n = x_{(n)}/(-x_{(1)}). \tag{6.2.3}$$

The absolute largest value, the range, the midrange, and the extremal quotient depend on the two extremes and are therefore called extremal functions.

Another notion is that of the *extreme distances* [10]. The first distance from the top, i_1, is defined as the difference

$$i_1 = x_{(n)} - x_{(n-1)}. \tag{6.2.4}$$

The *m*th distance from the top is

$$i_m = x_{(n-m+1)} - x_{(n-m)}. \tag{6.2.4a}$$

We now introduce two statistical functions, the return period and the intensity, needed for the analysis of the extremes. For observations which are equidistant in time, the number of observations has the dimension of time and the expression

$$T(x) = 1/[1 - F(x)] \tag{6.2.5}$$

is called the *return period* of a value equal to or larger than x. This is the expected number of observations necessary to obtain once a value exceeding x. The initial condition on $T(x)$ is

$$\lim_{x=-\infty} T(x) = 1. \tag{6.2.5a}$$

The return period increases with increasing values of x and without limit [1].

Related notions are the *characteristic* largest and smallest values $u_n(n) = u_n$ and $u_1(n) = u_1$. They are quantiles defined for a given initial distribution by

$$F(u_n) = 1 - 1/n, \qquad F(u_1) = 1/n. \tag{6.2.6}$$

The expected number of observations exceeding u_n or falling short of u_1 is equal to unity. By definition u_n increases and u_1 decreases with increasing sample sizes. For symmetrical distributions

$$u_1 = -u_n$$

and the same relation holds for two mutually symmetrical distributions.

The *intensity function* $\mu(x)$, defined by

$$\mu(x) = \frac{f(x)}{1 - F(x)} = -\frac{d}{dx} \lg [1 - F(x)], \tag{6.2.7}$$

where lg stands for the natural logarithm, becomes at the characteristic extreme values

$$\mu(u_n) = nf(u_n), \qquad \mu(u_1) = nf(u_1). \tag{6.2.7a}$$

These expressions are called *extremal intensities* and are written

$$\alpha_n = \mu(u_n), \qquad \alpha_1 = \mu(u_1). \tag{6.2.7b}$$

For symmetrical distributions the two values are equal. The intensity function may increase, remain constant, or decrease with increasing values of n.

Since for distributions which are unlimited in both directions the values u_n and u_1 increase in absolute size with increasing n and since $1/\alpha_n$ and $1/\alpha_1$ have the same dimension as x, they are used in order to reduce the extremes. The values y_n and y_1 defined by

$$y_n = \alpha_n(x_{(n)} - u_n), \qquad y_1 = \alpha_1(x_{(1)} - u_1) \tag{6.2.8}$$

are called *reduced extremes*. In contrast to the extremes proper, the reduced extremes have no dimensions. This linear reduction is preferable to the usual *standardization*

$$t_n = (x_{(n)} - \bar{x}_n)/\sigma_n, \qquad t_1 = (x_{(1)} - \bar{x}_1)/\sigma_1 \tag{6.2.8a}$$

where $\bar{x}_n$ and $\bar{x}_1$ and σ_n and σ_1 stand for the expectation and standard deviations of the extremes. The reduction (6.2.8) is always possible, whereas standardization is possible only when the first two moments of the variable exist. Since both procedures are linear, there is also a linear relation between y_n and t_n, y_1 and t_1.

For symmetrical distributions the reduction (6.2.8) may also be used for the range w_n which spreads in the two directions. The expression

$$R_n = \alpha_n(w_n - 2u_n) \tag{6.2.9}$$

is called the *reduced range*. The range w_n is nonnegative, but this is not so of the reduced range where

$$R_n \geq -2\alpha_n u_n. \tag{6.2.9a}$$

In addition to the extremes proper we introduce the notion of the *m*th *extremes*, that is, the second, third, fourth, etc. value from the top or from the bottom, especially when the rank m is small compared to the sample size n. For symmetrical initial distributions the distribution of the mth largest value is symmetrical to the distribution of the mth smallest value. Easy generalizations of (6.2.6) lead to the *characteristic* m*th extreme values*

$$u_m(n) = u_m, \qquad {}_mu(n) = {}_mu.$$

which are the quantiles defined by

$$F(u_m) = 1 - m/n, \qquad F({}_mu) = m/n. \tag{6.2.10}$$

For the largest (smallest) values m is counted here from the top (bottom).

The extremal mth intensities

$$\alpha_m(n) = \alpha_m, \qquad {}_m\alpha(n) = {}_m\alpha$$

are defined by

$$\alpha_m = nf(u_m)/m, \qquad {}_m\alpha = nf({}_mu)/m. \tag{6.2.11}$$

For symmetrical distributions the *m*th characteristic largest and smallest values are equal in magnitude and different in sign, whereas the intensities are equal. As before, the expressions

$$y_{m,n} = y_m, \qquad {}_my_n = {}_my$$

defined as

$$y_m = \alpha_m(x - u_m), \qquad {}_my = {}_m\alpha(x - {}_mu) \tag{6.2.12}$$

are called the *reduced* m*th extremes.*

The *m*th range w_m and the *m*th midsum v_m are defined [41, 53] as the difference and the sum of the *m*th extremes, respectively. The reduced *m*th range R_m is defined in analogy to (6.2.9) by

$$R_m = \alpha_m(w_m - 2u_m). \tag{6.2.13}$$

For symmetrical distributions the reduced V_m sum of the *m*th extremes is the sum v_m itself multiplied by α_m. If there is no ambiguity, complicated indices are omitted.

6.3 Exact and Asymptotic Properties

The probability that all *n* independent observations taken from a population with known probability function $F(x)$ are smaller than a certain value x is evidently $F^n(x)$. This is also the probability $\Phi_n(x)$ that the largest among *n* independent observations is smaller than x:

$$\Phi_n(x) = F^n(x). \tag{6.3.1}$$

In the following the condition of independence is assumed to hold, and this premise will not be repeated. But the reader should keep in mind that this assumption is an important restriction. The whole theory of extreme values consists in the analysis of the simple and exact expression (6.3.1). The first consequence is that the largest value of a statistical variable is not fixed but a new statistical variable, a triviality which some "practical" people often fail to realize. If the initial distribution is limited (or not), the same holds for the largest value.

The properties of $\Phi_n(x)$ depend mainly on the properties of $F(x)$ for large values of x. The larger *n* is, the smaller becomes the influence of the rest of the distribution. If *n* and $F(x)$ are known, analytically or numerically, all probability functions $\Phi_n(x)$ are known too. For increasing values of *n* they form a system of curves shifted to the right, and the question is whether they expand or contract with increasing *n* or tend to asymptotic forms.

The probability function $\Pi_n(x)$ for the smallest value to be larger than x is obtained in the same way as (6.3.1) from

$$\Pi_n(x) = [1 - F(x)]^n. \tag{6.3.2}$$

The density functions $\phi_n(x)$ and $\pi_n(x)$ corresponding to (6.3.1) and (6.3.2) are

$$\phi_n(x) = nF^{n-1}(x)f(x), \qquad \pi_n(x) = n[1 - F(x)]^{n-1}f(x). \qquad (6.3.3)$$

If the initial distribution is symmetrical, the distributions of the largest and of the smallest values are mutually symmetrical in the sense of (6.2.1*a*). Generally, for any given distribution of a largest value we can construct a distribution of a smallest value. If the initial distribution for which we constructed the distribution of the largest value is not symmetrical, the initial distribution corresponding to the second formula in (6.3.3) will be symmetrical to it. This relation is called the *symmetry principle*. The practical consequence is that the study of extreme values may be restricted to that of the largest value, and the same holds for the mth extremes.

If the initial distribution is symmetrical with respect to zero, the probability that the largest value will be positive (and the smallest value negative) converges quickly with increasing sample sizes toward unity.

Dugué [13] has proved three theorems for the quotients $x_{(n)}/n$ and $x_{(1)}/n$ valid if the sample size increases without limit.

1. An infinite sequence of random variables Z_v, with $v = 1, 2, \ldots$, is said to converge in probability to zero if there exists a number N such that for any $n > N$ the probability that $|Z_n|$ will be larger than zero is smaller than ϵ, where ϵ is arbitrarily small. Then his first theorem states: The quotients $x_{(n)}/n$ and $x_{(1)}/n$ both converge in probability to zero if

$$\lim_{x=\infty} x[1 - F(x) + F(-x)] = 0. \qquad (6.3.4)$$

2. Every outcome of the entire sequence of random variables Z_n, with $n \geq 1$, can be represented by a point in an Euclidian space of infinite dimension, the point having the coordinates $(Z_1, Z_2, \ldots, Z_n, \ldots)$. The sequence is said to converge almost surely to zero if the domain of points such that Z_n tends to zero as n becomes infinite has probability one. Then the second theorem states: The quotients $x_{(n)}/n$ and $x_{(1)}/n$ converge almost surely to zero if the first absolute moment exists.

3. The same sequence is said to converge with almost complete certainty to zero if any other sequence of random variable with the same marginal distribution (but with any other correlation) converges almost surely to zero. Then the third theorem states: The quotients $x_{(n)}/n$ and $x_{(1)}/n$ converge with almost complete certainty to zero if the second moment exists. The conditions in these theorems are necessary and sufficient.

Consider now the averages of the largest value. It is easy to calculate the median $\breve{x}_n$ of the largest value as a function of n and to obtain all quantiles of the extremes by an appropriate reduction. All these quantiles increase with n. From (6.3.1) it follows that

$$\Phi_n(u_n) \rightarrow 1/e \leftarrow \Pi_n(u_1) \tag{6.3.5}$$

and for the density functions that

$$\phi_n(u_n) \rightarrow \alpha/e \leftarrow \pi_n(u_1). \tag{6.3.6}$$

Hence, the characteristic values and the median of the extremes are such that

$$u_n < \breve{x}_n, \qquad u_1 > \breve{x}_1. \tag{6.3.7}$$

The mode of the largest value is, from (6.3.3), the solution $x = \tilde{x}_n$ of

$$\frac{n-1}{F(x)} f(x) = -\frac{f'(x)}{f(x)}. \tag{6.3.8}$$

If the initial distribution is such that L'Hôpital's rule holds in the form

$$-\frac{f'(x)}{f(x)} \rightarrow \frac{f(x)}{1-F(x)}, \tag{6.3.9}$$

the modal largest value converges toward the characteristic largest value. The condition (6.3.9) may also be written

$$\frac{\mu(x)}{-f'(x)/f(x)} \rightarrow \begin{cases} 1 + |\epsilon(x)| \\ 1 \\ 1 - |\epsilon(x)| \end{cases} \tag{6.3.9a}$$

with

$$\lim_{x=\infty} |\epsilon(x)| = 0. \tag{6.3.9b}$$

The condition (6.3.9) is exact for the exponential distribution. It holds asymptotically for the logistic, the normal, the log-normal, and the gamma distributions.

The calculation of the expected largest value $\bar{x}_n$ and of the moments requires, in general, complicated numerical procedures. If the mean μ and the standard deviation σ of the initial distribution exist, there is an upper limit for $\bar{x}_n$ as a function of the sample size, namely

$$\bar{x}_n \leq \mu + \sigma \frac{n-1}{\sqrt{2n-1}}. \tag{6.3.10}$$

If n is large, the expected largest value for any continuous variable which possesses the first two moments increases more slowly than $\sqrt{n/2}$ times the initial standard deviation. If the initial distribution is symmetrical, the limit can be narrowed down to

$$\bar{x}_n \leq \mu + \sigma(\sqrt{n})/2. \tag{6.3.10a}$$

The exact probability functions $\Phi_n(w_n)$ and $\Phi^*_n(v_n)$ of the range w_n and of the midsum v_n defined in (6.2.2) are

$$\Phi_n(w_n) = n\int_{-\infty}^{\infty} [F(x + w_n) - F(x)]^{n-1}\, dF(x) \qquad (6.3.11)$$

$$\Phi^*_n(v_n) = n\int_{-\infty}^{v/2} [F(v - x) - F(x)]^{n-1}\, dF(x). \qquad (6.3.11a)$$

These beautiful formulas are not of much use since, in general, the probability functions $F(x + w)$ and $F(v - x)$ cannot be expressed by $F(x)$.

The range increases with the sample size. For a symmetrical distribution the maximum of the mean range $\bar{w}_n$ as a function of the sample size is for unit standard deviation

$$\bar{w}_n \leq n\sqrt{2(1 - \epsilon_n)/(2n - 1)} \qquad (6.3.12)$$

where

$$\epsilon_n = \frac{(n - 1)!^2}{(2n - 2)!} \qquad (6.3.12a)$$

becomes very small if n is large. Asymptotically the mean range increases more slowly than $\sqrt{n}$.

The range and the initial mean are uncorrelated for symmetrical distributions. But the converse is not always true. Correlation zero does not imply symmetry [49].

To clarify the different results, consider some simple initial distributions. For the exponential distribution the averages of the largest value and its variance σ_n^2 are easily obtained as functions of n, namely

$$\begin{gathered} u_n = \tilde{x}_n = \lg n, \qquad \check{x}_n \to \lg n - \lg \lg 2, \\ \bar{x}_n \to \lg n + \gamma, \qquad \alpha_n = 1, \qquad \sigma_n \to \pi/\sqrt{6}, \end{gathered} \qquad (6.3.13)$$

where lg stands for the natural logarithm and γ is Euler's number. The most probable largest value is thus equal to the characteristic largest value, and the intensity function is constant and equal to unity. Similar properties hold for the logistic distribution where

$$\begin{gathered} u_n = \lg (n - 1), \qquad \tilde{x}_n \to \lg n, \qquad \check{x}_n = \lg n - \lg \lg 2, \\ \bar{x}_n \to \lg n + \gamma, \qquad \alpha_n = 1 - 1/n, \qquad \sigma_n \to \pi/\sqrt{6}. \end{gathered} \qquad (6.3.13a)$$

Since the initial variance is $\pi^2/3$, the asymptotic variance of the largest value is only one-half the initial one.

The smallest value for an exponential distribution behaves rather differently from the largest one since its probability function

$$\Pi_n(x) = e^{-nx} = \Pi(nx) \tag{6.3.14}$$

is the initial function itself, except for a linear transformation of the variable. If this property holds, a distribution of the extreme value is called *stable*.

For practical reasons most work on the exact distribution of extremes had been done for the normal distribution. Here the analytical properties are rather complicated, and no simple, general expressions can be obtained. The most probable largest value is derived from (6.3.8) as the solution $x = \tilde{x}_n$ of

$$n - 1 = xF(x)/f(x)$$

which converges slowly to

$$\tilde{x}_n = \sqrt{2 \lg 0.4n}. \tag{6.3.15}$$

The characteristic largest value can only be expressed by the series

$$1/n = f(u)[1 - u^{-2} + 3u^{-4} - 15u^{-6} + \ldots]/u \tag{6.3.16}$$

where $u = u_n$. The extremal intensity,

$$\alpha_n = u + u^{-1} - 2u^{-3} + 10u^{-5} - \ldots \tag{6.3.17}$$

increases with increasing sample size and converges very slowly to the characteristic largest value.

Tables for $\tilde{x}_n$, u_n, α_n are given in reference 27. A table for the expected largest value $\bar{x}_n$ as a function of n calculated by Tippett may be found in Karl Pearson's *Tables*, Volume 2 [50], which also gives an excellent summary on normal extremes. H. A. David [11] calculated tables of the upper percentage points for the extreme studentized normal values based on an independent estimate of the variance with $\nu = 10(1)20(10)100, 120, \infty$ degrees of freedom and for the sample sizes $n = 3(1)12$.

Dronkers [12] gave a new expansion for $1 - F(x)$ with the help of the function

$$\frac{d}{dx}\left[\frac{f(x)}{f'(x)}\right].$$

His work is closely related to the methods of R. von Mises [45]. In particular, he considered the largest values for the normal distribution where his expansion is identical with the classical one. He studied different transitional distributions of largest normal values valid for certain domains of n and justified them by comparing them to the numerical values of the exact distributions.

The normal range is often used as a substitute for the standard deviation, but the integration of (6.3.11) can be carried out exactly for normal ranges only if n equals 2 and 3. Therefore most work on normal ranges has been done by numerical methods [50].

Moore [46] gave tables for testing the equality of means of two samples taken from normal populations with a common unknown standard deviation σ. The two samples have different sizes varying from 2 to 20, and the estimate of σ is based on the range. Bliss [4] gave a rejection criterion for outlying normal observations, based on the value of the largest range as compared to the mean of the ranges, and tables to use this method for $k = 2(1)10$ samples each consisting of $n = 2(1)10$ independent observations.

Kudô [43] provided a test to be applied to a multivariate normal sample with known variance-covariance matrix; the test distinguishes an observation which is so extreme that it may be considered to be discordant from the rest and should, therefore, be rejected. The test is based on the maximum of

$$\sum_{i,j} \sigma^{ij}(x_i^{(\nu)} - \bar{x}_i)(x_j^{(\nu)} - \bar{x}_j), \qquad \nu = 1, 2, \ldots, n.$$

In a second article [44] he considers a normally distributed random vector $(x_1, x_2, \ldots, x_n)$ with mean zero and a covariance matrix such that the diagonal is σ^2 and all other cells are $\sigma^2\rho$. From the inversion of the characteristic function he derives an infinite series expansion for the density function of the vector. Finally he gives tables for the probability function of $\max\limits_{i \le n} x_{(i)}$. See also reference 55.

For the logarithmic normal distribution the characteristic largest value $u_{n,g}$ and the extremal intensity $\alpha_{n,g}$ are asymptotically related to the corresponding normal values u_n and α_n by

$$u_{n,g} = e^{u_n}, \qquad \alpha_{n,g} = \alpha_n e^{-u_n}. \tag{6.3.18}$$

In this case $\alpha_{n,g}$ decreases with increase in sample size, in contrast to the normal case.

6.4 Asymptotic Distributions

The exact distributions of extreme values are analytically simple but numerically complicated. The asymptotic distributions are analytically complicated but numerically simple. Within the exact theory of extreme values the initial parameters are preserved. In the asymptotic theory two new parameters enter, the characteristic extreme and the extremal intensity function, introduced in the second section. They depend on the asymptotic behavior of the initial distribution toward the extreme values of the variable.

The probability function $\Phi_n(x)$ of the largest value may be written from (6.3.1):

$$\Phi_n(x) = e^{n \lg F(x)}. \tag{6.4.1}$$

For large values of n the relevant part of $F(x)$ approaches unity and the exponent converges to the indeterminate product $\infty \cdot 0$. Therefore its value depends on the way $F(x)$ approaches unity. In order to obtain asymptotic expressions for the extreme value, we have to make certain assumptions about the asymptotic properties of the initial distribution. The existence of asymptotic expressions is thus linked to certain conditions. If they are not fulfilled, no asymptotic distribution of extreme values exists for a given initial distribution.

The asymptotic theory of extreme values has been studied from two angles. The first procedure, used by R. von Mises [45], starts from certain asymptotic properties of a given initial distribution at large values of the variable and shows that the corresponding distributions of the largest values converge to certain expressions.

In the second procedure a stability is postulated, namely, that the distribution of the maximum in a sample of size n taken from the distribution of the largest value should be this distribution itself except for a linear transformation of the variable. Thus the probability function $\Phi(x)$ of the largest value has to satisfy the functional equation

$$\Phi^n(x) = \Phi(a_n x + b_n) \tag{6.4.2}$$

for all integers $n \geq 2$, and for constants $a_n > 0$ and b_n to be determined.

The first solution was given by Fréchet [17]. Later the same solution and two others were found by Fisher and Tippett [16]. Finally Gnedenko [25] proved that only these three solutions exist. He found necessary and sufficient conditions on the initial distributions for the convergence of distributions of the largest value to one of the three asymptotic distributions.

The properties of the initial distributions will now be explained.

1. For the *exponential type* the probability $P(x) = 1 - F(x)$ of a value larger than x converges to zero for large values of the variable at least as strongly as the exponential function e^{-x} converges to zero. Most of the distributions used in statistics, such as the exponential, the normal, the log-normal, the logistic, and the gamma distribution, belong to this category. In these examples all moments of the initial variable and of its largest value exist. But the existence of all moments does not imply that the distribution is of the exponential type.

2. Other distributions, which are also unlimited, have a very long tail, such that the higher moments do not exist. Since this holds for Cauchy's distribution, it may be called the Cauchy type. It was first studied by Fréchet [17]. This type is rarely used in practical statistics.

3. There are certain distributions having an upper (or lower) limit ω (or ϵ). Then the largest value has this upper limit ω and the smallest value this lower limit ϵ. The limits enter as parameters in the distribution of the extremes.

A distribution may belong to a certain type from the standpoint of the largest value but need not belong to it from the standpoint of the smallest value and vice-versa.

The derivation of the three asymptotic distributions of largest values is explained in Table A. It shows the asymptotic properties of the intensity function $\mu(x)$, of the initial probability functions $F(x)$, and of the resulting asymptotic probability functions $\Phi(x)$. Gnedenko's [25] necessary and sufficient conditions on the initial distribution for the validity of the three types are given in the last line.

The three asymptotic distributions can be written down in closed form and are thus analytically simpler than, for example, the normal or the gamma distributions.

The parameters k for the second and third type are linked to the intensity function in Table A. Other interpretations are possible, however. For the third type it is the order of the first derivative of the probability function that does not vanish at the upper limit. The second type is often called Fréchet's type [17].

The approach of the exact distributions of largest values to their asymptotic forms are different for different initial distributions. It is quick for the exponential but slow for the normal distribution [16]. If the asymptotic distribution of extremes are considered as initial ones, the stability principle states that the asymptotic form is reached already for $n = 2$.

The symmetry principle explained previously leads from the asymptotic distributions of the largest value to the corresponding three asymptotic distributions of the smallest value.

The six asymptotic probability functions of extreme values are given in Table B. The first column gives the probabilities $\Phi_{(x)}$ of the largest value to be equal to or less than x. The second column gives the probabilities $\Pi(x)$ of the smallest value to be equal or greater than x. The corresponding density functions are then ϕ and π respectively. The transformations are obtained by introducing

$$y = -\lg\,[-\lg \Phi(x)], \qquad y = \lg\,[-\lg \Pi(x)] \tag{6.4.3}$$

in the first and second columns respectively.

The second and third distributions can be reduced to the first one by logarithmic transformations and by the limiting process $k \to \infty$. This is shown in Table C.

TABLE A

THE THREE ASYMPTOTIC PROBABILITY FUNCTIONS OF LARGEST VALUES

	Exponential Type	Cauchy Type	Limited Type
Intensity function	$\frac{\mu(x)}{f'(x)/f(x)} \to 1 + \epsilon$	$x\mu(x) \to k$	$\frac{\mu(x)}{\omega - x} \to k$
Condition	$\epsilon \to 0$	$k > 0$	$k > 0,\ x < \omega$
Initial probability for large x	$1 - \frac{1}{n} e^{-\alpha_n(x-u_n)}$	$1 - \frac{1}{n}\left(\frac{x - \epsilon}{u_n - \epsilon}\right)^{-k}$	$1 - \frac{1}{n}\left(\frac{\omega - x}{\omega - u_n}\right)^{k}$
Asymptotic probability $\Phi(x)$	$\exp(-e^{-\alpha_n(x-u_n)})$	$\exp\left[-\left(\frac{x - \epsilon}{u_n - \epsilon}\right)^{-k}\right]$	$\exp\left[-\left(\frac{\omega - x}{\omega - u_n}\right)^{k}\right]$
Gnedenko's condition	$\lim_{n=\infty} nP(u_n + x/\alpha_n) = e^{-x}$	$\lim_{x=\infty} \frac{P(x)}{P(cx)} = c^k$ $c > 0$	$\lim_{x=-0} \frac{P(cx + \omega)}{P(x + \omega)} = c^k$ $c > 0$

TABLE B

The Three Asymptotic Distributions of Extremes

	Largest Value	Smallest Value
Probability I	$\Phi^{(1)}(x) = \exp(-e^{-\alpha(x-u)})$	$\Pi^{(1)}(x) = \exp(-e^{\alpha(x-u)})$
Domain	$-\infty < x < \infty$	$-\infty < x < \infty$
Transformation	$x = u + y/\alpha$	$x = u + y/\alpha$
Curvature	$d^2x/dy^2 = 0$	$d^2x/dy^2 = 0$
Density I	$\phi^{(1)}(x) = \alpha e^{-\alpha(x-u)}\Phi^{(1)}(x)$	$\pi^{(1)}(x) = \alpha e^{\alpha(x-u)}\Pi^{(1)}(x)$
Probability II	$\Phi^{(2)}(x) = \exp\left[-\left(\frac{x-\epsilon}{u-\epsilon}\right)^{-k}\right]$	$\Pi^{(2)}(x) = \exp\left[-\left(\frac{\omega-x}{\omega-u}\right)^{-k}\right]$
Domain	$x \geq \epsilon,\ u > \epsilon,\ k > 0$	$x \leq \omega,\ u < \omega,\ k > 0$
Transformation	$x = \epsilon + (u-\epsilon)e^{y/k}$	$x = \omega + (\omega - u)e^{-y/k}$
Curvature	$d^2x/dy^2 > 0$	$d^2x/dy^2 < 0$
Density II	$\phi^{(2)}(x) = \frac{k}{u-\epsilon}\left(\frac{x-\epsilon}{u-\epsilon}\right)^{-k-1}\Phi^{(2)}(x)$	$\pi^{(2)}(x) = \frac{k}{\omega-u}\left(\frac{\omega-x}{\omega-u}\right)^{-k-1}\Pi^{(2)}(x)$
Probability III	$\Phi^{(3)}(x) = \exp\left[-\left(\frac{\omega-x}{\omega-u}\right)^{k}\right]$	$\Pi^{(3)}(x) = \exp\left[-\left(\frac{x-\epsilon}{u-\epsilon}\right)^{k}\right]$
Domain	$x \leq \omega,\ u < \omega,\ k > 0$	$x \geq \epsilon,\ u > \epsilon,\ k > 0$
Transformation	$x = \omega - (\omega - u)e^{-y/k}$	$x = \epsilon + (u-\epsilon)e^{y/k}$
Curvature	$d^2x/dy^2 < 0$	$d^2x/dy^2 > 0$
Density III	$\phi^{(3)}(x) = \frac{k}{\omega-u}\left(\frac{\omega-x}{\omega-u}\right)^{k-1}\Phi^{(3)}(x)$	$\pi^{(3)}(x) = \frac{k}{u-\epsilon}\left(\frac{x-\epsilon}{u-\epsilon}\right)^{k-1}\Pi^{(3)}(x)$

TABLE C

LOGARITHMIC TRANSFORMATIONS AND LIMITING TRANSITIONS FROM THE SECOND AND THIRD TO THE FIRST DISTRIBUTION

Transformation $\alpha = k$	Largest Values	Smallest Values
Second distribution	$u - \epsilon = e^{w}$	$\omega - u = e^{-w}$
Variable	$x - \epsilon = e^{z}$	$\omega - x = e^{-z}$
Result	$\exp(-e^{-\alpha(z-w)}) = \Phi^{(1)}(z)$	$\exp(-e^{\alpha(z-w)}) = \Pi^{(1)}(z)$
Third distribution	$\omega - u = e^{-v}$	$u - \epsilon = e^{v}$
Variable	$\omega - x = e^{-t}$	$x - \epsilon = e^{t}$
Result	$\exp(-e^{-\alpha(t-v)}) = \Phi^{(1)}(t)$	$\exp(-e^{\alpha(t-v)}) = \Pi^{(1)}(t)$
Limiting process	$1/k \to 0,\ k \to \infty$	
Second-distribution transformation	$\dfrac{u - \epsilon}{x - \epsilon} = \left(1 + \dfrac{z}{k}\right)^{-1}$	$\dfrac{\omega - x}{\omega - u} = \left(1 - \dfrac{z}{k}\right)$
Result	$\exp(-e^{-z}) = \Phi^{(1)}(z)$	$\exp(-e^{z}) = \Pi^{(1)}(z)$
Third-distribution transformation	$\dfrac{\omega - x}{\omega - u} = 1 - \dfrac{t}{k}$	$\dfrac{x - \epsilon}{u - \epsilon} = 1 + \dfrac{t}{k}$
Result	$\exp(-e^{-t}) = \Phi^{(1)}(t)$	$\exp(-e^{t}) = \Pi^{(1)}(t)$

6.5 The Three Types

The most important of the three asymptotic distributions is the first one. Most analytical, numerical, and practical studies on extreme values have been done for this type [28, 36]. It holds for the extremes of the normal and logistic distributions and for the largest values of the exponential, the logarithmic normal, and the gamma distributions.

The first asymptotic distribution is analytically very simple; the density function $\phi(y)$ is related to the probability function $\Phi(y)$ by

$$\phi(y) = \Phi(y)[-\lg \Phi(y)], \qquad y = \alpha_n(x - u_n). \tag{6.5.1}$$

Tables for Φ and ϕ as functions of y, for the inverse $y(\Phi)$, and for the relation (6.5.1) have been published by the National Bureau of Standards [48]. The return period T defined in (6.2.5) becomes asymptotically

$$\lg T(x) = y. \tag{6.5.2}$$

The two parameters u_n and α_n in the distribution of the largest value are positive and their product increases with n. However, $\alpha_n u_n/n$ converges to zero with increasing n.

The mean deviation ϑ_n taken about the median $\breve{x}_n$ is related to the parameter α_n by

$$\vartheta_n = \frac{0.96805}{\alpha_n}. \tag{6.5.3}$$

Thus $1/\alpha_n$ is a measure of dispersion. All moments exist. The moment generating functions $G_n(t)$ and $G_1(t)$ for the reduced largest and smallest values are

$$G_n(t) = \Gamma(1 - t), \qquad G_1(t) = \Gamma(1 + t). \tag{6.5.4}$$

Hence the expected values of the extremes are

$$\bar{x}_n = u_n + \frac{\gamma}{\alpha_n}, \qquad \bar{x}_1 = u_1 - \frac{\gamma}{\alpha_1} \tag{6.5.5}$$

where $\gamma = 0.57722$ stands for Euler's number. The standard deviations are

$$\sigma_n = \frac{\pi}{\sqrt{6}\alpha_n}, \qquad \sigma_1 = \frac{\pi}{\sqrt{6}\alpha_1}. \tag{6.5.6}$$

These relations have an interesting consequence. If α_n increases with n, the standard deviation of the largest value decreases with the size of the sample from which the largest value was taken. This holds, for example, for the normal distribution. However, if α_n is a constant, independent of n, as for the exponential distribution, we cannot decrease the standard deviation of the largest value by increasing the sample size. Finally if α_n decreases with increasing values of n (as for the logarithmic normal distribution), an increase of the sample size from which the largest value has been taken increases the standard deviation of the largest value. The same argument holds for α_1 and the smallest value.

The product $\alpha_n u_n$ is related to the coefficient of variation V_n of the largest values by

$$\alpha_n u_n = \frac{\pi}{\sqrt{6}V_n} - \gamma. \tag{6.5.7}$$

The usual standardized variable

$$t = \frac{x - \bar{x}_n}{\sigma_n} \tag{6.5.8}$$

is related to the reduced value y by

$$t = \frac{\sqrt{6}(y - \gamma)}{\pi}. \tag{6.5.9}$$

Formulas (6.5.6) to (6.5.9) have an important bearing on the nature of the parameters. Up to now they were related by (6.2.6) and (6.2.7*a*) to the initial distributions and to the sample size n, both of which were assumed to be known. Now they become part of the asymptotic distribution and may be estimated from the extreme values alone. This property is important since the initial distribution is unknown in most practical applications. In this case we omit the indices n.

The Gomperz formula for the probability $l(x)$ of surviving age x is a special case of an extremal distribution of the first type. Let u be the modal age at death and let α be the intensity function (force of mortality) at this age. Then the Gomperz formula

$$l(x) = l(u) \exp (1 - e^{\alpha(x-u)}) \tag{6.5.10}$$

is the first asymptotic probability function of smallest values with the boundary condition $x \geq 0$.

The simplest procedure for the estimation of parameters is based on the construction of a probability paper. The variable x is used as ordinate and the reduced variable y as abscissa, both in linear scales. A parallel to the abscissa shows the probability $\Phi(y)$. The largest observations x_m arranged in increasing magnitude are plotted at the positions $m/(N + 1)$ where N indicates the number of largest values. If the theory holds, the observations should be scattered closely about the increasing straight line

$$x = u + y/\alpha. \tag{6.5.11}$$

The same procedure may be applied to smallest values by changing y into $-y$. The observations are plotted in decreasing order of magnitude at $1 - m/(N + 1)$. Then the smallest values should be scattered about the decreasing straight line (6.5.11). Thus the use of the probability paper reduces the analysis of extreme values to the fitting of straight lines. If the return period is plotted on a second parallel to the abscissa, the paper leads, by the extrapolation of the straight line, to an easy forecast of extremes as functions of time.

The plotting position advocated here is based on the expectation $\bar{F}(x_m)$ of the cumulative frequency function at the mth value and is therefore distribution-free. This allows the comparison of observations plotted on different probability papers, that is, the comparison of different analytical interpretations. The method has the advantage that the return period of the largest value is $N + 1$, that is, near to the number of observations. This property is essential for the forecast of observations which are equidistant in time or for the extrapolation to larger sample sizes. Other considerations such as minimizing the errors of estimation of certain parameters lead to other plotting positions advocated by Blom [5], Chernoff [8], and Kimball [42]. Then the return period of the largest observation $T(x_N)$ is much larger than N. The plotting position acts as if we had a greater sample size than we actually do. Incidentally, no procedure should ever be used where the plotting position of the $(m + 1)$st value is smaller than that of the mth value.

The extremal probability paper is used by the Geological Survey for the analysis of floods and by the Weather Bureau for the analysis of climatological data such as largest rainfalls, snowfalls, atmospheric pressure, wind speeds, largest and smallest temperatures [58]. Hershfield and Kohler [40] studied the predictive value of the first-type distributions: "Thousands of station-years of rainfall data have been analysed in several ways in an attempt to evaluate this procedure. The results provide evidence for the acceptability of the Gumbel procedure for predicting the probability of occurrence of the extreme values of rainfall." Henry [39] used the first asymptotic distribution for the analysis of sickness data.

The second and third types possess upper or lower limits ω and ϵ, respectively. The characteristic values and the limits are independent except for the evident conditions $\omega > u > \epsilon$. The third parameter k is linked to the limits, however. In order to see this important relation, it is sufficient to consider the third asymptotic distribution of smallest values. The second transformation in (6.4.3) leads to

$$\lg (x - \epsilon) = \lg (u - \epsilon) + y/k. \qquad (6.5.12)$$

Thus $1/k$ measures the increase of $\lg (x - \epsilon)$ with increasing values of y. Assume now $\epsilon = 0$; then

$$\lg x = \lg u + y/k_1 \qquad (6.5.12a)$$

is linear in $\lg x$, and $1/k_1$ measures the increase of $\lg x$ with increasing values of y. Thus k and k_1 measure different relations. The same holds for any two different values $\epsilon_1 \neq \epsilon_2$. The value of $1/k_1$ may even have a smaller order of magnitude than $1/k$.

The first distribution can be reduced by a linear transformation to an expression which does not contain any parameters. This is not possible for the second and third distribution except in the trivial cases $k = 1$. However we may reduce these distributions to a form which contains only one parameter, namely k.

To make this clear consider the third distribution of smallest values. All moments $\overline{(x - \epsilon)^\nu}$ of order ν exist for any positive value of ν. They are

$$\overline{(x - \epsilon)^\nu} = (u - \epsilon)^\nu \Gamma(1 + \nu/k). \qquad (6.5.13)$$

If we write

$$B = B(k) = [\Gamma(1 + 2/k) - \Gamma^2(1 + 1/k)]^{-1/2}, \qquad (6.5.13a)$$

the expectation $\bar{x}$, the standard deviation σ, and the characteristic value u are related by

$$\bar{x} - \epsilon = (u - \epsilon)\Gamma(1 + 1/k), \qquad \sigma = (u - \epsilon)/B. \qquad (6.5.14)$$

The usual standardization leads to the probability function

$$\Pi(t) = \exp\{-[\Gamma(1 + 1/k) + t/B]^k\}, \qquad t = (x - \bar{x})/\sigma. \quad (6.5.15)$$

The lower limit and the characteristic value are eliminated, but the factor k remains. The probability function $\Pi(t)$ has the properties

$$\Pi(\infty) = 0, \qquad \Pi[B - B\Gamma(1 + 1/k)] = 1/e, \qquad \Pi[-B\Gamma(1 + 1/k)] = 1. \quad (6.5.15a)$$

A similar reduction is possible for the second distribution of largest values provided k is larger than 3.

For the analysis of observed extremes we need the estimation of the parameters (see Section 12C). The use of the probability paper reduces this problem for the second and third types to the fitting of straight lines for the logarithms if the limits are known. If we interpret y from (6.5.2) as the logarithm of the return period, the largest values increase in the first distribution as a linear function of the logarithm of time. In the second one the logarithms of the variables increase as linear functions of the logarithm of time. Therefore the second distribution leads to a larger forecast than the first one. This distribution has been used by Bernier [2, 3] and Gumbel et al. [36] for the analysis of floods.

The limits of the third distribution may be estimated by the method of moments, but the procedure is not quite satisfactory, especially for small samples. In particular, this method does not guarantee that the estimated lower limit falls short of the smallest observation. On the other hand, the method of maximum likelihood requires approximations that can barely be handled by standard equipment.

For $k = 1$ the third distribution of smallest values is the exponential function [7]. The case $k = 2$ is called Rayleigh's distribution. The extreme values taken from a uniform distribution have the third asymptotic distribution. The same holds for the smallest values taken from the exponential and the gamma distributions.

The third asymptotic distribution of the smallest values has two important practical applications. It has been used by W. Weibull [59] in a purely empirical way, with no connection to the theory of extreme values, for the analysis of breaking strengths and fatigue of metals. The lower limits in terms of life are the minimum life, in terms of stresses the endurances. Their estimation is essential for the safety of structures [19, 20]. The second application is the analysis of droughts [31, 36]. Velz [57] analyzed the droughts of 160 rivers in Michigan with the help of extreme-value paper. The estimation of the lower limit was made by graphical procedures. He obtained good results for the daily averages, 7 days, 15 days, 30 days, and monthly averages of the droughts and applied these methods to the solution of many hydrological problems.

If the analytical form of the initial distribution is unknown and only the extreme values are available, it is, in general, possible to decide the type of distribution to which the variable belongs. Physical conditions may indicate whether upper or lower limits exist and of what order of magnitude they are. A further indication of the type may be obtained by the use of probability paper. If the observations clearly depart from the straight line, the curvatures given in Table B may indicate which of the three distributions should be chosen. As with all graphical procedures, however, this method may not always lead to a clear decision, especially for small numbers of extremes.

6.6 Extreme Order Statistics

The previous considerations are now generalized to the *m*th extreme. The exact density function $\phi_n(x_m)$ of the *m*th value from the top among n observations is for any initial distribution

$$\phi_n(x_m) = \binom{n}{m} mF(x)^{n-m}[1 - F(x)]^{m-1}f(x). \tag{6.6.1}$$

The exact distribution of the *m*th value from the bottom is symmetrical to it. The mode $\tilde{x}_m$ is the solution of the equation

$$F(\tilde{x}_m) = \frac{n - m + \Delta(\tilde{x}_m)}{n + 1}, \qquad \Delta(\tilde{x}_m) = \left(\frac{f' \cdot F}{f\mu}\right)_{x=\tilde{x}_m}. \tag{6.6.2}$$

For distributions of the exponential type the asymptotic solution is from (6.3.9*a*),

$$F(\tilde{x}_m) = 1 - \frac{m}{n}, \tag{6.6.3}$$

that is, the characteristic *m*th largest value. It decreases for increasing values of m.

For initial distributions of the exponential type the expansion of the probability function about the characteristic *m*th largest value leads to the asymptotic density function $\phi_m(y_m)$ of the reduced *m*th largest value y_m,

$$\phi_m(y_m) = \frac{[m\phi(y_m)]^m}{(m - 1)!}, \tag{6.6.4}$$

where y_m is as defined in (6.2.12) and ϕ stands for the density function of the largest value given in Table B. The density function of the *m*th reduced smallest value is symmetrical to (6.6.4). Thus the density functions of the *m*th reduced extreme value can be expressed by the density function of the extreme value proper. The modes of the reduced mth extremes are zero, and the corresponding value of the density function becomes

$$\phi_m(\tilde{y}_m) = \frac{m^m e^{-m}}{(m-1)!}, \tag{6.6.5}$$

equal to the probability of the mean in Poisson's distribution.

The moment generating function $G_m(t)$ of the mth reduced largest value is

$$G_m(t) = \frac{m^t \Gamma(m-t)}{\Gamma(m)}. \tag{6.6.6}$$

Consequently the expectations $\bar{y}_m$ of the mth reduced largest value and the variances σ_m are

$$\bar{y}_m = \lg m + \gamma - \sum_{v=1}^{m-1} \frac{1}{v}, \qquad \sigma_m^{\ 2} = \sum_{v=m}^{\infty} v^{-2}. \tag{6.6.6a}$$

The asymptotic probability function $\Phi_m(y_m)$ of the mth largest value

$$\Phi_m(y_m) = \Phi^m(y_m) \sum_{v=0}^{m-1} \frac{m^v e^{-vy_m}}{v!} \tag{6.6.7}$$

cannot be reduced to the probability function $\Phi(y)$ of the extreme proper. Probability points for the mth extremes have been published by the National Bureau of Standards [48]. At the mode $\tilde{y}_m = 0$ the probability becomes

$$\Phi_m(\tilde{y}_m) = e^{-m} \sum_{v=0}^{m-1} \frac{m^v}{v!}. \tag{6.6.7a}$$

The distribution of the mth extremes contracts with increasing rank m and converges to the normal distribution as m approaches the order of magnitude $n/2$. These results hold for all distributions of the exponential type. In particular, the distribution of the mth extreme order statistic taken from N observations of the first asymptotic distribution of the largest value is again (6.6.4) if we write

$$y_m = y - \lg\left(\frac{N}{m} - \frac{1}{2} + \frac{1}{2m}\right). \tag{6.6.8}$$

The density function $\phi(i_m)$ of the extreme mth difference i_m [defined in (6.2.4a)] taken from an initial distribution of the exponential type converges toward the exponential function

$$\phi(i_m) = m\alpha_{m+1}\, e^{-mi_m\alpha_{m+1}}, \tag{6.6.9}$$

provided the difference between the characteristic values $u_m - u_{m+1}$ is small compared to the characteristic value u_{m+1} and the difference $\alpha_m - \alpha_{m+1}$ between the extremal intensities is small compared to α_{m+1}. The approximation becomes exact if the initial distribution is exponential [10, 60].

The distribution of the mth largest value taken from an initial distribution of the Cauchy type can be obtained by the same procedure as that for the exponential type. Let the variable x be so large that the initial probability and density functions given in Table A can be written for $\epsilon = 0$;

$$F(x) = 1 - Ax^{-k}, \qquad f(x) = Ax^{-k-1}.$$

If the characteristic mth largest value u_m defined in (6.2.10) is introduced, the initial functions become

$$F(x) = 1 - \frac{m}{n}\left(\frac{u_m}{x}\right)^k, \qquad f(x) = \frac{m}{n}\frac{k}{u_m}\left(\frac{u_m}{x}\right)^{k+1}$$

and the density $\phi_m^{(2)}(x_m)$ of the mth largest value $x_m = x$ for n observations obtained from (6.6.1),

$$\phi_m^{(2)}(x_m) = \binom{n}{m} m\left[1 - \frac{m}{n}\left(\frac{u_m}{x}\right)^k\right]^{n-m}\frac{m^m}{n^m}\frac{k}{u_m}\left(\frac{u_m}{x}\right)^{km+1},$$

converges, for increasing n and fixed m, to

$$\phi_m^{(2)}(x_m) = \frac{k}{u_m}\frac{m^m}{(m-1)!}\left(\frac{u_m}{x}\right)^{km+1} e^{-m(u_m/x)^k}. \tag{6.6.10}$$

For $m = 1$ we obtain, of course, the second asymptotic distribution of the largest values itself.

The modal mth largest value $\tilde{x}_m$, the solution of

$$\left(\frac{u_m}{\tilde{x}_m}\right)^k = 1 + \frac{1}{km} \tag{6.6.10a}$$

is smaller than the characteristic largest mth value u_m, whereas both coincide in the first asymptotic distribution. The difference between the two averages decreases if km increases.

The density of probability $\phi_m(u_m)$ at the characteristic mth largest value is, from (6.6.10),

$$\phi_m(u_m) = \frac{k}{u_m}\frac{m^m e^{-m}}{(m-1)!}. \tag{6.6.11}$$

This formula corresponds to (6.6.5) which is valid for the reduced value of the mth mode of the first asymptotic distribution.

Of course, formula (6.6.10) also holds, if we consider the mth largest value among N observations taken from the second asymptotic distribution itself. In this case the initial distribution in the basic formula (6.6.1) is

$$F(x) = e^{-(u/x)^k}, \qquad f(x) = \frac{k}{u}\left(\frac{u}{x}\right)^{k+1} e^{-(u/x)^k}.$$

An easy development leads to the approximation valid for large x

$$1 - F(x) = \left(\frac{u}{x}\right)^k e^{-\frac{1}{2}(u/x)^k}.$$

Introduction into (6.6.1) yields for N observations and $N \gg m$

$$\phi_m(x_m) = \frac{N^m}{(m-1)!}\frac{k}{u}\left(\frac{u}{x}\right)^{km+1} \exp\left[-\left(\frac{u}{x}\right)^k\left(N - \frac{m-1}{2}\right)\right]. \qquad (6.6.12)$$

The parameter u in this formula is the characteristic largest value. If we replace it by the characteristic mth largest value u_m, the relation between u and u_m is approximately

$$u = u_m(m/N)^{1/k}. \qquad (6.6.13)$$

Introduction of this value into (6.6.12) and the condition

$$N \gg (m-1)/2$$

leads immediately to (6.6.10). This result is intuitively evident: The asymptotic distribution of the mth largest value of an initial distribution of the Cauchy type holds also for the second asymptotic distributions of the largest value itself.

The distributions of the mth extremes for the exponential and the Cauchy types are linked by the same relation as the distribution of the largest values. If we write

$$(u_m/x)^k = e^{-y}, \qquad k = \alpha, \qquad (6.6.14)$$

the resulting density function $\phi(y)$ is the density function of the mth largest values of the exponential type. Consequently, the probability function $\Phi_m^{(2)}(x)$ of the mth largest value for initial distributions of the Cauchy type becomes

$$\Phi_m^{(2)}(x) = \Phi_m^{(1)}(u_m e^{y/k}). \qquad (6.6.15)$$

Since a similar logarithmic transformation reduces the third distribution to the first one, the analysis of the order statistics for the second and third type is reduced to the analysis of the order statistics of the exponential type.

Dronkers [12] studied the distribution of the mth largest values, the modes, and the corresponding values of the densities for varying n and m, derived transitional approximations, and gave their range of application.

6.7 Extremal Functions

The asymptotic probabilities $\Phi^*(z)$ of the absolute largest value z for a symmetrical initial distribution and for the three types is related to the asymptotic probabilities $\Phi(x)$ of the largest value by

$$\Phi^*(z) = \Phi^2(x). \tag{6.7.1}$$

Thus the probability function of the absolute largest value is equal to the probability function of the larger of two independent values taken from the distribution of the largest value.

For the study of the other extremal functions introduced in 6.2, we consider mainly unlimited symmetrical distributions of the first type.

The basic theorem is the asymptotic independence of the mth smallest and the mth largest values for $m \ll n$. It follows that the distribution of the extremal functions may be obtained from the convolution of the asymptotic distributions of the extremes, provided they exist.

Consider first the reduced range R defined in (6.2.9) and symmetrical distributions of the exponential type. Then (6.5.4) leads to the moment generating function $G_R(t)$:

$$G_R(t) = \Gamma^2(1 - t). \tag{6.7.2}$$

The asymptotic density function $\psi(R)$ obtained from the convolution of the density functions of the reduced largest and smallest values (see Table B) is

$$\psi(R) = e^{-R} \int_{-\infty}^{+\infty} \exp\left(-e^{-y} - e^{-y-R}\right) dy. \tag{6.7.3}$$

This integral can be expressed by the modified Bessel function of the second kind and of order zero (Hankel function), for which tables exist [6]. In the notation of the British tables

$$\psi(R) = 2e^{-R} K_0(2e^{-R/2}). \tag{6.7.4}$$

Hence the probability function $\Psi(R)$ is

$$\Psi(R) = 2e^{-R/2} K_1(2e^{-R/2}) \tag{6.7.5}$$

where K_1 is the same Bessel function of order one.

Tables of the asymptotic density and probability functions of the range have been published by [26, 48]. If 10^{-5} is neglected with respect to unity, the reduced range R is practically confined in the interval $-3.7 < R < 14$. The mode $\tilde{R}$, median $\breve{R}$, the expectation $\bar{R}$, and the variance $\sigma^2(R)$ are respectively

$$\tilde{R} = 0.50637, \qquad \breve{R} = 0.92860, \qquad \bar{R} = 2\gamma, \qquad \sigma^2(R) = \pi^2/3. \tag{6.7.6}$$

The last two formulae follow immediately from (6.7.2)

Since we assume that the initial distribution is symmetrical, the distribution of the smallest value is symmetrical to the distribution of the largest value. Therefore, the distribution of the range which is the sum $x_n + (-x_1)$ is the same as the distribution of the sum of two independent largest values, and the distribution of the sum of two independent smallest values is symmetrical to the distribution of the range.

The asymptotic distribution of the mth reduced range [32] for symmetrical distributions of the exponential type is obtained in the same way as in (6.7.3) by the convolution of the asymptotic distributions of the mth extremes from the top and from the bottom. This leads from (6.6.6) to the generating function $G_{R(m)}(t)$.

$$G_{R(m)}(t) = \frac{m^{2t}\Gamma^2(m-t)}{\Gamma^2(m)} \tag{6.7.7}$$

and from (6.6.4) to the density function $\psi_m(R_m)$

$$\psi_m(R_m) = m^{2m}\Gamma^{-2}(m)e^{mR_m}\int_{-\infty}^{+\infty} \exp\left(-me^{-y_m-R_m} - me^{y_m}\right) dy_m. \tag{6.7.8}$$

This density function of the mth reduced range can be reduced to the density function $\psi(R)$ of the reduced range proper by

$$\psi_m(R_m) = \Gamma^{-2}(m) \exp\left[-(m-1)(R_m - 2\lg m)\right] \psi(R_m - 2\lg m). \tag{6.7.9}$$

The probability function $\Psi_m(R_m)$ of the mth reduced range, however, cannot be reduced to the probability function of the range proper. Instead it is a series of functions involving the densities. The first two probability functions are

$$\Psi_2(R_2) = (1 + 4e^{-R_2})\,\Psi(R_2 - 2\lg 2) + \psi(R_2 - 2\lg 2), \tag{6.7.10}$$

$$\Psi_3(R_3) = (1 + 9e^{-R_3} + \tfrac{81}{4}e^{-2R_3})\,\Psi(R_3 - 2\lg 3) + (1 + \tfrac{9}{2}e^{-R_3})\,\psi(R_3 - 2\lg 3). \tag{6.7.11}$$

The general expressions for $\Psi_m(R_m)$ are given in reference 32. A table of the expectations, standard deviation, and the two Betas as functions of the rank m may also be found there. The skewness starts with $\beta_1 = 0.649$ for $m = 1$ and diminishes with m increasing to $\beta_1 = 0.053$ for $m = 10$.

The difference $\beta_2 - 3$ starts with 1.2 for $m = 1$ and diminishes with increasing m to 0.106 for $m = 10$. The asymptotic distributions of the mth ranges w_m ($m = 1, 2, \ldots$) are obtained from the distributions of the reduced ranges R_m by the transformation

$$w_m = u_m + \frac{R_m}{\alpha_m}. \tag{6.7.12}$$

The corresponding asymptotic expressions for the sum of the mth reduced extremes $V(m)$ for symmetrical distributions of the exponential type are much simpler than those for the range. The asymptotic generating function of $V(m)$ is from (6.6.6):

$$G_{V(m)}(t) = \Gamma(m + t)\frac{\Gamma(m - t)}{\Gamma^2(m)}. \tag{6.7.13}$$

The even semiinvariants of the reduced sum of the mth extremes and the mth reduced range coincide. The asymptotic distributions of the mth ranges are skewed, whereas the asymptotic distributions of the mth mid-sums are symmetrical. Indeed, the asymptotic density function $f(V_m)$ is

$$f(V_m) = \frac{(2m - 1)!}{(m - 1)!^2}\frac{e^{mV_m}}{(1 + e^{V_m})^{2m}} \tag{6.7.14}$$

with expectation zero and variance

$$\sigma^2(V_m) = 2\sum_{v=m}^{\infty} v^{-2}. \tag{6.7.15}$$

Formula (6.7.14) is a generalization of the so-called logistic function. The case $m = 1$ leads to the logistic function itself as the asymptotic distribution of the reduced midsum for initial symmetrical distributions of the exponential type. This result is interesting since it shows that not all measures of central tendency converge to normality.

The asymptotic distributions of v_m are obtained from those of the mth reduced midsum by the transformation

$$v_m = V_m/\alpha_m. \tag{6.7.16}$$

For increasing indices m the distributions of the mth extremes, mth ranges, and mth midranges converge to normality. Of course, the second and third statements follow immediately from the first one. It is interesting to study the three variances.

Consider a symmetrical distribution with median zero and unit variance, and let n be large. For increasing m we approach the middle of the distribution. Hence the expected mth values from the bottom ${}_m\bar{x}$ and from the top $\bar{x}_m$ are given by

$$F({}_m\bar{x}) = \tfrac{1}{2} - \epsilon, \qquad F(\bar{x}_m) = \tfrac{1}{2} + \epsilon, \qquad \epsilon^2 \ll \tfrac{1}{2}, \tag{6.7.17}$$

whereas the corresponding values of the densities are equal. The asymptotic distributions of these mth values are normal with variances

$$\sigma^2(x_m) = \sigma^2({}_mx) = 1/4nf^2(\bar{x}_m), \tag{6.7.18}$$

and the joint distribution has the coefficient of correlation

$$\rho = 2F({}_mx). \tag{6.7.19}$$

Then the asymptotic distributions of the mth range w_m and the mth midsum v_m are normal with expectations $\bar{w}_m$, $\bar{v}_m$ and variances $\sigma^2(w_m)$, $\sigma^2(v_m)$ given by

$$\bar{w}_m = 2\bar{x}_m, \qquad \bar{v}_m = 0, \tag{6.7.20}$$

$$nf^2(\bar{x}_m)\,\sigma^2(w_m) = 2F(\bar{x}_m) - 1, \tag{6.7.21}$$

$$nf^2(\bar{x}_m)\,\sigma^2(v_m) = 2F({}_m\bar{x}). \tag{6.7.21a}$$

The variance of the midsums is much larger than the variance of the range because the first is obtained by the addition, the second by the subtraction, of the covariance. The two variances are related by

$$nf^2(\bar{x}_m)[\sigma^2(w_m) + \sigma^2(v_m)] = 1. \tag{6.7.22}$$

The standard deviation of $(x_m + {}_mx)/2$ is of course one-half the value given by (6.7.21*a*).

The exact distribution of the extremal quotient q_n defined in (6.2.3) is complicated for small samples, even if the initial distribution is as simple as the rectangular one [37]. Murty [47] derived the distribution of the quotient of two largest values obtained from samples of sizes m and n, respectively, and taken from a rectangular distribution with known lower limit.

The asymptotic distribution of the extremal quotient [38] taken from unlimited symmetrical distributions is not too complicated. The logarithm of the extremal quotient for such distributions has a symmetrical asymptotic distribution.

Let x be a symmetrical variable of the exponential type and let

$$\lambda = e^{\alpha u}. \tag{6.7.23}$$

Then the extremal quotient q is nonnegative. The asymptotic probability function $H_\lambda(q)$ for sufficiently large values of λ, that is, of n, is

$$H_\lambda(q) = \int_0^1 \lambda e^{-\lambda(z+z^q)}\,dz \tag{6.7.24}$$

with

$$H_\lambda(0) = 0, \qquad H_\lambda(1) = \tfrac{1}{2}, \qquad H_\lambda(\infty) = 1. \tag{6.7.25}$$

This probability function and the density function $h_\lambda(q)$ have a symmetry relation about $q = 1$, namely

$$H_\lambda(1/q) = 1 - H_\lambda(q), \qquad h_\lambda(1/q) = q^2 h_\lambda(q). \tag{6.7.26}$$

No moments exist. The distribution of the extremal quotient contracts with increasing λ, that is, with the sample size from which the extremes were taken. The parameter λ may be estimated from the observed relative number of cases where q is contained between $\frac{1}{2}$ and 2. To this end a table of $H_\lambda(2) - H_\lambda(\frac{1}{2})$ as a function of λ was given in reference 38.

If the initial distribution is symmetrical and if the asymptotic distributions of the extremes are of the second or third type, the probability and density function $H_k(q)$ and $h_k(q)$ of the extremal quotient are much simpler than for the first type, namely,

$$H_k(q) = \frac{q^k}{1 + q^k}, \qquad h_k(q) = \frac{kq^{k-1}}{(1 + q^k)^2}. \tag{6.7.27}$$

The symmetry relations (6.7.26) hold here too. For increasing values of k the distribution contracts. The transformation

$$z = \lg q \tag{6.7.28}$$

leads to the probability function $H^*(z)$,

$$H^*(z) = \frac{1}{1 + e^{-kz}}, \tag{6.7.29}$$

that is, to the logistic function which also holds for the midrange of a distribution of the exponential type. The parameter k may thus be estimated from the sample standard deviation of the logarithms of the extremal quotients.

The study of sample values of the extremal quotient taken from one of the three types of initial symmetrical distributions thus also gives a criterion for the regularity of the extremes.

6.8 Bivariate Asymptotic Distributions of Extremes

To show the generalization of extreme values into several dimensions we have to state first some simple properties of bivariate distributions. A bivariate probability function $F(x, y)$ with margins $F_1(x)$ and $F_2(y)$ is a monotonically increasing function of x and y such that

$$0 \leq F(x, y) \leq 1 \tag{6.8.1}$$

and

$$\lim_{y=\infty} F(x, y) = F_1(x), \qquad \lim_{x=\infty} F(x, y) = F_2(y). \tag{6.8.1a}$$

If the margins are given, they do not determine the bivariate function. On the contrary, to given marginal functions corresponds an infinity of bivariate functions [18].

If the variables are independent, the bivariate function $F(x, y)$ splits into the product

$$F(x, y) = F_1(x)F_2(y). \tag{6.8.2}$$

The variables are said to have a positive (negative) association [54] if

$$\frac{F(x, y)}{F_1(x)F_2(y)} \gtrless 1. \tag{6.8.2a}$$

Let $P(x, y)$ be the probability function for the variables to exceed x and y; then

$$P(x, y) = 1 - F_1(x) - F_2(y) + F(x, y) \tag{6.8.3}$$

has the margins

$$\lim_{y=-\infty} P(x, y) = P_1(x), \qquad \lim_{x=-\infty} P(x, y) = P_2(y). \tag{6.8.3a}$$

Suppose n independent observations are made on such a bivariate population. Then the probability $\Phi_n(x, y)$ that the largest components do not exceed x and y is

$$\Phi_n(x, y) = F^n(x, y) \tag{6.8.4}$$

and the margins are $F_1{}^n(x)$ and $F_2{}^n(y)$. The probability $\Pi_n(x, y)$ that the smallest components in n independent observations exceed x and y is

$$\Pi_n(x, y) = P^n(x, y) \tag{6.8.4a}$$

and the margins are $P_1{}^n(x)$ and $P_2{}^n(y)$.

We are interested in the existence and analytic properties of the asymptotic probability functions $\Phi(x, y)$ and $\Pi(x, y)$ given by

$$\lim_{n=\infty} \Phi_n(x, y) = \Phi(x, y), \qquad \lim_{n=\infty} \Pi_n(x, y) = \Pi(x, y) \tag{6.8.5}$$

such that the margins are the univariate asymptotic functions $\Phi(x)$, $\Phi(y)$; $\Pi(x)$, $\Pi(y)$, respectively.

Since there are three such marginal distributions, the bivariate function [29] exists in six forms, $\Phi^{(K,\lambda)}(x, y)$ and $\Pi^{(K,\lambda)}(x, y)$ for $K, \lambda = 1, 2, 3$. For $K = \lambda = 1, 2, 3$ the marginal distributions are of the same type. For $K \neq \lambda$ they are of different types. To simplify the notation these indices will generally be omitted.

In addition, it is required that the bivariate extremal distributions be stable. This means that

$$\Phi^n(x, y) = \Phi(a_n x + b_n, a'_n y + b'_n) \tag{6.8.6}$$

must hold for suitably chosen values of

$$a_n, a'_n > 0, \qquad b_n, b'_n.$$

Since the marginal distributions do not determine the bivariate ones, we can not look for a finite number of solutions of this equation, as in the univariate case, but only for systems of bivariate extremal distributions.

Oddly enough the usual case is the trivial one, namely, that the bivariate extremal distribution is the product of the marginal ones. If a bivariate initial probability function $F(x, y)$ splits under certain conditions into the product of the two marginal functions $F_1(x)$ and $F_2(y)$, the same holds for the bivariate extremal distribution, provided it exists. If the initial variables are independent, their extremes are also independent. But Geffroy [24] has shown that the converse is not true. He gave a sufficient condition by which the joint probability function $\Phi(x, y)$ splits into the product of the marginal probability functions $\Phi_1(x)$ and $\Phi_2(y)$, although the initial bivariate function $F(x, y)$ does not split. The condition is

$$\lim_{x, y = \infty} \frac{P(x, y)}{1 - F(x, y)} = 0. \tag{6.8.7}$$

In this case the largest values of x and y are asymptotically independent, although the initial variables are dependent. This holds, for example, for the usual bivariate normal distribution and for $|r| \neq 1$; for bivariate distributions of the type [30]

$$F(x, y) = F_1(x)F_2(y)\{1 + \alpha[1 - F_1(x)][1 - F_2(y)]\}, \qquad -1 \leq \alpha \leq 1 \tag{6.8.8}$$

and its generalization given by Farlie [14]; for a bivariate exponential distribution [33]

$$F(x, y) = 1 - e^{-x} - e^{-y} + e^{-x-y-\delta xy}, \qquad x, y \geq 0, \qquad 0 \leq \delta \leq 1 \tag{6.8.8a}$$

and for a bivariate logistic distribution [35]

$$F(x, y) = (1 + e^{-x} + e^{-y})^{-1}, \qquad -\infty < x, \quad y < \infty \tag{6.8.8b}$$

and its generalization

$$1/F(x, y) = 1/F_1(x) + 1/F_2(y) - 1. \tag{6.8.8c}$$

If we write in (6.8.8) $\Phi^{(K)}(x)$ instead of $F_1(x)$ and similarly $\Phi^{(\lambda)}(y)$, the marginal distributions are extremal but the asymptotic bivariate distribution splits into the product of the marginal asymptotic distributions. The expressions (6.8.8) are bivariate initial distributions where the variables are dependent and the largest values are asymptotically independent. This trivial case is eliminated now. Therefore we require that the bivariate probability function not split into the product of the marginal extremal probability functions and that $\Phi(x, y)$ fulfill the stability condition (6.8.6), implying that it possesses the marginal functions

$$\lim_{x=\infty} \Phi(x, y) = \Phi(y), \qquad \lim_{y=\infty} \Phi(x, y) = \Phi(x). \tag{6.8.9}$$

If such functions $\Phi(x, y)$ exist, bivariate functions $\Pi(x, y)$ are obtained by the symmetry principle

$$\Pi(x, y) = \Phi(-x, -y). \tag{6.8.10}$$

Conversely if an expression $\Phi(x, y)$ is known, we obtain $\Pi(x, y)$. Both functions hold for the same population if the bivariate initial distribution is symmetrical.

We show first some specific families of bivariate symmetrical distributions resulting from given initial distributions; then we turn to general forms that contain an arbitrary function of the variables which remains to be specified.

An analytic expression for $\Pi(x, y)$ is obtained from the initial distribution (6.8.8*b*). In a previous article [35] it was shown that in this case

$$-\lg \Pi(x, y) = e^x + e^y - (e^{-x} + e^{-y})^{-1}.$$

Evidently its generalization

$$-\lg \Pi(x, y) = e^x + e^y - a(\bar{e}^x + e^{-y})^{-1}, \qquad 0 \leq a \leq 1 \tag{6.8.11}$$

is also a stable asymptotic bivariate extremal probability function, and $a = 0$ corresponds to independence. Since

$$e^x = -\lg \Pi^{(1)}(x), \qquad e^y = -\lg \Pi^{(2)}(y),$$

equation (6.8.11) can be written in a general form valid for the three types

$$-\lg \Pi^{(K,\lambda)}(x, y) = -\lg \Pi^{(K)}(x) - \lg \Pi^{(\lambda)}(y) + a \frac{\lg \Pi^{(K)}(x) \lg \Pi^{(\lambda)}(y)}{\lg \Pi^{(K)}(x) + \lg \Pi^{(\lambda)}(y)}. \tag{6.8.12}$$

From the symmetry principle (6.8.10) it follows that

$$\lg \Phi^{(K,\lambda)}(x, y) = \lg \Phi^{(K)}(x) + \lg \Phi^{(\lambda)}(y) - \frac{a \lg \Phi^{(K)}(x) \lg \Phi^{(\lambda)}(y)}{\lg \Phi^{(K)}(x) + \lg \Phi^{(\lambda)}(y)} \tag{6.8.12a}$$

is a bivariate probability function of largest values, a formula first given by Sibuya [54].

In order to find another system of bivariate extremal probability functions, consider the initial bivariate function

$$[-\lg F(x, y)]^m = [-\lg F_1(x)]^m + [-\lg F(y)]^m, \qquad m \geq 1. \quad (6.8.13)$$

The case $m = 1$ corresponds to independence. In the case $m = \infty$ the bivariate function degenerates into

$$\lim_{m=\infty} F(x, y) = \min [F_1(x), F_2(y)]$$

which is Frechet's [18] upper limit for bivariate probability functions with given margins. The corresponding bivariate extremal probability functions are

$$[-\lg \Phi^{(K,\lambda)}(x, y)]^m = [-\lg \Phi^{(K)}(x)]^m + [-\lg \Phi^{(\lambda)}(y)]^m, \quad (6.8.14)$$

$$[-\lg \Pi^{(K,\lambda)}(x, y)]^m = [-\lg \Pi^{(K)}(x)]^m + [-\lg \Pi^{(\lambda)}(y)]^m. \quad (6.8.14a)$$

To simplify the notation we write

$$\xi = -\lg \Phi^{(K)}(x), \qquad \eta = -\lg \Phi^{(\lambda)}(y), \qquad \zeta = -\lg \Phi^{(K,\lambda)}(x, y). \quad (6.8.15)$$

Then the system (6.8.12*a*) becomes

$$\zeta = \xi + \eta - a(1/\xi + 1/\eta)^{-1} \quad (6.8.16)$$

and the system (6.8.14) is

$$\zeta^m = \xi^m + \eta^m. \quad (6.8.17)$$

These two systems are the only ones known up to now that can be written down explicitly as known specific functions of x and y. They allow easy generalization into more than two dimensions.

We consider now more general systems containing functions of the variables that are not specified. The problem of the asymptotic distribution of the minima was first investigated by Finkelstein [15]. He derived an expression which in our notation and after the use of (6.8.3) may be written

$$\Pi^{(K,\lambda)}(x, y) = \Pi^{(K)}(x)\Pi^{(\lambda)}(y)e^{W(x,y)} \quad (6.8.18)$$

where $W(x, y)$ is a nondecreasing function in each of the variables with the boundary conditions

$$W(x, y) \leq -\lg \Pi^{(K)}(x), \qquad W(x, y) \leq -\lg \Pi^{(a)}(y),$$

$$W(x, \infty) \neq \infty, \qquad W(\infty, y) \neq \infty.$$

The expressions (6.8.12) and (6.8.14) are special cases of (6.8.18).

A general form of bivariate asymptotic distributions of largest values was found by Geffroy [24]. Since the marginal asymptotic probability functions are related by simple transformations (see Table C), it suffices to consider first only one type of margins. Geffroy found necessary and sufficient conditions that a bivariate probability function be a bivariate asymptotic probability function of largest values. His bivariate asymptotic probability function of largest values where the margins are the second asymptotic probability functions with $k = 1$ is

$$-\lg \Phi(x, y) = \frac{1}{y}\left[\phi\left(\frac{y}{x}\right) + 1\right], \qquad x \geq 0, \quad y \geq 0. \qquad (6.8.19)$$

Of course, ϕ is not a density function but a function such that for $t = y/x$

1. $\phi'(t)$ and $\phi''(t)$ exist for $t \geq 0$.
2. $\phi(0) = 0, \quad \phi'(0) \geq 0 \quad$ for $t \geq 0$.
3. The curve $\xi = \phi(t)$ has an asymptote $\xi = t + a$ with $-1 \leq a \leq 0$.

Roughly, $\phi(t)$ is an increasing convex function which behaves asymptotically like a straight line.

If $\phi(t)$ equals t the bivariate probability function splits into the product of the marginal functions. Geffroy's study is centered about the second asymptotic distribution of extreme values. The expression (6.8.19) can easily be generalized to the three asymptotic distributions. Since for the second distribution and $k = 1$,

$$\frac{1}{y} = -\lg \Phi^{(2)}(y) = \eta, \qquad (6.8.19a)$$

the introduction of this value into (6.8.19) and the use of the symbols (6.8.15) leads to the general formula

$$\zeta = \eta\left[1 + \phi\left(\frac{\xi}{\eta}\right)\right], \qquad (6.8.20)$$

which covers the three marginal distributions, that is the six cases.

If we write $t = \xi/\eta$, the systems (6.8.16) and (6.8.17) are special cases of (6.8.20) for

$$\phi(t) = t - \frac{at}{1 + t}$$

and

$$1 + \phi(t) = (1 + t^m)^{1/m}$$

respectively.

Tiago [56] showed independently of Geffroy that a bivariate extreme value distribution with type 1 margins has to be of the form

$$-\lg \Phi^{(1,1)}(x, y) = (e^{-x} + e^{-y})\, \psi(y - x) \qquad (6.8.21)$$

where the set of functions $\psi(\theta)$, for $\theta = y - x$, is convex, closed, and symmetric. He analyzed the nature of the function but gave only one analytic expression, namely the trivial case $\psi(\theta) = 1$, which corresponds to independence; of course $\psi(\theta)$ is not a density function.

Tiago's system is centered about the first asymptotic distribution. If we replace e^{-x} by ξ and e^{-y} by η and write

$$\psi(\lg \xi - \lg \eta) = \psi_1(t), \tag{6.8.21a}$$

the general system for the three types becomes

$$\zeta = \eta(1 + t)\, \psi_1(t). \tag{6.8.22}$$

This system is equivalent to Geffroy's systems if we write

$$\psi_1(t) = \frac{1 + \phi(t)}{1 + t}. \tag{6.8.22a}$$

Consequently the distributions (6.8.16) and (6.8.17) are also special cases of Tiago's systems.

Sibuya [54] proved on the basis of the stability postulate (6.8.6) that all bivariate asymptotic probability functions of largest values must be of the form

$$\Phi(x, y) = \Phi(y)[\Phi(x)]^{1+\chi(\eta/\xi)}. \tag{6.8.23}$$

From (6.8.2a) follows the important property that the extreme values in all bivariate distributions have a positive association.

If we introduce ξ, η, and ζ from (6.8.15) and write

$$t_1 = \eta/\xi \geq 0 \tag{6.8.23a}$$

the expression (6.8.23) becomes

$$\zeta = \xi[1 + t_1 + \chi(t_1)] \tag{6.8.24}$$

where $\chi(t_1)$ is a continuous convex function satisfying

$$\max(-t_1, -1) \leq \chi(t_1) \leq 0.$$

The case $\chi(t_1) = 0$ leads, of course, to independence.

Sibuya's function $\chi(t_1)$ is related to Geffroy's function $\phi(t)$ and Tiago's function $\psi_1(t)$ by

$$1 + \chi(t_1) = \frac{\phi(t)}{t} = \left(\frac{1}{t} + 1\right)\psi_1(t) - \frac{1}{t}. \tag{6.8.25}$$

The statements of Geffroy, Tiago, and Sibuya that the functions $\phi(t)$, $\psi_1(t)$, and $\chi(t_1)$ lead to all bivariate extremal distributions are thus compatible, and the families (6.8.16) and (6.8.17) are special cases of these systems. Let ζ_1 and ζ_2 correspond to two bivariate asymptotic stable probability functions with the same given margins. Then their mean

$$\zeta = \beta\zeta_1 + (1 - \beta)\zeta_2, \qquad \beta > 0 \tag{6.8.26}$$

corresponds also to a bivariate probability function of largest values, and the same holds for the sum of m such functions

$$\zeta = \sum_{v=1}^{m} \beta_v \zeta_v, \quad \sum_{v=1}^{m} \beta_v = 1, \quad \beta_v \geq 0. \tag{6.8.27}$$

This procedure allows the construction of additional systems of bivariate extremal stable distributions.

The correlation and regression analysis for these distributions remain to be done. In addition to (6.8.16) and (6.8.17) other explicit cases have to be found. The problem of n-dimensional extremal distributions of these kinds has not yet been studied.

In the preceding lines we have tried to state the main features of the present knowledge of the exact and asymptotic distributions of extremes, extreme order statistics, extremal functions, and bivariate extremal distributions. The choice made here may have a subjective bias. In view of the rapid recent development of mathematical statistics, further work will probably simplify and generalize the present knowledge and spread the applications of these methods in hydrology, climatology, civil and naval engineering, and into new fields.

I am indebted to Mr. Simeon Berman (Columbia University) for his help and to Professor H. Fairfield Smith (University of the Philippines) for his kind and acid criticism.

REFERENCES

In the following, some classical and recent publications are listed. A relatively complete bibliography is contained in reference 27.

1. G. N. Alexander, "Return period relationships," *J. Geophysical Res.*, Vol. 64, No. 6 (1959), pp. 675–682.
2. J. Bernier, "Sur l'application des diverses lois limites des valeurs extrêmes au problème des débits de crues," *Rev. Statist. Appl.*, Paris, Vol. 5 (1957), pp. 91–101.
3. J. Bernier, "Comparaison des lois de Gumbel et de Fréchet sur l'estimation des débits maxima," *La Houille Blanche*, Vol. 14 (1959), pp. 47–56.
4. C. I. Bliss, W. G. Cochran, and J. W. Tukey, "A rejection criterion based upon the range," *Biometrika*, Vol. 43 (1956), pp. 418–422.
5. Gunnar Blom, *Statistical Estimates and Transformed Beta Variables*, Almqvist and Wicksells, Uppsala, Sweden, 1958; John Wiley and Sons, New York, 1958.
6. British Association for the Advancement of Science, *Mathematical Tables*, Vol. 6, Part 1, Cambridge University Press, Cambridge, England, 1937.
7. P. G. Carlson, "Tests of hypothesis on the exponential lower limit," *Skand. Aktuartidskr.*, Vol. 41 (1958), pp. 47–54.
8. H. Chernoff, and G. J. Lieberman, "The use of generalized probability paper for continuous distributions," *Ann. Math. Statist.*, Vol. 27 (1956), pp. 806–818.
9. H. Cramér, *Mathematical Methods of Statistics*, Princeton, 1946.

10. J. H. Darwin, "The difference between consecutive members of a series of random variables arranged on order of size," *Biometrika*, Vol. 44 (1957), pp. 211–218.
11. H. A. David, "Revised upper percentage points of the extreme studentized deviate from the sample mean," *Biometrika*, Vol. 43 (1956), pp. 449–451.
12. J. J. Dronkers, "Approximate formulae for the statistical distribution of extreme values," *Biometrika*, Vol. 45 (1958), pp. 447–470.
13. Daniel Dugué, *Traité de Statistique Théorique et Appliquée*, Masson et Cie., Paris, 1958.
14. D. J. G. Farlie, "The performance of some correlation coefficients for a general bivariate distribution," *Biometrika*, Vol. 47 (1960), pp. 307–333.
15. B. V. Finkelstein, "On the limiting distributions of the extreme terms of a variational series of a two-dimensional random quantity," *Dokl. Akad. Nauk, SSSR* (N.S.), Vol. 91 (1953), p. 209 (Russian).
16. R. A. Fisher and L. H. C. Tippett, "Limiting forms of the frequency distribution of the largest or smallest member of a sample," *Proc. Camb. Phil. Soc.*, Vol. 24 (1928), pp. 180–190.
17. M. Fréchet, "Sur la loi de probabilité de l'écart maximum," *Ann. de la Soc. Polonaise de Math.*, Cracow, Vol. 6 (1927), pp. 93–116.
18. M. Fréchet, "Sur les tableaux de corrélation dont les marges sont données," *Ann. Univ. Lyon, A*, Vol. 14 (1951), pp. 53–77.
19. A. M. Freudenthal and E. J. Gumbel, "Physical and statistical aspects of fatigue," *Advanc. Appl. Mech.*, Vol. 4 (1956), pp. 117–158.
20. A. M. Freudenthal, and E. J. Gumbel, "Distribution functions for the prediction of fatigue life and fatigue strength," International Conference on Fatigue of Metals, London, 1957.
21. Jean Geffroy, "Sur la notion d'indépendence limite de deux variables aléatoires, application à l'étendue et au milieu d'un échantillon," *C.R. Acad. Sci., Paris*, Vol, 245 (1957), pp. 1291–1293.
22. Jean Geffroy, "Stabilité presque complète des valeurs extrêmes d'un échantillon et convergence presque compléte du milieu vers une limite certaine," *C.R. Acad. Sci., Paris*, Vol. 246 (1958), pp. 224–226.
23. Jean Geffroy, "Etude de la stabilité presque certaine des valeurs extrêmes d'un échantillon et de la convergence presque certaine de son milieu," *C.R. Acad. Sci., Paris*, Vol. 246 (1958), pp. 1154–1156.
24. Jean Geffroy, "Contributions à la théorie des valeurs extrêmes," *Publ. Inst. Statist. Paris*, Vol. 7 (1958), pp. 37–121, Vol. 8 (1959), pp. 123–184.
25. B. V. Gnedenko, "Sur la distribution limite du terme maximum d'une serie aléatoire," *Ann. Math.*, Vol. 44 (1943), pp. 423–453.
26. E. J. Gumbel, "Probability tables for the range," *Biometrika*, Vol. 36 (1949), pp. 142–148.
27. E. J. Gumbel, *Statistics of Extremes.* Columbia University Press, New York, 1958.
28. E. J. Gumbel, "Statistical theory of floods and droughts," *J. Inst. Water Engineers*, London, Vol. 12 (1958), pp. 157–184.
29. E. J. Gumbel, "Fonctions de probabilités à deux variables extrémales indépendantes," *C.R. Acad. Sci., Paris*, Vol. 246 (1958), pp. 49–50.
30. E. J. Gumbel, "Distributions à plusieurs variables dont les marges sont donées with remarks by M. Fréchet," *C.R. Acad. Sci., Paris*, Vol. 246 (1958), pp. 2717–2720.
31. E. J. Gumbel, "Théorie statistiqué des débits d'étiage," *La Houille Blanche*, Vol. 14 (1959), pp. 57–65.

32. E. J. Gumbel, "The *m*th range," *J. Math., Paris*, Tome 39, Fasc. 3 (1959), pp. 253–265.
33. E. J. Gumbel, "Bivariate exponential distributions," *J. Amer. Statist. Ass.*, Vol. 55 (1960), pp. 698–707.
34. E. J. Gumbel, "Distributions des valeurs extrêmes en plusieurs dimensions," *Publ. Inst. Statist., Paris*, Vol. 9 (1960), pp. 171–173.
35. E. J. Gumbel, "Bivariate logistic distributions," *J. Amer. Statist. Ass.*, Vol. 56 (1961), pp. 335–349.
36. E. J. Gumbel, A. D. Benham and D. H. Thomson, "Communications on the statistical theory of floods and droughts," *J. Inst. Water Engineers*, London, Vol. 13 (1959), pp. 71–102.
37. E. J. Gumbel and L. H. Herbach, "The exact distribution of the extremal quotient," *Ann. Math. Statist.*, Vol. 22 (1951), pp. 418–426.
38. E. J. Gumbel and R. D. Keeney, "The extremal quotient," *Ann. Math. Statist.*, Vol. 21 (1950), pp. 523–538.
39. H. W. Henry, "Evaluation of statistics of extremes for analysis of injury experience of industrial personnel," master's thesis, University of Tennessee, Knoxville, 1959.
40. D. M. Hershfield and M. A. Kohler, "An empirical appraisal of the Gumbel extreme-value procedure," *J. Geophysical Res.*, Vol. 64 (1959), p. 1106.
41. Hannes Hyrenius, "On the use of ranges, cross-ranges and extremes in comparing samples," *J. Amer. Statist. Ass.*, Vol. 48 (1953), pp. 534–545.
42. B. F. Kimball, "On the choice of plotting positions on probability paper," *J. Amer. Statist. Ass.*, Vol. 55 (1960), pp. 546–560.
43. A. Kudô, "On the testing of outlying observations," *Sankhyá*, Vol. 17 (1956), pp. 67–76.
44. A. Kudô, "On the distribution of the maximum value of an equally correlated sample from a normal population," *Sankhyá*, Vol. 20 (1958), pp. 309–316.
45. R. von Mises, "La distribution de la plus grande de *n* valeurs," *Rev. Math. de l'Union Interbalkanique*, Athens, No. 1 (1936), pp. 1–20.
46. P. G. Moore, "The two-sample *t*-test based on range," *Biometrika*, Vol. 44 (1957), pp. 482–489.
47. V. N. Murty, "The distribution of the quotient of maximum values in samples from a rectangular distribution," *J. Amer. Statist. Ass.*, Vol. 50 (1955), pp. 1136–1141.
48. National Bureau of Standards, "Probability tables for the analysis of extreme-value data," Appl. Math. Ser. 22, U.S. Dept. Commerce, Washington, D.C., 1953.
49. B. Ostle and G. P. Steck, "Correlation between sample means and sample ranges," *J. Amer. Statist. Ass.*, Vol. 54 (1959), pp. 465–471.
50. Karl Pearson, *Tables for Statisticians and Biometricians*, Vol. 11, third edition, London, 1931.
51. Paul R. Rider, "The midrange of a sample as an estimator of the population midrange," *J. Amer. Statist. Ass.*, Vol. 52 (1957), pp. 537–542.
52. Paul R. Rider, "Generalized Cauchy Distributions," *Ann. Inst. Statist. Math., Tokyo*, Vol. 9, No. 3 (1958), pp. 215–223.
53. Paul R. Rider, "Quasi-ranges of samples from an exponential population," *Ann. Math. Statist.*, Vol. 30 (1959), pp. 252–254.
54. M. Sibuya, "Bivariate extreme statistics I," *Ann. Inst. Statist. Math., Tokyo*, Vol. 11 (1960), pp. 195–210.
55. M. Siotani, "The extreme value of the generalized distances of the individual points in the multivariate normal sample," *Ann. Inst. Statist. Math., Tokyo*, Vol. 10 (1959), pp. 183–208.

56. J. Tiago de Oliveira, "Extremal distributions," *Faculdade de Ciencias de Lisboa*, No. 39 (1959).
57. C. J. Velz, *Drought Flow of Michigan Streams*, School of Public Health, University of Michigan, 1960.
58. Weather Bureau, "Rainfall intensity-frequency regime," Tech. Paper 29, Washington, D.C., 1958.
59. W. Weibull, "*Statistical evaluation of data from fatigue and creep-rupture tests. Fundamental concepts and general methods*," WADC Tech. Rep. 59–400, Part I, Wright Air Development Center, 1959.
60. Lionel Weiss, "The limiting joint distribution of the largest and smallest sample spacings," *Ann. Math. Statist.*, Vol. 30 (1959), pp. 590–593.

CHAPTER 7

Special Problems in Testing Hypotheses

H. A. DAVID

7A ORDER STATISTICS IN SHORT-CUT TESTS

7A.1 Introduction

The common tests of significance in samples from a normal population all depend either on sample means or sample variances or both. A good deal of work may be involved in the calculation of variances, and there are times when more simply computed statistics are desirable, even if they do not make quite as full use of the data. Such situations arise when data are "cheap" or when answers are required quickly, as in a preliminary survey of results, or when calculations have to be performed without the aid of machines, possibly by an untrained staff. A well-known example is the use of range w_n in quality control. It may be seen from Table 10D.2 that in small samples (say $n \leq 12$) little is lost in efficiency when w_n replaces the root-mean-square estimator s as a measure of spread. For this reason and because of the extreme arithmetic simplicity of the range, the root-mean-square estimator has been almost completely ousted from the quality control field.

The range w_n and also the mean range $\bar{w}_{n,k}$ (the mean of k ranges each taken over n observations, $n \leq 12$) have been applied to many other problems in recent years. With the aid of these statistics it is now possible to perform short-cut versions of all the commoner tests of significance, including the t-test, the F-test for equality of two variances, and Bartlett's test, and to deal with the simpler cases of the analysis of variance. Sequential tests on variances can also be based on range. It is the purpose of this chapter to describe these and similar tests and to discuss their merits. The related estimation procedures are also considered.

One point should be made clear at the outset. In view of the reduced efficiency of range estimators, it will perhaps be thought that if a short-cut test "establishes significance" when applied to some body of data, the corresponding orthodox test will do the same, but not necessarily vice versa. This is not so; except in very special cases the two tests are essentially different, and one test may establish significance where the other does not. (Of course, only one test should be carried out in practice). Such discrepant cases will be rare, however, since $\bar{w}_{n,k}$ and s are highly correlated. In fact we have (see, for example, reference 26)

$$\rho^2(\bar{w}_{n,k}, s) = \text{efficiency of } \bar{w}_{n,k}.$$

The reduced efficiency of range estimators will generally lead to a slightly lower power of range tests, but even this is not necessarily so in tests involving more than two samples. The question of power is examined in more detail later.

Another objection to the use of range which is sometimes voiced arises from the allegedly greater sensitivity of range to departures from normality in the parent population. We shall see that this objection is unfounded for small values of n.

Some other estimators of dispersion such as quasi-ranges

$$x_{(n-i+1)} - x_{(i)}, \quad i = 2, 3, \ldots$$

will also be considered briefly. Quasi-ranges (sometimes called pseudo-ranges) are particularly useful as the basis of a quick test when a known number of extreme individuals in a sample have been "censored." To deal with such a sample the mean will also have to be replaced by estimators of location, such as the median m or the quasi-midpoint $\frac{1}{2}(x_{(n-i+1)} + x_{(i)})$, which do not involve these extreme observations. Although the use of midpoint and median is sometimes advocated in complete samples, the rapidly declining efficiency of these statistics with increasing n (Table 10D.1) is a serious limitation, especially since they replace a quantity as simple as the sample mean.

For convenience, we summarize in the next section some basic results on the distribution of range.

7A.2 The Moments and Distribution of the Range and the Studentized Range

Let $W_n = w_n/\sigma$ be the standardized range of n continuous variates, each with variance σ^2 and cdf $F(x)$. The expectation of W_n is given by

$$E(W_n) = \int_{-\infty}^{\infty} \{1 - [1 - F(x)]^n - [F(x)]^n\}\, dx \qquad (7A.2.1)$$

as first established by Tippett [65] in a basic paper (see also reference 6, p. 471). When $F(x)$ is the cumulative normal distribution, $E(W_n)$ is generally denoted by d_n. This quantity was evaluated numerically by Tippett for $n = 2(1)1000$, and for $n \leq 20$ it is given in Table 7A.1. Similar but more complicated expressions can be obtained for the higher moments of W_n, but these are more conveniently found directly from the probability integral $P(W_n)$ of W_n, which is easily shown to be

$$P(W_n) = \int_{-\infty}^{\infty} n[F(x + W_n) - F(x)]^{n-1} f(x)\, dx. \quad (7A.2.2)$$

In the normal case Pearson and Hartley [47] have given four-decimal tables of this function for $n = 2(1)20$ as well as lower and upper percentage points. These tables are fundamental for all theoretical work on the range. The same authors have also tabulated the first six moments of range [49]. A much more detailed tabulation of cdf, percentage points, and moments up to $n = 100$ has recently been made by Harter and Clemm [21].

When σ is not known, the ratio of the range to an independent root-mean-square estimator s of σ which is based on ν DF is a natural generalization of W_n. Its possible usefulness was first pointed out by Student (see Newman [40]). The ratio is known as the studentized range and is denoted by $q_{n,\nu} \equiv w_n/s_\nu$. Hartley's [23] process of studentization allows the cdf of $q_{n,\nu}$ to be expressed in terms of $P(W_n)$ and a series in powers of $1/\nu$, namely

$$\Pr(q_{n,\nu} < q) = \Pr(W_n < q) + a_1\nu^{-1} + a_2\nu^{-2} + \dots, \quad (7A.2.3)$$

where a_1, a_2 are functions of n and q which have been tabulated by Pearson and Hartley [48] for $n = 2(1)20$ and $\nu \geq 10$. The representation of the left-hand side by only three terms is not altogether satisfactory, especially when $\nu \leq 20$. However, Harter et al. [22] have prepared very extensive tables of the probability integral of $q_{n,\nu}$, giving it (to six decimal places or six significant figures, whichever is less accurate) for $n = 2(1)20(2)40(10)100$ and $\nu = 1(1)20$, 24, 30, 40, 60, and 120. These authors have also tabulated for the same values of n and ν (to four-decimal places or four significant figures, whichever is less accurate) the percentage points of $q_{n,\nu}$ corresponding to cdf's 0.001, 0.005, 0.01, 0.025, 0.05, 0.1 (0.1) 0.9, 0.95, 0.975, 0.99, 0.995, and 0.999. We confine ourselves to reproducing in our Table 7A.2 upper 5 and 1% points.

The moments of $q_{n,\nu}$ have not been tabulated, but the rth moment about zero is readily obtainable from the relation

$$E(q_{n,\nu}^r) = E(s^{-r})E(w_n^{\ r}), \qquad r < \nu$$

$$= \frac{\nu^{r/2}\Gamma\left(\frac{\nu - r}{2}\right) E(w_n^{\ r})}{2^{r/2}\Gamma(\frac{1}{2}\nu)} .$$

7A.3 Approximations to Range and Mean Range in Small Samples

Early approximations to the distribution of range were based on Pearson-type curves fitted by the first four moments which were known either exactly or approximately (Pearson [43]). Tables of percentage points so constructed and used in quality control range charts were later seen to be remarkably accurate, as revealed by comparison with the exact values obtained by Pearson and Hartley [47]. For less direct applications of range, however, the need for a simple approximation became apparent. Various useful approximations are now available, and the following will be required later. We write them in terms of the mean range $\bar{w} = \bar{w}_{n,k}$:

(i) $\bar{w}/\sigma = c\chi_\nu/\sqrt{\nu}$ (Patnaik [42]).

(ii) $\bar{w}/\sigma = c\chi_\nu^{\ 2}/\nu$ (Cox [5]).

(iii) $\bar{w}/\sigma = (\chi_\nu^{\ 2}/c)^\alpha$ (Cadwell [3]).

Here χ_ν and $\chi_\nu^{\ 2}$ denote χ- and χ^2-variates with fractional degrees of freedom ν. The constants c and ν in (i) and (ii) are determined by equating the first two moments of left- and right-hand sides. For the three-parameter approximation (iii) third moments are also equated.

In general, the accuracy of the approximations increases with k (for a given n) as all of them and also $\bar{w}$ tend to normality; taking $\bar{w}$ to be normally distributed may indeed give sufficient accuracy for some purposes (compare Råde [55]). For the case of a single range ($k = 1$), when the approximations will be most severely tested, Pearson [45] has made a detailed comparison of (i) and (ii) for $n = 4, 6, 10$, and 15. He concludes that for $n < 10$ the χ-approximation is the more accurate, that there is little difference for $n = 10$, and that for $n > 10$ the χ^2-approximation becomes the better. Approximation (iii) is appreciably more accurate and seems adequate whenever a specially good representation of the range is required (see, for example, 7A.4, iii). Resnikoff [57] has tabulated the cdf of $\bar{w}_{5,k}$ for $k = 1(1)10$. The short table, Table A, gives the probability with which the various approximating variates exceed the exact 5% point of $\bar{w}_{5,k}$; the fourth decimal place is subject to some error.

With such a variety of reasonably accurate approximations available, considerable flexibility is possible. The χ-approximation has been the most popular since, in addition to its high accuracy, it takes $\bar{w}$ as proportional to $s_\nu \equiv \chi_\nu \sigma / \sqrt{\nu}$. It therefore permits at once the imitation of tests such as Student's t, the only change being a small reduction in the degrees of freedom. This will become clear in the next subsections. All approximations allow variance ratios to be replaced by range ratios or powers thereof, but the χ-approximation, applied only to the denominator of such a ratio, also gives an immediate reduction to the convenient studentized range form. It is, however, possible to proceed along similar lines with the χ^2-approximation (see Cox [6]).

TABLE A

k	Normal Approximation	χ-Approximation (i)	χ^2-Approximation (ii)	Three-Parameter Approximation (iii)
1	0.0382	0.0491	0.0542	0.0502
2	0.0413	0.0489	0.0536	0.0500
3	0.0427	0.0489	0.0531	0.0500
4	0.0435	0.0490	0.0528	0.0500
5	0.0441	0.0488	0.0525	0.0498
10	0.0454	0.0488	0.0516	0.0495

The usefulness of the three approximations rests, of course, on the availability of suitable tables. We now discuss their construction and use for the χ- and χ^2-approximations. Let M and V denote the mean and variance of $\bar{w}_{n,k}/\sigma$. (Here $M = d_n$, $V = V_n/k$). Then the χ-approximation gives

$$M = \frac{c\sqrt{2}}{\sqrt{\nu}}\,\Gamma\left(\frac{\nu+1}{2}\right)\Big/\Gamma\left(\frac{\nu}{2}\right)$$

$$= c\left(1 - \frac{1}{4\nu} + \frac{1}{32\nu^2} + \frac{5}{128\nu^3} - \frac{21}{2048\nu^4} - \cdots\right), \qquad (7A.3.1)$$

$$V = \mu'_2\left(\frac{\bar{w}}{\sigma}\right) - M^2 = c^2 - M^2. \qquad (7A.3.2)$$

Therefore c is easily found from (7A.3.2), whereas ν is most conveniently obtained by inversion of the series expansion (in powers of $1/\nu$) of V/M^2. This yields

$$\nu = A^{-1} + \frac{1}{4} - \frac{3}{16}A + \frac{3}{64}A^2 + \frac{33}{256}A^3 - \frac{1255}{4096}A^4 \ldots \qquad (7A.3.3)$$

where $A = 2V/M^2$.

Table 7A.8*b* gives c and ν for $n = 2(1)10$, $k = 1(1)10$ and to similar accuracy for all k. For example, for $n = 5$, $k = 12$ we have $c = 2.34$ and $\nu = 36.5 + 2(3.62) = 43.7$. An extended table ($n \leq 15$) has recently been given by Duncan [19]. If greater accuracy is required for special purposes, (7A.3.2) and (7A.3.3) should be used; for $k = 1$ see Thomson [64].

The χ^2-approximation gives c and ν in a particularly simple way. We have

$$M = c, \qquad V = 2c^2/\nu,$$

or

$$c = d_n, \qquad \nu = 2kd_n^{\,2}/V_n.$$

In Table 7A.1 d_n and $d_n^{\,2}/V_n$ are tabulated.

Table 7A.1 is also useful when σ has to be estimated from a number of ranges w_{n_t} of different sizes n_t. In this case the weighted mean range

$$\frac{\sum (d_{n_t}/V_{n_t}) w_{n_t}}{\sum d_{n_t}^{\,2}/V_{n_t}} \tag{7A.3.4}$$

is the best unbiased linear estimator of σ (see Grubbs and Weaver [20]). If in line with the above we require an estimator distributed as s, we can obtain an approximate value by adding one-half to the denominator of (7A.3.4) and attributing $\nu = \frac{1}{2}\Sigma d_{n_t}^{\,2}/V_{n_t}$ DF to the resulting ratio (David [14]).

A rather different approach has been adopted by Pillai [51, 52] who, starting from the joint distribution of the ith quasi-midpoint

$$M_i = \tfrac{1}{2}(x_{(n-i+1)} + x_{(i)})$$

and the ith quasi-half-range $W_i = \frac{1}{2}(x_{(n-i+1)} - x_{(i)})$, has developed series expansions for the pdf of both these statistics. For $W_1 = \frac{1}{2}(x_{(n)} - x_{(1)})$ the expansion is

$$f(W_1) = kW_1^{n-2}\, e^{-(n+4)W_1^2/6} \sum_{t=0}^{\infty} C_t^{(n)} W_1^{2t}$$

where

$$k = \frac{n-1}{2^4 n^{7/2}\Gamma(5)}\left(\frac{2}{\pi}\right)^{(n-1)/2}$$

and the C's are tabulated in reference 53 for $n = 3(1)8$.

7A.4 Tests on Variances

We show how range estimators of σ may be employed to test the usual null hypotheses.

(i) Single-sample test; $H_0: \sigma = \sigma_0$. Suppose a sample of n (≤ 100) is available for the estimation of σ. Grubbs and Weaver [20] have shown how to divide n into subgroups of n'_t, with $\Sigma n'_t = n$, so that a weighted mean $\Sigma a_t w_{n'_t}$ of the subgroup ranges gives the best unbiased estimator of σ. They have tabulated the a_t and also percentage points of $\Sigma a_t w_{n'_t}/\sigma$. Thus to test H_0 we simply refer $\Sigma a_t w_{n'_t}/\sigma_0$ to their tables. The optimal subgroup size is 8, with 6, 7, 9, 10 little inferior. Division of n into *equal* samples of 6 through 10 is much more convenient than forming a weighted mean range and generally little less efficient. Grubbs and Weaver also give tables of percentage points of $\bar{w}_{n',k}/d_{n'}\sigma$, with $n' = 6(1)10$, $k = 1(1)15$, for this purpose.

Alternatively, we may use Patnaik's approximation to $\bar{w}_{n',k}$. This has been done in Table 7A.3 to provide values of L, U by which $\bar{w}_{n',k}$ has to be multiplied to give 95 and 99% confidence intervals ($L\bar{w}$, $U\bar{w}$) for σ. Small values of n have been included, as the table applies equally when σ is estimated from a one-way classification of k groups of n' observations.

(ii) Two-sample tests; $H_0 : \sigma_1 = \sigma_2$. Link [31] has tabulated various upper percentage points of w_{n_1}/w_{n_2} for $n_1, n_2 = 1(1)10$. If n_1 (say) exceeds 10, a mean range ${}_1\bar{w}$ may be found from the first sample, and $w_{n_2}/{}_1\bar{w}/c$ may be referred to tables of the studentized range (Table 7A.2). If both n_1, $n_2 > 10$, then $({}_1\bar{w}c_2/{}_2\bar{w}c_1)^2$ is distributed approximately as F with ν_1, ν_2 DF.

(iii) k-sample tests; $H_0 : \sigma_1 = \sigma_2 = \ldots = \sigma_k$. Let s_t^2, $(t = 1, 2, \ldots, k)$ be a mean square estimator of σ_t^2 based on ν DF. Then H_0 may be tested very simply by referring $s^2_{\max}/s^2_{\min}$ to Table 7A.4 which gives upper 5 and 1% points of this ratio for $k = 2(1)12$ (Hartley [25], David [12]). The criterion is closely related to range since $\log (s^2_{\max}/s^2_{\min}) = \text{range} (\log s_t^2)$. In samples of 10 or less we may simplify further and use the ratio $w_{\max}/w_{\min}$ whose upper 5 and 1% points (Table 7A.5) were derived by Cadwell [3] from Table 7A.4 with the help of his approximation 3 (iii). If n is larger than 10, mean ranges can be used in conjunction with interpolation in Table 7A.4.

Example. Samples of 5 are taken from 5 machines at hourly intervals for 3 hours. There may be a change in the mean setting of a machine from hour to hour, but it is known that the variability remains constant. Test whether there is a significant difference in the variability of the 5 machines.

Let S_{ij} and w_{ij} be the sum of squares about the mean and the range in the jth sample ($j = 1, 2, 3$) of the ith machine ($i = 1, 2, \ldots, 5$). Then we may refer

$$\max \left(\sum_j S_{ij} \right) \Big/ \min \left(\sum_j S_{ij} \right)$$

to Table 7A.4 with $k = 5$ and $\nu = 12$. On the other hand, using ranges we base the test on the ratio

$$\max \left(\sum_j w_{ij} \right) \Big/ \min \left(\sum_j w_{ij} \right)$$

whose square we also refer to Table 7A.4 but with slightly reduced degrees of freedom $\nu = 11.1$ obtained from Table 7A.8*b*. The upper 5% points will be seen to be 5.30 and 5.8, respectively.

Other possible test statistics, which possess some advantages for certain alternatives to H_0, are $s^2_{max}/\Sigma s_t^2$ and correspondingly $w_{max}/\Sigma w_t$. See Chapter 9.

Sequential Tests. In view of its simplicity the range is particularly convenient in sequential tests on variances. For ease of application it is, however, advisable to base the estimation of σ on the sum of ranges from subgroups of equal size (say n'). In this way a decision is reached after a number of observations which is a multiple of n'. Using his approximation Cox [5] has given tests of $H_0 : \sigma = \sigma_0$ against $H_1 : \sigma = \delta\sigma_0$ (δ known) and of $H_0 : \sigma_1 = \sigma_2$ against $H_1 : \sigma_1 = \delta\sigma_2$. For the second test, which is of a composite hypothesis, Cox uses Wald's theory of "weight functions." His test has been re-examined from the point of view of the appropriate likelihood ratio criterion by Rushton [59]. Both authors give critical limits for $n = 4$ and 8, selected δ, and the most common combinations of Type I error α and Type II error β. Table 7A.6 is taken from Rushton's paper.

Example. To illustrate the sequential test for the equality of two variances, we have taken ranges w_{1t} and w_{2t} in samples of 8 down the first two columns of the Table of Gaussian Deviates in reference 56. The progressive sums of these ranges and their ratios are given in Table B. We test $H_0 : \sigma_1 = \sigma_2$ against

TABLE B

k	1	2	3	4	5
$\sum_{t=1}^{k} w_{1t}$	3.711	7.543	10.203	14.349	16.838
Σw_{2t}	1.899	5.659	8.572	11.784	14.594
$(\Sigma w_{1t})/(\Sigma w_{2t})$	1.954	1.333	1.190	1.218	1.154*

$H_1 : \sigma_1 = 2\sigma_2$ with $\alpha = 0.01$ $\beta = 0.05$. Table 7A.6 shows that the observed ratio first falls outside the critical limits after 5 trials when it is smaller than the tabulated lower limit of 1.205. H_0 is therefore accepted at this stage.

7A.5 Substitute t-Tests

We now turn to modifications of the t-test obtained by basing the estimation of σ on range. A fundamental result in this connection is that the sample mean is independent of any range estimator of σ. This was first established by Daly [7] and Lord [32]. We give a simple proof due to

Hartley [24]. The joint DF of n independent observations x_i from an $N(\mu, \sigma^2)$ population is

$$f(x_1, x_2, \ldots, x_n) = \text{const. exp}\left\{-\frac{1}{2\sigma^2}\left[n(\bar{x} - \mu)^2 + \sum_{i=1}^{n}(x_i - \bar{x})^2\right]\right\}$$

$$= \text{const. exp}\left[-\frac{n}{2\sigma^2}(\bar{x} - \mu)^2\right]$$

$$\times \exp\left\{-\frac{1}{2\sigma^2}\left[\sum_{j=1}^{n-1} y_j^2 + (\sum y_j)^2\right]\right\}$$

where $y_j = x_j - \bar{x}$, with $j = 1, 2, \ldots, n-1$. Clearly, any estimator of σ based on range (indeed, any function of the x_i invariant under a change of origin) can be expressed as a function of the y_j only and is therefore independent of $\bar{x}$.

Lord [32] considered as his basic test criterion the ratio

$$u_{n',k} = \frac{x}{\bar{w}_{n',k}/d_{n'}}$$

where x is $N(0, \sigma^2)$ and independent of $\bar{w}$. Using elaborate quadrature methods, Lord was able to tabulate upper 10, 5, 2, 1, 0.2, and 0.1% points of $u_{n',k}$. To test whether a sample mean $\bar{x}$ is significantly different from μ, the sample of size n is divided into k groups of n', and $\bar{w}_{n',k}$ is calculated. For greatest efficiency we take $n' = 8$ (a few observations may have to be ignored). The test is made by noting that $(\bar{x} - \mu)d_{n'}\sqrt{n}/\bar{w}$ is distributed as $u_{n',k}$. Likewise, for a two-sample test the samples are split into $k_1 + k_2$ $(=k_s)$ groups of n'. We now have

$$u_{n',k_s} = \frac{(\bar{x}_1 - \bar{x}_2)\, d_{n'}}{w_{n',k_s}(1/n_1 + 1/n_2)^{1/2}}.$$

In the same paper Lord also gave upper percentage points of $R_1 = |\bar{x} - \mu|/w$ and $R_2 = |\bar{x}_1 - \bar{x}_2|/\frac{1}{2}({}_1w + {}_2w)$ to provide immediate tests for the case when σ is estimated from single ranges in samples of n, with $n = 2(1)20$. In Table 7A.7 we reproduce his upper 5 and 1% points of R_1 and R_2 for $n \leq 12$. This approach has been taken further by Jackson and Ross [29] whose extensive tables, derived from Lord's, make the arithmetic of substitute t-tests extremely simple. They give upper 10, 5, and 1% points of

$$G_1 = \frac{|\bar{x} - \mu|}{\bar{w}_{n',k}} \qquad \text{and} \qquad G_2 = \frac{|\bar{x}_1 - \bar{x}_2|}{\frac{1}{2}(\bar{w}_{n',k_1} + \bar{w}_{n',k_2})}$$

for $n' = 2(1)15$ and $k, k_1, k_2 = 1(1)15$. It should be noted that $\bar{x}, \bar{x}_1, \bar{x}_2$ are here (but not in the u-test) the means of kn', k_1n', k_2n' observations, any remaining observations being ignored in the numerator as well as in the denominator to make this simple form of tabulation possible.

The need for new tables can be entirely avoided by the use of the χ-approximation. Consulting Table 7A.8*b*, as before, we find the values of ν and c appropriate to $\bar{w}$ and refer

$$t_1 = \frac{(\bar{x} - \mu)c\sqrt{n}}{\bar{w}} \qquad \text{and} \qquad t_2 = \frac{(\bar{x}_1 - \bar{x}_2)c}{\bar{w}(1/n_1 + 1/n_2)^{1/2}}$$

to tables of t with ν equivalent degrees of freedom (Patnaik [42]). See also Moore [36].

All these significance tests can easily be converted into confidence statements about either the single mean μ or the difference of two means (compare Noether [41]). In particular, $R_1(\alpha)$ and $R_2(\alpha)$, the upper α significance points of R_1 and R_2, give the confidence intervals $\bar{x} \mp R_1(\alpha)w$ and $\bar{x}_1 - \bar{x}_2 \mp \frac{1}{2}R_2(\alpha)({}_1w + {}_2w)$ which respectively cover μ and $\mu_1 - \mu_2$ with probability $1 - \alpha$.

Example. To test whether the means of the following two samples differ significantly.
First sample: 35.5, 23.4, 45.0, 20.4, 74.4, 46.7, 27.6, 47.6, 35.4, 38.9 ($n_1 = 10$, $\bar{x}_1 = 39.49$).
Second sample: 46.5, 63.9, 48.6, 43.6, 33.3, 38.7, 49.6, 56.1, 43.7, 51.3, 69.1, 51.8, 78.1, 57.2, 72.5, 74.2, 53.4, 66.9 ($n_2 = 18$, $\bar{x}_2 = 55.47$).

To achieve a common subgroup size we drop the last observation of the first sample and find the three ranges of 9 to be 54.0, 30.6, 26.4, giving $\bar{w} = 37.1$ and $G_2 = 15.98/37.1 = 0.43$ which exceeds the 1% point 0.38. For t_2 we find from Table 7A.8*b* $c = 3.01$, $\nu = 20.5$, giving

$$|t_2| = \frac{15.98 \times 3.01}{37.1 \times \sqrt{(\frac{1}{10} + \frac{1}{18})}} = 3.29$$

which again is significant at the 1% level (1% point = 2.84). The corresponding value of Student's t is -2.93 (1% point of $|t|$ is 2.78). Ninety-nine per cent confidence limits for $\mu_1 - \mu_2$ given by the first method are

$$(\bar{x} - G\bar{w}, \bar{x} + G\bar{w}) = (-30.1, -1.9).$$

Actually our samples have been artificially constructed from tables of random normal deviates to have $\mu_1 = 40$, $\mu_2 = 50$, and $\sigma = 10$. The true value $\mu_1 - \mu_2 = -10$ is therefore covered by the interval.

7A.6 The Use of Range in the Analysis of Variance

Standard tests of significance in the analysis of variance are often F-tests based on the ratio of a "treatment" mean square to an error mean square s^2. If the treatment means $\bar{x}_t$, with $t = 1, 2, \ldots, k$, are all calculated from the same number of observations n, a possible alternative criterion is

$$\sqrt{n} \text{ range } \bar{x}_t/s. \tag{7A.6.1}$$

The independence of numerator and denominator may be proved as before, so that (7A.6.1) is a studentized range q. In an over-all analysis of variance its use would save very little work; however, in procedures for ranking treatment means it plays a fundamental role (see Chapter 9).

For a one-way classification a computationally simple criterion is obtained if s in (7A.6.1) is replaced by $\bar{w}/c$. The ratio

$$c\sqrt{n} \text{ range } \bar{x}_t/\bar{w} \tag{7A.6.2}$$

is then distributed approximately as q with degrees of freedom ν and scale factor c obtainable from Table 7A.8b. This was first pointed out by Patnaik [42]. Simpler still, an immediate test can be made with the help of Table 7A.8a which gives upper 5 and 1% points of

$$Q = \text{range } X_t/W \tag{7A.6.3}$$

where

$$X_t = \sum_{i=1}^{n} x_{ti} \quad \text{and} \quad W = \sum_{t=1}^{k} w_t.$$

Example 1. Table C gives the yield of grain in bushels per acre, corresponding

TABLE C

	V_1	V_2	V_3	V_4	V_5	V_6	V_7
	13	15	14	14	17	15	16
	11	11	10	10	15	9	12
	10	13	12	15	14	13	13
	16	18	13	17	19	14	15
	12	12	11	10	12	10	11
Total X_t	62	69	60	66	77	61	67
Range w_t	6	7	4	7	7	6	5

to 7 varieties (compare [42]). We have $Q = (77 - 60)/42 = 0.405$ which is well below the 5% point (0.61) for $k = 7$, $n = 5$, so that the varieties do not differ significantly. If an estimate of the error SD is required, we use $W/7c = 42/(7 \times 2.35) = 2.55$ with c from Table 7A.8b which also gives $\nu = 25.6$. The root-mean-square estimate of σ is 2.49 with 28 DF.

If the cell frequencies n_t are unequal but not very different, the same procedure may be employed with $\bar{n}$, the average sample size, replacing n. This gives a test at a level of significance slightly less stringent than the nominal level (David [11]).

When we turn to a two-way classification, such as a randomized block experiment with k treatments and n blocks, a criterion of the form (7A.6.2) may still be used. The estimation of σ by the use of range is a little more complicated, however, since block constants as well as treatment constants have to be eliminated. The probability model is

$$x_{ti} = A_t + B_i + z_{ti}, \qquad i = 1, 2, \ldots, n$$

where the A_t, B_i may be "systematic" or "random" effects and the z_{ti} are independent $N(0, \sigma^2)$ variates. We first form residuals r_{ti} from the treatment means, obtaining

$$r_{ti} = x_{ti} - \bar{x}_t = B_i - \bar{B} + z_{ti} - \bar{z}_t$$

and then take ranges $w(i)$ of these residuals over the blocks, that is, $w(i) = \text{range}\,(r_{1i}, r_{2i}, \ldots, r_{ki})$. Clearly, $w(i)$ is equal to the range of the k independent normal deviates $z_{ti} - \bar{z}_t$, with $t = 1, 2, \ldots, k$, having mean zero and SD $\sigma\sqrt{1 - 1/n}$. The mean $\bar{w}$ of these n ranges will therefore provide an estimator of σ since

$$M \equiv E(\bar{w}) = \sqrt{1 - 1/n}\, d_k\sigma. \tag{7A.6.3}$$

However, the $w(i)$ are no longer independent but are intercorrelated with a common correlation coefficient ρ_w which is a complicated function of k and n. Hartley [24] has given a small table of ρ_w with the help of which Var w can be found from the relation

$$V \equiv \text{Var}\, \bar{w} = n^{-1}(1 - 1/n)[1 + (n - 1)\rho_w]V_k\sigma^2. \tag{7A.6.4}$$

Using (7A.3.2) and (7A.3.3), Hartley found the appropriate scale factors c and equivalent degrees of freedom ν as in Table 7A.8c. It will be noted that ν is now always somewhat less than $(k - 1)(n - 1)$. We have formed residuals from treatment means, which will be needed in any case in the assessment of the results. It is clear that residuals from block means might have been found instead. This would have led to a slightly different ν. From Table 7A.8c we see that $\nu(k, n) \geq \nu(n, k)$ for $k \geq n$.

Example 2. Consider again the previous example, but suppose that the 7 varieties have been laid out in 5 blocks. We first form the variety means $\bar{x}_t$

12.4, 13.8, 12.0, 13.2, 15.4, 12.2, 13.4

and set out the r_{ti} as well as the $w(i)$ in Table D. Note that each column sums to

TABLE D

r_{1i}	r_{2i}	r_{3i}	r_{4i}	r_{5i}	r_{6i}	r_{7i}	$w(i)$
0.6	1.2	2.0	0.8	1.6	2.8	2.6	2.2
−1.4	−2.8	−2.0	−3.2	−0.4	−3.2	−1.4	2.8
−2.4	−0.8	0.0	1.8	−1.4	0.8	−0.4	4.2
3.6	4.2	1.0	3.8	3.6	1.8	1.6	3.2
−0.4	−1.8	−1.0	−3.2	−3.4	−2.2	−2.4	3.0
							$\Sigma w(i) = 15.4$

zero. From Table 7A.8*c* we have $\nu = 22.4$ and $c = 2.45$. To test for differences between the treatments we calculate the studentized range

$$q_T = \frac{(\text{range } \bar{x}_t)\sqrt{n}}{\bar{w}/c}$$

$$= \frac{(15.4 - 12.0)\sqrt{5}}{3.08/2.45} = 6.05$$

which on reference to Table 7A.2 is seen to be highly significant (1% point = 5.6). If a test for block differences is required, we find

$$q_B = \frac{(\text{range } \bar{x}_i)\sqrt{k}}{\bar{w}/c} = 10.2$$

which is also highly significant. The same conclusions would be reached by the orthodox method of analysis.

For extensions of these techniques to more complicated situations such as a two-way classification with cell replication or a split-plot design, see David [11]. We may also mention Tukey's approach [66] which will be considered in Chapter 9.

An interesting use of range methods in quality control has been made by Seder and Cowan [61] in their "Span Plan Method" of process capability analysis.

7A.7 Other Short-cut Procedures Based on Order Statistics

Range-midrange Test. The single-sample substitute *t*-test has been taken a step further by Walsh [67], who considers for small *n* the ratio

$$\frac{\frac{1}{2}(x_{(1)} + x_{(n)}) - \mu}{x_{(n)} - x_{(1)}}.$$

He finds it reasonably efficient for $n \leq 8$.

Test of Homogeneity of Variance in a Two-Way Classification. Hartley [24] has given an interesting rough test of homogeneity of variance which can be carried out concurrently with his range analysis of a two-way classification. His criterion is, in the notation of Subsection 7A.6, range $w(i)/\bar{w}$ which on assuming a joint *normal* distribution of the $w(i)$ he shows to be essentially a studentized range.

Quasi-ranges and "Thickened" Ranges. Let the ith quasi-range be denoted by

$$w_{(i)} = x_{(n-i+1)} - x_{(i)}$$

where $2 \leq i \leq \frac{1}{2}n + 1$ or $\frac{1}{2}(n + 1)$, according as n is even or odd. Cadwell [4] has shown that the ordinary range w is a more efficient estimator of σ than any quasi-range for $n \leq 17$, but that thereafter $w_{(2)}$ is more efficient, to be in turn replaced by $w_{(3)}$ for $n \geq 32$, and so on.[1] He has tabulated moment constants and percentage points of $w_{(2)}$ and given a series expansion for $f(w_{(i)})$. Quasi-ranges are particularly useful in censored samples (see Subsection 7A.8). In complete samples their efficiency is not very high, but suitable linear combinations of w and $w_{(i)}$ can provide remarkably efficient estimators. A simple way of doing this is to use the "thickened" range

$$\begin{aligned} j_i &= x_{(n)} + x_{(n-1)} + \dots + x_{(n-i+1)} - x_{(i)} - \dots - x_{(2)} - x_{(1)} \\ &= w + w_{(2)} + \dots + w_{(i)} \end{aligned}$$

which was introduced by Jones [30]. The efficiencies of various j-statistics for $n \leq 10$ have been tabled by Nair [39]. Although these values are rather high, it has been shown by Dixon [18] that even better results can be obtained by summing over suitably selected quasi-ranges rather than consecutive quasi-ranges (see Table 10D.2). For example, it can be shown from Teichroew's tables [63] that for $n = 16$ the optimal thickened range is j_4 with efficiency 96.8%, whereas $w + w_{(2)} + w_{(4)}$ has efficiency 97.5%. It is clear from their high efficiencies that Dixon's statistics deserve more intensive study. Nothing is known about their distribution, but a χ-approximation may be expected to provide a reasonable fit.

Tolerance Factors for Normal Distributions Utilizing the Range. Two-sided tolerance limits L_1, L_2 are statistics calculated from a sample $x_1, x_2, \dots, x_n$ such that the probability is γ that at least a specified proportion P of the cdf $F(x)$ lies between L_1 and L_2. For a normal parent L_1, L_2 may be taken approximately as $\bar{x} \pm Ks$ where K is the tolerance factor and s the sample standard deviation. Mitra [34] and Resnikoff [58] have tabulated for $\gamma = 0.75, 0.90, 0.95, 0.975, 0.99, 0.995$ the approximate tolerance factors

[1] This question of the "optimal spacing" of the two order statistics providing the estimator of σ has been considered by Mosteller [38] and is discussed further in Section 10E.

K_1 and K_2 needed when s is replaced by a single range [$n = 2(1)20$] or by a mean range in samples of 4 or 5.

A Double-Limit Variables Sampling Plan in which a range estimate of σ is used has been put forward by Duncan [19].

7A.8 Significance Test in Censored Samples

Order statistics provide a simple approach to the otherwise difficult problem of making tests of significance in samples from which some extreme observations have been censored. Most of the following results are due to David and Johnson [8, 10].

The Probability Integral Transformation. Suppose that on the basis of a censored sample from a continuous population $f(x, \mu)$, which is completely specified except for the location parameter μ, we wish to test $H_0 : \mu = \mu_0$. Then the probability integral transformation

$$r_i = \int_{-\infty}^{x_i} f(x, \mu_0)\, dx$$

converts the original observations x_i into variates r_i uniformly distributed in (0, 1). Upper 5 and 1% points of the median of the r_i (in the *complete* sample of n), namely $r_{((n+1)/2)}$ (n odd) and $\frac{1}{2}(r_{(n/2)} + r_{(n/2+1)})$ (n even), are given in Table A7.9.

Example. In a life test on 26 electric light bulbs the experiment was terminated after 14 bulbs had failed, the last 2 bulbs burning out after 1625 and 1640 hours. Assuming that the lifetimes are normally distributed with $\sigma = 90$ hours, test whether this batch has fallen significantly below the standard of an average lifetime of 1700 hours.

We have $x_{(13)} = 1625$, $x_{(14)} = 1640$. Strictly speaking we should form $\frac{1}{2}(r_{(13)} + r_{(14)})$, but it will be sufficiently accurate simply to transform $m = 1632.5$. Thus we refer

$$\int_{-\infty}^{(1632.5-1700)/90} \frac{1}{\sqrt{2\pi}} e^{-t^2/2}\, dt = 0.227$$

to Table 7A.9 and find it below the lower 1% point (0.289).

Normal Populations with Known Variance. Although the procedure just given is applicable for any distribution, a $N(\mu, \sigma^2)$ parent can also be treated by taking m as approximately normal with mean μ and approximate variance $\pi/(2n + 1)$ (n odd), $\pi/(2n + 2.5)$ (n even). A test for differences in the location parameters of two censored samples from normal distributions with known variances can therefore easily be made. David and Johnson also consider more extreme censoring when the sample median is not available.

Normal Populations with Unknown Variance. The estimation of σ in censored samples may conveniently be based on the sample interquartile distance (sid) $x_u - x_l$, where x_u and x_l are the upper and lower sample quartiles, defined for sample size $n = 3(\text{mod } 4)$ as

$$x_u = x_{(3(n+1)/4)}, \qquad x_l = x_{((n+1)/4)}.$$

A χ-approximation to $x_u - x_l$ may be used to give approximate tests of significance, for example, for the equality of two variances [10].

To make tests analogous to the one and two-sample t-tests, we are led to the respective criteria (with obvious notation)

$$R = \frac{m - \mu_0}{x_u - x_l},$$

$$T = \frac{(m_1 - m_2)(n_1 + n_2)}{n_1(x_{u_1} - x_{l_1}) + n_2(x_{u_2} - x_{l_2})}.$$

Upper percentage points of R, based on its moments, are reproduced in Table 7A.10. Approximate percentage points of T are also given in reference 10.

Of course, the estimation of σ need not depend on the sid. When censoring has been sufficiently slight to permit its calculation, the optimal quasi-range (Subsection 7A.7) would be much more efficient, and its use in these tests seems to deserve investigation. To consider other quasi-ranges as well would, however, lead to too great a multiplicity of tests.

7A.9 The Power Function of Tests Based on Range

We have already seen what sort of efficiency range estimators of variance possess (Table 10D.2). Although a number of special studies have been made (e.g., references 16, 20), a good idea of efficiency can be gained in a wide variety of cases from the equivalent degrees of freedom ν of the estimator. Furthermore, it is clear that the power of tests such as the substitute t-test is, in view of Patnaik's approximation, reducible to the power of an ordinary t-test with slightly lowered degrees of freedom. The exact power has also been well tabulated by quadrature methods (Lord [32]). Table E (taken from Patnaik [42]) presents a comparison at significance level $\alpha = 0.05$ of the power of the approximate t-test with that of Lord's u-test for the case when the denominator is a single range of 10, and for various values of the noncentrality parameter μ/σ. Also shown is the power of the corresponding ordinary t-test. The choice of $n = 10$ is unfavorable both to the power of the range tests and to the χ-approximation. Nevertheless, the results may be regarded as very satisfactory. The general conclusion is that the use of range, especially mean range, leads to little loss in power and that, to the accuracy required of power functions, the

χ-approximation is quite adequate. If a few observations have to be neglected altogether, as may happen in the G-tests of Subsection 7A.5, the drop in power will, of course, be more substantial (Noether [41]).

TABLE E

POWER OF DOUBLE-TAILED TESTS AT SIGNIFICANCE LEVEL $\alpha = 0.05$

μ/σ	2	3	4
Approximate t-test ($\nu = 7.680$)	0.417	0.743	0.934
Lord's u-test	0.421	0.747	0.935
Ordinary t-test ($\nu = 9$)	0.431	0.761	0.944

When we turn to the power of range tests in the analysis of variance, we must distinguish between different probability models. For the simple random setup

$$x_{ti} = K + u_t + z_{ti}, \qquad t = 1, 2, \ldots, k, \quad i = 1, 2, \ldots, n$$

where K is a constant and the u_t, z_{ti} are all mutually independent normal deviates with respective variances σ'^2, σ^2, it is known that the standard F-tests are uniformly the most powerful tests of $H_0 : \sigma'^2 = 0$ against $H_1 : \sigma'^2 > 0$, Range tests, however, are little inferior (David [13]). In the multiparametric systematic case

$$x_{ti} = K + A_t + z_{ti}$$

where the A_t are constants subject to $\Sigma A_t = 0$, the situation is not so simple. The power of the range test, unlike that of the F-test, is not expressible as a function of a single parameter. Comparisons have been restricted to special cases (unless $k = 2$) in which σ is taken as known (i.e., $n = \infty$) and the alternative hypotheses specify a single outlying mean or two equal clusters. In the former case range tests are slightly *more* powerful, in the latter rather inferior. For details see references 13 and 17.

It is clear that if σ is taken as known, we are in the quality control situation. Investigations of power in the systematic case but relating specifically to this field have been made by Shimada [62] for $k = 4$. The power of range charts against changes in σ (the random setup with $n = \infty$) has been graphed by Scheffé [60].

David and Johnson [10] have computed the power of their R-test (Subsection 7A.8) and compared it with that of the single-sample t-test applied to the *uncensored* sample. Under these unfavorable conditions the R-test is, of course, greatly inferior.

7A.10 The Effect of Parent Nonnormality on Range Tests

The error made in incorrectly assuming parent normality is seldom easy to assess, and range tests are no exception to this. Although the subject has not been fully explored, it seems safe to sum up the position by stating that no great change in the robustness of a test is produced when root-mean-square estimators are replaced by range estimators, provided the latter are ranges or the mean of ranges taken over small samples ($n \leq 12$); there is indeed some evidence in favor of the greater stability of the range (Cox [6]). Broadly speaking, we find that tests for the equality of means are robust, but that tests for the equality of variances are not (see Box [2]).

Perhaps the result of greatest interest is the remarkable stability of the ratio $E(w_n/\sigma)$, the quantity whose normal-theory value d_n determines the width of control limits in quality control charts. Early work, mainly empirical, by Pearson and Adyanthāya [46] (see also [44] foreshadowed this finding. Plackett [54] has shown that there is in fact an upper bound to the value the ratio can assume, whatever the parent distribution may be, and that in small samples d_n falls little short of this maximum. There is, however, no lower bound other than zero unless some restrictions are placed on the parent distribution, as in reference 27. Table F (David [14]) gives $E[w_n/(d_n\sigma)]$ for a number of nonnormal populations (see also Moore [35] and, for $n = 5$, Moses [37]). Cox [6] shows that for $n \leq 5$ this quantity is generally slightly less than unity. Pooling a variety of results obtained both theoretically and empirically, he suggests that $E[w_n/(d_n\sigma)]$ does not depend on the parent β_1 and tabulates "average" values for a wide range of β_2's.

The dependence of the coefficient of variation of range on β_2 has been similarly examined by Cox. Here the changes are much more pronounced, and this is also true of upper percentage points (see Belz and Hooke [1], David [14]). If β_2 is known, approximate correction factors can be applied. Cox also indicates how rough percentage points of the ratio of two ranges and of the substitute t-test may be obtained in which the value of β_2 is taken into account.

Only one of the test ratios mentioned earlier appears to have been studied in detail for robustness. Walsh [67] has evaluated the probabilities in very small samples ($n = 3$, 4, 5) with which the ratio of midrange to range exceeds normal-theory upper percentage points for six populations, all very far from normal. The results indicate reasonable stability for this criterion. A number of significance tests for a rectangular parent have been considered by Hyrenius [28].

Although it takes us outside the aims of this section, we may also mention

TABLE F

EXPECTATION OF $w_n/(d_n\sigma)$, THE RATIO OF THE STANDARDIZED RANGE TO ITS NORMAL-THEORY EXPECTED VALUE

Type of Population $f(x)$	Rectangular $f(x) = 1$ $0 \leq x \leq 1$	Logistic $f(x) = e^{-x}(1 + e^{-x})^{-2}$ $-\infty \leq x \leq \infty$	Extreme Value $f(x) = \exp(-x - e^{-x})$ $-\infty \leq x \leq \infty$	$\frac{1}{2}\chi^2$ with 4 df $f(x) = xe^{-x}$ $x \geq 0$	Exponential $f(x) = e^{-x}$ $x \geq 0$	Maximum
β_1	0	0	1.30	2	4	
β_2	1.8	4.2	5.4	6	9	
n						
2	1.023	0.978	0.958	0.940	0.886	1.023
4	1.010	0.982	0.961	0.942	0.891	1.012
6	0.976	0.993	0.968	0.947	0.901	1.007
8	0.946	1.004	0.975	0.951	0.911	1.026
10	0.921	1.014	0.980	0.955	0.919	1.054
12	0.900	1.022	0.986	0.959	0.927	1.086

here that order statistics have been considered as possible tests of normality. The ratio of range to standard deviation calculated from the same *large* sample has been proposed as a test for kurtosis [15]. Other tests recently suggested include the ratios

$$J_r = \frac{x_{(r)} + x_{(n-r+1)} - 2m}{x_{(r)} - x_{(n-r+1)}}$$

and

$$H_{g,k} = \frac{x_{(g)} - x_{(n-g+1)}}{x_{(k)} - x_{(n-k+1)}}$$

as tests for skewness and kurtosis, respectively [9, 10].[1]

[1] I am indebted to Miss Betty Laby and Mrs. McDonald of the Department of Statistics, University of Melbourne, for computational assistance.

TABLE 7A.1

CONSTANTS CONNECTED WITH THE DISTRIBUTION OF THE RANGE w_n, IN SAMPLES OF n FROM A NORMAL POPULATION WITH VARIANCE σ^2:

$$d_n = E(w_n/\sigma),\ V_n = \text{Var}\ (w_n/\sigma)$$

n	d_n	$1/d_n$	$\sqrt{V_n}$	d_n/V_n	d_n^2/V_n
2	1.128	0.886	0.853	1.55	1.75
3	1.693	0.591	0.888	2.14	3.63
4	2.059	0.486	0.880	2.66	5.48
5	2.326	0.430	0.864	3.12	7.25
6	2.534	0.395	0.848	3.52	8.93
7	2.704	0.370	0.833	3.90	10.53
8	2.847	0.351	0.820	4.24	12.06
9	2.970	0.337	0.808	4.55	13.52
10	3.078	0.325	0.797	4.84	14.91
11	3.173	0.315	0.787	5.12	16.2
12	3.258	0.307	0.778	5.38	17.5
13	3.336	0.300	0.770	5.62	18.8
14	3.407	0.294	0.763	5.85	19.9
15	3.472	0.288	0.756	6.07	21.1
16	3.532	0.283	0.750	6.28	22.2
17	3.588	0.279	0.744	6.48	23.3
18	3.640	0.275	0.739	6.67	24.3
19	3.689	0.271	0.733	6.86	25.3
20	3.735	0.268	0.729	7.03	26.3

This table is reproduced from E. S. Pearson and H. O. Hartley, *Biometrika Tables for Statisticians*, Vol. 1, 1958, with permission of the Biometrika Trustees.

TABLE 7A.2

a. Upper 5% Points of the Studentized Range

ν \ n	2	3	4	5	6	7	8	9	10	11	12	13	14	15	16	17	18	19	20
1	17.97	26.98	32.82	37.08	40.41	43.12	45.40	47.36	49.07	50.59	51.96	53.20	54.33	55.36	56.32	57.22	58.04	58.83	59.56
2	6.08	8.33	9.80	10.88	11.74	12.44	13.03	13.54	13.99	14.39	14.75	15.08	15.38	15.65	15.91	16.14	16.37	16.57	16.77
3	4.50	5.91	6.82	7.50	8.04	8.48	8.85	9.18	9.46	9.72	9.95	10.15	10.35	10.52	10.69	10.84	10.98	11.11	11.24
4	3.93	5.04	5.76	6.29	6.71	7.05	7.35	7.60	7.83	8.03	8.21	8.37	8.52	8.66	8.79	8.91	9.03	9.13	9.23
5	3.64	4.60	5.22	5.67	6.03	6.33	6.58	6.80	6.99	7.17	7.32	7.47	7.60	7.72	7.83	7.93	8.03	8.12	8.21
6	3.46	4.34	4.90	5.30	5.63	5.90	6.12	6.32	6.49	6.65	6.79	6.92	7.03	7.14	7.24	7.34	7.43	7.51	7.59
7	3.34	4.16	4.68	5.06	5.36	5.61	5.82	6.00	6.16	6.30	6.43	6.55	6.66	6.76	6.85	6.94	7.02	7.10	7.17
8	3.26	4.04	4.53	4.89	5.17	5.40	5.60	5.77	5.92	6.05	6.18	6.29	6.39	6.48	6.57	6.65	6.73	6.80	6.87
9	3.20	3.95	4.41	4.76	5.02	5.24	5.43	5.59	5.74	5.87	5.98	6.09	6.19	6.28	6.36	6.44	6.51	6.58	6.64
10	3.15	3.88	4.33	4.65	4.91	5.12	5.30	5.46	5.60	5.72	5.83	5.93	6.03	6.11	6.19	6.27	6.34	6.40	6.47
11	3.11	3.82	4.26	4.57	4.82	5.03	5.20	5.35	5.49	5.61	5.71	5.81	5.90	5.98	6.06	6.13	6.20	6.27	6.33
12	3.08	3.77	4.20	4.51	4.75	4.95	5.12	5.27	5.39	5.51	5.61	5.71	5.80	5.88	5.95	6.02	6.09	6.15	6.21
13	3.06	3.73	4.15	4.45	4.69	4.88	5.05	5.19	5.32	5.43	5.53	5.63	5.71	5.79	5.86	5.93	5.99	6.05	6.11
14	3.03	3.70	4.11	4.41	4.64	4.83	4.99	5.13	5.25	5.36	5.46	5.55	5.64	5.71	[illegible]	5.85	5.91	5.97	6.03
15	3.01	3.67	4.08	4.37	4.59	4.78	4.94	5.08	5.20	5.31	5.40	5.49	5.57	5.65	5.72	5.78	5.85	5.90	5.96
16	3.00	3.65	4.05	4.33	4.56	4.74	4.90	5.03	5.15	5.26	5.35	5.44	5.52	5.59	5.66	5.73	5.79	5.84	5.90
17	2.98	3.63	4.02	4.30	4.52	4.70	4.86	4.99	5.11	5.21	5.31	5.39	5.47	5.54	5.61	5.67	5.73	5.79	5.84
18	2.97	3.61	4.00	4.28	4.49	4.67	4.82	4.96	5.07	5.17	5.27	5.35	5.43	5.50	5.57	5.63	5.69	5.74	5.79
19	2.96	3.59	3.98	4.25	4.47	4.65	4.79	4.92	5.04	5.14	5.23	5.31	5.39	5.46	5.53	5.59	5.65	5.70	5.75
20	2.95	3.58	3.96	4.23	4.45	4.62	4.77	4.90	5.01	5.11	5.20	5.28	5.36	5.43	5.49	5.55	5.61	5.66	5.71
24	2.92	3.53	3.90	4.17	4.37	4.54	4.68	4.81	4.92	5.01	5.10	5.18	5.25	5.32	5.38	5.44	5.49	5.55	5.59
30	2.89	3.49	3.85	4.10	4.30	4.46	4.60	4.72	4.82	4.92	5.00	5.08	5.15	5.21	5.27	5.33	5.38	5.43	5.47
40	2.86	3.44	3.79	4.04	4.23	4.39	4.52	4.63	4.73	4.82	4.90	4.98	5.04	5.11	5.16	5.22	5.27	5.31	5.36
60	2.83	3.40	3.74	3.98	4.16	4.31	4.44	4.55	4.65	4.73	4.81	4.88	4.94	5.00	5.06	5.11	5.15	5.20	5.24
120	2.80	3.36	3.68	3.92	4.10	4.24	4.36	4.47	4.56	4.64	4.71	4.78	4.84	4.90	4.95	5.00	5.04	5.09	5.13
∞	2.77	3.31	3.63	3.86	4.03	4.17	4.29	4.39	4.47	4.55	4.62	4.68	4.74	4.80	4.85	4.89	4.93	4.97	5.01

Tables 7A.2*a* and *b* are reproduced from *Biometrika*, Vol. 46 (1959), pp. 465–466, with permission of E. S. Pearson, editor of *Biometrika*.

b. Upper 1% Points of the Studentized Range

ν \ n	2	3	4	5	6	7	8	9	10	11	12	13	14	15	16	17	18	19	20
1	90.03	135.0	164.3	185.6	202.2	215.8	227.2	237.0	245.6	253.2	260.0	266.2	271.8	277.0	281.8	286.3	290.4	294.3	298.0
2	14.04	19.02	22.29	24.72	26.63	28.20	29.53	30.68	31.69	32.59	33.40	34.13	34.81	35.43	36.00	36.53	37.03	37.50	37.95
3	8.26	10.62	12.17	13.33	14.24	15.00	15.64	16.20	16.69	17.13	17.53	17.89	18.22	18.52	18.81	19.07	19.32	19.55	19.77
4	6.51	8.12	9.17	9.96	10.58	11.10	11.55	11.93	12.27	12.57	12.84	13.09	13.32	13.53	13.73	13.91	14.08	14.24	14.40
5	5.70	6.98	7.80	8.42	8.91	9.32	9.67	9.97	10.24	10.48	10.70	10.89	11.08	11.24	11.40	11.55	11.68	11.81	11.93
6	5.24	6.33	7.03	7.56	7.97	8.32	8.61	8.87	9.10	9.30	9.48	9.65	9.81	9.95	10.08	10.21	10.32	10.43	10.54
7	4.95	5.92	6.54	7.01	7.37	7.68	7.94	8.17	8.37	8.55	8.71	8.86	9.00	9.12	9.24	9.35	9.46	9.55	9.65
9	4.75	5.64	6.20	6.62	6.96	7.24	7.47	7.68	7.86	8.03	8.18	8.31	8.44	8.55	8.66	8.76	8.85	8.94	9.03
8	4.60	5.43	5.96	6.35	6.66	6.91	7.13	7.33	7.49	7.65	7.78	7.91	8.03	8.13	8.23	8.33	8.41	8.49	8.57
10	4.48	5.27	5.77	6.14	6.43	6.67	6.87	7.05	7.21	7.36	7.49	7.60	7.71	7.81	7.91	7.99	8.08	8.15	8.23
11	4.39	5.15	5.62	5.97	6.25	6.48	6.67	6.84	6.99	7.13	7.25	7.36	7.46	7.56	7.65	7.73	7.81	7.88	7.95
12	4.32	5.05	5.50	5.84	6.10	6.32	6.51	6.67	6.81	6.94	7.06	7.17	7.26	7.36	7.44	7.52	7.59	7.66	7.73
13	4.26	4.96	5.40	5.73	5.98	6.19	6.37	6.53	6.67	6.79	6.90	7.01	7.10	7.19	7.27	7.35	7.42	7.48	7.55
14	4.21	4.89	5.32	5.63	5.88	6.08	6.26	6.41	6.54	6.66	6.77	6.87	6.96	7.05	7.13	7.20	7.27	7.33	7.39
15	4.17	4.84	5.25	5.56	5.80	5.99	6.16	6.31	6.44	6.55	6.66	6.76	6.84	6.93	7.00	7.07	7.14	7.20	7.26
16	4.13	4.79	5.19	5.49	5.72	5.92	6.08	6.22	6.35	6.46	6.56	6.66	6.74	6.82	6.90	6.97	7.03	7.09	7.15
17	4.10	4.74	5.14	5.43	5.66	5.85	6.01	6.15	6.27	6.38	6.48	6.57	6.66	6.73	6.81	6.87	6.94	7.00	7.05
18	4.07	4.70	5.09	5.38	5.60	5.79	5.94	6.08	6.20	6.31	6.41	6.50	6.58	6.65	6.73	6.79	6.85	6.91	6.97
19	4.05	4.67	5.05	5.33	5.55	5.73	5.89	6.02	6.14	6.25	6.34	6.43	6.51	6.58	6.65	6.72	6.78	6.84	6.89
20	4.02	4.64	5.02	5.29	5.51	5.69	5.84	5.97	6.09	6.19	6.28	6.37	6.45	6.52	6.59	6.65	6.71	6.77	6.82
24	3.96	4.55	4.91	5.17	5.37	5.54	5.69	5.81	5.92	6.02	6.11	6.19	6.26	6.33	6.39	6.45	6.51	6.56	6.61
30	3.89	4.45	4.80	5.05	5.24	5.40	5.54	5.65	5.76	5.85	5.93	6.01	6.08	6.14	6.20	6.26	6.31	6.36	6.41
40	3.82	4.37	4.70	4.93	5.11	5.26	5.39	5.50	5.60	5.69	5.76	5.83	5.90	5.96	6.02	6.07	6.12	6.16	6.21
60	3.76	4.28	4.59	4.82	4.99	5.13	5.25	5.36	5.45	5.53	5.60	5.67	5.73	5.78	5.84	5.89	5.93	5.97	6.01
120	3.70	4.20	4.50	4.71	4.87	5.01	5.12	5.21	5.30	5.37	5.44	5.50	5.56	5.61	5.66	5.71	5.75	5.79	5.83
∞	3.64	4.12	4.40	4.60	4.76	4.88	4.99	5.08	5.16	5.23	5.29	5.35	5.40	5.45	5.49	5.54	5.57	5.61	5.65

TABLE 7A.3

FACTORS TO BE APPLIED TO THE MEAN RANGE $\bar{w}_{n,k}$ TO GIVE 95 AND 99% CONFIDENCE INTERVALS $(L\bar{w}, U\bar{w})$ FOR σ

k \ n	2		3		4		5		6		7		8		9		10	
	L	U	L	U	L	U	L	U	L	U	L	U	L	U	L	U	L	U
1	0.32	23	0.27	3.3	0.25	1.69	0.24	1.18	0.23	0.94	0.22	0.80	0.22	0.71	0.21	0.65	0.21	0.60
	0.25	113	0.23	7.7	0.21	2.9	0.20	1.81	0.20	1.33	0.194	1.09	0.190	0.93	0.187	0.83	0.185	0.75
2	0.40	5.3	0.33	1.61	0.30	1.05	0.28	0.82	0.27	0.70	0.25	0.62	0.25	0.56	0.24	0.53	0.24	0.49
	0.34	9.8	0.28	4.7	0.26	1.44	0.25	1.06	0.24	0.87	0.23	0.75	0.22	0.67	0.22	0.62	0.22	0.58
3	0.45	3.8	0.36	1.28	0.32	0.89	0.30	0.71	0.28	0.62	0.27	0.55	0.26	0.51	0.25	0.48	0.25	0.45
	0.39	7.0	0.32	1.76	0.29	1.12	0.27	0.86	0.26	0.73	0.25	0.64	0.24	0.59	0.24	0.54	0.23	0.51
4	0.49	2.5	0.38	1.13	0.34	0.80	0.31	0.66	0.29	0.58	0.28	0.52	0.27	0.48	0.26	0.45	0.26	0.43
	0.42	4.9	0.34	1.45	0.30	0.97	0.28	0.77	0.27	0.66	0.26	0.59	0.25	0.54	0.25	0.50	0.24	0.48
5	0.52	2.2	0.40	1.04	0.35	0.75	0.32	0.62	0.30	0.55	0.29	0.50	0.28	0.47	0.27	0.44	0.26	0.42
	0.45	3.2	0.36	1.29	0.32	0.88	0.30	0.72	0.28	0.62	0.27	0.56	0.26	0.51	0.25	0.48	0.25	0.45
6	0.54	2.0	0.41	0.98	0.36	0.72	0.33	0.60	0.31	0.53	0.29	0.49	0.28	0.45	0.28	0.43	0.27	0.41
	0.47	2.7	0.37	1.18	0.33	0.83	0.30	0.68	0.29	0.59	0.28	0.54	0.27	0.49	0.26	0.46	0.25	0.44
7	0.55	1.82	0.42	0.93	0.36	0.70	0.33	0.59	0.31	0.52	0.30	0.47	0.29	0.44	0.28	0.42	0.27	0.40
	0.49	2.4	0.38	1.11	0.34	0.79	0.31	0.65	0.29	0.57	0.28	0.52	0.27	0.48	0.26	0.45	0.26	0.43
8	0.57	1.72	0.43	0.90	0.37	0.68	0.34	0.57	0.32	0.51	0.30	0.47	0.29	0.44	0.28	0.41	0.27	0.39
	0.50	2.2	0.39	1.06	0.34	0.77	0.32	0.63	0.30	0.56	0.29	0.51	0.28	0.47	0.27	0.44	0.26	0.42
9	0.58	1.64	0.43	0.88	0.38	0.66	0.34	0.56	0.32	0.50	0.31	0.46	0.29	0.43	0.29	0.41	0.28	0.39
	0.52	2.1	0.40	1.01	0.35	0.74	0.32	0.62	0.30	0.54	0.29	0.50	0.28	0.46	0.27	0.44	0.26	0.41
10	0.59	1.58	0.44	0.86	0.38	0.65	0.35	0.55	0.33	0.49	0.31	0.45	0.30	0.43	0.29	0.40	0.28	0.39
	0.53	1.97	0.41	0.98	0.36	0.72	0.33	0.61	0.31	0.53	0.29	0.49	0.28	0.45	0.27	0.43	0.27	0.41

TABLE 7A.4

Percentage Points of the Ratio s^2_{max}/s^2_{min}

Upper 5% points

ν \ k	2	3	4	5	6	7	8	9	10	11	12
2	39.0	87.5	142	202	266	333	403	475	550	626	704
3	15.4	27.8	39.2	50.7	62.0	72.9	83.5	93.9	104	114	124
4	9.60	15.5	20.6	25.2	29.5	33.6	37.5	41.1	44.6	48.0	51.4
5	7.15	10.8	13.7	16.3	18.7	20.8	22.9	24.7	26.5	28.2	29.9
6	5.82	8.38	10.4	12.1	13.7	15.0	16.3	17.5	18.6	19.7	20.7
7	4.99	6.94	8.44	9.70	10.8	11.8	12.7	13.5	14.3	15.1	15.8
8	4.43	6.00	7.18	8.12	9.03	9.78	10.5	11.1	11.7	12.2	12.7
9	4.03	5.34	6.31	7.11	7.80	8.41	8.95	9.45	9.91	10.3	10.7
10	3.72	4.85	5.67	6.34	6.92	7.42	7.87	8.28	8.66	9.01	9.34
12	3.28	4.16	4.79	5.30	5.72	6.09	6.42	6.72	7.00	7.25	7.48
15	2.86	3.54	4.01	4.37	4.68	4.95	5.19	5.40	5.59	5.77	5.93
20	2.46	2.95	3.29	3.54	3.76	3.94	4.10	4.24	4.37	4.49	4.59
30	2.07	2.40	2.61	2.78	2.91	3.02	3.12	3.21	3.29	3.36	3.39
60	1.67	1.85	1.96	2.04	2.11	2.17	2.22	2.26	2.30	2.33	2.36
∞	1.00	1.00	1.00	1.00	1.00	1.00	1.00	1.00	1.00	1.00	1.00

Upper 1% points

ν \ k	2	3	4	5	6	7	8	9	10	11	12
2	199	448	729	1036	1362	1705	2063	2432	2813	3204	3605
3	47.5	85	120	151	184	21(6)	24(9)	28(1)	31(0)	33(7)	36(1)
4	23.2	37	49	59	69	79	89	97	106	113	120
5	14.9	22	28	33	38	42	46	50	54	57	60
6	11.1	15.5	19.1	22	25	27	30	32	34	36	37
7	8.89	12.1	14.5	16.5	18.4	20	22	23	24	26	27
8	7.50	9.9	11.7	13.2	14.5	15.8	16.9	17.9	18.9	19.8	21
9	6.54	8.5	9.9	11.1	12.1	13.1	13.9	14.7	15.3	16.0	16.6
10	5.85	7.4	8.6	9.6	10.4	11.1	11.8	12.4	12.9	13.4	13.9
12	4.91	6.1	6.9	7.6	8.2	8.7	9.1	9.5	9.9	10.2	10.6
15	4.07	4.9	5.5	6.0	6.4	6.7	7.1	7.3	7.5	7.8	8.0
20	3.32	3.8	4.3	4.6	4.9	5.1	5.3	5.5	5.6	5.8	5.9
30	2.63	3.0	3.3	3.4	3.6	3.7	3.8	3.9	4.0	4.1	4.2
60	1.96	2.2	2.3	2.4	2.4	2.5	2.5	2.6	2.6	2.7	2.7
∞	1.00	1.0	1.0	1.0	1.0	1.0	1.0	1.0	1.0	1.0	1.0

s^2_{max} is the largest and s^2_{min} the smallest in a set of k independent mean squares, each based on ν degrees of freedom.

Values in the column $k = 2$ and in the rows $\nu = 2$ and ∞ are exact. Elsewhere the third digit may be in error by a few units for the 5% points and several units for the 1% points. The third-digit figures in brackets for $\nu = 3$ are the most uncertain.

This table is reproduced from E. S. Pearson and H. O. Hartley, *Biometrika Tables for Statisticians*, Vol. 1, 1958, with permission of the Biometrika Trustees.

TABLE 7A.5

Approximate Upper 5 and 1% Points of the Ratio of Maximum Value to Minimum Value in a Set of k Independent Ranges. Each Range is for a Sample of Size n from a Normal Population of Fixed Standard Deviation

n \ k	2	3	4	5	6	7	8	9	10	11	12
						5%					
3	6.28	9.32	11.9	14.2	16.3	18.2	20.0	21.7	23.3	24.8	26.3
4	3.96	5.31	6.32	7.20	7.95	8.63	9.24	9.76	10.3	10.7	11.1
5	3.15	4.02	4.63	5.10	5.53	5.93	6.26	6.55	6.80	7.05	7.28
6	2.74	3.37	3.82	4.16	4.47	4.71	4.93	5.14	5.32	5.50	5.66
7	2.49	2.99	3.34	3.61	3.85	4.04	4.22	4.37	4.51	4.63	4.75
8	2.32	2.75	3.04	3.27	3.46	3.62	3.75	3.88	3.99	4.09	4.18
9	2.20	2.58	2.83	3.03	3.19	3.32	3.44	3.55	3.64	3.73	3.81
10	2.11	2.45	2.68	2.84	2.99	3.11	3.21	3.31	3.39	3.46	3.53
						1%					
3	14.1	21.0	26.7	31.8	36.4	40.7	44.8	48.5	52.1	55.4	58.7
4	6.91	9.28	11.0	12.4	13.7	14.8	15.8	16.7	17.6	18.5	19.1
5	4.87	6.16	7.06	7.76	8.44	9.04	9.51	9.93	10.5	10.8	11.2
6	3.96	4.80	5.40	5.86	6.30	6.66	6.99	7.25	7.51	7.76	7.96
7	3.44	4.08	4.52	4.86	5.16	5.43	5.66	5.86	6.06	6.26	6.46
8	3.11	3.63	3.98	4.27	4.50	4.71	4.88	5.05	5.18	5.31	5.44
9	2.88	3.33	3.62	3.86	4.05	4.20	4.34	4.47	4.60	4.71	4.81
10	2.71	3.10	3.35	3.56	3.73	3.87	4.00	4.10	4.20	4.29	4.38

This table is reproduced from J. H. Cadwell, "Approximation to the distribution of measures of dispersion by a power of χ^2," *Biometrika*, Vol. 40 (1953), pp. 336–346, with permission of the author and E. S. Pearson, editor of *Biometrika*.

TABLE 7A.6

CRITICAL LIMITS FOR A SEQUENTIAL RANGE TEST OF $H_0: \sigma_1 = \sigma_2$ AGAINST $H_1: \sigma_1 = \delta\sigma_2$
(SUBGROUP SIZE $n' = 8$)

Trial Number, k	$\delta = 1.5$				$\delta = 2$				$\delta = 3$			
	$\alpha = \beta = 0.05$		$\alpha = 0.01$ $\beta = 0.05$		$\alpha = \beta = 0.05$		$\alpha = 0.01$ $\beta = 0.05$		$\alpha = \beta = 0.05$		$\alpha = 0.01$ $\beta = 0.05$	
1	0.2878	4.097	0.2802	15.70	0.6337	2.633	0.6264	4.099	1.019	2.481	1.013	3.195
2	0.6361	2.157	0.6301	3.127	0.9533	1.928	0.9485	2.352	1.327	2.078	1.323	2.351
3	0.7957	1.781	0.7915	2.243	1.087	1.740	1.084	1.982	1.449	1.957	1.446	2.125
4	0.8870	1.621	0.8832	1.920	1.161	1.652	1.158	1.821	1.515	1.898	1.513	2.020
5	0.9470	1.533	0.9359	1.752	1.208	1.600	1.205	1.731	1.556	1.864	1.551	1.959
6	0.9884	1.476	0.9851	1.645	1.239	1.570	1.237	1.674	1.584	1.842	1.582	1.919
7	1.018	1.438	1.017	1.580	1.263	1.546	1.261	1.634	1.604	1.826	1.603	1.892
8	1.042	1.409	1.041	1.532	1.281	1.530	1.279	1.605	1.620	1.814	1.618	1.871
9	1.061	1.388	1.060	1.493	1.295	1.516	1.294	1.583	1.631	1.805	1.630	1.855
10	1.076	1.370	1.075	1.464	1.306	1.506	1.304	1.565	1.641	1.797	1.640	1.842
12	1.010	1.345	1.099	1.421	1.324	1.490	1.323	1.539	1.656	1.786	1.655	1.824
14	1.117	1.327	1.116	1.391	1.336	1.479	1.336	1.520	1.667	1.778	1.666	1.810
16	1.130	1.314	1.129	1.369	1.346	1.470	1.345	1.507	1.675	1.773	1.674	1.800
18	1.140	1.304	1.139	1.353	1.353	1.464	1.352	1.496	1.681	1.768	1.680	1.793
20	1.148	1.295	1.147	1.339	1.359	1.459	1.359	1.488	1.686	1.764	1.685	1.787

This table is reproduced from S. Rushton, "On sequential tests of the equality of variances of two normal populations with known means," *Sankhyā*, Vol. 12 (1952), pp. 63–78, with permission of P. C. Mahalanobis, editor of *Sankhyā*.

TABLE 7A.7

UPPER 5 AND 1% POINTS OF $R_1 = |\bar{x} - \mu|/w$ AND $R_2 = |\bar{x}_1 - \bar{x}_2|/\frac{1}{2}({}_1w + {}_2w)$, WHERE $\bar{x}$, w ARE THE MEAN AND THE RANGE IN NORMAL SAMPLES OF n

n	R_1		R_2	
	5%	1%	5%	1%
2	6.35	31.8	3.43	7.92
3	1.30	3.01	1.27	2.09
4	0.717	1.32	0.813	1.24
5	0.507	0.843	0.613	0.896
6	0.399	0.628	0.499	0.714
7	0.333	0.507	0.426	0.600
8	0.288	0.429	0.373	0.521
9	0.255	0.374	0.334	0.464
10	0.230	0.333	0.304	0.419
11	0.210	0.302	0.280	0.384
12	0.194	0.277	0.260	0.355

This table is reproduced from E. Lord, "Use of range in place of standard deviation in the t-test," *Biometrika*, Vol. 34 (1947), pp. 41–67, with permission of the author and E. S. Pearson, editor of *Biometrika*.

TABLE 7A.8

a. TABLES FOR ANALYSIS OF VARIANCE BASED ON RANGE

UPPER PERCENTAGE POINTS OF Q = RANGE OF GROUP TOTALS/SUM OF GROUP RANGES IN A ONE-WAY CLASSIFICATION INTO k GROUPS OF n OBSERVATIONS

k \ n	2		3		4		5		6		7		8		9		10	
	5%	1%	5%	1%	5%	1%	5%	1%	5%	1%	5%	1%	5%	1%	5%	1%	5%	1%
1	18.1	90.0	7.6	17.5	6.2	11.2	5.8	9.3	5.7	8.6	5.7	8.2	5.8	8.0	5.9	8.0	6.0	8.0
2	3.5	8.3	2.5	4.0	2.3	3.4	2.3	3.2	2.4	3.1	2.4	3.1	2.5	3.1	2.6	3.2	2.6	3.2
3	1.79	3.4	1.44	2.1	1.41	1.91	1.43	1.87	1.47	1.87	1.52	1.90	1.57	1.93	1.62	1.98	1.68	2.0
4	1.18	2.0	1.01	1.42	1.01	1.33	1.03	1.32	1.07	1.33	1.11	1.36	1.14	1.39	1.19	1.43	1.23	1.47
5	0.89	1.43	0.78	1.07	0.78	1.01	0.81	1.01	0.84	1.03	0.87	1.06	0.91	1.09	0.94	1.12	0.97	1.15
6	0.71	1.09	0.64	0.86	0.64	0.82	0.66	0.82	0.69	0.84	0.71	0.86	0.74	0.89	0.77	0.92	0.80	0.95
7	0.59	0.89	0.53	0.71	0.54	0.69	0.56	0.70	0.59	0.72	0.61	0.74	0.64	0.76	0.66	0.78	0.68	0.80
8	0.50	0.74	0.46	0.61	0.47	0.60	0.49	0.60	0.51	0.62	0.53	0.64	0.56	0.66	0.58	0.68	0.60	0.70
9	0.44	0.64	0.41	0.53	0.42	0.52	0.43	0.53	0.45	0.55	0.47	0.56	0.49	0.58	0.51	0.60	0.53	0.62
10	0.39	0.56	0.36	0.47	0.37	0.47	0.39	0.47	0.40	0.49	0.42	0.50	0.44	0.52	0.46	0.54	0.47	0.55

This table is reproduced from E. S. Pearson and H. O. Hartley, *Biometrika Tables for Statisticians*, Vol. 1, 1958, with permission of the Biometrika Trustees.

b. SCALE FACTOR *c* AND EQUIVALENT DEGREES OF FREEDOM ν APPROPRIATE TO A ONE-WAY CLASSIFICATION INTO *k* GROUPS OF *n* OBSERVATIONS

k \ *n*	2 ν	2 *c*	3 ν	3 *c*	4 ν	4 *c*	5 ν	5 *c*	6 ν	6 *c*	7 ν	7 *c*	8 ν	8 *c*	9 ν	9 *c*	10 ν	10 *c*
1	1.00	1.41	1.98	1.91	2.93	2.24	3.83	2.48	4.68	2.67	5.48	2.83	6.25	2.96	6.98	3.08	7.68	3.18
2	1.92	1.28	3.83	1.81	5.69	2.15	7.47	2.40	9.16	2.60	10.8	2.77	12.3	2.91	13.8	3.02	15.1	3.13
3	2.82	1.23	5.66	1.77	8.44	2.12	11.1	2.38	13.6	2.58	16.0	2.75	18.3	2.89	20.5	3.01	22.6	3.11
4	3.71	1.21	7.49	1.75	11.2	2.11	14.7	2.37	18.1	2.57	21.3	2.74	24.4	2.88	27.3	3.00	30.1	3.10
5	4.59	1.19	9.30	1.74	13.9	2.10	18.4	2.36	22.6	2.56	26.6	2.73	30.4	2.87	34.0	2.99	37.5	3.10
6	5.47	1.18	11.1	1.73	16.7	2.09	22.0	2.35	27.0	2.56	31.8	2.73	36.4	2.87	40.8	2.99	45.0	3.09
7	6.35	1.17	12.9	1.73	19.4	2.09	25.6	2.35	31.5	2.55	37.1	2.72	42.5	2.86	47.6	2.99	52.4	3.09
8	7.23	1.17	14.8	1.72	22.1	2.08	29.2	2.35	36.0	2.55	42.4	2.72	48.5	2.86	54.3	2.98	59.9	3.09
9	8.11	1.16	16.6	1.72	24.9	2.08	32.9	2.34	40.4	2.55	47.6	2.72	54.5	2.86	61.1	2.98	67.3	3.09
10	8.99	1.16	18.4	1.72	27.6	2.08	36.5	2.34	44.9	2.55	52.9	2.72	60.6	2.86	67.8	2.98	74.8	3.09
d_n		1.13		1.69		2.06		2.33		2.53		2.70		2.85		2.97		3.08
CD	0.88		1.82		2.74		3.62		4.47		5.27		6.03		6.76		7.45	

CD = constant difference

This table is reproduced (with extension) from E. S. Pearson and H. O. Hartley, *Biometrika Tables for Statisticians*, Vol. 1, 1958, with permission of the Biometrika Trustees.

c. Scale Factor c and Equivalent Degrees of Freedom ν for Analysis of Double Classification, with k Blocks and n Treatments

k \ n	2		3		4		5		6		7		8		9	
	ν	c	ν	c	ν	c	ν	c	ν	c	ν	c	ν	c	ν	c
2	1.0	1.00	2.0	1.35	2.9	1.58	3.8	1.75	4.7	1.89	5.5	2.00	6.3	2.10	7.0	2.18
3	1.9	1.05	3.7	1.48	5.6	1.76	7.4	1.96	9.3	2.12	11.3	2.26	13.4	2.37	15.7	2.46
4	2.7	1.07	5.4	1.54	8.2	1.84	11.0	2.06	13.9	2.23	16.9	2.38	20.1	2.50	23.6	2.60
5	3.6	1.08	7.2	1.57	10.9	1.88	14.6	2.12	18.5	2.30	22.4	2.45	26.6	2.57	31.1	2.68
6	4.5	1.09	8.9	1.59	13.6	1.91	18.2	2.15	23.0	2.34	27.9	2.49	33.0	2.62	38.3	2.73
7	5.4	1.09	10.7	1.61	16.3	1.93	21.8	2.18	27.6	2.37	33.3	2.52	39.3	2.65	45.4	2.76
8	6.3	1.10	12.5	1.62	19.0	1.95	25.4	2.20	32.1	2.39	38.7	2.55	45.6	2.68	52.5	2.79
9	7.1	1.10	14.3	1.63	21.7	1.96	29.0	2.21	36.6	2.41	44.0	2.57	51.8	2.70	59.6	2.81
10	8.1	1.10	16.1	1.63	24.4	1.97	32.6	2.22	41.0	2.42	49.3	2.58	57.9	2.71	66.6	2.83
20	16.7	1.11	33.9	1.66	51.5	2.02	68.8	2.28	86.0	2.48	103	2.64	119	2.78	134	2.90
d_n		1.13		1.69		2.06		2.33		2.53		2.70		2.85		2.97
CD	0.87		1.80		2.71		3.62		4.50		5.33		6.10		6.79	

This table is reproduced from E. S. Pearson and H. O. Hartley, *Biometrika Tables for Statisticians*, Vol. 1, 1958, with permission of the Biometrika Trustees.

TABLE 7A.9

UPPER 5 AND 1% POINTS OF THE MEDIAN IN A SAMPLE OF n DRAWN FROM $f(x) = 1$, $(0 \leq x \leq 1)$

n \ α	0.05	0.01	n \ α	0.05	0.01	n \ α	0.05	0.01
1	0.950	0.990	11	0.729	0.806	21	0.672	0.736
2	0.842	0.929	12	0.712	0.786	22	0.665	0.726
3	0.865	0.941	13	0.713	0.787	23	0.665	0.727
4	0.802	0.888	14	0.699	0.770	24	0.658	0.718
5	0.811	0.894	15	0.700	0.771	25	0.659	0.719
6	0.770	0.854	16	0.689	0.757	26	0.653	0.711
7	0.775	0.858	17	0.689	0.758	27	0.653	0.711
8	0.746	0.827	18	0.679	0.745	28	0.648	0.704
9	0.749	0.829	19	0.680	0.746	29	0.648	0.705
10	0.727	0.804	20	0.672	0.735	30	0.643	0.698

For n large use $\frac{1}{2}[1 + 1.645(n + 2)^{-1/2}]$, $\alpha = 0.05$
$\frac{1}{2}[1 + 2.326(n + 2)^{-1/2}]$, $\alpha = 0.01$.

TABLE 7A.10

UPPER PERCENTAGE POINTS OF $R = (m - \mu)/(x_u - x_l)$

n \ α	0.05	0.025	0.01
11	0.470	0.623	0.876
15	0.400	0.514	0.676
19	0.354	0.448	0.573
23	0.321	0.402	0.506
27	0.296	0.367	0.458
31	0.276	0.341	0.422
35	0.260	0.319	0.393
39	0.246	0.301	0.369
43	0.234	0.286	0.349
47	0.224	0.273	0.332
51	0.215	0.261	0.317

This table is reproduced from F. N. David and N. L. Johnson, "Some tests of significance with ordered variables," *J. R. Statist. Soc., B*, Vol. 18 (1956), pp. 1–20, with permission of the authors and the Royal Statistical Society.

REFERENCES

1. M. H. Belz and R. Hooke, "Approximate distribution of the range in the neighborhood of low percentage points," *J. Amer. Statist. Ass.*, Vol. 49 (1954), pp. 620–636.
2. G. E. P. Box, "Non-normality and tests on variances," *Biometrika*, Vol. 40 (1953), pp. 318–335.
3. J. H. Cadwell, "Approximating to the distributions of measures of dispersion by a power of χ^2," *Biometrika*, Vol. 40 (1953), pp. 336–346.
4. J. H. Cadwell, "The distribution of quasi-ranges in samples from a normal population," *Ann. Math. Statist.*, Vol. 24 (1953), pp. 603–613.
5. D. R. Cox, "The use of the range in sequential analysis," *J. R. Statist. Soc.*, *B*, Vol. 11 (1949), pp. 101–114.
6. D. R. Cox, "The mean and coefficient of variation of range in small samples from non-normal populations," *Biometrika*, Vol. 41 (1954), pp. 469–481.
7. J. F. Daly, "On the use of the sample range in an analogue of Student's t-test," *Ann. Math. Statist.*, Vol. 17 (1946), pp. 71–74.
8. F. N. David and N. L. Johnson, "Statistical treatment of censored data, Part I, Fundamental formulae," *Biometrika*, Vol. 41 (1954), pp. 228–240.
9. F. N. David and N. L. Johnson, "A test for skewness with ordered variables," *Ann. Eugen., London*, Vol. 18 (1954), pp. 351–353.
10. F. N. David and N. L. Johnson, "Some tests of significance with ordered variables," *J. R. Statist. Soc.*, *B*, Vol. 18 (1956), pp. 1–20.
11. H. A. David, "Further applications of range to the analysis of variance," *Biometrika*, Vol. 38 (1951), pp. 393–409.
12. H. A. David, "Upper 5 and 1% points of the maximum F-ratio," *Biometrika*, Vol. 39 (1952), pp. 422–424.
13. H. A. David, "The power function of some tests based on range," *Biometrika*, Vol. 40 (1953), pp. 347–353.
14. H. A. David, "The distribution of range in certain non-normal populations," *Biometrika*, Vol. 41 (1954), pp. 463–468.
15. H. A. David, H. O. Hartley, and E. S. Pearson, "The distribution of the ratio, in a single normal sample, of range to standard deviation," *Biometrika*, Vol. 41 (1954), pp. 482–493.
16. O. L. Davies and E. S. Pearson, "Methods of estimating from samples the population standard deviation," *J. R. Statist. Soc. Suppl.*, Vol. 1 (1934), pp. 76–93.
17. W. J. Dixon, "Analysis of extreme values," *Ann. Math. Statist.*, Vol. 21 (1950), pp. 488–506.
18. W. J. Dixon, "Estimates of the mean and standard deviation of a normal population," *Ann. Math. Statist.*, Vol. 28 (1957), pp. 806–809.
19. A. J. Duncan, "Design and operation of a double-limit variables sampling plan," *J. Amer. Statist. Ass.*, Vol. 53 (1958), pp. 543–550.
20. F. E. Grubbs and C. L. Weaver, "The best unbiased estimate of population standard deviation based on group ranges," *J. Amer. Statist. Ass.*, Vol. 42 (1947), pp. 224–241.
21. H. L. Harter and D. S. Clemm, "The probability integrals of the range and of the studentized range: probability integral, percentage points, and moments of the range." WADC Tech. Rep. 58–484, Vol. 1, 1959.
22. H. L. Harter, D. S. Clemm, and E. H. Guthrie, "The probability integrals of the range and of the studentized range: probability integral and percentage points of

the studentized range; critical values for Duncan's new multiple range test." WADC Tech. Rep. 58–484, Vol. 2, 1959.
23. H. O. Hartley, "Studentization," *Biometrika*, Vol. 33 (1944), pp. 173–180.
24. H. O. Hartley, "The use of range in analysis of variance," *Biometrika*, Vol. 37 (1950), pp. 271–280.
25. H. O. Hartley, "The maximum *F*-ratio as a short-cut test for heterogeneity of variance," *Biometrika*, Vol. 37 (1950), pp. 308–312.
26. H. O. Hartley, "Some recent developments in analysis of variance," *Comm. Pure and Appl. Math.*, Vol. 8 (1955), pp. 47–72.
27. H. O. Hartley and H. A. David, "Universal bounds for mean range and extreme observation," *Ann. Math. Statist.*, Vol. 25 (1954), pp. 85–99.
28. H. Hyrenius, "On the use of ranges, cross-ranges and extremes in comparing small samples," *J. Amer. Statist. Ass.*, Vol. 48 (1953), pp. 534–545.
29. J. E. Jackson and E. L. Ross, "Extended tables for use with the "G" test for means," *J. Amer. Statist. Ass.*, Vol. 50 (1955), pp. 416–433.
30. A. E. Jones, "A useful method for the routine estimation of dispersion from large samples," *Biometrika*, Vol. 33 (1946), pp. 274–282.
31. R. F. Link, "The sampling distribution of the ratio of two ranges from independent samples," *Ann. Math. Statist.*, Vol. 21 (1950), pp. 112–116.
32. E. Lord, "The use of range in place of standard deviation in the *t*-test," *Biometrika*, Vol. 34 (1947), pp. 41–67.
33. E. Lord, "Power of the modified *t*-test (*u*-test) based on range," *Biometrika*, Vol. 37 (1950), pp. 64–77.
34. S. K. Mitra, "Tables for tolerance limits for a normal population based on sample mean and range or mean range," *J. Amer. Statist. Ass.*, Vol. 52 (1957), pp. 88–94.
35. P. G. Moore, "Normality in quality control charts," *Appl. Statist.*, Vol. 6 (1957), pp. 171–179.
36. P. G. Moore, "The two sample *t*-test based on range," *Biometrika*, Vol. 44 (1957), pp. 482–489.
37. L. E. Moses, "Some theoretical aspects of the lot plot sampling inspection plan," *J. Amer. Statist. Ass.*, Vol. 51 (1956), pp. 84–107.
38. F. Mosteller, "On some useful 'inefficient' statistics," *Ann. Math. Statist.*, Vol. 17 (1946), pp. 377–408.
39. K. R. Nair, "Efficiencies of certain linear systematic statistics for estimating dispersion from normal samples," *Biometrika*, Vol. 37 (1950), pp. 182–183.
40. D. Newman, "Range in samples from a normal population," *Biometrika*, Vol. 31 (1939), pp. 20–30.
41. G. E. Noether, "Use of the range instead of the standard deviation," *J. Amer. Statist. Ass.*, Vol. 50 (1955), pp. 1040–1055.
42. P. B. Patnaik, "The use of mean range as an estimator of variance in statistical tests," *Biometrika*, Vol. 37 (1950), pp. 78–87.
43. E. S. Pearson, "Percentage limits for the distribution of range in samples from a normal population," *Biometrika*, Vol. 24 (1932), pp. 404–417.
44. E. S. Pearson, "Some notes on the use of range," *Biometrika*, Vol. 37 (1950), pp. 88–92.
45. E. S. Pearson, "Comparison of two approximations to the distribution of the range in small samples from normal populations," *Biometrika*, Vol. 39 (1952), pp. 130–136.
46. E. S. Pearson and N. K. Adyanthāya, "Distribution of frequency constants from symmetrical populations," *Biometrika*, Vol. 20A (1928), pp. 356–360.
47. E. S. Pearson and H. O. Hartley, "Probability integral of the range in samples of *n* observations from the normal population," *Biometrika*, Vol. 32 (1942), pp. 301–310.

48. E. S. Pearson and H. O. Hartley, "Tables of the probability integral of the studentized range," *Biometrika*, Vol. 33 (1943), pp. 89–99.
49. E. S. Pearson and H. O. Hartley, "Moment constants for the distribution of range," *Biometrika*, Vol. 38 (1951), pp. 463–464.
50. E. S. Pearson and H. O. Hartley, *Biometrika Tables for Statisticians*, Vol. 1, Cambridge University Press, Cambridge, England, 1958.
51. K. C. S. Pillai, "On the distribution of mid-range and semi-range in samples from a normal population," *Ann. Math. Statist.*, Vol. 21 (1950), pp. 100–105.
52. K. C. S. Pillai, "Some notes on ordered samples from a normal population," *Sankhyā*, Vol. 11 (1951), pp. 23–28.
53. K. C. S. Pillai, "On the distribution of 'Studentized' range," *Biometrika*, Vol. 39 (1952), pp. 194–195.
54. R. L. Plackett, "Limits of the ratio of mean range to standard deviation," *Biometrika*, Vol. 34 (1947), pp. 120–122.
55. L. Råde, "A note on a modified *t*-test," *Skand. Aktuartidskr.*, Vol. 37 (1954), pp. 65–70.
56. RAND Corporation, *A Million Random Digits with 100,000 Normal Deviates*, Free Press, Glencoe, Ill., 1955.
57. G. J. Resnikoff, "The distribution of the average-range for subgroups of five," Tech. Rep. 15, Appl. Math. and Statist. Lab., Stanford University, California, 1954, pp. 1–17.
58. G. J. Resnikoff, "Two-sided tolerance limits for normal distributions using the range," Tech. Rep. 33, Appl. Math. and Statist. Lab., Stanford University, California, 1957, pp. 1–18.
59. S. Rushton, "On sequential tests of the equality of variances of two normal populations with known means," *Sankhyā*, Vol. 12 (1952), pp. 63–78.
60. H. Scheffé, "Operating characteristics of average and range charts," *Industr. Qual. Contr.*, Vol. 6, No. 6 (1949), pp. 13–18.
61. L. A. Seder and D. Cowan, "The span plan method process capability analysis," A.S.Q.C. Gen. Publ. 3, 1956, pp. 1–59.
62. S. Shimada, "Power of *R*-chart," *Rep. Statist. Appl. Res.*, JUSE, Vol. 3, No. 3 (1954), pp. 14–18.
63. D. Teichroew, "Tables of expected values of order statistics and products of order statistics for samples of size twenty and less from the normal distribution," *Ann. Math. Statist.*, Vol. 27 (1956), pp. 410–426.
64. G. W. Thomson, "Scale factor and degrees of freedom for small sample sizes for χ-approximation to the range," *Biometrika*, Vol. 40 (1953), pp. 449–450.
65. L. H. C. Tippett, "On the extreme individuals and range of samples taken from a normal population," *Biometrika*, Vol. 17 (1925), pp. 364–387.
66. J. W. Tukey, "Some selected and easy methods of statistical analysis," *Trans. N.Y. Acad. Sci.* (Series II), Vol. 16 (1953), pp. 88–97.
67. J. E. Walsh, "On the range-midrange test and some tests with bounded significance levels," *Ann. Math. Statist.*, Vol. 23 (1952), pp. 257–267.

ADDITIONAL BIBLIOGRAPHY

1. S. H. Abdel-Aty, "Ordered variables in discontinuous distributions," *Statist. Neerlandica*, Vol. 8 (1954), pp. 61–82.
2. I. W. Burr, "Calculation of exact sampling distribution of ranges from a discrete population," *Ann. Math. Statist.*, Vol. 26 (1955), pp. 530–532.

3. J. T. Chu, "On the distribution of the sample median," *Ann. Math. Statist.*, Vol. 26 (1955), pp. 112–116.
4. J. T. Chu, "The inefficiency of the sample median for many familiar symmetric distributions," *Biometrika*, Vol. 42 (1955), pp. 520–521.
5. E. J. Gumbel, "The maxima of the mean largest value and of the range," *Ann. Math. Statist.*, Vol. 25 (1954), pp. 76–84.
6. A. Hald, *Statistical Theory with Engineering Applications*, John Wiley and Sons, New York, 1952.
7. B. I. Harley and E. S. Pearson, "The distribution of range in normal samples with $n = 200$," *Biometrika*, Vol. 44 (1957), pp. 257–260.
8. H. O. Hartley, "The range in random samples," *Biometrika*, Vol. 32 (1942), pp. 334–348.
9. E. P. King, "Estimating the standard deviation of a normal population," *Industr. Qual. Contr.*, Vol. 10, No. 2 (1953), pp. 1–4.
10. J. Machek, "On a two-sample procedure for testing Student's hypothesis using mean range," *Aplik. Mat.*, Vol. 4 (1959).
11. N. Mantel, "Rapid estimation of standard errors of means for small samples," *Amer. Statist.*, Vol. 5, No. 14 (1951), pp. 26–27.
12. M. Masuyama, "The use of sample range in estimating the standard deviation or the variance of any population," *Sankhyā*, Vol. 18 (1957), pp. 159–162.
13. P. G. Moore, "The ranges in small and correlated samples," *Trab. Estadist.*, Vol. 9 (1958), pp. 3–12.
14. S. Moriguti, "Extremal properties of extreme value distributions," *Ann. Math. Statist.*, Vol. 22 (1951), pp. 523–536.
15. S. Moriguti, "Bounds for second moments of the sample range," *Rep. Statist. Appl. Res.*, JUSE, Vol. 3, No. 3 (1954), pp. 57–64.
16. J. Moshman, "Testing a straggler mean in a two-way classification using the range," *Ann. Math. Statist.*, Vol. 23 (1952), pp. 126–132.
17. E. S. Pearson and J. Haines, "The use of range in place of standard deviation in small samples," *J. R. Statist. Soc.*, Suppl., Vol. 2 (1935), pp. 83–98.
18. P. R. Rider, "The distribution of the range in samples from a discrete rectangular population," *J. Amer. Statist. Ass.*, Vol. 46 (1951), pp. 375–378.
19. P. R. Rider, "The distribution of the quotient of ranges in samples from a rectangular population," *J. Amer. Statist. Ass.*, Vol. 46 (1951), pp. 502–507.
20. M. Siotani, "On the distribution of the sum of the positive or negative deviations from the mean in the sample drawn from the normal population," *Proc. Inst. Statist. Math., Tokyo*, Vol. 2 (1954), pp. 63–74 (Japanese).
21. M. Siotani, "An estimate of standard deviation of normal population based on the difference between means of two groups divided by sample mean," *Ann. Inst. Statist. Math., Tokyo*, Vol. 6 (1954), pp. 153–160.
22. M. Siotani, "Order statistics for discrete case with a numerical application to the binomial distribution," *Ann. Inst. Statist. Math., Tokyo*, Vol. 8 (1956), pp. 95–104.
23. T. J. Terpstra, "A confidence interval for the probability that a normally distributed variable exceeds a given value, based on the mean and the mean range of a number of samples," *Appl. Sci. Res.*, Section A, Vol. 3 (1953), pp. 297–307.
24. G. W. Thomson, "Bounds for the ratio of range to standard deviation," *Biometrika*, Vol. 42 (1955), pp. 268–269.
25. S. S. Wilks, "Order statistics," *Bull. Amer. Math. Soc.*, Vol. 54 (1948), pp. 6–50.
26. C. B. Winsten, "Inequalities in terms of mean range," *Biometrika*, Vol. 33 (1946), pp. 283–295.

JULIUS LIEBLEIN

7B THE CLOSEST TWO OUT OF THREE OBSERVATIONS[1]

Given the three order statistics in random samples of size three from a population with density function $f(x)$:

$$x_{(1)} \leq x_{(2)} \leq x_{(3)}. \tag{7B.1}$$

From these, a set of three new statistics,

$$x' \geq x'', \quad x''' \tag{7B.2}$$

are defined as follows:

$$\left.\begin{array}{ll} x' = x_{(2)}, \quad x'' = x_{(1)}, \quad x''' = x_{(3)}, & \textit{if } x_{(2)} - x_{(1)} < x_{(3)} - x_{(2)} \\ \text{and} & \\ x' = x_{(3)}, \quad x'' = x_{(2)}, \quad x''' = x_{(1)}, & \textit{if } x_{(2)} - x_{(1)} \geq x_{(3)} - x_{(2)} \end{array}\right\}. \tag{7B.3}$$

In other words, the pair (x', x'') are the two *closest* of the three, and x''' is a true outlier or extreme and is either the largest or smallest value, depending on the spacing.

Thus the new statistics in (7B.3) are not determined merely by their rank alone and are therefore somewhat more general than the usual order statistics. Unfortunately, the concept of "closeness" is not readily generalized to larger samples.

Triplicate determinations, that is, a set of three observations, are fairly common in the chemical laboratory inasmuch as a third one is occasionally taken to indicate which of the other two is more likely to be off the mark. And if only two of the three measurements are in close agreement, the worker is under strong temptation to discard completely the remaining distant one on the ground that evidence of gross error is present. A similar practice also appears to be encouraged by instruction methods in quantitative chemical analysis which grade students not only on the correctness of their results, made in duplicate, but also on their precision as measured by the difference between the two results. Thus a student might hope to improve his record by quietly making a third, uncalled-for analysis, giving himself the advantage of the closest two of all three, and omitting to mention the remaining one. This is a very striking example of the long-standing problem of the rejection of outlying observations and raises the statistical question of how estimates of the mean and variability of analyses are affected by such procedures.

[1] As explained in reference 2, the problem described in this section was proposed by Dr. W. J. Youden of the National Bureau of Standards.

This question suggests what combinations of (7B.2) would be of interest:

$$y_1 = \frac{x' - x''}{x_{(3)} - x_{(1)}}, \qquad y_2 = \frac{x' - x''}{2}, \qquad y_3 = \frac{x' + x''}{2}.$$

The first measures the ratio of the smaller gap to the range; the second measures the standard deviation of the two closest measurements, that is, half their difference; and the third is the mean of the two closest.

The sampling distributions and first two moments of y_1 are shown in Table 7B.1 for three parent populations. Some percentage points of y_1 are given in Table 7B.3. Similar features are shown in Table 7B.2 for y_2 and y_3 for two populations, together with a comparison of results for other measures that may be considered to be analogous to the statistics y_1, y_2, y_3 in some crude sense.

These tables may be used to answer questions such as the following: (1) In a random sample of three observations from a single (continuous) population what values of y_1 may be considered significant? (2) How does the range in a sample of true duplicate measurements compare with the difference between the two values in each of (*a*) the closest pair out of a sample of three measurements, (*b*) the lowest (or highest) pair out of such a sample, and (*c*) the pair of extremes (highest and lowest values) of the entire sample of three as regards several types of universes? (3) How do the means compare in each case?

The answers to these questions involve primarily the investigation of the distributions of the three statistics, y_1, y_2, and y_3, whose main properties are summarized in Tables 7B.1 and 7B.2.

The comparisons indicated in Tables 7B.1 and 7B.2 reveal the following facts for random samples of three measurements, where, unless otherwise stated, the statements apply to samples from a normal or a rectangular population.

1. The statistic y_1, which characterizes the partition of the range by the middle item in a random sample of three measurements, behaves remarkably alike for samples from three different basic populations, the normal, rectangular, and right triangular (Table 7B.1), suggesting that this ratio statistic would not be very useful as a criterion for discriminating between a normal population and some other population.

2. A set of two observations selected by taking the closest two out of three from a normal or a rectangular population differs from other pairs taken from the three or from a pair of true duplicates, as shown by the following.

(*a*) The average *difference* (as measured by y_2) between the selected pair is less than half that for the true duplicates, and the same is true of the variability of this distance as measured by the standard deviation (Table 7B.2, Part A, columns 1, 3, and 4, 6). Furthermore, the difference between the selected pair behaves (again in an average sense) very much like half the difference between the two lowest (or highest) in the full sample of three, and (in the same sense) is similar to one-quarter the difference between the two most extreme measurements in the sample. The standard deviation of the difference between the closest pair is, however, comparable to the standard deviation of half the range (Table 7B.2, Part *A*, columns 1, 2, and 4, 5).

(*b*) The mean (y_3) of a selected pair varies somewhat more than the mean of a true duplicate pair, the average value of both means being the same. Especially noteworthy is the fact that the true average of the population is *more precisely estimated by using the two most discrepant observations of the three in forming an average,* $\frac{1}{2}(x_1 + x_3)$, *then by taking the two that are most in agreement*, although, of course, neither method is as precise as taking the mean of all three (Table 7B.2, Part B, columns 1, 4). Thus, selection of measurements on the basis of close agreement *increases* rather than decreases the true error of measurement.

Results for the outlier, $\omega = x'''$, are particularly simple when the samples of three are from a rectangular population. Its density function is the flat nose of the parabola

$$p(\omega) = 3(\omega^2 - \omega + \tfrac{1}{2}), \qquad 0 \le \omega \le 1.$$

The moments are

$$E(\omega) = \tfrac{1}{2}, \qquad \sigma(\omega) = (10)^{-1/2} = 0.3162.$$

Some Relevant Literature. Section 7B has been abstracted from Lieblein [2]. A related discussion may be found in Seth [3]. Dixon [1] has studied (among others) the statistic

$$r_{10} = \frac{x_{(n)} - x_{(n-1)}}{x_{(n)} - x_{(1)}}$$

which for $n = 3$ may be considered to be "half" the definition of the ratio y_1. Tukey [4] has been concerned with the *largest*, rather than the smallest, gap in samples of 2 to 10. For the subject of outliers and rejection of observations in general, see Section 10H.

TABLE 7B.1

CHARACTERISTICS OF THE RATIO y_1 OF THE DISTANCE BETWEEN THE CLOSEST PAIR TO THE RANGE IN A SAMPLE OF THREE MEASUREMENTS

$$y_1 = \frac{x' - x''}{x_{(3)} - x_{(1)}}, \quad x'' \le x', \; x_{(1)} \le x_{(2)} \le x_{(3)}$$

	Normal Population	Rectangular Population	Right Triangular Population
Probability density function	$\frac{3\sqrt{3}}{\pi(y_1^2 - y_1 + 1)}, 0 \le y_1 \le \frac{1}{2}$	$2, 0 \le y_1 \le \frac{1}{2}$	$2, 0 \le y_1 \le \frac{1}{2}$
Mean	0.2621	0.25	0.25
Standard deviation	0.1428	0.1443	0.1443

This table is reproduced from J. Lieblein, "Properties of certain statistics involving the closest pair in a sample of three observations," *J. Res. Nat. Bur. Stand.*, Vol. 48 (1952), pp. 255–268, with permission of the National Bureau of Standards.

TABLE 7B.2

Characteristics of Other Statistics Related to the Closest Pair of Measurements in a Sample of Three

$x_{(1)} \leq x_{(2)} \leq \ldots \leq x_{(n)}$ denote the measurements in a sample of n ordered according to size. If $n = 3$, then x' and x'', $x' \geq x''$, denote the two *closest* measurements in the sample. The measurements before ordering are considered to be drawn independently at random from the populations designated. The rectangular population has been adjusted to unit variance and centered at the origin. Exact values and distribution functions are given when practical. Where the interval of nonzero probability density is omitted for a probability distribution, the variate is assumed to take all values from $-\infty$ to $+\infty$.

	Normal Population, $f(x) = \frac{1}{\sqrt{2\pi}} e^{-\frac{1}{2}x^2}$, $-\infty < x < \infty$			Rectangular Population with Unit Variance, $g(x) = \frac{1}{\sqrt{12}}$, $-\sqrt{3} \leq x \leq \sqrt{3}$		
	(1) Closest Pair in a Sample of 3	(2) Lowest Pair[a] in a Sample of 3	(3) Sample of 2 ("True Duplicates")	(4) Closest Pair in a Sample of 3	(5) Lowest Pair[a] in a Sample of 3	(6) Sample of 2 ("True Duplicates")
	A. Statistics Relative to the DISTANCE between Two Values					
Statistic	$x'-x''=2y_2=y'_2$	$(x_{(2)}-x_{(1)})/2=s$	$(x_{(2)}-x_{(1)})/2=p$	$x'-x''=2y_2=y'_2$	$(x_{(2)}-x_{(1)})/2=s$	$(x_{(2)}-x_{(1)})/2=p$
Probability density function	$\frac{3\sqrt{3}}{\pi}\int_{y'_2}^{\infty} e^{-\frac{1}{4}(3t^2+y'^2_2)}\,dt$	$\frac{6\sqrt{3}}{\pi}\int_{\frac{1}{3}s}^{\infty} e^{-(3t^2+s^2)}\,dt$	$\frac{2}{\sqrt{\pi}} e^{-p^2}$	$\frac{1}{\sqrt{3}}(\sqrt{3}-y'_2)^2$	$\frac{1}{\sqrt{3}}(\sqrt{3}-s)^2$	$\frac{2}{3}(\sqrt{3}-p)$
	$0 \leq y'_2 < \infty$	$0 \leq s < \infty$	$0 \leq p < \infty$	$0 \leq y'_2 \leq \sqrt{3}$	$0 \leq s \leq \sqrt{3}$	$0 \leq p \leq \sqrt{3}$
Mean	$E(y'_2)=0.4535$	$E(s)=\frac{3}{4\sqrt{\pi}}=0.4231$	$E(p)=\frac{1}{\sqrt{\pi}}=0.5642$	$E(y'_2)=\frac{\sqrt{3}}{4}=0.4330$	$E(s)=\frac{\sqrt{3}}{4}=0.4330$	$E(p)=\sqrt{\frac{1}{3}}=0.5774$
Other means for comparison	$E(x_{(3)}-x_{(1)})/4=\frac{3}{4\sqrt{\pi}}=0.4231$	$E(x_{(3)}-x_{(1)})/4=\frac{3}{4\sqrt{\pi}}$		$E(x_{(3)}-x_{(1)})/4=\frac{\sqrt{3}}{4}$	$E(x_{(3)}-x_{(1)})/4=\frac{\sqrt{3}}{4}$	
Standard deviation	$\sigma(y'_2)=0.3746$	$\sigma(s)=0.3379$	$\sigma(p)=\left(\frac{1}{2}-\frac{1}{\pi}\right)^{\frac{1}{2}}=0.4263$	$\sigma(y'_2)=\frac{3\sqrt{5}}{20}=0.3354$	$\sigma(s)=\frac{3\sqrt{5}}{20}=0.3354$	$\sigma(p)=\sqrt{\frac{1}{6}}=0.4082$
Other standard deviations for comparison	$\sigma(x_{(3)}-x_{(1)})/2=0.4442$	$\sigma(x_{(3)}-x_{(1)})/2=0.4442$		$\sigma(x_{(3)}-x_{(1)})/2=\frac{\sqrt{15}}{10}=0.3873$	$\sigma(x_{(3)}-x_{(1)})/2=\frac{\sqrt{15}}{10}=0.3873$	

TABLE 7B.2 *Continued*

B. Statistics Relative to the AVERAGE of Two Values

Statistic	$(x'+x'')/2=y_3$	$(x_{(1)}+x_{(2)})/2=q$	$(x_{(1)}+x_{(3)})/2=m$	$(x'+x'')/2=y_3$	$(x_{(1)}+x_{(2)})/2=q$	$(x_{(1)}+x_{(3)})/2=m$
Probability density function	$\frac{6}{\pi\sqrt{2\pi}}\int_0^{\infty}\int e^{-Q}\,dt\,dy_2$, where t ranges over $(-\infty, -3y_2+y_3)$ and $(3y_2+y_3, \infty)$ $Q=\frac{1}{2}t^2+y_2^2+y_3^2$	(*b*)	$\frac{1}{\sqrt{\pi}}e^{-m^2}$	(*b*)	(*b*)	$\frac{1}{3}(\sqrt{3}-\lvert m\rvert)$, $-\sqrt{3}\le m\le\sqrt{3}$
Mean	$E(y_3)=0$	$E(q)=-\frac{3}{4\sqrt{\pi}}=-0.4231$	$E(m)=0$	$E(y_3)=0$	$E(q)=-\frac{\sqrt{3}}{4}=-0.4330$	$E(m)=0$
Other means for comparison	$E(x_{(1)}+x_{(3)})/2=0$ $E(x_{(1)}+x_{(2)}+x_{(3)})/3=E\bar{x}=0$			$E(x_{(1)}+x_{(3)})/2=0$ $E(x_{(1)}+x_{(2)}+x_{(3)})/3=0$		
Standard deviation	$\sigma(y_3)=\left(\frac{1}{2}+\frac{\sqrt{3}}{4\pi}\right)^{1/2}=0.7986$	$\sigma(q)=0.6244$	$\sigma(m)=\sqrt{\frac{1}{2}}=0.7071$	$\sigma(y_3)=\sqrt{33/40}=0.9083$	$\sigma(q)=\sqrt{33/80}=0.6423$	$\sigma(m)=0.5$
Other standard deviations for comparison	$\sigma(x_{(1)}+x_{(3)})/2=\left(\frac{1}{2}-\frac{\sqrt{3}}{4\pi}\right)^{1/2}=0.6018$ $\sigma(x_{(1)}+x_{(2)}+x_{(3)})/3=\sigma_{\bar{x}}=\frac{1}{\sqrt{3}}=0.5774$	$\sigma(x_{(1)}+x_{(3)})/2=0.6018$		$\sigma(x_{(1)}+x_{(3)})/2=\sqrt{3/10}=0.5477$ $\sigma_{\bar{x}}=\frac{1}{\sqrt{3}}=0.5774$	$\sigma(x_{(1)}+x_{(2)})/3=\sqrt{3/10}=0.5477$	

[a] The characteristics of the *highest* pair are obtainable from symmetry considerations.
[b] These density functions have been omitted since they are rather complicated.
This table is reproduced from J. Lieblein, "Properties of certain statistics involving the closest pair in a sample of three observations," *J. Res. Nat. Bur. Stand.*, Vol. 48 (1952), pp. 255–268, with permission of the National Bureau of Standards.

TABLE 7B.3

PERCENTAGE POINTS OF y_1 FOR THE UNIT NORMAL

$$y_1 = \frac{x' - x''}{x_{(3)} - x_{(1)}}; \quad \Pr\{y_1 \le y_1^0\} = \frac{6}{\pi} \arctan\left(\frac{2y_1^0 - 1}{\sqrt{3}}\right) + 1$$

Probability P That y_1 Does Not Exceed Given Value of y_1^0		Critical Value y_1^0 Corresponding to Given Probability P	
y_1^0	P	P	y_1^0
0	0	0	0
1/11	0.1572	0.01	0.00603
1/6	0.2983	0.05	0.02979
1/3	0.6369	0.10	0.05874
		0.25	0.14128
		0.50	0.26795

This table is reproduced from J. Lieblein, "Properties of certain statistics involving the closest pair in a sample of three observations," *J. Res. Nat. Bur. Stand.*, Vol. 48 (1952), pp. 255–268, with permission of the National Bureau of Standards.

REFERENCES

1. W. J. Dixon, "Ratios involving extreme-values," *Ann. Math. Statist.*, Vol. 22 (1951), pp. 68–78.
2. J. Lieblein, "Properties of certain statistics involving the closest pair in a sample of three observations," *J. Res. Nat. Bur. Stand.*, Vol. 48, No. 3 (March 1952), pp. 255–268.
3. G. R. Seth, "On the distribution of the two closest among a set of three observations," *Ann. Math. Statist.*, Vol. 21 (1950), pp. 298–301.
4. J. W. Tukey, "Comparing individual means in the analysis of variance," *Biometrics*, Vol. 5 (1949), pp. 99–114.

JOHN E. WALSH

CHAPTER 8

Nonparametric Confidence Intervals and Tolerance Regions

8.1 Introduction

The use of order statistics is basic in determining nonparametric (distribution-free) confidence intervals for population percentage points and nonparametric tolerance regions for population distributions. This chapter deals mainly with the situation of a random sample from a continuous population. A short description of the fundamental theory is given for the univariate situation in which no further restrictions are imposed on the population sampled. This theory is used to obtain confidence intervals for percentage points and to obtain tolerance intervals.

If the univariate distribution satisfies the additional restriction of being symmetrical, confidence intervals for the population median can be obtained which tend to be more efficient than those for the general case. The derivation of this class of confidence intervals is outlined and a listing given for several of the less complicated types of intervals. Also a method is stated for obtaining confidence intervals on the basis of the Wilcoxon signed-rank test.

The tolerance interval concept extends to samples from multivariate distributions. These extensions are discussed and a method stated for determining tolerance regions in a general case.

8.2 Univariate Theory

Let $x_{(1)} \leq \ldots \leq x_{(n)}$ represent the values of a sample of size n from a continuous population with distribution function $F(x)$ while $x_{(0)} = -\infty$

and $x_{(n+1)} = \infty$. To follow the presentation of Wilks [14], the $n + 1$ random variables

$$C_i = \int_{x_{i-1}}^{x_i} dF(x), \qquad i = 1, 2, \ldots, n + 1$$

are called elementary coverages, and the joint frequency function of any n of these coverages, for convenience the first n, is

$$f(c_1, \ldots, c_n) = n!$$

where $c_i \geq 0$ and $\sum_{i=1}^{n} c_i \leq 1$. Thus the coverages for the intervals $I_i = (x_{(i-1)}, x_{(i)})$ are distribution-free, and their joint frequency function is of a reasonably uncomplicated form.

The distribution of various statistics of interest can be obtained on the basis of the joint distribution of any specified n of the elementary coverages. For example, if U is the set sum of any r $(r \leq n)$ of $C_1, \ldots, C_{n+1}$, then U has the frequency function

$$f(u) = \frac{n!}{(r-1)!\,(n-r)!} u^{r-1}(1-u)^{n-r}, \qquad 0 \leq u \leq 1$$

(see reference 14).

8.3 Confidence Intervals for Percentage Points

Let θ_p represent a $100p\%$ point of $F(x)$; that is, $F(\theta_p) = p$. Then, since $F(x)$ is a continuous monotonic increasing function of x, the theory of Subsection 8.2 shows that

$$\Pr(x_{(s)} < \theta_p) = \Pr[F(x_{(s)}) < p] = \frac{n!}{(s-1)!\,(n-s)!} \int_0^p u^{s-1}(1-u)^{n-s}\, du$$

$$= I_p(s, n-s+1) = \sum_{i=s}^{n} \binom{n}{i} p^i (1-p)^{n-i}, \tag{8.3.1}$$

$$\Pr(x_{(r)} > \theta_p) = \Pr[F(x_{(r)}) > p] = \frac{n!}{(r-1)!\,(n-r)!} \int_p^1 u^{r-1}(1-u)^{n-r}\, du$$

$$= 1 - I_p(r, n-r+1) = \sum_{i=0}^{r-1} \binom{n}{i} p^i (1-p)^{n-i}, \tag{8.3.2}$$

$$\Pr(x_{(r)} < \theta_p < x_{(s)}; r<s) = \Pr[F(x_{(r)}) < p < F(x_{(s)}); r < s]$$
$$= 1 - \Pr[F(x_{(r)}) > p] - \Pr[F(x_{(s)}) < p] \tag{8.3.3}$$

where $I_p(r, n-r+1)$ is Karl Pearson's incomplete beta function. Note that the two-sided confidence interval represents a nonoverlapping combination of two one-sided intervals.

Relations (8.3.1), (8.3.2), (8.3.3) define one-sided and two-sided confidence intervals for θ_p in terms of the order statistics $x_{(r)}$ and $x_{(s)}$. That is, $(x_{(s)}, \infty)$ is a one-sided confidence interval for θ_p with confidence coefficient given by (8.3.1), whereas $(-\infty, x_{(r)})$ is a one-sided confidence interval with confidence coefficient given by (8.3.2). Also $(x_{(r)}, x_{(s)})$ is a two-sided confidence interval for θ_p with confidence coefficient given by (8.3.3). For $n \leq 50$, these confidence coefficients can be evaluated by use of a table for the binomial distribution [2] or by a table of the incomplete beta function [3]. For $n \geq 10$, approximations [4] can be used to obtain reasonably accurate values.

8.4 Univariate Tolerance Intervals

Consider two functions of the sample values, denoted by L_1 and L_2, such that the random interval (L_1, L_2) has a probability β of containing at least $100\gamma\%$ of the population. That is,

$$\Pr[F(L_2) - F(L_1) \geq \gamma] = \beta. \tag{8.4.1}$$

The functions L_1, L_2 are called tolerance limits, and their probability properties for (8.4.1) usually depend on the form of $F(x)$. However, if $L_1 \not\equiv L_2$ and each of these functions is one of $x_{(0)}, x_{(1)}, \ldots, x_{(n+1)}$, the value of β is determined independently of the population distribution function (see reference 13). That is, this type of choice for the functions L_1, L_2 yields distribution-free tolerance intervals. Moreover, if $F(x)$ has a derivative (a practically unimportant restriction), this is the only type of distribution-free choice for one-sided tolerance intervals where the variable endpoint is a symmetric function of the sample values (see reference 5).

Letting $L_1 = x_{(r)}$ and $L_2 = x_{(s)}$ $(0 \leq r < s \leq n + 1)$, with the combination $r = 0$ and $s = n + 1$ excluded, the tolerance interval $(x_{(r)}, x_{(s)})$ equals the sum of *s-r* elementary coverages so that

$$\begin{aligned}\Pr[F(x_{(s)}) - F(x_{(r)}) \geq \gamma] &\\ &= \frac{n!}{(s-r-1)!\,(n-s+r)!}\int_\gamma^1 u^{s-r-1}(1-u)^{n-s+r}\,du\\ &= 1 - I_\gamma(s-r, n-s+r+1) = \sum_{i=0}^{s-r-1}\binom{n}{i}\gamma^i(1-\gamma)^{n-i},\end{aligned}$$

which determines β as a function of *s-r*, *n*, and γ. If a one-sided tolerance interval is considered (i.e., $L_1 = -\infty$ or $L_2 = \infty$), ordinarily one of the combinations $r = 0$, $s = n$ or $r = 1$, $s = n + 1$ is used. If a two-sided tolerance interval is considered, ordinarily $r = 1$ and $s = n$.

For both the one-sided and two-sided cases, the procedure (for specified γ) is to determine the smallest value of n such that

$$\Pr[F(x_{(s)}) - F(x_{(r)}) \geq \gamma] \geq \beta.$$

That is, the sample size is increased until the tolerance interval satisfies, or mildly improves, relation (8.4.1). For a specified type of one-sided tolerance interval and for two-sided tolerance intervals, the value required for n is minimized if the ordinarily adopted combinations of r, s values are used.

8.5 Confidence Intervals for Median of Symmetrical Population

In some cases the additional information of population symmetry may be available. That is, $x_{(1)} \leq \ldots \leq x_{(n)}$ are the values of a sample from a continuous symmetrical population. This additional knowledge can be used to obtain confidence intervals for $\phi = \theta_{1/2}$ that have a much wider choice of confidence coefficients and higher efficiencies (at least for approximate normality) than those derived in Subsection 8.3.

The confidence intervals considered are based on single order statistics of the $n(n + 1)/2$ averages $(x_{(i)} + x_{(j)})/2$, with $i \geq j$, or of any specified subset of these averages. Let $y'_{(1)} \leq \ldots \leq y'_{(h)}$ be the values of any given subset of h of the $(x_{(i)} + x_{(j)})/2$. Then exact confidence intervals of the forms $(-\infty, y'_{(r)})$, $(y'_{(r)}, \infty)$, $(y'_{(r)}, y'_{(s)})$ can be obtained for ϕ (see references 9, 10). These confidence intervals are derived by showing that the confidence coefficient has the same value for any continuous symmetrical population as it does for the rectangular population with nonzero range from 0 to 1. Table 8.1 contains a list of some probability relations that define many one-sided confidence intervals for ϕ. Two-sided confidence intervals can be obtained as nonoverlapping combinations of one-sided intervals. An efficiency analysis [9] indicates that the confidence intervals furnished by Table 8.1 have reasonably high efficiencies if $k \leq 3n/4$, at least for a normal population.

Use of Table 8.1 should be satisfactory if n is not very large (say $n \leq 20$). For larger values of n, a procedure based on the Wilcoxon signed-rank test [11, 12] can be used to furnish confidence intervals for ϕ. Tukey [8] showed that the Wilcoxon signed-rank test is equivalent to a subclass of the general results [9, 10]. Let $y_{(1)} \leq \ldots \leq y_{(n(n+1)/2)}$ be the values of the averages $(x_{(i)} + x_{(j)})/2$, with $i \geq j$. The one-sided confidence intervals of the forms $(-\infty, y_{(r)})$ and $(y_{(s)}, \infty)$ are equivalent to one-sided Wilcoxon signed-rank tests. Let T be the sum of the positive signed-ranks for the Wilcoxon test applied to the sample for the case of zero median. Then

$$\Pr(y_{(r)} > \phi) = \Pr[T \geq n(n+1)/2 - r + 1],$$

$$\Pr(y_{(s)} < \phi) = \Pr[T \leq n(n+1)/2 - s],$$

$$\Pr(y_{(r)} < \phi < y_{(s)};\, r < s) = 1 - \Pr(y_{(r)} > \phi) - \Pr(y_{(s)} < \phi).$$

For $n \geq 20$ the distribution of T is approximately normal with

$$E(T) = n(n+1)/4, \qquad V(T) = n(n+1)(2n+1)/24.$$

A continuity correction of one-half should be used in applying the normal approximation to determine probabilities for T.

The general class of confidence intervals [9, 10] are valid when the observations are not a random sample. Exact confidence intervals are obtained for ϕ if the n observations are independent and are from n continuous symmetrical populations for which ϕ is the common central value.

8.6 Multivariate Tolerance Regions

The data are a sample of size n from a continuous multivariate population with distribution function F. A tolerance region R is a function of the sample values with the property that

$$\Pr\left(\int_R dF \geq \gamma\right) = \beta. \tag{8.6.1}$$

Random regions R can be chosen so that the value of β is independent of F; that is, so that the tolerance regions are distribution-free. This can be accomplished by determining $(n + 1)$ basic random regions that are called statistical blocks. These statistical blocks, which correspond to the elementary coverages for the univariate case, can have a large number of different types of shapes. Let U be the set sum of any r of these $n + 1$ statistical blocks. Then, as for the univariate case, the frequency function of U is

$$f(u) = \frac{n!}{(r-1)!\,(n-r)!}\, u^{r-1}(1-u)^{n-r}, \qquad 0 \leq u \leq 1.$$

By suitable choice of the shapes for the statistical blocks and then appropriate selection of the r blocks to be used, the tolerance regions can be made to have a wide variety of shapes.

Now let us consider a procedure for determining statistical blocks [6]. The multivariate sample values are denoted by $w_1, \ldots, w_n$. First, without knowledge of the sample values, a function $g(w)$ is chosen for dividing the multivariate space into $k + 1$ "strips," where $0 \leq k \leq n$. The function $g(w)$ has different values for all possible different sample values. To determine the random "strips," k of the w_i are specified for use (without knowledge of their values). The actual values of these w_i are ordered in the sequence $w(1), \ldots, w(k)$ such that $g[w(j+1)] > g[w(j)]$.

Now statistical blocks are determined within each of these "strips" on the basis of the remaining sample values (i.e., the w_i not used in determining the "strips"). Here it is to be noted that some of the "strips" may contain no sample values. Let n_1 be the number of w_i such that $g(w_i) < g[w(1)]$, n_j the number of w_i such that $g[w(j-1)] < g(w_i) < g[w(j)]$ for $j = 2, \ldots, k$, and n_{k+1} the number of w_i such that $g(w_i) > g[w(k)]$. The "strip" for which n_j denotes the number of sample values is called the jth "strip." For the jth "strip" ($j = 1, \ldots, k+1$), choose at least n_j functions (n to be safe) without knowledge of the sample values. Let $g_j^{(1)}(w), g_j^{(2)}(w), \ldots, g_j^{(n_j)}(w)$ denote the first n_j of these functions for the jth "strip." To obtain the first block in the jth "strip," order the w_i for the jth "strip" in a sequence $w_{j1}^{(1)}, \ldots, w_{jn_j}^{(1)}$ such that $g_j^{(1)}(w_{j(t+1)}) \geq g_j^{(1)}(w_{jt}^{(1)})$. The first block for the jth strip is the set of points w which fall in the jth "strip" and also satisfy $g_j^{(1)}(w) < g_j^{(1)}(w_{j1}^{(1)})$. Then, discarding $w_{j1}^{(1)}$, order the remaining sample values into a sequence $w_{j1}^{(2)}, \ldots, w_{j(n_j-1)}^{(2)}$ such that $g_j^{(2)}(w_{j(t+1)}^{(2)}) \geq g_j^{(2)}(w_{jt}^{(2)})$. The second block for the jth "strip" is the set of points w which fall in the jth "strip" and also satisfy $g_j^{(2)}(w) < g_j^{(2)}(w_{j1}^{(2)})$. This process is continued until the function $g_j^{(n_j)}(w)$ is used; it yields $n_j + 1$ blocks for the jth "strip," the extra block being what is left over in the jth "strip" at the n_jth step in the process.

When this procedure is carried out for all the $k + 1$ "strips," a total of $n + 1 = (n_1 + 1) + \ldots + (n_{k+1} + 1)$ statistical blocks are obtained, since by the construction method chosen the sample is made up of the k points used to form the "strips" and the points falling within the strips. Note that the sample values are all different with probability one, so that the "strips" can be considered to have nonzero widths and the points not used in forming the "strips" can be considered not to fall on the "strip" boundaries.

For R equal to the set sum of a specified r of the statistical blocks, chosen without knowledge of the sample values,

$$\Pr\left(\int_R dF \geq \gamma\right) = \Pr(U \geq \gamma) = 1 - I_\gamma(r, n-r+1) = \sum_{i=0}^{r-1} \binom{n}{i} \gamma^i (1-\gamma)^{n-i}$$

so that β is completely determined by the values of r, γ, and n. These relations follow from the expression for the frequency function of U.

This method of obtaining distribution-free tolerance regions for the

TABLE 8.1

Some Probability Relations for Continuous Symmetrical Populations with Median ϕ

Probability Expression	$2^n \times$ Value	
$\Pr[(x_{(k)}+x_{(1)})/2 > \phi] = \Pr[(x_{(n)}+x_{(n+1-k)})/2 < \phi]$	2^{k-1}	
$\Pr\{\min[x_{(2)}, (x_{(k)}+x_{(1)})/2] > \phi\} = \Pr\{\max[x_{(n-1)}, (x_{(n)}+x_{(n+1-k)})/2] < \phi\}$	k	
$\Pr\{\min[(x_{(3)}+x_{(2)})/2, (x_{(k)}+x_{(1)})/2] > \phi\} = \Pr\{\max[(x_{(n-1)}+x_{(n-2)})/2, (x_{(n)}+x_{(n+1-k)})/2] < \phi\}$	$2(k-1)$	$(k>1)$
$\Pr\{\min[x_{(3)}, (x_{(k)}+x_{(1)})/2] > \phi\} = \Pr\{\max[x_{(n-2)}, (x_{(n)}+x_{(n+1-k)})/2] < \phi\}$	$1 + k(k-1)/2$	
$\Pr\{\min[(x_{(4)}+x_{(2)})/2, (x_{(k)}+x_{(1)})/2] > \phi\} = \Pr\{\max[(x_{(n-1)}+x_{(n-3)})/2, (x_{(n)}+x_{(n+1-k)})/2] < \phi\}$	$4(k-2)$	$(k>2)$
$\Pr\{\min[(x_{(4)}+x_{(3)})/2, (x_{(k)}+x_{(1)})/2] > \phi\} = \Pr\{\max[(x_{(n-2)}+x_{(n-3)})/2, (x_{(n)}+x_{(n+1-k)})/2] < \phi\}$	$2 + (k-1)(k-2)$	$(k>1)$
$\Pr\{\min[x_{(4)}, (x_{(k)}+x_{(1)})/2] > \phi\} = \Pr\{\max[x_{(n-3)}, (x_{(n)}+x_{(n+1-k)})/2] < \phi\}$	$k + k(k-1)(k-2)/6$	
$\Pr\{\min[(x_{(5)}+x_{(4)})/2, (x_{(k)}+x_{(1)})/2] > \phi\} = \Pr\{\max[(x_{(n-3)}+x_{(n-4)})/2, (x_{(n)}+x_{(n+1-k)})/2] < \phi\}$	$2(k-1) + (k-1)(k-2)(k-3)/6$	$(k>1)$
$\Pr\{\min[x_{(5)}, (x_{(k}+x_{(1)})/2] > \phi\} = \Pr\{\max[x_{(n-4)}, (x_{(n)}+x_{(n+1-k)})/2] < \phi\}$	$1 + k(k-1)/2 + k(k-1)(k-2)(k-3)/24$	
$\Pr\{\min[x_{(6)}, (x_{(k)}+x_{(1)})/2] > \phi\} = \Pr\{\max[x_{(n-5)}, (x_{(n)}+x_{(n+1-k)})/2] < \phi\}$	$k[1+(k-1)(k-2)/6 + (k-1)(k-2)(k-3)(k-4)/120]$	

multivariate case has been extended to discontinuous populations [7]. Sequential determination of multivariate tolerance regions has also been considered [1].

REFERENCES

1. D. A. S. Fraser, "Sequentially determined statistically equivalent blocks," *Ann. Math. Statist.*, Vol. 22 (1951), pp. 372–381.
2. National Bureau of Standards, "Tables of the binomial probability distribution," Appl. Math. Ser. 6, U.S. Dept. Commerce, Washington, D.C., 1950.
3. Karl Pearson, *Tables of the Incomplete Beta Function*, Cambridge University Press, Cambridge, England, 1932 and later.
4. M. S. Raff, "On approximating the point binomial," *J. Amer. Statist. Ass.*, Vol. 51 (1956), pp. 293–303.
5. Herbert Robbins, "On distribution-free tolerance limits in random sampling," *Ann. Math. Statist.*, Vol. 15 (1944), pp. 214–216.
6. John W. Tukey, "Non-parametric estimation, II. Statistically equivalent blocks and tolerance regions—the continuous case," *Ann. Math. Statist.*, Vol. 18 (1947), pp. 529–539.
7. John W. Tukey, "Non-parametric estimation, III. Statistically equivalent blocks and multivariate tolerance regions—the discontinuous case," *Ann. Math. Statist.*, Vol. 19 (1948), pp. 30–39.
8. John W. Tukey, "The simplest signed-rank tests," Memorandum Rep. 17, Statistical Research Group, Princeton University, Princeton, N.J., 1949 (duplicated).
9. John E. Walsh, "Some significance tests for the median which are valid under very general conditions," unpublished doctoral dissertation, Princeton University, Princeton, N.J., 1947.
10. John E. Walsh, "Some significance tests for the median which are valid under very general conditions," *Ann. Math. Statist.*, Vol. 20 (1949), pp. 64–81.
11. Frank Wilcoxon, "Individual comparisons of grouped data by ranking methods," *Biometrics Bull.*, Vol. 1 (1945), pp. 80–83.
12. Frank Wilcoxon, *Some Rapid Approximate Statistical Procedures*. Amer. Cyanamid Co., Stamford Research Laboratories, 1949.
13. S. S. Wilks, "On the determination of sample sizes for setting tolerance limits," *Ann. Math. Statist.*, Vol. 12 (1941), pp. 91–96.
14. S. S. Wilks, "Order statistics," *Bull. Amer. Math. Soc.*, Vol. 54 (1948), pp. 6–50.

H. A. DAVID

CHAPTER 9

Multiple Decisions and Multiple Comparisons

9.1 Introduction

The purpose of this chapter is to show how and why order statistics play an important part in the construction of multiple tests and of simultaneous confidence intervals. Subjects treated include the ranking of means and variances, multiple comparisons among a set of means, multiple comparisons with a standard, slippage tests, and short-cut procedures. Attention is drawn to a large number of statistics expressible as maxima and to methods often useful in handling these. Many of these statistics are also important in the problem of rejecting outlying observations, and reference should be made to Section 10H.

It is not our aim to deal comprehensively with the large field of multiple decisions and comparisons which has recently received much study. However, although we confine ourselves to approaches involving order statistics in a simple fashion, these do include a substantial proportion of the procedures developed. A more general earlier account has been given by Federer [14]. For a detailed treatment of various aspects of the subject and for further references, the following papers, listed in chronological order, may be consulted: Tukey [47], Scheffé [42], Roy and Bose [41], Bechhofer [1], Duncan [10], Hartley [25], Healy [26], and Lehmann [31].

9.2 The Ranking of Means

Suppose an experiment carried out to compare the yields of several varieties of wheat is to be analyzed. The usual method of doing this is by the analysis of variance; as the result of an F-ratio test we may accept or reject the null hypothesis H_0 that all the (true) mean yields are equal. What is frequently required, however, is not such an over-all test but rather a method to help us decide which means are different from which. A number of procedures with this aim will now be considered. It is assumed that we have available a set of independent sample means $\bar{x}_t$, with $t = 1, 2, \ldots, k$, following a $N(\mu_t, \sigma^2/n)$ law, and an independent mean-square estimator $s_m^2 = s^2/n$ of σ^2/n, based on ν degrees of freedom. The particular experimental design used need not concern us here.

Series of t-Tests. The simplest procedure is to replace the F-test by a series of t-tests. Two means $\bar{x}_t$, $\bar{x}_u$ are declared significantly different if

$$|\bar{x}_t - \bar{x}_u| > \sqrt{2}t_{\alpha/2}s_m \tag{9.2.1}$$

where $t_{\alpha/2}$ is the upper $\frac{1}{2}\alpha$ significance point of t with ν df. If all pairs of means are compared, the probability of making no incorrect statement by this procedure is, on H_0,

$$P = \Pr(\bar{x}_{\max} - \bar{x}_{\min} < \sqrt{2}t_{\alpha/2}s_m) = \Pr(q < \sqrt{2}t_{\alpha/2})$$

where q denotes a studentized range of k variates and with ν df. It will be seen from Table A, constructed from Pearson and Hartley's tabulation of

TABLE A

PROBABILITY P OF CORRECTLY ACCEPTING H_0 WHEN COMPARING k MEANS BY A SERIES OF t-TESTS, THE ESTIMATE OF ERROR HAVING ν DF

	ν \ k	2	3	4	5	6	8	10	12
	20	0.95	0.88	0.81	0.74	0.67	0.55	0.44	0.36
$\alpha = 0.05$	40	0.95	0.88	0.80	0.73	0.65	0.52	0.41	0.32
	∞	0.95	0.88	0.80	0.71	0.63	0.49	0.37	0.28
	20	0.99	0.97	0.95	0.93	0.91	0.86	0.81	0.77
$\alpha = 0.01$	40	0.99	0.97	0.95	0.93	0.90	0.85	0.79	0.74
	∞	0.99	0.97	0.95	0.93	0.90	0.84	0.77	0.71

the probability integral of q [37], that P declines rapidly with increasing k so that the probability, $1 - P$, of at least one incorrect declaration may be much greater than α.

To reduce the last probability, the series of t-tests is often not carried out at all unless a preliminary F-test has given a significant result. This procedure is satisfactory if H_0 holds but becomes increasingly less so the more the true situation departs from that specified by H_0. For example, if

$\mu_1 = \mu_2 = \ldots = \mu_{k-1} \ll \mu_k$, H_0 will, almost certainly, be rejected, and in dealing with the first $k - 1$ means we shall be back to the previous case, with $k - 1$ in place of k.

The Multiple Range Test. To overcome these difficulties Newman [34] put forward a method involving a multiple use of the studentized range. As modified by Keuls [27], this method leads to the following procedure (where "different" stands for "significantly different").

(i) Arrange the sample means in ascending order of magnitude as $\bar{x}_{(1)}, \bar{x}_{(2)}, \ldots, \bar{x}_{(k)}$.

(ii) Set out the "critical differences" $q_{p,\nu;\alpha}s_m$ for $p = 2, 3, \ldots, k$.

(iii) Declare $\bar{x}_{(1)}$ and $\bar{x}_{(k)}$ different if

$$\bar{x}_{(k)} - \bar{x}_{(1)} > q_{k,\nu;\alpha}s_m$$

where $q_{k,\nu;\alpha}$ is the upper α significance point of $q_{k,\nu}$ (Table 7A.2). If $\bar{x}_{(1)}, \bar{x}_{(k)}$ do not differ significantly, accept H_0 and stop the procedure; otherwise proceed to step iv.

(iv) Declare $\bar{x}_{(k)}$ different from $\bar{x}_{(2)}$ if

$$\bar{x}_{(k)} - \bar{x}_{(2)} > q_{k-1,\nu;\alpha}s_m;$$

if this is not true, state that $\bar{x}_{(k)}$ does not differ significantly from $\bar{x}_{(2)}, \bar{x}_{(3)}, \ldots, \bar{x}_{(k-1)}$.

(v) In this way deal, if necessary, with all the differences $\bar{x}_{(k)} - \bar{x}_{(u)}$, with $u = 1, 2, \ldots, k - 1$, by gauging them against $q_{k-u+1,\nu;\alpha}s_m$.

(vi) Proceed in the same way with the set of differences $\bar{x}_{(k-1)} - \bar{x}_{(v)}$, with $v = 1, 2, \ldots, k - 2$, by comparing them with $q_{k-v,\nu;\alpha}s_m$, and so on.

This procedure is quite simple to carry out. We apply it to an example, cited by Duncan [10], in which

$$k = 7, \qquad \nu = 30, \qquad s_m = 3.643$$

and the means, arranged in ascending order, are

49.6 58.1 61.0 61.5 67.6 71.2 71.3.

The critical differences $3.643q_{p,30;0.05}$ are found to be

10.53 12.71 13.99 14.94 15.66 16.25.

Applying steps iii through vi we obtain the following ranking:

49.6 <u>58.1 61.0 61.5 67.6 71.2 71.3</u>

where any two means are significantly different only if they are not underscored by the same line.

It will be seen that this procedure involves the testing of a sequence of null hypotheses, the first of which, H_0, is that all μ's are equal. If H_0 is true, the probability of rejecting it is clearly α. All later null hypotheses about the equality of a smaller number of μ's are also incorrectly rejected with probability α.

The Modified Multiple Range Test. The Newman-Keuls method is regarded by Duncan [10] as rather too stringent, in the sense that true differences between the means will tend to be missed too often. Duncan notes that in testing the equality of a subset of p, with $2 \leq p \leq k$, means ($H_{0,p}$), we are in fact testing whether $p - 1$ orthogonal contrasts between the μ's differ from zero. If these contrasts were tested in separate independent experiments, each at significance level α, the probability of incorrectly rejecting $H_{0,p}$ would be $\gamma_p = 1 - (1 - \alpha)^{p-1}$. This level of significance is also advocated by Duncan in the present situation, even though all tests are here based on a common-error mean square. His modified multiple range test proceeds exactly as the multible range test, except that $q_{p,\nu;\alpha}$ is replaced by $q_{p,\nu;\gamma_p}$. Values of this quantity for $\alpha = 0.05$, 0.01 are given in Table 9.1, a condensed version of tables prepared by Harter et al. [23]. For a special case they are compared in Table B with

TABLE B

COMPARISON OF CRITICAL DIFFERENCES (IN TERMS OF s_m) IN VARIOUS 5 PER CENT LEVEL PROCEDURES FOR THE RANKING OF 10 MEANS ($\nu = \infty$)

	Subset Size						
Test	2	3	4	5	6	8	10
Series of t-tests	2.77						2.77
Duncan's multiple range test	2.77	2.92	3.02	3.09	3.15	3.23	3.29
Newman-Keuls test	2.77	3.32	3.63	3.86	4.03	4.29	4.47
Tukey's test	4.47						4.47
Scheffé's test	5.82						5.82

the multipliers needed in several other tests. In Duncan's example the critical differences are now

10.53 11.07 11.37 11.66 11.84 11.99

and result in the following ranking:

49.6 58.1 61.0 61.5 67.6 71.2 71.3.

Generalization to Unequal Group Sizes. When the sample means are not based on the same number of observations, the foregoing procedures are no longer applicable. However, the critical difference corresponding to (9.2.1) is now simply

$$t_{\alpha/2}s\left(\frac{1}{n_t} + \frac{1}{n_u}\right)^{1/2}$$

where n_t, n_u are the numbers in the tth, uth group, respectively. Kramer [29] has proposed that the multiple range test and the modified multiple range test remain unchanged except for a modification of the critical difference. For example, in Duncan's method, if a set of p means is to be tested for equality, he replaces

$$q_{p,\nu;\gamma_p}s_m \qquad \text{by} \qquad q_{p,\nu;\gamma_p}s\left[\frac{1}{2}\left(\frac{1}{n_U} + \frac{1}{n_L}\right)\right]^{1/2}$$

where n_U, n_L are the number of observations corresponding to the largest and smallest means observed in the set. This procedure is clearly only approximate but will tend to be conservative, since means based on a small number of observations will tend to be overrepresented in the extremes of the group of means. That this results in a conservative test is readily seen from the limiting case where all n's except two are infinite. A less conservative but more elaborate method has also been given by Duncan [11].

For generalizations to other situations in which means have unequal variances (covariance analysis, higher designs), reference should be made to Kramer [30] and Duncan [11].

9.3 Simultaneous Confidence Intervals

Order statistics play a fundamental role in the construction of simultaneous confidence intervals for a set of parameters or functions thereof. The reason for this importance will be illustrated on the use of the studentized range for the case when the parametric functions are differences or contrasts (generalized differences) of means (Tukey [46]).

In the situation discussed in Subsection 9.2 we have seen that the statement

$$\frac{\bar{x}_{\max} - \bar{x}_{\min}}{s_m} < q_{k,\nu;\alpha} \tag{9.3.1}$$

holds with probability $1 - \alpha$, on the null hypothesis H_0 of equal means. Now (9.3.1) is clearly equivalent to the whole set of $\frac{1}{2}k(k - 1)$ statements,

$$\frac{|\bar{x}_t - \bar{x}_u|}{s_m} < q_{k,\nu;\alpha}, \qquad t, u = 1, 2, \ldots, k; \quad t \neq u, \tag{9.3.2}$$

which, therefore, on H_0, hold simultaneously with probability $1 - \alpha$.

When H_1 is true, so that $E(\bar{x}_t) = \mu_t$, we can simply replace (9.3.2) by

$$\frac{|\bar{x}_t - \bar{x}_u - \mu_t + \mu_u|}{s_m} < q_{k,\nu;\alpha}, \qquad (9.3.3)$$

and this, in turn, is equivalent to the required $\frac{1}{2}k(k - 1)$ confidence statements,

$$\bar{x}_t - \bar{x}_u - q_\alpha s_m < \mu_t - \mu_u < \bar{x}_t - \bar{x}_u + q_\alpha s_m, \qquad (9.3.4)$$

which must also hold with probability $1 - \alpha$. In particular, this set of statements will include the following test of significance: Declare any two means $\bar{x}_t$, $\bar{x}_u$ significantly different if

$$|\bar{x}_t - \bar{x}_u| > q_\alpha s_m. \qquad (9.3.5)$$

The resulting procedure gives the same test for the comparison of the largest and the smallest means as that of Newman and Keuls, but the critical difference is not reduced for other comparisons. The conservative nature of the method is illustrated in Table B.

It should be noted that we may replace

$$\bar{x}_t - \bar{x}_u \quad \text{by} \quad \sum c_t \bar{x}_t, \qquad \left(\sum c_t = 0, \quad \sum |c_t| = 2\right),$$

that is, by any contrast of the means (including one suggested by the results) which is suitably standardized. This follows at once from the inequality

$$\left|\sum c_t \bar{x}_t\right| \leq \bar{x}_{\max} - \bar{x}_{\min}.$$

Thus the *infinity* of confidence statements

$$\sum c_t \bar{x}_t - q_\alpha s_m < \sum c_t \mu_t < \sum c_t \bar{x}_t + q_\alpha s_m \qquad (9.3.6)$$

holds simultaneously with probability $1 - \alpha$.

For purposes of comparison we may also mention a different approach, not involving order statisics, to the problem of setting simultaneous confidence intervals to $\Sigma c_t \mu_t$. In this case, however, the c's must satisfy $\Sigma c_t^2 = 2$ in place of $\Sigma |c_t| = 2$. Using F-ratios in place of studentized ranges, Scheffé [42] obtains the inequalities

$$\sum c_t \bar{x}_t - s_m\sqrt{2(k - 1)F_\alpha} < \sum c_t \mu_t < \sum c_t \bar{x}_t + s_m\sqrt{2(k - 1)\, F_\alpha} \quad (9.3.7)$$

where F_α is the upper α significance point of the F-ratio with $k - 1$ and ν DF. Scheffé also shows that the intervals (9.3.7) are longer than those of (9.3.6) if the contrasts are differences of two means only, but that the situation is reversed if $\Sigma c_t \mu_t$ represents a contrast of one-half of the means with the other half. As in (9.3.5) we declare $\Sigma c_t \bar{x}_t$ significantly different from zero if

$$\left|\sum c_t \bar{x}_t\right| > s_m \sqrt{2(k - 1)F_\alpha}. \qquad (9.3.8)$$

This procedure is justified by the fact that the maximum value which $\frac{1}{2}n(\Sigma c_t\bar{x}_t)^2$ can assume is the whole of the between-groups sum of squares, so that on division by $n(k - 1)s_m{}^2$ the resulting maximum is distributed, on H_0, as F with $k - 1$ and ν DF. Order statistics do not enter since the maximum can be expressed in this simple fashion. It will also be seen that if $\Sigma c_t\bar{x}_t$ in (9.3.8) is replaced by the subset $\bar{x}_t - \bar{x}_u$, the proportion of experiments in which incorrect decisions are made will be *at most* equal to α, if H_0 is true.

Tukey's and Scheffé's methods are actually of somewhat wider application than we have indicated. A unified approach to the construction of simultaneous confidence intervals has been developed by Roy and Bose [41].

9.4 Multiple Procedures on Variances

The methods of Subsections 9.2 and 9.3 can readily be applied to variances instead of means, the role of the studentized range being taken over by the maximum F-ratio, $F_{\max} = s^2_{\max}/s^2_{\min}$. We assume that each s^2 is based on the same number of degrees of freedom. The logarithm of $F_{\max}$ is just the range of log s^2, no studentization being needed since the distribution of this range is clearly independent of σ^2. Against this simplification, however, must be set the greater sensitivity of tests on variances to departures from normality in the parent distribution.

Table C lists the corresponding tests on means and variances.

TABLE C

Tests on Means	Tests on Variances
F-test for homogeneity of means	Bartlett's test
q-test	$F_{\max}$-test
Battery of t-tests for difference of two means	Battery of F-tests for difference of two variances
Newman-Keuls multiple range test	Multiple $F_{\max}$-test
Duncan's modified range test	Modified $F_{\max}$-test

The multiple $F_{\max}$-test can be carried out exactly as the Newman-Keuls test, with the help of tables of upper percentage points $F_{\max}(\alpha)$ of $F_{\max}$ (Table 7A.4). For the modified $F_{\max}$-test, tables of $F_{\max}$ at significance level $\gamma_p = 1 - (1 - \alpha)^{p-1}$ are required; in the case $\alpha = 0.01$ these are given by David [6].

Multiple confidence intervals for a set of variance ratios $\sigma_t{}^2/\sigma_u{}^2$, with $t, u = 1, 2, \ldots, k$, can at once be set by means of the $F_{\max}$-ratio [39].

Corresponding to equation 9.3.4 we have the $\frac{1}{2}k(k-1)$ confidence statements,

$$\frac{s_t^2}{s_u^2 F_{\max}(\alpha)} < \frac{\sigma_t^2}{\sigma_u^2} < \frac{F_{\max}(\alpha) s_t^2}{s_u^2},$$

which hold simultaneously with probability $1 - \alpha$.

9.5 Short-cut Methods

In line with the approach used in Chapter 7A we can modify the tests of 9.2 and 9.3 by replacing the root-mean-square estimators of σ by range estimators. This has been done in detail by Tukey [48] in the problem of setting simultaneous confidence intervals to the differences of a set of means. In terms of s the solution is given by (9.3.4). For a one-way classification into k groups of n we replace the quantity (Tukey's "allowance")

$$q_{k,\nu;\alpha} \frac{s}{\sqrt{n}} \qquad \text{by} \qquad q_{k,\nu';\alpha} \frac{\bar{w}}{c\sqrt{n}}$$

where c, ν are the scale factor and degrees of freedom of Table 7A.8*b* and $\bar{w}$ is the mean of the group ranges. The factor $q_{k,\nu';\alpha}/c\sqrt{n}$ has been tabulated by Tukey for $\alpha = 0.05$ and $n, k \leq 20$; it equals nQ/k, with Q given in Table 7A.8*a*. We can proceed similarly for a two-way classification, using the method of Section 7A.6 to calculate $\bar{w}$, with c and ν from Table 7A.8*c*. Tukey proceeds by a slightly more convenient, but rather more inefficient, method and again gives the necessary tables. He also considers other experimental designs and such complications as "missing plots."

It seems less worthwhile to pursue this approach for the more elaborate multiple tests; for these the time required to calculate s is only a fairly small proportion of the time needed to carry out the battery of comparisons.

9.6 Selection Procedures Based on Multiple Comparisons with a Standard

Suppose we have in addition to a set of k treatment means $\bar{x}_t$ a control group mean $\bar{x}_0$, and that these $k + 1$ means $\bar{x}_u$, with $u = 0, 1, \ldots, k + 1$, are normally distributed with respective population means μ_u and variances σ^2/n_u. As before, an independent mean square estimate s^2 of σ^2 based on ν DF is also available. Interest centers on the discovery of treatments "better" or "superior" to the standard, which for definiteness we take to be treatments having $\mu_t > \mu_0$. The following are the main problems treated to date in which, in stating rules of procedure, we have made the simplifying assumption that $n_1 = n_2 = \ldots = n_k = n$.

1. Selection of the "best" treatment by a rule which guarantees with probability $1 - \alpha$ that the standard will be chosen if in fact all μ_u are equal. The probability of picking the standard will, of course, exceed $1 - \alpha$ if some or all the μ_t are actually smaller than μ_0 (Paulson [35]).

Rule: Select as best the treatment with the largest observed mean ($\bar{x}_{\max}$) if

$$\bar{x}_{\max} - \bar{x}_0 \geq v_\alpha s\left(\frac{1}{n} + \frac{1}{n_0}\right)^{1/2} \tag{9.6.1}$$

with v_α as defined later. Otherwise select the standard as best.

2. Selection of those, if any, of the $\bar{x}_t$ that are significantly greater than $\bar{x}_0$, under the same condition as those given in problem 1 (Dunnett [12]).

Rule: Accept as superior those treatments for which

$$\bar{x}_t - \bar{x}_0 > v_\alpha s\left(\frac{1}{n} + \frac{1}{n_0}\right)^{1/2}.$$

3. Selection of those, if any, of the $\bar{x}_t$ that are not significantly smaller than $\bar{x}_0$ by a rule which controls at $\geq 1 - \alpha$ the probability that the selected subset contains *all* the populations better than the standard, not only under the null hypothesis H_0 of equal μ_u's but for any possible true configuration of the μ_u's (Gupta and Sobel [21]).

Rule: Retain in the selected subset those treatments for which

$$\bar{x}_t - \bar{x}_0 \geq -v_\alpha s\left(\frac{1}{n} + \frac{1}{n_0}\right)^{1/2}.$$

The aim of both problems 2 and 3 is to obtain a group of reasonably good treatments which can be further investigated if the best one is required. Problem 3 may be regarded as a procedure for screening out inferior treatments. It has been applied to gamma-type and binomial populations.

It will be seen that the quantity v_α is required in all three cases. We turn now to its definition and consider problem 2 in some detail.

Define v_t by

$$v_t = \frac{\bar{x}_t - \bar{x}_0 - \mu_t + \mu_0}{s(1/n_t + 1/n_0)^{1/2}}.$$

Then lower confidence limits, with joint confidence coefficient $1 - \alpha$, for the k differences $\mu_t - \mu_0$ are clearly given by

$$\mu_t - \mu_0 > \bar{x}_t - \bar{x}_0 - v_{t,\alpha} s\left(\frac{1}{n_t} + \frac{1}{n_0}\right)^{1/2}, \tag{9.6.2}$$

provided the k constants $v_{t,\alpha}$ are chosen so that

$$\Pr(v_1 < v_{1,\alpha}, v_2 < v_{2,\alpha}, \ldots, v_k < v_{k,\alpha} \mid H_0) = 1 - \alpha. \qquad (9.6.3)$$

Equation (9.6.3) does not, of course, specify the $v_{t,\alpha}$ uniquely, but this may be remedied by also taking the k probabilities $\Pr(v_t < v_{t,\alpha})$ to be equal. If $n_1 = n_2 = \ldots = n_k = n$ we have

$$v_{1,\alpha} = v_{2,\alpha} = \ldots = v_{k,\alpha} = v_\alpha,$$

say, and (9.6.3) may be rewritten as

$$\Pr(\max v_t < v_\alpha) = 1 - \alpha.$$

Now v_t is a t-variate with ν DF and of the form x_t/s where x_t is $N(0, \sigma^2)$. Thus v_α is the upper α significance point of the largest of k studentized deviates x_t/s where the x_t are mutually correlated with $\rho = n/(n_0 + n)$. (Similarly, for two-sided simultaneous confidence intervals on the $\mu_t - \mu_0$ we are led to finding the upper percentage points of $\max |x_t|/s$.)

Tables of v_α. Tables have been constructed mainly for the case $n_0 = n_1 = \ldots = n_k$ (i.e., $\rho = \frac{1}{2}$). Dunnett [12] has tabulated upper 5 and 1% points of both $\max v_t$ and $\max |v_t|$ for $k = 1(1)9$ and $\nu \geq 5$. Further tables of $v_\alpha\sqrt{2}$ have been given by Gupta and Sobel [20] for $\alpha = 0.25$, 0.1, 0.05, 0.025, 0.01 and $k = 2$, 5, 10(1) 16(2) 20(5) 40, 50, and $\nu \geq 15$. The important case $n_0 = \infty$ (i.e., $\rho = 0$, control mean known) can be handled by means of tables due to Pillai and Ramachandran [38] who have tabulated upper 5% points of $\max v_t$ and $\max |v_t|$ for $k = 1(1)8$ and a wide range of ν-values.

9.7 Slippage Tests

Let $f_i = f(x, \theta_i, \tau_i, \ldots)$ denote the ith of k distributions and let H_0 be the null hypothesis

$$\theta_1 = \theta_2 = \ldots = \theta_k.$$

Slippage tests, in their simplest form, are concerned with the detection of a change in one of the θ_i, where i is *unknown.*

In a basic paper Paulson [36] considers the case of "slippage to the right" for $f_i = N(\mu_i, \sigma^2)$, that is, under H_i the μ's satisfy the relations

$$\mu_1 = \mu_2 = \ldots = \mu_{i-1} = \mu_{i+1} = \ldots = \mu_k$$

and

$$\mu_i = \mu_1 + \Delta, \qquad \Delta > 0.$$

He introduces the set of $k + 1$ decisions $(D_0, D_1, \ldots, D_k)$, corresponding to the acceptance of $H_0, H_1, \ldots, H_k$. The problem is then to choose one member of the set on the basis of a sample of n from each of the k distributions. Paulson imposes the following conditions:

1. When H_0 is true, D_0 should be selected with probability $1 - \alpha$.
2. The decision procedure must be invariant if a constant is added to all the observations or if all the observations are multiplied by a positive constant.
3. The decision procedure must be symmetric in the sense that the probability of selecting D_i when H_i is true should be independent of i.

Under these restrictions the procedure maximizing the probability of a correct decision when one of the distributions has slipped to the right is

$$\begin{cases} \text{If} \quad n(\bar{x}_M - \bar{x}) > \lambda_\alpha S, & \text{select } D_M \\ \text{If} \quad n(\bar{x}_M - \bar{x}) \le \lambda_\alpha S, & \text{select } D_0 \end{cases} \tag{9.7.1}$$

where $\bar{x}_M = \bar{x}_{\max} \quad (M = 1, 2, \ldots, k)$,

$\bar{x}$ is the grand mean,

S^2 is the *total* sum of squares $\sum_{i=1}^{k} \sum_{j=1}^{n} (x_{ij} - \bar{x})^2$, and

λ_α is a constant determined by condition 1, that is, λ_α is the upper α significance point of

$$n(\bar{x}_{\max} - \bar{x})/S. \tag{9.7.2}$$

If F_0 is the upper $2\alpha/k$ significance point of the F-distribution with 1 and $nk - 2$ df, λ_α is given approximately by

$$\lambda_\alpha = \left[\frac{n(k - 1)F_0}{k(nk - 2 + F_0)}\right]^{1/2}.$$

For $\Delta < 0$, the test criterion would, of course, be

$$n(\bar{x} - \bar{x}_{\min})/S$$

which has the same null distribution as (9.7.2).

Corresponding tests have been constructed to detect the slippage of a variance for $f_i = N(\mu_i, \sigma_i^2)$. Here H_i takes the form

$$\sigma_1^2 = \sigma_2^2 = \ldots = \sigma_{i-1}^2 = \sigma_{i+1}^2 = \ldots = \sigma_k^2$$

and

$$\sigma_i^2 = k^2\sigma_1^2, \qquad k^2 \neq 1.$$

Under restrictions almost identical with conditions 1–3, procedures entirely analogous to (9.7.1) have been proved to be optimal. These are given by replacing the criterion of (9.7.2) by

$$s_{\max}^2/\sum s_i^2 \qquad \text{for } k^2 > 1 \text{ (Truax [45])}, \tag{9.7.3}$$

$$s_{\min}^2/\sum s_i^2 \qquad \text{for } k^2 < 1 \text{ (Doornbos [7])}. \tag{9.7.4}$$

A more general slippage test for gamma distributions has also been discussed by Doornbos and Prins [8].

Reference should also be made to the last two authors [9] for other slippage tests, including some on discrete distributions.

A related approach may be mentioned here, although it does not fall in the category of slippage problems. Seal [43, 44] deals with the choice of a decision rule yielding a subset of means or Type III variates, respectively, which is "most likely" to contain the population having the largest or smallest μ or scale parameter.

Detection of slippage of two μ's by an equal amount, but in opposite directions, has been considered by Ramachandran and Khatri [40] who find that the studentized range of the sample means provides the optimal criterion; that is, the distributions giving rise to the smallest and largest means are declared to have slipped if

$$kn(\bar{x}_{\max} - \bar{x}_{\min}) > q_{k,k(n-1);\alpha} \left(\sum s_i^2\right)^{1/2},$$

whereas in the contrary case H_0 is accepted. Evidently $s^2_{\max}/s^2_{\min}$ will provide a corresponding optimal procedure for testing equality of variances when the alternatives H_{ij} $(i \neq j)$ to H_0 are

$$\sigma_1^2 = \ldots = \sigma_{i-1}^2 = \sigma_{i+1}^2 = \ldots = \sigma_{j-1}^2 = \sigma_{j+1}^2 = \ldots = \sigma_k^2$$

and

$$\sigma_i^2 = k^2\sigma_1^2, \quad \sigma_j^2 = \sigma_1^2/k^2, \qquad k^2 \neq 1.$$

9.8 Other Multiple-Decision Procedures

A situation constantly occurring in the analysis of variance is that a number of "treatment" mean squares s_t^2, with $t = 1, 2, \ldots, k$, are tested against a common residual mean square s_0^2. If the tth treatment effect is zero, $F_t = s_t^2/s_0^2$ is an F-ratio with, say, ν_t, ν_0 DF. It is clear that if all treatment effects are zero (H_0), the probability of returning at least one of them as significant may be much greater than α. The position is, in fact, closely analogous to the problem, discussed in Subsection 9.6, of comparing a number of treatment means with the mean of a control group. Corresponding to equations (9.6.2) and (9.6.3), the lower confidence limits with joint confidence coefficient $1 - \alpha$, for the k ratios of the population variances σ_t^2 to σ_0^2, are given by

$$\sigma_t^2/\sigma_0^2 > s_t^2/(F_{t,\alpha}s_0^2) \qquad (9.8.1)$$

where the $F_{t,\alpha}$ satisfy the equation

$$\Pr(F_1 < F_{1,\alpha}, F_2 < F_{2,\alpha}, \ldots, F_k < F_{k,\alpha}) = 1 - \alpha. \qquad (9.8.2)$$

As in (9.6.3) this condition does not define the $F_{t,\alpha}$ uniquely; their choice is considered in detail in references 25 and 4. If $\nu_1 = \nu_2 = \ldots = \nu_k = \nu$, we are led to finding the upper α significance point of $s^2_{\max}/s_0^2$. This has been tabled by Nair [32] for $\nu = 1$, the case useful for testing the treatments in a 2^n factorial experiment. Finney [15] and David [4] have dealt with the case of even ν.

Multiple tests of significance are easily made when all the ν_t are equal (Hartley [25]). Let $s^2_{(1)}, s^2_{(2)}, \ldots, s^2_{(k)}$ be the mean squares arranged in ascending order of magnitude and denote the upper α significance point of $s^2_{(k)}/s_0{}^2$ by $F_{(k),\alpha}$. Then $s^2_{(k)}$ is declared significant if it exceeds $F_{(k),\alpha}s_0{}^2$, in which case we proceed to test $s^2_{(k-1)}$ which is gauged against $F_{(k-1),\alpha}s_0{}^2$, and so on.

Closely related to $s^2_{\max}/s_0{}^2$ is the statistic $s^2_{\max}/\Sigma s_t{}^2$ already referred to in Section 9.7. For $\nu = 2$ this provides an appropriate test for the largest of k components in harmonic analysis. The test is due to Fisher [16] who later [17] also discussed the testing of the second largest component. Cochran [3] has extended some of Fisher's results to other even values of ν and has proposed the use of $s^2_{\max}/\Sigma s_t{}^2$ as a possible test for the equality of k variances in normal populations. Upper percentage points have been tabulated by Eisenhart and Solomon [13]. Bliss et al. [2] have also given upper 5% points of the corresponding short-cut criterion $w_{\max}/\Sigma w_t$.

9.9 Approximations to Upper Significance Points of Statistics Expressible as Maxima

The test criteria we have considered in this section are all expressible as maxima; for example, the studentized range is the largest value in a set of $k(k-1)$ studentized differences. Upper percentage points of a number of these statistics have been tabulated by various special methods. There is, however, a general approach often useful in providing good approximations.[1] As an illustration we shall apply it to the extreme deviate from the sample mean (normal parent, $\sigma = 1$), namely

$$x_{\max} - \bar{x} = \max_{t=1,2,\ldots,k} (x_t - \bar{x}).$$

Now if $x_{\max} - \bar{x}$ exceeds some value Y, at least one of the $x_t - \bar{x}$ must exceed Y. By the method of inclusion and exclusion it follows that (cf. [4])

$$\begin{aligned}\Pr(x_{\max}-\bar{x}>Y) &\\ = \binom{k}{1}\Pr(x_1-\bar{x}>Y) &- \binom{k}{2}\Pr(x_1-\bar{x}>Y,\, x_2-\bar{x}>Y) + \ldots\\ &+ (-1)^{k-1}\Pr(x_1-\bar{x}>Y,\, x_2-\bar{x}>Y, \ldots, x_k-\bar{x}>Y). \qquad (9.9.1)\end{aligned}$$

For sufficiently large values of Y a first approximation to the left-hand side is given by the first term on the right, with later terms as successive correction terms. We have, therefore, that $(x_{\max} - \bar{x})_\alpha$, the upper α significance point of $x_{\max} - \bar{x}$, is approximately equal to the upper α/k significance point Y_1, say, of the normal variate $x_1 - \bar{x}$, the approximation being

[1] Lower percentage points of statistics expressible as minima can be found in the same way; for $s^2_{\min}/\Sigma s_t{}^2$ see Doornbos [7].

very good for $\alpha \leq 0.05$ [19]. The procedure is particularly successful in this case since $x_1 - \bar{x}$, $x_2 - \bar{x}$ are negatively correlated normal deviates so that the joint probability of their exceeding a large value Y is very small. In fact, since

$$\Pr(x_1 - \bar{x} > Y, x_2 - \bar{x} > Y) < [\Pr(x_1 - \bar{x} > Y)]^2, \qquad (9.9.2)$$

it follows from (9.9.1) and the definition of Y_1 that

$$\alpha - \tfrac{1}{2}\alpha^2 < \alpha - \tfrac{1}{2}(k-1)\alpha^2/k < \Pr(x_{\max} - \bar{x} > Y_1) < \alpha. \qquad (9.9.3)$$

Doornbos and Prins [8, 9] have investigated conditions under which counterparts of (9.9.2) and hence (9.9.3) hold when statistics other than $x_{\max} - \bar{x}$ are considered.

Closer approximations to the upper percentage points of statistics expressible as maxima may be obtained if the second and possibly later terms on the right-hand side of the equation corresponding to (9.9.1) can be evaluated. For examples, see references 2–5, 8, 9, 13, 15–17, 22, 28, 35, and 36.

Generalizations to the rth largest value ($2 \leq r \leq k$) and to the determination of power functions are also possible [17, 4, 8, 9].

Another approach which is occasionally useful is to assume that the variates in whose maximum we are interested may be taken as approximately independent [24, 15]. This assumption may also be used to approximate to the second and later terms on the right-hand side of the analogue of equation (9.9.1).

We list below the various approximations considered above, illustrating them on $x_{\max} - \bar{x}$, and indicate also whether they provide upper or lower bounds for $\Pr(x_{\max} - \bar{x} > Y)$. The signs in (9.9.6) and (9.9.7) need separate investigation in each application. To obtain an approximation to $(x_{\max} - \bar{x})_\alpha$, we simply equate the selected right-hand side to α and solve for Y. The solution will be an overestimate for (9.9.4) and an underestimate otherwise. Which of (9.9.4) through (9.9.7) should be used in any particular instance depends on ease of application and accuracy required:

$$\Pr(x_{\max} - \bar{x} > Y) < k \Pr(x_1 - \bar{x} > Y), \qquad (9.9.4)$$

$$\Pr(x_{\max} - \bar{x} > Y) > k \Pr(x_1 - \bar{x} > Y) - \binom{k}{2} \Pr(x_1 - \bar{x} > Y, x_2 - \bar{x} > Y), \qquad (9.9.5)$$

$$\Pr(x_{\max} - \bar{x} > Y) = 1 - \Pr(x_{\max} - \bar{x} < Y) > 1 - [\Pr(x_1 - \bar{x} < Y)]^k, \qquad (9.9.6)$$

$$\Pr(x_{\max} - \bar{x} > Y) > k \Pr(x_1 - \bar{x} > Y) - \binom{k}{2} [\Pr(x_1 - \bar{x} > Y)]^2. \qquad (9.9.7)$$

TABLE 9.1

a. SIGNIFICANT STUDENTIZED RANGES FOR DUNCAN'S 5%-LEVEL MULTIPLE RANGE TEST

ν \ k	2	3	4	5	6	7	8	9	10	12	14	16	18	20	50	100
1	17.97	17.97	17.97	17.97	17.97	17.97	17.97	17.97	17.97	17.97	17.97	17.97	17.97	17.97	17.97	17.97
2	6.08	6.08	6.08	6.08	6.08	6.08	6.08	6.08	6.08	6.08	6.08	6.08	6.08	6.08	6.08	6.08
3	4.50	4.52	4.52	4.52	4.52	4.52	4.52	4.52	4.52	4.52	4.52	4.52	4.52	4.52	4.52	4.52
4	3.93	4.01	4.03	4.03	4.03	4.03	4.03	4.03	4.03	4.03	4.03	4.03	4.03	4.03	4.03	4.03
5	3.64	3.75	3.80	3.81	3.81	3.81	3.81	3.81	3.81	3.81	3.81	3.81	3.81	3.81	3.81	3.81
6	3.46	3.59	3.65	3.68	3.69	3.70	3.70	3.70	3.70	3.70	3.70	3.70	3.70	3.70	3.70	3.70
7	3.34	3.48	3.55	3.59	3.61	3.62	3.63	3.63	3.63	3.63	3.63	3.63	3.63	3.63	3.63	3.63
8	3.26	3.40	3.48	3.52	3.55	3.57	3.58	3.58	3.58	3.58	3.58	3.58	3.58	3.58	3.58	3.58
9	3.20	3.34	3.42	3.47	3.50	3.52	3.54	3.54	3.55	3.55	3.55	3.55	3.55	3.55	3.55	3.55
10	3.15	3.29	3.38	3.43	3.46	3.49	3.50	3.52	3.52	3.53	3.53	3.53	3.53	3.53	3.53	3.53
11	3.11	3.26	3.34	3.40	3.44	3.46	3.48	3.49	3.50	3.51	3.51	3.51	3.51	3.51	3.51	3.51
12	3.08	3.22	3.31	3.37	3.41	3.44	3.46	3.47	3.48	3.50	3.50	3.50	3.50	3.50	3.50	3.50
13	3.06	3.20	3.29	3.35	3.39	3.42	3.44	3.46	3.47	3.48	3.49	3.49	3.49	3.49	3.49	3.49
14	3.03	3.18	3.27	3.33	3.37	3.40	3.43	3.44	3.46	3.47	3.48	3.48	3.48	3.48	3.48	3.48
15	3.01	3.16	3.25	3.31	3.36	3.39	3.41	3.43	3.45	3.46	3.48	3.48	3.48	3.48	3.48	3.48
16	3.00	3.14	3.24	3.30	3.34	3.38	3.40	3.42	3.44	3.46	3.47	3.48	3.48	3.48	3.48	3.48
17	2.98	3.13	3.22	3.28	3.33	3.37	3.39	3.41	3.43	3.45	3.46	3.47	3.48	3.48	3.48	3.48
18	2.97	3.12	3.21	3.27	3.32	3.36	3.38	3.40	3.42	3.44	3.46	3.47	3.47	3.47	3.47	3.47
19	2.96	3.11	3.20	3.26	3.31	3.35	3.38	3.40	3.42	3.44	3.46	3.47	3.47	3.47	3.47	3.47
20	2.95	3.10	3.19	3.26	3.30	3.34	3.37	3.39	3.41	3.44	3.45	3.46	3.47	3.47	3.47	3.47
24	2.92	3.07	3.16	3.23	3.28	3.32	3.34	3.37	3.39	3.42	3.44	3.46	3.46	3.47	3.48	3.48
30	2.89	3.04	3.13	3.20	3.25	3.29	3.32	3.35	3.37	3.40	3.43	3.45	3.46	3.47	3.49	3.49
40	2.86	3.01	3.10	3.17	3.22	3.27	3.30	3.33	3.35	3.39	3.42	3.44	3.46	3.47	3.50	3.50
60	2.83	2.98	3.07	3.14	3.20	3.24	3.28	3.31	3.33	3.37	3.41	3.43	3.45	3.47	3.54	3.54
120	2.80	2.95	3.04	3.12	3.17	3.22	3.25	3.29	3.31	3.36	3.39	3.42	3.45	3.47	3.58	3.60
∞	2.77	2.92	3.02	3.09	3.15	3.19	3.23	3.26	3.29	3.34	3.38	3.41	3.44	3.47	3.64	3.74

Tables 9.1*a* and *b* are condensed tables from H. L. Harter, D. S. Clemm, and E. H. Guthrie, "The probability integrals of the range and of the studentized range; probability integral and percentage points of the studentized range; critical values for Duncan's new multiple range test." WADC Tech. Rep. 58-484, Vol. 2, 1959. The tables are reproduced with permission of the authors.

b. SIGNIFICANT STUDENTIZED RANGES FOR DUNCAN'S 1%-LEVEL MULTIPLE RANGE TEST

ν \ k	2	3	4	5	6	7	8	9	10	12	14	16	18	20	50	100
1	90.03	90.03	90.03	90.03	90.03	90.03	90.03	90.03	90.03	90.03	90.03	90.03	90.03	90.03	90.03	90.03
2	14.04	14.04	14.04	14.04	14.04	14.04	14.04	14.04	14.04	14.04	14.04	14.04	14.04	14.04	14.04	14.04
3	8.26	8.32	8.32	8.32	8.32	8.32	8.32	8.32	8.32	8.32	8.32	8.32	8.32	8.32	8.32	8.32
4	6.51	6.68	6.74	6.76	6.76	6.76	6.76	6.76	6.76	6.76	6.76	6.76	6.76	6.76	6.76	6.76
5	5.70	5.89	5.99	6.04	6.06	6.07	6.07	6.07	6.07	6.07	6.07	6.07	6.07	6.07	6.07	6.07
6	5.24	5.44	5.55	5.61	5.66	5.68	5.69	5.70	5.70	5.70	5.70	5.70	5.70	5.70	5.70	5.70
7	4.95	5.14	5.26	5.33	5.38	5.42	5.44	5.45	5.46	5.47	5.47	5.47	5.47	5.47	5.47	5.47
8	4.75	4.94	5.06	5.14	5.19	5.23	5.26	5.28	5.29	5.31	5.32	5.32	5.32	5.32	5.32	5.32
9	4.60	4.79	4.91	4.99	5.04	5.09	5.12	5.14	5.16	5.18	5.20	5.20	5.21	5.21	5.21	5.21
10	4.48	4.67	4.79	4.87	4.93	4.98	5.01	5.04	5.06	5.09	5.11	5.12	5.12	5.12	5.12	5.12
11	4.39	4.58	4.70	4.78	4.84	4.89	4.92	4.95	4.98	5.01	5.03	5.04	5.05	5.06	5.06	5.06
12	4.32	4.50	4.62	4.71	4.77	4.82	4.85	4.88	4.91	4.94	4.97	4.99	5.00	5.01	5.01	5.01
13	4.26	4.44	4.56	4.64	4.71	4.76	4.79	4.82	4.85	4.89	4.92	4.94	4.95	4.96	4.97	4.97
14	4.21	4.39	4.51	4.59	4.65	4.70	4.74	4.78	4.80	4.84	4.87	4.89	4.91	4.92	4.94	4.94
15	4.17	4.35	4.46	4.55	4.61	4.66	4.70	4.73	4.76	4.80	4.83	4.86	4.87	4.89	4.91	4.91
16	4.13	4.31	4.42	4.51	4.57	4.62	4.66	4.70	4.72	4.77	4.80	4.82	4.84	4.86	4.89	4.89
17	4.10	4.28	4.39	4.48	4.54	4.59	4.63	4.66	4.69	4.74	4.77	4.80	4.82	4.83	4.87	4.87
18	4.07	4.25	4.36	4.44	4.51	4.56	4.60	4.64	4.66	4.71	4.74	4.77	4.79	4.81	4.86	4.86
19	4.05	4.22	4.34	4.42	4.48	4.53	4.58	4.61	4.64	4.69	4.72	4.75	4.77	4.79	4.84	4.84
20	4.02	4.20	4.31	4.40	4.46	4.51	4.55	4.59	4.62	4.66	4.70	4.73	4.75	4.77	4.83	4.83
24	3.96	4.13	4.24	4.32	4.39	4.44	4.48	4.52	4.55	4.60	4.63	4.66	4.69	4.71	4.80	4.80
30	3.89	4.06	4.17	4.25	4.31	4.37	4.41	4.44	4.48	4.53	4.57	4.60	4.63	4.65	4.77	4.78
40	3.82	3.99	4.10	4.18	4.24	4.30	4.34	4.38	4.41	4.46	4.50	4.54	4.57	4.59	4.74	4.76
60	3.76	3.92	4.03	4.11	4.17	4.23	4.27	4.31	4.34	4.39	4.44	4.47	4.50	4.53	4.71	4.76
120	3.70	3.86	3.96	4.04	4.11	4.16	4.20	4.24	4.27	4.33	4.37	4.41	4.44	4.47	4.67	4.77
∞	3.64	3.80	3.90	3.98	4.04	4.09	4.14	4.17	4.20	4.26	4.31	4.34	4.38	4.41	4.64	4.78

REFERENCES

1. R. E. Bechhofer, "A single-sample multiple decision procedure for ranking means of normal populations with known variances," *Ann. Math. Statist.*, Vol. 25 (1954), pp. 16–39.
2. C. I. Bliss, W. G. Cochran, and J. W. Tukey, "A rejection criterion based upon the range," *Biometrika*, Vol. 43 (1956), pp. 418–422.
3. W. G. Cochran, "The distribution of the largest of a set of estimated variances as a fraction of their total," *Ann. Eugen., London*, Vol. 11 (1941), pp. 47–52.
4. H. A. David, "On the application to statistics of an elementary theorem in probability," *Biometrika*, Vol. 43 (1956), pp. 85–91.
5. H. A. David, "Revised upper percentage points of the extreme studentized deviate from the sample mean," *Biometrika*, Vol. 43 (1956), pp. 449–451.
6. H. A. David, "The ranking of variances in normal populations," *J. Amer. Statist. Ass.*, Vol. 51 (1956), pp. 621–626.
7. R. Doornbos, "Significance of the smallest of a set of estimated normal variances," *Statist. Neerlandica*, Vol. 10 (1956), pp. 117–126.
8. R. Doornbos and H. J. Prins, "Slippage tests for a set of Gamma-variates," *Indag. Math.*, Vol. 18 (1956), pp. 329–337.
9. R. Doornbos and H. J. Prins, "On slippage tests," *Indag. Math.*, Vol. 20 (1958), I, pp. 38–46; II, pp. 47–55.
10. D. B. Duncan, "Multiple range and multiple *F* tests," *Biometrics*, Vol. 11 (1955), pp. 1–42.
11. D. B. Duncan, "Multiple range tests for correlated and heteroscedastic means," *Biometrics*, Vol. 13 (1957), pp. 164–176.
12. C. W. Dunnett, "A multiple comparison procedure for comparing several treatments with a control," *J. Amer. Statist. Ass.*, Vol. 50 (1955), pp. 1096–1121.
13. C. Eisenhart, M. W. Hastay, and W. A. Wallis, editors, *Selected Techniques of Statistical Analysis*, McGraw-Hill Book Co., New York, 1947, pp. 384–394.
14. W. T. Federer, *Experimental Design*, Macmillan, New York, 1955, pp. 18–45.
15. D. J. Finney, "The joint distribution of variance ratios based on a common error mean square," *Ann. Eugen., London*, Vol. 11 (1941), pp. 136–140.
16. R. A. Fisher, "Tests of significance in harmonic analysis," *Proc. Roy. Soc. A.*, Vol. 125 (1929), pp. 54–59; reprinted with an extended table as Paper 16 in [18].
17. R. A. Fisher, "On the similarity of the distributions found for the test of significance in harmonic analysis, and in Stevens's problem in geometrical probability," *Ann. Eugen., London*, Vol. 10 (1940), pp. 14–17; reprinted as Paper 37 in [18].
18. R. A. Fisher, *Contributions to Mathematical Statistics*, John Wiley and Sons, New York, 1950.
19. F. E. Grubbs, "Sample criteria for testing outlying observations," *Ann. Math. Statist.*, Vol. 21 (1950), pp. 27–58.
20. S. S. Gupta and M. Sobel, "On a statistic which arises in selection and ranking problems," *Ann. Math. Statist.*, Vol. 28 (1957), pp. 957–967.
21. S. S. Gupta and M. Sobel, "On selecting a subset which contains all populations better than a standard," *Ann. Math. Statist.*, Vol. 29 (1958), pp. 235–244.
22. M. Halperin, S. W. Greenhouse, J. Cornfield, and Julia Zalokar, "Tables of percentage points for the studentized maximum absolute deviate in normal samples," *J. Amer. Statist. Ass.*, Vol. 50 (1955), pp. 185–195.

23. H. L. Harter, D. S. Clemm, and E. H. Guthrie, "The probability integrals of the range and of the studentized range: probability integral and percentage points of the studentized range; critical values for Duncan's new multiple range test," WADC Tech. Rep. 58–484, Vol. 2, 1959.
24. H. O. Hartley, "Studentization and large-sample theory," *J. R. Statist. Soc.*, Suppl., Vol. 5 (1938), pp. 80–88.
25. H. O. Hartley, "Some recent developments in analysis of variance," *Comm. Pure and Appl. Math.*, Vol. 8 (1955), pp. 47–72.
26. W. C. Healy, "Two-sample procedures in simultaneous estimation," *Ann. Math. Statist.*, Vol. 27 (1956), pp. 687–702.
27. M. Keuls, "The use of studentized range in connection with an analysis of variance," *Euphytica*, Vol. 1 (1952), pp. 112–122.
28. R. M. Kozelka, "Approximate upper percentage points for extreme values in multinomial sampling," *Ann. Math. Statist.*, Vol. 27 (1956), pp. 507–512.
29. C. Y. Kramer, "Extension of multiple range tests to group means with unequal numbers of replications," *Biometrics*, Vol. 12 (1956), pp. 307–310.
30. C. Y. Kramer, "Extension of multiple range tests to group correlated adjusted means," *Biometrics*, Vol. 13 (1957), pp. 13–18.
31. E. L. Lehmann, "A theory of some multiple decision problems," *Ann. Math. Statist.*, Vol. 28 (1957), I, pp. 1–25; II, pp. 547–572.
32. K. R. Nair, "The studentized form of the extreme mean square test in the analysis of variance," *Biometrika*, Vol. 35 (1948), pp. 16–31.
33. K. R. Nair, "The distribution of the extreme deviate from the sample mean and its studentized form," *Biometrika*, Vol. 35 (1948), pp. 118–144.
34. D. Newman, "Range in samples from a normal population," *Biometrika*, Vol. 31 (1939), pp. 20–30.
35. E. Paulson, "On the comparison of several experimental categories with a control," *Ann. Math. Statist.*, Vol. 23 (1952), pp. 239–246.
36. E. Paulson, "An optimum solution to the k-sample slippage problem for the normal distribution," *Ann. Math. Statist.*, Vol. 23 (1952), pp. 610–616.
37. E. S. Pearson and H. O. Hartley, "Tables of the probability integral of the studentized range," *Biometrika*, Vol. 33 (1943), pp. 89–99.
38. K. C. S. Pillai and K. V. Ramachandran, "On the distribution of the ratio of the ith observation in an ordered sample from a normal population to an independent estimate of the standard deviation," *Ann. Math. Statist.*, Vol. 25 (1954), pp. 565–572.
39. K. V. Ramachandran, "Contributions to simultaneous confidence interval estimation," *Biometrics*, Vol. 12 (1956), pp. 51–56.
40. K. V. Ramachandran and C. G. Khatri, "On a decision procedure based on the Tukey statistic," *Ann. Math. Statist.*, Vol. 28 (1957), pp. 802–806.
41. S. N. Roy and R. C. Bose, "Simultaneous confidence interval estimation," *Ann. Math. Statist.*, Vol. 24 (1953), pp. 513–536.
42. H. Scheffé, "A method for judging all contrasts in the analysis of variance," *Biometrika*, Vol. 40 (1953), pp. 87–104.
43. K. C. Seal, "On a class of decision procedures for ranking means of normal populations," *Ann. Math. Statist.*, Vol. 26 (1955), pp. 387–398.
44. K. C. Seal, "On ranking parameters of scale in Type III populations," *J. Amer. Statist. Ass.*, Vol. 53 (1958), pp. 164–175.
45. D. R. Truax, "An optimum slippage test for the variances of k normal distributions," *Ann. Math. Statist.*, Vol. 24 (1953), pp. 669–674.

46. J. W. Tukey, "Quick and dirty methods in statistics, Part II, Simple analyses for standard designs," *Proceedings Fifth Annual Convention, American Society for Quality Control* (1951), pp. 189–197.
47. J. W. Tukey, "The problem of multiple comparisons," unpublished memorandum, Princeton University, Princeton, N.J., 1953, 396 pp.
48. J. W. Tukey, "Some selected and easy methods of statistical analysis," *Trans. N.Y. Acad. Sci.*, Ser. II, Vol. 16 (1953), pp. 88–97.

PART II

Specific Applications

CHAPTER 10

ECONOMICS LIBRARY AND STATISTICS

Normal Distribution

H. RUBEN

10A THE MOMENTS OF THE ORDER STATISTICS AND OF THE RANGE IN SAMPLES FROM NORMAL POPULATIONS

10A.1 Introduction

The problem of the distribution of order statistics in normal populations has been extensively considered in the literature. For example,[1] Tippett [23] gives the second, third, and fourth moments of the extreme order statistics for a few sample sizes. Hojo [10] examines the sampling variation of the median, quartiles, and interquartile distance in samples from normal populations and computes a large number of integrals for this purpose. Cole [1] produces a very simple recurrence relationship between certain simple multiples of the moments, termed normalized moments, which enables the normalized moments for all samples of size no greater than n to be obtained, by successive differencing, from the normalized moments of the extreme order statistics in samples of size $m \leq n$.[2] Hastings, Mosteller, Tukey, and Winsor [9] give, among other results, the means, variances, covariances, and correlations of order statistics in samples of ten or less from a normal population, some of the results being given to only two decimal places because of the extreme amount of computation necessary. Jones [12] and Godwin [6, 7] have

[1] The references given are not intended to provide an exhaustive bibliography.

[2] I have found that the cumulative error induced by the differencing increases too rapidly for the moments of the order statistics, except for those that are only a few places removed from the extremes, to be computed with a reasonable degree of accuracy.

obtained exact values for some of the lower moments. In particular, Godwin [6, p. 283] proceeds in a more systematic manner and approaches very closely the essential idea upon which this brief discussion is based. (For fuller details, see Ruben [18].)

In general, it may be said that many statisticians have attacked the problem in a rather disjointed and fragmentary manner, usually from the small sample end, but have failed to develop a systematic attack which at the same time throws light on the interconnection between the moments and enables the computation of the moments to become an economic proposition. It is believed that these conditions are met by the present approach which attempts to reveal the geometrical significance of the moments. It appears, in fact, that these, together with the moment generating function of the *square* of any order statistic, are intimately related to the contents of the members of a singly infinite class A of hyperspherical simplices, specifically simplices whose primary angles are all either θ or $\pi - \theta$. The moments are represented as linear functions of these contents [equations (10A.3.18) and (10A.3.19)].

The problem of the distribution of the range in normal samples has also been rather extensively studied. The reader's attention is directed particularly to the papers by Tippett [23] and E. S. Pearson [13, 14], the tables by Pearson and Hartley [15], as well as to some recent work by Cox [2] and Harley and Pearson [8] on the asymptotic distribution and the distribution for the single case $n = 200$, respectively, of the range in normal samples. Tippett's paper gives the expected value of the range in standardized normal samples for $n = 2(1)1000$ to five decimal places and the values of the standard deviation and the two beta coefficients for $n = 2$, 10, 20, 60, 100, 200, 500, 1000, the standard deviation being accurately presented to two decimal places and the beta coefficients effectively so to the same number of decimal places, Pearson and Hartley's tables give the actual probability integral of the range to four decimal places for $n = 2(1)20$. Finally, Ruben [20] has shown that the moments of the range, together with the product moments of the extreme order statistics, may be expressed as linear functions of the products of the contents of spherical hypersimplices of class A (10A.4.2 *et seq.*). These relationships may be exploited for a detailed numerical study of the moment characteristics of the range in samples of small or moderate size, but they are not so directly convenient when n is large because of the alternating signs and the binomial coefficients of the terms in the relationships. The expected value of the range for all n and the second moment for an even n are derived explicitly. The variances for $n = 2$ and 4 are seen to be functions of elementary trigonometric functions, but for $n \geq 6$ the results are more complex.

10A.2 Hyperspherical Simplices and Their Relation to Truncated[3] Multivariate Normal Distributions

Hyperspherical simplices (Somerville [22]) are the simplest geometrical figures that may be constructed on the surfaces of hyperspheres. Let $\mathbf{x} = (x_1, x_2, \ldots, x_k)$ represent the coordinates of a point in k-dimensional Euclidean space ($k = 1, 2, \ldots$). A $(k - 1)$-dimensional hyperspherical surface consists of the set of points x which satisfy the relationship

$$Q(\mathbf{x}) \equiv x_1^2 + x_2^2 + \ldots + x_k^2 = a^2, \qquad (10A.2.1)$$

a being a positive constant which represents the radius of the corresponding *hypersphere* centered at the origin. For $k = 1$, the spherical surface consists of the *two points* $x_1 = -a$, $x_1 = +a$; for $k = 2$, the surface is the *circle* $x_1^2 + x_2^2 = a^2$; for $k = 3$, the *surface is that of an "ordinary" sphere*; and for $k = 4, 5, \ldots$ the surfaces are (by analogy) those of *hyperspheres.*

A hyperspherical simplex consists of the $(k-1)$-dimensional set of points $\mathbf{x}$ on a hyperspherical surface which (in addition to 10A.2.1) satisfy the relationships

$$\left.\begin{array}{l} L_1(\mathbf{x}) \equiv b_{11}x_1 + b_{12}x_2 + \ldots + b_{1k}x_k \geq 0 \\ \quad\cdot \qquad \cdot \qquad \cdot \qquad\qquad \cdot \\ \quad\cdot \qquad \cdot \qquad \cdot \qquad\qquad \cdot \\ \quad\cdot \qquad \cdot \qquad \cdot \qquad\qquad \cdot \\ L_k(\mathbf{x}) \equiv b_{k1}x_1 + b_{k2}x_2 + \ldots + b_{kk}x_k \geq 0 \end{array}\right\}, \qquad (10A.2.2)$$

the k linear functions $L_1(\mathbf{x}), \ldots, L_k(\mathbf{x})$ supposedly being essentially distinct.

A relationship such as $L_1(\mathbf{x}) = 0$ defines a $(k-1)$-dimensional hyperplane or $(k-1)$-flat (the generalization of an ordinary plane in three-dimensional space), immersed in k-dimensional space, through the origin, whereas $L_1(\mathbf{x}) \geq 0$ defines a half-space, that is, the set of points on one side of the flat. It follows that the k-relationships (10A.2.2) represent the set of points in a corner K of the k-dimensional space, formed by k distinct flats through the origin. Furthermore, the intersection of the flat $L_1(\mathbf{x}) = 0$ with the spherical surface $Q(\mathbf{x}) = a^2$ is a spherical surface but of dimensionality $k - 2$; such a surface is called a great sphere (the generalization of a great circle on an "ordinary" spherical surface). More generally, the set of points common to m ($m < k$) such flats and the surface $Q(\mathbf{x}) = a^2$ is a great sphere of dimensionality $k-1-m$. The *edges* of the simplex described jointly by (10A.2.1) and (10A.2.2) are themselves simplices and

[3] The sense in which the distribution is truncated will be apparent from (10A.2.3) and (10A.2.4).

are portions of great spheres, with dimensionality $k-2, k-3, \ldots, 0$, and the basic simplex is a portion of the original $(k-1)$-dimensional spherical surface $Q(\mathbf{x}) = a^2$. The number of edges of dimensionality $k-1-m$ is $\binom{k}{m}$. The simplices corresponding to $k = 1, 2, 3, 4, \ldots$ are a point, arc of a circle, spherical triangle, spherical tetrahedron, etc. Thus, the spherical tetrahedron hax 4 edges of dimensionality 2 (4 spherical triangles), 6 edges of dimensionality 1 (6 arcs of great circles), and 4 edges of dimensionality 0 (4 points or vertices).

The concept of the *content* of a k-dimensional geometric entity is the natural generalization of the length, area, and volume of geometrical entities in one, two and three dimensions respectively. Formally, the content of the general $(k-1)$-dimensional hyperspherical simplex is

$$a^{k-1}\int \ldots \int \sin^{k-2}\theta_1 \sin^{k-3}\theta_2 \ldots \sin\theta_{k-2}\, d\theta_1\, d\theta_2 \ldots d\theta_{k-1},$$

the region of integration being that common to the sets of points characterized by (10A.2.1) and (10A.2.2). The angles $\theta_1, \theta_2, \ldots, \theta_{k-1}$ are the polar angles of a point of the hyperspherical surface in (10A.2.1) relative to the coordinate reference frame $x_1, x_2, \ldots, x_k$, the relationship between the two sets of quantities being provided by

$$\left.\begin{aligned} x_i &= a \sin\theta_1 \sin\theta_2 \ldots \sin\theta_{i-1} \cos\theta_i, \qquad i = 1, 2, \ldots, k-1 \\ x_k &= a \sin\theta_1 \sin\theta_2 \ldots \sin\theta_{k-1} \end{aligned}\right\}$$

for a point $(x_1, x_2, \ldots, x_k)$ on the hyperspherical surface.

The expression $a^{k-1} \sin^{k-2}\theta_1 \sin^{k-3}\theta_2 \ldots \sin\theta_{k-2}\, d\theta_1\, d\theta_2 \ldots d\theta_{k-1}$ represents an infinitesimal solid angle or, equivalently, the content of an infinitesimal region on the hyperspherical surface in (10A.2.1). Clearly the content of the simplex is the product of a^{k-1} and some function of the $\binom{k}{2}$ angles, here termed *primary angles*, between the k flats which demarcate the simplex. The angle between the flats $L_i(\mathbf{x}) = 0$ and $L_j(\mathbf{x}) = 0$ $(j \neq i)$ interior to the region K will be denoted by (ij). The ratio of the content of the simplex to the total content of the hyperspherical surface $Q(\mathbf{x}) = a^2$ on which it is constructed will be denoted by

$$C_k \equiv C_k[(12), (13), \ldots, (\overline{k-1k})]$$

and will be referred to as the *relative content*.

It is instructive to relate C_k to a suitably truncated multivariate normal distribution. By this is meant a distribution in which $\mathbf{x}$ is constrained to lie in the region K and in which the density function of $\mathbf{x}$ is proportional to $(2\pi)^{-k/2}\exp\left(-\sum_1^k x_i^2/2\right)$. It is not difficult to show that the proportionality, or normalizing, constant is $1/C_k$, that is,

$$C_k = (2\pi)^{-k/2}\int_K\cdots\int \exp\left(-\sum_1^k x_i^2/2\right) dx_1\, dx_2 \ldots dx_k, \quad (10A.2.3)$$

which follows directly from the symmetry of the spherical (non-truncated) normal distribution in k dimensions. This distribution has $(2\pi)^{-k/2}\exp\left(-\sum_1^k x_i^2/2\right)$ for its density function, and the surfaces of constant density are the hyperspherical surfaces represented by (10A.2.1), with $0 < a < \infty$. Consider two such contiguous surfaces. Clearly the ratio of the integral of $(2\pi)^{-k/2}\exp\left(-\sum_1^k x_i^2/2\right)$ over the part of the annular region between these two spherical surfaces that lies in the region K to the integral over the entire annulus is equal to the ratio of the content of the corresponding simplex to the content of the total spherical surface, that is, it is equal to C_k. The result (10A.2.3) follows on noting that

$$(2\pi)^{-k/2}\int_{-\infty}^{\infty}\cdots\int_{-\infty}^{\infty} \exp\left(-\sum_1^k x_i^2/2\right) dx_1\, dx_2 \ldots dx_k = 1.$$

Equation (10A.2.3) may be applied to the determination of the total probability in a corner and, in particular in one of the generalized quadrants, of the multivariate nonsingular normal distribution with variance-covariance matrix $\mathbf{V}$. This determination is effected by a linear orthogonal transformation chosen so as to orient the new axes along the axes of the ellipsoids of constant density of the distribution, followed by a simple scaling transformation to convert the ellipsoids into spheres. Thus

$$(2\pi)^{-k/2}\,|\mathbf{V}|^{-1/2}\int_{\mathbf{x}\geq\mathbf{0}}\cdots\int \exp\left(-\tfrac{1}{2}\mathbf{x}'\mathbf{V}^{-1}\mathbf{x}\right) d\mathbf{x}$$

$$= (2\pi)^{-k/2}\,|\mathbf{V}|^{-1/2}\int_{\mathbf{Ry}\geq\mathbf{0}}\cdots\int \exp\left(-\tfrac{1}{2}\mathbf{y}'\mathbf{K}\mathbf{y}\right) d\mathbf{y}$$

$$= (2\pi)^{-k/2}\int_{\mathbf{RK}^{-1/2}\boldsymbol{\xi}\geq\mathbf{0}}\cdots\int \exp\left(-\tfrac{1}{2}\boldsymbol{\xi}'\boldsymbol{\xi}\right) d\boldsymbol{\xi} \quad (10A.2.4)$$

with $\mathbf{x} = \mathbf{Ry}$, $\boldsymbol{\xi} = \mathbf{K}^{1/2}\mathbf{y}$, $\mathbf{R}$ being the (orthogonal) matrix of the latent vectors of $\mathbf{V}^{-1}$ and $\mathbf{K}$ the diagonal matrix with diagonal elements equal to the latent roots of $\mathbf{V}^{-1}$. The right-hand member of (10A.2.4) is of the same form as the right-hand member of (10A.2.3), and the angle (ij) of the simplex to which it corresponds is $\cos^{-1}(-\rho_{ij})$, where ρ_{ij} is the correlation between x_i and x_j. The latter statement does not follow easily from (10A.2.4) but may be proved by an alternative method relating the probability contained in K under the multivariate normal distribution to the content of an appropriate hyperspherical simplex. By means of triangular resolution $\mathbf{V}$ may be written in the form

$$\mathbf{V} = \mathbf{LL}' \tag{10A.2.5}$$

where $\mathbf{L}$ is a $k\times k$ lower triangular matrix, from which

$$(2\pi)^{-k/2}\,|\mathbf{V}|^{-\frac{1}{2}} \int_{\mathbf{x}\geq\mathbf{0}}\!\!\!\cdots\!\int \exp\left(-\tfrac{1}{2}\mathbf{x}'\mathbf{V}^{-1}\mathbf{x}\right) d\mathbf{x} = (2\pi)^{-k/2} \int_{\mathbf{L}\boldsymbol{\xi}\geq\mathbf{0}}\!\!\!\cdots\!\int \exp\left(-\tfrac{1}{2}\boldsymbol{\xi}'\boldsymbol{\xi}\right) d\boldsymbol{\xi} \tag{10A.2.6}$$

on setting $\mathbf{x} = \mathbf{L}\boldsymbol{\xi}$. To determine the angles (ij) interior to the region K between the k flats represented by $\mathbf{L}\boldsymbol{\xi} = \mathbf{0}$, note that

$$\begin{aligned}\cos(ij) &= -\sum_{r=1}^{k} l_{ir}l_{jr}\Big/\left[\left(\sum_{r=1}^{k} l_{ir}^{\,2}\right)\left(\sum_{r=1}^{k} l_{jr}^{\,2}\right)\right]^{\frac{1}{2}} \\ &= -v_{ij}/(v_{ii}v_{jj})^{\frac{1}{2}}, \qquad j\neq i\end{aligned}$$

by (10A.2.5). Hence, since v_{ij} is the covariance between x_i and x_j, with $i, j = 1, 2, \ldots, k$,

$$(ij) = \cos^{-1}(-\rho_{ij}), \qquad j\neq i \tag{10A.2.7}$$

as stated.

A fundamental differential relationship for C_k has been obtained by Schläfli [21].[4] The infinitesimal change dC_k in the relative content corresponding to infinitesimal changes $d(ij)$ in the angles (ij) is given by

$$dC_k = \frac{1}{2\pi}\sum_{j>i}\sum C_{k-2}(\overline{ij})\,d(ij), \qquad k = 2, 3, \ldots \tag{10A.2.8}$$

$C_0(\theta)$ being interpreted identically as 1. In (10A.2.8) $(\overline{ij})$ denotes the edge of dimensionality $k-3$, formed by the flats $L_i(\mathbf{x}) = 0$ and $L_j(\mathbf{x}) = 0$, and $C_{k-2}(\overline{ij})$ its content (e.g., for $k = 5$, $C_3(\overline{ij})$ is the relative area of a spherical triangle). The simplex (ij) is a function of *its* primary angles, of which there are $\binom{k-2}{2}$ in number, and a typical such primary angle,

[4] For a more recent attack on Schläfli's problem see Van der Vaart [24, 25].

formed by the flats $L_p(\mathbf{x}) = 0$ and $L_q(\mathbf{x}) = 0$, with $q \neq p$, will be denoted by $(\overline{ij}\, pq)$. The relationship between the two sets of angles is given by

$$\cos(\overline{ij}\, pq) = -\Delta\begin{pmatrix} p & \\ q & ij \end{pmatrix} \Big/ [\Delta(p\, ij)\, \Delta(q\, ij)]^{1/2} \qquad (10A.2.9)$$

where

$$\Delta\begin{pmatrix} p & \\ q & ij \end{pmatrix} = \begin{vmatrix} -\cos(pq) & -\cos(pi) & -\cos(pj) \\ -\cos(iq) & 1 & -\cos(ij) \\ -\cos(jq) & -\cos(ji) & 1 \end{vmatrix}, \qquad (10A.2.9a)$$

$$\Delta(p\, ij) = \begin{vmatrix} 1 & -\cos(pi) & -\cos(pj) \\ -\cos(ip) & 1 & -\cos(ij) \\ -\cos(jp) & -\cos(ji) & 1 \end{vmatrix}. \qquad (10A.2.9b)$$

The first few values for C_k are

$$C_0 = 1, \quad C_1 = \tfrac{1}{2}, \quad C_2 = (12)/(2\pi), \quad C_3 = [(12) + (13) + (23) - \pi]/)4\pi), \qquad (10A.2.10)$$

the expression for C_3 corresponding to the area of a spherical triangle in terms of its "excess." For dimensionality greater than three, C_k can no longer be expressed in terms of elementary functions because of the intractability of (10A.2.8) (Hoppe [11], Richmond [17], Coxeter [3]).

Schläfli's proof of (10A.2.8) is based on geometrical considerations. A recent elegant proof of a nongeometrical character due to Plackett [16] is worth noting. We have seen that the relative content of a hyperspherical simplex may always be expressed as the total probability contained in the positive orthant under a normal multivariate distribution (10A.2.4 and 10A.2.3) and that this is a function solely of the $\tfrac{1}{2}k(k-1)$ primary angles (ij) (the angles between the k bounding planes which define the simplex) or equivalently the $\tfrac{1}{2}k(k-1)$ correlations ρ_{ij} in the corresponding multivariate normal distribution (10A.2.7). Plackett's argument exploits the following two properties of the multivariate normal distribution. Let the probability density function for a multivariate normal distribution with unit standard deviations be denoted by

$$\phi_k \equiv \phi_k(\mathbf{x}, \mathbf{V}) = (2\pi)^{-k/2}\, |\mathbf{V}|^{-1/2} \exp(-\tfrac{1}{2}\mathbf{x}'\mathbf{V}^{-1}\mathbf{x}),$$

and let

$$\phi_k \equiv \phi_k(\mathbf{V}) = (2\pi)^{-k/2}\, |\mathbf{V}|^{-1/2} \int_{\mathbf{x} \geq \mathbf{0}} \!\!\cdots\! \int \exp(-\tfrac{1}{2}\mathbf{x}'\mathbf{V}^{-1}\mathbf{x})\, d\mathbf{x}.$$

Then

$$\text{(i)} \quad \partial\phi_k/\partial\rho_{ij} = \partial^2\phi_k/\partial x_i \partial x_j,$$

and (ii) the conditional distributions of the normal multivariate distribution are expressible in terms of deviation from regression.

A differential relationship connecting $d\Phi_k$ with the infinitesimal changes $d\rho_{ij}$ in the correlation coefficients is then obtained fairly readily from (i) and (ii). This relationship is equivalent to Schläfli's relationship (10A.2.8) on noting that $(ij) = \cos^{-1}(-\rho_{ij})$. In this connection, (10A.2.9), (10A.2.9*a*), and (10A.2.9*b*) are equivalent to the relation between the partial correlation coefficients of order two and the total correlation coefficients (of order zero), obtained by successive application of the reduction formula

$$\rho_{ij\cdot pq} = \frac{\rho_{ij\cdot q} - \rho_{ip\cdot q}\rho_{jp\cdot q}}{[(1 - \rho^2_{ip\cdot q})(1 - \rho^2_{jp\cdot q})]^{1/2}}$$

and the analogous formula with q deleted, $\rho_{ij\cdot pq}$ being equal to $-\cos(\overline{pq}\,ij)$.

The spherical simplices which occur in the distributional theory of order statistics in normal samples are the skew members for which the primary angles are either θ or $\pi - \theta$. Specifically, setting $k = \beta + \gamma$, the simplices are demarcated by $\beta+\gamma$ flats, each of dimensionality $\beta+\gamma-1$, which may be divided into two sets, $\{1, 2, \ldots, \beta\}$ and $\{\beta+1, \beta+2, \ldots, \beta+\gamma\}$, in such a way that

$$\begin{aligned}(ij) &= \theta, \qquad i, j \text{ in same set}, \qquad \neq i \\ &= \pi - \theta, \quad i, j \text{ in opposite sets}, \quad \tfrac{1}{2}\pi \leq \theta \leq \pi.\end{aligned} \qquad (10A.2.11)$$

Such a simplex will be referred to as a type A simplex and its relative content denoted by $V_{\beta,\beta+\gamma}(\theta)$. Examination of the third-order determinants involved in (10A.2.9), (10A.2.9*a*), and (10A.2.9*b*) reveals that

$$\begin{aligned}(\overline{ij}\,pq) &= \phi(\theta), \qquad p, q \text{ in same set, all } i, j, j \neq i, q \neq p \\ &= \pi - \phi(\theta), \quad p, q \text{ in opposite sets, all } i, j, j \neq i\end{aligned} \qquad (10A.2.12)$$

where

$$\phi(\theta) = \cos^{-1}\frac{\cos\theta}{1 - 2\cos\theta}. \qquad (10A.2.12a)$$

The significance of (10A.2.12) is that $(\overline{ij})$ is itself a type A simplex, from which (10A.2.8) supplies a differential recurrence relationship which allows the evaluation of the contents of simplices of type A (Ruben [18]). Consider in fact $(\overline{ij})$ where i and j belong to the first set $\{1, 2, \ldots, \beta\}$ with $j \neq i$. This is a skew simplex of type A with dimensionality reduced by two. It may be regarded as demarcated by $\beta+\gamma-2$ flats of dimensionality $\beta+\gamma-3$ which divide into two groups,

$$\{1, 2, \ldots, i-1, i+1, \ldots, j-1, j+1, \ldots, \beta\}$$

and

$$\{\beta+1, \beta+2, \ldots, \beta+\gamma\},$$

such that the angle between any two distinct flats in the same group is $\phi(\theta)$ and that between any two flats in distinct groups is $\pi - \phi(\theta)$. There are $\binom{\beta}{2}$ such simplices, and $d(ij) = d\theta$. Consider now $(\overline{ij})$ where i and j belong to the second set, $\{\beta+1, \beta+2, \ldots, \beta+\gamma\}$, with $j \neq i$. This is also a skew simplex of type A with dimensionality reduced by two. It may be regarded as demarcated by $\beta+\gamma-2$ flats of dimensionality $\beta+\gamma-3$ which divide into two groups, $\{1, 2, \ldots, \beta\}$ and

$$\{\beta+1, \ldots, i-1, i+1, \ldots, j-1, j+1, \ldots, \beta+\gamma\},$$

such that the angle between any two distinct flats in the same group is $\phi(\theta)$ and that between any two flats in different groups is $\pi - \phi(\theta)$. There are $\binom{\gamma}{2}$ such simplices, and $d(ij) = d\theta$. Consider, finally, $(\overline{ij})$ where i and j are in opposite sets. This is once again a type A simplex with dimensionality reduced by two. It may be regarded as demarcated by $\beta+\gamma-2$ flats of dimensionality $\beta+\gamma-3$ which divide into two groups, $\{1, 2, \ldots, i-1, i+1, \ldots, \beta\}$ and $\{\beta+1, \ldots, j-1, j+1, \ldots, \beta+\gamma\}$, such that the angle between any two distinct flats in the same group is $\phi(\theta)$ and that between any two flats in different groups is $\pi - \phi(\theta)$. There are $\beta\gamma$ such simplices, and $d(ij) = -d\theta$. By combining these results and applying them in (10A.2.8),

$$dV_{\beta,\beta+\gamma}(\theta) = \frac{1}{2\pi}\left[\binom{\beta}{2} V_{\beta-2,\beta+\gamma-2}(\phi(\theta)) - \beta\gamma V_{\beta-1,\beta+\gamma-2}(\phi(\theta)) + \binom{\gamma}{2} V_{\beta,\beta+\gamma-2}(\phi(\theta))\right] d\theta. \quad (10A.2.13)$$

Hence,

$$V_{\beta,\beta+\gamma}(\theta) = \frac{1}{2^{\beta+\gamma}} + \frac{1}{2\pi}\int_{\frac{1}{2}\pi}^{\theta}\left[\binom{\beta}{2} V_{\beta-2,\beta+\gamma-2}(\phi(\theta')) - \beta\gamma V_{\beta-1,\beta+\gamma-2}(\phi(\theta')) + \binom{\gamma}{2} V_{\beta,\beta+\gamma-2}(\phi(\theta'))\right] d\theta', \qquad \beta, \gamma = 0, 1, 2 \ldots . \quad (10A.2.14)$$

Equation (10A.2.14) may be expressed compactly in symbolical form as follows:

$$V_{\beta,\beta+\gamma}(\theta) = \frac{1}{2^{\beta+\gamma}} + \frac{1}{4\pi} L^2 \int_{\frac{1}{2}\pi}^{\theta} V_{\beta,\beta+\gamma}(\phi(\theta'))\, d\theta', \qquad \beta, \gamma = 0, 1, 2, \ldots \tag{10A.2.15}$$

where

$$\mathbf{L} = \beta\mathbf{B} - \gamma\mathbf{\Gamma} \tag{10A.2.15a}$$

and $\boldsymbol{B}$ and $\mathbf{\Gamma}$ are the operators which *decrease* β and γ, respectively, by 1.

Successive application of (10A.2.15) yields[5]

$$V_{\beta,\beta+\gamma}(\theta) = \frac{1}{2^{\beta+\gamma}} \sum_{k=0}^{[(\beta+\gamma)/2]} \mathbf{L}^{2k}\psi_k(\theta), \qquad \beta, \gamma = 0, 1, 2, \ldots \tag{10A.2.16}$$

where $[m]$ denotes, as usual, the integral part of m and the auxiliary functions $\psi_k(\theta)$ are defined by

$$\psi_0(\theta) = 1,$$
$$\psi_k(\theta) = \frac{1}{\pi}\int_{\pi/2}^{\theta} \psi_{k-1}(\phi(\theta'))\, d\theta', \qquad \tfrac{1}{2}\pi \le \theta \le \pi, \quad k = 1, 2, \ldots. \tag{10A.2.16a}$$

In particular, for regular simplices ($\gamma = 0$),

$$V_{\beta,\beta}(\theta) = \frac{1}{2^\beta} + \frac{\beta(\beta-1)}{4\pi}\int_{\pi/2}^{\theta} V_{\beta-2,\beta-2}(\phi(\theta'))\, d\theta', \qquad \beta = 0, 1, 2, \ldots \tag{10A.2.17}$$

$$V_{\beta,\beta}(\theta) = \frac{1}{2^\beta}\sum_{k=0}^{[\beta/2]} \beta^{(2k)}\psi_k(\theta), \qquad \beta = 0, 1, 2, \ldots \tag{10A.2.18}$$

where

$$\beta^{(0)} = 1,$$
$$\beta^{(m)} = \beta(\beta-1)\ldots(\beta-m+1), \qquad m = 1, 2, \ldots. \tag{10A.2.18a}$$

Equations (10A.2.15) and (10A.2.17) may be expressed in a slightly different form, which is perhaps more convenient for computational purposes, by setting

$$\theta' = \cos^{-1}(-1/x'), \quad (x' \ge 1) \qquad \text{and} \qquad \bar{V}_{\beta,\beta+\gamma}(x) \equiv V_{\beta,\beta+\gamma}(\theta).$$

This gives

$$\bar{V}_{\beta,\beta+\gamma}(x) = \frac{1}{2^{\beta+\gamma}} + \frac{1}{4\pi}\mathbf{L}^2\int_x^\infty \bar{V}_{\beta,\beta+\gamma}(x'+2)\frac{dx'}{x'\sqrt{x'^2-1}}, \qquad \beta, \gamma = 0, 1, 2, \ldots \tag{10A.2.19}$$

[5] See (10A.3.11) for the interpretation of $\boldsymbol{L}^{2k}\psi_k(\theta)$ in (10A.2.16).

and

$$\bar{V}_{\beta,\beta}(x) = \frac{1}{2^\beta} + \frac{\beta(\beta-1)}{4\pi}\int_x^\infty \bar{V}_{\beta-2,\beta-2}(x'+2)\frac{dx'}{x'\sqrt{x'^2-1}},$$

$$\beta = 0, 1, 2, \ldots. \quad (10A.2.20)$$

Tables of $\bar{V}_{\beta,\beta}(x)$, denoted there by $\bar{u}_\beta(x)$, for $x = 2(1)12$, $\beta = 0(1)51 - x$, and generally accurate to ten decimal places, have been supplied by Ruben [18, pp. 222–223].

10A.3 Relation between Moments of Order Statistics in Normal Samples and Hyperspherical Simplices

The probability density function of the rth order statistic, counting from the lowest member, in a random independent sample of size n from a continuous distribution with probability density function $f(x)$ and cumulative distribution function $F(x)$ is readily obtainable as a particular application of the multinomial distribution (Wilks [26]). The required density function is

$$n\binom{n-1}{r-1} f(x)[F(x)]^{r-1}[1 - F(x)]^{n-r} \quad (10A.3.1)$$

and the moments about the origin are therefore

$$s_{r/n}^{\mu'} = n\binom{n-1}{r-1}\int_{-\infty}^{\infty} x^s f(x)[F(x)]^{r-1}[1 - F(x)]^{n-r}\,dx, \qquad s = 1, 2, \ldots$$

$$(10A.3.2)$$

[The limits of integration in (10A.3.2) are taken as $-\infty$ and $+\infty$, for convenience, by defining $f(x)$ as zero in the range of values of x not assumed by the random variable.] We consider here the case in which the parent distribution is normal and standardized, for which

$$f(x) = \frac{1}{\sqrt{2\pi}} e^{-x^2/2}, \quad (10A.3.3)$$

$$F(x) = \frac{1}{\sqrt{2\pi}}\int_{-\infty}^{x} e^{-\xi^2/2} d\xi. \quad (10A.3.4)$$

In order to study the properties of integrals of the type given in (10A.3.2) we find it fruitful to consider a more inclusive class of integrals. Define

$$\phi(s; \alpha; \beta, \gamma) = \int_{-\infty}^{\infty} x^s [f(x)]^\alpha [F(x)]^\beta [1 - F(x)]^\gamma\,dx \quad (10A.3.5)$$

where s, β, and γ are nonnegative integers and α is real and positive. This equation gives the general form of integral needed in the derivation of the series [see (10A.3.18)] for the moments of the order statistics. We show first that any member of the more general class of integrals can be expressed as the series (10A.3.7) depending on functions $\phi(0;\ \alpha;\ \beta, \gamma)$ and containing coefficients whose values depend only on α.

An auxiliary but important application of the integral in (10A.3.5) is that the latter arises in connection with the moment generating function of the square of the general order statistic in samples from normal populations. In this instance $s = 0$ [see (10A.3.21)].

Integrating by parts, and noting that

$$\frac{df(x)}{dx} = -xf(x),$$

we obtain

$$\phi(s;\alpha;\beta,\gamma) = \frac{s-1}{\alpha}\,\phi(s-2;\alpha;\beta,\gamma) + \frac{\beta}{\alpha}\,\phi(s-1;\alpha+1;\beta-1,\gamma)$$
$$-\frac{\gamma}{\alpha}\,\phi(s-1;\alpha+1;\beta,\gamma-1), \qquad s = 1, 2, \ldots. \tag{10A.3.6}$$

It is convenient to represent the reduction formula in (10A.3.6) in symbolical form.[6] It may in fact then be shown by induction that $\phi(s;\ \alpha;\ \beta, \gamma)$ can be expressed as a linear combination of ϕ's in which $s = 0$. The formulas in question are

$$\phi(2k+1;\alpha;\beta,\gamma) = \sum_{i=0}^{k} a_{2k+1,2i+1}(\alpha)(\mathbf{PL})^{2i+1}\phi(0;\alpha;\beta,\gamma),$$
$$\phi(2k;\alpha;\beta,\gamma) = \sum_{i=0}^{k} a_{2k,2i}(\alpha)(\mathbf{PL})^{2i}\phi(0;\alpha;\beta,\gamma), \qquad k = 0, 1, 2, \ldots \tag{10A.3.7}$$

where

$$\mathbf{P} = \frac{1}{\alpha}\,\mathbf{A} \tag{10A.3.7a}$$

and **A** is the operator which *increases* α by 1. The a's are functions of the α's and are given as far as $a_{10,10}(\alpha)$ by Ruben [18] together with their numerical values when $\alpha = 1$. In the application of the formulas in

[6] The symbolic form is

$$\phi(s;\ \alpha;\ \beta,\gamma) = \frac{s-1}{\alpha}\,\phi(s-2;\ \alpha;\ \beta,\gamma) + \mathbf{PL}\,\phi(s-1;\ \alpha;\ \beta,\gamma), \qquad s = 1, 2, \ldots$$

where **P** is defined in (10A.3.7a).

(10A.3.7) the following relationships should be noted:

$$\mathbf{P}^m \equiv \frac{1}{\alpha^{-(m)}} \mathbf{A}^m, \qquad m = 0, 1, 2, \ldots \tag{10A.3.8}$$

where

$$u^{-(0)} = 1 \tag{10A.3.8a}$$

$$u^{-(m)} = u(u+1)\ldots(u+m-1), \qquad m = 1, 2, \ldots$$

$$L^m \equiv \sum_{j=0}^{m} (-)^j \gamma^{(j)} \beta^{(m-j)} \mathbf{\Gamma}^j \mathbf{B}^{m-j}, \qquad m = 0, 1, 2, \ldots \tag{10A.3.9}$$

and

$$L^m \equiv 0, \qquad m > \beta + \gamma; \quad \beta, \gamma = 0, 1, 2, \ldots \tag{10A.3.10}$$

m being integral.

Finally, although this is needed for (10A.2.16) rather than for (10A.3.7), if ω is independent of β and γ, then

$$L^m \omega = \omega \sum_{j=0}^{m} (-)^j \binom{m}{j} \gamma^{(j)} \beta^{(m-j)}. \tag{10A.3.11}$$

A simple numerical example will make the use of the formulas (10A.3.7) sufficiently clear. The second of the two formulas gives, for $k = 2$,

$$\phi(4; \alpha; \beta, \gamma) = [a_{4,0}(\alpha) + a_{4,2}(\alpha)(PL)^2 + a_{4,4}(\alpha)(\mathbf{PL})^4]\phi(0; \alpha; \beta, \gamma).$$

Suppose now $\beta + \gamma < 4$. Then, by (10A.3.10), the last term in this expansion vanishes for all permissible values of α. Hence, on using (10A.3.9) together with (10A.3.8) and substituting for the required $a(\alpha)$,

$$\begin{aligned}
&\phi(4; \alpha; \beta, \gamma) \\
&\quad = a_{4,0}(\alpha)\phi(0; \alpha; \beta, \gamma) + a_{4,2}(\alpha)\mathbf{P}^2\mathbf{L}^2\phi(0; \alpha; \beta, \gamma) \\
&\quad = a_{4,0}(\alpha)\phi(0; \alpha; \beta, \gamma) \\
&\qquad + a_{4,2}(\alpha)P^2[\beta(\beta-1)B^2 - 2\beta\gamma B\Gamma + \gamma(\gamma-1)\Gamma^2]\phi(0; \alpha; \beta, \gamma) \\
&\quad = a_{4,0}(\alpha)\phi(0; \alpha; \beta, \gamma) + a_{4,2}(\alpha)\mathbf{P}^2[\beta(\beta-1)\phi(0; \alpha; \beta-2, \gamma) \\
&\qquad - 2\beta\gamma\phi(0; \alpha; \beta-1, \gamma-1) + \gamma(\gamma-1)\phi(0; \alpha; \beta, \gamma-2)] \\
&\quad = a_{4,0}(\alpha)\phi(0; \alpha; \beta, \gamma) + a_{4,2}(\alpha)\frac{1}{\alpha(\alpha+1)} \\
&\qquad \times [\beta(\beta-1)\phi(0; \alpha+2; \beta-2, \gamma) - 2\beta\gamma\phi(0; \alpha+2; \beta-1, \gamma-1) \\
&\qquad + \gamma(\gamma-1)\phi(0; \alpha+2; \beta, \gamma-2)] \\
&\quad = \frac{3}{\alpha^2}\phi(0; \alpha; \beta, \gamma) + \left(\frac{1}{\alpha+2} + \frac{2}{\alpha+1} + \frac{3}{\alpha}\right)\frac{1}{\alpha(\alpha+1)} \\
&\qquad \times [\beta(\beta-1)\phi(0; \alpha+2; \beta-2, \gamma) - 2\beta\gamma\phi(0; \alpha+2; \beta-1, \gamma-1) \\
&\qquad + \gamma(\gamma-1)\phi(0; \alpha+2; \beta, \gamma-2)], \qquad \beta + \gamma < 4.
\end{aligned}$$

In particular,

$$\phi(4;1;\beta,\gamma) = 3\phi(0;1;\beta,\gamma) + \frac{13}{3}\cdot\frac{1}{2}$$
$$\times [\beta(\beta-1)\phi(0;3;\beta-2,\gamma) - 2\beta\phi(0;3;\beta-1,\gamma-1)$$
$$+ \gamma(\gamma-1)\phi(0;3;\beta,\gamma-2)], \qquad \beta+\gamma<4.$$

Comparison of (10A.3.2) and (10A.3.7) indicates that the required moments are expressible as linear combinations of $\phi(0;\alpha;\beta,\gamma)$. It now remains to evaluate the latter function. We show that

$$\phi(0;\alpha;\beta,\gamma) = (2\pi)^{-(\alpha-1)/2}\alpha^{-1/2}V_{\beta,\beta+\gamma}\left(\cos^{-1} - \frac{1}{1+\alpha}\right). \qquad (10A.3.12)$$

The essential artifice is to express the integral in (10A.3.5), with $s = 0$, as a multiple integral in $\beta+\gamma$ variables of the form (10A.2.4). In fact,

$$\phi(0;\alpha;\beta,\gamma)$$
$$= \int_{-\infty}^{\infty} \frac{1}{(2\pi)^{\alpha/2}} e^{-\alpha x^2/2} \prod_{i=1}^{\beta}\left(\int_{-\infty}^{x} \frac{1}{(2\pi)^{1/2}} e^{-u_i^2/2}\,du_i\right)$$
$$\times \prod_{j=\beta+1}^{\beta+\gamma}\left(\int_{x}^{\infty} \frac{1}{(2\pi)^{1/2}} e^{-u_j^2/2}\,du_j\right) dx$$
$$= \frac{1}{(2\pi)^{(\alpha+\beta+\gamma)/2}} \int_{u_1=-\infty}^{x} \cdots \int_{u_\beta=-\infty}^{x} \int_{u_{\beta+1}=x}^{\infty} \cdots \int_{u_{\beta+\gamma}=x}^{\infty} \int_{x=-\infty}^{\infty}$$
$$\exp\left[-\tfrac{1}{2}\left(\alpha x^2 + \sum_{1}^{\beta+\gamma} u_i^2\right)\right] dx\,du_1\ldots du_{\beta+\gamma}. \qquad (10A.3.13)$$

On applying the transformation

$$y_i = u_i - x, \qquad i = 1, 2, \ldots, \beta+\gamma, \qquad (10A.3.14)$$
$$x' = x,$$

$$\phi(0;\alpha;\beta,\gamma)$$
$$= \frac{1}{(2\pi)^{(\alpha+\beta+\gamma)/2}} \int_{y_1=-\infty}^{0} \cdots \int_{y_\beta=-\infty}^{0} \int_{y_{\beta+1}=0}^{\infty} \cdots \int_{y_{\beta+\gamma}=0}^{\infty} \int_{x'=-\infty}^{\infty}$$
$$\times \exp\left\{-\tfrac{1}{2}(\alpha+\beta+\gamma)\left[x' + \sum_{1}^{\beta+\gamma} \frac{y_i}{\alpha+\beta+\gamma}\right]^2 - \frac{Q}{2(\alpha+\beta+\gamma)}\right\}$$
$$\times dx'\,dy_1\ldots dy_{\beta+\gamma} \qquad (10A.3.15)$$

where Q is the positive definite quadratic form

$$Q \equiv Q(y_1, y_2, \ldots, y_{\beta+\gamma}) = (\alpha + \beta + \gamma - 1) \sum y_i^2 - \sum' \sum' y_i y_j,$$

the accented summations indicating that $j \neq i$. By integrating with respect to x',

$$\begin{aligned} &\phi(0; \alpha; \beta, \gamma) \\ &= \frac{1}{(2\pi)^{(\alpha-1)/2}\alpha^{1/2}} \cdot \frac{[\alpha/(\alpha+\beta+\gamma)]^{1/2}}{(2\pi)^{(\beta+\gamma)/2}} \int_{y_1=-\infty}^{0} \cdots \int_{y_\beta=-\infty}^{0} \int_{y_{\beta+1}=0}^{\infty} \cdots \int_{y_{\beta+\gamma}=0}^{\infty} \\ &\qquad \exp\left[-\frac{Q}{2(\alpha+\beta+\gamma)}\right] dy_1 \ldots dy_{\beta+\gamma}. \end{aligned} \tag{10A.3.16}$$

The second term of the right-hand member of (10A.3.16) is to be compared with the left-hand member of (10A.2.4). The correlation matrix of the multivariate normal distribution in the former expression, after y_i $(i = 1, 2, \ldots, \beta)$ has been changed to $-y_i$ in order to make the range of integration coincide with the generalized positive quadrant, has its off-diagonal elements ρ_{ij} equal to $1/(1 + \alpha)$ if i and j are in the same sets, $\{1, 2, \ldots, \beta\}$ and $\{\beta + 1, \beta + 2, \ldots, \beta + \gamma\}$, and to $-1/(1 + \alpha)$ if they are in different sets. (The appropriate orthogonal transformation, referred to after (10A.2.4), for Q in (10A.3.16) is the one that orients one axis along the line $y_1 = y_2 = \ldots = y_{\beta+\gamma}$ whereas the remaining $\beta+\gamma-1$ orthogonal axes may be chosen arbitrarily in the plane perpendicular to the latter line.) Equation (10A.3.12) then follows without difficulty. On substituting in (10A.3.7) the expression given for $(0;\ \alpha; \beta, \gamma)$ in (10A.3.12),

$$\left.\begin{aligned} &\phi(2k+1; \alpha; \beta, \gamma) \\ &= \sum_{i=0}^{k} a_{2k+1,2i+1}(\alpha) \frac{1}{(2\pi)^{(2i+\alpha)/2}(2i+\alpha+1)^{1/2}\alpha^{-(2i+1)}} \\ &\qquad \times \mathbf{L}^{2i+1} V_{\beta,\beta+\gamma}\left(\cos^{-1} - \frac{1}{2i+\alpha+2}\right), \quad k = 0, 1, 2, \ldots \\ &\phi(2k; \alpha; \beta, \gamma) \\ &= \sum_{i=0}^{k} a_{2k,2i}(\alpha) \frac{1}{(2\pi)^{(2i+\alpha-1)/2}(2i+\alpha)^{1/2}\alpha^{-(2i)}} \\ &\qquad \times \mathbf{L}^{2i} V_{\beta,\beta+\gamma}\left(\cos^{-1} - \frac{1}{2i+\alpha+1}\right), \quad k = 0, 1, 2, \ldots \end{aligned}\right\} \tag{10A.3.17}$$

where, as in (10A.3.10) $\mathbf{L}^m V_{\beta,\beta+\gamma}(\theta)$ is to be equated to zero for $m = \beta + \gamma + 1, \beta + \gamma + 2, \ldots.$

On substituting further $\alpha = 1$, $\beta \equiv r - 1$, $\gamma \equiv n - r$,

$$\left.\begin{aligned}
&{}_{2k+1}\mu'_{r|n} \\
&\quad = n\binom{n-1}{r-1}\sum_{i=0}^{k} a_{2k+1,2i+1}(1)\frac{1}{(2\pi)^{i+\frac{1}{2}}\sqrt{2i+2}(2i+1)!} \\
&\qquad \times \mathrm{L}^{2i+1}V_{r-1,n-1}\left(\cos^{-1}-\frac{1}{2i+3}\right), \qquad k = 0, 1, 2, \ldots \\
&{}_{2k}\mu'_{r|n} \\
&\quad = n\binom{n-1}{r-1}\sum_{i=0}^{k} a_{2k,2i}(1)\frac{1}{(2\pi)^{i}\sqrt{2i+1}(2i)!} \\
&\qquad \times \mathrm{L}^{2i}V_{r-1,n-1}\left(\cos^{-1}-\frac{1}{2i+2}\right), \qquad k = 0, 1, 2, \ldots.
\end{aligned}\right\} \tag{10A.3.18}$$

The case of the extreme members of the sample ($\gamma = 0$, $r = n$) is of special interest. Equations (10A.3.18) reduce to

$$\left.\begin{aligned}
&{}_{2k+1}\mu'_{n|n} \\
&\quad = n\sum_{i=0}^{k} a_{2k+1,2i+1}(1)\binom{n-1}{2i+1}\frac{1}{(2\pi)^{i+\frac{1}{2}}\sqrt{2+2i}} \\
&\qquad \times V_{n-2-2i,n-2-2i}\left(\cos^{-1}-\frac{1}{3+2i}\right), \quad k = 0, 1, 2, \ldots \\
&{}_{2k}\mu'_{n|n} \\
&\quad = n\sum_{i=0}^{k} a_{2k,2i}(1)\binom{n-1}{2i}\frac{1}{(2\pi)^{i}\sqrt{1+2i}} \\
&\qquad \times V_{n-1-2i,n-1-2i}\left(\cos^{-1}-\frac{1}{2+2i}\right), \quad k = 0, 1, 2, \ldots
\end{aligned}\right\} \tag{10A.3.19}$$

where the combinatorial coefficients $\binom{r}{s}$ are to be interpreted as zero if $s > r$. The simplices involved in (10A.3.19) are *regular* with primary bounding angles $\cos^{-1}(-\frac{1}{3})$, $\cos^{-1}(-\frac{1}{5}), \ldots,$ and $\cos^{-1}(-\frac{1}{2})$, $\cos^{-1}(-\frac{1}{4}), \ldots.$ (It may be shown that $V_{k,k}(2\pi/3) = 1/(k+1)$, Ruben [18]). Equations (10A.3.18) and (10A.3.19) may be expressed more conveniently in terms of the $\bar{V}$'s by substituting $\bar{V}_{r-1,n-1}(2i+3)$ for $V_{r-1,n-1}\left(\cos^{-1}-\dfrac{1}{2i+3}\right)$, etc. Tables for ${}_r\mu'_{n|n}$, $n = 1(1)50$, $r = 1(1)10$, to ten figure accuracy, as well as tables of the moments about the mean, the measures of skewness and of kurtosis, and the standard deviation of the extreme order statistics for $n = 1(1)50$, accurate to seven or eight decimal places, have been provided by Ruben [18]. These tables are reproduced as Tables 10A.1 and 10A.2.

The character of the double series in (10A.3.18) may be represented graphically (Fig. 10A.1). For

$$\mathbf{L}^m V_{\beta,\beta+\gamma}(\theta) = \sum_{j=0}^{m} (-)^j \binom{m}{j} \beta^{(m-j)} \gamma^{(j)} V_{\beta+j-m,\beta+\gamma-m}(\theta), \quad (10A.3.20)$$

and therefore the typical term on the right-hand side of (10A.3.20) does not vanish if, and only if, $m - \beta \leq j \leq \gamma$.

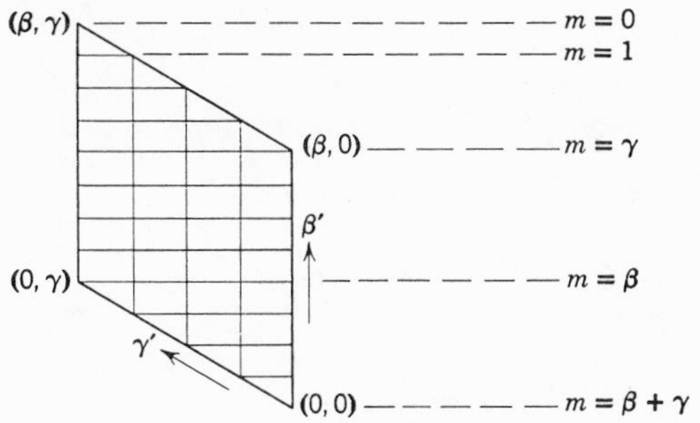

Fig. 10A.1 Illustrating the character and the possible mode of summation of the series in (10A.3.18) and (10A.3.20).

Let (β', γ') represent the coordinates of a point relative to two axes in a plane. Associate with each such point the function $V_{\beta',\beta'+\gamma'}$. Consider the nonnegative points contained within and on the sides of the parallelogram with vertices (0, 0), $(\beta, 0)$, $(0, \gamma)$, (β, γ). Then the value of the series in (10A.3.20) is obtained by summation along the nonnegative integral points on the portion of the line $\beta' + \gamma' = \beta + \gamma - m$ that lies within and on the sides of the parallelogram. Correspondingly, the value of the series in (10A.3.18) is obtained by summation along a set of alternately spaced lines. For the extreme members, γ equals zero and the parallelogram shrinks into the line with end points (0, 0) and $(\beta, 0)$, summation then being effected along the appropriate nonnegative integral points on this line segment. This summation corresponds to (10A.3.19).

For purposes of illustration, consider the trivial yet illuminating case where $n = 4$, $r = 3$ $(\beta = 2, \gamma = 1)$, and $k = 1$ in the second part of (10A.3.18). This will show how the exact values of all the moments of order statistics, in samples of size $n \leq 4$, some of which were first obtained by Jones [12], may be devised immediately from the fundamental formulas (10A.3.18), once the values of the coefficients $a(1)$ are known. At the same time it will illustrate the use of these formulas in more difficult cases.

On substitution,

$$
\begin{aligned}
{}_2\mu'_{3|4} &= 4\binom{3}{2}\left[a_{2,0}(1)V_{2,3}(\cos^{-1}-\tfrac{1}{2}) + a_{2,2}(1)\frac{1}{2\pi\sqrt{3}\cdot 2!}\mathbf{L}^2V_{2,3}(\cos^{-1}-\tfrac{1}{4})\right] \\
&= 4\binom{3}{2}\left\{1\cdot\frac{1}{4}\frac{2!\,1!}{3!} + 1\cdot\frac{1}{4\pi\sqrt{3}}\left[2\cdot 1\cdot V_{0,1}(\cos^{-1}-\tfrac{1}{4})\right.\right. \\
&\qquad \left.\left. - 2\cdot 2\cdot 1\cdot V_{1,1}(\cos^{-1}-\tfrac{1}{4}) + 1\cdot 0\cdot V_{2,1}(\cos^{-1}-\tfrac{1}{4})\right]\right\},
\end{aligned}
$$

having used the formula

$$V_{\beta,\beta+\gamma}(\tfrac{2}{3}\pi) = \frac{1}{\beta+\gamma+1}\cdot\frac{\beta!\,\gamma!}{(\beta+\gamma)!}$$

which follows directly from (10A.3.12), by noting that (10A.3.1), being a density function, must integrate out to 1 over the entire range of x.

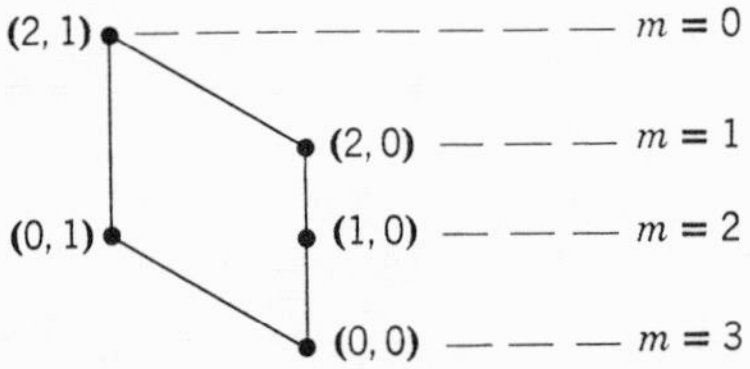

Fig. 10A.2

We would expect to interpret $V_{2,1}(\theta)$ as being identically zero [more generally, $V_{h,k}(\theta) \equiv 0 \quad (h > k)$]. Such an interpretation is not strictly needed, however, since $V_{2,1}(\cos^{-1}-\tfrac{1}{4})$ is preceded in this expansion by a zero coefficient (more generally $V_{h,k}(\theta)$ will always be preceded in the series expansion for the moments by a zero coefficient whenever $h > k$). Since

$$V_{0,1}(\theta) = \tfrac{1}{2} = V_{1,1}(\theta),$$

we obtain

$${}_2\mu'_{3|4} = 1 - \frac{\sqrt{3}}{\pi},$$

in agreement with Jones's result.

The terms needed in the expansion can be obtained more expeditiously from the parallelogram diagram, the coefficients being derived from the values of the $a(1)$'s and by the use of (10A.3.20). The parallelogram appropriate to the case $\beta = 2$, $\gamma = 1$ is depicted in Fig. 10A.2. The points along which summation is effected are (2, 1) (corresponding to $m = 0$), and (0, 1) and (1, 0) (corresponding to $m = 2$). The associated V's are $V_{2,3}$ and $V_{0,1}$ and $V_{1,1}$, respectively, as in the expansion for ${}_2\mu'_{4|3}$.

Finally, the moment generating function of the square of the rth order statistic may also be obtained from (10A.3.12):

$$\begin{aligned}M_{r|n}(\theta) &= E(e^{\theta x^2})\\ &= (2\pi)^{-\theta}E\{[f(x)]^{-2\theta}\}\\ &= (2\pi)^{-\theta}n\binom{n-1}{r-1}\phi(0;1-2\theta;r-1,n-r), \qquad \theta<\tfrac{1}{2}\\ &= n\binom{n-1}{r-1}V_{r-1,n-1}\left[\cos^{-1}\left(-\frac{1}{2-2\theta}\right)\right](1-2\theta)^{-\frac{1}{2}}.\end{aligned} \tag{10A.3.21}$$

For $n \le 4$, $M_{r|n}(\theta)$ may be expressed in terms of elementary trigonometric functions with the aid of (10A.2.10). Thus,

$$M_{r|2}(0) = (1-2\theta)^{-\frac{1}{2}}, \qquad r = 1, 2, \tag{10A.3.22}$$

that is, the even moments of either the smaller or of the greater member in a random sample of two items from a normal population are identical with the even moments relating to a sample of one item, and

$$M_{1|3}(\theta) = \frac{3\left[\cos^{-1}\left(-\dfrac{1}{2-2\theta}\right)\right]}{2\pi}(1-2\theta)^{-\frac{1}{2}} = M_{3|3}(\theta), \tag{10A.3.23}$$

$$M_{2|3}(\theta) = 3\left[1 - \frac{\cos^{-1}\left(-\dfrac{1}{2-2\theta}\right)}{\pi}\right](1-2\theta)^{-\frac{1}{2}}, \tag{10A.3.24}$$

$$M_{1|4}(\theta) = \left[\frac{3\cos^{-1}\left(-\dfrac{1}{2-2\theta}\right)}{\pi} - 1\right](1-2\theta)^{-\frac{1}{2}} = M_{4|4}(\theta), \tag{10A.3.25}$$

$$M_{2|4}(\theta) = 3\left[1 - \frac{\cos^{-1}\left(-\dfrac{1}{2-2\theta}\right)}{\pi}\right](1-2\theta)^{-\frac{1}{2}} = M_{3|4}(\theta). \tag{10A.3.26}$$

10A.4 Relation of the Moments of the Range and Product Moments of Extreme Order Statistics in Normal Samples to Hyperspherical Simplices[7]

We have seen in Section 10A.3 that the moments of order statistics in normal samples are expressible as linear functions of the contents of hyperspherical simplices of type A. This section will demonstrate that the product moments of the extreme order statistics are expressible as linear functions of the *products* of the contents of these simplices. The odd moments of the range when the number of items is odd, and the even

[7] For yet another application of our simplices to the explicit evaluation of the sum of squares of normal scores, used in the analysis of ranked data (Fisher and Yates [5]), see Ruben [19].

moments when the number of items is even, may be expressed in a similar manner.

The joint probability density function of the extreme order statistics in normal samples of size n is

$$n(n-1)[F(v)-F(u)]^{n-2}f(u)f(v), \qquad v \geq u \qquad (10A.4.1)$$

where $f(x)$ and $F(x)$ are as defined in (10A.3.3) and (10A.3.4). Hence, for n even (when the integrand defining $E(uv)$ is symmetric in u and v),

$$\begin{aligned}
E(uv) &= n(n-1)\iint_{v\geq u}[F(v)-F(u)]^{n-2}f(u)f(v)uv\,du\,dv \\
&= \tfrac{1}{2}n(n-1)\int_{-\infty}^{\infty}\int_{-\infty}^{\infty}[F(v)-F(u)]^{n-2}f(u)f(v)uv\,du\,dv \\
&= \tfrac{1}{2}n(n-1)\int_{-\infty}^{\infty}\int_{-\infty}^{\infty}\sum_{k=0}^{n-2}(-)^k\binom{n-2}{k}[F(u)]^k[F(v)]^{n-2-k} \\
&\quad \times f(u)f(v)uv\,du\,dv \\
&= \tfrac{1}{2}n(n-1)\sum_{k=0}^{n-2}(-)^k\binom{n-2}{k}\int_{-\infty}^{\infty}u[F(u)]^k f(u)\,du \\
&\quad \times \int_{-\infty}^{\infty}v[F(v)]^{n-2-k}f(v)\,dv \\
&= \frac{1}{8\pi}n(n-1)\sum_{k=0}^{n-2}(-)^k\binom{n-2}{k}k(n-k-2) \\
&\quad u_{k-1}(\cos^{-1}-\tfrac{1}{3})u_{n-k-3}(\cos^{-1}-\tfrac{1}{3}), \quad n = 2, 4, 6\ldots
\end{aligned} \qquad (10A.4.2)$$

where $u_m(\theta) \equiv V_{m,m}(\theta)$, use having been made of the result from (10A.3.19) that the expectation of the upper extreme statistic in a normal sample of size N is

$$N\int_{-\infty}^{\infty}\xi[F(\xi)]^{N-1}f(\xi)\,d\xi = \frac{N(N-1)}{2\sqrt{\pi}}u_{N-2}(\cos^{-1}-\tfrac{1}{3}), \quad N = 1, 2, \ldots. \qquad (10A.4.2a)$$

The relation between the present u's and the $\bar{u}$'s defined after (10A.2.20) is $u_m(\cos^{-1}-1/x) \equiv \bar{u}_m(x)$.

A similar argument may be used to derive $E(v-u)^m$, the moments of the range R_n based on a sample of size n from a normal population, when m and n are both odd and when m and n are both even. These moments are expressed as sums of products of contents of simplices whose angles are either θ or $\pi-\theta$, where

$$\theta = \cos^{-1}(-\tfrac{1}{3}), \cos^{-1}(-\tfrac{1}{4}), \ldots, \cos^{-1}\left(-\frac{1}{m+2}\right).$$

We shall not, however, derive the relevant expressions here but shall instead use (10A.4.2) to obtain the second moment only of R_n for even n.

We have

$$\begin{aligned}E(R_n^2) &= E(v-u)^2\\ &= 2E(v^2) - 2E(uv)\\ &= 2 + \frac{n(n-1)(n-2)}{2\pi\sqrt{3}}\, u_{n-3}(\cos^{-1} - \tfrac{1}{4})\\ &\quad + \frac{n(n-1)(n-2)(n-3)}{4\pi} \sum_{k=0}^{n-4} (-)^k \binom{n-4}{k} u_k(\cos^{-1} - \tfrac{1}{3})\\ &\quad \times u_{n-4-k}(\cos^{-1} - \tfrac{1}{3}), \qquad n = 2, 4, \ldots \qquad (10A.4.3)\end{aligned}$$

on applying (10A.3.19) to express $E(v^2)$ in the form used in (10A.4.3). It should be noted incidentally that for *all n*

$$\begin{aligned}E(R_n) &= E(v-u)\\ &= 2E(v)\\ &= \frac{n(n-1)}{\sqrt{\pi}}\, u_{n-2}(\cos^{-1} - \tfrac{1}{3}), \qquad n = 1, 2, \ldots \qquad (10A.4.4)\end{aligned}$$

on using (10A.4.2*a*).

Equations (10A.4.3) and (10A.4.4) may be used to devise explicit expressions for the variances of R_2 and R_4 in terms of elementary trigonometric functions. Similar expressions for the variance of R_n when $n = 6, 8, \ldots$ are not possible, since the formulas for these variances involve the contents of spherical tetrahedra, pentahedra, etc., and these (as indicated earlier) cannot be expressed in terms of elementary trigonometric functions. On the other hand $E(R_6^2)$, as opposed to VR_6, can be expressed in the desired form. In fact,

$$E(R_2) = \frac{2}{\sqrt{\pi}}, \qquad (10A.4.5)$$

$$E(R_4) = \frac{12}{\sqrt{\pi}}\, \frac{\cos^{-1} - \tfrac{1}{3}}{2\pi}, \qquad (10A.4.6)$$

$$E(R_6) = \frac{30}{\sqrt{\pi}}\, u_4(\cos^{-1} - \tfrac{1}{3}), \qquad (10A.4.7)$$

$$E(R_2^2) = 2, \qquad (10A.4.8)$$

$$E(R_4^2) = 2 + \frac{6}{\pi\sqrt{3}} + \frac{6}{\pi}, \qquad (10A.4.9)$$

$$E(R_6^2) = 2 - \frac{15}{\pi\sqrt{3}} - \frac{45}{\pi} + \frac{15}{\pi^2}[\sqrt{3}\cos^{-1}(-\tfrac{1}{4}) + 6\cos^{-1}(-\tfrac{1}{3})], \qquad (10A.4.10)$$

$$VR_2 = 2 - \frac{4}{\pi}, \qquad (10A.4.11)$$

$$VR_4 = 2 + \frac{6}{\pi} + \frac{2\sqrt{3}}{\pi} - \frac{36}{\pi^3}[\cos^{-1}(-\tfrac{1}{3})]^2. \qquad (10A.4.12)$$

TABLE 10A.1

Moments of Extreme Members, ${}_r\mu'_{n|n}$, in Samples of Size n Drawn from Normal Populations

n \ r	1	2	3	4	5
1	0	1·00000 0000	0	3·00000 0000	0
2	0·56418 9584	1·00000 0000	1·41047 3959	3·00000 0000	6·06503 8023
3	0·84628 4377	1·27566 4448	2·11571 0938	4·19454 5940	9·09755 7036
4	1·02937 5374	1·55132 8896	2·70042 5704	5·38909 1881	11·88062 0268
5	1·16296 4474	1·80002 0436	3·22487 9364	6·52339 5486	14·53895 5578
6	1·26720 6361	2·02173 9069	3·70526 1794	7·59745 6758	17·09454 9080
7	1·35217 8376	2·22030 4136	4·14966 7934	8·61704 4920	19·55839 3798
8	1·42360 0306	2·39953 4975	4·56358 1597	9·58792 9198	21·93884 615
9	1·48501 3162	2·56261 7418	4·95118 1032	10·51515 5116	24·24294 426
10	1·53875 2731	2·71210 3790	5·31580 4079	11·40304 4507	26·47678 168
11	1·58643 6352	2·85002 7742	5·66018 0737	12·25530 1015	28·64569 426
12	1·62922 7640	2·97801 9090	5·98657 7532	13·07511 5628	30·75438 816
13	1·66799 0177	3·09739 6615	6·29689 7766	13·86525 5250	32·80703 849
14	1·70338 1554	3·20923 8822	6·59275 5132	14·62813 4342	34·80736 837
15	1·73591 3445	3·31443 7059	6·87552 9415	15·36587 2528	36·75871 365
16	1·76599 1393	3·41373 5410	7·14640 9450	16·08034 1083	38·66407 622
17	1·79394 1981	3·50776 0835	7·40642 6717	16·77320 0671	40·52616 843
18	1·82003 1879	3·59704 6171	7·65648 1911	17·44593 2213	42·34745 031
19	1·84448 1512	3·68204 7852	7·89736 6170	18·09986 2296	44·13016 084
20	1·86747 5060	3·76315 9715	8·12977 8192	18·73618 4245	45·87634 459
21	1·88916 7917	3·84072 3854	8·35433 8148	19·35597 5699	47·58787 434
22	1·90969 2325	3·91503 9251	8·57159 9074	19·96021 3381	49·26647 044
23	1·92916 1713	3·98636 8684	8·78205 6290	20·54978 5557	50·91371 752
24	1·94767 4075	4·05494 4325	8·98615 5205	21·12550 263	52·53107 895
25	1·96531 4610	4·12097 2294	9·18429 7863	21·68810 616	54·11990 930
26	1·98215 7840	4·18463 6408	9·37684 8436	22·23827 665	55·68146 535
27	1·99826 9303	4·24610 1279	9·56413 7882	22·77664 017	57·21691 556
28	2·01370 6925	4·30551 4889	9·74646 7901	23·30377 420	58·72734 852
29	2·02852 2147	4·36301 0759	9·92411 4318	23·82021 261	60·21378 036
30	2·04276 0845	4·41870 9768	10·09732 9992	24·32645 008	61·67716 127
31	2·05646 4099	4·47272 1701	10·26634 7323	24·82294 588	63·11838 132
32	2·06966 8829	4·52514 6562	10·43138 0426	25·31012 735	64·53827 561
33	2·08240 8337	4·57607 5706	10·59262 7020	25·78839 276	65·93762 894
34	2·09471 2757	4·62559 2804	10·75027 0082	26·25811 404	67·31717 988
35	2·10660 9441	4·67377 4683	10·90447 9295	26·71963 905	68·67762 449
36	2·11812 3288	4·72069 2054	11·05541 2315	27·17329 371	70·01961 969
37	2·12927 7027	4·76641 0142	11·20321 5903	27·61938 383	71·34378 620
38	2·14009 1456	4·81098 9241	11·34802 6914	28·05819 679	72·65071 130
39	2·15058 5659	4·85448 5197	11·48997 3178	28·49000 300	73·94095 130
40	2·16077 7179	4·89694 9839	11·62917 4294	28·91505 728	75·21503 372
41	2·17068 2186	4·93843 1351	11·76574 2323	29·33360 007	76·47345 938
42	2·18031 5609	4·97897 4611	11·89978 2420	29·74585 847	77·71670 421
43	2·18969 1262	5·01862 1481	12·03139 3399	30·15204 729	78·94522 094
44	2·19882 1950	5·05741 1077	12·16066 8233	30·55236 992	80·15944 068
45	2·20771 9565	5·09538 0002	12·28769 4522	30·94701 916	81·35977 429
46	2·21639 5169	5·13256 2557	12·41255 4895	31·33617 792	82·54661 372
47	2·22485 9069	5·16899 0930	12·53532 7387	31·72001 998	83·72033 315
48	2·23312 0882	5·20469 5366	12·65608 5780	32·09871 054	84·88129 016
49	2·24118 9599	5·23970 4322	12·77489 9908	32·47240 679	86·02982 667
50	2·24907 3631	5·27404 4605	12·89183 5941	32·84125 849	87·16626 994

This table is reproduced from H. Ruben, "On the moments of order statistics in samples from normal populations," *Biometrika*, Vol. 41 (1954), pp. 200–227, with permission of E. S. Pearson, editor of *Biometrika*.

TABLE 10A.1 *Continued*

n \ r	6	7	8	9	10
1	15·00000 000	0	105·00000 0	0	945·00000
2	15·00000 000	37·44808 36	105·00000 0	303·28716 3	945·00000
3	21·79972 305	56·17212 54	155·23218 8	454·93074 5	1407·98355
4	28·59944 610	74·16003 19	205·46437 7	603·73513 9	1870·96710
5	35·22660 772	91·77987 07	255·06652 6	751·11993 7	2331·11618
6	41·68120 792	109·07401 19	304·03863 8	897·19147 1	2788·43082
7	47·97432 643	126·06364 04	352·40762 6	1042·00290 7	3242·99105
8	54·11704 295	142·76617 39	400·20040 7	1185·60041 6	3694·87692
9	60·11939 069	159·19714 68	447·44198 8	1328·02667 6	4144·16423
10	65·99035 636	175·37063 38	494·15547 2	1469·32149 3	4590·92456
11	71·73800 254	191·29946 19	540·36223 3	1609·52211 3	5035·22556
12	77·36959 015	206·99536 78	586·08209 7	1748·66346 5	5477·13127
13	82·89168 443	222·46912 62	631·33349 6	1886·77837 6	5916·70244
14	88·31024 450	237·73065 92	676·13361 2	2023·89775 2	6353·99673
15	93·63069 901	252·78913 03	720·49849 5	2160·05074 7	6789·06900
16	98·85801 015	267·65302 48	764·44316 9	2295·26490 1	7221·97147
17	103·99672 809	282·33021 97	807·98172 9	2429·56628 0	7652·75394
18	109·05103 766	296·82804 46	851·12741 8	2562·97958 8	8081·46396
19	114·02479 836	311·15333 50	893·89270 6	2695·52826 2	8508·14696
20	118·92157 897	325·31247 89	936·28934 9	2827·23458 7	8932·84640
21	123·74468 755	339·31145 76	978·32845 4	2958·11976 4	9355·60392
22	128·49719 757	353·15588 21	1020·02052 5	3088·20399 1	9776·45944
23	133·18197 078	366·85102 56	1061·37551 5	3217·50653 5	10195·45124
24	137·80167 727	380·40185 19	1102·40286 1	3346·04579 3	10612·61612
25	142·35881 312	393·81304 07	1143·11152 9	3473·83935 1	11027·98943
26	146·85571 609	407·08901 08	1183·51004 4	3600·90403 7	11441·60519
27	151·29457 942	420·23394 06	1223·60652 3	3727·25596 8	11853·49616
28	155·67746 420	433·25178 61	1263·40870 2	3852·91059 3	12263·69389
29	160·00631 037	446·14629 83	1302·92396 2	3977·88273 7	12672·22882
30	164·28294 657	458·92103 76	1342·15935 3	4102·18663 7	13079·13032
31	168·50909 90	471·57938 78	1381·12161 5	4225·83597 5	13484·42672
32	172·68639 92	484·12456 81	1419·81719 7	4348·84391 1	13888·14543
33	176·81639 16	496·55964 50	1458·25227 8	4471·22311 0	14290·31294
34	180·90053 95	508·88754 19	1496·43277 8	4592·98577 6	14690·95486
35	184·94023 16	521·11104 91	1534·36438 0	4714·14366 8	15090·09599
36	188·93678 64	533·23283 20	1572·05253 8	4834·70813 0	15487·76036
37	192·89145 81	545·25543 90	1609·50249 4	4954·69011 0	15883·97122
38	196·80544 02	557·18130 91	1646 71928 9	5074·10018 2	16278·75114
39	200·67987 00	569·01277 81	1683·70777 2	5192·94856 3	16672·12201
40	204·51583 21	580·75208 53	1720·47261 3	5311·24513 1	17064·10506
41	208·31436 17	592·40137 87	1757·01831 5	5428·99944 4	17454·72091
42	212·07644 81	603·96272 02	1793·34921 5	5546·22075 1	17843·98959
43	215·80303 72	615·43809 10	1829·46950 0	5662·91801 2	18231·93056
44	219·49503 42	626·82939 59	1865·38321 0	5779·09990 6	18618·56273
45	223·15330 61	638·13846 69	1901·09424 9	5894·77484 8	19003·90451
46	226·77868 38	649·36706 80	1936·60639 0	6009·95099 8	19387·97380
47	230·37196 46	660·51689 81	1971·92327 9	6124·63627 3	19770·78803
48	233·93391 36	671·58959 50	2007·04844 5	6238·83836 1	20152·36417
49	237·46526 56	682·58673 78	2041·98530 5	6352·56472 5	20532·71874
50	240·96672 72	693·50985 06	2076·73716 4	6465·82261 9	20911·86784

TABLE 10A.2

The Moments about the Mean, the Measures of Skewness and of Kurtosis, and the Standard Deviation of Extreme Members in Samples of Size n Drawn from Normal Populations

n	μ_2	μ_3	μ_4	β_1	$\beta_2 - 3$	$\sqrt{\mu_2}$
1	1·00000 000	0	3·00000 00	0	0	1·00000 00
2	0·68169 011	0·07707 945	1·42279 69	0·01875 50	0·06174 43	0·82564 53
3	0·55946 720	0·08919 934	0·97955 22	0·04543 59	0·12952 43	0·74797 54
4	0·49171 524	0·09120 683	0·76459 74	0·06997 03	0·16231 77	0·70122 41
5	0·44753 407	0·09058 710	0·64107 54	0·09154 92	0·20078 82	0·66897 99
6	0·41592 711	0·08917 023	0·55943 20	0·11050 66	0·23379 78	0·64492 41
7	0·39191 778	0·08753 521	0·50113 26	0·12728 60	0·26259 20	0·62603 34
8	0·37289 714	0·08588 990	0·45721 20	0·14227 12	0·28805 84	0·61065 30
9	0·35735 333	0·08431 165	0·42279 90	0·15576 92	0·31084 08	0·59779 04
10	0·34434 382	0·08282 697	0·39501 52	0·16802 22	0·33141 89	0·58680 82
11	0·33324 744	0·08144 141	0·37204 79	0·17922 15	0·35015 75	0·57727 59
12	0·32363 639	0·08015 182	0·35269 69	0·18951 99	0·36733 95	0·56889 05
13	0·31520 538	0·07895 167	0·33613 48	0·19904 06	0·38318 91	0·56143 15
14	0·30773 010	0·07783 336	0·32177 24	0·20788 42	0·39788 63	0·55473 43
15	0·30104 157	0·07678 934	0·30917 77	0·21613 37	0·41157 72	0·54867 26
16	0·29500 981	0·07581 253	0·29802 68	0·22385 80	0·42438 30	0·54314 81
17	0·28953 300	0·07489 647	0·28807 16	0·23111 52	0·43640 41	0·53808 27
18	0·28453 013	0·07403 540	0·27911 89	0·23795 45	0·44772 53	0·53341 37
19	0·27993 580	0·07322 415	0·27101 57	0·24441 81	0·45841 87	0·52908 96
20	0·27569 662	0·07245 817	0·26363 94	0·25054 19	0·46854 62	0·52506 82
21	0·27176 844	0·07173 345	0·25689 02	0·25635 77	0·47816 00	0·52131 41
22	0·26811 447	0·07104 635	0·25068 64	0·26189 23	0·48730 80	0·51779 77
23	0·26470 377	0·07039 370	0·24496 01	0·26716 97	0·49603 01	0·51449 37
24	0·26151 002	0·06977 268	0·23965 45	0·27221 11	0·50436 15	0·51138 05
25	0·25851 078	0·06918 079	0·23472 16	0·27703 53	0·51233 28	0·50843 96
26	0·25568 671	0·06861 576	0·23012 06	0·28165 88	0·51997 21	0·50565 47
27	0·25302 107	0·06807 556	0·22581 68	0·28609 63	0·52730 46	0·50301 20
28	0·25049 931	0·06755 837	0·22178 02	0·29036 13	0·53435 19	0·50049 91
29	0·24810 866	0·06706 255	0·21798 48	0·29446 55	0·54113 42	0·49810 51
30	0·24583 790	0·06658 663	0·21440 79	0·29841 97	0·54766 97	0·49582 04
31	0·24367 711	0·06612 926	0·21102 97	0·30223 38	0·55397 34	0·49363 66
32	0·24161 750	0·06568 923	0·20783 28	0·30591 67	0·56006 08	0·49154 60
33	0·23965 122	0·06526 541	0·20480 20	0·30947 61	0·56594 66	0·48954 19
34	0·23777 127	0·06485 680	0·20192 34	0·31291 97	0·57164 13	0·48761 80
35	0·23597 135	0·06446 249	0·19918 49	0·31625 42	0·57715 59	0·48576 88
36	0·23424 579	0·06408 161	0·19657 59	0·31948 58	0·58250 37	0·48398 95
37	0·23258 948	0·06371 339	0·19408 62	0·32262 00	0·58768 62	0·48227 53
38	0·23099 780	0·06335 710	0·19170 75	0·32566 20	0·59272 11	0·48062 23
39	0·22946 652	0·06301 212	0·18943 18	0·32861 71	0·59761 04	0·47902 66
40	0·22799 182	0·06267 778	0·18725 20	0·33148 92	0·60236 66	0·47748 49
41	0·22657 020	0·06235 357	0·18516 15	0·33428 30	0·60699 15	0·47599 39
42	0·22519 846	0·06203 894	0·18315 46	0·33700 20	0·61149 41	0·47455 08
43	0·22387 366	0·06173 341	0·18122 58	0·33964 99	0·61587 96	0·47315 29
44	0·22259 311	0·06143 652	0·17937 03	0·34222 99	0·62015 48	0·47179 77
45	0·22135 432	0·06114 786	0·17758 36	0·34474 54	0·62432 34	0·47048 31
46	0·22015 501	0·06086 702	0·17586 17	0·34719 89	0·62839 06	0·46920 68
47	0·21899 305	0·06059 368	0·17420 05	0·34959 37	0·63235 93	0·46796 69
48	0·21786 649	0·06032 745	0·17259 69	0·35193 19	0·63623 67	0·46676 17
49	0·21677 350	0·06006 804	0·17104 75	0·35421 62	0·64002 38	0·46558 94
50	0·21571 241	0·05981 512	0·16954 94	0·35644 83	0·64372 80	0·46444 85

This table is reproduced from H. Ruben, "On the moments of order statistics in samples from normal populations," *Biometrika*, Vol. 41 (1954), pp. 200–227, with permission of E. S. Pearson, editor of *Biometrika*.

REFERENCES

1. R. H. Cole, "Relations between moments of order statistics," *Ann. Math. Statist.*, Vol. 22 (1951), pp. 308–310.
2. D. R. Cox, "A note on the asymptotic distribution of range," *Biometrika*, Vol. 35 (1948), pp. 310–315.
3. H. S. M. Coxeter, "The functions of Schläfli and Lobachewski," *Quart. J. Math.*, Vol. 6 (1935), pp. 13–29.
4. H. S. M. Coxeter, *Regular Polytopes*, Methuen and Co. Ltd., London, 1948.
5. R. A. Fisher and F. Yates, *Statistical Tables for Biological, Agricultural and Medical Research*, Oliver and Boyd Ltd., London, 1949.
6. H. J. Godwin, "Some low moments of order statistics," *Ann. Math. Statist.*, Vol. 20 (1949), pp. 279–285.
7. H. J. Godwin, "On the estimation of dispersion by linear systematic statistics," *Biometrika*, Vol. 36 (1949), pp. 92–100.
8. B. I. Harley and E. S. Pearson, "The distribution of range in normal samples with $n = 200$," *Biometrika*, Vol. 44 (1957), pp. 257–260.
9. C. Hastings, Jr., F. Mosteller, J. W. Tukey, and C. P. Winsor, "Low moments for small samples: a comparative study of order statistics," *Ann. Math. Statist.*, Vol. 18 (1947), pp. 413–426.
10. T. Hojo, "Distribution of the median, quartiles and interquartile distance in samples from a normal population," *Biometrika*, Vol. 23 (1931), pp. 315–360.
11. E. R. E. Hoppe, "Berechnung einiger viehrdehnigen Winkel," *Arch. Math. Phys.*, Vol. 67 (1882), pp. 269–290.
12. H. L. Jones, "Exact lower moments of order statistics in small samples from a normal population," *Ann. Math. Statist.*, Vol. 19 (1948), pp. 270–273.
13. E. S. Pearson, "A further note on the distribution of range in samples taken from a normal population," *Biometrika*, Vol. 18 (1926), pp. 173–194.
14. E. S. Pearson, "The percentage limits for the distribution of range in samples from a normal population," *Biometrika*, Vol. 24 (1932), pp. 404–417.
15. E. S. Pearson and H. O. Hartley, "The probability integral of the range in samples of n observations from the normal population," *Biometrika*, Vol. 32 (1942), pp. 301–310.
16. R. L. Plackett, "A reduction formula for normal multivariate integrals," *Biometrika*, Vol. 41 (1954), pp. 351–360.
17. H. W. Richmond, "The volume of a tetrahedron in elliptic space," *Quart. J. Pure Appl. Math.*, Vol. 34 (1903), pp. 175–177.
18. H. Ruben, "On the moments of order statistics in samples from normal populations," *Biometrika*, Vol. 41 (1954), pp. 200–227.
19. H. Ruben, "On the sum of squares of normal scores," *Biometrika*, Vol. 43 (1956), pp. 456–458.
20. H. Ruben, "On the moments of the range and product moments of extreme order statistics in normal samples," *Biometrika*, Vol. 43 (1956), pp. 458–460.
21. L. Schläfli, "On the multiple integral $\int^n dx\, dy \ldots dz$ whose limits are $p_1 = a_1x + b_1y + \ldots + h_1z > 0, p_2 > 0, \ldots, p_n > 0$, and $x^2 + y^2 + \ldots + z^2 < 1$," *Quart. J. Pure Appl. Math.*, Vol. 2 (1858), pp. 269–301, Vol. 3 (1858), pp. 54–68, 97–108. See also *Gesammelle Mathematische Abhandlugen*, Vol. 1, Lehre von der Sphärischen Kontinuen, pp. 227–298, Verlag Birkhäuser Basel.
22. D. M. Y. Sommerville, *An Introduction to the Geometry of N Dimensions*, Methuen and Co. Ltd., London, 1929.

23. L. H. C. Tippett, "On the extreme individuals and the range of samples taken from a normal population," *Biometrika*, Vol. 17 (1925), pp. 364–387.
24. H. R. Van der Vaart, "The content of certain spherical polyhedra for any number of dimensions," *Experentia*, Vol. 9 (1953), pp. 88–89.
25. H. R. Van der Vaart, "The content of some classes of non-Euclidean polyhedra for any number of dimensions with several applications," *Proc. Kon. Ned. Akad. Wetensch. A.*, Amsterdam, Vol. 58 (1955), pp. 199–221.
26. S. S. Wilks, *Mathematical Statistics*, Princeton University Press, Princeton, N.J., 1946.

D. TEICHROEW

10B TABLES OF LOWER MOMENTS OF ORDER STATISTICS FOR SAMPLES FROM THE NORMAL DISTRIBUTION

10B.1 Introduction

Let $x_1, x_2, \ldots, x_n$ be a sample from $N(0, 1)$ arranged in order of size so that

$$x_{(1)} \leq x_{(2)} \leq x_{(3)} \leq \ldots \leq x_{(n)}.$$

The means, variances, and covariances of these "order statistics" may be obtained from the formulas given by (2.1.9*a*, *b*, *c*).

10B.2 Computation

The means and variances are relatively simple to compute since they require merely the evaluation of one-dimensional integrals in which the integrands vanish at both ends of the range of integration. The values given in Tables 10B.1 and 10B.2 were computed by the method developed by Rosser [2]. Rosser's method is applicable to higher moments; for the means and variances, it is equivalent to the formulas given by Godwin [1]. The numerical integration was performed on values of the normal integral obtained from Sheppard's table [4], and the values were checked by sum checks. In addition the integrals

$$D(m, n) = \int_{-\infty}^{+\infty} x^2 f(x)[F(x)]^m[1 - F(x)]^n \, dx \qquad (10B.2.1)$$

appear in the computation of the integrals

$$G(m, n, p) = \int_{-\infty}^{+\infty} \int_{-\infty}^{y} xyf(x)f(y)[F(x)]^m[1 - F(y)]^n \times [F(y) - F(x)]^P \, dx \, dy, \qquad (10B.2.2)$$

and the integrals

$$B(m, n) = \int_{-\infty}^{+\infty} xf(x)[F(x)]^m[1 - F(x)]^n \, dx \qquad (10B.2.3)$$

appear in the checks for the G's just given.

The computation of the covariances is more complicated because it involves either the evaluation of a large number of double integrals $G(m, n, p)$ or the more accurate evaluation of a smaller number of double integrals $\psi(a, b)$ which require more elaborate integration formulas. Godwin [1] has given a method for the computation of the B's, D's, and G's which is based on two basic sets of integrals $\psi(a)$ and $\psi(a, b)$ where

$$\psi(a) = \int_{-\infty}^{+\infty} [F(x)]^a[1 - F(x)]^a \, dx, \qquad (10B.2.4)$$

$$\psi(a, b) = \int_{-\infty}^{+\infty} [F(x)]^a \, dx \int_{x}^{\infty} [1 - F(y)]^b \, dy. \qquad (10B.2.5)$$

All the computations were performed on the SWAC, using fixed-point, triple-precision arithmetic; tables are available in Teichroew [5].

Using the tables of expected values of order statistics and products of order statistics, Sarhan and Greenberg [3] calculated the variances and covariances for the same order statistics. Their table is reproduced as Table 10B.3.

10B.3 Tables

Table 10B.1 gives the expected values $E(x_i)$.

Table 10B.2 gives $E(x_i, x_j)$ rounded to ten decimal places.

Table 10B.3 gives $V(x_i)$ and Cov $(x_i x_j)$ rounded to 10 decimal places. Missing values may be obtained by symmetry relations, for example,

1. $E(x_{(i)}) = -E(x_{(n-i+1)})$.
2. If n is odd, the center order statistic has its mean equal to zero.
3. $E(x_{(i)}x_{(j)}) = E(x_{(j)}x_{(i)}) = E(x_{(n-i+1)}\, x_{(n-j+1)})$.
4. Cov $(x_{(i)}x_{(j)}) =$ Cov $(x_{(n-i+1)}\, x_{(n-j+1)})$.

Note: Ruben has considered the moments of order statistics in samples from normal populations more generally and in a geometrical approach (cf. Section 10A).

REFERENCES

1. H. J. Godwin, "Some low moments of order statistics," *Ann. Math. Statist.*, Vol. 20 (1949), pp. 279–285.
2. Barkley Rosser, "Numerical computation of low moments of order statistics from a normal population," Nat. Bur. of Stand. Rep., 1951.
3. A. E. Sarhan and B. G. Greenberg, "Estimation of location and scale parameters by order statistics from singly and doubly censored samples, Part I, "The normal distribution up to samples of size 10," *Ann. Math. Statist.*, Vol. 27 (1956), pp. 427–451.
4. W. F. Sheppard, *The Probability Integral, British Associated Mathematical Tables*, Cambridge University Press, Cambridge, England, 1939.
5. D. Teichroew, "Tables of expected values of order statistics and products of order statistics for samples of size 20 and less from the normal distribution," *Ann. Math. Statist.*, Vol. 27 (1956), pp. 410–426.

TABLE 10B.1

Expected Values of Order Statistics*

n	i	$E(x_{(i)}, n)$	n	i	$E(x_{(i)}, n)$	n	i	$E(x_{(i)}, n)$
2	1	.56418 95835	12	5	.31224 88787	17	5	.61945 76511
3	1	.84628 43753	12	6	.10258 96798	17	6	.45133 34467
4	1	1.02937 53730	13	1	1.66799 01770	17	7	.29518 64872
4	2	.29701 13823	13	2	1.16407 71937	17	8	.14598 74231
5	1	1.16296 44736	13	3	.84983 46324	18	1	1.82003 18790
5	2	.49501 89705	13	4	.60285 00882	18	2	1.35041 37134
6	1	1.26720 63606	13	5	.38832 71210	18	3	1.06572 81829
6	2	.64175 50388	13	6	.19052 36911	18	4	.84812 50190
6	3	.20154 68338	14	1	1.70338 15541	18	5	.66479 46127
7	1	1.35217 83756	14	2	1.20790 22754	18	6	.50158 15510
7	2	.75737 42706	14	3	.90112 67039	18	7	.35083 72382
7	3	.35270 69592	14	4	.66176 37035	18	8	.20773 53071
8	1	1.42360 03060	14	5	.45556 60500	18	9	.06880 25682
8	2	.85222 48625	14	6	.26729 70489	19	1	1.84448 15116
8	3	.47282 24949	14	7	.08815 92141	19	2	1.37993 84915
8	4	.15251 43995	15	1	1.73591 34449	19	3	1.09945 30994
9	1	1.48501 31622	15	2	1.24793 50823	19	4	.88586 19615
9	2	.93229 74567	15	3	.94768 90303	19	5	.70661 14847
9	3	.57197 07829	15	4	.71487 73983	19	6	.54770 73710
9	4	.27452 59191	15	5	.51570 10430	19	7	.40164 22742
10	1	1.53875 27308	15	6	.33529 60639	19	8	.26374 28909
10	2	1.00135 70446	15	7	.16529 85263	19	9	.13072 48795
10	3	.65605 91057	16	1	1.76599 13931	20	1	1.86747 50598
10	4	.37576 46970	16	2	1.28474 42232	20	2	1.40760 40959
10	5	.12266 77523	16	3	.99027 10960	20	3	1.13094 80522
11	1	1.58643 63519	16	4	.76316 67458	20	4	.92098 17004
11	2	1.06191 65201	16	5	.57000 93557	20	5	.74538 30058
11	3	.72883 94047	16	6	.39622 27551	20	6	.59029 69215
11	4	.46197 83072	16	7	.23375 15785	20	7	.44833 17532
11	5	.22489 08792	16	8	.07728 74593	20	8	.31493 32416
12	1	1.62922 76399	17	1	1.79394 19809	20	9	.18695 73647
12	2	1.11573 21843	17	2	1.31878 19878	20	10	.06199 62865
12	3	.79283 81991	17	3	1.02946 09889			
12	4	.53684 30214	17	4	.80738 49287			

* Since $x_{(1)} \leqslant x_{(2)} \cdots \leqslant x_{(n)}$, all expected values shown in this table are negative. Their counterparts on the other side are positive since $E(x_{(i)} = -E(x_{(n-i+1)})$.

This table is reproduced from D. Teichroew, "Tables of expected values of order statistics and products of order statistics from samples of size 20 and less from the normal distribution," *Ann. Math. Statist.*, Vol. 27 (1956), pp. 410–426, with permission of W. Kruskal, editor of the *Annals of Mathematical Statistics*.

TABLE 10B.2

Expected Values of Products of Normal Order Statistics

n	i	j	$E(x_{(i)}x_{(j)};n)$	n	i	j	$E(x_{(i)}x_{(j)};n)$	n	i	j	$E(x_{(i)}x_{(j)};n)$
1	1	1	1.00000 00000	8	1	1	2.39953 49747	10	1	6	−.13035 66254
2	1	1	1.00000 00000	8	1	2	1.39953 49747	10	1	7	−.52928 83257
2	2	2	1.00000 00000	8	1	3	.79907 62783	10	1	8	−.96842 82811
3	1	1	1.27566 44477	8	1	4	.31184 25735	10	1	9	−1.50680 02399
3	1	2	.27566 44477	8	1	5	−.14235 45216	10	1	10	−2.34106 10315
3	1	3	−.55132 88954	8	1	6	−.61290 27315	10	2	2	1.21724 00737
3	2	2	.44867 11046	8	1	7	−1.16492 90242	10	2	3	.80357 20248
4	1	1	1.55132 88954	8	1	8	−1.98980 25239	10	2	4	.48797 62226
4	1	2	.55132 88954	8	2	2	.96568 82621	10	2	5	.21257 70424
4	1	3	−.14772 81323	8	2	3	.56614 69584	10	2	6	−.04863 46765
4	1	4	−.95492 96586	8	2	4	.25323 98948	10	2	7	−.31404 67778
4	2	2	.44867 11046	8	2	5	−.03241 18438	10	2	8	−.60464 26847
4	2	3	.14772 81323	8	2	6	−.32422 86175	10	2	9	−.95934 47746
5	1	1	1.80002 04360	8	2	7	−.66304 06044	10	3	3	.60541 68331
5	1	2	.80002 04360	8	3	3	.42432 99017	10	3	4	.38032 60958
5	1	3	.14814 77252	8	3	4	.22447 06701	10	3	5	.18822 18294
5	1	4	−.46991 74988	8	3	5	.04885 15166	10	3	6	.00874 81054
5	1	5	−1.27827 10984	8	3	6	−.12574 39762	10	3	7	−.17160 54566
5	2	2	.55656 27332	8	4	4	.21044 68615	10	3	8	−.36738 03049
5	2	3	.20843 54440	8	4	5	.12591 48488	10	4	4	.29913 80219
5	2	4	−.09510 11144	9	1	1	2.56261 74183	10	4	5	.17360 31403
5	3	3	.28683 36616	9	1	2	1.56261 74183	10	4	6	.05969 16062
6	1	1	2.02173 90694	9	1	3	.97012 95851	10	4	7	−.05225 29049
6	1	2	1.02173 90694	9	1	4	.49898 17432	10	5	5	.16610 12814
6	1	3	.39483 66863	9	1	5	.07274 22354	10	5	6	.11055 15903
6	1	4	−.15297 20358	9	1	6	−.34819 14908	11	1	1	2.85002 77414
6	1	5	−.73587 22832	9	1	7	−.80030 77349	11	1	2	1.85002 77414
6	1	6	−1.54947 05060	9	1	8	−1.34438 03016	11	1	3	1.26861 57614
6	2	2	.69142 72690	9	1	9	−2.17420 88731	11	1	4	.81841 62399
6	2	3	.31832 96521	9	2	2	1.09487 54256	11	1	5	.42562 33724
6	2	4	.01032 03642	9	2	3	.68736 32588	11	1	6	.05720 07586
6	2	5	−.30594 40716	9	2	4	.37294 55079	11	1	7	−.30839 96597
6	3	3	.28683 36616	9	2	5	.09344 77394	11	1	8	−.69165 68331
6	3	4	.14265 16716	9	2	6	−.17939 36730	11	1	9	−1.12114 69906
7	1	1	2.22030 41356	9	2	7	−.47001 14367	11	1	10	−1.65524 31199
7	1	2	1.22030 41356	9	2	8	−.81746 39387	11	1	11	−2.49346 50118
7	1	3	.60903 83042	9	3	3	.51353 31898	11	2	2	1.33286 42755
7	1	4	.09848 68607	9	3	4	.29909 87825	11	2	3	.91427 62554
7	1	5	−.40036 28885	9	3	5	.11376 80176	11	2	4	.59773 16558
7	1	6	−.96418 63986	9	3	6	−.06365 82663	11	2	5	.32525 83655
7	1	7	−1.78358 41490	9	3	7	−.24991 53959	11	2	6	.07192 05024
7	2	2	.83034 86720	9	4	4	.24592 33257	11	2	7	−.17792 83736
7	2	3	.44161 45034	9	4	5	.13699 13669	11	2	8	−.43863 19457
7	2	4	.13072 98656	9	4	6	.03730 27039	11	2	9	−.72971 16588
7	2	5	−.16517 61670	9	5	5	.16610 12814	11	2	10	−1.09056 36980
7	2	6	−.49363 46110	10	1	1	2.71210 37899	11	3	3	.69693 11658
7	3	3	.34412 37617	10	1	2	1.71210 37899	11	3	4	.46367 52869
7	3	4	.16555 98429	10	1	3	1.12577 18388	11	3	5	.26655 00636
7	3	5	.00520 26434	10	1	4	.66645 83784	11	3	6	.08551 78832
7	4	4	.21044 68615	10	1	5	.25949 67065	11	3	7	−.09143 52295

This table is reproduced from D. Teichroew, "Tables of expected values of order statistics and products of order statistics from order samples of size 20 and less from the normal distribution," *Ann. Math. Statist.*, Vol. 27 (1956), pp. 410–426, with permission of W. Kruskal, editor of the *Annals of Mathematical Statistics*.

TABLE 10B.2 *Continued*

n	i	j	$E(x_{(i)}x_{(j)}; n)$	n	i	j	$E(x_{(i)}x_{(j)}; n)$	n	i	j	$E(x_{(i)}x_{(j)}; n)$
11	3	8	−.27482 06666	12	6	6	.13716 24335	14	1	1	3.20923 88213
11	3	9	−.47845 18709	12	6	7	.09786 99407	14	1	2	2.20923 88213
11	4	4	.36137 86128	13	1	1	3.09739 66149	14	1	3	1.63813 45584
11	4	5	.22376 99938	13	1	2	2.09739 66149	14	1	4	1.20610 76773
11	4	6	.10003 46585	13	1	3	1.52340 67031	14	1	5	.83996 85490
11	4	7	−.01901 81895	13	1	4	1.08641 29990	14	1	6	.50901 53339
11	4	8	−.14087 88129	13	1	5	.71318 92732	14	1	7	.19625 86980
11	5	5	.19021 69879	13	1	6	.37261 38249	14	1	8	−.11005 46103
11	5	6	.11674 49805	13	1	7	.04688 33088	14	1	9	−.42009 46865
11	5	7	.04861 76885	13	1	8	−.27717 83904	14	1	10	−.74496 56899
11	6	6	.13716 24335	13	1	9	−.61230 31771	14	1	11	−1.09989 97992
12	1	1	2.97801 90896	13	1	10	−.97461 57510	14	1	12	−1.51105 65052
12	1	2	1.97801 90896	13	1	11	−1.39066 20939	14	1	13	−2.03701 04294
12	1	3	1.40064 48721	13	1	12	−1.91878 35177	14	1	14	−2.88488 07386
12	1	4	.95770 81654	13	1	13	−2.76375 64087	14	2	2	1.64344 79321
12	1	5	.57581 29501	13	2	2	1.54548 87851	14	2	3	1.21455 21950
12	1	6	.22313 53113	13	2	3	1.11947 86969	14	2	4	.89599 83466
12	1	7	−.11947 98445	13	2	4	.80149 03085	14	2	5	.62879 95664
12	1	8	−.46770 36483	13	2	5	.53292 13392	14	2	6	.38887 15475
12	1	9	−.83919 55827	13	2	6	.28959 88669	14	2	7	.16317 73868
12	1	10	−1.26121 26489	13	2	7	.05804 57285	14	2	8	−.05711 69005
12	1	11	−1.79198 71742	13	2	8	−.17146 74891	14	2	9	−.27950 69979
12	1	12	−2.63376 05793	13	2	9	−.40813 32366	14	2	10	−.51204 55279
12	2	2	1.44212 29110	13	2	10	−.66340 38591	14	2	11	−.76565 95612
12	2	3	1.01949 71285	13	2	11	−.95595 83375	14	2	12	−1.05900 48647
12	2	4	.70216 89575	13	2	12	−1.32667 39000	14	2	13	−1.43374 15141
12	2	5	.43189 07057	13	3	3	.87361 06037	14	3	3	.95773 39030
12	2	6	.18424 85733	13	3	4	.62859 26962	14	3	4	.70831 46326
12	2	7	−.05500 35423	13	3	5	.42447 04964	14	3	5	.50164 08601
12	2	8	−.29717 48037	13	3	6	.24120 59303	14	3	6	.31754 40043
12	2	9	−.55469 83245	13	3	7	.06792 82354	14	3	7	.14535 11045
12	2	10	−.84647 59479	13	3	8	−.10299 14878	14	3	8	−.02200 85032
12	2	11	−1.21260 75731	13	3	9	−.27856 77916	14	3	9	−.19040 07284
12	3	3	.78657 10977	13	3	10	−.46735 91289	14	3	10	−.36600 58138
12	3	4	.54683 59754	13	3	11	−.68315 45225	14	3	11	−.55709 77133
12	3	5	.34582 33989	13	4	4	.49643 94108	14	3	12	−.77769 71294
12	3	6	.16355 98631	13	4	5	.34235 43058	14	4	4	.56515 85063
12	3	7	−.01121 56206	13	4	6	.20584 27845	14	4	5	.40517 01872
12	3	8	−.18712 43766	13	4	7	.07801 73339	14	4	6	.26424 37333
12	3	9	−.37334 70932	13	4	8	−.04713 55097	14	4	7	.13349 25589
12	3	10	−.58355 66485	13	4	9	−.17494 01662	14	4	8	.00719 05256
12	4	4	.42801 13701	13	4	10	−.31169 54238	14	4	9	−.11927 53893
12	4	5	.28119 74136	13	5	5	.27404 82785	14	4	10	−.25063 68524
12	4	6	.15023 90816	13	5	6	.17772 22865	14	4	11	−.39310 68524
12	4	7	.02616 74273	13	5	7	.08904 34754	14	5	5	.32464 16720
12	4	8	−.09754 90483	13	5	8	.00336 97700	14	5	6	.22054 62157
12	4	9	−.22753 83422	13	5	9	−.08317 48535	14	5	7	.12521 59995
12	5	5	.22811 30981	13	6	6	.15461 68094	14	5	8	.03405 57967
12	5	6	.14165 47372	13	6	7	.10168 24204	14	5	9	−.05648 46831
12	5	7	.06166 16395	13	6	8	.05212 01841	14	5	10	−.14990 02795
12	5	8	−.01660 20662	13	7	7	.11679 89950	14	6	6	.18298 01703

TABLE 10B.2 *Continued*

n	i	j	$E(x_{(i)}x_{(j)}; n)$	n	i	j	$E(x_{(i)}x_{(j)}; n)$	n	i	j	$E(x_{(i)}x_{(j)}; n)$
14	6	7	.11970 52573	15	4	9	−.06206 91293	16	2	15	−1.62998 91758
14	6	8	.06039 70132	15	4	10	−.18987 67942	16	3	3	1.11697 54048
14	6	9	.00245 92097	15	4	11	−.32433 82747	16	3	4	.86061 26454
14	7	7	.11679 89950	15	4	12	−.47169 95126	16	3	5	.64998 26930
14	7	8	.08753 66786	15	5	5	.37781 74644	16	3	6	.46457 54507
15	1	1	3.31443 70586	15	5	6	.26743 31303	16	3	7	.29383 42833
15	1	2	2.31443 70586	15	5	7	.16683 37346	16	3	8	.13121 04477
15	1	3	1.74582 84742	15	5	8	.07143 31681	16	3	9	−.02809 89274
15	1	4	1.31802 46931	15	5	9	−.02212 21836	16	3	10	−.18827 94941
15	1	5	.95779 69592	15	5	10	−.11683 30234	16	3	11	−.35370 26425
15	1	6	.63469 79582	15	5	11	−.21603 47915	16	3	12	−.52983 60638
15	1	7	.33225 18229	15	6	6	.21829 00871	16	3	13	−.72482 70563
15	1	8	.03957 36673	15	6	7	.14689 22656	16	3	14	−.95327 73058
15	1	9	−.25204 03438	15	6	8	.08014 07559	16	4	4	.70028 92373
15	1	10	−.55108 35331	15	6	9	.01543 42647	16	4	5	.53126 35264
15	1	11	−.86769 12702	15	6	10	−.04944 10103	16	4	6	.38373 20754
15	1	12	−1.21655 26558	15	7	7	.13001 52951	16	4	7	.24869 15226
15	1	13	−1.62362 41465	15	7	8	.09004 99964	16	4	8	.12065 61178
15	1	14	−2.14777 39615	15	7	9	.05235 02295	16	4	9	−.00432 37162
15	1	15	−2.99828 17812	15	8	8	.10169 46521	16	4	10	−.12962 66569
15	2	2	1.73646 34988	16	1	1	3.41373 54094	16	4	11	−.25872 32978
15	2	3	1.30507 20833	16	1	2	2.41373 54094	16	4	12	−.39590 09182
15	2	4	.98602 72992	16	1	3	1.84731 12087	16	4	13	−.54749 81070
15	2	5	.71995 26573	16	1	4	1.42314 99069	16	5	5	.43226 23745
15	2	6	.48276 68106	16	1	5	1.06794 02886	16	5	6	.31667 39395
15	2	7	.26168 92701	16	1	6	.75138 84716	16	5	7	.21178 86399
15	2	8	.04842 38833	16	1	7	.45735 36462	16	5	8	.11300 34551
15	2	9	−.16355 24188	16	1	8	.17550 84595	16	5	9	.01708 18433
15	2	10	−.38050 99695	16	1	9	−.10195 11721	16	5	10	−.07867 66926
15	2	11	−.60984 62515	16	1	10	−.38202 22664	16	5	11	−.17698 22446
15	2	12	−.86220 53501	16	1	11	−.67219 06141	16	5	12	−.28112 23697
15	2	13	−1.15632 39995	16	1	12	−.98198 37155	16	6	6	.25803 86623
15	2	14	−1.53462 06103	16	1	13	−1.32575 02291	16	6	7	.18008 04100
15	3	3	1.03884 67484	16	1	14	−1.72935 17286	16	6	8	.10744 70169
15	3	4	.78569 53136	16	1	15	−2.25197 62116	16	6	9	.03753 15039
15	3	5	.57688 47969	16	1	16	−3.10489 68626	16	6	10	−.03176 42139
15	3	6	.39208 32453	16	2	2	1.82496 17979	16	6	11	−.10247 13993
15	3	7	.22070 74184	16	2	3	1.39138 59986	16	7	7	.15204 24618
15	3	8	.05601 36122	16	2	4	1.07191 00598	16	7	8	.10368 42572
15	3	9	−.10720 30892	16	2	5	.80677 53414	16	7	9	.05793 54921
15	3	10	−.27386 03347	16	2	6	.57185 42866	16	7	10	.01325 33917
15	3	11	−.44968 15299	16	2	7	.35451 43842	16	8	8	.10169 46521
15	3	12	−.64283 01302	16	2	8	.14679 55938	16	8	9	.07905 57704
15	3	13	−.86760 84623	16	2	9	−.05723 07939	17	1	1	3.50776 08345
15	4	4	.63328 25216	16	2	10	−.26280 91651	17	1	2	2.50776 08345
15	4	5	.46839 54140	16	2	11	−.47548 74045	17	1	3	1.94326 81594
15	4	6	.32386 61474	16	2	12	−.70227 00971	17	1	4	1.52228 66799
15	4	7	.19076 28673	16	2	13	−.95365 51101	17	1	5	1.17139 83159
15	4	8	.06351 75907	16	2	14	−1.24851 49137	17	1	6	.86039 87122

TABLE 10B.2 *Continued*

n	i	j	$E(x_{(i)}x_{(j)}; n)$	n	i	j	$E(x_{(i)}x_{(j)}; n)$	n	i	j	$E(x_{(i)}x_{(j)}; n)$
17	1	7	.57337 10807	17	4	14	−.62058 23190	18	2	7	.52579 71599
17	1	8	.30036 02504	17	5	5	.48712 82192	18	2	8	.32629 69700
17	1	9	.03414 41055	17	5	6	.36715 49498	18	2	9	.13364 37283
17	1	10	−.23135 40122	17	5	7	.25870 89814	18	2	10	−.05636 68282
17	1	11	−.50210 08789	17	5	8	.15715 34507	18	2	11	−.24755 81181
17	1	12	−.78494 23030	17	5	9	.05931 87706	18	2	12	−.44393 11712
17	1	13	−1.08900 90086	17	5	10	−.03730 72491	18	2	13	−.65029 63787
17	1	14	−1.42843 26533	17	5	11	−.13505 67988	18	2	14	−.87326 71257
17	1	15	−1.82904 55966	17	5	12	−.23648 48775	18	2	15	−1.12325 89453
17	1	16	−2.35036 31645	17	5	13	−.34489 02158	18	2	16	−1.41948 44863
17	1	17	−3.20550 13557	17	6	6	.30058 43470	18	2	17	−1.80640 17049
17	2	2	1.90932 86076	17	6	7	.21720 87085	18	3	3	1.26467 64541
17	2	3	1.47382 12827	17	6	8	.13980 20328	18	3	4	1.00305 35893
17	2	4	1.15396 29569	17	6	9	.06574 42736	18	3	5	.78948 03338
17	2	5	.88962 66310	17	6	10	−.00698 59665	18	3	6	.60308 20649
17	2	6	.65661 02659	17	6	11	−.08021 38072	18	3	7	.43325 69926
17	2	7	.44236 27797	17	6	12	−.15588 96202	18	3	8	.27363 82127
17	2	8	.23913 96759	17	7	7	.18003 82402	18	3	9	.11984 10480
17	2	9	.04139 28192	17	7	8	.12491 29753	18	3	10	−.03157 75063
17	2	10	−.15549 06731	17	7	9	.07281 54074	18	3	11	−.18371 62727
17	2	11	−.35599 25332	17	7	10	.02217 32128	18	3	12	−.33978 91153
17	2	12	−.56521 21375	17	7	11	−.02837 24403	18	3	13	−.50363 38299
17	2	13	−.78991 25546	17	8	8	.11204 84927	18	3	14	−.68050 28532
17	2	14	−1.04052 60200	17	8	9	.08080 00267	18	3	15	−.87864 62568
17	2	15	−1.33608 86697	17	8	10	.05114 76686	18	3	16	−1.11326 04489
17	2	16	−1.72042 01008	17	9	9	.09004 65814	18	4	4	.82988 20810
17	3	3	1.19221 07252	18	1	1	3.59704 61702	18	4	5	.65422 63222
17	3	4	.93305 05306	18	1	2	2.59704 61702	18	4	6	.50196 17902
17	3	5	.72084 96577	18	1	3	2.03427 65308	18	4	7	.36390 60479
17	3	6	.53491 52167	18	1	4	1.61609 97450	18	4	8	.23461 65634
17	3	7	.36467 94144	18	1	5	1.26897 78155	18	4	9	.11039 26076
17	3	8	.20370 91772	18	1	6	.96275 44762	18	4	10	−.01163 48391
17	3	9	.04745 55487	18	1	7	.68166 51889	18	4	11	−.13401 60252
17	3	10	−.10781 56686	18	1	8	.41601 09008	18	4	12	−.25936 68761
17	3	11	−.26569 04144	18	1	9	.15896 16815	18	4	13	−.39078 45980
17	3	12	−.43021 07197	18	1	10	−.09496 18007	18	4	14	−.53248 36936
17	3	13	−.60670 27090	18	1	11	−.35079 10772	18	4	15	−.69106 12193
17	3	14	−.80335 02164	18	1	12	−.61383 47108	18	5	5	.54186 03092
17	3	15	−1.03505 57182	18	1	13	−.89051 42554	18	5	6	.41813 66297
17	4	4	.76587 72428	18	1	14	−1.18969 36460	18	5	7	.30668 07870
17	4	5	.59330 28054	18	1	15	−1.52536 57101	18	5	8	.20281 14988
17	4	6	.44322 64848	18	1	16	−1.92337 42230	18	5	9	.10339 39287
17	4	7	.30655 90118	18	1	17	−2.44355 91207	18	5	10	.00603 60908
17	4	8	.17785 06544	18	1	18	−3.30074 41351	18	5	11	−.09135 44997
17	4	9	.05330 57575	18	2	2	1.98991 01268	18	5	12	−.19089 31496
17	4	10	−.07014 40479	18	2	3	1.55267 97662	18	5	13	−.29505 55083
17	4	11	−.19540 29393	18	2	4	1.23247 94168	18	5	14	−.40718 36001
17	4	12	−.32570 55597	18	2	5	.96883 03606	18	6	6	.34482 47854
17	4	13	−.46527 83685	18	2	6	.73744 01802	18	6	7	.25689 37505

TABLE 10B.2 *Continued*

n	i	j	$E(x_{(i)}x_{(j)}; n)$	n	i	j	$E(x_{(i)}x_{(j)}; n)$	n	i	j	$E(x_{(i)}x_{(j)}; n)$
18	6	8	.17553 00021	19	2	14	−.73123 82925	19	6	11	−.02134 96632
18	6	9	.09809 30677	19	2	15	−.95274 96978	19	6	12	−.09877 04413
18	6	10	.02260 96299	19	2	16	−1.20223 32941	19	6	13	−.17836 20745
18	6	11	−.05260 93423	19	2	17	−1.49908 24322	19	6	14	−.26205 43418
18	6	12	−.12923 63965	19	2	18	−1.88835 35110	19	7	7	.24693 38145
18	6	13	−.20919 60677	19	3	3	1.33451 10082	19	7	8	.18154 56358
18	7	7	.21210 34702	19	3	4	1.07070 03889	19	7	9	.12004 79540
18	7	8	.15139 92491	19	3	5	.85591 60662	19	7	10	.06082 97030
18	7	9	.09415 84056	19	3	6	.66910 59363	19	7	11	.00259 85845
18	7	10	.03878 84044	19	3	7	.49962 04556	19	7	12	−.05582 13320
18	7	11	−.01603 11780	19	3	8	.34112 70806	19	7	13	−.11565 43329
18	7	12	−.07156 68585	19	3	9	.18934 87555	19	8	8	.15239 43086
18	8	8	.12965 00217	19	3	10	.04103 65629	19	8	9	.10850 51122
18	8	9	.09146 89512	19	3	11	−.10659 12312	19	8	10	.06669 58229
18	8	10	.05509 64106	19	3	12	−.25623 38217	19	8	11	.02595 95147
18	8	11	.01955 77328	19	3	13	−.41086 52514	19	8	12	−.01458 51042
18	9	9	.09004 65814	19	3	14	−.57419 50647	19	9	9	.09837 66271
18	9	10	.07201 04387	19	3	15	−.75144 37762	19	9	10	.07327 03911
19	1	1	3.68204 78516	19	3	16	−.95094 41729	19	9	11	.04933 12957
19	1	2	2.68204 78516	19	3	17	−1.18817 56533	19	10	10	.08079 09751
19	1	3	2.12082 70910	19	4	4	.89222 54987	20	1	1	3.76315 97146
19	1	4	1.70514 62523	19	4	5	.71386 54325	20	1	2	2.76315 97146
19	1	5	1.36134 13030	19	4	6	.55969 65138	20	1	3	2.20334 06878
19	1	6	1.05927 66874	19	4	7	.42044 02316	20	1	4	1.78989 83552
19	1	7	.78329 22736	19	4	8	.29064 30231	20	1	5	1.44904 08118
19	1	8	.52386 95189	19	4	9	.16666 14590	20	1	6	1.15063 48881
19	1	9	.27445 15628	19	4	10	.04575 76598	20	1	7	.87909 21502
19	1	10	.02996 34144	19	4	11	−.07438 76891	20	1	8	.62502 36800
19	1	11	−.21401 84895	19	4	12	−.19600 29194	20	1	9	.38206 78460
19	1	12	−.46185 59408	19	4	13	−.32152 30588	20	1	10	.14543 27711
19	1	13	−.71841 79950	19	4	14	−.45396 68711	20	1	11	−.08889 26380
19	1	14	−.98983 53826	19	4	15	−.59756 57833	20	1	12	−.32465 42591
19	1	15	−1.28478 86665	19	4	16	−.75905 79000	20	1	13	−.56576 49939
19	1	16	−1.61718 28951	19	5	5	.59609 42648	20	1	14	−.81678 99399
19	1	17	−2.01289 86080	19	5	6	.46912 18881	20	1	15	−1.08365 51006
19	1	18	−2.53209 20354	19	5	7	.35508 47179	20	1	16	−1.37491 30326
19	1	19	−3.39117 37939	19	5	8	.24925 07652	20	1	17	−1.70441 51707
19	2	2	2.06701 59055	19	5	9	.14849 89037	20	1	18	−2.09809 45742
19	2	3	1.62823 66660	19	5	10	.05051 41639	20	1	19	−2.61641 25315
19	2	4	1.30772 81241	19	5	11	−.04663 86868	20	1	20	−3.47725 83786
19	2	5	1.04467 74622	19	5	12	−.14479 56323	20	2	2	2.14092 24544
19	2	6	.81469 35030	19	5	13	−.24594 14349	20	2	3	1.70074 14812
19	2	7	.60527 67432	19	5	14	−.35251 67925	20	2	4	1.37995 34182
19	2	8	.40891 41917	19	5	15	−.46792 44975	20	2	5	1.11742 89274
19	2	9	.22048 14684	19	6	6	.39000 52335	20	2	6	.88867 43301
19	2	10	.03604 90040	19	6	7	.29818 53404	20	2	7	.68118 45644
19	2	11	−.14777 85386	19	6	8	.21348 33614	20	2	8	.48750 54400
19	2	12	−.33432 31434	19	6	9	.13323 26697	20	2	9	.30263 12966
19	2	13	−.52726 99747	19	6	10	.05548 77905	20	2	10	.12282 27822

TABLE 10B.2 *Concluded*

n	i	j	$E(x_{(i)}x_{(j)}; n)$	n	i	j	$E(x_{(i)}x_{(j)}; n)$	n	i	j	$E(x_{(i)}x_{(j)}; n)$
20	2	11	−.05502 56801	20	4	6	.61628 48185	20	6	9	.17022 63337
20	2	12	−.23379 34563	20	4	7	.47597 85179	20	6	10	.09058 72810
20	2	13	−.41646 98104	20	4	8	.34573 32605	20	6	11	.01240 45909
20	2	14	−.60652 56628	20	4	9	.22193 82389	20	6	12	−.06569 00797
20	2	15	−.80845 17036	20	4	10	.10194 29857	20	6	13	−.14506 55681
20	2	16	−1.02871 53688	20	4	11	−.01641 62785	20	6	14	−.22726 43343
20	2	17	−1.27777 82114	20	4	12	−.13511 33623	20	6	15	−.31423 93531
20	2	18	−1.57521 34603	20	4	13	−.25616 84132	20	7	7	.28361 37564
20	2	19	−1.96663 85237	20	4	14	−.38190 08258	20	7	8	.21423 29399
20	3	3	1.40185 69655	20	4	15	−.51528 76108	20	7	9	.14914 96896
20	3	4	1.13608 73612	20	4	16	−.66059 43627	20	7	10	.08673 36466
20	3	5	.92022 49684	20	4	17	−.82470 02582	20	7	11	.02571 07728
20	3	6	.73304 61715	20	5	5	.64959 18260	20	7	12	−.03503 06974
20	3	7	.56384 55907	20	5	6	.51977 46692	20	7	13	−.09658 24633
20	3	8	.40630 41631	20	5	7	.40349 64454	20	7	14	−.16015 53620
20	3	9	.25621 53876	20	5	8	.29597 10292	20	8	8	.17881 39224
20	3	10	.11046 28149	20	5	9	.19407 70951	20	8	9	.13013 82496
20	3	11	−.03352 11508	20	5	10	.09554 84059	20	8	10	.08383 50290
20	3	12	−.17809 92725	20	5	11	−.00144 47474	20	8	11	.03887 50395
20	3	13	−.32570 85570	20	5	12	−.09855 34351	20	8	12	−.00561 46394
20	3	14	−.47916 42651	20	5	13	−.19745 10463	20	8	13	−.05046 69633
20	3	15	−.64209 57155	20	5	14	−.30004 37127	20	9	9	.11276 48879
20	3	16	−.81971 78215	20	5	15	−.40876 40897	20	9	10	.08184 33087
20	3	17	−1.02045 47229	20	5	16	−.52708 49053	20	9	11	.05222 70111
20	3	18	−1.26005 60520	20	6	6	.43560 15809	20	9	12	.02326 98571
20	4	4	.95288 39168	20	6	7	.34041 91897	20	10	10	.08079 09751
20	4	5	.77212 83437	20	6	8	.25285 97019	20	10	11	.06608 30803

TABLE 10B.3

Variances and Covariances of Order Statistics in Sample of Sizes up to 20 from a Normal Population

n	i	j	Value	n	i	j	Value	n	i	j	Value
2	1	1	.6816901139	7				9			
		2	.3183098861		3	3	.2197215626		4	4	.1705588454
	2	2	.6816901139			4	.1655598429			5	.1369913669
3	1	1	.5594672038			5	.1296048425			6	.1126671842
		2	.2756644477		4	4	.2104468615		5	5	.1661012814
		3	.1648683485	8	1	1	.3728971434	10	1	1	.3443438233
	2	2	.4486711046			2	.1863073997			2	.1712629030
4	1	1	.4917152369			3	.1259660300			3	.1162590989
		2	.2455926930			4	.0947230277			4	.0882494247
		3	.1580080701			5	.0747650242			5	.0707413677
		4	.1046840000			6	.0602075169			6	.0583987134
	2	2	.3604553434			7	.0482985508			7	.0489206279
		3	.2359438935			8	.0368353073			8	.0410844589
5	1	1	.4475340691		2	2	.2394010458			9	.0340406470
		2	.2243309596			3	.1631958727			10	.0266989351
		3	.1481477252			4	.1232633317		2	2	.2145241430
		4	.1057719776			5	.0975647193			3	.1466226180
		5	.0742152685			6	.0787224662			4	.1117015961
	2	2	.3115189521			7	.0632466118			5	.0897428245
		3	.2084354440		3	3	.2007687900			6	.0741995414
		4	.1499426668			4	.1523584312			7	.0622278486
	3	3	.2868336616			5	.1209637555			8	.0523067222
6	1	1	.4159271090			6	.0978171355			9	.0433711561
		2	.2085030023		4	4	.1871862195		3	3	.1750032834
		3	.1394352565			5	.1491754908			4	.1338022448
		4	.1024293940	9	1	1	.3573533264			5	.1077445336
		5	.0773637839			2	.1781434240			6	.0892254012
		6	.0563414544			3	.1207454442			7	.0749183943
	2	2	.2795777392			4	.0913071400			8	.0630332449
		3	.1889859560			5	.0727422354		4	4	.1579389144
		4	.1396640604			6	.0594831125			5	.1275089295
		5	.1059054582			7	.0490764061			6	.1057858169
	3	3	.2462125354			8	.0400936927			7	.0889462026
		4	.1832727978			9	.0310552188		5	5	.1510539039
7	1	1	.3919177761		2	2	.2256968778			6	.1255989678
		2	.1961990246			3	.1541163526	11	1	1	.3332474428
		3	.1321155811			4	.1170056918			2	.1653647712
		4	.0984868607			5	.0934477394			3	.1123584351
		5	.0765598346			6	.0765461431			4	.0855170596
		6	.0599187124			7	.0632354695			5	.0688483064
		7	.0448022105			8	.0517146091			6	.0572007586
	2	2	.2567328862		3	3	.1863826133			7	.0483754063
		3	.1744833274			4	.1420779776			8	.0412423472
		4	.1307298656			5	.1137680176			9	.0351103357
		5	.1019550089			6	.0933625386			10	.0294198503
		6	.0799811748			7	.0772351806			11	.0233152868

This table is reproduced from A. E. Sarhan and B. G. Greenberg, "Estimation of location and scale parameters by order statistics from simply and doubly censored samples, Part I, The normal distribution up to samples of size 10," *Ann. Math. Statist.*, Vol. 27 (1956), pp. 427–451, with permission of the authors and W. Kruskal, editor of the *Annals of Mathematical Statistics.*

TABLE 10B.3 *Continued*

n	*i*	*j*	Value	*n*	*i*	*j*	Value	*n*	*i*	*j*	Value
11				12	3			13	3		
	2	2	.2051975798			4	.1212063211			8	.0589221432
		3	.1403096511			5	.0982605602			9	.0514460445
		4	.1071492595			6	.0822228461			10	.0449637542
		5	.0864430257			7	.0701213964			11	.0390643799
		6	.0719305024			8	.0604384621		4	4	.1330111820
		7	.0608869662			9	.0522825611			5	.1082512667
		8	.0519504506			10	.0450357615			6	.0909855605
		9	.0442549455		4	4	.1398109405			7	.0780173339
		10	.0371029977			5	.1135687821			8	.0677217143
	3	3	.1657242880			6	.0951645279			9	.0591628729
		4	.1269672925			7	.0812419810			10	.0517328050
		5	.1026407291			8	.0700795832		5	5	.1232503256
		6	.0855178832			9	.0606620874			6	.1037367701
		7	.0724741050		5	5	.1306137359			7	.0890434754
		8	.0618873278			6	.1096212247			8	.0773552864
		9	.0527550069			7	.0936951520			9	.0676230994
	4	4	.1479546565			8	.0808972960		6	6	.1183175325
		5	.1198752861		6	6	.1266377911			7	.1016824204
		6	.1000346585			7	.1083945831			8	.0884194610
		7	.0848765182	13	1	1	.3152053842		7	7	.1167989950
		8	.0725451434			2	.1557272904	14	1	1	.3077301026
	5	5	.1396410804			3	.1058908842			2	.1517203662
		6	.1167449805			4	.0808649736			3	.1031719531
		7	.0991935960			5	.0654634499			4	.0788715916
	6	6	.1371624335			6	.0548221797			5	.0639657428
12	1	1	.3236363870			7	.0468833088			6	.0537064714
		2	.1602373762			8	.0406132548			7	.0460899189
		3	.1089309641			9	.0354226462			8	.0401141688
		4	.0830686767			10	.0309322744			9	.0352141760
		5	.0670884464			11	.0268537250			10	.0310371163
		6	.0559933694			12	.0228858068			11	.0273362865
		7	.0476620974			13	.0184348220			12	.0239061001
		8	.0410208554		2	2	.1904130721			13	.0205080257
		9	.0354439060			3	.1302055829			14	.0166279801
		10	.0305012591			4	.0997262696		2	2	.1844200252
		11	.0257945392			5	.0808785938			3	.1260791989
		12	.0206221233			6	.0678145832			4	.0966524633
	2	2	.1972646039			7	.0580457285			5	.0785202981
		3	.1349020328			8	.0503167946			6	.0660028340
		4	.1031959206			9	.0439095087			7	.0566896715
		5	.0835045822			10	.0383601798			8	.0493708148
		6	.0697859658			11	.0333147765			9	.0433617156
		7	.0594590652			12	.0284018130			10	.0382337404
		8	.0512113198		3	3	.1513917013			11	.0336863221
		9	.0442747124			4	.1162698131			12	.0294681314
		10	.0381191478			5	.0944566603			13	.0252863928
		11	.0322507340			6	.0792922993		3	3	.1457045665
	3	3	.1579786877			7	.0679282354			4	.1119816877

TABLE 10B.3 *Continued*

n	i	j	Value	n	i	j	Value	n	i	j	Value
14	3			15	2			16	1		
		5	.0911181271			6	.0643390895			3	.0985009764
		6	.0766754957			7	.0554074400			4	.0754040023
		7	.0659084825			8	.0484238833			5	.0613086724
		8	.0574341188			9	.0427294113			6	.0516624963
		9	.0504677802			10	.0379177516			7	.0445503705
		10	.0445169192			11	.0337151721			8	.0390194716
		11	.0392352316			12	.0299152347			9	.0345378158
		12	.0343322071			13	.0263303885			10	.0307810093
	4	4	.1272273070			14	.0227213594			11	.0275353612
		5	.1036931108		3	3	.1407322502			12	.0246479007
		6	.0873562483			4	.1082138452			13	.0219956755
		7	.0751519909			5	.0881605755			14	.0194585037
		8	.0655310936			6	.0743268436			15	.0168710289
		9	.0576120957			7	.0640558183			16	.0138287378
		10	.0508402240			8	.0560136122		2	2	.1743940788
		11	.0448243469			9	.0494485109			3	.1191409287
	5	5	.1171012461			10	.0438960670			4	.0914359918
		6	.0987747550			11	.0390426915			5	.0744591145
		7	.0850536546			12	.0346513382			6	.0628093909
		8	.0742181416			13	.0305060359			7	.0542033941
		9	.0652867776		4	4	.1222328270			8	.0475009769
		10	.0576401464			5	.0997323941			9	.0420638230
	6	6	.1115324579			6	.0841705696			10	.0375018250
		7	.0961405595			7	.0725946869			11	.0335574912
		8	.0839617110			8	.0635175907			12	.0300461298
		9	.0739069221			9	.0560990511			13	.0268189579
	7	7	.1090269480			10	.0498187836			14	.0237301562
		8	.0953087256			11	.0443247452			15	.0205785433
15	1	1	.3010415703			12	.0393501820		3	3	.1363385612
		2	.1481297708		5	5	.1118698986			4	.1048706756
		3	.1007223449			6	.0945206004			5	.0855189036
		4	.0770594060			7	.0815891122			6	.0722075087
		5	.0625845851			8	.0714331681			7	.0623568515
		6	.0526530129			9	.0631224388			8	.0546749107
		7	.0453078886			10	.0560795065			9	.0484366096
		8	.0395736673			11	.0499127743			10	.0431979377
		9	.0349035905		6	6	.1058666366			11	.0386652995
		10	.0309614122			7	.0914683204			12	.0346277256
		11	.0275211039			8	.0801407559			13	.0309149135
		12	.0244126313			9	.0708582099			14	.0273595378
		13	.0214819828			10	.0629824402		4	4	.1178657554
		14	.0185333263		7	7	.1026916923			5	.0962513413
		15	.0151137071			8	.0900499964			6	.0813480448
	2	2	.1791215291			9	.0796738323			7	.0703000911
		3	.1224176953		8	8	.1016946521			8	.0616728990
		4	.0939067144	16	1	1	.2950098090			9	.0546595026
		5	.0763912337			2	.1448881689			10	.0487647746

TABLE 10B.3 *Continued*

n	i	j	Value	n	i	j	Value	n	i	j	Value
16	4			17	2			17	6		
		11	.0436607328			9	.0413928192			12	.0478122599
		12	.0391112669			10	.0370349110		7	7	.0929031780
		13	.0349253749			11	.0332940892			8	.0818194607
	5	5	.1073517089			12	.0299982825			9	.0728154074
		6	.0908232622			13	.0270170379			10	.0652667274
		7	.0785480532			14	.0242386812			11	.0587626219
		8	.0689488802			15	.0215459396		8	8	.0907361650
		9	.0611364182			16	.0187658306			9	.0808000267
		10	.0545638941		3	3	.1324207975			10	.0724599963
		11	.0488684327			4	.1018792434		9	9	.0900465814
		12	.0437882959			5	.0831421716	18	1	1	.2845301297
	6	6	.1010461906			6	.0702850403			2	.1392501620
		7	.0874627156			7	.0607964413			3	.0946172637
		8	.0768239668			8	.0534208202			4	.0724851730
		9	.0681545540			9	.0474555487			5	.0590304274
		10	.0608534805			10	.0424726884			6	.0498600635
		11	.0545210724			11	.0381925587			7	.0431302310
	7	7	.0974026613			12	.0344194567			8	.0379260195
		8	.0856181916			13	.0310047771			9	.0337388141
		9	.0760015577			14	.0278210708			10	.0302610667
		10	.0678931922			15	.0247342095			11	.0272938041
	8	8	.0957213007		4	4	.1140068197			12	.0247002471
		9	.0850291218			5	.0931620339			13	.0223801573
17	1	1	.2895330037			6	.0788266621			14	.0202537421
		2	.1419424629			7	.0682298909			15	.0182488619
		3	.0964748737			8	.0599826092			16	.0162850441
		4	.0738849615			9	.0533057575			17	.0142368875
		5	.0601272302			10	.0477239973			18	.0117719054
		6	.0507326948			11	.0429261816		2	2	.1662929294
		7	.0438236491			12	.0386942630			3	.1135058132
		8	.0384672834			13	.0348624030			4	.0871597604
		9	.0341441055			14	.0312881041			5	.0710825990
		10	.0305389548		5	5	.1034004377			6	.0600975754
		11	.0274465527			6	.0875729930			7	.0520217423
		12	.0247237144			7	.0758534534			8	.0457683625
		13	.0222620771			8	.0667204245			9	.0407317967
		14	.0199690651			9	.0593187706			10	.0365451034
		15	.0177476891			10	.0531257771			11	.0329704894
		16	.0154552071			11	.0477987292			12	.0298442464
		17	.0127264751			12	.0430970793			13	.0270462261
	2	2	.1701426762			13	.0388375657			14	.0244806359
		3	.1161866734		6	6	.0968824669			15	.0220607111
		4	.0891982557			7	.0839811738			16	.0196894667
		5	.0726970385			8	.0739130260			17	.0172154925
		6	.0613998459			9	.0657442736		3	3	.1288998943
		7	.0530761573			10	.0589030403			4	.0991828539
		8	.0466140918			11	.0530137275			5	.0809899792

TABLE 10B.3 *Continued*

n	*i*	*j*	Value	*n*	*i*	*j*	Value	*n*	*i*	*j*	Value
18	3			18				19	3		
		6	.0685324700		8	8	.0864960639			8	.0511541418
		7	.0593598602			9	.0771762286			9	.0456228816
		8	.0522488413			10	.0693891332			10	.0410365629
		9	.0465162123			11	.0627116906			11	.0371346427
		10	.0417473296		9	9	.0853127880			12	.0337391171
		11	.0376730987			10	.0767442321			13	.0307215918
		12	.0341080171	19	1	1	.2799358050			14	.0279835020
		13	.0309157650			2	.1367768168			15	.0254424108
		14	.0279875014			3	.0929061763			16	.0230195063
		15	.0252244786			4	.0711902425			17	.0206214645
		16	.0225161109			5	.0580094835		4	4	.1074740839
	4	4	.1105660331			6	.0490405678			5	.0879051965
		5	.0903973787			7	.0424705246			6	.0745033878
		6	.0765579277			8	.0374006329			7	.0646406188
		7	.0663522086			9	.0333319395			8	.0570032284
		8	.0584310521			10	.0299634144			9	.0508572608
		9	.0520394281			11	.0271011338			10	.0457576598
		10	.0467183404			12	.0246129452			11	.0414165091
		11	.0421694861			13	.0224037540			12	.0376368753
		12	.0381869632			14	.0204007370			13	.0342765540
		13	.0346192645			15	.0185431530			14	.0312262549
		14	.0313452497			16	.0167731147			15	.0283944527
		15	.0282548286			17	.0150223067			16	.0256935148
	5	5	.0999084321			18	.0131789994		5	5	.0967944745
		6	.0846879168			19	.0109382527			6	.0821055695
		7	.0734460811		2	2	.1627856651			7	.0712796742
		8	.0647101858			3	.1110590145			8	.0628870095
		9	.0576543520			4	.0852931053			9	.0561272025
		10	.0517756675			5	.0695970759			10	.0505141639
		11	.0467468133			6	.0588910196			11	.0457330144
		12	.0423415563			7	.0510351093			12	.0415681234
		13	.0383932046			8	.0449652247			13	.0378636088
		14	.0347682770			9	.0400891754			14	.0344995261
	6	6	.0932407331			10	.0360490040			15	.0313752928
		7	.0809202644			11	.0326137544		6	6	.0900218693
		8	.0713338046			12	.0296258236			7	.0782029063
		9	.0635829688			13	.0269716592			8	.0690294360
		10	.0571197288			14	.0245641909			9	.0616336896
		11	.0515868552			15	.0223306885			10	.0554877905
		12	.0467370896			16	.0202017247			11	.0502493169
		13	.0423879846			17	.0180952193			12	.0456834841
	7	7	.0890167025			18	.0158767294			13	.0416203596
		8	.0785179677		3	3	.1257138904			14	.0379290224
		9	.0700199026			4	.0967367097		7	7	.0856172981
		10	.0629269074			5	.0790298792			8	.0756153413
		11	.0568501034			6	.0669273696			9	.0675433161
		12	.0515199092			7	.0580336124			10	.0608297030

TABLE 10B.3 *Concluded*

n	i	j	Value	n	i	j	Value	n	i	j	Value
19	7			20	2			20	5		
		11	.0551032224			11	.0322405467			7	.0693175756
		12	.0501089625			12	.0293684960			8	.0612251429
		13	.0456621835			13	.0268315105			9	.0547222526
	8	8	.0828339961			14	.0245479493			10	.0493374275
		9	.0740273546			15	.0224526609			11	.0447662310
		10	.0666958229			16	.0204888032			12	.0408014074
		11	.0604372723			17	.0185994024			13	.0372948400
		12	.0549752083			18	.0167136502			14	.0341351571
	9	9	.0812876330			19	.0147107671			15	.0312332040
		10	.0732703911		3	3	.1228134687			16	.0285109200
		11	.0664202898			4	.0945049010		6	6	.0871511254
	10	10	.0807909751			5	.0772355098			7	.0757703360
20	1	1	.2756966156			6	.0654510179			8	.0669555789
		2	.1344941714			7	.0568056677			9	.0598659769
		3	.0913234064			8	.0501310269			10	.0539910639
		4	.0699879991			9	.0447763202			11	.0490008080
		5	.0570566384			10	.0403482354			12	.0446702771
		6	.0482701093			11	.0365934287			13	.0408385549
		7	.0418437826			12	.0333397949			14	.0373845194
		8	.0368937058			13	.0304645792			15	.0342111024
		9	.0329296302			14	.0278756579		7	7	.0826123955
		10	.0296562523			15	.0254994381			8	.0730383676
		11	.0268838808			16	.0232716371			9	.0653307665
		12	.0244839567			17	.0211277373			10	.0589387428
		13	.0223649803			18	.0189874448			11	.0535056766
		14	.0204584277		4	4	.1046766243			12	.0487882257
		15	.0187096782			5	.0856442356			13	.0446121090
		16	.0170711408			6	.0726321560			14	.0408459989
		17	.0154951854			7	.0630731775		8	8	.0796309757
		18	.0139227072			8	.0556855081			9	.0712591607
		19	.0122530117			9	.0497539273			10	.0643103375
		20	.0102047204			10	.0448455403			11	.0583997310
	2	2	.1595731636			11	.0406811669			12	.0532644495
		3	.1088143707			12	.0370709493			13	.0487159834
		4	.0835758044			13	.0338793392		9	9	.0778118317
		5	.0682247554			14	.0310045146			10	.0702526464
		6	.0577699656			15	.0283650517			11	.0638176734
		7	.0501109523			16	.0258897454			12	.0582229133
		8	.0442041191			17	.0235070343		10	10	.0769474356
		9	.0394693443		5	5	.0939960007			11	.0699266198
		10	.0355565554			6	.0797773755				

A. E. SARHAN AND B. G. GREENBERG

10C THE BEST LINEAR ESTIMATES FOR THE PARAMETERS OF THE NORMAL DISTRIBUTION

10C.1 Exact Estimates

The use of order statistics for estimating parameters of the normal distribution in small samples is advantageous because the method combines highly efficient linear estimates with a simplicity of calculation. The benefits of this method of estimation, however, are very apparent when one or more portions of the sample observations have been censored from the observer.

In order to understand the way in which the term censored is being used here, it is well to set down some definitions.

A sample is said to have type I censoring at the extremes when there is a fixed point on the abscissa beyond which the exact magnitude of an observation is not determinable. This fixed point may be selected in advance by the investigator when the errors of measurement at the extremes are known to be large relative to those in the central portion of the distribution. Censorship points may also be selected in advance when the costs of determining the exact size of such an extremal observation may not be justified by its relative value in reducing the imprecision of estimates. Regardless of the reason for trimming the data this way, the point of censorship is fixed and known as well as the percentage of observations censored from the sample, Sometimes, however, because of a limitation in the sensitivity of the measuring device, this fixed point of screening may or may not be known to the investigator. (He will, of course, know the proportion of observations trimmed from the sample.) As long as the method of censoring is based on the use of a fixed point along the abscissa, the sample is referred to as type I censored, regardless of whether or not the investigator knows this point.

A different method of trimming observations from the extremes of a sample is based on a predetermined proportion of censoring. This is referred to as type II censoring and may be utilized for the same reasons as those for using type I censoring. For instance, if experience has shown that observations at the extremes are not worth the effort, the investigator may decide in advance to screen out fixed proportions at either end. Other occasions may arise when wild or contaminated observations are discarded and are considered censored for purposes of estimation. *The distinguishing characteristic in type II censoring is that the point of censorship is a random one.* Moreover, it is always unknown to the investigator, except that he knows its position is beyond the magnitude of the first or last known observation.

The methods of estimation for type I censored samples should take into consideration the fixed point of censorship on the abscissa whenever it is known. Sampling studies [2] demonstrated that ignoring such information would lead to little or negligible bias in the estimates themselves. The variances of the estimates, however, will be affected, particularly the one for the location parameter. We might speculate that ignoring the knowledge about point of censorship and substituting the methods for type II samples would lead to a loss of information equivalent to a fraction of one additional observation in the sample.

To illustrate the advantages of best linear estimates in small censored samples, consider a sample in which r_1 observations on the left-hand side of the distribution have been trimmed at an unknown point on the abscissa and r_2 observations have been similarly censored from the other extreme. If maximum-likelihood estimates are sought by conventional methods, the first drawback is the computational unattractiveness of the procedure itself. The procedure would be justified in spite of the computational unattractiveness if we were certain that the extra labor would produce an estimate greatly superior to the simple linear one. Such assurance in increased efficiency is not available and is, in fact, unknown with small samples.

The foregoing illustration was based on a doubly censored sample. We can expand this by saying that the general case of the type II censored sample, whether doubly, singly, or uncensored, is worth studying from the point of view of order statistics for the numerical results to be achieved therein. These numerical results enable the drawing of inferences concerning patterns in the relative influence of observations on the estimates and their variances. These latter features can be revealed very easily in a study based on order statistics.

Estimates of the parameters using the best linear unbiased systematic statistics are obtained simply by multiplying each known observation by an appropriate coefficient (see Chapter 3) such that

$$\mu^* = \sum_{i=r_1+1}^{n-r_2} a_{1i}x_{(i)} \qquad (10C.1.1)$$

and

$$\sigma^* = \sum_{i=r_1+1}^{n-r_2} a_{2i}x_{(i)}. \qquad (10C.1.2)$$

The coefficients a_{ki} were obtained by arranging the uncensored elements in a sample of size n in ascending order (i.e., $x_{(1)} \leq x_{(2)} \leq \ldots \leq x_{(n)}$) and then applying the method of least squares to obtain the linear combination of the elements that would produce estimates of the parameters with no bias and minimum variance. These coefficients have been calculated and tabulated by Sarhan and Greenberg [2, 3, 4] for samples of size 20 and less for all conditions of censoring at the extremes. These coefficients are reproduced here in Table 10C.1.

The variances (and covariances) of the estimates and their efficiencies relative to the corresponding best *linear* estimates using complete samples are given in Tables 10C.2 and 10C.3.

10C.2 Alternative Estimates

Gupta [1] suggested alternative linear estimates for the mean and standard deviation of a normal population to be used for samples of a size greater than 10 because the exact estimate is tedious to calculate and because the exact variances and covariances of the order statistics for larger samples are unavailable. He calculated the variances and relative efficiencies of these alternative estimates for a sample of size 10. Gupta's alternative linear estimates were intended for the special case of singly censored samples. His work has been extended to permit its use in the general case of doubly censored samples [2] to give

$$\mu^{*\prime} = \sum_{i=r_1+1}^{n-r_2} b_i x_{(i)} \qquad (10C.2.1)$$

where $\mu^{*\prime}$ is the alternative estimate of the population mean, and

$$\sigma^{*\prime} = \sum_{i=r_1+1}^{n-r_2} c_i x_{(i)} \qquad (10C.2.2)$$

where $\sigma^{*\prime}$ is the alternative estimate of the population standard deviation- The values of b_i and c_i in $\mu^{*\prime}$ and $\sigma^{*\prime}$ are determined by

$$b_i = \frac{1}{n - r_1 - r_2} - \frac{\bar{u}_k(u_i - \bar{u}_k)}{\sum_{j=r_1+1}^{n-r_2} (u_j - \bar{u}_k)^2} \qquad (10C.2.3)$$

and

$$c_i = \frac{u_i - \bar{u}_k}{\sum_{j=r_1+1}^{n-r_2} (u_j - \bar{u}_k)^2} \qquad (10C.2.4)$$

where

$$\bar{u}_k = \frac{1}{n - r_1 - r_2} \sum_{j=r_1+1}^{n-r_2} u_j \tag{10C.2.5}$$

or the arithmetic mean of the expected values of the uncensored sample elements. The estimates (10C.2.1) and (10C.2.2) are unbiased estimates of the mean and standard deviation, respectively.

Table 10C.4 gives the variances and relative efficiencies of the alternative estimates for samples of sizes 10, 12, and 15.

Figures 10C.1 and 10C.2 show the efficiencies of the alternative estimate from a sample of size 15 in relation to the correspondingly best linear estimate for the mean and the standard deviation, respectively. From the figures it is clear that the alternative estimate is relatively more precise when applied to doubly censored samples. The present graphs show that the alternative estimate is even better than previously supposed. Furthermore, the alternative estimate appears better if we judge its value or efficiency in estimating the standard deviation rather than the mean alone.

The use of exact estimates and the alternative estimate will be illustrated in (10C.3). Other estimators of the parameters for the singly censored sample can be found in Gupta [1] where the maximum-likelihood estimates were obtained. A recent paper by Saw [5] proposed another nonlinear estimator for σ^* which is unbiased and asymptotically efficient. Its calculation is limited to special cases of single censoring.

A recent contribution by Watterson [6] extended the methods of linear estimation with censored samples from multivariate normal populations. The sample is ordered with respect to one variate, and the remaining variables are associated with this arrangement. Censoring can occur in one of three ways.

1. The censoring is complete on both the ordered variate and its associated values.
2. The censoring may occur only on the associated variates.
3. The censoring may be limited to the ordered variate.

Samples that have been censored in one of these three ways provide sufficient information to estimate all parameters in the bivariate case. The latter has, of course, five parameters since there are two means, two standard deviations, and a covariance. The estimators considered by Watterson correspond to minimum variance linear unbiased estimates and "alternative" estimates.

The multivariate case is deducible by applying the theory to each pair of variates.

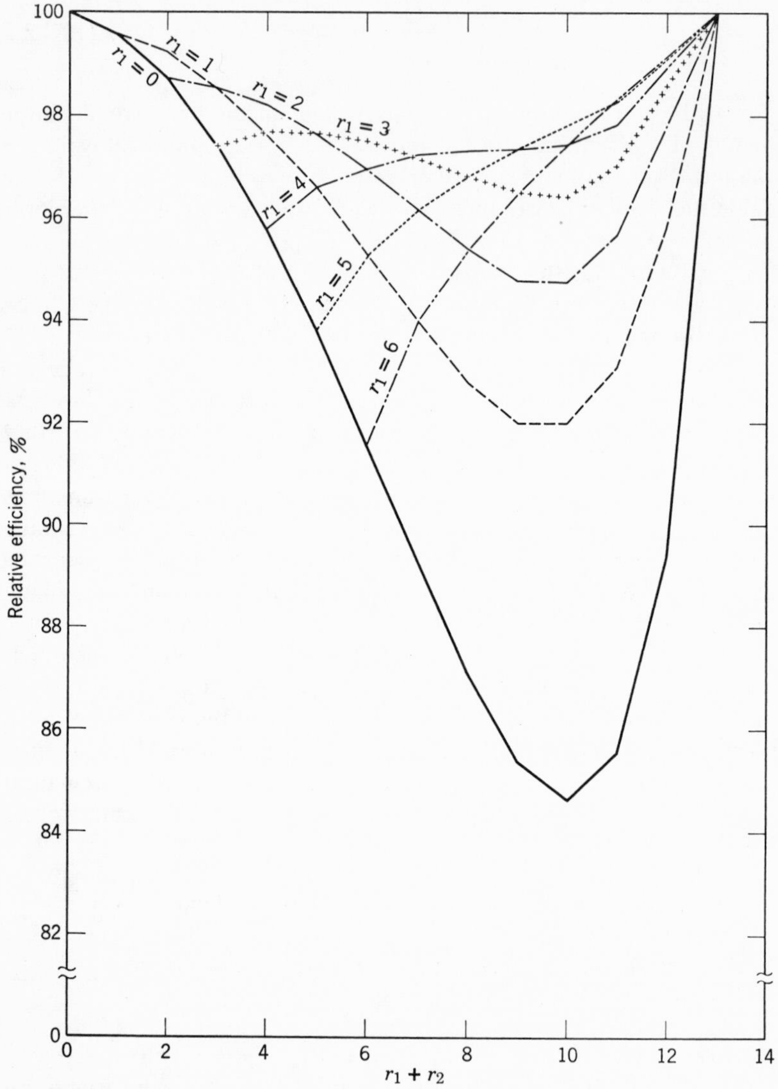

Fig. 10C.1 Relative efficiency of the alternative estimate of μ under conditions of censoring a sample of size 15 from the normal population. Reproduced from A. E. Sarhan and B. G. Greenberg, "Estimation of location and scale parameters by order statistics from singly and doubly censored samples, Part II," *Ann. Math. Statist.*, Vol. 29 (1958), pp. 79–105, with permission of W. Kruskal, editor of the *Annals of Mathematical Statistics*.

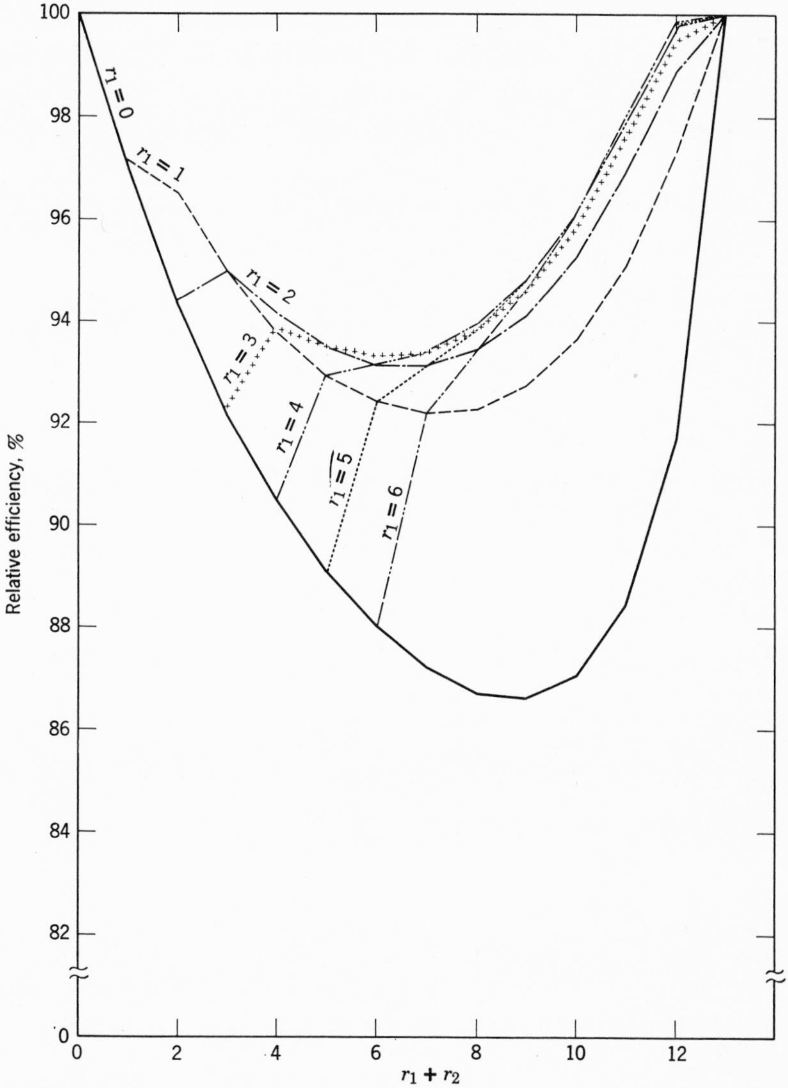

Fig. 10C.2 Relative efficiency of the alternative estimate of σ under conditions of censoring a sample of size 15 from the normal population. Reproduced from A. E. Sarhan and B. G. Greenberg from "Estimation of location and scale parameters by order statistics from singly and doubly censored samples, Part II," *Ann. Math. Statist.*, Vol. 29 (1958), pp. 79–105, with permission of W. Kruskal, editor of the *Annals of Mathematical Statistics.*

10C.3 Numerical Example

Students were learning to measure strontium-90 concentrations in samples of milk; measurement involved readings and calculations. The test substance was supposed to contain 9.22 micromicrocuries per liter. Poor technique was present in all observations, but the skill of the observers in using the measuring device was limited probably to the central portion of the range. Owing to the relatively larger measurement error

TABLE A

	Coefficients			
	Exact Estimate		Alternative Estimate	
Ordered Observations	μ^*	σ^*	$\mu^{*\prime}$	$\sigma^{*\prime}$
1. —	0	0	0	0
2. —	0	0	0	0
3. 8.2	0.20496319	−0.88982266	0.09515275	−0.79906860
4. 8.4	0.10382533	−0.11005067	0.15114637	−0.37232645
5. 9.1	0.11220127	−0.02620385	0.20170682	0.01300816
6. 9.8	0.11982080	0.05494874	0.25071680	0.38652614
7. 9.9	0.45918942	0.97112842	0.30127725	0.77186075
8. —	0	0	0	0
9. —	0	0	0	0
10. —	0	0	0	0
Estimate of parameter by linear systematic statistics	9.29	1.69	9.33	1.87

known to exist at the extremes, particularly at the upper end, it was decided to trim the two smallest observations (on the left) and the three largest (on the right) in a sample of ten.

The data, when arranged in an array, appear as the first column in Table A.

If we assume that the sample was drawn from a normal universe, the exact coefficients (a_{1i} and a_{2i}) for the best linear estimate, obtained from reference 2 or Table 10C.1 for the case $n = 10$, $r_1 = 2$, $r_2 = 3$, are those shown in the second and third columns. If the alternative estimate is desired, the coefficients are obtainable from (10C.2.3) and (10C.2.4) in combination with a table for the values of u_i.

The exact and alternative estimates of the mean and standard deviation are provided. They are similar, as they should be according to the relative efficiencies given in Table 10C.4, namely 97.95% for the mean and 96.88% for the standard deviation.

10C.4 Comments

Certain characteristic features which can be gleaned from the tables are discussed in references 2 and 3. One comment worthy of repetition here is that when the sample size is odd, and all the sample elements are censored except the middle one and its neighbor on either side, the central observation will have all the weight in estimating the mean (i.e., the other observation is of no value). If the sample size is even under the same circumstances of censoring, each middle observation has one-half the weight in estimating the mean.

Table 10C.3 shows that the relative efficiency of μ^* holds up (about 65% or better) as long as the sample median value remains known, no matter how many values below (or above) this one are missing. (For an even n, the relative efficiency is about 70% or better as long as the two middle values are uncensored.)

Thus, for $n = 10$, even if only the two values $x_{(5)}$ and $x_{(6)}$ are known, with the other eight missing ($r_1 = r_2 = 4$), the efficiency is still 72%. But if one of these midvalues, $x_{(6)}$, is lost, all the other values (to one side) $x_{(1)}, x_{(2)}, x_{(3)}, x_{(4)}, x_{(5)}$ (i.e., $r_1 = 0$, $r_2 = 5$) cannot make up for it. They produce an efficiency no better than 60%. In other words, "a single central value is worth more than half the sample in estimating the mean" [2].

This result was anticipated because the asymptotic efficiency of the median is $2/\pi = 63.7\%$.

Figure 10C.3 shows the relative efficiency of the best linear estimate of μ under all conditions of censoring a sample of size 20 from the normal distribution. Each one of the curves shows the efficiency of the estimate of the mean for a certain number of known elements $[k = n - (r_1 + r_2)]$ for all possible values of r_1 and r_2. The efficiency attains its maximum whenever the middle element is known.

Figure 10C.4 shows the relative efficiency of the best linear estimate of σ under all conditions of censoring a sample of 20 from the normal distribution. In this figure the graphs for $r_1 = 0, 1, \ldots, 17$ show a parallelism as r_1 changes. Thus, for any corresponding value of r_2 the efficiency decreases by about the same amount for each change in the value of r_1.

From Table 10C.3 we note that for a given n and fixed uncensored

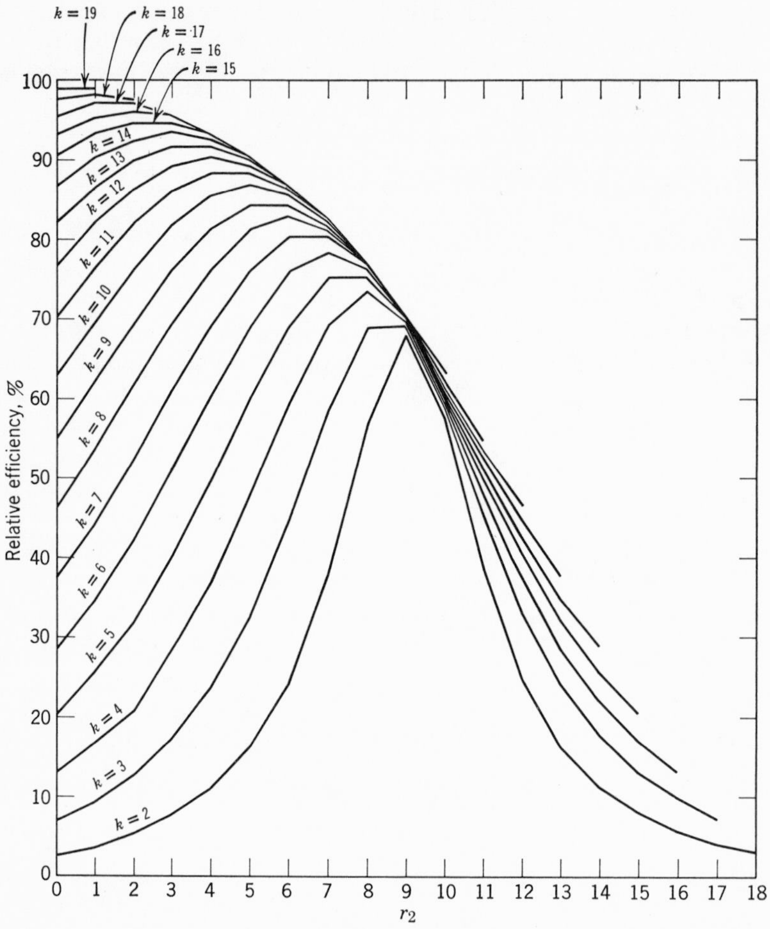

Fig. 10C.3 Relative efficiency of the best linear estimate of μ under all conditions of censoring a sample of size 20 from the normal distribution. Reproduced from A. E. Sarhan and B. G. Greenberg, "Estimation of location and scale parameters by order statistics from singly and doubly censored samples, Part II," Tech. Rep. 4, OOR Project 1597, 1958, with permission of the Commanding Officer, U.S. Army Research Office.

sample size ($r_1 + r_2 =$ constant), the efficiency of the best estimate of σ is remarkably constant independently of how r_1 and r_2 are chosen. In other words, there is practically no difference in efficiency whatever the proportion of the relative censoring from either side.

The constancy of the efficiency can be observed very clearly in Fig. 10C.4. The approximate horizontal lines show constancy of the relative efficiencies of σ^* for the known elements k of the sample whatever may be

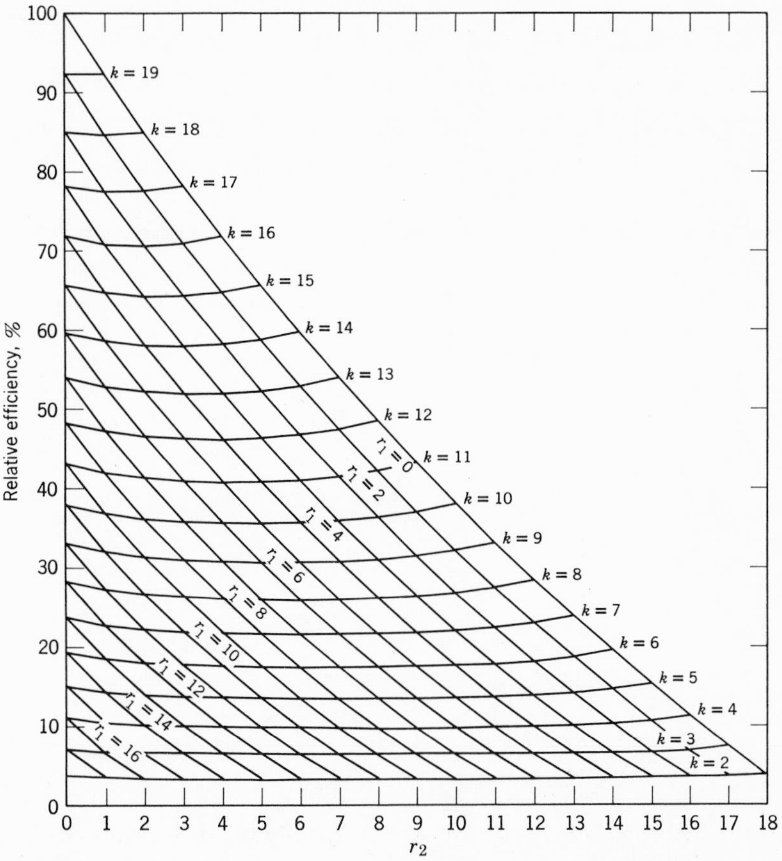

Fig. 10C.4 Relative efficiency of the best linear estimate of σ under all conditions of censoring a sample of size 20 from the normal distributions. Reproduced from A. E. Sarhan and B. G. Greenberg, "Estimation of location and scale parameters by order statistics from singly and doubly censored samples, Part II," Tech. Rep. 4, OOR Project 1597, 1958, with permission of the Commanding Officer, U.S. Army Research Office.

the individual values of r_1 and r_2. From Table 10C.3 (and graphs similar to Fig. 10C.4), Table B is constructed to show how the efficiency in estimating σ^* varies with the number of known values for each sample size to serve as a rough guide in censoring. This table is useful for practical work in censoring.

In estimating the standard deviation, hardly any censoring is tolerable even in the most favorable cases. Thus for $n = 20$, it can be seen from the table that for as few as two missing observations ($r_1 + r_2 = 2$), whether at the same or opposite ends of the sample, the efficiency barely

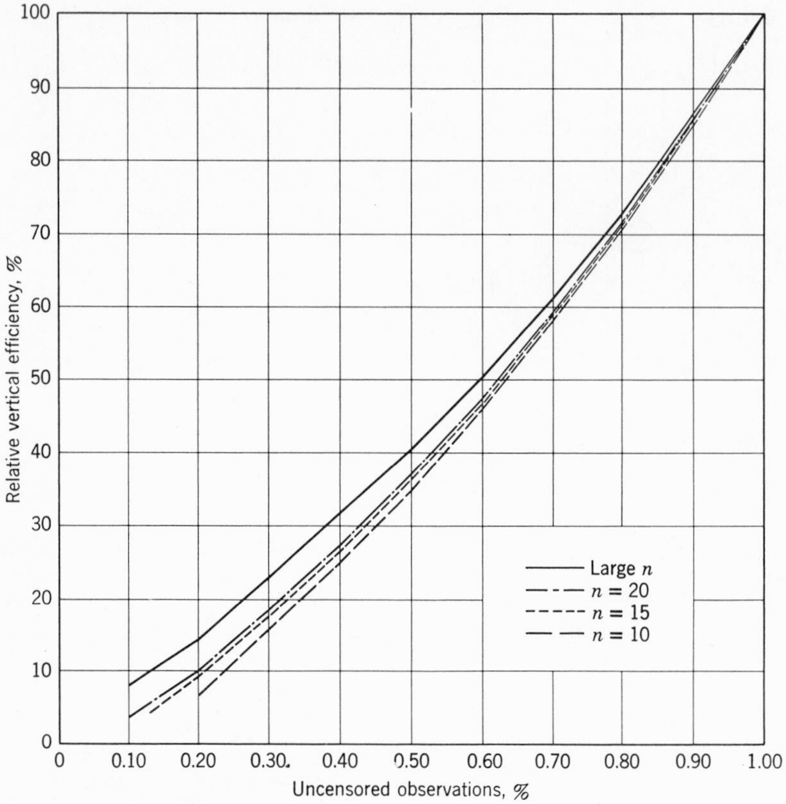

Fig. 10C.5 Approximate efficiencies in estimating σ^* for censored samples of size 10, 15, 20, and large n. Reproduced from A. E. Sarhan and B. G. Greenberg, "Estimation of location and scale parameters by order statistics from singly and doubly censored samples, Part II," *Ann. Math. Statist.*, Vol. 29, 1958, pp. 79–105, with permission of W. Kruskal, editor of the *Annals of Mathematical Statistics*.

attains 85%. For more missing elements the efficiency drops rapidly from a value under 78% to as little as 3%.

Figure 10C.5 gives the relative efficiency of the standard deviation with the proportion of uncensored sample elements for samples of size 10, 15, 20, and large n. Because the efficiency in estimation of the standard deviation depends primarily on the known number of elements rather than from which side the censoring occurred, graphs of $n = 10, 15, 20$ can be compared with that of large n obtained from Gupta [1] for singly censored samples.

TABLE B

ROUGH GUIDE FOR ASSESSING APPROXIMATE EFFICIENCY (PER CENT)* OF ESTIMATES OF σ

Sample Size	Number of Uncensored Observations in Sample, or $k = n - r_1 - r_2$																		
n	2	3	4	5	6	7	8	9	10	11	12	13	14	15	16	17	18	19	20
2	100																		
3	45	100																	
4	25	60	100																
5	20	40	70	100															
6	15	30	50	75	100														
7	11	25	40	60	75	100													
8	9	20	35	45	60	80	100												
9	8	17	30	40	50	65	80	100											
10	7	15	25	35	45	55	70	85	100										
11	6	13	21	30	39	50	61	73	86	100									
12	6	12	19	27	35	44	54	64	75	89	100								
13	5	11	17	24	31	39	48	57	67	77	88	100							
14	5	10	15	22	28	36	43	51	59	69	78	89	100						
15	4	9	14	20	26	32	39	46	54	62	71	80	90	100					
16	4	8	13	18	24	30	36	43	50	57	65	73	81	90	100				
17	4	8	12	17	22	27	33	39	46	52	59	66	74	82	91	100			
18	3	7	11	16	20	25	31	36	42	48	54	61	68	76	83	91	100		
19	3	7	11	16	19	24	29	34	39	45	50	57	63	70	77	84	92	100	
20	3	6	10	14	18	22	27	31	36	42	47	53	59	65	71	78	85	92	100

* These values are rounded averages of different combinations of censoring and are within 2 or 3% in almost all cases.

TABLE 10C.1

The Coefficients of the Best Linear Estimates of the Mean and Standard Deviation in Censored Samples up to Size 20 from a Normal Population

$n = 2$

$r_1 = 0$, r_2		$x_{(1)}$	$x_{(2)}$	$x_{(3)}$
0	μ^*	.5000	.5000	
	σ^*	−.8862	.8862	

$n = 3$

$r_1 = 0$, r_2		$x_{(1)}$	$x_{(2)}$	$x_{(3)}$
0	μ^*	.3333	.3333	.3333
	σ^*	−.5908	.0000	.5908
1	μ^*	.0000	1.0000	
	σ^*	−1.1816	1.1816	

$n = 4$

$r_1 = 0$, r_2		$x_{(1)}$	$x_{(2)}$	$x_{(3)}$	$x_{(4)}$		$r_1 = 1$, r_2
0	μ^*	.2500	.2500	.2500	.2500		
	σ^*	−.4539	−.1102	.1102	.4539		
1	μ^*	.1161	.2408	.6431			
	σ^*	−.6971	−.1268	.8239			
2	μ^*	−.4056	1.4056	.5000	.5000	μ^*	1
	σ^*	−1.3654	1.3654	1.6834	−1.6834	σ^*	
				$x_{(3)}$	$x_{(2)}$		

$n = 5$

$r_1 = 0$, r_2		$x_{(1)}$	$x_{(2)}$	$x_{(3)}$	$x_{(4)}$	$x_{(5)}$		$r_1 = 1$, r_2
0	μ^*	.2000	.2000	.2000	.2000	.2000		
	σ^*	−.3724	−.1352	.0000	.1352	.3724		
1	μ^*	.1252	.1830	.2147	.4771			
	σ^*	−.5117	−.1668	.0274	.6511			
2	μ^*	−.0638	.1498	.9139	1.0000	.0000	μ^*	2
	σ^*	−.7696	−.2121	.9817	2.0201	−2.0201	σ^*	
3	μ^*	−.7411	1.7411	.3893	.2214	.3893	μ^*	1
	σ^*	−1.4971	1.4971	1.0101	.0000	−1.0101	σ^*	
				$x_{(4)}$	$x_{(3)}$	$x_{(2)}$		

Up to $n = 15$ of this table is reproduced from A. E. Sarhan and B. G. Greenberg, "Estimation of location and scale parameters by order statistics from singly and doubly censored samples, Parts I and II," *Ann. Math. Statist.*, Vol. 27 (1956), pp. 427–451 and Vol. 29 (1958), pp. 79–105, with permission of W. Kruskal, editor of the *Annals of Mathematical Statistics*.

The rest of the table is reproduced from A. E. Sarhan and B. G. Greenberg, "Estimation of location and scale parameters by order statistics from singly and doubly censored samples, Part III, "Tech. Rep. 4, OOR Project 1597, with permission of the Commanding Officer, U.S. Army Research Office.

$n = 6$

$r_1 = 0$ r_2		$x_{(1)}$	$x_{(2)}$	$x_{(3)}$	$x_{(4)}$	$x_{(5)}$	$x_{(6)}$		$r_1 = 1$ r_2
0	μ^*	.1667	.1667	.1667	.1667	.1667	.1667		
	σ^*	−.3175	−.1386	−.0432	.0432	.1386	.3175		
1	μ^*	.1183	.1510	.1680	.1828	.3799			
	σ^*	−.4097	−.1685	−.0406	.0740	.5448			
2	μ^*	.0185	.1226	.1761	.6828	1.4578	−.4578	μ^*	3
	σ^*	−.5528	−.2091	−.0290	.7909	2.2717	−2.2717	σ^*	
3	μ^*	−.2159	.0649	1.1511	.6680	.1781	.1539	μ^*	2
	σ^*	−.8244	−.2760	1.1004	1.2317	−.0878	−1.1438	σ^*	
4	μ^*	−1.0261	2.0261	.3198	.1802	.1802	.3198	μ^*	1
	σ^*	−1.5988	1.5988	.7531	.0829	−.0829	−.7531	σ^*	
				$x_{(5)}$	$x_{(4)}$	$x_{(3)}$	$x_{(2)}$		

$n = 6$

$r_1 = 2$ r_2		$x_{(1)}$	$x_{(2)}$	$x_{(3)}$	$x_{(4)}$	$x_{(5)}$	$x_{(6)}$
2	μ^*			.5000	.5000		
	σ^*			−2.4808	2.4808		

$n = 7$

$r_1 = 0$ r_2		$x_{(1)}$	$x_{(2)}$	$x_{(3)}$	$x_{(4)}$	$x_{(5)}$	$x_{(6)}$	$x_{(7)}$		$r_1 = 1$ r_2
0	μ^*	.1429	.1429	.1429	.1429	.1429	.1429	.1429		
	σ^*	−.2778	−.1351	−.0625	.0000	.0625	.1351	.2778		
1	μ^*	.1088	.1295	.1400	.1487	.1571	.3159			
	σ^*	−.3440	−.1610	−.0681	.0114	.0901	.4716			
2	μ^*	.0465	.1072	.1375	.1626	.5462	1.8716	−.8716	μ^*	4
	σ^*	−.4370	−.1943	−.0718	.0321	.6709	2.4712	−2.4712	σ^*	
3	μ^*	−.0738	.0677	.1375	.8686	.9321	.1270	−.0592	μ^*	3
	σ^*	−.5848	−.2428	−.0717	.8994	1.4030	−.1548	−1.2483	σ^*	
4	μ^*	−.3474	−.0135	1.3609	.5186	.1634	.1432	.1748	μ^*	2
	σ^*	−.8682	−.3269	1.1951	.9298	.0248	−.1258	−.8288	σ^*	
5	μ^*	−1.2733	2.2733	.2718	.1520	.1524	.1520	.2718	μ^*	1
	σ^*	−1.6812	1.6812	.6108	.1061	.0000	−.1061	−.6108	σ^*	
				$x_{(6)}$	$x_{(5)}$	$x_{(4)}$	$x_{(3)}$	$x_{(2)}$		

$n = 7$

$r_1 = 2$ r_2		$x_{(1)}$	$x_{(2)}$	$x_{(3)}$	$x_{(4)}$	$x_{(5)}$	$x_{(6)}$	$x_{(7)}$
2	μ^*			.4157	.1686	.4157		
	σ^*			−1.4176	.0000	1.4176		
3	μ^*			.0000	1.0000			
	σ^*			−2.8352	2.8352			

$n = 8$

$r_1 = 0$, r_2		$x_{(1)}$	$x_{(2)}$	$x_{(3)}$	$x_{(4)}$	$x_{(5)}$	$x_{(6)}$	$x_{(7)}$	$x_{(8)}$		$r_1 = 1$, r_2
0	μ^*	.1250	.1250	.1250	.1250	.1250	.1250	.1250	.1250		
	σ^*	−.2476	−.1294	−.0713	−.0230	.0230	.0713	.1294	.2476		
1	μ^*	.0997	.1139	.1208	.1265	.1318	.1370	.2704			
	σ^*	−.2978	−.1515	−.0796	−.0200	.0364	.0951	.4175			
2	μ^*	.0569	.0962	.1153	.1309	.1451	.4555	2.2462	−1.2462	μ^*	5
	σ^*	−.3638	−.1788	−.0881	−.0132	.0570	.5868	2.6357	−2.6357	σ^*	
3	μ^*	−.0167	.0677	.1084	.1413	.6993	1.1778	.0741	−.2519	μ^*	4
	σ^*	−.4586	−.2156	−.0970	.0002	.7709	1.5423	−.2086	−1.3337	σ^*	
4	μ^*	−.1549	.0176	.1001	1.0372	.7102	.1406	.1061	.0431	μ^*	3
	σ^*	−.6110	−.2707	−.1061	.9878	1.0696	−.0197	−.1605	−.8894	σ^*	
5	μ^*	−.4632	−.0855	1.5487	.4282	.1442	.1338	.1222	.1716	μ^*	2
	σ^*	−.9045	−.3690	1.2735	.7615	.0630	−.0318	−.1319	−.6608	σ^*	
6	μ^*	−1.4915	2.4915	.2367	.1315	.1319	.1319	.1315	.2367	μ^*	1
	σ^*	−1.7502	1.7502	.5184	.1115	.0361	−.0361	−.1115	−.5184	σ^*	
				$x_{(7)}$	$x_{(6)}$	$x_{(5)}$	$x_{(4)}$	$x_{(3)}$	$x_{(2)}$		

$n = 8$

$r_1 = 2$, r_2		$x_{(1)}$	$x_{(2)}$	$x_{(3)}$	$x_{(4)}$	$x_{(5)}$	$x_{(6)}$		$r_1 = 3$, r_2
2	μ^*			.3569	.1431	.1431	.3569		
	σ^*			−1.0357	−.0674	.0674	1.0357		
3	μ^*			.1742	.1429	.6829			
	σ^*			−1.5661	−.0678	1.6338			
4	μ^*			−.4761	1.4761	.5000	.5000	μ^*	3
	σ^*			−3.1220	3.1220	3.2784	−3.2784	σ^*	
						$x_{(5)}$	$x_{(4)}$		

$n = 9$

$r_1 = 0$ r_2		$x_{(1)}$	$x_{(2)}$	$x_{(3)}$	$x_{(4)}$	$x_{(5)}$	$x_{(6)}$	$x_{(7)}$	$x_{(8)}$	$x_{(9)}$		$r_1 = 1$ r_2
0	μ^*	.1111	.1111	.1111	.1111	.1111	.1111	.1111	.1111	.1111		
	σ^*	−.2237	−.1233	−.0751	−.0360	.0000	.0360	.0751	.1233	.2237		
1	μ^*	.0915	.1018	.1067	.1106	.1142	.1177	.1212	.2365			
	σ^*	−.2633	−.1421	−.0841	−.0370	.0062	.0492	.0954	.3757			
2	μ^*	.0602	.0876	.1006	.1110	.1204	.1294	.3909	2.5874	−1.5874	μ^*	6
	σ^*	−.3129	−.1647	−.0938	−.0364	.0160	.0678	.5239	2.7753	−2.7753	σ^*	
3	μ^*	.0104	.0660	.0923	.1133	.1320	.5860	1.4054	.0218	−.4272	μ^*	5
	σ^*	−.3797	−.1936	−.1048	−.0333	.0317	.6797	1.6591	−.2534	−1.4057	σ^*	
4	μ^*	−.0731	.0316	.0809	.1199	.8408	.8916	.1153	.0699	−.0768	μ^*	4
	σ^*	−.4766	−.2335	−.1181	−.0256	.8537	1.1852	−.0558	−.1896	−.9399	σ^*	
5	μ^*	−.2272	−.0284	.0644	1.1912	.5804	.1321	.1140	.0936	.0799	μ^*	3
	σ^*	−.6330	−.2944	−.1348	1.0622	.8828	.0299	−.0578	−.1535	−.7015	σ^*	
6	μ^*	−.5664	−.1521	1.7185	.3663	.1275	.1214	.1148	.1074	.1626	μ^*	2
	σ^*	−.9355	−.4047	1.3402	.6514	.0775	.0109	−.0563	−.1291	−.5544	σ^*	
7	μ^*	−1.6868	2.6868	.2097	.1159	.1162	.1163	.1162	.1159	.2097	μ^*	1
	σ^*	−1.8092	1.8092	.4527	.1107	.0532	.0000	−.0532	−.1107	−.4527	σ^*	
				$x_{(8)}$	$x_{(7)}$	$x_{(6)}$	$x_{(5)}$	$x_{(4)}$	$x_{(3)}$	$x_{(2)}$		

$n = 9$

$r_1 = 2$ r_2		$x_{(1)}$	$x_{(2)}$	$x_{(3)}$	$x_{(4)}$	$x_{(5)}$	$x_{(6)}$	$x_{(7)}$		$r_1 = 3$ r_2
2	μ^*			.3134	.1243	.1246	.1243	.3134		
	σ^*			−.8317	−.0885	.0000	.0885	.8317		
3	μ^*			.2040	.1191	.1330	.5440			
	σ^*			−1.1222	−.1023	.0223	1.2022			
4	μ^*			−.0527	.1098	.9429	1.0000	.0000	μ^*	4
	σ^*			−1.6894	−.1227	1.8122	3.6426	−3.6426	σ^*	
5	μ^*			−.9229	1.9229	.4315	.1370	.4315	μ^*	3
	σ^*			−3.3620	3.3620	1.8213	.0000	−1.8213	σ^*	
						$x_{(6)}$	$x_{(5)}$	$x_{(4)}$		

$n = 10$

$r_1 = 0$, r_2		$x_{(1)}$	$x_{(2)}$	$x_{(3)}$	$x_{(4)}$	$x_{(5)}$	$x_{(6)}$	$x_{(7)}$	$x_{(8)}$	$x_{(9)}$	$x_{(10)}$		$r_1 = 1$, r_2
0	μ^*	.1000	.1000	.1000	.1000	.1000	.1000	.1000	.1000	.1000	.1000		
	σ^*	−.2044	−.1172	−.0763	−.0436	−.0142	.0142	.0436	.0763	.1172	.2044		
1	μ^*	.0843	.0921	.0957	.0986	.1011	.1036	.1060	.1085	.2101			
	σ^*	−.2364	−.1334	−.0851	−.0465	−.0119	.0215	.0559	.0937	.3423			
2	μ^*	.0605	.0804	.0898	.0972	.1037	.1099	.1161	.3424	2.9000	−1.9000	μ^*	7
	σ^*	−.2753	−.1523	−.0947	−.0488	−.0077	.0319	.0722	.4746	2.8960	−2.8960	σ^*	
3	μ^*	.0244	.0636	.0818	.0962	.1089	.1207	.5045	1.6166	−.0289	−.5877	μ^*	6
	σ^*	−.3252	−.1758	−.1058	−.0502	−.0006	.0469	.6107	1.7595	−.2918	−1.4678	σ^*	
4	μ^*	−.0316	.0383	.0707	.0962	.1185	.7078	1.0623	.0892	.0351	−.1866	μ^*	5
	σ^*	−.3930	−.2063	−.1192	−.0501	.0111	.7576	1.2835	−.0859	−.2145	−.9831	σ^*	
5	μ^*	−.1240	−.0016	.0549	.0990	.9718	.7261	.1179	.0938	.0665	−.0043	μ^*	4
	σ^*	−.4919	−.2491	−.1362	−.0472	.9243	.9844	.0031	−.0797	−.1719	−.7359	σ^*	
6	μ^*	−.2923	−.0709	.0305	1.3327	.4933	.1204	.1095	.0979	.0846	.0942	μ^*	3
	σ^*	−.6520	−.3150	−.1593	1.1263	.7599	.0514	−.0097	−.0734	−.1440	−.5842	σ^*	
7	μ^*	−.6596	−.2138	1.8734	.3209	.1138	.1098	.1057	.1013	.0961	.1525	μ^*	2
	σ^*	−.9625	−.4357	1.3981	.5726	.0827	.0325	−.0166	−.0674	−.1235	−.4803	σ^*	
8	μ^*	−1.8634	2.8634	.1884	.1036	.1040	.1041	.1041	.1040	.1036	.1884	μ^*	1
	σ^*	−1.8608	1.8608	.4034	.1074	.0616	.0201	−.0201	−.0616	−.1074	−.4034	σ^*	
				$x_{(9)}$	$x_{(8)}$	$x_{(7)}$	$x_{(6)}$	$x_{(5)}$	$x_{(4)}$	$x_{(3)}$	$x_{(2)}$		

$n = 10$

$r_1 = 2$ r_2		$x_{(1)}$	$x_{(2)}$	$x_{(3)}$	$x_{(4)}$	$x_{(5)}$	$x_{(6)}$	$x_{(7)}$	$x_{(8)}$		$r_1 = 3$ r_2
2	μ^*			.2798	.1099	.1103	.1103	.1099	.2798		
	σ^*			−.7021	−.0947	−.0310	.0310	.0947	.7021		
3	μ^*			.2050	.1038	.1122	.1198	.4592			
	σ^*			−.8898	−.1101	−.0262	.0549	.9711			
4	μ^*			.0606	.0935	.1178	.7281	1.4847	−.4847	μ^*	5
	σ^*			−1.1952	−.1318	−.0144	1.3415	3.9511	−3.9511	σ^*	
5	μ^*			−.2648	.0735	1.1914	.6930	.1198	.1871	μ^*	4
	σ^*			−1.7947	−.1688	1.9635	2.0344	−.0553	−1.9791	σ^*	
6	μ^*			−1.3406	2.3406	.3807	.1193	.1193	.3807	μ^*	3
	σ^*			−3.5677	3.5677	1.2832	.0559	−.0559	−1.2832	σ^*	
						$x_{(7)}$	$x_{(6)}$	$x_{(5)}$	$x_{(4)}$		

$n = 10$

$r_1 = 4$ r_1		$x_{(1)}$	$x_{(2)}$	$x_{(3)}$	$x_{(4)}$	$x_{(5)}$	$x_{(6)}$	$x_{(7)}$
4	μ^*					.5000	.5000	
	σ^*					−4.0761	4.0761	

$n = 11$

$r_1 = 0$ r_2		$x_{(1)}$	$x_{(2)}$	$x_{(3)}$	$x_{(4)}$	$x_{(5)}$	$x_{(6)}$	$x_{(7)}$	$x_{(8)}$	$x_{(9)}$	$x_{(10)}$	$x_{(11)}$		$r_1 = 1$ r_2
0	μ^*	.0909	.0909	.0909	.0909	.0909	.0909	.0909	.0909	.0909	.0909	.0909		
	σ^*	−.1883	−.1115	−.0760	−.0481	−.0234	.0000	.0234	.0481	.0760	.1115	.1883		
1	μ^*	.0781	.0841	.0869	.0891	.0910	.0928	.0945	.0963	.0982	.1891			
	σ^*	−.2149	−.1256	−.0843	−.0519	−.0233	.0038	.0309	.0593	.0911	.3149			
2	μ^*	.0592	.0744	.0814	.0869	.0917	.0962	.1005	.1049	.3047	3.1882	−2.1882	μ^*	8
	σ^*	−.2463	−.1417	−.0934	−.0555	−.0220	.0095	.0409	.0736	.4349	3.0023	−3.0023	σ^*	
3	μ^*	.0320	.0609	.0741	.0845	.0935	.1020	.1101	.4430	1.8131	−.0776	−.7355	μ^*	7
	σ^*	−.2852	−.1610	−.1038	−.0589	−.0194	.0178	.0545	.5562	1.8473	−.3251	−1.5222	σ^*	
4	μ^*	−.0082	.0415	.0642	.0820	.0974	.1116	.6116	1.2227	.0631	.0019	−.2877	μ^*	6
	σ^*	−.3357	−.1854	−.1163	−.0621	−.0146	.0299	.6842	1.3689	−.1119	−.2362	−1.0208	σ^*	
5	μ^*	−.0698	.0128	.0504	.0797	.1049	.8220	.8646	.1026	.0738	.0407	−.0818	μ^*	5
	σ^*	−.4045	−.2175	−.1317	−.0647	−.0061	.8246	1.0717	−.0195	−.0985	−.1881	−.7656	σ^*	
6	μ^*	−.1702	−.0323	.0303	.0786	1.0937	.6157	.1116	.0971	.0813	.0632	.0311	μ^*	4
	σ^*	−.5053	−.2627	−.1519	−.0657	.9857	.8517	.0301	−.0272	−.0882	−.1569	−.6095	σ^*	
7	μ^*	−.3516	−.1104	−.0016	1.4636	.4301	.1093	.1022	.0948	.0868	.0776	.0992	μ^*	3
	σ^*	−.6687	−.3331	−.1807	1.1825	.6715	.0611	.0154	−.0307	−.0796	−.1345	−.5032	σ^*	
8	μ^*	−.7445	−.2712	2.0157	.2859	.1025	.0998	.0970	.0941	.0909	.0872	.1426	μ^*	2
	σ^*	−.9862	−.4630	1.4492	.5130	.0836	.0440	.0061	−.0320	−.0722	−.1173	−.4252	σ^*	
9	μ^*	−2.0245	3.0245	.1710	.0938	.0940	.0941	.0942	.0941	.0940	.0938	.1710	μ^*	1
	σ^*	−1.9065	1.9065	.3647	.1033	.0656	.0320	.0000	−.0320	−.0656	−.1033	−.3647	σ^*	
				$x_{(10)}$	$x_{(9)}$	$x_{(8)}$	$x_{(7)}$	$x_{(6)}$	$x_{(5)}$	$x_{(4)}$	$x_{(3)}$	$x_{(2)}$		

$n = 11$

$r_1 = 2$ r_2		$x_{(3)}$	$x_{(4)}$	$x_{(5)}$	$x_{(6)}$	$x_{(7)}$	$x_{(8)}$	$x_{(9)}$		$r_1 = 3$ r_2
2	μ^*	.2529	.0986	.0990	.0990	.0990	.0986	.2529		
	σ^*	−.6113	−.0952	−.0465	.0000	.0465	.0952	.6113		
3	μ^*	.1978	.0927	.0983	.1032	.1079	.4001			
	σ^*	−.7445	−.1095	−.0482	.0102	.0682	.8239			
4	μ^*	.1031	.0834	.0981	.1117	.6036	1.9486	−.9486	μ^*	6
	σ^*	−.9395	−.1287	−.0484	.0276	1.0890	4.2179	−4.2179	σ^*	
5	μ^*	−.0736	.0675	.0999	.9062	.9504	.0966	−.0470	μ^*	5
	σ^*	−1.2584	−.1573	−.0453	1.4610	2.2169	−.1019	−2.1150	σ^*	
6	μ^*	−.4631	.0359	1.4273	.5616	.1125	.1024	.2235	μ^*	4
	σ^*	−1.8863	−.2083	2.0946	1.4723	.0202	−.0867	−1.4057	σ^*	
7	μ^*	−1.7312	2.7312	.3413	.1057	.1059	.1057	.3413	μ^*	3
	σ^*	−3.7473	3.7473	1.0451	.0764	.0000	−.0764	−1.0451	σ^*	
				$x_{(8)}$	$x_{(7)}$	$x_{(6)}$	$x_{(5)}$	$x_{(4)}$		

$n = 11$

$r_1 = 4$ r_2		$x_{(5)}$	$x_{(6)}$	$x_{(7)}$
4	μ^*	.4421	.1157	.4421
	σ^*	−2.2233	.0000	2.2233
5	μ^*	.0000	1.0000	
	σ^*	−4.4466	4.4466	

$n = 12$

$r_1 = 0$ r_2		$x_{(1)}$	$x_{(2)}$	$x_{(3)}$	$x_{(4)}$	$x_{(5)}$	$x_{(6)}$	$x_{(7)}$	$x_{(8)}$	$x_{(9)}$	$x_{(10)}$	$x_{(11)}$	$x_{(12)}$		$r_1 = 0$ r_2
0	μ^*	.0833	.0833	.0833	.0833	.0833	.0833	.0833	.0833	.0833	.0833	.0833	.0833		
	σ^*	−.1748	−.1061	−.0749	−.0506	−.0294	−.0097	.0097	.0294	.0506	.0749	.1061	.1748		
1	μ^*	.0726	.0775	.0796	.0813	.0828	.0842	.0855	.0868	.0882	.0896	.1719			
	σ^*	−.1972	−.1185	−.0827	−.0548	−.0305	−.0079	.0142	.0367	.0608	.0881	.2919			
2	μ^*	.0574	.0693	.0747	.0789	.0825	.0859	.0891	.0923	.0956	.2745	3.4554	−2.4554	μ^*	9
	σ^*	−.2232	−.1324	−.0911	−.0590	−.0310	−.0050	.0203	.0461	.0733	.4020	3.0970	−3.0970	σ^*	
3	μ^*	.0360	.0581	.0682	.0759	.0827	.0888	.0948	.1006	.3950	1.9966	−.1242	−.8725	μ^*	8
	σ^*	−.2545	−.1487	−.1007	−.0633	−.0308	−.0007	.0286	.0582	.5119	1.9252	−.3546	−1.5706	σ^*	
4	μ^*	.0057	.0428	.0595	.0724	.0836	.0938	.1036	.5386	1.3737	.0373	−.0298	−.3812	μ^*	7
	σ^*	−.2937	−.1686	−.1119	−.0678	−.0296	.0058	.0400	.6259	1.4442	−.1345	−.2554	−1.0542	σ^*	
5	μ^*	−.0382	.0210	.0477	.0684	.0861	.1022	.7128	.9961	.0870	.0542	.0162	−.1536	μ^*	6
	σ^*	−.3448	−.1939	−.1255	−.0726	−.0267	.0155	.7479	1.1482	−.0390	−.1151	−.2024	−.7918	σ^*	
6	μ^*	−.1048	−.0109	.0313	.0637	.0915	.9292	.7331	.1018	.0844	.0652	.0430	−.0275	μ^*	5
	σ^*	−.4146	−.2274	−.1428	−.0774	−.0210	.8833	.9313	.0121	−.0423	−.1011	−.1684	−.6316	σ^*	
7	μ^*	−.2125	−.0609	.0070	.0589	1.2075	.5361	.1035	.0939	.0839	.0729	.0601	.0496	μ^*	4
	σ^*	−.5171	−.2749	−.1659	−.0820	1.0399	.7559	.0435	.0009	−.0430	−.0903	−.1442	−.5228	σ^*	
8	μ^*	−.4059	−.1472	−.0321	1.5852	.3819	.0996	.0946	.0896	.0843	.0785	.0717	.0998	μ^*	3
	σ^*	−.6836	−.3493	−.1996	1.2324	.6042	.0654	.0295	−.0059	−.0423	−.0814	−.1259	−.4435	σ^*	
9	μ^*	−.8225	−.3249	2.1474	.2580	.0932	.0912	.0892	.0872	.0851	.0827	.0798	.1336	μ^*	2
	σ^*	−1.0075	−.4874	1.4948	.4660	.0827	.0503	.0198	−.0102	−.0410	−.0738	−.1112	−.3825	σ^*	
10	μ^*	−2.1728	3.1728	.1566	.0856	.0858	.0859	.0860	.0860	.0859	.0858	.0856	.1566	μ^*	1
	σ^*	−1.9474	1.9474	.3334	.0989	.0671	.0391	.0128	−.0128	−.0391	−.0671	−.0989	−.3334	σ^*	
				$x_{(11)}$	$x_{(10)}$	$x_{(9)}$	$x_{(8)}$	$x_{(7)}$	$x_{(6)}$	$x_{(5)}$	$x_{(4)}$	$x_{(3)}$	$x_{(2)}$		

$n = 12$

$r_1 = 2$ r_2		$x_{(3)}$	$x_{(4)}$	$x_{(5)}$	$x_{(6)}$	$x_{(7)}$	$x_{(8)}$	$x_{(9)}$	$x_{(10)}$		$r_1 = 3$ r_2
2	μ^*	.2309	.0895	.0898	.0899	.0899	.0898	.0895	.2309		
	σ^*	−.5437	−.0933	−.0545	−.0179	.0179	.0545	.0933	.5437		
3	μ^*	.1883	.0840	.0880	.0914	.0947	.0978	.3558			
	σ^*	−.6440	−.1061	−.0587	−.0142	.0292	.0733	.7204			
4	μ^*	.1206	.0759	.0858	.0947	.1032	.5197	2.3903	−1.3903	μ^*	7.
	σ^*	−.7811	−.1225	−.0631	−.0076	.0465	.9278	4.4525	−4.4525	σ^*	
5	μ^*	.0076	.0633	.0832	.1015	.7444	1.2001	.0699	−.2700	μ^*	6
	σ^*	−.9829	−.1451	−.0676	.0045	1.1911	2.3763	−.1421	−2.2342	σ^*	
6	μ^*	−.1993	.0417	.0806	1.0771	.7412	.1016	.0836	.0736	μ^*	5
	σ^*	−1.3139	−.1796	−.0719	1.5654	1.6109	−.0111	−.1124	−1.4874	σ^*	
7	μ^*	−.6489	−.0018	1.6507	.4812	.1029	.0970	.0907	.2282	μ^*	4
	σ^*	−1.9673	−.2429	2.2102	1.1775	.0488	−.0223	−.0950	−1.1090	σ^*	
8	μ^*	−2.0971	3.0971	.3097	.0950	.0953	.0953	.0950	.3097	μ^*	3
	σ^*	−3.9063	3.9063	.8780	.0828	.0273	−.0273	−.0828	−.8780	σ^*	
				$x_{(9)}$	$x_{(8)}$	$x_{(7)}$	$x_{(6)}$	$x_{(5)}$	$x_{(4)}$		

$n = 12$

$r_1 = 4$ r_2		$x_{(5)}$	$x_{(6)}$	$x_{(7)}$	$x_{(8)}$		$r_1 = 5$ r_2
4	μ^*	.3973	.1027	.1027	.3973		
	σ^*	−1.5849	−.0497	.0497	1.5849		
5	μ^*	.1962	.1034	.7004			
	σ^*	−2.3874	−.0468	2.4342			
6	μ^*	−.4893	1.4893	.5000	.5000	μ^*	5
	σ^*	−4.7696	4.7696	4.8738	−4.8738	σ^*	
				$x_{(7)}$	$x_{(6)}$		

$n = 13$

$r_1 = 0$ r_2		$x_{(1)}$	$x_{(2)}$	$x_{(3)}$	$x_{(4)}$	$x_{(5)}$	$x_{(6)}$	$x_{(7)}$	$x_{(8)}$	$x_{(9)}$	$x_{(10)}$	$x_{(11)}$	$x_{(12)}$	$x_{(13)}$		$r_1 = 1$ r_2
0	μ^*	.0769	.0769	.0769	.0769	.0769	.0769	.0769	.0769	.0769	.0769	.0769	.0769	.0769		
	σ^*	−.1632	−.1013	−.0735	−.0520	−.0335	−.0164	.0000	.0164	.0335	.0520	.0735	.1013	.1632		
1	μ^*	.0679	.0718	.0735	.0749	.0761	.0771	.0781	.0792	.0802	.0813	.0824	.1576			
	σ^*	−.1824	−.1122	−.0806	−.0563	−.0353	−.0160	.0026	.0212	.0404	.0612	.0850	.2724			
2	μ^*	.0552	.0648	.0691	.0724	.0752	.0778	.0803	.0827	.0852	.0877	.2497	3.7044	−2.7044	μ^*	10
	σ^*	−.2043	−.1243	−.0884	−.0607	−.0368	−.0148	.0063	.0273	.0490	.0723	.3743	3.1823	−3.1823	σ^*	
3	μ^*	.0380	.0555	.0633	.0693	.0745	.0792	.0836	.0880	.0924	.3564	2.1686	−.1687	−.9999	μ^*	9
	σ^*	−.2301	−.1382	−.0970	−.0653	−.0379	−.0128	.0113	.0352	.0598	.4750	1.9951	−.3810	−1.6141	σ^*	
4	μ^*	.0144	.0430	.0557	.0655	.0739	.0816	.0888	.0958	.4813	1.5160	.0123	−.0600	−.4683	μ^*	8
	σ^*	−.2616	−.1549	−.1071	−.0703	−.0386	−.0095	.0182	.0456	.5781	1.5114	−.1546	−.2727	−1.0841	σ^*	
5	μ^*	−.0185	.0259	.0457	.0610	.0740	.0857	.0968	.6294	1.1209	.0712	.0352	−.0070	−.2203	μ^*	7
	σ^*	−.3011	−.1754	−.1191	−.0758	−.0386	−.0046	.0278	.6867	1.2161	−.0561	−.1298	−.2151	−.8151	σ^*	
6	μ^*	−.0659	.0020	.0322	.0553	.0750	.0928	.8085	.8453	.0916	.0716	.0496	.0239	−.0820	μ^*	6
	σ^*	−.3528	−.2015	−.1339	−.0819	−.0374	.0032	.8042	1.0015	−.0034	−.0556	−.1127	−.1786	−.6512	σ^*	
7	μ^*	−.1371	−.0330	.0132	.0484	.0784	1.0301	.6382	.0969	.0853	.0730	.0595	.0437	.0035	μ^*	5
	σ^*	−.4236	−.2363	−.1528	−.0888	−.0341	.9355	.8296	.0287	−.0116	−.0538	−.0998	−.1528	−.5401	σ^*	
8	μ^*	−.2516	−.0876	−.0151	.0400	1.3143	.4755	.0955	.0889	.0820	.0746	.0666	.0572	.0597	μ^*	4
	σ^*	−.5276	−.2859	−.1785	−.0964	1.0884	.6826	.0505	.0172	−.0164	−.0515	−.0896	−.1335	−.4594	σ^*	
9	μ^*	−.4561	−.1817	−.0610	1.6988	.3439	.0912	.0876	.0840	.0802	.0763	.0719	.0668	.0983	μ^*	3
	σ^*	−.6969	−.3638	−.2165	1.2773	.5509	.0669	.0377	.0093	−.0192	−.0489	−.0811	−.1181	−.3976	σ^*	
10	μ^*	−.8946	−.3753	2.2699	.2353	.0853	.0839	.0824	.0809	.0794	.0778	.0759	.0737	.1254	μ^*	2
	σ^*	−1.0266	−.5094	1.5360	.4278	.0808	.0536	.0283	.0039	−.0207	−.0462	−.0738	−.1055	−.3483	σ^*	
11	μ^*	−2.3101	3.3101	.1445	.0788	.0790	.0791	.0791	.0791	.0791	.0791	.0790	.0788	.1445	μ^*	1
	σ^*	−1.9845	1.9845	.3076	.0947	.0673	.0434	.0213	.0000	−.0213	−.0434	−.0673	−.0947	−.3076	σ^*	
				$x_{(12)}$	$x_{(11)}$	$x_{(10)}$	$x_{(9)}$	$x_{(8)}$	$x_{(7)}$	$x_{(6)}$	$x_{(5)}$	$x_{(4)}$	$x_{(3)}$	$x_{(2)}$		

$n = 13$

$r_1 = 2$, r_2		$x_{(3)}$	$x_{(4)}$	$x_{(5)}$	$x_{(6)}$	$x_{(7)}$	$x_{(8)}$	$x_{(9)}$	$x_{(10)}$	$x_{(11)}$		$r_1 = 3$, r_2
2	μ^*	.2125	.0819	.0822	.0823	.0823	.0823	.0822	.0819	.2125		
	σ^*	−.4911	−.0904	−.0584	−.0287	.0000	.0287	.0584	.0904	.4911		
3	μ^*	.1784	.0770	.0799	.0825	.0848	.0871	.0892	.3211			
	σ^*	−.5698	−.1017	−.0636	−.0283	.0058	.0398	.0748	.6431			
4	μ^*	.1272	.0700	.0770	.0833	.0892	.0949	.4584	2.8102	−1.8102	μ^*	8
	σ^*	−.6724	−.1157	−.0695	−.0266	.0146	.0555	.8142	4.6615	−4.6615	σ^*	
5	μ^*	.0479	.0597	.0732	.0854	.0969	.6370	1.4405	.0415	−.4820	μ^*	7
	σ^*	−.8133	−.1341	−.0763	−.0229	.0282	1.0184	2.5175	−.1774	−2.3402	σ^*	
6	μ^*	−.0822	.0437	.0680	.0901	.8805	.9169	.0883	.0639	−.0691	μ^*	6
	σ^*	−1.0214	−.1597	−.0846	−.0154	1.2810	1.7328	−.0380	−.1350	−1.5598	σ^*	
7	μ^*	−.3174	.0164	.0607	1.2404	.6209	.0970	.0865	.0752	.1204	μ^*	5
	σ^*	−1.3635	−.1994	−.0952	1.6581	1.2929	.0255	−.0417	−.1115	−1.1652	σ^*	
8	μ^*	−.8233	−.0391	1.8624	.4246	.0939	.0902	.0862	.0820	.2231	μ^*	4
	σ^*	−2.0397	−.2735	2.3132	.9927	.0610	.0095	−.0423	−.0958	−.9251	σ^*	
9	μ^*	−2.4408	3.4408	.2838	.0863	.0866	.0866	.0866	.0863	.2838	μ^*	3
	σ^*	−4.0488	4.0488	.7622	.0841	.0414	.0000	−.0414	−.0841	−.7622	σ^*	
				$x_{(10)}$	$x_{(9)}$	$x_{(8)}$	$x_{(7)}$	$x_{(6)}$	$x_{(5)}$	$x_{(4)}$		

$n = 13$

$r_1 = 4$, r_2		$x_{(5)}$	$x_{(6)}$	$x_{(7)}$	$x_{(8)}$	$x_{(9)}$		$r_1 = 5$, r_2
4	μ^*	.3615	.0923	.0924	.0923	.3615		
	σ^*	−1.2545	−.0674	.0000	.0674	1.2545		
5	μ^*	.2377	.0900	.0977	.5745			
	σ^*	−1.6839	−.0755	.0184	1.7410			
6	μ^*	−.0422	.0861	.9562	1.0000	.0000	μ^*	6
	σ^*	−2.5323	−.0873	2.6196	5.2487	−5.2487	σ^*	
7	μ^*	−.9632	1.9632	.4498	.1003	.4498	μ^*	5
	σ^*	−5.0555	5.0555	2.6243	.0000	−2.6243	σ^*	
				$x_{(8)}$	$x_{(7)}$	$x_{(6)}$		

$n = 14$

$r_1 = 0$ r_2		$x_{(1)}$	$x_{(2)}$	$x_{(3)}$	$x_{(4)}$	$x_{(5)}$	$x_{(6)}$	$x_{(7)}$	$x_{(8)}$	$x_{(9)}$	$x_{(10)}$	$x_{(11)}$	$x_{(12)}$	$x_{(13)}$	$x_{(14)}$		$r_1 = 1$ r_2
0	μ^*	.0714	.0714	.0714	.0714	.0714	.0714	.0714	.0714	.0714	.0714	.0714	.0714	.0714	.0714		
	σ^*	−.1532	−.0968	−.0717	−.0526	−.0362	−.0212	−.0070	.0070	.0212	.0362	.0526	.0717	.0968	.1532		
1	μ^*	.0637	.0669	.0683	.0694	.0704	.0712	.0721	.0728	.0736	.0745	.0753	.0762	.1455			
	σ^*	−.1698	−.1065	−.0784	−.0568	−.0384	−.0216	−.0056	.0100	.0259	.0426	.0609	.0820	.2556			
2	μ^*	.0530	.0609	.0643	.0670	.0692	.0713	.0732	.0751	.0770	.0789	.0809	.2291	3.9374	−2.9374	μ^*	11
	σ^*	−.1885	−.1171	−.0854	−.0612	−.0404	−.0215	−.0036	.0140	.0319	.0505	.0707	.3506	3.2597	−3.2597	σ^*	
3	μ^*	.0388	.0529	.0592	.0639	.0680	.0717	.0752	.0785	.0819	.0852	.3247	2.3304	−.2112	−1.1191	μ^*	10
	σ^*	−.2102	−.1292	−.0933	−.0658	−.0423	−.0209	−.0006	.0192	.0393	.0601	.4438	2.0584	−.4048	−1.6536	σ^*	
4	μ^*	.0199	.0426	.0526	.0602	.0667	.0726	.0782	.0835	.0887	.4350	1.6505	−.0121	−.0888	−.5496	μ^*	9
	σ^*	−.2361	−.1434	−.1023	−.0709	−.0440	−.0196	.0035	.0260	.0487	.5382	1.5721	−.1726	−.2882	−1.1112	σ^*	
5	μ^*	−.0057	.0288	.0440	.0557	.0655	.0744	.0828	.0908	.5637	1.2394	.0556	.0167	−.0291	−.2827	μ^*	8
	σ^*	−.2678	−.1604	−.1129	−.0765	−.0455	−.0174	.0092	.0350	.6363	1.2771	−.0713	−.1430	−.2267	−.8362	σ^*	
6	μ^*	−.0411	.0102	.0328	.0500	.0646	.0777	.0899	.7159	.9525	.0811	.0591	.0345	.0057	−.1329	μ^*	7
	σ^*	−.3077	−.1815	−.1256	−.0829	−.0466	−.0137	.0172	.7407	1.0642	−.0171	−.0675	−.1231	−.1878	−.6688	σ^*	
7	μ^*	−.0915	−.0158	.0175	.0429	.0643	.0835	.8992	.7365	.0897	.0765	.0623	.0466	.0281	−.0397	μ^*	6
	σ^*	−.3599	−.2084	−.1414	−.0903	−.0469	−.0077	.8546	.8949	.0158	−.0227	−.0635	−.1084	−.1606	−.5555	σ^*	
8	μ^*	−.1670	−.0537	−.0040	.0338	.0655	1.1255	.5661	.0908	.0827	.0743	.0652	.0552	.0435	.0222	μ^*	5
	σ^*	−.4317	−.2444	−.1618	−.0990	−.0457	.9825	.7515	.0379	.0065	−.0256	−.0596	−.0970	−.1402	−.4734	σ^*	
9	μ^*	−.2879	−.1127	−.0360	.0218	1.4148	.4277	.0883	.0834	.0784	.0733	.0677	.0616	.0544	.0651	μ^*	4
	σ^*	−.5372	−.2959	−.1898	−.1094	1.1322	.6244	.0540	.0270	.0003	−.0271	−.0560	−.0876	−.1242	−.4107	σ^*	
10	μ^*	−.5027	−.2142	−.0886	1.8054	.3129	.0840	.0812	.0785	.0758	.0729	.0699	.0665	.0625	.0957	μ^*	3
	σ^*	−.7091	−.3771	−.2318	1.3180	.5075	.0669	.0426	.0191	−.0040	−.0276	−.0525	−.0797	−.1112	−.3610	σ^*	
11	μ^*	−.9616	−.4228	2.3843	.2163	.0787	.0776	.0765	.0753	.0742	.0730	.0717	.0703	.0685	.1180	μ^*	2
	σ^*	−1.0441	−.5293	1.5734	.3961	.0785	.0552	.0338	.0133	−.0070	−.0275	−.0492	−.0728	−.1002	−.3203	σ^*	
12	μ^*	−2.4378	3.4378	.1341	.0730	.0731	.0732	.0733	.0733	.0733	.0733	.0732	.0731	.0730	.1341	μ^*	1
	σ^*	−2.0182	2.0182	.2858	.0907	.0667	.0459	.0270	.0089	−.0089	−.0270	−.0459	−.0667	−.0907	−.2858	σ^*	
				$x_{(13)}$	$x_{(12)}$	$x_{(11)}$	$x_{(10)}$	$x_{(9)}$	$x_{(8)}$	$x_{(7)}$	$x_{(6)}$	$x_{(5)}$	$x_{(4)}$	$x_{(3)}$	$x_{(2)}$		

$n = 14$

$r_1 = 2$, r_2		$x_{(3)}$	$x_{(4)}$	$x_{(5)}$	$x_{(6)}$	$x_{(7)}$	$x_{(8)}$	$x_{(9)}$	$x_{(10)}$	$x_{(11)}$	$x_{(12)}$		$r_1 = 3$, r_2
2	μ^*	.1969	.0755	.0758	.0759	.0759	.0759	.0759	.0758	.0755	.1969		
	σ^*	−.4488	−.0872	−.0602	−.0354	−.0117	.0017	.0354	.0602	.0872	.4488		
3	μ^*	.1689	.0711	.0734	.0753	.0771	.0788	.0804	.0820	.2930			
	σ^*	−.5125	−.0972	−.0656	−.0367	−.0090	.0182	.0457	.0744	.5827			
4	μ^*	.1287	.0651	.0703	.0749	.0792	.0834	.0874	.4111	3.2094	−2.2094	μ^*	9
	σ^*	−.5926	−.1092	−.0718	−.0375	−.0048	.0273	.0596	.7291	4.8497	−4.8497	σ^*	
5	μ^*	.0695	.0565	.0661	.0748	.0829	.0907	.5593	1.6712	.0123	−.6835	μ^*	8
	σ^*	−.6975	−.1244	−.0791	−.0376	.0018	.0403	.8965	2.6442	−.2087	−2.4355	σ^*	
6	μ^*	−.0206	.0440	.0606	.0755	.0895	.7510	1.0874	.0734	.0439	−.2047	μ^*	7
	σ^*	−.8420	−.1444	−.0881	−.0365	.0123	1.0987	1.8416	−.0617	−.1552	−1.6247	σ^*	
7	μ^*	−.1668	.0247	.0527	.0779	1.0115	.7583	.0893	.0750	.0596	.0178	μ^*	6
	σ^*	−1.0559	−.1728	−.0996	−.0330	1.3612	1.3951	.0053	−.0588	−.1262	−1.2153	σ^*	
8	μ^*	−.4285	−.0084	.0405	1.3964	.5397	.0905	.0837	.0766	.0690	.1405	μ^*	5
	σ^*	−1.4081	−.2172	−.1160	1.7413	1.0932	.0424	−.0061	−.0555	−.1074	−.9667	σ^*	
9	μ^*	−.9875	−.0756	2.0631	.3818	.0860	.0835	.0809	.0781	.0750	.2147	μ^*	4
	σ^*	−2.1051	−.3010	2.4061	.8643	.0660	.0266	−.0125	−.0522	−.0937	−.7987	σ^*	
10	μ^*	−2.7647	3.7647	.2621	.0791	.0794	.0795	.0795	.0794	.0791	.2621	μ^*	3
	σ^*	−4.1778	4.1778	.6765	.0831	.0489	.0162	−.0162	−.0489	−.0831	−.6765	σ^*	
				$x_{(11)}$	$x_{(10)}$	$x_{(9)}$	$x_{(8)}$	$x_{(7)}$	$x_{(6)}$	$x_{(5)}$	$x_{(4)}$		

$n = 14$

$r_1 = 4$, r_2		$x_{(5)}$	$x_{(6)}$	$x_{(7)}$	$x_{(8)}$	$x_{(9)}$	$x_{(10)}$		$r_1 = 5$, r_2
4	μ^*	.3320	.0839	.0841	.0841	.0839	.3320		
	σ^*	−1.0495	−.0738	−.0244	.0244	.0738	1.0495		
5	μ^*	.2456	.0807	.0857	.0903	.4978			
	σ^*	−1.3227	−.0839	−.0195	.0439	1.3821			
6	μ^*	.0837	.0755	.0895	.7512	1.4921	−.4921	μ^*	7
	σ^*	−1.7721	−.0983	−.0088	1.8791	5.5823	−5.5823	σ^*	
7	μ^*	−.2720	.0657	1.2063	.7061	.0910	.2029	μ^*	6
	σ^*	−2.6618	−.1229	2.7848	2.8338	−.0406	−2.7931	σ^*	
8	μ^*	−1.4198	2.4198	.4098	.0902	.0902	.4098	μ^*	5
	σ^*	−5.3115	5.3115	1.8560	.0441	−.0441	−1.8560	σ^*	
				$x_{(9)}$	$x_{(8)}$	$x_{(7)}$	$x_{(6)}$		

$n = 14$

$r_1 = 6$, r_2		$x_{(7)}$	$x_{(8)}$
6	μ^*	.5000	.5000
	σ^*	−5.6716	5.6716

$n = 15$

$r_1 = 0$ r_2		$x_{(1)}$	$x_{(2)}$	$x_{(3)}$	$x_{(4)}$	$x_{(5)}$	$x_{(6)}$	$x_{(7)}$	$x_{(8)}$	$x_{(9)}$	$x_{(10)}$	$x_{(11)}$	$x_{(12)}$	$x_{(13)}$	$x_{(14)}$	$x_{(15)}$		$r_1 = 1$ r_2
0	μ^*	.0667	.0667	.0667	.0667	.0667	.0667	.0667	.0667	.0667	.0667	.0667	.0667	.0667	.0667	.0667		
	σ^*	−.1444	−.0927	−.0699	−.0526	−.0379	−.0247	−.0122	.0000	.0122	.0247	.0379	.0526	.0699	.0927	.1444		
1	μ^*	.0599	.0627	.0639	.0648	.0655	.0662	.0669	.0675	.0682	.0688	.0695	.0702	.0709	.1351			
	σ^*	−.1590	−.1013	−.0760	−.0568	−.0404	−.0256	−.0116	.0019	.0154	.0293	.0440	.0602	.0791	.2409			
2	μ^*	.0508	.0574	.0602	.0624	.0642	.0659	.0675	.0690	.0704	.0719	.0735	.0751	.2116	4.1564	−3.1564	μ^*	12
	σ^*	−.1752	−.1108	−.0825	−.0610	−.0427	−.0262	−.0106	.0044	.0195	.0349	.0512	.0690	.3300	3.3306	−3.3306	σ^*	
3	μ^*	.0390	.0506	.0556	.0595	.0628	.0657	.0685	.0711	.0737	.0763	.0790	.2982	2.4829	−.2519	−1.2311	μ^*	11
	σ^*	−.1937	−.1214	−.0897	−.0655	−.0450	−.0265	−.0091	.0078	.0246	.0417	.0598	.4169	2.1162	−.4265	−1.6897	σ^*	
4	μ^*	.0234	.0418	.0498	.0560	.0611	.0658	.0701	.0743	.0784	.0824	.3969	1.7779	−.0356	−.1163	−.6260	μ^*	10
	σ^*	−.2154	−.1336	−.0977	−.0705	−.0473	−.0264	−.0068	.0122	.0310	.0502	.5042	1.6273	−.1890	−.3024	−1.1359	σ^*	
5	μ^*	.0030	.0305	.0425	.0516	.0593	.0663	.0727	.0789	.0849	.5104	1.3522	.0403	−.0011	−.0501	−.3413	μ^*	9
	σ^*	−.2414	−.1481	−.1071	−.0760	−.0496	−.0258	−.0035	.0180	.0393	.5940	1.3324	−.0850	−.1549	−.2373	−.8553	σ^*	
6	μ^*	−.0244	.0155	.0330	.0462	.0574	.0674	.0767	.0856	.6425	1.0549	.0706	.0467	.0200	−.0115	−.1807	μ^*	8
	σ^*	−.2733	−.1654	−.1181	−.0822	−.0518	−.0244	.0012	.0258	.6882	1.1208	−.0293	−.0781	−.1325	−.1963	−.6847	σ^*	
7	μ^*	−.0621	−.0046	.0205	.0395	.0555	.0698	.0830	.7983	.8308	.0823	.0677	.0519	.0342	.0134	−.0803	μ^*	7
	σ^*	−.3136	−.1870	−.1315	−.0894	−.0538	−.0219	.0079	.7892	.9536	.0045	−.0326	−.0722	−.1162	−.1677	−.5694	σ^*	
8	μ^*	−.1155	−.0326	.0036	.0309	.0539	.0743	.9854	.6537	.0857	.0764	.0666	.0561	.0443	.0305	−.0131	μ^*	6
	σ^*	−.3664	−.2146	−.1482	−.0979	−.0555	−.0174	.9001	.8129	.0269	−.0029	−.0339	−.0670	−.1036	−.1464	−.4859	σ^*	
9	μ^*	−.1950	−.0732	−.0203	.0196	.0531	1.2157	.5093	.0848	.0789	.0728	.0664	.0595	.0518	.0428	.0338	μ^*	5
	σ^*	−.4390	−.2518	−.1700	−.1082	−.0562	1.0252	.6892	.0430	.0177	−.0078	−.0342	−.0624	−.0935	−.1298	−.4223	σ^*	
10	μ^*	−.3217	−.1364	−.0560	.0043	1.5097	.3890	.0818	.0781	.0744	.0706	.0666	.0623	.0575	.0519	.0677	μ^*	4
	σ^*	−.5459	−.3050	−.2002	−.1211	1.1722	.5767	.0555	.0331	.0111	−.0110	−.0339	−.0582	−.0850	−.1163	−.3721	σ^*	
11	μ^*	−.5462	−.2448	−.1148	1.9058	.2873	.0777	.0756	.0735	.0714	.0693	.0671	.0647	.0620	.0587	.0927	μ^*	3
	σ^*	−.7201	−.3892	−.2458	1.3552	.4712	.0661	.0453	.0256	.0062	−.0131	−.0331	−.0543	−.0778	−.1050	−.3311	σ^*	
12	μ^*	−1.0242	−.4676	2.4918	.2002	.0730	.0721	.0712	.0704	.0695	.0686	.0676	.0666	.0654	.0640	.1113	μ^*	2
	σ^*	−1.0601	−.5477	1.6077	.3693	.0761	.0558	.0373	.0197	.0026	−.0145	−.0321	−.0508	−.0714	−.0954	−.2968	σ^*	
13	μ^*	−2.5574	3.5574	.1252	.0679	.0681	.0682	.0682	.0682	.0682	.0682	.0682	.0682	.0681	.0679	.1252	μ^*	1
	σ^*	−2.0493	2.0493	.2672	.0869	.0656	.0474	.0308	.0152	.0000	−.0152	−.0308	−.0474	−.0656	−.0869	−.2672	σ^*	
				$x_{(14)}$	$x_{(13)}$	$x_{(12)}$	$x_{(11)}$	$x_{(10)}$	$x_{(9)}$	$x_{(8)}$	$x_{(7)}$	$x_{(6)}$	$x_{(5)}$	$x_{(4)}$	$x_{(3)}$	$x_{(2)}$		

$n = 15$

$r_1 = 2$ r_2		$x_{(3)}$	$x_{(4)}$	$x_{(5)}$	$x_{(6)}$	$x_{(7)}$	$x_{(8)}$	$x_{(9)}$	$x_{(10)}$	$x_{(11)}$	$x_{(12)}$	$x_{(13)}$		$r_1 = 3$ r_2
2	μ^*	.1835	.0701	.0703	.0704	.0705	.0705	.0705	.0704	.0703	.0701	.1835		
	σ^*	−.4139	−.0838	−.0607	−.0395	−.0195	.0000	.0195	.0395	.0607	.0838	.4139		
3	μ^*	.1601	.0662	.0679	.0695	.0708	.0721	.0734	.0746	.0758	.2697			
	σ^*	−.4668	−.0927	−.0660	−.0417	−.0187	.0037	.0261	.0490	.0730	.5341			
4	μ^*	.1274	.0609	.0649	.0684	.0717	.0748	.0778	.0808	.3734	3.5892	−2.5892	μ^*	10
	σ^*	−.5314	−.1032	−.0721	−.0438	−.0170	.0090	.0349	.0612	.6624	5.0207	−5.0207	σ^*	
5	μ^*	.0815	.0536	.0608	.0673	.0733	.0790	.0845	.5000	1.8923	−.0171	−.8752	μ^*	9
	σ^*	−.6129	−.1160	−.0792	−.0457	−.0142	.0164	.0468	.8049	2.7587	−.2368	−2.5219	σ^*	
6	μ^*	.0150	.0436	.0555	.0662	.0762	.0857	.6579	1.2523	.0577	.0238	−.3338	μ^*	8
	σ^*	−.7200	−.1323	−.0878	−.0475	−.0095	.0272	.9699	1.9396	−.0828	−.1734	−1.6834	σ^*	
7	μ^*	−.0854	.0289	.0481	.0654	.0815	.8614	.8925	.0804	.0629	.0441	−.0799	μ^*	7
	σ^*	−.8679	−.1539	−.0987	−.0486	−.0017	1.1708	1.4867	−.0125	−.0741	−.1395	−1.2605	σ^*	
8	μ^*	−.2467	.0063	.0375	.0655	1.1375	.6535	.0857	.0764	.0666	.0561	.0617	μ^*	6
	σ^*	−1.0872	−.1847	−.1132	−.0486	1.4336	1.1828	.0264	−.0198	−.0674	−.1178	−1.0042	σ^*	
9	μ^*	−.5335	−.0324	.0205	1.5454	.4801	.0840	.0793	.0745	.0694	.0639	.1487	μ^*	5
	σ^*	−1.4486	−.2334	−.1346	1.8166	.9544	.0508	.0137	−.0235	−.0619	−.1023	−.8312	σ^*	
10	μ^*	−1.1426	−.1111	2.2537	.3478	.0792	.0775	.0756	.0737	.0716	.0693	.2054	μ^*	4
	σ^*	−2.1646	−.3259	2.4905	.7692	.0678	.0363	.0055	−.0254	−.0571	−.0905	−.7058	σ^*	
11	μ^*	−3.0706	4.0706	.2436	.0731	.0733	.0734	.0734	.0734	.0733	.0731	.2436	μ^*	3
	σ^*	−4.2953	4.2953	.6102	.0810	.0528	.0261	.0000	−.0261	−.0528	−.0810	−.6102	σ^*	
				$x_{(12)}$	$x_{(11)}$	$x_{(10)}$	$x_{(9)}$	$x_{(8)}$	$x_{(7)}$	$x_{(6)}$	$x_{(5)}$	$x_{(4)}$		

$n = 15$

$r_1 = 4$ r_2		$x_{(5)}$	$x_{(6)}$	$x_{(7)}$	$x_{(8)}$	$x_{(9)}$	$x_{(10)}$	$x_{(11)}$		$r_1 = 5$ r_2
4	μ^*	.3073	.0770	.0772	.0772	.0772	.0770	.3073		
	σ^*	−.9085	−.0756	−.0374	.0000	.0374	.0756	.9085		
5	μ^*	.2424	.0736	.0770	.0802	.0832	.4435			
	σ^*	−1.1001	−.0854	−.0377	.0088	.0552	1.1592			
6	μ^*	.1339	.0686	.0774	.0859	.6342	1.9724	−.9724	μ^*	8
	σ^*	−1.3838	−.0987	−.0367	.0236	1.4956	5.8824	−5.8824	σ^*	
7	μ^*	−.0644	.0601	.0791	.9252	.9607	.0776	−.0383	μ^*	7
	σ^*	−1.8515	−.1186	−.0327	2.0028	3.0212	−.0764	−2.9448	σ^*	
8	μ^*	−.4928	.0435	1.4494	.5846	.0865	.0804	.2486	μ^*	6
	σ^*	−2.7788	−.1547	2.9335	2.0090	.0169	−.0670	−1.9590	σ^*	
9	μ^*	−1.8586	2.8586	.3769	.0820	.0821	.0820	.3769	μ^*	5
	σ^*	−5.5431	5.5431	1.4614	.0604	.0000	−.0604	−1.4614	σ^*	
				$x_{(10)}$	$x_{(9)}$	$x_{(8)}$	$x_{(7)}$	$x_{(6)}$		

$n = 15$

$r_1 = 6$ r_2		$x_{(7)}$	$x_{(8)}$	$x_{(9)}$
6	μ^*	.4557	.0887	.4557
	σ^*	−3.0248	.0000	3.0248
7	μ^*	.0000	1.0000	
	σ^*	−6.0497	6.0497	

$n = 16$

$r_1 = 0$ | $r_1 = 1$

r_2		$x_{(1)}$	$x_{(2)}$	$x_{(3)}$	$x_{(4)}$	$x_{(5)}$	$x_{(6)}$	$x_{(7)}$	$x_{(8)}$	$x_{(9)}$	$x_{(10)}$	$x_{(11)}$	$x_{(12)}$	$x_{(13)}$	$x_{(14)}$	$x_{(15)}$	$x_{(16)}$		r_2
0	μ^*	.0625	.0625	.0625	.0625	.0625	.0625	.0625	.0625	.0625	.0625	.0625	.0625	.0625	.0625	.0625	.0625		
	σ^*	−.1366	−.0889	−.0681	−.0524	−.0391	−.0272	−.0160	−.0053	.0053	.0160	.0272	.0391	.0524	.0681	.0889	.1366		
1	μ^*	.0566	.0589	.0599	.0607	.0613	.0619	.0625	.0630	.0635	.0640	.0645	.0651	.0657	.0663	.1261			
	σ^*	−.1495	−.0967	−.0737	−.0563	−.0416	−.0284	−.0161	−.0042	.0075	.0193	.0316	.0447	.0593	.0763	.2279			
2	μ^*	.0487	.0543	.0566	.0585	.0600	.0614	.0626	.0638	.0650	.0662	.0674	.0687	.0700	.1967	4.3629	−3.3629	μ^*	13
	σ^*	−.1637	−.1051	−.0797	−.0604	−.0441	−.0294	−.0158	−.0027	.0103	.0233	.0369	.0513	.0671	.3120	3.3959	−3.3959	σ^*	
3	μ^*	.0386	.0483	.0525	.0557	.0584	.0608	.0630	.0652	.0673	.0693	.0714	.0736	.2757	2.6273	−.2907	−1.3366	μ^*	12
	σ^*	−.1797	−.1145	−.0862	−.0647	−.0466	−.0303	−.0151	−.0006	.0138	.0282	.0432	.0590	.3935	2.1693	−.4464	−1.7229	σ^*	
4	μ^*	.0257	.0408	.0474	.0524	.0566	.0604	.0638	.0671	.0704	.0736	.0768	.3649	1.8989	−.0584	−.1425	−.6979	μ^*	11
	σ^*	−.1982	−.1252	−.0935	−.0694	−.0491	−.0310	−.0140	.0022	.0182	.0343	.0508	.4748	1.6779	−.2039	−.3155	−1.1585	σ^*	
5	μ^*	.0090	.0313	.0410	.0484	.0545	.0601	.0652	.0700	.0747	.0794	.4664	1.4596	.0253	−.0183	−.0702	−.3964	μ^*	10
	σ^*	−.2200	−.1376	−.1018	−.0747	−.0518	−.0313	−.0123	.0060	.0239	.0419	.5577	1.3830	−.0974	−.1659	−.2469	−.8728	σ^*	
6	μ^*	−.0129	.0191	.0329	.0434	.0522	.0601	.0673	.0742	.0808	.5829	1.1529	.0601	.0347	.0060	−.0280	−.2257	μ^*	9
	σ^*	−.2461	−.1523	−.1114	−.0806	−.0546	−.0313	−.0097	.0110	.0312	.6439	1.1724	−.0402	−.0878	−.1411	−.2040	−.6992	σ^*	
7	μ^*	−.0420	.0030	.0225	.0373	.0496	.0606	.0707	.0803	.7180	.9214	.0748	.0589	.0417	.0223	−.0007	−.1185	μ^*	8
	σ^*	−.2782	−.1700	−.1229	−.0874	−.0575	−.0307	−.0059	.0177	.7350	1.0068	−.0056	−.0415	−.0801	−.1233	−.1742	−.5821		
8	μ^*	−.0817	−.0185	.0089	.0295	.0467	.0621	.0762	.8769	.7381	.0802	.0699	.0590	.0472	.0339	.0182	−.0464	μ^*	7
	σ^*	−.3189	−.1920	−.1369	−.0954	−.0604	−.0292	−.0004	.8333	.8682	.0173	−.0114	−.0414	−.0737	−.1097	−.1520	−.4973	σ^*	
9	μ^*	−.1379	−.0484	−.0096	.0194	.0438	.0653	1.0674	.5883	.0810	.0741	.0670	.0596	.0515	.0425	.0317	.0044	μ^*	6
	σ^*	−.3723	−.2204	−.1545	−.1049	−.0632	−.0262	.9415	.7473	.0336	.0095	−.0150	−.0407	−.0682	−.0988	−.1348	−.4328	σ^*	
10	μ^*	−.2211	−.0916	−.0358	.0061	.0410	1.3015	.4632	.0792	.0747	.0701	.0654	.0604	.0550	.0490	.0418	.0413	μ^*	5
	σ^*	−.4457	−.2586	−.1776	−.1167	−.0657	1.0642	.6381	.0459	.0249	.0040	−.0173	−.0395	−.0634	−.0898	−.1209	−.3820	σ^*	
11	μ^*	−.3534	−.1587	−.0750	−.0125	1.5996	.3569	.0761	.0732	.0704	.0674	.0644	.0613	.0579	.0541	.0495	.0688	μ^*	4
	σ^*	−.5538	−.3134	−.2097	−.1319	1.2088	.5368	.0560	.0369	.0184	−.0000	−.0187	−.0382	−.0590	−.0822	−.1093	−.3406	σ^*	
12	μ^*	−.5869	−.2739	−.1398	2.0006	.2656	.0723	.0706	.0690	.0673	.0657	.0640	.0622	.0603	.0581	.0554	.0895	μ^*	3
	σ^*	−.7303	−.4004	−.2586	1.3894	.4404	.0649	.0469	.0299	.0134	−.0029	−.0195	−.0367	−.0551	−.0756	−.0995	−.3062	σ^*	
13	μ^*	−1.0829	−.5101	2.5931	.1865	.0681	.0674	.0667	.0660	.0653	.0645	.0638	.0630	.0622	.0612	.0600	.1054	μ^*	2
	σ^*	−1.0748	−.5645	1.6394	.3463	.0736	.0557	.0395	.0242	.0095	−.0050	−.0198	−.0351	−.0515	−.0697	−.0910	−.2768	σ^*	
14	μ^*	−2.6696	3.6696	.1174	.0636	.0637	.0638	.0638	.0638	.0639	.0639	.0638	.0638	.0638	.0637	.0636	.1174	μ^*	1
	σ^*	−2.0779	2.0779	.2511	.0834	.0643	.0481	.0334	.0197	.0065	−.0065	−.0197	−.0334	−.0481	−.0643	−.0834	−.2511	σ^*	
				$x_{(15)}$	$x_{(14)}$	$x_{(13)}$	$x_{(12)}$	$x_{(11)}$	$x_{(10)}$	$x_{(9)}$	$x_{(8)}$	$x_{(7)}$	$x_{(6)}$	$x_{(5)}$	$x_{(4)}$	$x_{(3)}$	$x_{(2)}$		

$n = 16$

$r_1 = 2$ r_2		$x_{(3)}$	$x_{(4)}$	$x_{(5)}$	$x_{(6)}$	$x_{(7)}$	$x_{(8)}$	$x_{(9)}$	$x_{(10)}$	$x_{(11)}$	$x_{(12)}$	$x_{(13)}$	$x_{(14)}$		$r_1 = 3$ r_2
2	μ^*	.1718	.0654	.0656	.0657	.0657	.0658	.0658	.0657	.0657	.0656	.0654	.1718		
	σ^*	−.3847	−.0806	−.0604	−.0421	−.0248	−.0082	.0082	.0248	.0421	.0604	.0806	.3847		
3	μ^*	.1519	.0619	.0633	.0645	.0656	.0666	.0676	.0686	.0695	.0704	.2500			
	σ^*	−.4293	−.0885	−.0655	−.0447	−.0251	−.0062	.0124	.0312	.0507	.0713	.4939			
4	μ^*	.1249	.0572	.0604	.0631	.0657	.0681	.0704	.0727	.0750	.3424	3.9510	−2.9510	μ^*	11
	σ^*	−.4827	−.0977	−.0713	−.0474	−.0249	−.0033	.0180	.0394	.0615	.6086	5.1771	−5.1771	σ^*	
5	μ^*	.0880	.0510	.0566	.0615	.0661	.0704	.0746	.0788	.4529	2.1043	−.0465	−1.0578	μ^*	10
	σ^*	−.5482	−.1087	−.0780	−.0502	−.0242	.0008	.0254	.0501	.7331	2.8633	−.2623	−2.6010	σ^*	
6	μ^*	.0367	.0427	.0517	.0597	.0671	.0741	.0809	.5870	1.4113	.0415	.0039	−.4568	μ^*	9
	σ^*	−.6312	−.1222	−.0860	−.0532	−.0226	.0068	.0356	.8728	2.0287	−.1019	−.1899	−1.7370	σ^*	
7	μ^*	−.0367	.0311	.0451	.0576	.0691	.0801	.7537	1.0229	.0707	.0506	.0288	−.1731	μ^*	8
	σ^*	−.7404	−.1394	−.0958	−.0564	−.0196	.0156	1.0359	1.5696	−.0284	−.0879	−.1516	−1.3017	σ^*	
8	μ^*	−.1467	.0143	.0359	.0553	.0731	.9680	.7650	.0799	.0685	.0565	.0435	−.0135	μ^*	7
	σ^*	−.8915	−.1625	−.1084	−.0596	−.0142	1.2361	1.2635	.0122	−.0321	−.0782	−.1273	−1.0381	σ^*	
9	μ^*	−.3223	−.0115	.0225	.0528	1.2585	.5776	.0808	.0744	.0677	.0607	.0531	.0856	μ^*	6
	σ^*	−1.1158	−.1955	−.1255	−.0626	1.4995	1.0350	.0375	.0023	−.0335	−.0706	−.1102	−.8605	σ^*	
10	μ^*	−.6328	−.0557	.0007	1.6878	.4339	.0780	.0746	.0712	.0676	.0638	.0597	.1511	μ^*	5
	σ^*	−1.4858	−.2481	−.1515	1.8854	.8514	.0548	.0253	−.0040	−.0337	−.0645	−.0973	−.7321	σ^*	
11	μ^*	−1.2894	−.1456	2.4350	.3199	.0734	.0721	.0707	.0693	.0678	.0662	.0644	.1960	μ^*	4
	σ^*	−2.2193	−.3485	2.5678	.6955	.0678	.0419	.0168	−.0080	−.0332	−.0593	−.0870	−.6344	σ^*	
12	μ^*	−3.3604	4.3604	.2276	.0679	.0681	.0682	.0682	.0682	.0682	.0681	.0679	.2276	μ^*	3
	σ^*	−4.4033	4.4033	.5571	.0785	.0548	.0324	.0107	−.0107	−.0324	−.0548	−.0785	−.5571	σ^*	
				$x_{(13)}$	$x_{(12)}$	$x_{(11)}$	$x_{(10)}$	$x_{(9)}$	$x_{(8)}$	$x_{(7)}$	$x_{(6)}$	$x_{(5)}$	$x_{(4)}$		

$n = 16$

$r_1 = 4$ r_2		$x_{(5)}$	$x_{(6)}$	$x_{(7)}$	$x_{(8)}$	$x_{(9)}$	$x_{(10)}$	$x_{(11)}$	$x_{(12)}$		$r_1 = 5$ r_2
4	μ^*	.2862	.0711	.0713	.0714	.0714	.0713	.0711	.2862		
	σ^*	−.8047	−.0751	−.0445	−.0147	.0147	.0445	.0751	.8047		
5	μ^*	.2352	.0679	.0704	.0727	.0748	.0769	.4021			
	σ^*	−.9480	−.0842	−.0470	−.0111	.0244	.0602	1.0057			
6	μ^*	.1562	.0632	.0693	.0751	.0807	.5555	2.4387	−1.4387	μ^*	9
	σ^*	−1.1458	−.0959	−.0496	−.0050	.0390	1.2573	6.1549	−6.1549	σ^*	
7	μ^*	.0265	.0561	.0683	.0798	.7693	1.2110	.0615	−.2725	μ^*	8
	σ^*	−1.4392	−.1121	−.0521	.0057	1.5977	3.1906	−.1084	−3.0823	σ^*	
8	μ^*	−.2068	.0441	.0673	1.0954	.7592	.0801	.0689	.0918	μ^*	7
	σ^*	−1.9237	−.1370	−.0540	2.1147	2.1467	−.0071	−.0874	−2.0521	σ^*	
9	μ^*	−.7049	.0201	1.6848	.5107	.0805	.0768	.0728	.2591	μ^*	6
	σ^*	−2.8854	−.1832	3.0686	1.5854	.0400	−.0173	−.0752	−1.5330	σ^*	
10	μ^*	−2.2799	3.2799	.3493	.0753	.0754	.0754	.0753	.3493	μ^*	5
	σ^*	−5.7542	5.7542	1.2182	.0667	.0221	−.0221	−.0667	−1.2182	σ^*	
				$x_{(11)}$	$x_{(10)}$	$x_{(9)}$	$x_{(8)}$	$x_{(7)}$	$x_{(6)}$		

$n = 16$

$r_1 = 6$ r_2		$x_{(7)}$	$x_{(8)}$	$x_{(9)}$	$x_{(10)}$		$r_1 = 7$ r_2
6	μ^*	.4194	.0806	.0806	.4194		
	σ^*	−2.1259	−.0397	.0397	2.1259		
7	μ^*	.2081	.0813	.7106			
	σ^*	−3.1972	−.0359	3.2331			
8	μ^*	−.4940	1.4940	.5000	.5000	μ^*	7
	σ^*	−6.3912	6.3912	6.4694	−6.4694	σ^*	
				$x_{(9)}$	$x_{(8)}$		

$n = 17$

$r_1 = 0$ r_2		$x_{(1)}$	$x_{(2)}$	$x_{(3)}$	$x_{(4)}$	$x_{(5)}$	$x_{(6)}$	$x_{(7)}$	$x_{(8)}$	$x_{(9)}$	$x_{(10)}$	$x_{(11)}$	$x_{(12)}$	$x_{(13)}$	$x_{(14)}$	$x_{(15)}$	$x_{(16)}$	$x_{(17)}$		$r_1 = 1$ r_2
0	μ^*	.0588	.0588	.0588	.0588	.0588	.0588	.0588	.0588	.0588	.0588	.0588	.0588	.0588	.0588	.0588	.0588	.0588		
	σ^*	−.1297	−.0854	−.0663	−.0519	−.0398	−.0290	−.0189	−.0094	.0000	.0094	.0189	.0290	.0398	.0519	.0663	.0854	.1297		
1	μ^*	.0536	.0556	.0565	.0571	.0577	.0582	.0586	.0590	.0595	.0599	.0603	.0607	.0612	.0617	.0622	.1183			
	σ^*	−.1412	−.0925	−.0715	−.0556	−.0423	−.0304	−.0194	−.0089	.0014	.0117	.0222	.0332	.0450	.0582	.0737	2164			
2	μ^*	.0468	.0515	.0535	.0550	.0563	.0574	.0585	.0595	.0605	.0615	.0624	.0634	.0645	.0656	.1837	4.5582	−3.5582	μ^*	14
	σ^*	−.1537	−.1001	−.0769	−.0595	−.0448	−.0317	−.0196	−.0080	.0033	.0146	.0261	.0381	.0510	.0653	.2960	3.4564	−3.4564	σ^*	
3	μ^*	.0381	.0463	.0498	.0525	.0547	.0567	.0585	.0603	.0620	.0636	.0653	.0670	.0688	.2564	2.7643	−.3280	−1.4364	μ^*	13
	σ^*	−.1677	−.1085	−.0829	−.0636	−.0474	−.0329	−.0196	−.0068	.0057	.0181	.0308	.0439	.0580	.3728	2.2184	−.4648	−1.7536	σ^*	
4	μ^*	.0271	.0398	.0453	.0494	.0528	.0559	.0588	.0615	.0641	.0666	.0692	.0718	.3378	2.0140	.0804	−.1676	−.7659	μ^*	12
	σ^*	−.1837	−.1179	−.0895	−.0681	−.0501	−.0341	−.0192	−.0051	.0087	.0225	.0364	.0509	.4491	1.7246	−.2176	−.3275	−1.1795	σ^*	
5	μ^*	.0131	.0317	.0397	.0457	.0507	.0552	.0593	.0632	.0670	.0707	.0744	.4294	1.5621	.0106	.0349	−.0894	−.4485	μ^*	11
	σ^*	−.2022	−.1287	−.0969	−.0730	−.0529	−.0351	−.0185	−.0028	.0126	.0278	.0433	.5263	1.4295	−.1087	−.1760	−.2559	−.8890	σ^*	
6	μ^*	−.0047	.0214	.0327	.0411	.0482	.0545	.0603	.0658	.0710	.0762	.5334	1.2467	.0497	.0229	.0075	−.0436	−.2682	μ^*	10
	σ^*	−.2241	−.1412	−.1055	−.0786	−.0560	−.0359	−.0173	.0004	.0176	.0346	.6059	1.2197	−.0502	−.0967	−.1491	−.2111	−.7126	σ^*	
7	μ^*	−.0278	.0083	.0239	.0356	.0454	.0540	.0620	.0695	.0767	.6525	1.0084	.0673	.0503	.0318	.0109	−.0140	−.1545	μ^*	9
	σ^*	−.2504	−.1561	−.1154	−.0849	−.0592	−.0364	−.0154	.0046	.0240	.6892	1.0554	−.0147	−.0496	−.0874	−.1299	−.1801	−.5936	σ^*	
8	μ^*	−.0585	−.0088	.0126	.0286	.0421	.0539	.0648	.0750	.7903	.8194	.0746	.0634	.0515	.0385	.0239	.0054	−.0778	μ^*	8
	σ^*	−.2828	−.1742	−.1274	−.0922	−.0627	−.0365	−.0124	.0105	.7777	.9186	.0087	−.0190	−.0483	−.0799	−.1153	−.1572	−.5076	σ^*	
9	μ^*	−.1002	−.0317	−.0022	.0199	.0383	.0545	.0694	.9521	.6648	.0768	.0692	.0613	.0529	.0438	.0335	.0212	−.0235	μ^*	7
	σ^*	−.3238	−.1967	−.1419	−.1009	−.0665	−.0359	−.0079	.8736	.7999	.0252	.0021	−.0216	−.0466	−.0735	−.1037	−.1394	−.4423	σ^*	
10	μ^*	−.1589	−.0633	−.0223	.0084	.0340	.0565	1.1456	.5353	0763	.0710	.0657	.0602	.0543	.0480	.0408	.0323	.0162	μ^*	6
	σ^*	−.3777	−.2257	−.1603	−.1113	−.0704	−.0341	.9796	.6933	.0375	.0176	.0024	−.0230	−.0447	−.0581	−.0942	−.1251	−.3909	σ^*	
11	μ^*	−.2457	−.1091	−.0506	−.0070	.0293	1.3831	.4250	.0741	.0706	.0670	.0634	.0596	.0557	.0514	.0465	.0407	.0460	μ^*	5
	σ^*	−.4519	−.2649	−.1846	−.1245	−.0744	1.1002	.5952	.0474	.0296	.0120	−.0057	−.0238	−.0428	−.0633	−.0862	−.1133	−.3491	σ^*	
12	μ^*	−.3832	−.1799	−.0932	−.0287	1.6850	.3299	.0711	.0688	.0665	.0642	.0619	.0595	.0569	.0542	.0511	.0473	.0688	μ^*	4
	σ^*	−.5612	−.3212	−.2185	−.1418	1.2427	.5029	.0557	.0393	.0234	.0077	−.0080	−.0240	−.0409	−.0591	−.0793	−.1032	−.3144	σ^*	
13	μ^*	−.6253	−.3014	−.1637	2.0904	.2471	.0676	.0662	.0649	.0636	.0622	.0609	.0595	.0581	.0565	.0547	.0525	.0863	μ^*	3
	σ^*	−.7398	−.4108	−.2705	1.4211	.4139	.0634	.0476	.0327	.0185	.0045	−.0096	−.0240	−.0390	−.0552	−.0733	−.0949	−.2850	σ^*	
14	μ^*	−1.1383	−.5506	2.6888	.1745	.0638	.0632	.0626	.0620	.0615	.0609	.0603	.0597	.0591	.0584	.0576	.0565	.1000	μ^*	2
	σ^*	−1.0885	−.5802	1.6687	.3262	.0712	.0552	.0408	.0274	.0145	.0019	−.0107	−.0236	−.0371	−.0516	−.0679	−.0870	−.2595	σ^*	
15	μ^*	−2.7754	3.7754	.1105	.0597	.0599	.0599	.0600	.0600	.0600	.0600	.0600	.0600	.0600	.0599	.0599	.0597	.1105	μ^*	1
	σ^*	−2.1046	2.1046	.2370	.0801	.0629	.0483	.0352	.0230	.0114	.0000	−.0114	−.0230	−.0352	−.0483	−.0629	−.0801	−.2370	σ^*	
				$x_{(16)}$	$x_{(15)}$	$x_{(14)}$	$x_{(13)}$	$x_{(12)}$	$x_{(11)}$	$x_{(10)}$	$x_{(9)}$	$x_{(8)}$	$x_{(7)}$	$x_{(6)}$	$x_{(5)}$	$x_{(4)}$	$x_{(3)}$	$x_{(2)}$		

$n = 17$

$r_1 = 2$ r_2		$x_{(3)}$	$x_{(4)}$	$x_{(5)}$	$x_{(6)}$	$x_{(7)}$	$x_{(8)}$	$x_{(9)}$	$x_{(10)}$	$x_{(11)}$	$x_{(12)}$	$x_{(13)}$	$x_{(14)}$	$x_{(15)}$		$r_1 = 3$ r_2
2	μ^*	.1616	.0613	.0615	.0616	.0616	.0616	.0616	.0616	.0616	.0616	.0615	.0613	.1616		
	σ^*	−.3597	−.0776	−.0597	−.0436	−.0285	−.0141	.0000	.0141	.0285	.0436	.0597	.0776	.3597		
3	μ^*	.1444	.0581	.0593	.0603	.0612	.0620	.0628	.0636	.0643	.0651	.0658	.2331			
	σ^*	−.3980	−.0847	−.0645	−.0464	−.0294	−.0132	.0026	.0184	.0346	.0514	.0693	.4600			
4	μ^*	.1216	.0540	.0566	.0588	.0608	.0627	.0646	.0664	.0682	.0699	.3165	4.2963	−3.2963	μ^*	12
	σ^*	−.4430	−.0928	−.0699	−.0494	−.0302	−.0118	.0061	.0240	.0421	.0610	.5640	5.3212	−5.3212	σ^*	
5	μ^*	.0913	.0486	.0531	.0570	.0605	.0639	.0672	.0704	.0735	.4145	2.3075	−.0755	−1.2319	μ^*	11
	σ^*	−.4970	−.1023	−.0762	−.0526	−.0307	−.0097	.0107	.0311	.0517	.6749	2.9593	−.2856	−2.6737	σ^*	
6	μ^*	.0505	.0416	.0486	.0548	.0605	.0659	.0711	.0761	.5310	1.5646	.0252	−.0157	−.5740	μ^*	10
	σ^*	−.5635	−.1138	−.0834	−.0561	−.0308	−.0065	.0170	.0405	.7966	2.1104	−.1191	−.2050	−1.7863	σ^*	
7	μ^*	−.0058	.0322	.0428	.0522	.0608	.0690	.0769	.6719	1.1493	.0606	.0382	.0138	−.2619	μ^*	9
	σ^*	−.6479	−.1279	−.0922	−.0601	−.0302	−.0018	.0258	.9343	1.6454	−.0427	−.1005	−.1627	−1.3394	σ^*	
8	μ^*	−.0858	.0192	.0349	.0490	.0619	.0741	.8466	.8738	.0735	.0603	.0463	.0312	−.0852	μ^*	8
	σ^*	−.7591	−.1460	−.1031	−.0645	−.0287	.0053	1.0961	1.3368	−.0005	−.0432	−.0880	−.1361	−1.0691	σ^*	
9	μ^*	−.2048	.0003	.0240	.0451	.0645	1.0709	.6735	.0769	.0690	.0607	.0520	.0425	.0254	μ^*	7
	σ^*	−.9132	−.1704	−.1172	−.0695	−.0254	1.2957	1.1079	.0257	−.0079	−.0425	−.0787	−.1174	−.8872	σ^*	
10	μ^*	−.3940	−.0287	.0078	.0402	1.3747	.5195	.0759	.0712	.0664	.0614	.0561	.0504	.0991	μ^*	6
	σ^*	−1.1420	−.2055	−.1368	−.0754	1.5598	.9252	.0435	.0156	−.0125	−.0412	−.0713	−.1035	−.7559	σ^*	
11	μ^*	−.7271	−.0782	−.0187	1.8240	.3967	.0727	.0701	.0676	.0649	.0622	.0593	.0561	.1504	μ^*	5
	σ^*	−1.5200	−.2617	−.1670	1.9486	.7714	.0565	.0324	.0086	−.0153	−.0397	−.0652	−.0924	−.6562	σ^*	
12	μ^*	−1.4288	−.1790	2.6078	.2966	.0683	.0673	.0663	.0653	.0641	.0630	.0617	.0603	.1871	μ^*	4
	σ^*	−2.2697	−.3694	2.6391	.6363	.0668	.0451	.0242	.0036	−.0170	−.0381	−.0600	−.0834	−.5776	σ^*	
13	μ^*	−3.6356	4.6356	.2137	.0634	.0636	.0637	.0637	.0638	.0637	.0637	.0636	.0634	.2137	μ^*	3
	σ^*	−4.5030	4.5030	.5135	.0759	.0555	.0363	.0180	.0000	−.0180	−.0363	−.0555	−.0759	−.5135	σ^*	
				$x_{(14)}$	$x_{(13)}$	$x_{(12)}$	$x_{(11)}$	$x_{(10)}$	$x_{(9)}$	$x_{(8)}$	$x_{(7)}$	$x_{(6)}$	$x_{(5)}$	$x_{(4)}$		

$n = 17$

$r_1 = 4$, r_2		$x_{(5)}$	$x_{(6)}$	$x_{(7)}$	$x_{(8)}$	$x_{(9)}$	$x_{(10)}$	$x_{(11)}$	$x_{(12)}$	$x_{(13)}$		$r_1 = 5$, r_2
4	μ^*	.2680	.0661	.0663	.0664	.0664	.0664	.0663	.0661	.2680		
	σ^*	−.7248	−.0737	−.0483	−.0239	.0000	.0239	.0483	.0737	.7248		
5	μ^*	.2266	.0631	.0650	.0667	.0683	.0699	.0714	.3689			
	σ^*	−.8367	−.0819	−.0519	−.0230	.0052	.0334	.0621	.8927			
6	μ^*	.1658	.0589	.0633	.0675	.0715	.0754	.4975	2.8904	−1.8904	μ^*	10
	σ^*	−.9838	−.0921	−.0559	−.0211	.0129	.0468	1.0930	6.4042	−6.4042	σ^*	
7	μ^*	.0732	.0528	.0612	.0692	.0769	.6667	1.4558	.0436	−.4994	μ^*	9
	σ^*	−1.1874	−.1055	−.0605	−.0174	.0247	1.3459	3.3451	−.1372	−3.2079	σ^*	
8	μ^*	−.0767	.0435	.0585	.0727	.9020	.9319	.0718	.0564	−.0601	μ^*	8
	σ^*	−1.4898	−.1243	−.0661	−.0104	1.6906	2.2717	−.0286	−.1059	−2.1371	σ^*	
9	μ^*	−.3434	.0277	.0546	1.2611	.6450	.0771	.0702	.0630	.1447	μ^*	7
	σ^*	−1.9898	−.1537	−.0733	2.2168	1.6975	.0220	−.0328	−.0887	−1.5980	σ^*	
10	μ^*	−.9085	−.0038	1.9123	.4585	.0748	.0723	.0697	.0669	.2577	μ^*	6
	σ^*	−2.9831	−.2092	3.1923	1.3242	.0505	.0083	−.0341	−.0772	−1.2717	σ^*	
11	μ^*	−2.6845	3.6845	.3258	.0696	.0697	.0698	.0697	.0696	.3258	μ^*	5
	σ^*	−5.9480	5.9480	1.0518	.0688	.0341	.0000	−.0341	−.0688	−1.0518	σ^*	
				$x_{(12)}$	$x_{(11)}$	$x_{(10)}$	$x_{(9)}$	$x_{(8)}$	$x_{(7)}$	$x_{(6)}$		

$n = 17$

$r_1 = 6$, r_2		$x_{(7)}$	$x_{(8)}$	$x_{(9)}$	$x_{(10)}$	$x_{(11)}$		$r_1 = 7$, r_2
6	μ^*	.3891	.0739	.0740	.0739	.3891		
	σ^*	−1.6667	−.0548	.0000	.0548	1.6667		
7	μ^*	.2571	.0727	.0776	.5926			
	σ^*	−2.2320	−.0602	.0156	2.2766			
8	μ^*	−.0349	.0706	.9643	1.0000	.0000	μ^*	8
	σ^*	−3.3541	−.0680	3.4220	6.8499	−6.8499	σ^*	
9	μ^*	−.9785	1.9785	.4603	.0795	.4603	μ^*	7
	σ^*	−6.7025	6.7025	3.4250	.0000	−3.4250	σ^*	
				$x_{(10)}$	$x_{(9)}$	$x_{(8)}$		

$n = 18$

$r_1 = 0$ r_2		$x_{(1)}$	$x_{(2)}$	$x_{(3)}$	$x_{(4)}$	$x_{(5)}$	$x_{(6)}$	$x_{(7)}$	$x_{(8)}$	$x_{(9)}$	$x_{(10)}$	$x_{(11)}$	$x_{(12)}$	$x_{(13)}$	$x_{(14)}$	$x_{(15)}$	$x_{(16)}$	$x_{(17)}$	$x_{(18)}$		$r_1 = 1$ r_2
0	μ^*	.0556	.0556	.0556	.0556	.0556	.0556	.0556	.0556	.0556	.0556	.0556	.0556	.0556	.0556	.0556	.0556	.0556	.0556		
	σ^*	−.1235	−.0822	−.0645	−.0512	−.0401	−.0302	−.0211	−.0125	−.0041	.0041	.0125	.0211	.0302	.0401	.0512	.0645	.0822	.1235		
1	μ^*	.0509	.0526	.0534	.0540	.0544	.0548	.0552	.0556	.0559	.0563	.0566	.0570	.0574	.0577	.0582	.0586	.1113			
	σ^*	−.1338	−.0887	−.0693	−.0548	−.0426	−.0318	−.0219	−.0124	−.0033	.0058	.0149	.0243	.0342	.0450	.0570	.0712	.2061			
2	μ^*	.0449	.0489	.0507	.0520	.0531	.0540	.0549	.0558	.0566	.0574	.0582	.0590	.0598	.0607	.0616	.1723	4.7435	−3.7435	μ^*	15
	σ^*	−.1449	−.0955	−.0743	−.0584	−.0451	−.0333	−.0224	−.0121	−.0021	.0078	.0178	.0281	.0389	.0505	.0634	.2818	3.5126	−3.5126	σ^*	
3	μ^*	.0373	.0443	.0474	.0496	.0515	.0532	.0547	.0562	.0576	.0589	.0603	.0617	.0631	.0646	.2396	2.8947	−.3637	−1.5309	μ^*	14
	σ^*	−.1573	−.1030	−.0798	−.0623	−.0477	−.0347	−.0228	−.0115	−.0005	.0103	.0213	.0325	.0442	.0568	.3545	2.2640	−.4819	−1.7821	σ^*	
4	μ^*	.0279	.0387	.0433	.0468	.0497	.0522	.0546	.0568	.0589	.0610	.0631	.0652	.0674	.3144	2.1237	−.1017	−.1917	−.8303	μ^*	13
	σ^*	−.1713	−.1114	−.0858	−.0665	−.0504	−.0361	−.0230	−.0105	.0015	.0135	.0254	.0377	.0505	.4264	1.7678	−.2302	−.3387	−1.1989	σ^*	
5	μ^*	.0161	.0317	.0384	.0434	.0475	.0512	.0546	.0578	.0609	.0639	.0669	.0698	.3979	1.6601	−.0036	−.0510	−.1077	−.4978	μ^*	12
	σ^*	−.1872	−.1209	−.0925	−.0711	−.0533	−.0375	−.0230	−.0092	.0042	.0173	.0305	.0440	.4988	1.4726	−.1191	−.1853	−.2642	−.9040	σ^*	
6	μ^*	.0013	.0230	.0323	.0392	.0450	.0502	.0549	.0593	.0636	.0677	.0718	.4918	1.3366	.0395	.0114	−.0205	−.0586	−.3084	μ^*	11
	σ^*	−.2058	−.1318	−.1001	−.0763	−.0564	−.0388	−.0226	−.0073	.0075	.0221	.0367	.5728	1.2634	−.0593	−.1049	−.1564	−.2177	−.7250	σ^*	
7	μ^*	−.0176	.0121	.0247	.0342	.0421	.0491	.0555	.0615	.0673	.0729	.5980	1.0920	.0597	.0418	.0221	−.0002	−.0268	−.1887	μ^*	10
	σ^*	−.2278	−.1445	−.1089	−.0821	−.0598	−.0400	−.0219	−.0047	.0119	.0282	.6497	1.1002	−.0230	−.0571	−.0941	−.1360	−.1857	−.6043	σ^*	
8	μ^*	−.0419	−.0019	.0153	.0281	.0387	.0482	.0568	.0648	.0726	.7194	.8979	.0690	.0570	.0441	.0301	.0142	−.0048	−.1076	μ^*	9
	σ^*	−.2543	−.1597	−.1191	−.0888	−.0635	−.0411	−.0205	−.0011	.0176	.7305	.9649	.0009	−.0260	−.0545	−.0856	−.1205	−.1620	−.5171	σ^*	
9	μ^*	−.0741	−.0200	.0031	.0204	.0348	.0474	.0590	.0698	.8597	.7388	.0726	.0643	.0556	.0464	.0363	.0249	.0112	−.0499	μ^*	8
	σ^*	−.2869	−.1781	−.1315	−.0966	−.0676	−.0418	−.0183	.0039	.8168	.8479	.0177	−.0045	−.0276	−.0520	−.0785	−.1083	−.1437	−.4510	σ^*	
10	μ^*	−.1176	−.0441	−.0128	.0106	.0300	.0471	.0627	1.0241	.6053	.0731	.0672	.0613	.0550	.0484	.0412	.0330	.0232	−.0076	μ^*	7
	σ^*	−.3283	−.2010	−.1466	−.1059	−.0720	−.0421	−.0147	.9107	.7434	.0301	.0111	−.0082	−.0283	−.0495	−.0725	−.0983	−.1290	−.3990	σ^*	
11	μ^*	−.1788	−.0775	−.0343	−.0022	.0245	.0479	1.2204	.4913	.0718	.0677	.0636	.0593	.0549	.0502	.0451	.0393	.0324	.0244	μ^*	6
	σ^*	−.3827	−.2307	−.1657	−.1173	−.0770	−.0414	1.0148	.6479	.0399	.0231	.0063	−.0108	−.0284	−.0471	−.0673	−.0900	−.1168	−.3568	σ^*	
12	μ^*	−.2689	−.1257	−.0648	−.0195	.0180	1.4609	.3928	.0695	.0667	.0639	.0610	.0581	.0551	.0518	.0483	.0444	.0396	.0490	μ^*	5
	σ^*	−.4576	−.2707	−.1911	−.1317	−.0824	1.1335	.5586	.0480	.0326	.0176	.0026	−.0125	−.0282	−.0448	−.0627	−.0828	−.1066	−.3219	σ^*	
13	μ^*	−.4113	−.2001	−.1106	−.0442	1.7662	.3067	.0666	.0648	.0629	.0611	.0592	.0573	.0554	.0533	.0510	.0484	.0453	.0681	μ^*	4
	σ^*	−.5681	−.3285	−.2266	−.1509	1.2741	.4735	.0551	.0407	.0268	.0133	−.0001	−.0137	−.0278	−.0426	−.0586	−.0766	−.0978	−.2923	σ^*	
14	μ^*	−.6615	−.3276	−.1867	2.1758	.2310	.0634	.0623	.0612	.0601	.0590	.0580	.0569	.0557	.0545	.0532	.0517	.0498	.0832	μ^*	3
	σ^*	−.7486	−.4205	−.2815	1.4505	.3908	.0619	.0478	.0346	.0221	.0099	−.0022	−.0145	−.0271	−.0404	−.0548	−.0710	−.0901	−.2668	σ^*	
15	μ^*	−1.1905	−.5891	2.7796	.1640	.0599	.0595	.0590	.0585	.0581	.0576	.0571	.0566	.0561	.0556	.0550	.0543	.0535	.0951	μ^*	2
	σ^*	−1.1013	−.5948	1.6960	.3086	.0689	.0545	.0416	.0296	.0182	.0072	−.0038	−.0149	−.0263	−.0384	−.0514	−.0660	−.0833	−.2445	σ^*	
16	μ^*	−2.8756	3.8756	.1043	.0564	.0565	.0565	.0566	.0566	.0566	.0566	.0566	.0566	.0566	.0566	.0565	.0565	.0564	.1043	μ^*	1
	σ^*	−2.1294	2.1294	.2245	.0771	.0614	.0482	.0363	.0254	.0151	.0050	−.0050	−.0151	−.0254	−.0363	−.0482	−.0614	−.0771	−.2245	σ^*	
				$x_{(17)}$	$x_{(16)}$	$x_{(15)}$	$x_{(14)}$	$x_{(13)}$	$x_{(12)}$	$x_{(11)}$	$x_{(10)}$	$x_{(9)}$	$x_{(8)}$	$x_{(7)}$	$x_{(6)}$	$x_{(5)}$	$x_{(4)}$	$x_{(3)}$	$x_{(2)}$		

$n = 18$

$r_1 = 2$ r_2		$x_{(3)}$	$x_{(4)}$	$x_{(5)}$	$x_{(6)}$	$x_{(7)}$	$x_{(8)}$	$x_{(9)}$	$x_{(10)}$	$x_{(11)}$	$x_{(12)}$	$x_{(13)}$	$x_{(14)}$	$x_{(15)}$	$x_{(16)}$		$r_1 = 3$ r_2
2	μ^*	.1525	.0577	.0579	.0579	.0580	.0580	.0580	.0580	.0580	.0580	.0579	.0579	.0577	.1525		
	σ^*	−.3381	−.0747	−.0587	−.0443	−.0310	−.0184	−.0061	.0061	.0184	.0310	.0443	.0587	.0747	.3381		
3	μ^*	.1375	.0548	.0558	.0566	.0574	.0581	.0587	.0593	.0599	.0605	.0611	.0617	.2185			
	σ^*	−.3714	−.0811	−.0632	−.0472	−.0324	−.0183	−.0046	.0090	.0227	.0367	.0514	.0672	.4310			
4	μ^*	.1180	.0511	.0532	.0551	.0567	.0583	.0598	.0612	.0626	.0641	.0655	.2944	4.6262	−3.6262	μ^*	13
	σ^*	−.4099	−.0883	−.0683	−.0503	−.0337	−.0178	−.0025	.0127	.0280	.0437	.0600	.5263	5.4546	−5.4546	σ^*	
5	μ^*	.0926	.0465	.0500	.0532	.0561	.0588	.0613	.0639	.0664	.0689	.3824	2.5024	−.1041	−1.3984	μ^*	12
	σ^*	−.4553	−.0967	−.0740	−.0537	−.0348	−.0170	.0004	.0175	.0347	.0522	.6266	3.0481	−.3071	−2.7410	σ^*	
6	μ^*	.0593	.0404	.0460	.0509	.0554	.0596	.0637	.0677	.0716	.4854	1.7123	.0088	−.0350	−.6861	μ^*	11
	σ^*	−.5099	−.1065	−.0806	−.0574	−.0359	−.0155	.0042	.0237	.0432	.7347	2.1856	−.1349	−.2189	−1.8318	σ^*	
7	μ^*	.0147	.0326	.0409	.0482	.0549	.0612	.0672	.0731	.6074	1.2717	.0502	.0257	−.0009	−.3468	μ^*	10
	σ^*	−.5774	−.1184	−.0884	−.0616	−.0367	−.0132	.0095	.0319	.8542	1.7150	−.0557	−.1120	−.1729	−1.3743	σ^*	
8	μ^*	−.0463	.0221	.0341	.0448	.0545	.0637	.0725	.7546	.9798	.0666	.0519	.0362	.0192	−.1537	μ^*	9
	σ^*	−.6631	−.1331	−.0979	−.0663	−.0372	−.0096	.0170	.9904	1.4040	−.0119	−.0533	−.0970	−.1441	−1.0977	σ^*	
9	μ^*	−.1325	.0076	.0251	.0405	.0547	.0680	.9367	.7674	.0724	.0632	.0536	.0434	.0323	−.0322	μ^*	8
	σ^*	−.7763	−.1521	−.1098	−.0719	−.0370	−.0041	1.1512	1.1744	.0152	−.0172	−.0507	−.0860	−.1241	−.9117	σ^*	
10	μ^*	−.2602	−.0132	.0124	.0350	.0558	1.1702	.6039	.0730	.0673	.0613	.0552	.0486	.0414	.0494	μ^*	7
	σ^*	−.9332	−.1777	−.1254	−.0787	−.0357	1.3506	.9922	.0335	.0069	−.0202	−.0481	−.0775	−.1092	−.7776	σ^*	
11	μ^*	−.4622	−.0453	−.0066	.0277	1.4864	.4731	.0712	.0676	.0641	.0604	.0566	.0525	.0480	.1066	μ^*	6
	σ^*	−1.1664	−.2148	−.1472	−.0871	1.6155	.8398	.0467	.0239	.0012	−.0219	−.0456	−.0706	−.0975	−.6760	σ^*	
12	μ^*	−.8168	−.1000	−.0378	1.9545	.3660	.0679	.0660	.0640	.0620	.0599	.0578	.0555	.0529	.1480	μ^*	5
	σ^*	−1.5517	−.2742	−.1812	2.0071	.7071	.0569	.0367	.0169	−.0028	−.0228	−.0433	−.0648	−.0880	−.5960	σ^*	
13	μ^*	−1.5616	−.2114	2.7728	.2767	.0639	.0631	.0623	.0615	.0607	.0598	.0588	.0578	.0566	.1786	μ^*	4
	σ^*	−2.3165	−.3886	2.7051	.5877	.0655	.0468	.0290	.0116	−.0056	−.0231	−.0410	−.0598	−.0800	−.5311	σ^*	
14	μ^*	−3.8976	4.8976	.2014	.0595	.0597	.0598	.0598	.0598	.0598	.0598	.0598	.0597	.0595	.2014	μ^*	3
	σ^*	−4.5955	4.5955	.4770	.0732	.0554	.0388	.0230	.0076	−.0076	−.0230	−.0388	−.0554	−.0732	−.4770	σ^*	
				$x_{(15)}$	$x_{(14)}$	$x_{(13)}$	$x_{(12)}$	$x_{(11)}$	$x_{(10)}$	$x_{(9)}$	$x_{(8)}$	$x_{(7)}$	$x_{(6)}$	$x_{(5)}$	$x_{(4)}$		

$n = 18$

$r_1 = 4$ r_2		$x_{(5)}$	$x_{(6)}$	$x_{(7)}$	$x_{(8)}$	$x_{(9)}$	$x_{(10)}$	$x_{(11)}$	$x_{(12)}$	$x_{(13)}$	$x_{(14)}$		$r_1 = 5$ r_2
4	μ^*	.2521	.0618	.0620	.0621	.0621	.0621	.0621	.0620	.0618	.2521		
	σ^*	−.6611	−.0717	−.0503	−.0298	−.0099	.0099	.0298	.0503	.0717	.6611		
5	μ^*	.2177	.0590	.0605	.0618	.0631	.0643	.0655	.0666	.3416			
	σ^*	−.7513	−.0791	−.0542	−.0304	−.0073	.0157	.0387	.0623	.8055			
6	μ^*	.1691	.0552	.0586	.0618	.0648	.0677	.0705	.4523	3.3274	−2.3274	μ^*	11
	σ^*	−.8657	−.0880	−.0587	−.0306	−.0033	.0236	.0507	.9720	6.6338	−6.6338	σ^*	
7	μ^*	0990	.0500	.0562	.0620	.0675	.0730	.5924	1.6944	.0245	−.7189	μ^*	10
	σ^*	−1.0165	−.0993	−.0639	−.0301	.0026	.0350	1.1723	3.4870	−.1634	−3.3235	σ^*	
8	μ^*	−.0067	.0424	.0529	.0628	.0723	.7763	1.1017	.0621	.0433	−.2071	μ^*	9
	σ^*	−1.2255	−.1143	−.0704	−.0286	.0119	1.4268	2.3860	−.0480	−.1228	−2.2152	σ^*	
9	μ^*	−.1758	.0308	.0483	.0648	1.0318	.7784	.0722	.0627	.0527	.0340	μ^*	8
	σ^*	−1.5364	−.1355	−.0788	−.0248	1.7755	1.7996	.0059	−.0468	−.1010	−1.6576	σ^*	
10	μ^*	−.4747	.0113	.0413	1.4221	.5683	.0728	.0682	.0634	.0584	.1689	μ^*	7
	σ^*	−2.0508	−.1691	−.0908	2.3106	1.4204	.0361	−.0042	−.0449	−.0868	−1.3206	σ^*	
11	μ^*	−1.1041	−.0279	2.1320	.4184	.0696	.0679	.0661	.0642	.0621	.2517	μ^*	6
	σ^*	−3.0733	−.2329	3.3062	1.1454	.0553	.0226	−.0100	−.0429	−.0766	−1.0938	σ^*	
12	μ^*	−3.0732	4.0732	.3055	.0647	.0649	.0649	.0649	.0649	.0647	.3055	μ^*	5
	σ^*	−6.1270	6.1270	.9300	.0687	.0408	.0135	−.0135	−.0408	−.0687	−.9300	σ^*	
				$x_{(13)}$	$x_{(12)}$	$x_{(11)}$	$x_{(10)}$	$x_{(9)}$	$x_{(8)}$	$x_{(7)}$	$x_{(6)}$		

$n = 18$

$r_1 = 6$ r_2		$x_{(7)}$	$x_{(8)}$	$x_{(9)}$	$x_{(10)}$	$x_{(11)}$	$x_{(12)}$
6	μ^*	.3632	.0683	.0684	.0684	.0683	.3632
	σ^*	−1.3851	−.0610	−.0202	.0202	.0610	1.3851
7	μ^*	.2699	.0664	.0697	.0728	.5212	
	σ^*	−1.7410	−.0683	−.0155	.0367	1.7880	
8	μ^*	.0985	.0633	.0725	.7657		
	σ^*	−2.3291	−.0788	−.0059	2.4138		
9	μ^*	−.2723	.0576	1.2147			
	σ^*	−3.4979	−.0970	3.5949			
10	μ^*	−1.4517	2.4517				
	σ^*	−6.9880	6.9880				

$n = 18$

$r_1 = 7$ r_2		$x_{(8)}$	$x_{(9)}$	$x_{(10)}$	$x_{(11)}$		$r_1 = 8$ r_2
7	μ^*	.4271	.0729	.0729	.4271		
	σ^*	−2.3949	−.0361	.0361	2.3949		
8	μ^*	.2122	.0736	.7142			
	σ^*	−3.6001	−.0321	3.6323			
9	μ^*	−.4952	1.4952	.5000	.5000	μ^*	8
	σ^*	−7.1977	7.1977	7.2672	−7.2672	σ^*	
				$x_{(10)}$	$x_{(9)}$		

$n = 19$

$r_1 = 0$, r_2		$x_{(1)}$	$x_{(2)}$	$x_{(3)}$	$x_{(4)}$	$x_{(5)}$	$x_{(6)}$	$x_{(7)}$	$x_{(8)}$	$x_{(9)}$	$x_{(10)}$	$x_{(11)}$	$x_{(12)}$	$x_{(13)}$	$x_{(14)}$	$x_{(15)}$	$x_{(16)}$	$x_{(17)}$	$x_{(18)}$	$x_{(19)}$		$r_1 = 1$, r_2
0	μ^*	.0526	.0526	.0526	.0526	.0526	.0526	.0526	.0526	.0526	.0526	.0526	.0526	.0526	.0526	.0526	.0526	.0526	.0526	.0526		
	σ^*	−.1178	−.0792	−.0628	−.0505	−.0402	−.0312	−.0228	−.0150	−.0074	.0000	.0074	.0150	.0228	.0312	.0402	.0505	.0628	.0792	.1178		
1	μ^*	.0485	.0500	.0506	.0511	.0515	.0519	.0522	.0525	.0528	.0531	.0534	.0537	.0540	.0543	.0547	.0550	.0554	.1052			
	σ^*	−.1272	−.0851	−.0672	−.0538	−.0427	−.0328	−.0238	−.0152	−.0070	.0011	.0092	.0174	.0259	.0349	.0447	.0558	.0689	.1969			
2	μ^*	.0431	.0467	.0482	.0493	.0502	.0511	.0518	.0525	.0532	.0539	.0546	.0552	.0559	.0566	.0574	.0581	.1623	4.9198	−3.9198	μ^*	16
	σ^*	−.1372	−.0914	−.0719	−.0573	−.0451	−.0344	−.0245	−.0152	−.0063	.0025	.0113	.0202	.0295	.0392	.0498	.0616	.2690	3.5652	−3.5652	σ^*	
3	μ^*	.0365	.0426	.0451	.0471	.0487	.0501	.0514	.0526	.0538	.0550	.0561	.0572	.0584	.0596	.0608	.2249	3.0189	−.3980	−1.6209	μ^*	15
	σ^*	−.1482	−.0982	−.0769	−.0609	−.0477	−.0359	−.0252	−.0150	−.0053	.0043	.0139	.0236	.0336	.0442	.0556	.3381	2.3065	−.4977	−1.8088	σ^*	
4	μ^*	.0283	.0376	.0415	.0445	.0469	.0491	.0510	.0529	.0547	.0564	.0582	.0599	.0616	.0634	.2940	2.2286	−.1222	−.2148	−.8916	μ^*	14
	σ^*	−.1605	−.1057	−.0823	−.0649	−.0504	−.0375	−.0257	−.0146	−.0040	.0065	.0170	.0276	.0385	.0499	.4062	1.8082	−.2420	−.3491	−1.2171	σ^*	
5	μ^*	.0182	.0315	.0371	.0413	.0448	.0479	.0507	.0534	.0559	.0584	.0609	.0633	.0658	.3707	1.7540	−.0175	−.0665	−.1253	−.5447	μ^*	13
	σ^*	−.1744	−.1141	−.0884	−.0692	−.0532	−.0391	−.0262	−.0140	−.0022	.0093	.0207	.0323	.0442	.4744	1.5126	−.1288	−.1939	−.2719	−.9179	σ^*	
6	μ^*	.0057	.0240	.0318	.0376	.0424	.0467	.0506	.0542	.0577	.0611	.0644	.0678	.4561	1.4228	.0295	.0003	−.0330	−.0730	−.3467	μ^*	12
	σ^*	−.1905	−.1237	−.0952	−.0740	−.0563	−.0407	−.0264	−.0129	.0000	.0127	.0253	.0380	.5437	1.3039	−.0678	−.1125	−.1632	−.2239	−.7365	σ^*	
7	μ^*	−.0100	.0147	.0253	.0331	.0396	.0453	.0506	.0554	.0601	.0647	.0691	.5520	1.1724	.0522	.0334	.0128	−.0108	−.0390	−.2211	μ^*	11
	σ^*	−.2091	−.1347	−.1030	−.0794	−.0597	−.0423	−.0264	−.0114	.0029	.0170	.0309	.6152	1.1416	−.0307	−.0639	−.1003	−.1416	−.1908	−.6142	σ^*	
8	μ^*	−.0298	−.0032	.0172	.0276	.0363	.0439	.0509	.0574	.0636	.0696	.6603	.9736	.0633	.0506	.0369	.0220	.0050	−.0154	−.1358	μ^*	10
	σ^*	−.2312	−.1476	−.1120	−.0855	−.0634	−.0439	−.0261	−.0093	.0067	.0224	.6898	1.0075	−.0062	−.0324	−.0603	−.0908	−.1253	−.1665	−.5260	σ^*	
9	μ^*	−.0553	−.0115	.0070	.0209	.0324	.0425	.0516	.0602	.0684	.7839	.8103	.0682	.0593	.0500	.0400	.0290	.0166	.0017	−.0750	μ^*	9
	σ^*	−.2578	−.1630	−.1226	−.0925	−.0675	−.0454	−.0252	−.0063	.0118	.7685	.8920	.0109	−.0106	−.0331	−.0570	−.0830	−.1125	−.1476	−.4591	σ^*	
10	μ^*	−.0888	−.0306	−.0059	.0125	.0277	.0411	.0532	.0646	.9264	.6732	.0697	.0634	.0568	.0500	.0426	.0346	.0255	.0145	−.0302	μ^*	8
	σ^*	−.2907	−.1817	−.1353	−.1007	−.0720	−.0468	−.0237	−.0021	.8530	.7894	.0235	.0052	−.0135	−.0331	−.0539	−.0765	−.1021	−.1326	−.4064	σ^*	
11	μ^*	−.1341	−.0560	−.0229	.0017	.0221	.0399	.0561	1.0931	.5558	.0693	.0647	.0601	.0553	.0503	.0449	.0391	.0324	.0244	.0038	μ^*	7
	σ^*	−.3324	−.2051	−.1509	−.1106	−.0772	−.0478	−.0210	.9450	.6959	.0333	.0173	.0011	−.0155	−.0327	−.0510	−.0709	−.0934	−.1202	−.3639	σ^*	
12	μ^*	−.1976	−.0910	−.0459	−.0124	.0153	.0395	1.2920	.4542	.0677	.0644	.0611	.0578	.0543	.0507	.0469	.0427	.0379	.0322	.0301	μ^*	6
	σ^*	−.3873	−.2353	−.1708	−.1228	−.0831	−.0482	1.0474	.6091	.0413	.0268	.0124	−.0020	−.0167	−.0321	−.0483	−.0660	−.0860	−.1097	−.3286	σ^*	
13	μ^*	−.2909	−.1415	−.0783	−.0316	.0070	1.5353	.3652	.0654	.0631	.0608	.0585	.0562	.0538	.0513	.0486	.0457	.0424	.0384	.0507	μ^*	5
	σ^*	−.4629	−.2762	−.1971	−.1384	−.0898	1.1645	.5269	.0481	.0346	.0216	.0087	−.0043	−.0175	−.0313	−.0458	−.0617	−.0796	−.1008	−.2989	σ^*	
14	μ^*	−.4379	−.2194	−.1273	−.0593	1.8438	.2867	.0627	.0611	.0596	.0581	.0566	.0551	.0535	.0519	.0501	.0482	.0460	.0434	.0671	μ^*	4
	σ^*	−.5744	−.3353	−.2342	−.1594	1.3034	.4479	.0542	.0414	.0292	.0174	.0057	−.0060	−.0180	−.0304	−.0435	−.0578	−.0739	−.0930	−.2733	σ^*	
15	μ^*	−.6958	−.3527	−.2086	2.2572	.2169	.0597	.0588	.0579	.0570	.0561	.0552	.0543	.0534	.0524	.0514	.0503	.0490	.0474	.0802	μ^*	3
	σ^*	−.7568	−.4295	−.2918	1.4781	.3705	.0603	.0476	.0359	.0247	.0139	.0033	−.0073	−.0181	−.0294	−.0413	−.0542	−.0688	−.0861	−.2510	σ^*	
16	μ^*	−1.2401	−.6258	2.8659	.1547	.0566	.0562	.0558	.0554	.0550	.0546	.0542	.0538	.0534	.0530	.0525	.0520	.0515	.0507	.0906	μ^*	2
	σ^*	−1.1132	−.6084	1.7216	.2930	.0666	.0536	.0419	.0312	.0210	.0111	.0015	−.0082	−.0181	−.0283	−.0391	−.0509	−.0642	−.0799	−.2312	σ^*	
17	μ^*	−2.9705	3.9705	.0989	.0533	.0534	.0535	.0535	.0535	.0535	.0535	.0535	.0535	.0535	.0535	.0535	.0535	.0534	.0533	.0989	μ^*	1
	σ^*	−2.1527	2.1527	.2134	.0742	.0599	.0478	.0371	.0272	.0178	.0088	.0000	−.0088	−.0178	−.0272	−.0371	−.0478	−.0599	−.0742	−.2134	σ^*	
				$x_{(18)}$	$x_{(17)}$	$x_{(16)}$	$x_{(15)}$	$x_{(14)}$	$x_{(13)}$	$x_{(12)}$	$x_{(11)}$	$x_{(10)}$	$x_{(9)}$	$x_{(8)}$	$x_{(7)}$	$x_{(6)}$	$x_{(5)}$	$x_{(4)}$	$x_{(3)}$	$x_{(2)}$		

$n = 19$

$r_1 = 2$ r_2		$x_{(3)}$	$x_{(4)}$	$x_{(5)}$	$x_{(6)}$	$x_{(7)}$	$x_{(8)}$	$x_{(9)}$	$x_{(10)}$	$x_{(11)}$	$x_{(12)}$	$x_{(13)}$	$x_{(14)}$	$x_{(15)}$	$x_{(16)}$	$x_{(17)}$		$r_1 = 3$ r_2
2	μ^*	.1444	.0545	.0546	.0547	.0548	.0548	.0548	.0548	.0548	.0548	.0548	.0547	.0546	.0545	.1444		
	σ^*	−.3192	−.0719	−.0575	−.0447	−.0328	−.0215	−.0107	.0000	.0107	.0215	.0328	.0447	.0575	.0719	.3192		
3	μ^*	.1312	.0519	.0527	.0534	.0540	.0546	.0551	.0557	.0562	.0567	.0572	.0576	.0581	.2056			
	σ^*	−.3484	−.0777	−.0618	−.0475	−.0344	−.0219	−.0099	.0019	.0137	.0257	.0381	.0511	.0652	.4059			
4	μ^*	.1143	.0486	.0503	.0519	.0532	.0545	.0557	.0569	.0581	.0592	.0604	.0615	.2754	4.9420	−3.9420	μ^*	14
	σ^*	−.3818	−.0842	−.0665	−.0506	−.0359	−.0221	−.0087	.0044	.0175	.0307	.0444	.0588	.4940	5.5788	−5.5788	σ^*	
5	μ^*	.0927	.0445	.0474	.0500	.0523	.0545	.0566	.0587	.0607	.0627	.0647	.3552	2.6897	−.1321	−1.5576	μ^*	13
	σ^*	−.4206	−.0916	−.0717	−.0539	−.0375	−.0220	−.0071	.0075	.0222	.0369	.0521	.5857	3.1305	−.3269	−2.8036	σ^*	
6	μ^*	.0649	.0392	.0438	.0478	.0514	.0548	.0580	.0612	.0643	.0673	.4474	1.8547	−.0075	−.0538	−.7933	μ^*	12
	σ^*	−.4664	−.1002	−.0777	−.0576	−.0391	−.0217	−.0048	.0117	.0281	.0446	.6832	2.2553	−.1495	−.2318	−1.8741	σ^*	
7	μ^*	.0287	.0326	.0392	.0450	.0503	.0553	.0601	.0647	.0692	.5549	1.3902	.0396	.0134	−.0152	−.4280	μ^*	11
	σ^*	−.5218	−.1104	−.0847	−.0618	−.0407	−.0208	−.0017	.0171	.0357	.7892	1.7793	−.0677	−.1226	−.1824	−1.4066	σ^*	
8	μ^*	−.0194	.0239	.0334	.0417	.0493	.0564	.0632	.0698	.6819	1.0828	.0595	.0434	.0262	.0075	−.2104	μ^*	10
	σ^*	−.5902	−.1227	−.0930	−.0666	−.0422	−.0193	.0027	.0242	.9070	1.4659	−.0223	−.0626	−.1053	−.1516	−1.1241	σ^*	
9	μ^*	−.0849	.0124	.0257	.0375	.0482	.0583	.0679	.8348	.8591	.0675	.0572	.0464	.0349	.0223	−.0874	μ^*	9
	σ^*	−.6772	−.1380	−.1032	−.0721	−.0436	−.0168	.0090	1.0419	1.2356	.0057	−.0256	−.0582	−.0928	−.1303	−.9344	σ^*	
10	μ^*	−.1770	−.0034	.0155	.0322	.0474	.0616	1.0238	.6867	.0698	.0631	.0561	.0489	.0411	.0327	.0017	μ^*	8
	σ^*	−.7922	−.1578	−.1160	−.0788	−.0447	−.0126	1.2020	1.0535	.0246	−.0010	−.0272	−.0545	−.0833	−.1144	−.7977	σ^*	
11	μ^*	−.3129	−.0262	.0010	.0251	.0471	1.2659	.5487	.0691	.0647	.0603	.0557	.0509	.0458	.0402	.0646	μ^*	7
	σ^*	−.9517	−.1846	−.1329	−.0871	−.0451	1.4014	.9021	.0381	.0163	−.0056	−.0279	−.0511	−.0756	−.1021	−.6942	σ^*	
12	μ^*	−.5272	−.0613	−.0206	.0153	1.5938	.4352	.0668	.0641	.0614	.0586	.0557	.0526	.0494	.0458	.1106	μ^*	6
	σ^*	−1.1890	−.2234	−.1569	−.0979	1.6672	.7711	.0483	.0292	.0103	−.0087	−.0280	−.0481	−.0693	−.0921	−.6128	σ^*	
13	μ^*	−.9023	−.1210	−.0564	2.0797	.3401	.0637	.0621	.0606	.0590	.0574	.0558	.0541	.0522	.0501	.1448	μ^*	5
	σ^*	−1.5813	−.2859	−.1943	2.0614	.6541	.0566	.0393	.0225	.0059	−.0108	−.0277	−.0453	−.0638	−.0838	−.5469	σ^*	
14	μ^*	−1.6880	−.2427	2.9307	.2595	.0600	.0594	.0588	.0581	.0575	.0568	.0560	.0553	.0544	.0534	.1707	μ^*	4
	σ^*	−2.3601	−.4065	2.7666	.5469	.0639	.0477	.0322	.0173	.0025	−.0122	−.0272	−.0428	−.0591	−.0768	−.4923	σ^*	
15	μ^*	−4.1475	4.1475	.1905	.0561	.0562	.0563	.0563	.0564	.0564	.0564	.0563	.0563	.0562	.0561	.1905	μ^*	3
	σ^*	−4.6818	4.6818	.4460	.0707	.0549	.0404	.0265	.0132	.0000	−.0132	−.0265	−.0404	−.0549	−.0707	−.4460	σ^*	
				$x_{(16)}$	$x_{(15)}$	$x_{(14)}$	$x_{(13)}$	$x_{(12)}$	$x_{(11)}$	$x_{(10)}$	$x_{(9)}$	$x_{(8)}$	$x_{(7)}$	$x_{(6)}$	$x_{(5)}$	$x_{(4)}$		

$n = 19$

$r_1 = 4$ r_2		$x_{(5)}$	$x_{(6)}$	$x_{(7)}$	$x_{(8)}$	$x_{(9)}$	$x_{(10)}$	$x_{(11)}$	$x_{(12)}$	$x_{(13)}$	$x_{(14)}$	$x_{(15)}$		$r_1 = 5$ r_2
4	μ^*	.2380	.0580	.0582	.0583	.0583	.0583	.0583	.0583	.0582	.0580	.2380		
	σ^*	−.6089	−.0696	−.0512	−.0337	−.0167	.0000	.0167	.0337	.0512	.0696	.6089		
5	μ^*	.2089	.0555	.0567	.0577	.0587	.0597	.0606	.0615	.0623	.3185			
	σ^*	−.6835	−.0762	−.0551	−.0351	−.0156	.0035	.0225	.0419	.0617	.7359			
6	μ^*	.1691	.0520	.0547	.0572	.0595	.0617	.0639	.0661	.4158	3.7497	−2.7497	μ^*	12
	σ^*	−.7755	−.0841	−.0596	−.0364	−.0139	.0082	.0302	.0525	.8785	6.8463	−6.8463	σ^*	
7	μ^*	.1137	.0475	.0522	.0566	.0608	.0649	.0689	.5354	1.9264	.0047	−.9311	μ^*	11
	σ^*	−.8923	−.0937	−.0649	−.0375	−.0111	.0148	.0406	1.0442	3.6180	−.1875	−3.4305	σ^*	
8	μ^*	.0346	.0412	.0489	.0561	.0631	.0698	.6863	1.2679	.0517	.0297	−.3493	μ^*	10
	σ^*	−1.0466	−.1060	−.0713	−.0384	−.0067	.0244	1.2447	2.4914	−.0657	−.1383	−2.2874	σ^*	
9	μ^*	−.0834	.0321	.0444	.0560	.0670	.8840	.9099	.0664	.0546	.0422	−.0731	μ^*	9
	σ^*	−1.2607	−.1224	−.0795	−.0388	.0004	1.5010	1.8933	−.0087	−.0596	−.1123	−1.7127	σ^*	
10	μ^*	−.2711	.0183	.0380	.0564	1.1585	.6776	.0698	.0634	.0567	.0497	.0829	μ^*	8
	σ^*	−1.5795	−.1459	−.0904	−.0380	1.8538	1.5083	.0233	−.0154	−.0549	−.0957	−1.3655	σ^*	
11	μ^*	−.6009	−.0050	.0277	1.5782	.5117	.0685	.0652	.0618	.0583	.0546	.1799	μ^*	7
	σ^*	−2.1073	−.1832	−.1068	2.3973	1.2306	.0434	.0122	−.0191	−.0510	−.0839	−1.1323	σ^*	
12	μ^*	−1.2920	−.0521	2.3441	.3862	.0650	.0638	.0624	.0611	.0596	.0580	.2439	μ^*	6
	σ^*	−3.1570	−.2547	3.4118	1.0144	.0573	.0310	.0050	−.0211	−.0476	−.0749	−.9641	σ^*	
13	μ^*	−3.4468	4.4468	.2878	.0605	.0606	.0607	.0607	.0607	.0606	.0605	.2878	μ^*	5
	σ^*	−6.2931	6.2931	.8365	.0677	.0446	.0221	.0000	−.0221	−.0446	−.0677	−.8365	σ^*	
				$x_{(14)}$	$x_{(13)}$	$x_{(12)}$	$x_{(11)}$	$x_{(10)}$	$x_{(9)}$	$x_{(8)}$	$x_{(7)}$	$x_{(6)}$		

$n = 19$

$r_1 = 6$ r_2		$x_{(7)}$	$x_{(8)}$	$x_{(9)}$	$x_{(10)}$	$x_{(11)}$	$x_{(12)}$	$x_{(13)}$		$r_1 = 7$ r_2
6	μ^*	.3409	.0635	.0637	.0637	.0637	.0635	.3409		
	σ^*	−1.1932	−.0632	−.0314	.0000	.0314	.0632	1.1932		
7	μ^*	.2702	.0614	.0637	.0659	.0680	.4707			
	σ^*	−1.4409	−.0706	−.0311	.0078	.0466	1.4882			
8	μ^*	.1537	.0583	.0642	.0700	.6539	1.9828	−.9828	μ^*	10
	σ^*	−1.8092	−.0806	−.0296	.0206	1.8988	7.5178	−7.5178	σ^*	
9	μ^*	−.0562	.0530	.0657	.9375	.9673	.0648	−.0321	μ^*	9
	σ^*	−2.4186	−.0958	−.0254	2.5398	3.8225	−.0612	−3.7612	σ^*	
10	μ^*	−.5036	.0428	1.4607	.5991	.0705	.0664	.2641	μ^*	8
	σ^*	−3.6306	−.1234	3.7540	2.5438	.0145	−.0547	−2.5036	σ^*	
11	μ^*	−1.9126	2.9126	.3990	.0673	.0674	.0673	.3990	μ^*	7
	σ^*	−7.2517	7.2517	1.8709	.0502	.0000	−.0502	−1.8709	σ^*	
				$x_{(12)}$	$x_{(11)}$	$x_{(10)}$	$x_{(9)}$	$x_{(8)}$		

$n = 19$

$r_1 = 8$ r_2		$x_{(9)}$	$x_{(10)}$	$x_{(11)}$
8	μ^*	.4640	.0720	.4640
	σ^*	−3.8248	.0000	3.8248
9	μ^*	.0000	1.0000	
	σ^*	−7.6497	7.6497	

$n = 20$

$r_1 = 0$ / r_2		$x_{(1)}$	$x_{(2)}$	$x_{(3)}$	$x_{(4)}$	$x_{(5)}$	$x_{(6)}$	$x_{(7)}$	$x_{(8)}$	$x_{(9)}$	$x_{(10)}$	$x_{(11)}$	$x_{(12)}$	$x_{(13)}$	$x_{(14)}$	$x_{(15)}$	$x_{(16)}$	$x_{(17)}$	$x_{(18)}$	$x_{(19)}$	$x_{(20)}$		$r_1 = 1$ / r_2
0	μ^*	.0500	.0500	.0500	.0500	.0500	.0500	.0500	.5000	.0500	.0500	.0500	.0500	.0500	.0500	.0500	.0500	.0500	.0500	.0500	.0500		
	σ^*	−.1128	−.0765	−.0611	−.0497	−.0402	−.0318	−.0241	−.0169	−.0101	−.0033	.0033	.0101	.0169	.0241	.0318	.0402	.0497	.0611	.0765	.1128		
1	μ^*	.0462	.0476	.0482	.0486	.0489	.0493	.0495	.0498	.0501	.0503	.0506	.0508	.0511	.0513	.0516	.0519	.0522	.0525	.0996			
	σ^*	−.1212	−.0819	−.0652	−.0528	−.0425	−.0335	−.0252	−.0174	−.0099	−.0026	.0046	.0119	.0193	.0271	.0354	.0444	.0546	.0667	.1884			
2	μ^*	.0415	.0446	.0459	.0469	.0477	.0484	.0491	.0497	.0502	.0508	.0514	.0519	.0525	.0531	.0537	.0544	.0550	.1533	5.0879	−4.0879	μ^*	17
	σ^*	−.1303	−.0876	−.0695	−.0561	−.0449	−.0351	−.0261	−.0177	−.0096	−.0017	.0061	.0140	.0221	.0305	.0394	.0491	.0599	.2574	3.6146	−3.6146	σ^*	
3	μ^*	.0356	.0409	.0431	.0448	.0462	.0474	.0485	.0496	.0506	.0516	.0525	.0535	.0544	.0554	.0564	.0575	.2119	3.1377	−.4310	−1.7066	μ^*	16
	σ^*	−.1401	−.0938	−.0741	−.0595	−.0474	−.0367	−.0269	−.0178	−.0090	−.0004	.0080	.0166	.0253	.0344	.0440	.0543	.3233	2.3464	−.5126	−1.8338	σ^*	
4	μ^*	.0284	.0365	.0399	.0424	.0445	.0463	.0480	.0496	.0511	.0526	.0540	.0554	.0569	.0584	.0599	.2762	2.3290	−.1421	−.2370	−.9499	μ^*	15
	σ^*	−.1511	−.1006	−.0792	−.0632	−.0500	−.0384	−.0277	−.0178	−.0082	.0011	.0103	.0196	.0291	.0389	.0492	.3880	1.8459	−.2530	−.3588	−1.2341	σ^*	
5	μ^*	.0197	.0311	.0359	.0395	.0425	.0451	.0475	.0497	.0519	.0539	.0560	.0580	.0600	.0621	.3470	1.8440	−.0311	−.0815	−.1422	−.5893	μ^*	14
	σ^*	−.1634	−.1081	−.0847	−.0673	−.0528	−.0401	−.0285	−.0176	−.0071	.0030	.0131	.0232	.0335	.0441	.4526	1.5500	−.1378	−.2020	−.2792	−.9310	σ^*	
6	μ^*	.0090	.0246	.0312	.0361	.0402	.0438	.0470	.0501	.0530	.0558	.0586	.0613	.0640	.4254	1.5058	.0197	−.0105	−.0451	−.0867	−.3831	μ^*	13
	σ^*	−.1773	−.1166	−.0908	−.0717	−.0558	−.0418	−.0291	−.0171	−.0057	.0055	.0165	.0275	.0387	.5179	1.3416	−.0756	−.1195	−.1696	−.2297	−.7472	σ^*	
7	μ^*	−.0042	.0167	.0255	.0321	.0375	.0423	.0466	.0507	.0545	.0583	.0619	.0656	.5126	1.2499	.0449	.0253	.0036	−.0210	−.0507	−.2520	μ^*	12
	σ^*	−.1934	−.1262	−.0978	−.0766	−.0591	−.0437	−.0296	−.0164	−.0038	.0085	.0206	.0327	.5848	1.1802	−.0377	−.0703	−.1061	−.1469	−.1957	−.6235	σ^*	
8	μ^*	−.0206	.0069	.0185	.0272	.0343	.0406	.0463	.0517	.0567	.0616	.0664	.6103	1.0466	.0576	.0442	.0299	.0141	−.0040	−.0257	−.1627	μ^*	11
	σ^*	−.2121	−.1374	−.1057	−.0822	−.0627	−.0455	−.0299	−.0153	−.0013	.0123	.0257	.6541	1.0472	−.0128	−.0383	−.0657	−.0957	−.1298	−.1706	−.5342	σ^*	
9	μ^*	−.0414	−.0053	.0099	.0213	.0306	.0388	.0463	.0532	.0598	.0662	.7205	.8796	.0638	.0543	.0444	.0337	.0220	.0086	−.0075	−.0989	μ^*	10
	σ^*	−.2343	−.1504	−.1149	−.0886	−.0667	−.0475	−.0300	−.0136	.0020	.0172	.7268	.9329	.0047	−.0162	−.0382	−.0616	−.0873	−.1165	−.1513	−.4665	σ^*	
10	μ^*	−.0680	−.0208	−.0008	.0140	.0262	.0369	.0466	.0557	.0642	.8460	.7390	.0662	.0594	.0524	.0450	.0370	.0282	.0182	.0062	−.0517	μ^*	9
	σ^*	−.2612	−.1660	−.1258	−.0959	−.0712	−.0494	−.0296	−.0111	.0065	.8038	.8318	.0175	−.0002	−.0184	−.0375	−.0579	−.0803	−.1056	−.1359	−.4133	σ^*	
11	μ^*	−.1028	−.0408	−.0146	.0048	.0209	.0349	.0476	.0594	.9905	.6186	.0666	.0616	.0565	.0512	.0457	.0397	.0332	.0258	.0168	−.0158	μ^*	8
	σ^*	−.2943	−.1850	−.1389	−.1046	−.0762	−.0513	−.0287	−.0076	.8866	.7400	.0274	.0120	−.0037	−.0198	−.0367	−.0546	−.0743	−.0966	−.1232	−.3704	σ^*	
12	μ^*	−.1498	−.0673	−.0326	−.0068	.0144	.0329	.0497	1.1595	.5141	.0656	.0620	.0583	.0545	.0506	.0465	.0421	.0373	.0318	.0252	.0121	μ^*	7
	σ^*	−.3363	−.2088	−.1550	−.1151	−.0820	−.0531	−.0268	.9771	.6552	.0353	.0215	.0077	−.0063	−.0206	−.0356	−.0516	−.0691	−.0890	−.1126	−.3348	σ^*	
13	μ^*	−.2154	−.1039	−.0569	−.0222	.0064	.0313	1.3607	.4225	.0639	.0612	.0585	.0558	.0531	.0503	.0473	.0441	.0406	.0367	.0318	.0341	μ^*	6
	σ^*	−.3916	−.2396	−.1755	−.1280	−.0888	−.0544	1.0779	.5754	.0419	.0293	.0168	.0044	−.0081	−.0210	−.0345	−.0489	−.0646	−.0823	−.1035	−.3048	σ^*	
14	μ^*	−.3117	−.1565	−.0914	−.0433	−.0037	1.6066	.3414	.0616	.0597	.0579	.0560	.0541	.0522	.0502	.0481	.0459	.0434	.0406	.0372	.0517	μ^*	5
	σ^*	−.4679	−.2813	−.2028	−.1447	−.0967	1.1934	.4991	.0478	.0359	.0244	.0131	.0018	−.0095	−.0212	−.0334	−.0463	−.0605	−.0765	−.0956	−.2792	σ^*	
15	μ^*	−.4632	−.2378	−.1433	−.0738	1.9180	.2692	.0591	.0578	.0566	.0553	.0541	.0528	.0515	.0502	.0489	.0474	.0458	.0439	.0416	.0658	μ^*	4
	σ^*	−.5804	−.3417	−.2414	−.1673	1.3308	.4252	.0532	.0417	.0309	.0204	.0101	−.0002	−.0105	−.0211	−.0322	−.0439	−.0568	−.0713	−.0887	−.2568	σ^*	
16	μ^*	−.7284	−.3766	−.2298	2.3348	.2045	.0564	.0556	.0548	.0541	.0534	.0526	.0519	.0511	.0504	.0496	.0487	.0477	.0466	.0453	.0773	μ^*	3
	σ^*	−.7645	−.4380	−.3014	1.5039	.3524	.0587	.0472	.0366	.0266	.0170	.0076	−.0018	−.0112	−.0209	−.0310	−.0417	−.0534	−.0667	−.0825	−.2371	σ^*	
17	μ^*	−1.2872	−.6610	2.9482	.1464	.0535	.0532	.0529	.0525	.0522	.0519	.0516	.0512	.0509	.0506	.0502	.0498	.0494	.0489	.0482	.0865	μ^*	2
	σ^*	−1.1244	−.6212	1.7456	.2791	.0645	.0526	.0420	.0322	.0230	.0142	.0056	−.0030	−.0116	−.0205	−.0297	−.0395	−.0503	−.0624	−.0768	−.2195	σ^*	
18	μ^*	−3.0609	4.0609	.0939	.0506	.0507	.0508	.0508	.0508	.0508	.0508	.0508	.0508	.0508	.0508	.0508	.0508	.0508	.0507	.0506	.0939	μ^*	1
	σ^*	−2.1745	2.1745	.2034	.0716	.0584	.0473	.0375	.0285	.0200	.0119	.0039	−.0039	−.0119	−.0200	−.0285	−.0375	−.0473	−.0584	−.0716	−.2034	σ^*	
				$x_{(19)}$	$x_{(18)}$	$x_{(17)}$	$x_{(16)}$	$x_{(15)}$	$x_{(14)}$	$x_{(13)}$	$x_{(12)}$	$x_{(11)}$	$x_{(10)}$	$x_{(9)}$	$x_{(8)}$	$x_{(7)}$	$x_{(6)}$	$x_{(5)}$	$x_{(4)}$	$x_{(3)}$	$x_{(2)}$		

$n = 20$

$r_1 = 2$ r_2		$x_{(3)}$	$x_{(4)}$	$x_{(5)}$	$x_{(6)}$	$x_{(7)}$	$x_{(8)}$	$x_{(9)}$	$x_{(10)}$	$x_{(11)}$	$x_{(12)}$	$x_{(13)}$	$x_{(14)}$	$x_{(15)}$	$x_{(16)}$	$x_{(17)}$	$x_{(18)}$		$r_1 = 3$ r_2
2	μ^*	.1372	.0516	.0518	.0518	.0519	.0519	.0519	.0519	.0519	.0519	.0519	.0519	.0518	.0518	.0516	.1372		
	σ^*	−.3025	−.0694	−.0563	−.0447	−.0339	−.0239	−.0142	−.0047	.0047	.0142	.0239	.0339	.0447	.0563	.0694	.3025		
3	μ^*	.1254	.0492	.0500	.0506	.0511	.0516	.0520	.0525	.0529	.0533	.0537	.0541	.0545	.0549	.1943			
	σ^*	−.3284	−.0747	−.0603	−.0474	−.0357	−.0246	−.0139	−.0035	.0068	.0172	.0278	.0389	.0506	.0632	.3839			
4	μ^*	.1106	.0463	.0478	.0491	.0502	.0513	.0523	.0533	.0542	.0552	.0561	.0571	.0580	.2587	5.2448	−4.2448	μ^*	15
	σ^*	−.3577	−.0805	−.0646	−.0504	−.0374	−.0252	−.0134	−.0019	.0095	.0209	.0326	.0447	.0575	.4660	5.6948	−5.6948	σ^*	
5	μ^*	.0920	.0426	.0451	.0472	.0492	.0510	.0527	.0544	.0560	.0577	.0593	.0609	.3318	2.8697	−.1594	−1.7103	μ^*	14
	σ^*	−.3912	−.0871	−.0694	−.0537	−.0392	−.0256	−.0126	.0002	.0128	.0254	.0383	.0517	.5506	3.2074	−.3453	−2.8621	σ^*	
6	μ^*	.0684	.0380	.0418	.0451	.0480	.0508	.0535	.0560	.0585	.0610	.0635	.4153	1.9919	−.0237	−.0722	−.8961	μ^*	13
	σ^*	−.4303	−.0947	−.0749	−.0573	−.0411	−.0259	−.0114	.0028	.0169	.0310	.0453	.6397	2.3203	−.1629	−.2437	−1.9136	σ^*	
7	μ^*	.0383	.0323	.0377	.0425	.0468	.0508	.0546	.0583	.0619	.0655	.5112	1.5048	.0290	.0012	−.0292	−.5058	μ^*	12
	σ^*	−.4767	−.1035	−.0812	−.0613	−.0431	−.0260	−.0096	.0064	.0221	.0379	.7350	1.8391	−.0787	−.1325	−.1912	−1.4367	σ^*	
8	μ^*	−.0006	.0250	.0326	.0393	.0453	.0510	.0564	.0616	.0666	.6228	1.1828	0521	.0349	.0164	−.0039	−.2822	μ^*	11
	σ^*	−.5327	−.1140	−.0885	−.0659	−.0452	−.0257	−.0071	.0110	.0289	.8392	1.5234	−.0319	−.0712	−.1130	−.1586	−1.1487	σ^*	
9	μ^*	−.0521	.0156	.0261	.0353	.0437	.0516	.0590	.0662	.7545	.9485	.0623	.0511	.0392	.0265	.0127	−.1403	μ^*	10
	σ^*	−.6020	−.1267	−.0973	−.0712	−.0473	−.0249	−.0035	.0173	.9557	1.2921	−.0029	−.0334	−.0652	−.0991	−.1360	−.9554	σ^*	
10	μ^*	−.1218	.0031	.0176	.0304	.0420	.0528	.0631	.9128	.7679	.0661	.0586	.0508	.0426	.0338	.0242	−.0440	μ^*	9
	σ^*	−.6903	−.1426	−.1081	−.0775	−.0495	−.0233	.0017	1.0896	1.1100	.0165	−.0083	−.0337	−.0603	−.0886	−.1194	−.8162	σ^*	
11	μ^*	−.2195	−.0141	.0061	.0239	.0402	.0553	1.1082	.6230	.0666	.0616	.0564	.0510	.0453	.0392	.0326	.0244	μ^*	8
	σ^*	−.8070	−.1631	−.1218	−.0852	−.0517	−.0204	1.2492	.9593	.0303	.0094	−.0117	−.0335	−.0562	−.0803	−.1064	−.7109	σ^*	
12	μ^*	−.3633	−.0388	−.0100	.0153	.0384	1.3584	.5036	.0653	.0619	.0585	.0550	.0513	.0475	.0434	.0389	.0745	μ^*	7
	σ^*	−.9690	−.1909	−.1400	−.0949	−.0537	1.4485	.8295	.0407	.0225	.0043	−.0140	−.0329	−.0525	−.0734	−.0960	−.6283	σ^*	
13	μ^*	−.5893	−.0768	−.0343	.0031	1.6973	.4034	.0629	.0607	.0586	.0564	.0541	.0518	.0493	.0467	.0438	.1123	μ^*	6
	σ^*	−1.2101	−.2314	−.1658	−.1079	1.7153	.7144	.0490	.0327	.0166	.0006	−.0155	−.0321	−.0493	−.0676	−.0874	−.5614	σ^*	
14	μ^*	−.9839	−.1414	−.0746	2.1999	.3180	.0599	.0587	.0575	.0562	.0549	.0536	.0523	.0509	.0493	.0476	.1411	μ^*	5
	σ^*	−1.6089	−.2967	−.2065	2.1121	.6096	.0559	.0409	.0263	.0121	−.0021	−.0165	−.0311	−.0464	−.0625	−.0801	−.5061	σ^*	
15	μ^*	−1.8089	−.2731	3.0819	.2445	.0566	.0561	.0556	.0550	.0545	.0540	.0534	.0528	.0521	.0514	.0506	.1634	μ^*	4
	σ^*	−2.4009	−.4231	2.8240	.5121	.0621	.0479	.0343	.0213	.0085	−.0042	−.0170	−.0301	−.0437	−.0581	−.0738	−.4594	σ^*	
16	μ^*	−4.3863	5.3863	.1808	.0530	.0531	.0532	.0533	.0533	.0533	.0533	.0533	.0533	.0532	.0531	.0530	.1808	μ^*	3
	σ^*	−4.7627	4.7627	.4191	.0682	.0542	.0412	.0290	.0172	.0057	−.0057	−.0172	−.0290	−.0412	−.0542	−.0682	−.4191	σ^*	
				$x_{(17)}$	$x_{(16)}$	$x_{(15)}$	$x_{(14)}$	$x_{(13)}$	$x_{(12)}$	$x_{(11)}$	$x_{(10)}$	$x_{(9)}$	$x_{(8)}$	$x_{(7)}$	$x_{(6)}$	$x_{(5)}$	$x_{(4)}$		

$n = 20$

$r_1 = 4$, r_2		$x_{(5)}$	$x_{(6)}$	$x_{(7)}$	$x_{(8)}$	$x_{(9)}$	$x_{(10)}$	$x_{(11)}$	$x_{(12)}$	$x_{(13)}$	$x_{(14)}$	$x_{(15)}$	$x_{(16)}$		$r_1 = 5$, r_2
4	μ^*	.2255	.0547	.0549	.0549	.0550	.0550	.0550	.0550	.0549	.0549	.0547	.2255		
	σ^*	−.5653	−.0674	−.0513	−.0361	−.0215	−.0071	.0071	.0215	.0361	.0513	.0674	.5653		
5	μ^*	.2004	.0523	.0533	.0542	.0550	.0558	.0565	.0572	.0579	.0586	.2987			
	σ^*	−.6282	−.0733	−.0552	−.0380	−.0214	−.0052	.0109	.0271	.0436	.0607	.6789			
6	μ^*	.1671	.0493	.0514	.0534	.0552	.0570	.0587	.0604	.0621	.3855	4.1580	−3.1580	μ^*	13
	σ^*	−.7040	−.0803	−.0595	−.0399	−.0209	−.0024	.0159	.0343	.0531	.8038	7.0440	−7.0440	σ^*	
7	μ^*	.1222	.0452	.0490	.0524	.0557	.0558	.0619	.0649	.4899	2.1517	−.0155	−1.1362	μ^*	12
	σ^*	−.7977	−.0887	−.0646	−.0419	−.0200	.0014	.0226	.0438	.9451	3.7396	−.2096	−3.5300	σ^*	
8	μ^*	.0604	.0399	.0458	.0513	.0566	.0616	.0666	.6178	1.4302	.0405	.0160	−.4867	μ^*	11
	σ^*	−.9169	−.0990	−.0707	−.0439	−.0182	.0068	.0316	1.1104	2.5889	−.0819	−.1526	−2.3544	σ^*	
9	μ^*	−.0273	.0325	.0416	.0501	.0582	.0660	.7787	1.0392	.0598	.0461	.0317	−.1767	μ^*	10
	σ^*	−1.0745	−.1122	−.0782	−.0461	−.0152	.0148	1.3115	1.9799	−.0220	−.0714	−.1227	−1.7637	σ^*	
10	μ^*	−.1573	.0220	.0359	.0489	.0612	.9893	.7858	.0660	.0580	.0497	.0410	−.0004	μ^*	9
	σ^*	−1.2934	−.1300	−.0879	−.0482	−.0102	1.5697	1.5892	.0116	−.0257	−.0640	−.1039	−1.4072	σ^*	
11	μ^*	−.3629	.0059	.0275	.0477	1.2818	.6048	.0665	.0619	.0572	.0523	.0471	.1102	μ^*	8
	σ^*	−1.6196	−.1555	−.1012	−.0501	1.9264	1.3086	.0328	.0028	−.0274	−.0584	−.0906	−1.1678	σ^*	
12	μ^*	−.7224	−.0212	.0139	1.7297	.4675	.0644	.0620	.0595	.0569	.0542	.0514	.1841	μ^*	7
	σ^*	−2.1599	−.1963	−.1216	2.4778	1.0914	.0472	.0221	−.0028	−.0281	−.0539	−.0806	−.9954	σ^*	
13	μ^*	−1.4729	−.0761	2.5490	.3594	.0610	.0600	.0590	.0580	.0569	.0558	.0545	.2354	μ^*	6
	σ^*	−3.2350	−.2750	3.5100	.9137	.0578	.0360	.0146	−.0066	−.0281	−.0500	−.0727	−.8648	σ^*	
	μ^*	−3.8063	4.8063	.2721	.0568	.0570	.0570	.0571	.0571	.0570	.0570	.0568	.2721	μ^*	5
14	σ^*	−6.4480	6.4480	.7622	.0662	.0466	.0277	.0092	−.0092	−.0277	−.0466	−.0662	−.7622	σ^*	
				$x_{(15)}$	$x_{(14)}$	$x_{(13)}$	$x_{(12)}$	$x_{(11)}$	$x_{(10)}$	$x_{(9)}$	$x_{(8)}$	$x_{(7)}$	$x_{(6)}$		

$n = 20$

$r_1 = 6$ / r_2		$x_{(7)}$	$x_{(8)}$	$x_{(9)}$	$x_{(10)}$	$x_{(11)}$	$x_{(12)}$	$x_{(13)}$	$x_{(14)}$		$r_1 = 7$ / r_2
6	μ^*	.3214	.0594	.0595	.0596	.0596	.0595	.0594	.3214		
	σ^*	−1.0532	−.0634	−.0377	−.0125	.0125	.0377	.0634	1.0532		
7	μ^*	.2653	.0573	.0590	.0606	.0622	.0637	.4319			
	σ^*	−1.2372	−.0704	−.0395	−.0091	.0210	.0512	1.2839			
8	μ^*	.1794	.0543	.0585	.0625	.0664	.5789	2.4609	−1.4609	μ^*	11
	σ^*	−1.4924	−.0794	−.0411	−.0035	.0336	1.5828	7.8140	−7.8140	σ^*	
9	μ^*	.0405	.0497	.0580	.0660	.7859	1.2178	.0540	−.2718	μ^*	10
	σ^*	−1.8723	−.0920	−.0425	.0059	2.0008	3.9980	−.0878	−3.9102	σ^*	
10	μ^*	−.2067	.0421	.0577	1.1069	.7712	.0662	.0586	.1040	μ^*	9
	σ^*	−2.5015	−.1114	−.0432	2.6561	2.6807	−.0050	−.0718	−2.6040	σ^*	
11	μ^*	−.7285	.0270	1.7015	.5299	.0664	.0638	.0611	.2789	μ^*	8
	σ^*	−3.7537	−.1476	3.9013	1.9900	.0340	−.0141	−.0626	−1.9473	σ^*	
12	μ^*	−2.3608	3.3608	.3747	.0626	.0627	.0627	.0626	.3747	μ^*	7
	σ^*	−7.4963	7.4963	1.5506	.0562	.0186	−.0186	−.0562	−1.5506	σ^*	
				$x_{(13)}$	$x_{(12)}$	$x_{(11)}$	$x_{(10)}$	$x_{(9)}$	$x_{(8)}$		

$n = 20$

$r_1 = 8$ / r_2		$x_{(9)}$	$x_{(10)}$	$x_{(11)}$	$x_{(12)}$		$r_1 = 9$ / r_2
8	μ^*	.4335	.0665	.0665	.4335		
	σ^*	−2.6634	−.0332	.0332	2.6634		
9	μ^*	.2156	.0672	.7173			
	σ^*	−4.0023	−.0291	4.0314			
10	μ^*	−.4961	1.4961	.5000	.5000	μ^*	9
	σ^*	−8.0025	8.0025	8.0650	−8.0650	σ^*	
				$x_{(11)}$	$x_{(10)}$		

TABLE 10C.2

Variances and Covariances of the Best Linear Estimates of the Mean (μ^*) and Standard Deviation (σ^*) for Censored Samples up to Size 20 from a Normal Population

n	r_1		r_2 = 0	1	2	3	4	5	6	7	8	9	10	11	12
2	0	$V(\mu^*)$	.5000												
		$V(\sigma^*)$	.5708												
		Cov (μ^*, σ^*)	0												
3	0	$V(\mu^*)$	.3333	.4487											
		$V(\sigma^*)$	.2755	.6378											
		Cov (μ^*, σ^*)	0	.2044											
4	0	$V(\mu^*)$	.2500	.2870	.5130										
		$V(\sigma^*)$	.1801	.3021	.6730										
		Cov (μ^*, σ^*)	0	.0672	.3567										
	1	$V(\mu^*)$		.2982											
		$V(\sigma^*)$		.7057											
		Cov (μ^*, σ^*)		0											
5	0	$V(\mu^*)$	.2000	.2177	.2839	.6112									
		$V(\sigma^*)$	.1333	.1948	.3181	.6957									
		Cov (μ^*, σ^*)	0	.0330	.1234	.4749									
	1	$V(\mu^*)$		.2258	.2868										
		$V(\sigma^*)$		.3297	.7406										
		Cov (μ^*, σ^*)		0	.1584										
6	0	$V(\mu^*)$	.1667	.1769	.2068	.2999	.7186								
		$V(\sigma^*)$	.1057	.1428	.2044	.3292	.7119								
		Cov (μ^*, σ^*)	0	.0195	.0624	.1702	.5705								
	1	$V(\mu^*)$		.1825	.2070	.3296									
		$V(\sigma^*)$		.2102	.3460	.7628									
		Cov (μ^*, σ^*)		0	.0577	.2837									
	2	$V(\mu^*)$			.2147										
		$V(\sigma^*)$			.7747										
		Cov (μ^*, σ^*)			0										
7	0	$V(\mu^*)$	.1429	.1494	.1660	.2071	.3248	.8264							
		$V(\sigma^*)$	.0875	.1123	.1493	.2114	.3375	.7243							
		Cov (μ^*, σ^*)	0	.0128	.0375	.0881	.2099	.6503							
	1	$V(\mu^*)$		.1535	.1668	.2095	.3954								
		$V(\sigma^*)$		.1527	.2201	.3572	.7785								
		Cov (μ^*, σ^*)		0	.0300	.1065	.3864								
	2	$V(\mu^*)$			.1731	.2104									
		$V(\sigma^*)$			.3622	.7962									
		Cov (μ^*, σ^*)			0	.1273									

Up to $n = 15$ of this table is reproduced from A. E. Sarhan and B. G. Greenberg, "Estimation of location and scale parameters by order statistics from singly and doubly censored samples, Parts I and II," *Ann. Math. Statist.*, Vol. 27 (1956), pp. 427–451, and Vol. 29 (1958), pp. 79–105, with permission of W. Kruskal, editor of the *Annals of Mathematical Statistics*. The rest of the table is reproduced from A. E. Sarhan and B. G. Greenberg "Estimation of location and scale parameters by order statistics from singly and doubly censored samples, Part III," Tech. Rep. 4-OOR, Project 1597, with permission of the Commanding Officer, U.S. Army Research Office.

8	0	$V(\mu^*)$	.1250	.1295	.1399	.1623	.2138	.3541	.9310		
		$V(\sigma^*)$	.0746	.0924	.1171	.1542	.2168	.3441	.7342		
		Cov (μ^*, σ^*)	0	.0090	.0250	.0538	.1106	.2442	.7186		
	1	$V(\mu^*)$		.1326	.1409	.1623	.2233	.4711			
		$V(\sigma^*)$		.1193	.1594	.2272	.3655	.7904			
		Cov (μ^*, σ^*)		0	.0183	.0564	.1483	.4728			
	2	$V(\mu^*)$			.1457	.1627	.2392				
		$V(\sigma^*)$			.2300	.3732	.8113				
		Cov (μ^*, σ^*)			0	.0494	.2325				
	3	$V(\mu^*)$				.1682					
		$V(\sigma^*)$				.8171					
		Cov (μ^*, σ^*)				0					
9	0	$V(\mu^*)$	.1111	.1144	.1214	.1352	.1629	.2241	.3854	1.0313	
		$V(\sigma^*)$	.0650	.0784	.0960	.1207	.1581	.2212	.3494	.7423	
		Cov (μ^*, σ^*)	0	.0067	.0178	.0362	.0684	.1305	.2743	.7781	
	1	$V(\mu^*)$		.1167	.1224	.1352	.1647	.2435	.5505		
		$V(\sigma^*)$		.0976	.1242	.1645	.2327	.3720	.7998		
		Cov (μ^*, σ^*)		0	.0123	.0350	.0798	.1846	.5470		
	2	$V(\mu^*)$			.1261	.1361	.1657	.2851			
		$V(\sigma^*)$			.1662	.2371	.3814	.8227			
		Cov (μ^*, σ^*)			0	.0267	.0920	.3216			
	3	$V(\mu^*)$				.1410	.1661				
		$V(\sigma^*)$				.3841	.8317				
		Cov (μ^*, σ^*)				0	.1060				
10	0	$V(\mu^*)$	.1000	.1025	.1075	.1167	.1336	.1664	.2366	.4174	1.1269
		$V(\sigma^*)$	.0576	.0681	.0813	.0989	.1237	.1613	.2248	.3539	.7491
		Cov (μ^*, σ^*)	0	.0051	.0132	.0260	.0465	.0816	.1483	.3011	.8306
	1	$V(\mu^*)$		.1043	.1085	.1168	.1339	.1712	.2672	.6304	
		$V(\sigma^*)$		.0824	.1014	.1280	.1685	.2371	.3773	.8075	
		Cov (μ^*, σ^*)		0	.0088	.0238	.0500	.1007	.2167	.6120	
	2	$V(\mu^*)$			.1113	.1180	.1339	.1767	.3401		
		$V(\sigma^*)$			.1292	.1713	.2426	.3877	.8316		
		Cov (μ^*, σ^*)			0	.0168	.0505	.1293	.3986		
	3	$V(\mu^*)$				.1218	.1343	.1866			
		$V(\sigma^*)$				.2442	.3921	.8426			
		Cov (μ^*, σ^*)				0	.0429	.1964			
	4	$V(\mu^*)$					.1383				
		$V(\sigma^*)$					.8458				
		Cov (μ^*, σ^*)					0				

			r_2													
n	r_1		0	1	2	3	4	5	6	7	8	9	10	11	12	13
11	0	$V(\mu^*)$	.0909	.0929	.0966	.1031	.1143	.1342	.1718	.2504	.4493	1.2179				
		$V(\sigma^*)$	.0517	.0601	.0704	.0836	.1013	.1262	.1640	.2279	.3577	.7550				
		Cov (μ^*, σ^*)	0	.0041	.0102	.0195	.0336	.0559	.0936	.1644	.3251	.8777				
	1	$V(\mu^*)$		.0943	.0975	.1033	.1143	.1356	.1805	.2929	.7093					
		$V(\sigma^*)$		.0712	.0854	.1043	.1311	.1717	.2408	.3817	.8140					
		Cov (μ^*, σ^*)		0	.0066	.0172	.0343	.0637	.1194	.2453	.6696					
	2	$V(\mu^*)$			.0997	.1044	.1144	.1364	.1926	.3997						
		$V(\sigma^*)$			.1052	.1330	.1753	.2469	.3928	.8389						
		Cov (μ^*, σ^*)			0	.0115	.0321	.0718	.1623	.4662						
	3	$V(\mu^*)$				.1075	.1153	.1369	.2202							
		$V(\sigma^*)$				.1764	.2496	.3982	.8512							
		Cov (μ^*, σ^*)				0	.0239	.0806	.2748							
	4	$V(\mu^*)$					.1191	.1372								
		$V(\sigma^*)$					.3999	.8564								
		Cov (μ^*, σ^*)					0	.0908								
12	0	$V(\mu^*)$	.0833	.0849	.0878	.0926	.1004	.1136	.1363	.1784	.2650	.4809	1.3044			
		$V(\sigma^*)$	.0469	.0538	.0620	.0723	.0855	.1033	.1283	.1663	.2305	.3610	.7601			
		Cov (μ^*, σ^*)	0	.0033	.0081	.0152	.0254	.0406	.0645	.1045	.1791	.3469	.9202			
	1	$V(\mu^*)$		.0861	.0885	.0929	.1004	.1139	.1393	.1915	.3195	.7864				
		$V(\sigma^*)$		.0627	.0737	.0878	.1067	.1336	.1745	.2438	.3854	.8195				
		Cov (μ^*, σ^*)		0	.0052	.0130	.0250	.0440	.0762	.1364	.2710	.7212				
	2	$V(\mu^*)$			.0903	.0939	.1007	.1140	.1421	.2115	.4614					
		$V(\sigma^*)$			.0884	.1082	.1361	.1786	.2505	.3971	.8450					
		Cov (μ^*, σ^*)			0	.0084	.0222	.0460	.0909	.1918	.5263					
	3	$V(\mu^*)$				.0963	.1018	.1140	.1457	.2617						
		$V(\sigma^*)$				.1369	.1804	.2539	.4032	.8581						
		Cov (μ^*, σ^*)				0	.0153	.0454	.1141	.3438						
	4	$V(\mu^*)$					.1049	.1144	.1524							
		$V(\sigma^*)$					.2549	.4059	.8647							
		Cov (μ^*, σ^*)					0	.0379	.1699							
	5	$V(\mu^*)$						.1175								
		$V(\sigma^*)$						.8667								
		Cov (μ^*, σ^*)						0								
13	0	$V(\mu^*)$	.0769	.0782	.0805	.0841	.0899	.0991	.1141	.1395	.1858	.2799	.5118	1.3868		
		$V(\sigma^*)$	.0429	.0486	.0554	.0636	.0739	.0872	.1050	.1302	.1688	.2329	.3640	.7646		
		Cov (μ^*, σ^*)	0	.0027	.0066	.0121	.0198	.0309	.0472	.0725	.1146	.1925	.3668	.9589		

13	1	$V(\mu^*)$		.0792	.0811	.0845	.0900	.0992	.1152	.1444	.2036	.3466	.8613			
		$V(\sigma^*)$		.0559	.0647	.0756	.0898	.1088	.1358	.1768	.2465	.3886	.8243			
		Cov (μ^*, σ^*)		0	.0041	.0101	.0190	.0322	.0530	.0876	.1518	.2944	.7679			
	2	$V(\mu^*)$			.0826	.0854	.0903	.0992	.1159	.1500	.2324	.5237				
		$V(\sigma^*)$			.0761	.0909	.1106	.1387	.1813	.2536	.4007	.8502				
		Cov (μ^*, σ^*)			0	.0064	.0162	.0320	.0587	.1084	.2184	.5803				
	3	$V(\mu^*)$				.0874	.0914	.0993	.1164	.1584	.3078					
		$V(\sigma^*)$				.1112	.1399	.1836	.2574	.4073	.8639					
		Cov (μ^*, σ^*)				0	.0107	.0294	.0648	.1442	.4054					
	4	$V(\mu^*)$					.0939	.1002	.1167	.1780						
		$V(\sigma^*)$					.1843	.2591	.4108	.8714						
		Cov (μ^*, σ^*)					0	.0216	.0716	.2397						
	5	$V(\mu^*)$						.1032	.1168							
		$V(\sigma^*)$						.4118	.8747							
		Cov (μ^*, σ^*)						0	.0793							
14	0	$V(\mu^*)$	.0714	.0725	.0743	.0772	.0816	.0883	.0988	.1155	.1435	.1938	.2950	.5419	1.4654	
		$V(\sigma^*)$	.0395	.0444	.0500	.0568	.0650	.0753	.0886	.1065	.1318	.1702	.2350	.3666	.7687	
		Cov (μ^*, σ^*)	0	.0023	.0055	.0099	.0159	.0242	.0360	.0533	.0799	.1239	.2048	.3851	.9945	
	1	$V(\mu^*)$		.0733	.0749	.0775	.0817	.0883	.0992	.1175	.1505	.2164	.3736	.9337		
		$V(\sigma^*)$		.0505	.0576	.0664	.0773	.0915	.1106	.1376	.1789	.2488	.3914	.8284		
		Cov (μ^*, σ^*)		0	.0034	.0081	.0149	.0246	.0390	.0612	.0981	.1660	.3158	.8105		
	2	$V(\mu^*)$			.0762	.0784	.0821	.0884	.0993	.1193	.1594	.2543	.5858			
		$V(\sigma^*)$			.0668	.0781	.0929	.1127	.1408	.1836	.2561	.4038	.8547			
		Cov (μ^*, σ^*)			0	.0050	.0124	.0236	.0411	.0704	.1243	.2427	.6293			
	3	$V(\mu^*)$				.0800	.0831	.0887	.0993	.1212	.1737	.3567				
		$V(\sigma^*)$				.0933	.1137	.1425	.1863	.2604	.4108	.8689				
		Cov (μ^*, σ^*)				0	.0079	.0206	.0422	.0825	.1714	.4609				
	4	$V(\mu^*)$					.0852	.0896	.0994	.1237	.2104					
		$V(\sigma^*)$					.1430	.1875	.2626	.4148	.8770					
		Cov (μ^*, σ^*)					0	.0141	.0411	.1020	.3022					
	5	$V(\mu^*)$						.0922	.0997	.1286						
		$V(\sigma^*)$						.2633	.4166	.8812						
		Cov (μ^*, σ^*)						0	.0338	.1496						
	6	$V(\mu^*)$							.1022							
		$V(\sigma^*)$							.8825							
		Cov (μ^*, σ^*)							0							
15	0	$V(\mu^*)$	.0667	.0676	.0691	.0714	.0748	.0799	.0875	.0992	.1176	.1480	.2022	.3101	.5713	1.5404
		$V(\sigma^*)$	.0366	.0408	.0456	.0512	.0580	.0662	.0765	.0899	.1078	.1332	.1718	.2368	.3689	.7723
		Cov (μ^*, σ^*)	0	.0019	.0046	.0082	.0130	.0195	.0284	.0409	.0590	.0868	.1325	.2163	.4020	1.0273

n	r_1		r_2 = 0	1	2	3	4	5	6	7	8	9	10	11	12	13	14	15	16
15	1	$V(\mu^*)$		.0683	.0696	.0717	.0749	.0799	.0877	.1001	.1207	.1574	.2296	.4004	1.0037				
		$V(\sigma^*)$		.0460	.0519	.0590	.0678	.0787	.0929	.1121	.1393	.1807	.2508	.3939	.8322				
		Cov (μ^*, σ^*)		0	.0028	.0067	.0120	.0194	.0299	.0453	.0689	.1079	.1791	.3355	.8496				
	2	$V(\mu^*)$			.0706	.0724	.0753	.0800	.0877	.1007	.1239	.1697	.2769	.6471					
		$V(\sigma^*)$			.0594	.0684	.0798	.0946	.1145	.1427	.1856	.2584	.4065	.8586					
		Cov (μ^*, σ^*)			0	.0040	.0098	.0181	.0304	.0496	.0812	.1389	.2649	.6740					
	3	$V(\mu^*)$				.0738	.0762	.0804	.0877	.1011	.1279	.1908	.4069						
		$V(\sigma^*)$				.0802	.0953	.1157	.1446	.1886	.2629	.4138	.8731						
		Cov (μ^*, σ^*)				0	.0061	.0153	.0298	.0541	.0987	.1962	.5112						
	4	$V(\mu^*)$					.0780	.0813	.0879	.1014	.1340	.2472							
		$V(\sigma^*)$					.1161	.1455	.1901	.2655	.4182	.8817							
		Cov (μ^*, σ^*)					0	.0099	.0270	.0590	.1295	.3585							
	5	$V(\mu^*)$						.0835	.0886	.1016	.1487								
		$V(\sigma^*)$						.1906	.2667	.4205	.8866								
		Cov (μ^*, σ^*)						0	.0196	.0644	.2126								
	6	$V(\mu^*)$							.0911	.1017									
		$V(\sigma^*)$							.4212	.8888									
		Cov (μ^*, σ^*)							0	.0704									
16	0	$V(\mu^*)$	.0625	.0633	.0645	.0664	.0692	.0731	.0789	.0874	.1002	.1202	.1529	.2107	.3250	.5998	1.6121		
		$V(\sigma^*)$	.0341	.0378	.0419	.0467	.0523	.0590	.0672	.0776	.0910	.1090	.1345	.1732	.2385	.3710	.7756		
		Cov (μ^*, σ^*)	0	.0017	.0039	.0069	.0109	.0160	.0229	.0323	.0454	.0644	.0933	.1406	.2269	.4177	1.0578		
	1	$V(\mu^*)$		.0639	.0650	.0667	.0693	.0732	.0789	.0878	.1017	.1245	.1647	.2431	.4269	1.0713			
		$V(\sigma^*)$		.0422	.0472	.0532	.0603	.0690	.0800	.0942	.1135	.1407	.1823	.2527	.3962	.8355			
		Cov (μ^*, σ^*)		0	.0024	.0055	.0098	.0156	.0236	.0348	.0512	.0761	.1170	.1913	.3537	.8858			
	2	$V(\mu^*)$			.0659	.0674	.0697	.0733	.0789	.0880	.1029	.1294	.1808	.2998	.7073				
		$V(\sigma^*)$			.0534	.0608	.0699	.0813	.0961	.1160	.1443	.1874	.2604	.4089	.8621				
		Cov (μ^*, σ^*)			0	.0033	.0079	.0143	.0234	.0369	.0574	.0912	.1525	.2854	.7151				
	3	$V(\mu^*)$				.0685	.0705	.0737	.0790	.0880	.1042	.1359	.2091	.4578					
		$V(\sigma^*)$				.0701	.0819	.0970	.1175	.1465	.1905	.2651	.4164	.8768					
		Cov (μ^*, σ^*)				0	.0048	.0118	.0222	.0384	.0651	.1136	.2189	.5573					
	4	$V(\mu^*)$					.0720	.0746	.0793	.0880	.1056	.1466	.2867						
		$V(\sigma^*)$					.0973	.1182	.1476	.1924	.2680	.4211	.8858						
		Cov (μ^*, σ^*)					0	.0074	.0192	.0390	.0753	.1546	.4098						
	5	$V(\mu^*)$						.0764	.0802	.0881	.1074	.1747							
		$V(\sigma^*)$						.1480	.1933	.2695	.4238	.8911							
		Cov (μ^*, σ^*)						0	.0130	.0375	.0921	.2695							
	6	$V(\mu^*)$							.0824	.0884	.1110								
		$V(\sigma^*)$							.2700	.4250	.8941								
		Cov (μ^*, σ^*)							0	.0306	.1337								
	7	$V(\mu^*)$								.0904									
		$V(\sigma^*)$								.8950									
		Cov (μ^*, σ^*)								0									

17	0	$V(\mu^*)$	.0588	.0595	.0605	.0621	.0644	.0675	.0720	.0784	.0877	.1016	.1231	.1581	.2194	.3398	.6274	1.6808	
		$V(\sigma^*)$	.0320	.0352	.0387	.0428	.0476	.0532	.0599	.0682	.0786	.0920	.1101	.1357	.1745	.2400	.3729	.7786	
		Cov (μ^*, σ^*)	0	.0015	.0034	.0059	.0092	.0134	.0189	.0262	.0360	.0497	.0694	.0993	.1481	.2369	.4324	1.0862	
	1	$V(\mu^*)$		.0600	.0610	.0624	.0645	.0676	.0720	.0786	.0885	.1038	.1288	.1723	.2566	.4529	1.1366		
		$V(\sigma^*)$		.0390	.0433	.0483	.0542	.0613	.0701	.0811	.0954	.1147	.1420	.1837	.2543	.3982	.8385		
		Cov (μ^*, σ^*)		0	.0020	.0047	.0082	.0129	.0191	.0276	.0395	.0567	.0829	.1254	.2026	.3706	.9193		
	2	$V(\mu^*)$			.0617	.0630	.0649	.0677	.0720	.0786	.0890	.1059	.1354	.1923	.3227	.7662			
		$V(\sigma^*)$			.0485	.0547	.0620	.0711	.0825	.0974	.1174	.1458	.1890	.2622	.4110	.8652			
		Cov (μ^*, σ^*)			0	.0028	.0065	.0116	.0186	.0285	.0429	.0648	.1005	.1650	.3044	.7531			
	3	$V(\mu^*)$				.0640	.0656	.0681	.0722	.0786	.0894	.1083	.1447	.2281	.5086				
		$V(\sigma^*)$				.0623	.0716	.0833	.0985	.1190	.1481	.1923	.2670	.4187	.8801				
		Cov (μ^*, σ^*)				0	.0039	.0093	.0172	.0287	.0463	.0752	.1275	.2399	.5997				
	4	$V(\mu^*)$					.0669	.0690	.0725	.0787	.0897	.1112	.1609	.3280					
		$V(\sigma^*)$					.0835	.0990	.1199	.1495	.1943	.2701	.4236	.8893					
		Cov $(\mu^*, \sigma^*$					0	.0057	.0144	.0278	.0500	.0905	.1778	.4567					
	5	$V(\mu^*)$						.0705	.0734	.0788	.0899	.1159	.2046						
		$V(\sigma^*)$						.1202	.1501	.1955	.2719	.4266	.8951						
		Cov (μ^*, σ^*)						0	.0093	.0250	.0540	.1175	.3213						
	6	$V(\mu^*)$							.0753	.0795	.0900	.1273							
		$V(\sigma^*)$							.1958	.2728	.4282	.8985							
		Cov (μ^*, σ^*)							0	.0180	.0584	.1909							
	7	$V(\mu^*)$								.0815	.0900								
		$V(\sigma^*)$								.4288	.9001								
		Cov (μ^*, σ^*)								0	.0633								
18	0	$V(\mu^*)$	.0556	.0561	.0570	.0584	.0602	.0628	.0664	.0713	.0784	.0885	.1034	.1264	.1635	.2282	.3544	.6543	1.7467
		$V(\sigma^*)$	.0301	.0329	.0360	.0395	.0436	.0483	.0540	.0607	.0690	.0794	.0929	.1111	.1368	.1757	.2414	.3746	.7814
		Cov (μ^*, σ^*)	0	.0013	.0030	.0051	.0079	.0114	.0158	.0216	.0293	.0395	.0538	.0742	.1050	.1552	.2463	.4462	1.1127
	1	$V(\mu^*)$		.0566	.0574	.0586	.0604	.0628	.0664	.0714	.0787	.0896	.1064	.1334	.1802	.2702	.4783	1.1996	
		$V(\sigma^*)$		.0362	.0400	.0442	.0492	.0551	.0622	.0710	.0821	.0964	.1158	.1432	.1850	.2558	.4000	.8413	
		Cov (μ^*, σ^*)		0	.0017	.0040	.0070	.0108	.0158	.0224	.0314	.0439	.0619	.0892	.1334	.2132	.3865	.9506	
	2	$V(\mu^*)$			.0581	.0591	.0607	.0630	.0664	.0714	.0789	.0906	.1094	.1420	.2041	.3456	.8237		
		$V(\sigma^*)$			.0444	.0496	.0557	.0631	.0722	.0836	.0985	.1186	.1470	.1904	.2638	.4130	.8680		
		Cov (μ^*, σ^*)			0	.0023	.0054	.0096	.0151	.0227	.0332	.0485	.0717	.1093	.1768	.3221	.7885		

n	r_1		r_2 = 0	1	2	3	4	5	6	7	8	9	10	11	12	13	14	15	16	17	18
18	3	$V(\mu^*)$				.0600	.0614	.0634	.0666	.0714	.0790	.0915	.1131	.1543	.2476	.5592					
		$V(\sigma^*)$				.0559	.0635	.0728	.0846	.0998	.1204	.1495	.1938	.2688	.4208	.8831					
		Cov (μ^*, σ^*)				0	.0032	.0076	.0137	.0223	.0348	.0538	.0847	.1403	.2594	.6389					
	4	$V(\mu^*)$					.0624	.0642	.0670	.0715	.0791	.0924	.1180	.1763	.3703						
		$V(\sigma^*)$					.0730	.0850	.1005	.1214	.1511	.1961	.2720	.4258	.8924						
		Cov (μ^*, σ^*)					0	.0046	.0112	.0209	.0359	.0603	.1045	.1991	.5000						
	5	$V(\mu^*)$						.0655	.0678	.0718	.0791	.0934	.1265	.2373							
		$V(\sigma^*)$						.1008	.1220	.1519	.1974	.2741	.4290	.8985							
		Cov (μ^*, σ^*)						0	.0070	.0179	.0361	.0693	.1408	.3689							
	6	$V(\mu^*)$							.0694	.0725	.0791	.0948	.1486								
		$V(\sigma^*)$							.1522	.1980	.2752	.4310	.9023								
		Cov (μ^*, σ^*)							0	.0120	.0345	.0839	.2432								
	7	$V(\mu^*)$								.0744	.0794	.0977									
		$V(\sigma^*)$								.2756	.4319	.9044									
		Cov (μ^*, σ^*)								0	.0279	.1208									
	8	$V(\mu^*)$									.0810										
		$V(\sigma^*)$									.9050										
		Cov (μ^*, σ^*)									0										
19	0	$V(\mu^*)$	.0526	.0531	.0539	.0550	.0566	.0587	.0616	.0656	.0710	.0787	.0895	.1055	.1299	.1691	.2369	.3687	.6804	1.8101	
		$V(\sigma^*)$	.0284	.0309	.0336	.0367	.0403	.0443	.0491	.0547	.0614	.0698	.0802	.0938	.1120	.1377	.1768	.2426	.3763	.7839	
		Cov (μ^*, σ^*)	0	.0011	.0026	.0045	.0068	.0098	.0135	.0182	.0242	.0322	.0429	.0576	.0787	.1104	.1619	.2551	.4591	1.1377	
	1	$V(\mu^*)$		.0536	.0543	.0553	.0568	.0588	.0616	.0656	.0712	.0793	.0911	.1093	.1383	.1882	.2836	.5032	1.2606		
		$V(\sigma^*)$		.0338	.0371	.0408	.0451	.0500	.0560	.0631	.0719	.0829	.0973	.1167	.1443	.1862	.2571	.4017	.8438		
		Cov (μ^*, σ^*)		0	.0015	.0035	.0060	.0092	.0133	.0186	.0256	.0350	.0481	.0669	.0951	.1409	.2232	.4013	.9799		
	2	$V(\mu^*)$			.0549	.0558	.0571	.0590	.0617	.0656	.0713	.0797	.0926	.1133	.1488	.2160	.3682	.8797			
		$V(\sigma^*)$			.0410	.0454	.0505	.0567	.0641	.0731	.0846	.0995	.1197	.1482	.1917	.2652	.4147	.8705			
		Cov (μ^*, σ^*)			0	.0020	.0046	.0080	.0125	.0185	.0265	.0377	.0539	.0782	.1174	.1877	.3386	.8214			
	3	$V(\mu^*)$				.0565	.0577	.0594	.0619	.0656	.0713	.0801	.0942	.1184	.1643	.2673	.6091				
		$V(\sigma^*)$				.0507	.0570	.0646	.0739	.0857	.1010	.1216	.1508	.1952	.2703	.4226	.8857				
		Cov (μ^*, σ^*)				0	.0027	.0063	.0111	.0178	.0271	.0405	.0608	.0936	.1523	.2776	.6754				
	4	$V(\mu^*)$					.0586	.0601	.0623	.0658	.0713	.0803	.0960	.1257	.1925	.4131					
		$V(\sigma^*)$					.0647	.0743	.0863	.1018	.1228	.1525	.1976	.2737	.4278	.8952					
		Cov (μ^*, σ^*)					0	.0037	.0089	.0163	.0270	.0434	.0700	.1175	.2190	.5401					
	5	$V(\mu^*)$						.0612	.0631	.0661	.0713	.0805	.0983	.1385	.2718						
		$V(\sigma^*)$						.0864	.1022	.1235	.1535	.1991	.2759	.4312	.9015						
		Cov (μ^*, σ^*)						0	.0054	.0135	.0260	.0465	.0834	.1624	.4128						

	6	$V(\mu^*)$							.0644	.0669	.0715	.0807	.1019	.1734							
		$V(\sigma^*)$							.1237	.1540	.1999	.2773	.4334	.9056							
		Cov (μ^*, σ^*)							0	.0087	.0232	.0498	.1074	.2912							
	7	$V(\mu^*)$								.0685	.0721	.0808	.1111								
		$V(\sigma^*)$								.2002	.2779	.4346	.9081								
		Cov (μ^*, σ^*)								0	.0166	.0535	.1733								
	8	$V(\mu^*)$									.0738	.0808									
		$V(\sigma^*)$									.4350	.9092									
		Cov (μ^*, σ^*)									0	.0575									
20	0	$V(\mu^*)$	.0500	.0504	.0511	.0521	.0534	.0552	.0576	.0608	.0651	.0710	.0792	.0909	.1078	.1335	.1747	.2456	.3828	.7056	1.8710
		$V(\sigma^*)$	.0268	.0291	.0316	.0343	.0374	.0409	.0450	.0497	.0553	.0621	.0705	.0810	.0945	.1128	.1386	.1778	.2438	.3778	.7863
		Cov (μ^*, σ^*)	0	.0010	.0023	.0039	.0060	.0085	.0116	.0155	.0204	.0267	.0350	.0460	.0612	.0829	.1155	.1682	.2634	.4713	1.1613
	1	$V(\mu^*)$		.0508	.0514	.0523	.0536	.0553	.0576	.0608	.0652	.0714	.0801	.0930	.1124	.1434	.1963	.2970	.5275	1.3194	
		$V(\sigma^*)$		.0317	.0346	.0378	.0415	.0458	.0508	.0567	.0638	.0726	.0838	.0982	.1176	.1452	.1872	.2584	.4032	.8461	
		Cov (μ^*, σ^*)		0	.0013	.0030	.0052	.0079	.0113	.0156	.0212	.0286	.0385	.0521	.0715	.1008	.1479	.2325	.4153	1.0075	
	2	$V(\mu^*)$			.0520	.0528	.0539	.0555	.0577	.0608	.0652	.0716	.0809	.0950	.1176	.1559	.2280	.3905	.9343		
		$V(\sigma^*)$			.0380	.0418	.0462	.0514	.0575	.0649	.0740	.0855	.1005	.1206	.1493	.1928	.2665	.4163	.8728		
		Cov (μ^*, σ^*)			0	.0017	.0040	.0068	.0105	.0153	.0217	.0302	.0420	.0589	.0843	.1251	.1981	.3541	.8523		
	3	$V(\mu^*)$				.0534	.0544	.0558	.0579	.0609	.0652	.0717	.0816	.0974	.1242	.1746	.2870	.6583			
		$V(\sigma^*)$				.0464	.0517	.0579	.0655	.0749	.0867	.1020	.1226	.1519	.1965	.2717	.4243	.8881			
		Cov (μ^*, σ^*)				0	.0023	.0053	.0092	.0145	.0217	.0316	.0459	.0674	.1020	.1636	.2946	.7095			
	4	$V(\mu^*)$					.0552	.0564	.0583	.0611	.0652	.0717	.0822	.1002	.1340	.2092	.4561				
		$V(\sigma^*)$					.0581	.0658	.0754	.0874	.1030	.1240	.1537	.1989	.2752	.4296	.8977				
		Cov (μ^*, σ^*)					0	.0031	.0073	.0130	.0211	.0328	.0505	.0790	.1297	.2375	.5775				
	5	$V(\mu^*)$						.0574	.0590	.0614	.0653	.0718	.0829	.1041	.1516	.3076					
		$V(\sigma^*)$						.0755	.0877	.1035	.1248	.1549	.2006	.2775	.4331	.9042					
		Cov (μ^*, σ^*)						0	.0044	.0106	.0197	.0336	.0562	.0966	.1825	.4536					
	6	$V(\mu^*)$							.0602	.0622	.0656	.0718	.0837	.1109	.2009						
		$V(\sigma^*)$							.1037	.1252	.1556	.2016	.2791	.4355	.9085						
		Cov (μ^*, σ^*)							0	.0066	.0168	.0336	.0640	.1292	.3355						
	7	$V(\mu^*)$								.0636	.0663	.0718	.0848	.1288							
		$V(\sigma^*)$								.1558	.2021	.2799	.4369	.9113							
		Cov (μ^*, σ^*)								0	.0112	.0319	.0771	.2216							
	8	$V(\mu^*)$									.0679	.0721	.0871								
		$V(\sigma^*)$									.2802	.4376	.9128								
		Cov $(\mu^*, \sigma^*$									0	.0256	.1102								
	9	$V(\mu^*)$										.0734									
		$V(\sigma^*)$										.9133									
		Cov (μ^*, σ^*)										0									

TABLE 10C.3

PERCENTAGE EFFICIENCIES OF THE BEST LINEAR ESTIMATES OF THE MEAN (μ^*) AND STANDARD DEVIATION (σ^*) FOR CENSORED SAMPLES RELATIVE TO UNCENSORED SAMPLES IN A NORMAL POPULATION UP TO SIZE 20

n	r_1		r_2 = 0	1	2	3	4	5	6	7	8	9	10	11	12	13
2	0	μ^*	100.00													
		σ^*	100.00													
3	0	μ^*	100.00	74.29												
		σ^*	100.00	43.19												
4	0	μ^*	100.00	87.10	48.73											
		σ^*	100.00	59.60	26.75											
	1	μ^*		83.84												
		σ^*		25.51												
5	0	μ^*	100.00	91.86	70.44	32.72										
		σ^*	100.00	68.45	41.91	19.16										
	1	μ^*		88.58	69.73											
		σ^*		40.44	18.00											
6	0	μ^*	100.00	94.23	80.58	55.58	23.19									
		σ^*	100.00	74.03	51.72	32.11	14.85									
	1	μ^*		91.32	80.52	50.57										
		σ^*		50.29	30.55	13.86										
	2	μ^*			77.61											
		σ^*			13.64											
7	0	μ^*	100.00	95.61	86.06	68.97	43.98	17.29								
		σ^*	100.00	77.89	58.61	41.40	25.92	12.08								
	1	μ^*		93.09	85.64	68.20	36.13									
		σ^*		57.30	39.76	24.50	11.24									
	2	μ^*			82.52	67.88										
		σ^*			24.16	10.99										
8	0	μ^*	100.00	96.50	89.36	77.04	58.48	35.30	13.43							
		σ^*	100.00	80.73	63.73	48.39	34.42	21.68	10.16							
	1	μ^*		94.30	88.70	77.00	55.97	26.53								
		σ^*		62.55	46.80	32.84	20.41	9.44								
	2	μ^*			85.81	76.83	52.25									
		σ^*			32.44	19.99	9.20									
	3	μ^*				74.32										
		σ^*				9.13										

9	0	μ^*	100.00	97.11	91.52	82.21	68.20	49.59	28.83	10.77		
		σ^*	100.00	82.90	67.69	53.84	41.12	29.40	18.61	8.76		
	1	μ^*		95.18	90.74	82.19	67.48	45.63	20.18			
		σ^*		66.62	52.34	39.53	27.94	17.48	8.13			
	2	μ^*			88.14	81.62	67.07	38.97				
		σ^*			39.11	27.42	17.05	7.90				
	3	μ^*				78.81	66.89					
		σ^*				16.93	7.82					
10	0	μ^*	100.00	97.56	93.03	85.72	74.85	60.09	42.27	23.96	8.87	
		σ^*	100.00	84.62	70.85	58.23	46.55	35.70	25.62	16.27	7.69	
	1	μ^*		95.85	92.20	85.60	74.69	58.40	37.42	15.86		
		σ^*		69.88	56.83	45.00	34.19	24.29	15.27	7.13		
	2	μ^*			89.87	84.78	74.69	56.61	29.40			
		σ^*			44.58	33.62	23.74	14.85	6.93			
	3	μ^*				82.09	74.48	53.60				
		σ^*				23.59	14.69	6.84				
	4	μ^*					72.29					
		σ^*					6.81					
11	0	μ^*	100.00	97.89	94.13	88.20	79.55	67.74	52.92	36.31	20.23	7.46
		σ^*	100.00	86.02	73.43	61.82	51.04	40.95	31.51	22.68	14.45	6.85
	1	μ^*		96.36	93.29	87.98	79.54	67.06	50.37	31.04	12.82	
		σ^*		72.55	60.53	49.55	39.44	30.10	21.47	13.54	6.35	
	2	μ^*			91.20	87.04	79.46	66.64	47.21	22.75		
		σ^*			49.14	38.86	29.48	20.93	13.16	6.16		
	3	μ^*				84.56	78.84	66.39	41.29			
		σ^*				29.31	20.71	12.98	6.07			
	4	μ^*					76.32	66.28				
		σ^*					12.93	6.04				

Up to $n = 15$ of this table is reproduced from A. E. Sarhan and B. G. Greenberg, "Estimation of location and scale parameters by order statistics from singly and doubly censored samples, Parts I and II," *Ann. Math. Statist.*, Vol. 27 (1956), pp. 427–451, and Vol. 29 (1958), pp. 79–105, with permission of W. Kruskal, editor of the *Annals of Mathematical Statistics*. The rest of the table is reproduced from A. E. Sarhan and B. G. Greenberg, "Estimation of location and scale parameters by order statistics from singly and doubly censored samples, Part III," Tech. Rep. 4-OOR, Project 1597, with permission of the Commanding Officer, U.S. Army Research Office.

n	r_1		r_2: 0	1	2	3	4	5	6	7	8	9	10	11	12	13	14
12	0	μ^*	100.00	98.16	94.95	90.04	82.98	73.38	61.13	46.72	31.45	17.33	6.39				
		σ^*	100.00	87.18	75.57	64.84	54.80	45.39	36.53	28.18	20.33	12.98	6.17				
	1	μ^*		96.78	94.13	89.74	82.97	73.14	59.83	43.52	26.08	10.60					
		σ^*		74.78	63.63	53.40	43.92	35.09	26.87	19.22	12.16	5.72					
	2	μ^*			92.25	88.75	82.75	73.08	58.63	39.40	18.06						
		σ^*			53.01	43.33	34.44	26.25	18.71	11.81	5.55						
	3	μ^*				86.49	81.89	73.08	57.21	31.85							
		σ^*				34.25	25.99	18.47	11.63	5.46							
	4	μ^*					79.43	72.84	54.68								
		σ^*					18.39	11.55	5.42								
	5	μ^*						70.91									
		σ^*						5.41									
13	0	μ^*	100.00	98.36	95.60	91.44	85.55	77.61	67.43	55.13	41.39	27.48	15.03	5.55			
		σ^*	100.00	88.16	77.39	67.39	58.02	49.19	40.84	32.94	25.47	18.41	11.78	5.61			
	1	μ^*		97.11	94.80	91.08	85.51	77.55	66.80	53.27	37.78	22.19	8.93				
		σ^*		76.66	66.28	56.70	47.77	39.42	31.59	24.25	17.40	11.03	5.20				
	2	μ^*			93.10	90.09	85.17	77.55	66.38	51.28	33.10	14.69					
		σ^*			56.32	47.20	38.76	30.93	23.65	16.91	10.70	5.04					
	3	μ^*				88.03	84.20	77.43	66.10	48.58	24.99						
		σ^*				38.56	30.65	23.36	16.66	10.53	4.96						
	4	μ^*					81.88	76.80	65.93	43.21							
		σ^*					23.27	16.55	10.44	4.92							
	5	μ^*						74.54	65.86								
		σ^*						10.41	4.90								
14	0	μ^*	100.00	98.53	96.11	92.53	87.54	80.87	72.31	61.85	49.78	36.85	24.21	13.18	4.87		
		σ^*	100.00	89.00	78.95	69.59	60.79	52.48	44.59	37.10	29.98	23.22	16.82	10.78	5.14		
	1	μ^*		97.39	95.34	92.14	87.45	80.86	72.03	60.79	47.45	33.01	19.12	7.65			
		σ^*		78.28	68.56	59.55	51.12	43.20	35.74	28.71	22.09	15.88	10.09	4.77			
	2	μ^*			93.79	91.16	87.03	80.82	71.92	59.86	44.82	28.08	12.19				
		σ^*			59.19	50.57	42.55	35.06	28.06	21.52	15.43	9.79	4.62				
	3	μ^*				89.29	86.00	80.55	71.90	58.92	41.12	20.03					
		σ^*				42.35	34.76	27.73	21.21	15.18	9.62	4.55					
	4	μ^*					83.86	79.70	71.88	57.75	33.95						
		σ^*					27.63	21.08	15.05	9.53	4.51						
	5	μ^*						77.44	71.64	55.56							
		σ^*						15.01	9.49	4.48							
	6	μ^*							69.91								
		σ^*							4.48								

15	0	μ^*	100.00	98.68	96.52	93.40	89.11	83.42	76.15	67.21	56.70	45.04	32.97	21.50	11.67	4.33	
		σ^*	100.00	89.72	80.30	71.51	63.21	55.35	47.88	40.76	33.97	27.49	21.33	15.47	9.93	4.74	
	1	μ^*		97.62	95.79	92.99	88.97	83.42	76.04	66.62	55.23	42.36	29.03	16.65	6.64		
		σ^*		79.69	70.54	62.04	54.06	46.54	39.42	32.68	26.30	20.28	14.60	9.30	4.40		
	2	μ^*			94.37	92.04	88.50	83.31	76.02	66.22	53.79	39.28	24.07	10.30			
		σ^*			61.70	53.53	45.89	38.73	32.00	25.68	19.73	14.18	9.01	4.27			
	3	μ^*				90.33	87.46	82.93	76.01	65.93	52.12	34.94	16.38				
		σ^*				45.70	38.43	31.66	25.33	19.43	13.93	8.85	4.20				
	4	μ^*					85.49	81.95	75.86	65.73	49.75	26.97					
		σ^*					31.55	25.18	19.27	13.80	8.76	4.15					
	5	μ^*						79.80	75.25	65.61	44.82						
		σ^*						19.22	13.74	8.71	4.13						
	6	μ^*							73.19	65.56							
		σ^*							8.70	4.12							
16	0	μ^*	100.00	98.79	96.87	94.11	90.37	85.46	79.21	71.51	62.38	52.01	40.87	29.66	19.23	10.42	3.88
		σ^*	100.00	90.35	81.49	73.19	65.34	57.89	50.79	44.00	37.52	31.31	25.38	19.71	14.32	9.20	4.40
	1	μ^*		97.82	96.16	93.69	90.19	85.44	79.18	71.20	61.47	50.19	37.95	25.71	14.64	5.83	
		σ^*		80.92	72.29	64.24	56.66	49.50	42.70	36.24	30.09	24.26	18.73	13.51	8.62	4.09	
	2	μ^*			94.85	92.78	89.69	85.27	79.17	71.05	60.71	48.31	34.57	20.85	8.84		
		σ^*			63.92	56.15	48.87	42.02	35.55	29.43	23.66	18.22	13.11	8.35	3.96		
	3	μ^*				91.20	88.67	84.80	79.10	70.99	59.98	46.00	29.89	13.65			
		σ^*				48.68	41.71	35.19	29.06	23.31	17.92	12.88	8.20	3.89			
	4	μ^*					86.84	83.78	78.80	70.98	59.20	42.62	21.80				
		σ^*					35.08	28.89	23.13	17.75	12.74	8.11	3.85				
	5	μ^*						81.76	77.97	70.96	58.21	35.78					
		σ^*						23.07	17.67	12.67	8.06	3.83					
	6	μ^*							75.89	70.71	6.28						
		σ^*							12.65	8.03	3.82						
	7	μ^*								69.16							
		σ^*								3.81							

			r_2																		
n	r_1		0	1	2	3	4	5	6	7	8	9	10	11	12	13	14	15	16	17	18
17	0	μ^*	100.00	98.89	97.15	94.70	91.40	87.11	81.68	75.01	67.04	57.87	47.77	37.20	26.81	17.31	9.38	3.50			
		σ^*	100.00	90.91	82.54	74.68	67.23	60.15	53.38	46.90	40.69	34.74	29.03	23.56	18.32	13.32	8.57	4.11			
	1	μ^*		97.99	96.48	94.27	91.20	87.07	81.68	74.86	66.49	56.66	45.67	34.14	22.92	12.99	5.18				
		σ^*		82.00	73.83	66.19	58.98	52.14	45.64	39.43	33.52	27.88	22.51	17.40	12.57	8.03	3.81				
	2	μ^*			95.27	93.40	90.68	86.85	81.66	74.81	66.11	55.54	43.43	30.59	18.23	7.68					
		σ^*			65.89	58.49	51.54	44.97	38.74	32.84	27.24	21.93	16.92	12.19	7.78	3.70					
	3	μ^*				91.94	89.68	86.32	81.51	74.81	65.82	54.33	40.64	25.79	11.57						
		σ^*				51.35	44.66	38.38	32.45	26.86	21.59	16.63	11.97	7.63	3.63						
	4	μ^*					87.99	85.29	81.10	74.79	65.60	52.88	36.56	17.93							
		σ^*					38.27	32.28	26.66	21.39	16.45	11.84	7.55	3.59							
	5	μ^*						83.41	80.15	74.62	65.45	50.75	28.75								
		σ^*						26.59	21.30	16.35	11.76	7.49	3.57								
	6	μ^*							78.15	74.02	65.36	46.20									
		σ^*							16.32	11.72	7.47	3.56									
	7	μ^*								72.15	65.33										
		σ^*								7.46	3.55										
18	0	μ^*	100.00	98.98	97.40	95.19	92.26	88.47	83.71	77.87	70.89	62.79	53.71	43.95	33.97	24.35	15.68	8.49	3.18		
		σ^*	100.00	91.41	83.47	76.00	68.92	62.17	55.70	49.51	43.56	37.84	32.34	27.05	21.98	17.11	12.45	8.02	3.85		
	1	μ^*		98.13	96.76	94.76	92.03	88.40	83.71	77.81	70.57	61.99	52.23	41.64	30.83	20.56	11.62	4.63			
		σ^*		82.97	75.21	67.94	61.06	54.52	48.28	42.33	36.63	31.18	25.96	20.99	16.25	11.75	7.51	3.57			
	2	μ^*			95.63	93.93	91.49	88.14	83.65	77.80	70.39	61.34	50.77	39.14	27.22	16.08	6.74				
		σ^*			67.65	60.59	53.93	47.63	41.64	35.94	30.51	25.35	20.44	15.79	11.39	7.28	3.46				
	3	μ^*				92.57	90.53	87.58	83.44	77.79	70.29	60.73	49.14	36.01	22.44	9.94					
		σ^*				53.75	47.33	41.27	35.54	30.11	24.97	20.10	15.51	11.18	7.14	3.40					
	4	μ^*					88.97	86.56	82.95	77.70	70.26	60.13	47.07	31.51	15.00						
		σ^*					41.16	35.36	29.90	24.75	19.90	15.33	11.05	7.06	3.37						
	5	μ^*						84.81	81.95	77.38	70.26	59.47	43.93	23.41							
		σ^*						29.83	24.65	19.78	15.23	10.97	7.01	3.35							
	6	μ^*							80.06	76.58	70.23	58.61	37.39								
		σ^*							19.75	15.18	10.92	6.97	3.33								
	7	μ^*								74.66	69.98	56.89									
		σ^*								10.91	6.96	3.32									
	8	μ^*									68.56										
		σ^*									3.32										

19	0	μ^*	100.00	99.06	97.61	95.61	92.98	89.61	85.40	80.25	74.09	66.91	58.78	49.88	40.52	31.13	22.21	14.27	7.74	2.91	
		σ^*	100.00	91.85	84.30	77.20	70.44	63.99	57.80	51.86	46.15	40.65	35.35	30.24	25.32	20.59	16.04	11.69	7.54	3.62	
	1	μ^*		98.26	96.99	95.18	92.73	89.51	85.39	80.22	73.91	66.40	57.75	48.17	38.06	27.97	18.56	10.46	4.18		
		σ^*		83.84	76.45	69.51	62.93	56.67	50.68	44.95	39.46	34.19	29.13	24.29	19.66	15.23	11.03	7.06	3.36		
	2	μ^*			95.94	94.38	92.19	89.22	85.29	80.22	73.84	66.03	56.82	46.44	35.37	24.36	14.30	5.98			
		σ^*			69.24	62.48	56.10	50.04	44.27	38.77	33.51	28.49	23.70	19.13	14.80	10.69	6.84	3.26			
	3	μ^*				93.12	91.27	88.64	85.03	80.18	73.82	65.74	55.88	44.45	32.04	19.69	8.64				
		σ^*				55.93	49.75	43.91	38.37	33.10	28.09	23.33	18.81	14.53	10.49	6.71	3.20				
	4	μ^*					89.82	87.64	84.48	80.01	73.82	65.52	54.85	41.88	27.34	12.74					
		σ^*					43.80	38.18	32.88	27.85	23.10	18.60	14.35	10.36	6.63	3.17					
	5	μ^*						86.01	83.47	79.58	73.79	65.36	53.56	38.00	19.36						
		σ^*						32.80	27.74	22.97	18.47	14.24	10.28	6.58	3.15						
	6	μ^*							81.69	78.66	73.61	65.24	51.63	30.35							
		σ^*							22.93	18.41	14.18	10.23	6.54	3.13							
	7	μ^*								76.80	73.03	65.17	47.38								
		σ^*								14.16	10.20	6.52	3.12								
	8	μ^*									71.31	65.15									
		σ^*									6.52	3.12									
20	0	μ^*	100.00	99.12	97.79	95.97	93.59	90.56	86.81	82.24	76.78	70.39	63.11	55.03	46.38	37.44	28.62	20.36	13.06	7.09	2.67
		σ^*	100.00	92.25	85.06	78.27	71.81	65.63	59.70	54.00	48.51	43.21	38.09	33.15	28.39	23.79	19.36	15.10	11.01	7.11	3.41
	1	μ^*		98.38	97.20	95.55	93.33	90.45	86.79	82.23	76.68	70.07	62.40	53.79	44.48	34.88	25.48	16.84	9.48	3.79	
		σ^*		84.62	77.57	70.93	64.63	58.62	52.86	47.34	42.04	36.95	32.05	27.34	22.81	18.48	14.33	10.39	6.66	3.17	
	2	μ^*			96.22	94.78	92.80	90.14	86.66	82.22	76.66	69.87	61.82	52.61	42.53	32.08	21.93	12.80	5.35		
		σ^*			70.67	64.20	58.07	52.24	46.68	41.36	36.26	31.39	26.71	22.25	17.98	13.92	10.07	6.45	3.07		
	3	μ^*				93.61	91.91	89.55	86.36	82.13	76.66	69.75	61.30	51.36	40.26	28.64	17.42	7.60			
		σ^*				57.90	51.96	46.32	40.96	35.85	30.97	26.32	21.88	17.67	13.66	9.88	6.33	3.02			
	4	μ^*					90.55	88.58	85.78	81.89	76.64	69.69	60.80	49.90	37.33	23.90	10.96				
		σ^*					46.21	40.77	35.62	30.72	26.07	21.65	17.46	13.49	9.75	6.25	2.99				
	5	μ^*						87.06	84.76	81.39	76.53	69.67	60.29	48.01	32.98	16.26					
		σ^*						35.54	30.60	25.93	21.51	17.33	13.38	9.67	6.20	2.97					
	6	μ^*							83.10	80.42	76.21	69.67	59.72	45.09	24.89						
		σ^*							25.89	21.44	17.25	13.31	9.62	6.16	2.95						
	7	μ^*								78.64	75.43	69.63	58.96	38.82							
		σ^*								17.23	13.28	9.59	6.14	2.95							
	8	μ^*									73.65	69.39	57.41								
		σ^*									9.58	6.13	2.94								
	9	μ^*										68.09									
		σ^*										2.94									

TABLE 10C.4

Variances and Relative Efficiencies[a] of Alternative Estimates of the Mean ($\mu^{*\prime}$) and Standard Deviation ($\sigma^{*\prime}$) for Censored Samples of Size 10, 12, and 15 from a Normal Population

n	r_1			r_2: 0	1	2	3	4	5	6	7	8	9	10
10	0	$\mu^{*\prime}$	V	0.1000	0.1031	0.1096	0.1215	0.1428	0.1826	0.2634	0.4561	1.1269		
			R.E.	100.00	99.43	98.06	96.03	93.54	91.13	89.83	91.50	100.00		
		$\sigma^{*\prime}$	V	0.0577	0.0702	0.0864	0.1075	0.1364	0.1789	0.2480	0.3807	0.7491		
			R.E.	99.87	96.92	94.07	92.03	90.72	90.17	90.66	92.97	100.00		
	1	$\mu^{*\prime}$	V		0.1053	0.1103	0.1201	0.1390	0.1786	0.2753	0.6304			
			R.E.		99.04	89.29	97.28	96.29	95.89	97.06	100.00			
		$\sigma^{*\prime}$	V		0.0849	0.1055	0.1338	0.1759	0.2453	0.3841	0.8075			
			R.E.		97.08	96.11	95.64	95.80	96.65	98.22	100.00			
	2	$\mu^{*\prime}$	V			0.1133	0.1204	0.1368	0.1792	0.3401				
			R.E.			98.20	97.95	97.85	98.57	100.00				
		$\sigma^{*\prime}$	V			0.1341	0.1768	0.2475	0.3894	0.8316				
			R.E.			96.32	96.88	98.02	99.56	100.00				
	3	$\mu^{*\prime}$	V				0.1238	0.1356	0.1866					
			R.E.				98.43	99.03	100.00					
		$\sigma^{*\prime}$	V				0.2484	0.3922	0.8426					
			R.E.				96.16	99.96	100.00					
	4	$\mu^{*\prime}$	V					0.1383						
			R.E.					100.00						
		$\sigma^{*\prime}$	V					0.8458						
			R.E.					100.00						

12	0	$\mu^{*\prime}$	V	0.0833	0.0853	0.0892	0.0957	0.1062	0.1233	0.1520	0.2029	0.3023	0.5317	1.3044
			R.E.	100.00	99.51	98.38	96.72	94.59	92.13	89.71	87.90	87.64	90.44	100.00
		$\sigma^{*\prime}$	V	0.0469	0.0554	0.0658	0.0786	0.0946	0.1157	0.1447	0.1876	0.2573	0.3909	0.7601
			R.E.	99.89	97.03	94.20	92.04	90.42	89.29	88.66	88.66	89.60	92.36	100.00
	1	$\mu^{*\prime}$	V		0.0869	0.0900	0.0954	0.1044	0.1199	0.1478	0.2026	0.3312	0.7864	
			R.E.		99.11	98.38	97.39	96.20	95.03	94.25	94.50	96.48	100.00	
		$\sigma^{*\prime}$	V		0.0648	0.0772	0.0928	0.1134	0.1418	0.1841	0.2542	0.3940	0.8195	
			R.E.		96.77	95.48	94.58	94.15	94.19	94.75	95.93	97.81	100.00	
	2	$\mu^{*\prime}$	V			0.0921	0.0961	0.1037	0.1179	0.1468	0.2154	0.4614		
			R.E.			98.13	97.67	97.11	96.68	96.85	98.21	100.00		
		$\sigma^{*\prime}$	V			0.0930	0.1139	0.1428	0.1857	0.2569	0.4000	0.8450		
			R.E.			95.09	94.97	95.30	96.14	97.51	99.28	100.00		
	3	$\mu^{*\prime}$	V				0.0985	0.1041	0.1164	0.1473	0.2617			
			R.E.				97.77	97.79	97.99	98.85	100.00			
		$\sigma^{*\prime}$	V				0.1433	0.1868	0.2589	0.4040	0.8581			
			R.E.				95.53	96.54	98.04	99.80	100.00			
	4	$\mu^{*\prime}$	V					0.1066	0.1155	0.1524				
			R.E.					98.38	99.08	100.00				
		$\sigma^{*\prime}$	V					0.2596	0.4060	0.8647				
			R.E.					98.17	99.98	100.00				
	5	$\mu^{*\prime}$	V						0.1175					
			R.E.						100.00					
		$\sigma^{*\prime}$	V						0.8667					
			R.E.						100.00					

[a] The percentage efficiency is calculated relative to the corresponding best linear systematic statistic.

This table is reproduced from A. E. Sarhan and B. G. Greenberg, "Estimation of location and scale parameters by order statistics from singly and doubly censored samples, Parts I and II," *Ann. Math. Statist.*, Vol. 27 (1956), pp. 427–451 and Vol. 29 (1958), pp. 79–105, with permission of W. Kruskal, editor of the *Annals of Mathematical Statistics*.

n	r_1			r_2 = 0	1	2	3	4	5	6	7	8	9	10	11	12	13
15	0	$\mu^{*\prime}$	V	0.0668	0.0578	0.0700	0.0732	0.0781	0.0851	0.0955	0.1111	0.1350	0.1733	0.2388	0.3623	0.6385	1.5404
			R.E.	100.00	99.60	98.71	97.46	95.84	93.88	91.66	89.32	87.12	85.40	84.66	85.58	89.47	100.00
		$\sigma^{*\prime}$	V	0.0367	0.0420	0.0483	0.0555	0.0639	0.0741	0.0868	0.1029	0.1242	0.1536	0.1970	0.2674	0.4021	0.7723
			R.E.	99.90	97.23	94.53	92.38	90.64	89.25	88.15	87.35	86.85	86.75	87.19	88.54	91.74	100.00
	1	$\mu^{*\prime}$	V		0.0688	0.0706	0.0734	0.0775	0.0838	0.0932	0.1077	0.1311	0.1710	0.2465	0.4173	1.0037	
			R.E.		99.22	98.57	97.70	96.63	95.38	94.08	92.88	92.06	92.01	93.17	95.95	100.00	
		$\sigma^{*\prime}$	V		0.0476	0.0546	0.0629	0.0728	0.0851	0.1007	0.1213	0.1500	0.1927	0.2635	0.4045	0.8322	
			R.E.		96.62	95.12	93.93	93.08	92.54	92.31	92.40	92.86	93.75	95.21	97.38	100.00	
	2	$\mu^{*\prime}$	V			0.0719	0.0741	0.0776	0.0831	0.0919	0.1061	0.1307	0.1773	0.2829	0.6471		
			R.E.			98.23	97.70	97.02	96.23	95.45	94.86	94.81	95.72	97.89	100.00		
		$\sigma^{*\prime}$	V			0.0630	0.0731	0.0856	0.1014	0.1223	0.1514	0.1946	0.2664	0.4107	0.8586		
			R.E.			94.28	93.63	93.28	93.26	93.57	94.26	95.38	96.99	98.98	100.00		
	3	$\mu^{*\prime}$	V				0.0757	0.0784	0.0830	0.0909	0.1048	0.1318	0.1934	0.4069			
			R.E.				97.54	97.25	96.88	96.54	96.46	97.05	98.65	100.00			
		$\sigma^{*\prime}$	V				0.0858	0.1019	0.1232	0.1527	0.1965	0.2692	0.4156	0.8731			
			R.E.				93.42	93.50	93.93	94.73	95.97	97.66	99.58	100.00			
	4	$\mu^{*\prime}$	V					0.0801	0.0835	0.0901	0.1036	0.1354	0.2472				
			R.E.					97.36	97.40	97.49	97.89	98.99	100.00				
		$\sigma^{*\prime}$	V					0.1235	0.1533	0.1976	0.2711	0.4188	0.8817				
			R.E.					94.02	94.90	96.20	97.94	99.85	100.00				
	5	$\mu^{*\prime}$	V						0.0854	0.0901	0.1025	0.1487					
			R.E.						97.86	98.35	99.13	100.00					
		$\sigma^{*\prime}$	V						0.1980	0.2720	0.4206	0.8866					
			R.E.						96.26	98.05	99.97	100.00					
	6	$\mu^{*\prime}$	V							0.0918	0.1017						
			R.E.							99.17	100.00						
		$\sigma^{*\prime}$	V							0.4212	0.8888						
			R.E.							100.00	100.00						

REFERENCES

1. A. K. Gupta, "Estimation of the mean and standard deviation of a normal population from a censored sample," *Biometrika*, Vol. 39 (1952), pp. 260–273.
2. A. E. Sarhan and B. G. Greenberg, "Estimation of location and scale parameters by order statistics from singly and doubly censored samples, Part 1, The normal distribution up to samples of size 10," *Ann. Math. Statist.*, Vol. 27 (1956), pp. 427–451.
3. A. E. Sarhan and B. G. Greenberg, "Estimation of location and scale parameters by order statistics from singly and doubly censored samples, Part II," *Ann. Math. Statist.*, Vol. 29 (1958), pp. 79–105.
4. A. E. Sarhan and B. G. Greenberg, "Estimation of location and scale parameters by order statistics from singly and doubly censored samples, Part III," Tech. Rep. 4, OOR Project 1597.
5. J. G. Saw, "Estimation of the normal population parameters given a singly censored sample," *Biometrika*, Vol. 46 (1959), pp. 150–159.
6. G. A. Watterson, "Linear estimation in censored samples from multivariate normal populations," *Ann. Math. Statist.*, Vol. 30 (1959), pp. 814–824.

A. E. SARHAN and B. G. GREENBERG

10D SIMPLE ESTIMATES OF THE MEAN AND STANDARD DEVIATION OF A NORMAL POPULATION

Dixon [1] suggested simple estimates of the mean and standard deviation of a normal population which are highly efficient. For the mean he suggested

1. The mean of the best two observations.
2. $\bar{x}_{(2,n-1)} = \sum_{i=2}^{n-1} \frac{x_{(i)}}{(n-2)}$.

Estimate 1, mean of the best two observations, denotes an equivalent of the estimate commonly used in large samples, the mean of the twenty-seventh and seventy-third percentiles. Dixon used the best linear systematic statistics as well as the median and midrange for comparing the efficiencies. Table 10D.1 from [1] gives the variances and efficiencies for the median, midrange, the mean of best two, and $\bar{x}_{2,n-1}$ for samples of sizes 2 to 20 and ∞.

The efficiency reported for the median, midrange, and the mean of the best two is the ratio of the variance of the arithmetic mean to the variance of the statistic.

Estimate 2 is the mean of all observations except the largest and the smallest. The column termed "Eff" for this estimate as given in Table 10D.1 represents the efficiencies relative to the mean of all observations. The last column marked "Eff*" gives the efficiency of this particular estimate relative to the BLE based on the same observations given in Sarhan and Greenberg [2].

It can be seen from the table that for sample sizes larger than five the two best-ordered observations are not far from the twenty-seventh and seventy-third percentiles, and efficiencies are close to the asymptotic efficiency of the latter (0.810).

The efficiency of $\bar{x}_{(2,n-1)}$ relative to the BLE based on the same observations are high. In no case is the loss in efficiency more than 1% since the last column in the table does not show any value less than 0.990. This efficiency would not be expected because in the case of censoring the largest and smallest observations the weights for the BLE of the mean are

TABLE 10D.1

SEVERAL ESTIMATES OF MEAN OF NORMAL POPULATION WITH EFFICIENCIES
(Variances to be multiplied by σ^2)

	Median		Midrange		$(x_{(i)} + x_{(j)})/2$			$\bar{x}_{2,n-1}$		
n	Var.	Eff.	Var.	Eff.	i, j	Var.	Eff.	Var.	Eff.	Eff.*
2	0.500	1.00	0.500	1.00	1, 2	0.500		1.00		
3	0.449	0.743	0.362	0.920	1, 3	0.362	0.920	0.449	0.743	1.000
4	0.298	0.838	0.298	0.838	2, 3	0.298	0.838	0.298	0.838	1.000
5	0.287	0.697	0.261	0.767	2, 4	0.231	0.867	0.227	0.881	0.994
6	0.215	0.776	0.236	0.706	2, 5	0.193	0.865	0.184	0.906	0.992
7	0.210	0.679	0.218	0.654	2, 6	0.168	0.849	0.155	0.922	0.990
8	0.168	0.743	0.205	0.610	3, 6	0.149	0.837	0.134	0.934	0.990
9	0.166	0.669	0.194	0.572	3, 7	0.132	0.843	0.118	0.942	0.990
10	0.138	0.723	0.186	0.539	3, 8	0.119	0.840	0.105	0.949	0.990
11	0.137	0.663	0.178	0.510	3, 9	0.109	0.832	0.0952	0.955	0.991
12	0.118	0.709	0.172	0.484	4, 9	0.100	0.831	0.0869	0.959	0.991
13	0.117	0.659	0.167	0.461	4, 10	0.0924	0.833	0.0799	0.963	0.991
14	0.102	0.699	0.162	0.440	4, 11	0.0860	0.830	0.0739	0.966	0.992
15	0.102	0.656	0.158	0.422	4, 12	0.0808	0.825	0.0688	0.969	0.992
16	0.0904	0.692	0.154	0.392	5, 12	0.0756	0.827	0.0644	0.971	0.993
17	0.0901	0.653	0.151	0.389	5, 13	0.0711	0.827	0.0605	0.973	0.993
18	0.0810	0.686	0.148	0.375	5, 14	0.0673	0.825	0.0570	0.975	0.993
19	0.0808	0.651	0.145	0.363	6, 14	0.0640	0.823	0.0539	0.976	0.993
20	0.0734	0.681	0.143	0.350	6, 15	0.0607	0.824	0.0511	0.978	0.994
∞		0.637		0.000	0.27, 0.73		0.810		1.000	1.000

Eff.* = $V(\text{BLSS})V(\bar{x}_{2,n-1})$.

This table is reproduced from W. J. Dixon, "Estimation of the mean and standard deviation of a normal population," *Ann. Math. Statist.*, Vol. 28 (1957), pp. 806–809, with permission of the author and W. Kruskal, editor of the *Annals of Mathematical Statistics*.

not close to $1/(n-2)$, but the symmetry of the distribution corrects for this.

Dixon [1] also suggested the use of the subranges $x_{n-i+1} - x_i = w_{(i)}$ (and $w_{(1)} = w$, the range) as simple estimates of the population standard deviation. He calculated the unbiased estimate of the type $s' = k'(\Sigma w_{(i)})$ (where the summation is over the subset of all $w_{(i)}$ which give minimum variance) for samples of size 20 or smaller. This estimate is given in Table 10D.2. The column headed "Eff" refers to the efficiency relative to the unbiased sample standard deviation. The final column "Eff*" compares the efficiency of this statistic to the best linear estimate as given in Sarhan and Greenberg [2]. By examining this ratio we can see that the loss in efficiency is not great when use is made of "zero or one" weights for each range instead of optimum weights from the BLE.

The same table gives the variances and efficiency of the range (relative to the unbiased sample standard deviation) as well as the value of k which satisfies $E(kw) = \sigma$ up to samples of size 20 for reference.

TABLE 10D.2

A LINEAR ESTIMATE OF THE STANDARD DEVIATION
(Variances to be multiplied by σ^2)

Sample Size	Range k	Range Var.	Range Eff.	Estimate	s' Var.	s' Eff.	s' Eff.*
2	0.886	0.571	1.000	$0.8862w$	0.571	1.000	1.000
3	0.591	0.275	0.992	$0.5908w$	0.275	0.992	1.000
4	0.486	0.183	0.975	$0.4857w$	0.183	0.975	0.986
5	0.430	0.138	0.955	$0.4299w$	0.138	0.955	0.966
6	0.395	0.112	0.933	$0.2619(w + w_{(2)})$	0.109	0.957	0.968
7	0.370	0.0949	0.911	$0.2370(w + w_{(2)})$	0.0895	0.967	0.978
8	0.351	0.0829	0.890	$0.2197(w + w_{(2)})$	0.0761	0.970	0.980
9	0.337	0.0740	0.869	$0.2068(w + w_{(2)})$	0.0664	0.968	0.979
10	0.325	0.0671	0.850	$0.1968(w + w_{(2)})$	0.0591	0.964	0.974
11	0.315	0.0616	0.831	$0.1608(w + w_{(2)} + w_{(4)})$	0.0529	0.967	0.977
12	0.307	0.0571	0.814	$0.1524(w + w_{(2)} + w_{(4)})$	0.0478	0.972	0.981
13	0.300	0.0533	0.797	$0.1456(w + w_{(2)} + w_{(4)})$	0.0436	0.975	0.984
14	0.294	0.0502	0.781	$0.1399(w + w_{(2)} + w_{(4)})$	0.0401	0.977	0.985
15	0.288	0.0474	0.766	$0.1352(w + w_{(2)} + w_{(4)})$	0.0372	0.977	0.985
16	0.283	0.0451	0.751	$0.1311(w + w_{(2)} + w_{(4)})$	0.0347	0.975	0.983
17	0.279	0.0430	0.738	$0.1050(w + w_{(2)} + w_{(3)} + w_{(5)})$	0.0325	0.978	0.985
18	0.275	0.0412	0.725	$0.1020(w + w_{(2)} + w_{(3)} + w_{(5)})$	0.0305	0.978	0.986
19	0.271	0.0395	0.712	$0.09939(w + w_{(2)} + w_{(3)} + w_{(5)})$	0.0288	0.979	0.986
20	0.268	0.0381	0.700	$0.10446(w + w_{(2)} + w_{(4)} + w_{(6)})$	0.0272	0.980	0.987

Eff.* = $V(\text{BLSS})/V(s')$.

This table is reproduced from W. J. Dixon, "Estimation of the mean and standard deviation of a normal population," *Ann. Math. Statist.*, Vol. 28 (1957), pp. 806–809, with permission of the author and W. Kruskal, editor of the *Annals of Mathematical Statistics*.

REFERENCES

1. W. J. Dixon, "Estimates of the mean and standard deviation of a normal population," *Ann. Math. Statist.*, Vol. 28 (1957), pp. 806–809.
2. A. E. Sarhan and B. G. Greenberg, "Estimation of location and scale parameters by order statistics from singly and doubly censored samples," Parts II and III, *Ann. Math. Statist.*, Vol. 29 (1958), pp. 79–105; Tech. Rep. 4, OOR Project 1597, 1958.

JUNJIRO OGAWA

10E DETERMINATIONS OF OPTIMUM SPACINGS IN THE CASE OF NORMAL DISTRIBUTION

10E.1 Introduction

We have seen in Chapter 5 that the best linear unbiased estimators μ^*_0 and σ^*_0 are efficient for a given spacing $\lambda_1, \lambda_2, \ldots, \lambda_k$; we may, however, raise their efficiencies by choosing the spacing suitably. The values of $\lambda_1, \lambda_2, \ldots, \lambda_k$ for which the relative efficiency of an estimator attains its maximum value are called an *optimum spacing*. In this section we consider the problems of determining the optimum spacings in the case of the normal distribution.

10E.2 Location Parameter μ

In this case

$$f_i \equiv f(u_i) = \frac{1}{\sqrt{2\pi}} e^{-\frac{1}{2}u_i^2}, \qquad i = 1, 2, \ldots, k$$

and the frequency function is clearly symmetric with respect to the origin. Since the relative efficiency is

$$\eta(\mu) = K_1,$$

the required optimum spacing is such that it makes K_1 maximum.

Since

$$\frac{df_i}{du_i} = -u_i f_i, \qquad \frac{d\lambda_i}{du_i} = f_i, \qquad i = 1, 2, \ldots, k \tag{10E.2.1}$$

we have the following by differentiating K_1 with respect to u_i:

$$\frac{\partial K_1}{\partial u_i} = f_i\left(\frac{f_{i+1} - f_i}{\lambda_{i+1} - \lambda_i} - \frac{f_i - f_{i-1}}{\lambda_i - \lambda_{i-1}}\right)\left(2u_i + \frac{f_{i+1} - f_i}{\lambda_{i+1} - \lambda_i} + \frac{f_i - f_{i-1}}{\lambda_i - \lambda_{i-1}}\right), \quad i = 1, 2, \ldots, k. \quad (10E.2.2)$$

Thus we have the following 2^k systems of k equations, whose ith constituent is either

$$\frac{f_{i+1} - f_i}{\lambda_{i+1} - \lambda_i} - \frac{f_i - f_{i-1}}{\lambda_i - \lambda_{i-1}} = 0 \quad (10E.2.3)$$

or

$$2u_i + \frac{f_{i+1} - f_i}{\lambda_{i+1} - \lambda_i} + \frac{f_i - f_{i-1}}{\lambda_i - \lambda_{i-1}} = 0, \quad (10E.2.4)$$

and the relevant solution must satisfy the following order condition:

$$-\infty \equiv u_0 < u_1 < u_2 < \ldots < u_k < u_{k+1} \equiv +\infty. \quad (10E.2.5)$$

If we regard the ordinate f of the standard normal frequency function, that is,

$$f(u) = \frac{1}{\sqrt{2\pi}} e^{-\frac{1}{2}u^2}$$

as a function of the probability

$$\lambda = \frac{1}{\sqrt{2\pi}} \int_{-\infty}^{u} e^{-\frac{1}{2}t^2}\, dt,$$

its graph is convex upward and takes its maximum value $1/\sqrt{2\pi}$ at $\lambda = 0.5$ and is symmetric with respect to $\lambda = 0.5$. Hence equation (10E.2.3) is not satisfied unless any two of f_{i-1}, f_i, f_{i+1} coincide. Consequently, the required optimum spacing should be searched among the solutions of the simultaneous equations

$$2u_i + \frac{f_{i+1} - f_i}{\lambda_{i+1} - \lambda_i} + \frac{f_i - f_{i-1}}{\lambda_i - \lambda_{i-1}} = 0, \qquad i = 1, 2, \ldots, k \quad (10E.2.6)$$

which satisfy the order condition (10E.2.5).

In connection with this we can prove the following.

Theorem 1. The system of simultaneous equations (10E.2.6) has one and only one solution which satisfies the order condition (10E.2.5) [3].

From this theorem we can conclude that in the normal distribution *the optimum spacing for the location parameter μ is necessarily a symmetric one.* In fact, if

$$0 < \lambda_1 < \lambda_2 < \ldots < \lambda_k < 1$$

is a spacing satisfying the system of equations (10E.2.6), we can show that the spacing

$$0 < 1 - \lambda_k < 1 - \lambda_{k-1} < \ldots < 1 - \lambda_1 < 1$$

also satisfies the equations (10E.2.6). This can easily be seen as follows: put

$$\lambda'_i = 1 - \lambda_{k-i+1}, \qquad i = 1, 2, \ldots, k.$$

Then, by the symmetry of $f(u)$, the corresponding λ'_i-quantile of the population is

$$u'_i = -u_{k-i+1}, \qquad i = 1, 2, \ldots, k$$

and

$$f'_i \equiv f(u'_i) = f(-u_{k-i+1}) = f(u_{k-i+1}) \equiv f_{k-i+1}.$$

Thus we have

$$2u'_i + \frac{f'_{i+1} - f'_i}{\lambda'_{i+1} - \lambda'_i} + \frac{f'_i - f'_{i-1}}{\lambda'_i - \lambda'_{i-1}}$$

$$= -\left(2u_{k-i+1} + \frac{f_{k-i+1} - f_{k-i}}{\lambda_{k-i+1} - \lambda_{k-i}} + \frac{f_{k-i} - f_{k-i-1}}{\lambda_{k-i} - \lambda_{k-i-1}}\right),$$

$$i = 1, 2, \ldots, k. \qquad (10E.2.7)$$

By the uniqueness of the solution (as shown by Theorem 1), we can see that

$$u'_i = u_i, \qquad i = 1, 2, \ldots, k$$

or

$$u_i + u_{k-i+1} = 0, \qquad i = 1, 2, \ldots, k$$

and correspondingly we have

$$\lambda_i + \lambda_{k-i+1} = 1, \qquad i = 1, 2, \ldots, k$$

which means that the spacing is symmetric.

Ogawa [6] solved the system of equations (10E.2.6) numerically, and the results are given in Table 10E.1.

Mosteller [4] considered only the estimator

$$\bar{\mu} = \frac{1}{k}\sum_{i=1}^{k} x_{(n_i)}, \qquad (10E.2.8)$$

and he determined the optimum spacings for $k = 1, 2, 3$. For example,

$$k = 3, \qquad \lambda_1 = 0.1826, \qquad \lambda_2 = 0.5000,$$
$$\lambda_3 = 0.8174, \qquad \text{and} \quad K_1 = 0.879.$$

On the other hand, our best linear unbiased estimate gives $\lambda_1 = 0.163$, $\lambda_2 = 0.500$, $\lambda_3 = 0.837$, $K_1 = 0.880$, which is a little higher than that obtained by Mosteller [4].

Corresponding to these optimum spacings we have Table 10E.2 for explicit expressions of the best linear unbiased estimator based on selected values.

Table 10E.3 compares the efficiencies of various spacings in estimating the mean. The last column in the table represents an intuitive plausible spacing.

Yost [8] has obtained some closely connected results which are slightly less efficient.

10E.3 Scale Parameter σ

In this case the required optimum spacing is such that it makes the relative efficiency $\eta(\sigma) = \frac{1}{2}K_2$ maximum. As for the location parameter μ, by differentiating K_2 with repsect to u_i, we obtain

$$\frac{\partial K_2}{\partial u_i} = f_i\left(\frac{f_{i+1}u_{i+1} - f_iu_i}{\lambda_{i+1} - \lambda_i} - \frac{f_iu_i - f_{i-1}u_{i-1}}{\lambda_i - \lambda_{i-1}}\right)$$

$$\cdot\left(2u_i^2 - 2 + \frac{f_{i+1}u_{i+1} - f_iu_i}{\lambda_{i+1} - \lambda_i} + \frac{f_iu_i - f_{i-1}u_{i-1}}{\lambda_i - \lambda_{i-1}}\right). \quad (10E.3.1)$$

Hence we have 2^k systems of k equations whose ith constituent is either

$$G_i \equiv \frac{f_{i+1}u_{i+1} - f_iu_i}{\lambda_{i+1} - \lambda_i} - \frac{f_iu_i - f_{i-1}u_{i-1}}{\lambda_i - \lambda_{i-1}} = 0 \quad (10E.3.2)$$

or

$$F_i \equiv 2u_i^2 - 2 + \frac{f_{i+1}u_{i+1} - f_iu_i}{\lambda_{i+1} - \lambda_i} + \frac{f_iu_i - f_{i-1}u_{i-1}}{\lambda_i - \lambda_{i-1}} = 0. \quad (10E.3.3)$$

The graph of $uf(u)$, that is,

$$uf(u) = -f'(u)$$

as a function of the probability

$$\lambda = \frac{1}{\sqrt{2\pi}}\int_{-\infty}^{u} e^{-\frac{1}{2}t^2}\, dt$$

is symmetric with respect to the point $\lambda = 0.5$ on the λ-axis and in the interval $0 \leq \lambda \leq 0.5$ is convex downward.

Concerning the solutions of these 2^k systems of k equations we can prove the following.

Theorem 2. (*a*) Any system of 2^k equations which involves more than two constituents $G_i = 0$ has no solution which satisfies the order condition (10E.2.5). (*b*) A solution satisfying the order condition (10E.2.5) of any system of k equations which involves only one constituent $G_i = 0$ does not give a maximum point for K_2 [3].

Thus we may consider only solutions of the system of equations

$$F_1 = 0, \quad F_2 = 0, \quad \ldots, \quad F_k = 0. \tag{10E.3.4}$$

About the nature of the solution of (10E.2.4) we can prove the following.

Theorem 3. (*a*) There exists no solution that has zero among its constituents. (*b*) There exists one and only one solution in which each constituent has any prescribed sign. Accordingly, the system has just 2^k solutions. (*c*) Among these 2^k solutions, those whose constituents have the property that, for any fixed j, u_i with $i > j$ are all positive and u_i with $i \leq j$ are all negative satisfy the order condition (10E.2.5) and give the maximum points for K_2 [3].

Ogawa [5] solved the system of equations (10E.3.4) numerically, and the results are shown in Table 10E.4. It is to be noted that the function K_2 has many maxima, and the one that gives the greatest maximum among them is not yet theoretically known. In the table, however, different spacings are given, and among these the greatest value of K_2 is selected. Ogawa also obtained the explicit expressions for the best linear unbiased estimators which give the maximum efficiency (Table 10E.5), and he compared the efficiencies of various spacings (Table 10E.6).

Mosteller [4] was concerned mainly with the use of *quasi-ranges.* We summarize his results as follows.

Theorem 4. In estimating the standard deviation σ of a normal distribution from a large sample of size n, an unbiased estimator $\sigma^{*\prime}$ is

$$\sigma^{*\prime} = \frac{1}{c}\,(x_{(n-r+1)} - x_{(r)}) \tag{10E.3.5}$$

where $c = E(Y_{(n-r+1)} - Y_{(r)})$, and where the Y's are the order statistics drawn from $N(0,1)$. The estimator $\sigma^{*\prime}$ is asymptotically normally distributed with variance

$$\sigma^2(\sigma^{*\prime}) = \frac{2\sigma^2}{nc^2}\,\frac{\lambda_1(1 - 2\lambda_1)}{f_1^{\,2}} \tag{10E.3.6}$$

where $\lambda_1 = r/n$ and $f_1 = (1/\sqrt{2\pi})e^{-u_1^2/2}$. We minimize $\sigma^2(\sigma^{*\prime})$ for large samples when $\lambda_1 = 0.0694$, and for that value of λ_1 we have

$$\sigma^2_{\text{opt}}(\sigma^{*\prime}) \approx \frac{0.767\sigma^2}{n}. \tag{10E.3.7}$$

The unbiased estimator

$$\sigma^{*\prime\prime} = \frac{1}{c'}\,(x_{(n-r+1)} + x_{(n-s+1)} - x_{(s)} - x_{(r)}) \tag{10E.3.8}$$

where $c' = E(Y_{(n-r+1)} + Y_{(n-s+1)} - Y_{(s)} - Y_{(r)})$ may be used in lieu of $\sigma^{*\prime}$. The minimum value of the variance is

$$\sigma^2(\sigma^{*\prime} \mid \lambda_1 = 0.07, \lambda_2 = 0.20) \approx \frac{0.66\sigma^2}{n}. \tag{10E.3.9}$$

10E.4 When Both the Location Parameter μ and the Scale Parameter σ Are Unknown

In this case the situation is far more complicated, and we do not yet have any answer concerning the general behavior of the optimum spacings.

If we consider the special case of $k = 2$ and assume the symmetric spacing, we obtain the following solution, that is,

$$\lambda_1 = 0.134, \qquad \lambda_2 = 0.866, \tag{10E.4.1}$$

which gives the efficiency

$$0.4066. \tag{10E.4.2}$$

This value of relative efficiency is greater than those that are given in Tables 10E.1 and 10E.4 for $k = 2$.

For practical purposes, we may adopt the following compromising method. If we compare the two Tables 10E.1 and 10E.4, we find that the values of $\frac{1}{2}\Delta$ in Table 10E.1 are greater than the corresponding values of $\frac{1}{2}\Delta$ in Table 10E.4 for $k = 3, 4, 5, 6$; hence, if there is no special emphasis on the accuracy of estimate of σ, it will be better to take the optimum spacings which were originally obtained for the estimation of the mean μ.

10E.5 Optimum Grouping

Strictly speaking, any measurements or observations should be regarded as grouped data, but here we are concerned with much more coarse grouping.

Mathematically, the random variables in the grouped observations are the frequencies obeying a multinomial probability distribution. Here, naturally, arises a problem of optimum grouping. This problem was treated by Gjeddebaek [2] and Cox [1] for the case of a normal distribution. Walker [7] gave a general discussion with examples of a normal distribution.

It should be pointed out that the asymptotic results for optimum grouping coincide with the asymptotic optimum spacing of sample quantiles, as would be expected. The reason for this will be seen by considering a problem belonging to the class known as "dosage-mortality curve method" or "generalized probability paper method" [6].

TABLE 10E.1

Optimum Spacings for Estimating the Mean μ and the Corresponding Maximum Relative Efficiencies

k	1	2	3	4	5	6	7	8	9	10
λ_1	0.500	0.270	0.163	0.107	0.074	0.055	0.040	0.031	0.024	0.020
u_1	0.000	−0.613	−0.982	−1.243	−1.447	−1.598	−1.751	−1.866	−1.977	−2.054
λ_2		0.730	0.500	0.351	0.255	0.195	0.147	0.115	0.092	0.076
u_2		0.613	0.000	−0.383	−0.659	−0.860	−1.049	−1.200	−1.329	−1.433
λ_3			0.837	0.649	0.500	0.395	0.308	0.247	0.202	0.167
u_3			0.982	0.383	0.000	−0.266	−0.502	−0.684	−0.834	−0.966
λ_4				0.893	0.745	0.605	0.500	0.412	0.343	0.288
u_4				1.243	0.659	0.266	0.000	−0.222	−0.404	−0.559
λ_5					0.926	0.805	0.692	0.588	0.500	0.427
u_5					1.447	0.860	0.502	0.222	0.000	−0.184
λ_6						0.945	0.852	0.753	0.657	0.573
u_6						1.598	1.049	0.684	0.404	0.184
λ_7							0.960	0.885	0.798	0.712
u_7							1.751	1.200	0.834	0.559
λ_8								0.969	0.908	0.833
u_8								1.866	1.329	0.966
λ_9									0.976	0.924
u_9									1.977	1.433
λ_{10}										0.980
u_{10}										2.054
K_1	0.6366	0.8097	0.8800	0.9342	0.9420	0.9559	0.9654	0.9722	0.9771	0.9808
$\frac{1}{2}K_2$	0.0000	0.3303	0.5326	0.6566	0.7392	0.7902	0.8516	0.8620	0.8858	0.9016
$\frac{1}{2}\Delta$	0.000	0.267	0.469	0.614	0.696	0.752	0.822	0.838	0.866	0.884

This table is reproduced from Junjiro Ogawa, "Contributions to the theory of systematic statistics, I," *Osaka Math. J.*, Vol. 3 (1951), pp. 175–213, with permission of the editor of *Osaka Mathematical Journal*.

TABLE 10E.2

EXPLICIT EXPRESSIONS OF THE BEST LINEAR UNBIASED ESTIMATORS OF THE MEAN WITH OPTIMUM SPACINGS

k	Expressions
2	$\frac{1}{2}\{x([0.270n] + 1) + x([0.730n] + 1)\}$
3	$0.297\{x([0.163n] + 1) + x([0.837n] + 1)\} + 0.407x([0.500n] + 1)$
4	$0.197\{x([0.107n] + 1) + x([0.893n] + 1)\} + 0.308\{x([0.351n] + 1) + x([0.649n] + 1)\}$
5	$0.133\{x([0.074n] + 1) + x([0.926n] + 1)\} + 0.233\{x([0.255n] + 1) + x([0.745n] + 1)\} + 0.269x([0.500n] + 1)$
6	$0.099\{x([0.055n] + 1) + x([0.945n] + 1)\} + 0.181\{x([0.195n] + 1) + x([0.805n] + 1)\}$ $+ 0.220\{x([0.395n] + 1) + x([0.605n] + 1)\}$
7	$0.071\{x([0.040n] + 1) + x([0.960n] + 1) + 0.140\{x([0.147n] + 1) + x([0.853n] + 1)\}$ $+ 0.186\{x([0.308n] + 1) + x([0.692n] + 1)\} + 0.203x([0.500n] + 1)$
8	$0.049\{x([0.031n] + 1) + x([0.969n] + 1)\} + 0.111\{x([0.115n] + 1) + x([0.885n] + 1)\}$ $+ 0.155\{x([0.247n] + 1) + x([0.753n] + 1)\} + 0.178\{x([0.412n] + 1) + x([0.588n] + 1)\}$
9	$0.044\{x([0.024n] + 1) + x([0.976n] + 1)\} + 0.091\{x([0.092n] + 1) + x([0.908n] + 1)\}$ $+ 0.130\{x([0.202n] + 1) + x([0.798n] + 1)\} + 0.155\{x([0.343n] + 1) + x([0.657n] + 1)\} + 0.163x([0.500n] + 1)$
10	$0.036\{x([0.020n] + 1) + x([0.980n] + 1)\} + 0.075\{x([0.076n] + 1) + x([0.924n] + 1)\}$ $+ 0.109\{x([0.167n] + 1) + x([0.833n] + 1)\} + 0.133\{x([0.288n] + 1) + x([0.712n] + 1)\}$ $+ 0.147\{x([0.427n] + 1) + x([0.573n] + 1)\}$

[a] In this table *n* denotes the sample size.

This table is reproduced from Junjiro Ogawa, "Contributions to the theory of systematic statistics, I," *Osaka Math. J.*, Vol. 3 (1951), pp. 175–213, with permission of the editor of *Osaka Mathematical Journal.*

TABLE 10E.3

COMPARISON OF EFFICIENCIES OF VARIOUS SPACINGS IN ESTIMATING THE MEAN WITH THE LAST COLUMN REPRESENTING AN INTUITIVE PLAUSIBLE SPACING

k	Optimum Spacing	Equal-Probability Spacing	Expected Values Spacing	$\lambda_i = \frac{i - \frac{1}{2}}{k}$
1	0.6366	0.6366	0.637	0.637
2	0.8097	0.7926	0.809	0.808
3	0.8800	0.8606	0.878	0.878
4	0.9342	0.8969	0.914	0.913
5	0.9420	0.9172	0.933	0.934
6	0.9559	0.9352	0.948	0.948
7	0.9654	0.9450	0.956	0.957
8	0.9722	0.9521	0.963	0.963
9	0.9771	0.9591	0.968	0.969
10	0.9808	0.9634	0.972	0.973

This table is reproduced from Junjiro Ogawa, "Contributions to the theory of systematic statistics, I," *Osaka Math. J.*, Vol. 3 (1951), pp. 175–213, with permission of the editor of *Osaka Mathematical Journal.*

TABLE 10E.4

OPTIMUM SPACINGS FOR ESTIMATING THE SCALAR PARAMETER σ AND THE CORRESPONDING MAXIMUM RELATIVE EFFICIENCIES

k	1		2			3				4			5		6
λ_1	0.058	0.942	0.069	0.905[a]	0.018	0.021	0.072	0.007[b]	0.882	0.023	0.009[a]	0.072	0.010	0.025	0.010
u_1	−1.572	1.572	−1.483	1.311	−2.097	−2.034	−1.468	−2.457	1.185	−1.995	−2.366	−1.461	−2.326	−1.960	−2.318
λ_2			0.931	0.982	0.095	0.118	0.882	0.039	0.961	0.127	0.048	0.852	0.053	0.133	0.056
u_2			1.483	2.097	−1.311	−1.185	1.185	−1.762	1.762	−1.141	−1.665	1.045	−1.618	−1.112	−1.589
λ_3						0.928	0.979	0.118	0.993	0.873	0.148	0.952	0.163	0.837	0.171
u_3						1.468	2.034	−1.185	2.457	1.141	−1.045	1.665	−0.982	0.982	−0.950
λ_4										0.977	0.928	0.991	0.867	0.947	0.829
u_4										1.995	1.461	2.366	1.112	1.618	0.950
λ_5													0.975	0.990	0.944
u_5													1.960	2.326	1.589
λ_6															0.990
u_6															2.318
$\frac{1}{2}K_2$	0.304		0.653		0.374	0.729		0.399		0.824	0.745		0.858		0.893
K_1	0.246		0.512		0.352	0.605		0.370		0.715	0.658		0.764		0.814
K_3	0.387		0		±0.482	0.393		±0.500		0	0.823		±0.035		0
$\frac{1}{2}\Delta$	0.003		0.334		0.061	0.367		0.002		0.589	0.151		0.656		0.727

[a] Nonsymmetric solutions for even k, which gives smaller maximum efficiencies.
[b] A one-sided solution for $k = 3$ (odd), which gives smaller maximum efficiency.
This table is reproduced from Junjiro Ogawa, "Contributions to the theory of systematic statistics, I, *Osaka Math. J.*, Vol. 3 (1951), pp. 175–213, with permission of the editor of *Osaka Mathematical Journal*.

TABLE 10E.5

EXPLICIT EXPRESSIONS OF THE BEST LINEAR UNBIASED ESTIMATOR FOR THE SCALAR PARAMETER (σ) WITH OPTIMUM SPACINGS

k	Expressions
2	$0.674\{x([0.931n]+1) - x([0.069n]+1)\}$
3	$0.070 \cdot \mu + 0.305 \cdot x([0.928n]+1) - 0.253 \cdot x([0.118n]+1) - 0.123 \cdot x([0.021n]+1)$ $-0.070 \cdot \mu - 0.305 \cdot x([0.072n]+1) + 0.253 \cdot x([0.882n]+1) + 0.123 \cdot x([0.979n]+1)$
4	$0.115\{x([0.977n]+1) - x([0.023n]+1)\} + 0.237\{x([0.873n]+1) - x([0.127n]+1)\}$
5	$0.020\mu + 0.117x([0.975n]+1) + 0.230x([0.867n]+1) - 0.186x([0.169n]+1)$ $- 0.126x([0.053n]+1) - 0.056x([0.010n]+1)$ $-0.020\mu - 0.117x([0.025n]+1) - 0.230x([0.133n]+1) + 0.186x([0.831n]+1)$ $+ 0.126x([0.947n]+1) + 0.056x([0.990n]+1)$
6	$0.056\{x([0.990n]+1) - x([0.011n]+1)\} + 0.126\{x([0.944n]+1) - x([0.056n]+1)\}$ $+ 0.181\{x([0.829n]+1) - x([0.171n]+1)\}$

[a] Here n denotes the sample size.

TABLE 10E.6

COMPARISON OF EFFICIENCIES OF VARIOUS SPACINGS IN ESTIMATING σ

k \ Spacing	Optimum Spacing	Equal-Probability Spacing	$\lambda_i = \frac{i - \frac{1}{2}}{k}$
1	0.304	0.000	0.000
2	0.653	0.221	0.413
3	0.729	0.368	0.526
4	0.824	0.468	0.619
5	0.858	0.541	0.681
6	0.893	0.595	0.725

These tables are reproduced from J. Ogawa, "Contributions to the theory of systematic statistics, I," *Osaka Math. J.*, Vol. 3 (1951), pp. 175–213, with permission of the editor of *Osaka Mathematical Journal.*

REFERENCES

1. D. R. Cox, "Note on grouping," *J. Amer. Statist. Ass.*, Vol. 52 (1957), pp. 543–547.
2. N. F. Gjeddebaek, "Contributions to the study of grouped observations, application of the method of maximum likelihood in case of normally distributed observations," *Skand. Aktuartidskr.*, Vol. 42 (1949), pp. 136–159.
3. I. Higuchi, "On the solutions of certain simultaneous equations in the theory of systematic statistics," *Ann. Inst. Statist. Math., Tokyo*, Vol. 5, No. 2 (1956), pp. 77–90.
4. F. Mosteller, "On some useful 'inefficient' statistics," *Ann. Math. Statist.*, Vol. 17 (1948), pp. 377–407.
5. J. Ogawa, "Contributions to the theory of systematic statistics, I," *Osaka Math. J.*, Vol. 3, No. 2 (1951), pp. 175–213.
6. J. Ogawa, "Contributions to the theory of systematic statistics, II, Large sample theoretical treatments of some problems arising from dosage and time-mortality curves," *Osaka Math. J.*, Vol. 4 (1952), pp. 41–61.
7. J. Walker, "Optimum decomposition of sample space," doctoral thesis, University of North Carolina, Chapel Hill, 1957.
8. E. K. Yost, "Joint estimation of mean and standard deviation of percentiles," unpublished master's thesis, University of Oregon, Eugene, Oregon, 1948.

JUNJIRO OGAWA

10F ESTIMATION OF CORRELATION COEFFICIENT BY ORDER STATISTICS

10F.1 Introduction

In the present section our concern is the estimation of the correlation coefficient ρ of a bivariate normal distribution, whose frequency function is given by

$$f(x, y) = \frac{1}{2\pi\sigma_1\sigma_2\sqrt{1-\rho^2}} \times \exp\left\{-\frac{1}{2(1-\rho^2)}\left[\frac{(x-\mu_1)^2}{\sigma_1^{\,2}} - 2\rho\,\frac{(x-\mu_1)(y-\mu_2)}{\sigma_1\sigma_2} + \frac{(y-\mu_2)^2}{\sigma_2^{\,2}}\right]\right\}. \tag{10F.1.1}$$

The usual estimator based on a random sample

$$(X_1, Y_1), (X_2, Y_2), \ldots, (X_n, Y_n)$$

is

$$r = \frac{\sum_{i=1}^{n} (x_i - \bar{x})(y_i - \bar{y})}{\left[\sum_{i=1}^{n} (x_i - \bar{x})^2 \cdot \sum_{i=1}^{n} (y_i - \bar{y})^2\right]^{1/2}}, \tag{10F.1.2}$$

and it is well known that this is an efficient estimator. There are numerous other techniques in the literature for estimating ρ. Mosteller [1] proposed another estimate which is particularly well adapted for use with punched-card equipment.

10F.2 Estimation of ρ When Means and Standard Deviations Are Known

In this case we can assume, without any loss of generality, that

$$\mu_1 = \mu_2 = 0 \qquad \text{and} \qquad \sigma_1 = \sigma_2 = 1.$$

Hence the frequency function of the population becomes

$$f(x, y) = \frac{1}{2\pi\sqrt{1 - \rho^2}} \exp\left[-\frac{1}{2(1 - \rho^2)}(x^2 - 2\rho xy + y^2)\right]. \tag{10F.2.1}$$

The technique used will be to construct lines $y = 0$ and $x = \pm k$, which cut the xy-plane into six parts. We shall form an estimate of ρ based on

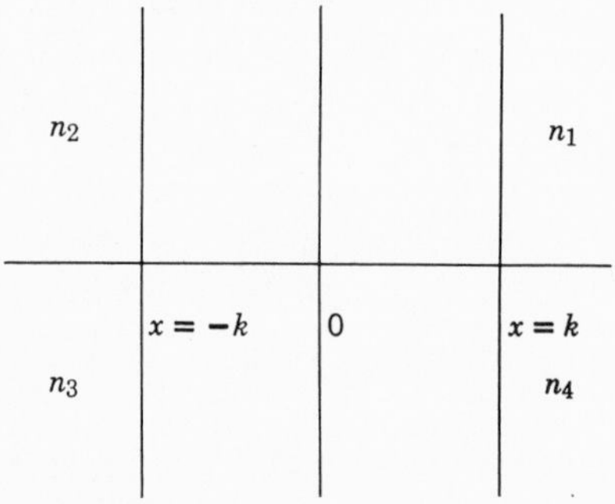

Fig. 10F.1. Construction of the lines $y = 0$ and $x = \pm k$.

the number of observations falling in the four corners. Figure 10F.1 represents the lines laid out. We shall denote the frequencies as in the figure.

Put

$$p_1 = \int_0^\infty \int_k^\infty f(x, y)\, dx\, dy, \qquad p_2 = \int_0^\infty \int_{-\infty}^{-k} f(x, y)\, dx\, dy,$$
$$p_3 = \int_{-\infty}^0 \int_{-\infty}^{-k} f(x, y)\, dx\, dy, \qquad p_4 = \int_{-\infty}^0 \int_k^\infty f(x, y)\, dx\, dy, \tag{10F.2.2}$$

and

$$p_5 = \int_{-\infty}^\infty \int_{-k}^k f(x, y)\, dx\, dy = \int_{-k}^k f(t)\, dt.$$

Then the likelihood (or probability) is

$$g(n_1, n_2, n_3, n_4) = \frac{n!}{\prod_{i=1}^5 n_i!} \prod_{i=1}^5 p_i^{n_i} \tag{10F.2.3}$$

where

$$n_5 = n - \sum_{i=1}^4 n_i. \tag{10F.2.4}$$

The maximum-likelihood estimate of ρ can be obtained by solving the equation

$$\frac{d(\log g)}{d\rho} = 0$$

which turns out to be

$$\sum_{i=1}^4 \frac{n_i}{p_i} \frac{dp_i}{d\rho} = 0. \tag{10F.2.5}$$

Equation (10F.2.5) can be rewritten as follows:

$$\frac{p_1}{\lambda - p_1} = \frac{n_1 + n_3}{n_2 + n_4} \tag{10F.2.6}$$

where

$$\lambda = p_1 + p_4 = p_2 + p_3 = \int_k^\infty f(t)\, dt. \tag{10F.2.7}$$

Since the variance of the maximum-likelihood estimate is given by

$$-1 \Big/ E\left(\frac{d^2 \log g}{d\rho^2}\right)$$

asymptotically, we have

$$V(\hat{\rho}) = \frac{p_1(\lambda - p_1)}{2n\lambda \dot{p}_1^{\,2}}. \tag{10F.2.8}$$

Hence

$$V(\hat{\rho} \mid \rho = 0) = \frac{\pi\lambda}{4n} [f(k)]^{-2} \tag{10F.2.9}$$

which is minimized for $\lambda \approx 0.2702$ and $k = 0.6121$, and for these values we obtain

$$V_{\text{opt}}(\hat{\rho} \mid \rho = 0) \approx \frac{1.939}{n}. \tag{10F.2.10}$$

Theorem 1. If a sample of size n is drawn from a bivariate normal population with known means μ_1, μ_2 and variances $\sigma_1{}^2$ and $\sigma_2{}^2$, but unknown correlation coefficient ρ, the maximum-likelihood estimator $\hat{\rho}$ of ρ based on the number of observations falling in the four corners of the plane determined by the lines $x = \mu_1 \pm k\sigma_1$, $y = \mu_2$ is found by solving for $\hat{\rho}$ the equation

$$\frac{n_1 + n_3}{n_1 + n_2 + n_3 + n_4} = \left(\frac{p_1}{\lambda}\right)_{\rho=\hat{\rho}} \tag{10F.2.11}$$

where n_1 is the number of observations falling in the upper right, n_2 in the upper left, n_3 in the lower left, n_4 in the lower right-hand corner, and p_i is the probability of the region into which n_i observations fall, $\lambda = p_1 + p_4$. The variance of this estimator $\hat{\rho}$ is given by

$$\sigma^2(\hat{\rho}) = \frac{p_1(\lambda - p_1)}{2n\lambda\, \dot{p}_1{}^2} \tag{10F.2.12}$$

which is minimized for $\rho = 0$ by setting $k = 0.6121$, $\lambda = 0.2702$, giving

$$\sigma^2_{\text{opt}}(\hat{\rho} \mid \rho = 0) \approx \frac{1.939}{n}.$$

10F.3 Estimation of ρ When the Parameters Are Unknown

This case is more practical than that treated in Subsection 10F.2. The procedure of constructing the estimator of ρ is as follows. Each of the N observations in the sample has an x coordinate and a y coordinate: (i) order the observations with respect to the x coordinate; (ii) discard all observations except the n with the largest x coordinates called the *right set* and the n with the smallest x coordinates called the *left set*, retaining, therefore, $2n$ observations; (iii) order the pooled $2n$ observations with respect to the y coordinate; (iv) break the $2n$ observations into two sets of n observations each, the *upper set* containing the n observations with the greatest y coordinates, and the *lower set* containing the n observations with the smallest y coordinates; (v) reorder the upper set of observations with respect to the x coordinate. The n observations will be divided into those whose x coordinates belong to the right set and those whose x coordinates belong to the left set; the situation is illustrated in Table A.

Then the estimator $\hat{\rho}'$ of ρ can be obtained by solving the equations

$$\frac{n'_1}{n'_2} = \frac{p'_1}{\lambda'_1 - p'_1} \tag{10F.3.1}$$

TABLE A

	Left Set	Right Set	Totals
Upper set	n'_2	n'_1	n
Lower set	n'_3	n'_4	n
Totals	n	n	$2n$

where n'_1 is the number of observations in the upper set which are also members of the right set, and $n'_2 = n - n'_1$ and

$$p'_1 = \int_0^\infty \int_{k'}^\infty f(x, y)\, dx\, dy \tag{10F.3.2}$$

and

$$\lambda'_1 = n/N \tag{10F.3.3}$$

where $f(x, y)$ are given by (10F.2.1).

Concerning this estimator of ρ we can prove the following.

Theorem 2. If a sample of size N is drawn from a bivariate normal population with unknown parameters, the maximum-likelihood estimator $\hat{\rho}'$ of ρ based on the $2n$ observations composed of those observations with the n largest x coordinates and the n smallest x coordinates may be obtained by solving for $\hat{\rho}'$ the equation

$$\frac{n - c}{n} = \left(\frac{p'_1}{\lambda'_1}\right)_{\rho=\hat{\rho}'} \tag{10F.3.4}$$

where $\frac{1}{2} > \lambda'_1 = n/N > 0$

$$p'_1 = \int_0^\infty \int_k^\infty \frac{1}{2\pi\sqrt{1 - \rho^2}} \exp\left[-\frac{1}{2(1 - \rho^2)}(x^2 - 2\rho xy + y^2)\right] dx\, dy$$

and

$$\lambda'_1 = \frac{1}{\sqrt{2\pi}} \int_{k'}^\infty e^{-t^2/2}\, dt,$$

and $n - c$ is the number of the $2n$ observations with largest y coordinates which also have the largest x coordinates. The variance of this estimator $\hat{\rho}'$ is given by

$$V(\hat{\rho}') = \frac{p'_1(\lambda'_1 - p'_1)}{2N\lambda'_1 \dot{p}'^2_1} \tag{10F.3.5}$$

and for $\rho = 0$ this is minimized by choosing

$$\lambda'_1 = 0.2702. \tag{10F.3.6}$$

That is, by choosing that 27% of the observations with largest x coordinates, and that 27% with smallest x coordinates, for these values of λ'_1 we have

$$V_{\text{opt}}(\hat{\rho}' \mid \rho = 0) \approx \frac{1.939}{N}. \tag{10F.3.7}$$

Figure 10F.2 shows the curve for estimating the correlation coefficient, and it may be used to obtain the estimates when the methods of Subsections 10F.2 and 10F.3 are used.

We shall explain the method of obtaining the solutions of (10F.2.6) and (10F.3.4) graphically by using Fig. 10F.2.

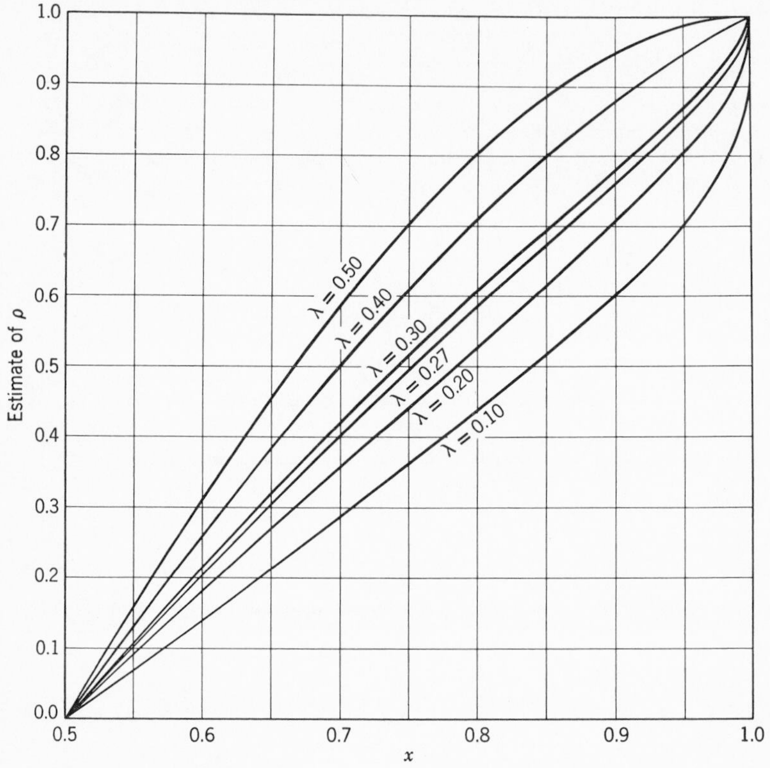

Fig. 10F.2 Curve for estimating the correlation coefficient. Reproduced from F. Mosteller, "On some useful inefficient statistics," *Ann. Math. Statist.*, Vol. 17 (1946), pp. 394–407, with permission of the author and W. Kruskal, editor of the *Annals of Mathematical Statistics*.

Procedure for Solving Equation (10F.2.6). (i) When $n_1 + n_3$ is larger than $n_2 + n_4$, evaluate the ratio $\dfrac{(n_1 + n_3)}{(n_1 + n_2 + n_3 + n_4)} = x_0$ and find the intersection of the line $x = x_0$ with the curve for the particular λ being used.

(ii) Through the point of intersection of the vertical line $x = x_0$ and the λ curve draw a horizontal line.

(iii) The value of $\hat{\rho}$ is indicated on the vertical axis at the point of intersection of the horizontal line and the vertical axis.

(iv) When $n_1 + n_3$ is smaller than $n_2 + n_4$, use the ratio $x_0 = \dfrac{(n_2 + n_4)}{(n_1 + n_2 + n_3 + n_4)}$ and follow the same procedure; $\hat{\rho}$ will be the negative of the number appearing on the vertical axis.

Example (Mosteller [1]). Suppose a sample of 1000 is drawn from a bivariate normal population for which the mean of x is a, the mean of y is b, and the variance of x is σ_x^2, and all three parameters are known (it is not necessary to know σ_y^2). The xy-plane is cut by the three lines $x = a \pm k\sigma_x$, $y = b$, where, say, $k = 0.612$, so that $\lambda = 0.27$. Suppose we find the observations are distributed as follows:

in the upper right-hand corner: $n_1 = 160$
in the lower left-hand corner: $n_3 = 170$
in the upper left-hand corner: $n_2 = 110$
in the lower right-hand corner: $n_4 = 110$

To estimate p we set up $x_0 = (n_1 + n_3)/(n_1 + n_2 + n_3 + n_4) = 330/550 = 0.6$. Referring to Fig. 10F.2, we find that the estimate of ρ is

$$\hat{\rho} = 0.20$$

Remarks. In using Fig. 10F.2 for this case it will be useful to know the following:

$\lambda = 0.50$; $k = 0.000$; $\lambda = 0.40, k = 0.253$; $\lambda = 0.30, k = 0.524$;
$\lambda = 0.27$; $k = 0.612$; $\lambda = 0.20, k = 0.841$; $\lambda = 0.10, k = 1.282$.

Procedure for Solving Equation (10F.3.4). (i) When $n - c$ is larger than c, evaluate the ratio $x_0 = (n - c)/n$ and find the intersection of the line $x = x_0$ with the curve for the particular λ_1 being used.

(ii) Through the point of intersection of the vertical line $x = x_0$ and the λ_1 curve draw a horizontal line.

(iii) The value of $\hat{\rho}'$ is indicated on the vertical axis at the point of intersection of the horizontal line and the vertical axis.

(iv) When $n - c < c$, use the ratio $x_0 = c/n$ and follow the same procedure; $\hat{\rho}'$ will be the negative of the number appearing in the vertical axis.

Example (Mosteller [1]). Suppose a sample of $N = 1000$ is drawn from a bivariate normal population with all parameters unknown. Suppose we set $n = 200$ and follow the procedure given in the beginning of this paragraph, and suppose we find the observations are distributed as follows:

in the upper right-hand corner: $n - c = 50$

then of course

in the lower left-hand corner: $n - c = 50$
in the upper left-hand corner: $c = 150$
in the lower right-hand corner: $c = 150$

Since $n - c = 50$ is smaller than $c = 150$, the estimate this time is negative, so we set $x_0 = c/n = 150/200 = 0.75$. Referring to Fig. 10F.2, we find, using the curve corresponding to $\lambda = 0.20$, that the estimate of ρ is

$$\hat{\rho}' = -0.44$$

10F.4 The Use of Averages for Estimating ρ When the Variance Ratio Is Known [1]

In an unpublished manuscript George Brown has proposed an estimator of the correlation coefficient. Suppose x and y are distributed according to (10F.1.1) with equal variances σ^2 and means equal to zero. Here the ratio of variances must be known; equality of variances is not necessary. Retain only those observations for which $x_i \geq k\sigma$, and from them for the statistics

$$\rho_B = \frac{\bar{y}_+ - \bar{y}_-}{\bar{x}_+ - \bar{x}_-} \tag{10F.4.1}$$

where $\bar{y}_+$ and $\bar{x}_+$ are the average of the n_1 x's and y's for which $x_i > k\sigma$, and $\bar{y}_-$ and $\bar{x}_-$ are similarly defined for the n_2 observations for which $x_i < -k\sigma$. Then ρ_B is an unbiased estimator of ρ. Regarding the x's as fixed variates it follows that

$$\sigma^2(\rho_B \mid x) = \frac{(1 - \rho^2)\sigma^2}{(\bar{x}_+ - \bar{x}_-)^2}\left(\frac{1}{n_1} + \frac{1}{n_2}\right). \tag{10F.4.2}$$

If we approximate by substituting expected values for observed values, equation (10F.4.2) turns out to be

$$\sigma^2(\rho_B) \approx \frac{(1 - \rho^2)\sigma^2\lambda}{2N\left(\frac{1}{\sqrt{2\pi}}e^{-k^2/2}\right)^2} \tag{10F.4.3}$$

where

$$\lambda = \frac{1}{\sqrt{2\pi}}\int_{-\infty}^{-k} e^{-t^2/2}\,dt.$$

The value of k which minimizes the expression given by (10F.4.3) is

$$k = 0.6121$$

which gives

$$\lambda = 0.2702.$$

Therefore, for $\rho = 0$ and large samples, the minimum variance is approximately

$$\frac{1.23\sigma^2}{N}$$

for an efficiency of about 0.81. The relative efficiency of the methods of Subsections 10F.2 and 10F.3 is 0.635 compared with the present method.

REFERENCES

1. F. Mosteller, "On some useful 'inefficient' statistics," *Ann. Math. Statist.*, Vol. 17 (1946), pp. 377–407.

JUNJIRO OGAWA

10G TESTS OF SIGNIFICANCE USING SAMPLE QUANTILES [2]

10G.1 Introduction

The following arguments will be valid for rather general populations whose probability density function depends only on the location parameter μ and the scale parameter σ and satisfies a certain general condition. For the time being, however, we shall, for practical reasons, restrict ourselves to the normal population $N(\mu, \sigma^2)$.

The limiting distribution of k sample quantiles

$$X_{(n_1)}, X_{(n_2)}, \ldots, X_{(n_k)}$$

where

$$n_i = [n\lambda_i] + 1, \qquad i = 1, 2, \ldots, k$$

and

$$0 < \lambda_1 < \lambda_2 \ldots < \lambda_k < 1$$

are given k real numbers, has the density function

$$\begin{aligned} h(x_{(n_1)}, x_{(n_2)}, \ldots, x_{(n_k)}) &= (2\pi\sigma^2)^{-k/2} f_1 f_2 \ldots f_k [\lambda_1(\lambda_2 - \lambda_1) \ldots (\lambda_k - \lambda_{k-1})(1 - \lambda_k)]^{-1/2} n^{k/2} \\ &\times \exp\left\{-\frac{n}{2\sigma^2}\left[\sum_{i=1}^{k} \frac{\lambda_{i+1} - \lambda_{i-1}}{(\lambda_{i+1} - \lambda_i)(\lambda_i - \lambda_{i-1})} f_i^2 (x_{(n_i)} - \mu - u_i\sigma)^2 \right.\right. \\ &\left.\left. - 2\sum_{i=2}^{k} \frac{f_i \cdot f_{i-1}}{\lambda_i - \lambda_{i-1}} (x_{(n_i)} - \mu - u_i\sigma)(x_{(n_i-1)} - \mu - u_{i-1}\sigma)\right]\right\}. \end{aligned} \tag{10G.1.1}$$

where we have put

$$\lambda_0 = 0, \qquad \lambda_{k+1} = 1.$$

10G.2 Student's Hypothesis, H_1: $\mu = \mu_0$

Let

$$\Omega \equiv \sum_{i=1}^{k} \frac{\lambda_{i+1} - \lambda_{i-1}}{(\lambda_{i+1} - \lambda_i)(\lambda_i - \lambda_{i-1})} f_i^2(x_{(n_i)} - \mu - u_i\sigma)^2$$
$$- 2\sum_{i=2}^{k} \frac{f_i f_{i-1}}{\lambda_i - \lambda_{-1}} (x_{(n_i)} - \mu - u_i\sigma)(x_{(n_{i-1})} - \mu - u_{i-1}\sigma) \quad (10G.2.1)$$

and determine μ^* and σ^* for which

$$K_1 \cdot \mu^* + K_3 \cdot \sigma^* = X, \qquad K_3 \cdot \mu^* + K_2 \cdot \sigma^* = Y, \quad (10G.2.2)$$

where

$$K_1 = \sum_{i=1}^{k+1} \frac{(f_i - f_{i-1})^2}{\lambda_i - \lambda_{i-1}}, \qquad K_2 = \sum_{i=1}^{k+1} \frac{(f_i u_i - f_{i-1}u_{i-1})^2}{\lambda_i - \lambda_{i-1}},$$
$$K_3 = \sum_{i=1}^{k+1} \frac{(f_i - f_{i-1})(f_i u_i - f_{i-1}u_{i-1})}{\lambda_i - \lambda_{i-1}}, \quad (10G.2.3)$$

and

$$X = \sum_{i=1}^{k+1} \frac{(f_i - f_{i-1})(f_i x_{(n_i)} - f_{i-1}x_{(n_{i-1})})}{\lambda_i - \lambda_{i-1}},$$
$$Y = \sum_{i=1}^{k+1} \frac{(f_i u_i - f_{i-1}u_{i-1})(f_i x_{(n_i)} - f_{i-1}x_{(n_{i-1})})}{\lambda_i - \lambda_{i-1}}, \quad (10G.2.4)$$

where

$$f_0 = f_{k+1} = 0.$$

These values of μ^*, σ^* give the minimum value Ω_0 of Ω, which turns out to be

$$\Omega_0 = \sum_{i=1}^{k+1} \frac{(f_i x_{(n_i)} - f_{i-1}x_{(n_{i-1})})^2}{\lambda_i - \lambda_{i-1}} - (K_1\mu^{*2} + 2K_3\mu^*\sigma^* + K_2\sigma^{*2}). \quad (10G.2.5)$$

The next step is as follows: let

$$\Omega' \equiv \sum_{i=1}^{k} \frac{\lambda_{i+1} - \lambda_{i-1}}{(\lambda_{i+1} - \lambda_i)(\lambda_i - \lambda_{i-1})} f_i^2(x_{(n_i)} - \mu_0 - u_i\sigma)^2$$
$$- 2\sum_{i=2}^{k} \frac{f_i f_{i-1}}{\lambda_i - \lambda_{i-1}} (x_{(n_i)} - \mu_0 - u_i\sigma)(x_{(n_{i-1})} - \mu_0 - u_{i-1}\sigma); \quad (10G.2.6)$$

then it is minimized at $\sigma = \hat{\sigma}^*$, where

$$K_2\hat{\sigma}^* + K_3\mu_0 = Y \quad (10G.2.7)$$

and, after some calculations, the minimum value Ω'_0 of Ω' is

$$\Omega'_0 = \sum_{i=1}^{k+1} \frac{(f_i x_{(n_i)} - f_{i-1} x_{(n_{i-1})})^2}{\lambda_i - \lambda_{i-1}} - 2\mu_0(K_1\mu^* - K_3\sigma^*)$$

$$- \frac{[K_3(\mu^* - \mu_0) + K_2\sigma^*]^2}{K_2} + K_1\mu_0^2. \quad (10G.2.8)$$

Hence the statistic

$$t = \sqrt{k-2} \cdot \sqrt{(\Omega'_0 - \Omega_0)/\Omega_0} = \sqrt{(k-2)\Delta/K_2}\,\frac{\mu^* - \mu_0}{\sqrt{\Omega_0}} \quad (10G.2.9)$$

is distributed according to the Student t-distribution with degrees of freedom $k - 2$.

In particular, if the spacing of $X_{(n_1)}, X_{(n_2)}, \ldots, X_{(n_k)}$ is symmetric, then $K_3 = 0$. Hence (10G.2.9) becomes

$$t = \sqrt{(k-2) \cdot K_1} \cdot \frac{\mu^* - \mu_0}{\sqrt{\Omega_0}} \quad (10G.2.10)$$

where

$$\Omega_0 = \sum_{i=1}^{k+1} \frac{(f_i x_{(n_i)} - f_{i-1} x_{(n_{i-1})})^2}{\lambda_i - \lambda_{i-1}} - K_1\mu^{*2} - K_2\mu^{*2}. \quad (10G.2.11)$$

The confidence interval of the confidence coefficient $100\,(1 - \alpha)\%$ for the true mean μ is

$$\mu^* - t_{k-2}(100\alpha)\sqrt{\Omega_0/(k-2)K_1} < \mu < \mu^* + t_{k-2}(100\alpha)\sqrt{\Omega_0/k-2)K_1} \quad (10G.2.12)$$

where $t_{k-2}(100\alpha)$ is the $100\alpha\%$ point of the t-distribution of degrees of freedom $k - 2$.

10G.3 Test of the Homogeneity of Several Means

Suppose that there are given l normal populations $N(\mu_\alpha, \sigma^2)$, with $\alpha = 1, 2, \ldots, l$, with unknown common variance σ^2 and unknown means μ_α, with $\alpha = 1, 2, \ldots, l$, and let

$$X_{(1)}^{(\alpha)}, X_{(2)}^{(\alpha)}, \ldots, X_{(n)}^{(\alpha)}, \qquad \alpha = 1, 2, \ldots, l$$

be order statistics of size n (common to all populations) drawn from $N(\mu_\alpha, \sigma^2)$, with $\alpha = 1, 2, \ldots, l$, respectively. Of course, the sample sizes may vary from population to population, but for simplicity of explanation we have here assumed the common sample size for all populations.

In addition, let

$$\lim_{n\to\infty} \frac{n_i}{n} = \lambda_i, \qquad i = 1, 2, \ldots, k$$

and

$$0 < \lambda_1 < \lambda_2 < \ldots < \lambda_k < 1.$$

We are concerned with the test of homogeneity of means, that is, the test of the generalized Student hypothesis

$$H_2\colon\ \mu_1 = \mu_2 = \ldots = \mu_l \tag{10G.3.1}$$

based on the limiting distribution of the selected sample quantiles

Now let

$$\Omega = \sum_{\alpha=1}^{l}\Bigg[\sum_{i=1}^{k} \frac{\lambda_{i+1} - \lambda_{i-1}}{(\lambda_{i+1} - \lambda_i)(\lambda_i - \lambda_{i-1})} f_i^2(x_{(n_i)}^{(\alpha)} - \mu_\alpha - u_i\sigma)^2$$
$$- 2\sum_{i=2}^{k} \frac{f_i f_{i-1}}{\lambda_i - \lambda_{i-1}} (x_{(n_i)}^{(\alpha)} - \mu_\alpha - u_i\sigma)(x_{(n_{i-1})}^{(\alpha)} - \mu_\alpha - u_{i-1}\sigma)\Bigg], \tag{10G.3.2}$$

and let $\mu^*_1, \ldots, \mu^*_l, \sigma^*$ be such that

$$\left.\frac{\partial\Omega}{\partial\mu_\alpha}\right|_{\substack{\mu=\mu^*\\ \sigma=\sigma^*}} = 0; \qquad \alpha = 1, 2, \ldots, l; \qquad \left.\frac{\partial\Omega}{\alpha\sigma}\right|_{\substack{\mu=\mu^*\\ \sigma=\sigma^*}} = 0$$

$$\mu' = (\mu_1, \mu_2, \ldots, \mu_l), \quad \mu^{*\prime} = (\mu^*_1\mu^*_2 \ldots \mu_l^*).$$

These turn out to be

$$\left.\begin{array}{l} K_1\mu_1^* + \qquad\qquad\qquad + K_3\sigma^* = X_1 \\ \qquad K_1\mu_2^* \qquad\quad + K_3\sigma^* = X_2 \\ \qquad\quad \cdot \qquad\qquad\quad \cdot \qquad \cdot \\ \qquad\qquad \cdot \qquad\qquad \cdot \qquad \cdot \\ \qquad\qquad\quad \cdot \qquad\quad \cdot \qquad \cdot \\ \qquad\qquad\qquad K_1\mu_l^* + K_3\sigma^* = X_l \\ K_3(\mu_1^* + \ldots \mu_l^*) + lK_2\sigma^* = Y_1 + Y_2 + \ldots + Y_l \end{array}\right\} \tag{10G.3.3}$$

where K_1, K_2, K_3 are given by (10G.2.3) and

$$X_\alpha = \sum_{i=1}^{k+1} \frac{(f_i - f_{i-1})(f_i x_{(n_i)}^{(\alpha)} - f_{i-1} x_{(n_{i-1})}^{(\alpha)})}{\lambda_i - \lambda_{i-1}} \qquad \alpha = 1, 2, \ldots, l. \tag{10G.3.4}$$
$$Y_\alpha = \sum_{i=1}^{k+1} \frac{(f_i u_i - f_{i-1} u_{i-1})(f_i x_{(n_i)}^{(\alpha)} - f_{i-1} x_{(n_{i-1})}^{(\alpha)})}{\lambda_i - \lambda_{i-1}}.$$

Let the minimum value of Ω be Ω_0, which can be obtained from (10G.2.11) by substituting μ^*, σ^* for μ, σ, respectively.

Under the null hypothesis H_2: $\mu_1 = \ldots = \mu_l = \mu$, for example, we can minimize Ω for the values of $\mu = \hat{\mu}^*$ and $\sigma = \hat{\sigma}^*$, which should be determined such that

$$\begin{aligned} lK_1 \cdot \hat{\mu}^* + lK_3 \cdot \hat{\sigma}^* &= X_1 + \ldots + X_l, \\ lK_3 \cdot \hat{\mu}^* + lK_2 \cdot \hat{\sigma}^* &= Y_1 + \ldots + Y_l. \end{aligned} \quad (10G.3.5)$$

And if we denote the minimum value of Ω under H_2 by Ω'_0 the statistic

$$F_{(l-1, lk-l-1)} = \frac{lk - l - 1}{l - 1} \frac{\Omega'_0 - \Omega_0}{\Omega_0} \quad (10G.3.6)$$

is distributed according to the Snedecor F-distribution of degrees of freedom $(l - 1, lk - l - 1)$.

In particular, for $l = 2$ the statistic (10G.3.6) becomes

$$F_{(1,2k-3)} = \frac{2k - 3}{2} K_1 \frac{(\mu^*_1 - \mu^*_2)^2}{\Omega_0}.$$

Hence the statistic

$$t = \sqrt{F_{(1,2k-3)}} = \sqrt{(2k - 3)K_1/2}\, \frac{\mu^*_1 - \mu^*_2}{\sqrt{\Omega_0}} \quad (10G.3.7)$$

is distributed according to the Student t-distribution with degrees of freedom $2k - 3$. Whence we get the confidence interval of confidence coefficient $100(1 - \alpha)\%$ for the difference of true means of the two populations

$$\begin{aligned} \mu^*_1 - \mu^*_2 - t_{2k-3}(100\alpha)\sqrt{2\Omega/(2k - 3)K_1} < \mu_1 - \mu_2 < \mu^*_1 - \mu^*_2 \\ + t_{2k-3}(100\alpha)\sqrt{2\Omega_0/(2K_1k - 3)}. \end{aligned} \quad (10G.3.8)$$

10G.4 Selection of the Optimum Spacing for Testing Purposes

For the practical application of these test procedures we must determine the spacing of the sample quantiles which makes the power of the test being used as large as possible.

It is well known that the statistic

$$t = \frac{z + \delta}{\sqrt{w/f}}, \qquad \delta \neq 0 \quad (10G.4.1)$$

where z is distributed as $N(0, 1)$ and w is distributed as the chi-square distribution of degrees of freedom f and independently of z, is distributed as the so-called "noncentral t-distribution" of degrees of freedom f, with the noncentrality parameter δ and

$$P[|t| \leq t_f(100\alpha)] = e^{-\delta^2/2} \sum_{\nu=0}^{\infty} \frac{(\delta^2/2)^\nu}{\nu!} I\left[\nu + \frac{1}{2}, \frac{f}{2}; \frac{t_f^2(100\alpha)}{f + t_f^2(100\alpha)}\right] \quad (10G.4.2)$$

where $I(p, q; x)$ is the Pearson incomplete beta function, that is,

$$I(p, q; x) = \frac{\int_0^x t^{p-1}(1-t)^{q-1}\, dt}{B(p, q)}.$$

It can be shown that the right-hand side of (10G.4.2) for fixed f and α is a decreasing function of $|\delta|$. Hence the power function of the t-test

$$P\{|t| > t_f(100\alpha)\} = 1 - e^{-\delta^2/2} \sum_{\nu=0}^{\infty} \frac{(\delta^2/2)^\nu}{\nu!} I\left[\nu + \frac{1}{2}, \frac{f}{2}; \frac{t_f^2(100\alpha)}{f + t_f^2(100\alpha)}\right] \quad (10G.4.3)$$

is an increasing function of $|\delta|$ for fixed f and α.

It can easily be seen that in the t-test (10G.2.10) we obtain

$$\delta = \sqrt{\Delta/K_2}\,\frac{\mu' - \mu_0}{\sigma} \quad \text{and} \quad f = k - 2 \quad (10G.4.4)$$

and in the test for homogeneity of several means (10G.3) (and for $l = 2$) we obtain

$$\delta = \sqrt{K_1/2}\,\frac{\mu'}{\sigma} \quad \text{and} \quad f = 2k - 3, \quad (10G.4.5)$$

$$\mu' = \mu_1 - \mu_2 \neq 0.$$

If we restrict ourselves to the symmetric spacings, then (10G.4.4) becomes

$$\delta = \sqrt{K_1}\,\frac{\mu' - \mu_0}{\sigma} \quad \text{and} \quad f = k - 2. \quad (10G.4.6)$$

Hence in any case we must choose spacing so that K_1 is maximum. Thus we can use the table given in reference 2.

Let us show one example of testing Student's hypothesis. This example is concerned with a sample of size 50 and is not a good one since the labor necessary for calculations of our test procedure is almost comparable to that necessary for usual t-test procedure. It should be remembered that this example is given only to illustrate the test procedure.

Example. Suppose we have a sample of size $n = 50$ drawn from a univariate normal population $N(\mu,\sigma^2)$. The elements are ordered in ascending order of magnitude as shown in Table A.

TABLE A

−2.714	−1.400	−1.169	−1.083	−1.017
−1.016	−0.837	−0.828	−0.710	−0.644
−0.597	−0.539	−0.432	−0.416	−0.378
−0.318	−0.313	−0.310	−0.305	−0.275
−0.220	−0.078	−0.068	−0.059	−0.007
0.019	0.060	0.071	0.121	0.194
0.209	0.229	0.239	0.266	0.311
0.471	0.506	0.606	0.610	0.733
0.738	0.744	0.824	0.921	0.925
1.045	1.115	1.254	1.747	1.774

If we take the case $k = 4$, we can see the following from the table given in reference 2:

$$\lambda_1 = 0.107 \qquad \lambda_2 = 0.351 \qquad \lambda_3 = 0.649 \qquad \lambda_4 = 0.893$$
$$n_1 = 5 \qquad n_2 = 18 \qquad n_3 = 32 \qquad n_4 = 45$$
$$X_1 = X_{(n_1)} = -1.017, \qquad X_2 = X_{(n_2)} = -0.310,$$
$$X_3 = X_{(n_3)} = 0.229, \qquad X_4 = X_{(n_4)} = 0.925.$$

The corresponding abscissas and ordinates are

$$f_1 = 0.1849 \qquad f_2 = 0.3712 \qquad f_3 = 0.3712 \qquad f_4 = 0.1849$$
$$u_1 = -1.24 \qquad u_2 = -0.38 \qquad u_3 = 0.38 \qquad u_4 = 1.24$$

and

$$K_1 = 0.9324, \qquad K_2 = 1.3132, \qquad K_3 = 0,$$

$$\Omega_0 = \frac{f_1^2 x_1^2}{\lambda_1} + \frac{(f_2x_2 - f_1x_1)^2}{\lambda_2 - \lambda_1} + \frac{(f_3x_3 - f_2x_2)^2}{\lambda_3 - \lambda_2} + \frac{(f_4x_4 - f_3x_3)^2}{\lambda_4 - \lambda_3} + \frac{f_4x_4^2}{1 - \lambda_4}$$
$$- K_1\mu^{*2} - K_2\sigma^{*2}, \qquad K_1\mu^* = X, \quad K_2\sigma^* = Y.$$

Hence we have the scheme given in Table 10G.1 for calculating t.

In this example we can suppose that t is distributed approximately as Student's t-distribution with degrees of freedom 2, and thus we have $t_2(10) = 2.92$; so the result is not significant. As a matter of fact, we constructed this example by taking 50 samples from the random normal number $\mu = 0$, $\sigma = 1$ of Table 2 in reference 1, and the result was as expected.

TABLE 10G.1

CALCULATING SCHEME OF THE STATISTIC t

λ_0 .000		f_0 .0000											
	$\lambda_1 - \lambda_0$ .107		$f_1 - f_0$ .1849			f_1u_1 −.229276			f_1x_1 −.1880433	$\frac{f_1x_1}{\lambda_1}$ −1.75741	$f_1\frac{f_1x_1}{\lambda_1}$ −.3249451	$f_1u_1\frac{f_1x_1}{\lambda_1}$ .4029319	$f_1x_1\frac{f_1x_1}{\lambda_1}$ .3304692
λ_1 .107		f_1 .1849		u_1 −1.24	f_1u_1 −.229276		x_1 −1.017	f_1x_1 −.1880433					
	$\lambda_2 - \lambda_1$ .244		$f_2 - f_1$ .1863			$f_2u_2 - f_1u_1$ .088220			$f_2x_2 - f_1x_1$ .0729713	$\frac{f_2x_2 - f_1x_1}{\lambda_2 - \lambda_1}$ .299063	$(f_2 - f_1)\frac{f_2x_2 - f_1x_1}{\lambda_2 - \lambda_1}$ .0557154	$(f_2u_2 - f_1u_1)\frac{f_2x_2 - f_1x_1}{\lambda_2 - \lambda_1}$ .0263833	$(f_2x_2 - f_1x_1)\frac{f_2x_2 - f_1x_1}{\lambda_2 - \lambda_1}$ .0218230
λ_2 .351		f_2 .3712		u_2 −.38	f_2u_2 −.141056		x_2 −.310	f_2x_2 −.1150720					
	$\lambda_3 - \lambda_2$ .298		$f_3 - f_2$ .0000			$f_3u_3 - f_2u_2$ .282112			$f_3x_3 - f_2x_2$ .2000768	$\frac{f_3x_3 - f_2x_2}{\lambda_3 - \lambda_2}$ .67140	$(f_3 - f_2)\frac{f_3x_3 - f_2x_2}{\lambda_3 - \lambda_2}$ −.0000000	$(f_3u_3 - f_2u_2)\frac{f_3x_3 - f_2x_2}{\lambda_3 - \lambda_2}$ .1894100	$(f_3x_3 - f_2x_2)\frac{f_3x_3 - f_2x_2}{\lambda_3 - \lambda_2}$ .1343316
λ_3 .649		f_3 .3712		u_3 .38	f_3u_3 .141056		x_3 .229	f_3x_3 .0850048					
	$\lambda_4 - \lambda_3$ 0.244		$f_4 - f_3$ −.1863			$f_4u_4 - f_3u_3$ .088220			$f_4x_4 - f_3x_3$ .0860277	$\frac{f_4x_4 - f_3x_3}{\lambda_4 - \lambda_3}$ .35275	$(f_4 - f_3)\frac{f_4x_4 - f_3x_3}{\lambda_4 - \lambda_3}$ −.0656838	$(f_4u_4 - f_3u_3)\frac{f_4x_4 - f_3x_3}{\lambda_4 - \lambda_3}$ .0311037	$(f_4x_4 - f_3x_3)\frac{f_4x_4 - f_3x_3}{\lambda_4 - \lambda_3}$ .0303308
λ_4 .893		f_4 .1849		u_4 1.24	f_4u_4 .229276		x_4 .925	f_4x_4 .1710325					
	$\lambda_5 - \lambda_4$ 0.107		$f_5 - f_4$ −.1849			$-f_4u_4$ −.229276			$-f_4x_4$ −.1710325	$\frac{-f_4x_4}{\lambda_5 - \lambda_4}$ −1.59843	$(f_5 - f_4)\frac{-f_4x_4}{\lambda_5 - \lambda_4}$ .2955497	$-f_4u_4\frac{-f_4x_4}{\lambda_5 - \lambda_4}$ .3664816	$-f_4x_4\frac{-f_4x_4}{\lambda_5 - \lambda_4}$ .2733835
λ_5 1.000		f_5 .0000											
									Total		−.0393638	1.0163105	.7903381
									$(\text{Total})^2$		.001549509	1.032887032	
									$(\text{Total})^2/K$		.0016586	.7865421	

$$\Omega_0 = \sum_{i=0}^{k} \frac{(f_{i+1}x_{i+1} - f_ix_i)^2}{\lambda_{i+1} - \lambda_i} - \frac{1}{K_1}\left[\sum_{i=0}^{k} \frac{(f_{i+1} - f_i)(f_{i+1}x_{i+1} - f_ix_i)}{\lambda_{i+1} - \lambda_i}\right]^2 - \frac{1}{K_2}\left[\sum_{i=0}^{k} \frac{(f_{i+1}u_{i+1} - f_iu_i)(f_{i+1}x_{i+1} - f_ix_i)}{\lambda_{i+1} - \lambda_i}\right]^2 = .7903381 - .0016586 - .7865421$$

$$t = \sqrt{2 \cdot K_1}\,\frac{\frac{1}{K_1}\sum_{i=0}^{k} \frac{(f_{i+1} - f_i)(f_{i+1}x_{i+1} - f_ix_i)}{\lambda_{i+1} - \lambda_i}}{\sqrt{\Omega_0}} = \sqrt{2 \times 0.9342} \times \frac{\frac{.2955497}{.9342}}{\sqrt{.7903381 - .0016586 - .786542}} = 1.2457$$

REFERENCES

1. W. J. Dixon and F. J. Massey, Jr., *Introduction to Statistical Analysis*, second edition, McGraw-Hill Book Co., New York, 1957.
2. J. Ogawa, "Contributions to the theory of systematic statistics, I," *Osaka Math. J.*, Vol. 3, No. 2 (1951), pp. 175–213.

W. J. DIXON

10H REJECTION OF OBSERVATIONS

10H.1 Tests Designed for Specific Types of Departures from Normality

Under this main heading there are problems which are often discussed under the following headings.

1. Rejection of observations.
2. Tests for outliers, aberrant or extreme values, or gross errors.
3. Analysis of contaminated data, that is, data not all arising from the desired population, that is, heterogeneity of data.
4. General departures from normality, for example, skewness or kurtosis.

Most attempts at solving problems in this area have relied on the use of order statistics in some form.

10H.2 General Discussion

It is well recognized by those who collect or analyze data that values occur in a sample of n observations which are so far removed from the remaining values that the analyst is not willing to believe that these values have come from the same population. Many times values occur which are "dubious" in the eyes of the analyst and he feels that he should make a decision whether to accept or reject these values as part of his sample. If the observation is valid and he rejects it, or if it is invalid and he accepts it, his results will be biased. However, he may not be looking for an error but may wish to recognize a situation when an occasional observation occurs which is from a different population. He may wish to discover whether a significant analysis of variance indicates an extreme value significantly different from the remainder. Also, of course, the extreme value may differ significantly without causing a significant analysis of variance, and he may wish to discover this. It is reasonable to suppose that a criterion for rejecting observations introduces a number of questions.

1. Should any observations be removed if we wish a representative sample including whatever contamination arises naturally? In other words, it may be desirable to describe the population including *all* observations, for only in that way do we describe what is actually happening.

2. If the analyst wishes to sample the population unaffected by contamination, he must either remove the contaminating items or employ statistical procedures which reduce to a minimum the effect of the contamination on the estimates of the population. That is, he may wish to describe only 95% of his population if the description is altered radically by the remaining 5% of the observations. He may have external reasons which are good and sufficient for wishing to describe only 95% of his observations. Suppose he wishes to use the sample for a statistical inference; the inclusion of all the data may sufficiently violate the assumptions underlying the inference to exclude the possibility of making a valid inference.

If we wish to follow some procedure which attempts to remove contamination, we must consider the performance of any proposed criterion with respect to the proportion of contamination the criterion will discover, and, of course, the proportion of the "good" observations that are removed by the use of the criterion. But, perhaps more important, we must consider what sort of bias will result when the standard statistical procedures are applied to samples of observations which have been processed in this manner.

If we wish to follow a procedure that will not search for particular values to be excluded but will minimize their effect if present, we must investigate the sampling distributions of these modified statistics and estimate the loss in information resulting from their use when all observations are "good." We must also investigate the expected bias which will result when "bad" items are present even though essentially excluded. Perhaps the most disturbing fact about the avoidance of "bad" items is that a decision must still be made whether a "bad" item was present or not in order to know in which way our estimates may be biased. For example, a sample mean computed by avoiding the two end observations will not be a biased estimate of the mean of a symmetric population if both end items should actually be included or if both end items should not be included. If only one of the two should not be included, however, this estimate of the mean will be biased.

10H.3 Sampling Assumptions

Assumptions will be referred to by the following numbers.

1. The sample size n is assumed fixed.
2. A proportion $1-\gamma$ of the observations are from a population $N(\mu, \sigma^2)$.
3. A proportion γ of the observations are either
   (*a*) $N(\mu + \lambda\sigma, \sigma^2)$, sampling denoted by $C_+(n, \gamma, \lambda)$.
   (*b*) $N(\mu, \lambda^2\sigma^2)$, sampling denoted by $C_\times(n, \gamma, \lambda)$.
4. The observational information available is one of those given in Table A.

TABLE A

Sample	Known μ	Known σ	Independent s	Available Statistic (see below)
(*a*) one sample of n	yes	yes	–	χ^2, B_0
(*b*) one sample of n	no	yes	–	χ^2, B_1, B_2, C_1
(*c*) one sample of n	no	no	yes	B_3, C_2
(*d*) one sample of n	no	no	no	B'_1, C'_1, D_1, D_2, r's
(*e*) k samples of r_i each	no	yes	–	same as above, but based on $\bar{x}$'s of each sample
(*f*)	no	no	yes	same as above, but based on $\bar{x}$'s of each sample
(*g*)	no	no	no	F_1, F_2

Assumption 3*a* represents the occurrence of an "error" in mean value such as will occur in dial readings when errors are made in reading incorrectly digits other than the last one or two. Errors of this sort may result from momentary shifts in line voltage or from the inclusion among a group of objects of one or two items of completely different origin. This type of contamination will be referred to as "location error." The symbol B represents the occurrence of an "error" from a population with the same mean but with a greater variance than the remainder of the sample. This type of error will be referred to as a "scalar error." It is likely that many errors could be better described as a combination of A and B, but a study of these two errors separately should throw considerable light on the question of "gross errors" or "blunders."

Many authors have written on the subject of the rejection of outlying observations. Apparently none has been successful in obtaining a general solution to the problem. Nor has there been success in the development of a criterion for discovery of outliers by means of a general statistical theory, for example, maximum likelihood. A large number of criteria have been advanced on more or less intuitive grounds as appropriate criteria for this purpose. In no case other than Dixon [7, 9] and David [6] was investigation made of the performance of these criteria except for a few illustrative examples.

References for the criteria discussed in the next section are given at the end of this chapter. Indications are given about the significance values available in these papers.

The various criteria that will be discussed are

A. χ^2-test

$$\chi^2 = \frac{\sum (x - \bar{x})^2}{\sigma^2} \tag{10H.3.1}$$

B. Extreme deviation

$$B_0 = \frac{x_{(n)} - \mu}{\sigma} \quad \left(\text{or } \frac{\mu - x_{(1)}}{\sigma}\right) \tag{10H.3.2}$$

$$B_1 = \frac{x_{(n)} - \bar{x}}{\sigma} \quad \left(\text{or } \frac{\bar{x} - x_{(1)}}{\sigma}\right) \tag{10H.3.3}$$

$$B'_1 = \frac{x_{(n)} - \bar{x}}{s} \quad \left(\text{or } \frac{\bar{x} - x_{(1)}}{s}\right) \tag{10H.3.4}$$

$$B_2 = \frac{x_{(n)} - x_{(n-1)}}{\sigma} \quad \left(\text{or } \frac{x_{(2)} - x_{(1)}}{\sigma}\right) \tag{10H.3.5}$$

$$B_3 = \frac{x_{(n)} - \bar{x}}{s} \quad \left(\text{or } \frac{\bar{x} - x_{(1)}}{s}\right)$$

(s independently estimated) (10H.3.6)

C. Range

$$C_1 = \frac{w}{\sigma} \tag{10H.3.7}$$

$$C'_1 = \frac{w}{s} \tag{10H.3.8}$$

$$C_2 = q = \frac{w}{s}$$

(s independently estimated) (10H.3.9)

D. Modified F-tests

1. For single outlier $x_{(1)}$,

$$D_1 = \frac{S_1^{\,2}}{S^2} \tag{10H.3.10}$$

where

$$S_1^{\,2} = \sum_2^n (x - \bar{x}_1)^2, \qquad \bar{x}_1 = \sum_2^n \frac{x}{n-1}$$

$$S^2 = \sum_1^n (x - \bar{x})^2, \qquad \bar{x} = \sum_1^n \frac{x}{n}$$

$$\left(\text{or for } x_n,\ D_1 = \frac{S_n^{\,2}}{S^2}\right)$$

2. For double outliers $x_{(1)}$, $x_{(2)}$,

$$D_2 = \frac{S_{1,2}^2}{S^2} \tag{10H.3.11}$$

where

$$S_{1,2}^2 = \sum_3^n (x - \bar{x}_{1,2})^2, \qquad \bar{x}_{1,2} = \sum_3^n \frac{x}{n-2}$$

$$\left(\text{or for } x_{(n)},\ x_{(n-1)},\ D_2 = \frac{S_{n,n-1}^2}{S^2}\right)$$

E. Various ratios of ranges and subranges

1. For single outlier $x_{(1)}$,

$$r_{10} = \frac{x_{(2)} - x_{(1)}}{x_{(n)} - x_{(1)}} \tag{10H.3.12}$$

$$\left(\text{or for } x_{(n)},\ r_{10} = \frac{x_{(n)} - x_{(n-1)}}{x_{(n)} - x_{(1)}}\right)$$

2. For single outlier $x_{(1)}$ avoiding $x_{(n)}$,

$$r_{11} = \frac{x_{(2)} - x_{(1)}}{x_{(n-1)} - x_{(1)}} \tag{10H.3.13}$$

$$\left(\text{or for } x_{(n)} \text{ avoiding } x_{(1)},\ r_{11} = \frac{x_{(n)} - x_{(n-1)}}{x_{(n)} - x_{(2)}}\right)$$

3. For single outlier $x_{(1)}$, avoiding $x_{(n)}$, $x_{(n-1)}$,

$$r_{12} = \frac{x_{(2)} - x_{(1)}}{x_{(n-2)} - x_{(1)}} \tag{10H.3.14}$$

$$\left(\text{or for } x_{(n)} \text{ avoiding } x_{(1)},\ x_{(2)},\ r_{12} = \frac{x_{(n)} - x_{(n-1)}}{x_{(n)} - x_{(3)}}\right)$$

4. For outlier $x_{(1)}$ avoiding $x_{(2)}$,

$$r_{20} = \frac{x_{(3)} - x_{(1)}}{x_{(n)} - x_{(1)}} \tag{10H.3.15}$$

$$\left(\text{or for } x_{(n)} \text{ avoiding } x_{(n-1)},\ r_{20} = \frac{x_{(n)} - x_{(n-2)}}{x_{(n)} - x_{(1)}}\right)$$

5. For outlier $x_{(1)}$ avoiding $x_{(2)}$ and $x_{(n)}$,

$$r_{21} = \frac{x_{(3)} - x_{(1)}}{x_{(n-1)} - x_{(1)}} \tag{10H.3.16}$$

$$\left(\text{or for } x_{(n)} \text{ avoiding } x_{(n-1)}, x_{(1)},\ r_{21} = \frac{x_{(n)} - x_{(n-2)}}{x_{(n)} - x_{(2)}}\right)$$

6. For outlier $x_{(1)}$ avoiding $x_{(2)}$ and $x_{(n)}$, $x_{(n-1)}$,

$$r_{22} = \frac{x_{(3)} - x_{(1)}}{x_{(n-2)} - x_{(1)}} \tag{10H.3.17}$$

$$\left(\text{or for } x_{(n)} \text{ avoiding } x_{(n-1)}, x_{(1)}, x_{(2)},\ r_{22} = \frac{x_{(n)} - x_{(n-2)}}{x_{(n)} - x_{(3)}}\right)$$

F. Criteria based on k samples of equal size n

$$F_1 = \frac{\max(w_i)}{\sum w_i} = T_k \tag{10H.3.18}$$

$$F_2 = \frac{\max(s_i^2)}{\sum s_i^2} \tag{10H.3.19}$$

10H.4 Distributions of the Various Criteria

In order to use any of these criteria we must have available at least a few percentiles of the distributions.

Tables of Percentiles for Various Criteria

B_0	Table 10H.1	Percentiles 0.1, 0.5, 1, 2.5, 5, 10, 90, 95, 97.5, 99, 99.5, 99.9 for $n = 1(1)30$. (Reproduced from reference 19.) *Note.* These are percentiles of the extreme order statistic.
B_1	Table 10H.2	Percentiles as for B_0 for $n = 3(1)9$. (Reproduced from reference 15.) This table is also in reference 19 as Table 25.
	Table 10H.3	Percentiles 90, 95, 99, 99.5 for $n = 2(1)25$. (Reproduced from reference 12.) Procedures for obtaining percentiles are given in reference 14.

B'_1	Table 10H.4	Percentiles 90, 95, 97.5, 99 for $n = 3(1)25$. (Reproduced from reference 12.) These percentiles for $n = 3(1)19$ are in reference 20, and percentiles 90, 95, 97.5 for $n = 3(1)22$, 32, 42, 102, 202, 502, 1002 are in reference 21.
B_2	Table 10H.5	$\Pr(B_2 > \lambda)$, $\lambda = 0.1\ (0.1)\ 5.0$ for $n = 2, 3, 10(10)$ $100(100)1000$. (Reproduced from reference 13.) The same reference also contains tables for second and third ordered observations.
B_3	Table 10H.6	Percentiles 1, 5 for $n = 3(1)9$ and $\nu = 10, 15, 30, \infty$; percentiles 90, 95 for $n = 3(1)9$ and $\nu = 10(1)20$, 24, 30, 40, 60, 120. (Lower per cent points are reproduced from reference 19 and upper points are reproduced from reference 5.)
C_1	Table 10H.7	Percentiles 0.1, 0.5, 1, 2.5, 5, 10, 90, 95, 97.5, 99, 99.5, 99.9 for $n = 2(1)20$. (Reproduced from reference 19.)
C'_1	Table 10H.8 (and Table 10H.8a)	Percentiles 0, 0.5, 1, 2.5, 5, 10, 90, 95, 97.5, 99, 99.5, 100 for $n = 3(1)20(10)60$, 80, 100, 150, 200, 500, 1000 except percentiles 0.5 to 10 for $n = 3(1)9$. (Reproduced from references 4 and 22.)
C_2	Table 7A.2	Percentiles 95, 99 for $n = 2(1)20$; $\nu = 1(1)20$, 24, 30, 40, 60, 120, ∞ except percentiles 1 and 5 for $\nu = 1(1)9$.
D_1	Table 10H.9	Percentiles 90, 95, 97.5, 99 for $n = 3(1)25$. (Reproduced from reference 12.)
D_2	Table 10H.10	Percentiles 90, 95, 97.5, 99 for $n = 4(1)20$. (Reproduced from reference 12.)
E	Table 10H.11	Percentiles 5, 10(10)90, 95, 98, 99, 99.5 of r_{10} for $n = 3(1)30$; of r_{11}, r_{20} for $n = 4(1)30$; of r_{12}, r_{21} for $n = 5(1)30$; of r_{22} for $n = 6(1)30$. (Reproduced from reference 8.)
F_1	Table 10H.12	Percentile 95 for $k = 2(1)10$, 12, 15, 20, 50 and $n = 2(1)10$. (Reproduced from reference 1.)
F_2	Tables 10H.13*a* and *b*	Percentiles 95, 99 for $k = 2(1)10$, 12, 15, 20, 24, 30, 40, 60, 120, ∞ and each s_i^2 having df $= 1(1)10$, 16, 36, 144, ∞. (Reproduced from reference 11.)

10H.5 Power of the Various Criteria or "Which Should I Use?"

It is easy to see from the preceding sections that various writers have shown great imagination in defining criteria which it is assumed satisfy their intuition about the type of criterion which has some optimum properties for the purpose in mind. In general, adequate percentiles have been computed so that we may choose one of several levels of significance for a test of the null hypothesis that all observations are from a single normal population. Most articles on this subject have stopped at this point except for the discussion of several illustrative examples and perhaps an examination of a few samples from other populations (e.g., see reference 4). To carry the problem further we must consider the following questions.

1. What will a rejection of the null hypothesis lead us to do?
   (*a*) State that the sample is "nonnormal." This is a straightforward and simple test of hypothesis.
   (*b*) Reject the likely looking "criminal," or perhaps several "criminals," and proceed with the usual statistical procedures on the remainder of the sample. This requires a rule for deciding which of the observations are the "criminals."
   (*c*) Reject the likely looking "criminal" and select a new "recruit" at random. This requires a rule for selecting the observation to be rejected and an observational situation comparable to that existing when the original observations were made.
   (*d*) Change to an alternate statistical technique which is less affected by the presence of a "criminal," or perhaps a better statement is, "Use an alternate technique which has less bias in samples that lead to rejection of the null hypothesis." For example, we may estimate the population mean from the sample median.
   (*e*) Reject a suspected observation and retest the remaining sample for homogeneity, continuing until no rejection occurs. This alters the level of significance if we consider the sample remaining after each rejection as a new sample.
2. What considerations are used in a choice of the level of significance to be used in the test? These considerations, of course, depend on which of these procedures is contemplated. However, several examples are stated to indicate the problems involved.
   (*a*) Desire to fix the proportions of homogeneous samples which will lose one observation.
   (*b*) Desire to identify all observations which are from another population. This is impossible.
   (*c*) Desire to obtain an unbiased estimate of a population parameter. If we perform this test only as an aid to minimizing bias, the level of significance cannot be freely chosen but is determined by specification of the population being sampled from.
3. For what kind of nonnormality do we desire maximum power?

   (*a*) Presence of a specified number, say, one or two observations from another population.
   (*b*) Populations as specified in assumptions 2 and 3.
   (*c*) Some mixture of the two types indicated in *b*.
   (*d*) Other functional forms.
4. For what kind of nonnormality do we desire minimum bias in estimation of population parameters?
5. If a test is performed on a sample, what rule is followed in selecting the observation to reject?
   (*a*) By inspection. This does not answer the question.
   (*b*) The observation most distant from the mean.
   (*c*) The largest (or smallest) observation.

It is an understatement to say that the present literature does not provide answers to all these questions. However, in the framework of these questions and defining the problem as 1*b*, 3*a* and *b*, 5*b* and *c*, the criteria A, B_1, B_2, C_1, C_2, $D_1 \equiv B'_1$, D_2, r_{10}, r_{11}, r_{12}, r_{20}, r_{21}, r_{22} have been investigated [7]. David [6] has powers of B_1 for problems 1*b*, 2*a*, 3*a*, 5*b*.

Also defining the problem as choosing alternatives among 1*b*, *d*, and *e* to answer 2*c* for alternatives 3*b* with rule 5*b* for rejection, some answers are known [9]. Bias was measured by mean square error of the resulting estimate. A synopsis of the results of these two studies will be given in the following subsections.

10H.6 Performance of Criteria under Assumptions 4*b* and *c*

The χ^2-test will, of course, give an indication of a large dispersion, and since the extreme values are likely to be chief contributors to the sum of squares, it is possible to use this test as a criterion for rejecting a value or values which are at the greatest distance from the mean. It might be supposed that B_1 and B_2 would give better results since particular attention is paid to the end item. The same argument would influence us in favor of C_1 or C_2. The performance of C_2 can, of course, be expected to vary with the degrees of freedom in the independent estimate of σ. For this study the degrees of freedom for this estimate were held to the single value 9 DF.

We may use χ^2 since if the value of χ^2 is too large (greater than some upper percentage point for χ^2) we may reject the value most distant from the mean, χ^2 tables may be used for percentage points.

Criteria A, B_1, B_2, C_1, C_2 were investigated for $\alpha = 1\%$, 5%, and 10%, for $\lambda = 2, 3, 5, 7$, where one or more items are selected from a population $N(\mu+\lambda\sigma, \sigma^2)$ and the remainder from $N(\mu, \sigma^2)$. Investigations were also made for one item from $N(\mu, \lambda^2\sigma^2)$ for $\lambda = 2, 4, 8, 12$. The investigation was carried out by sampling methods. The performances of different criteria were assessed for the same group of samples in order to obtain more precision in the comparison of the different tests. All the points appearing on the graphs in the subsequent sections of this paper were based on from 66 to 200 determinations for each of two sizes.

The performances of these criteria were measured by computing the chance that the contaminating distribution provides an extreme value and the test discovers this value. Of course, performance could be measured by the chance that the test gives a significant value when a member of the contaminating population is present in the sample, even though not at an extreme. However, since it was assumed that discovery of an outlier would frequently be followed by the rejection of an extreme, a success was recorded only when the extreme value was from the contaminating distribution.

The performance was judged by applying the criterion to each sample, always suspecting an outlier in the direction of the shifted mean for location error. Since the location errors were inserted by adding a fixed value to one or more of the observations, the largest value was tested as an outlier. The measure of performance was the percentage of location errors identified. When the location error was not an outlier, no test was performed and a failure for the test was recorded.

When the model of contamination involved the scalar error, the value farthest from the mean was suspected. This step of course alters somewhat the level of significance, but this procedure was followed alike for all criteria investigated. The performance was measured in the same fashion as for location errors.

Considering, first location errors, a study of the performance curves showing the per cent discovery of contaminators plotted against λ (the number of standard deviation units the population of contaminators is removed from the remainder) showed that the level of performance for σ known is considerably above the level of performance when σ is not known. The difference is greater for $n = 5$ than for $n = 15$ and, of course, the difference will diminish as the sample size increases. Figure 10H.1 shows the performance curves for $\alpha = 5\%$ (5% significance level for the test for an outlier) of $B_1 = (x_{(n)} - \bar{x})/\sigma$ for $n = 5$ and $n = 15$ and of

$$r_{10} = \frac{x_{(n)} - x_{(n-1)}}{x_{(n)} - x_{(1)}} \text{ for } n = 5 \text{ and } n = 15.$$

The curves for different levels of significance were similar in shape, exhibiting only the expected changes with changes in the level of significance.

Test B_1 in Fig. 10H.1 was found to give the best performance of all criteria considered if a single location error is present. The curves showing the comparative performance of these criteria are given in reference 7, from which we may conclude:

1. The differences among A, B_1, B_2, and C_1 are not great.
2. The knowledge of σ is less important in larger samples.
3. The curve for C_2 lies above that of r_{10} for $n = 5$ and below that of r_{10} for $n = 15$. This is consistent with the use of 9 DF in the independent estimate of σ.

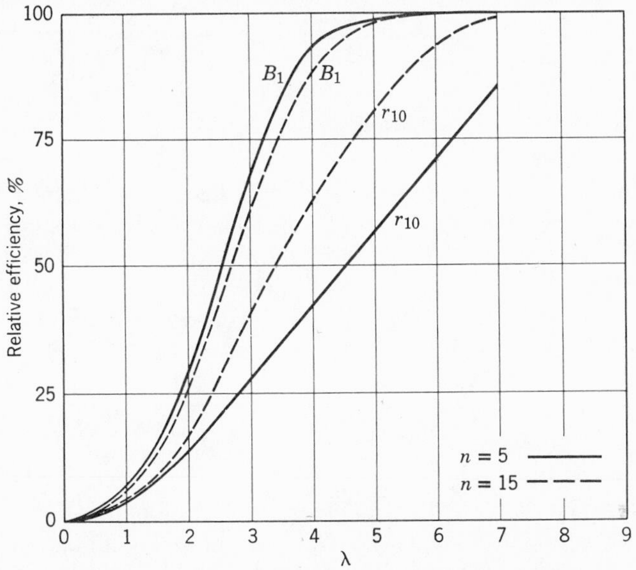

Fig. 10H.1 Improvement in performance obtained with knowledge of σ, $\alpha = 5\%$, $n = 5, 15$.

If the question of ease in computation or application is important, it may be desirable to use B_2 or C_1 in place of B_1, for they are slightly easier to compute and it is not necessary to measure all observations to obtain the value of these statistics. If two outliers may be expected in a single sample, the performance of B_2 will be lowered and the performance of B_1 and C_1 will be improved. Any difference between the performance of B_1 and the performance of C_1 when two outliers are present was not discernible for $n = 5$ or 15.

H. A. David [5] has computed the power function of B_1 for alternatives $\mu + \lambda$ for $n = 3(1)10$, 12, 15, 20, 25 and $\lambda = 1, 2, 3, 4$ for rejecting an extreme observation when exactly one observation from the alternative distribution is present ($\alpha = 0.05$).

The performance curves of these criteria if a scalar error is present are very similar to those given except that:

1. A high level of performance is approached very slowly. For example, from Fig. 5 of reference 7 showing the performance of B_1 and r_{10} for $n = 15$ and $\alpha = 5\%$, for $\lambda = 4$ only 50% of the extraneous observations are discovered.

2. There is a smaller difference in the performance between the criteria with σ known and σ unknown (see reference 7, Fig. 5).

The performance values of B_1 and C_1 are noticeably increased by the introduction of more contaminators, whereas that of B_2 decreases. No difference in the performance of B_1 and C_1 was noted for either $n = 5$ or $n = 15$.

The performance of C_2 approaches that of B_1 as the number of degrees of freedom increases.

The general recommendations for possibilities of either type of contamination, location, or scalar errors would lead us to the use of B_1 or C_1 if σ is known.

Criterion C_1 is recommended since its performance is almost as good as the performance of B_1 for a single outlier. Their performances are about equal for two outliers, and C_1 affords protection for outliers either above or below the mean.

10H.7 Performance of Criteria under Assumption 4*d*

Criteria D_1 and D_2 have strong intuitive reasons for their use since the dispersion is estimated by s^2. The ratios are attractive because of their simplicity and their preoccupation with the extreme values. Test B'_1 is the "studentized" ratio corresponding to B_1 and is equivalent to D_1 since $D_1 = 1 - B_1'^2/(n-1)$. There is no apparent difference in the performance of D_1 and r_{10} when one outlier is present and no apparent difference in D_2 and r_{20} when two outliers are present. This is true for both models of contamination and for the three levels of significance investigated. The comparison of D_2 and r_{20} was made only for $n = 5$, however (critical values were not available for D_2 for $n = 15$ at that time).

The performance of D_1 and r_{10} under the two models of contamination can be obtained by reference to the curve for r_{10} in Fig. 10H.1. The curve for D_1 is practically identical with the curve for r_{10}.

There is no question that r_{10} is simpler to use, so that if this condition of contamination (scalar errors) exists, r_{10} will probably be chosen. As before, however, we should investigate what happens when more than one error is present. Criterion D_2 is designed for this case as is r_{20}. Since the performance of these two criteria is approximately the same, r_{20} would probably be chosen because of its simplicity. Critical values for this statistic are available for $n \leq 30$.

Criteria r_{11}, r_{12}, r_{20}, r_{21}, r_{22} were designed for use in situations where additional outliers may occur and we wish to minimize the effect of these outliers on the investigation of the particular value being tested.

It has been suggested that D_1 could be used repeatedly to remove more than one outlier from a sample. This procedure cannot be recommended since the presence of additional outliers handicaps the performance of both D_1 and r_{10} for small sample sizes, and therefore the process of rejection might never get started. For larger sample sizes the performance of D_1 is affected much less by the presence of two errors than is the performance of r_{10}. The repetitive use of D_1 is not recommended either since r_{20} performs in a superior manner to D_1 in such situations. This difference in performance of D_1 and r_{10} depends markedly on the level of significance used as well as the sample size. For small samples there is little difference in performance for any of the levels of significance we might use. For the larger sample sizes there is no appreciable difference for very high levels of significance. The difference is very great for lower levels of significance, however. In fact as λ increases for two errors of the location type, the level of significance which divides the region of approach to zero performance from the region of approach to perfect performance of D_1 is given by the level of significance corresponding to a significance value of $\frac{1}{2}\frac{n}{n-1}$ for D_1. Thus, for example, in samples of size 15, $\frac{1}{2}\frac{n}{n-1} = \frac{15}{28} = 0.536$. This value lies between the values for the 2.5% and 5% levels of significance. These values are 0.503 and 0.556 respectively. Therefore the use of the 1% or 2.5% levels will give poorer and poorer performance as λ increases, and the use of the 5% or 10% levels will give better and better performance as λ increases when two errors are present. The dividing point is such that for samples of size 11 or less the use of any of the given levels of significance will cause the performance to decrease as λ increases. For samples of size $n \leq 14$ the 1%, 2.5%, and 5% levels have the same effect, for samples of size $n \leq 16$ the 1% and 2.5% levels, and for samples of size $n \leq 19$ just the 1% level. For three such errors the limit approached by D_1 as λ increases is $\frac{2}{3}\frac{n}{n-1}$. Therefore, the performance of D_1 will approach zero for all levels of significance and for all sample sizes for which critical values are known except the 10% level of significance for sample sizes larger than 21. An indication of these limiting values $\frac{k-1}{k}\frac{n}{n-1}$

for k contaminators present can be obtained by considering these k-values to be at a distance k from the population mean, computing D_1 and allowing λ to increase indefinitely.

The comparative performance of the r-criteria, $\alpha = 5\%$, in samples of size 5 for the two models of contamination (one contaminator present) are given in Figs. 7 and 8 of reference 7. For samples of size 15 the curves are given in Figs. 9 and 10 of reference 7. A single curve suffices here since there is no discernible difference in the curves for the different r-criteria. There is considerable difference in the performance curves if more than one outlier is present. However, the performances of r_{10}, r_{11}, r_{12} are essentially the same when two location outliers are present as the performances of r_{20}, r_{21}, r_{22}.

Additional curves were presented showing the performance of all six of the r-criteria for both one and two outliers of location and scalar types in samples of size 5 and 15.

It should be noted in the comparisons that no model of contamination was investigated which would cause one or more errors at both extremes in the sample. It is obvious that the performance of D_1 and D_2 would be considerably decreased, but the performance of r_{11}, r_{12} and r_{21}, r_{22} would not be materially affected since these criteria avoid values at the opposite extreme. Their repeated use might discover most of such outliers, whereas D_1 or D_2 is likely to fail on the first trial.

10H.8 Sampling from a Contaminated Population

In the previous sections the performances of the various criteria were assessed for samples where a certain number of contaminators were present. We might well ask why a test is needed if it is known that contaminators are present. It would seem more realistic to state that a certain per cent of contamination will occur in the long run, and that we will not know in any particular case whether 0, 1, 2, . . . contaminators will be present. We would then wish a criterion to indicate the presence of contamination in a particular sample.

The performances of these criteria were investigated for the same two models of contamination and reported as per cent of total contamination discovered. The tests were applied only once to each sample.

Investigation was made for 5, 10, and 20% contamination. For example, in samples of size 5 which have 10% contamination, on the average, 59.0% of the samples will contain no "errors," 32.8% will contain one, 7.3% two, 0.8% three, 0.1% four, and 0.0% five. Thus in 100 samples of 5 which are 10% contaminated with location errors having mean $\mu + 5\sigma$, about 59 contain no errors. If the r_{10}-criterion is used with a 5% level of significance, one value will be "discovered" in 3.0 of the samples containing no errors. Of the 33 samples containing one "error," the "error" would be discovered in 18 of these samples This criterion would discover none of the '"errors" in samples containing more than one "error." We would have obtained 18 of the 50 contaminating values and 3 that were members of the original population.

When σ is known the performance will increase when more contaminators are present. Performance, however, has been measured in terms of

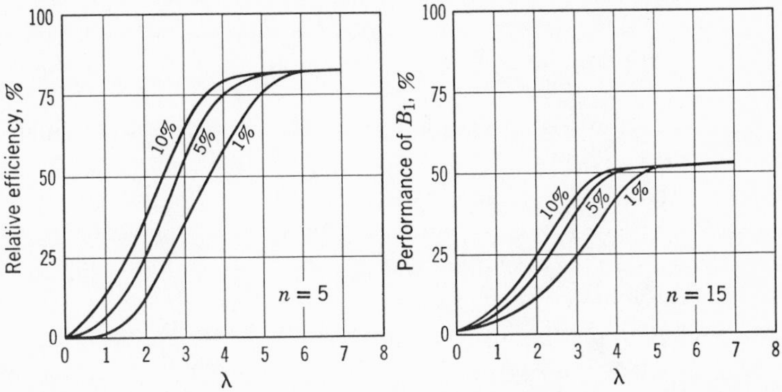

Fig. 10H.2 Performance of B_1 for various levels of significance when the population is 10% contaminated with location errors.

finding a single contaminator; that is, the test has been used only once. Therefore even with increasing per cent contamination, the level of performance measured in this way will decrease with increasing contamination. Repeated use of the test criteria was not investigated.

Criterion B_1 gives the best performance for both location and scalar errors for the levels of contamination and levels of significance considered. A and C_1 are only slightly inferior. Criterion B_2 is handicapped when more than one error is present; thus its performance is poorer for heavier contamination. Figure 10H.2 shows the performance of B_1 for the different levels of significance, 10% contamination, and the two sample sizes 5 and 15 for location errors. Reference 7 also contains figures for the other criteria showing the effects on performance of changes in level of significance, amounts of contamination, type of contamination, and sample sizes 5 and 15.

When σ is not known, the performance of various criteria will eventually decrease as more and more contaminators are present in the sample, even though several of the criteria show improvement in discovering a single error if two are present. The performance of these criteria is greatly affected by the size of the sample. For samples of size 5, r_{10} and D_1

perform alike, r_{10} being superior to the other r's (r_{20} second best) for the levels of contamination considered, and D_2 is inferior to r_{20}.

For samples of size 15, r_{20}, r_{21}, r_{22} perform alike as do r_{10}, r_{11}, and r_{12}. Criteria D_1 and r_{20}, r_{21}, r_{22} perform approximately the same and are superior to r_{10}, r_{11}, r_{12}.

Throughout the investigation of performance, location errors were placed only at one extreme and scalar errors at either extreme. The test for an error was made using as a suspected value the extreme value in the direction of the location error or for the scalar error the value most distant from the mean. It can be expected then that if performance were assessed when location errors could occur in either direction, different results would be obtained. In addition, for scalar errors, if errors were always sought at one particular extreme or at both extremes, different results would be obtained. If these changes were made in the models of contamination, those criteria designed to avoid errors at the other extreme would have an advantage over those not so designed for σ unknown. If σ is known, the criteria that do not avoid the other extreme would have an advantage over those that do avoid the other extreme. These points were used to discriminate among the criteria that were judged to be equal in performance under the models used in the sampling study.

1. For σ known: B_1 or C_1 should be used, or in small samples A, B_1, or C_1 should be used.

2. For σ unknown: r_{10} should be used for very small samples (7 or less), r_{22} should be used for sample sizes over 13. Probably r_{21} would be best for sample sizes from about 11 to 13, and r_{11} for those from 8 to 10.

10H.9 Attempts to Remove Bias [9]

We may not be primarily concerned with tagging the particular observation which is from a different population but may wish to use a procedure of analysis not appreciably affected by the presence of such observations, for example, to estimate the mean or variance of the basic distribution in a situation where unavoidable contamination occasionally occurs.

10H.10 Effects of Contamination on the Mean and Median

The median has often been proposed as an estimator for μ under certain conditions of contamination. The ability of the mean and median to estimate μ can be compared by computing the mean square error (MSE) of the estimates for various types of contamination. The biases will be listed in several cases. The bias of the arithmetic mean is defined as

$E(\bar{x} - \mu)/\sigma$ and the MSE is defined as $E(\bar{x} - \mu)^2/\sigma^2$. The criterion of *better* estimate of mean to be used here is *smaller* MSE.

From Table B, it can be concluded that the median is superior to the mean of untreated data for 10% contamination in samples of size 5, only if contamination is centered about 3.3σ or further from the mean. For 1% contamination the untreated mean is superior to the median for λ as large as 7.

The curves labeled $\alpha = 0$ in Fig. 10H.3 show the frequency and extent of contamination that can be tolerated before the MSE of the mean exceeds the MSE of the median. Curves are given for samples of size 5

TABLE B

SAMPLES NOT TREATED FOR CONTAMINATION

	$C_+(5, 0.10, \lambda)$					$C_+(5, 0.01, \lambda)$			
	Mean		Median			Mean		Median	
λ	Bias	MSE	Bias	MSE	λ	Bias	MSE	Bias	MSE
0	0	0.200	0	0.287	0	0	0.200	0	0.287
2	0.2	0.313	0.15	0.41	2	0.02	0.208	0.02	0.30
3	0.3	0.455	0.18	0.48	3	0.03	0.219	0.02	0.30
5	0.5	0.908	0.20	0.61	5	0.05	0.252	0.02	0.30
7	0.7	1.588	0.22	0.80	7	0.07	0.302	0.02	0.30

and 15 and for location and scalar contamination. For example, for samples of size 5 which are 5% contaminated, the MSE for $\bar{x}$ is smaller when the contaminating distribution is shifted 3σ but not when it is shifted 4σ.

Let us now consider changes in these results when some of the contamination has been removed by the use of one of the r-criteria of reference 20.

Investigation was made using the 1, 5, and 10% levels of significance. The sample was tested until no further observations could be removed; that is, if a rejection was obtained at a certain level of significance, the reduced sample was again tested for outlier using the same level for α. This means, of course, that α should no longer be called a level of significance.

The additional curves in Fig. 10H.3 indicate the larger regions in which the MSE of $\bar{x}$ for treated samples is smaller than the MSE of the median for untreated samples when larger values of α are used. For extreme contamination an $\alpha = 0.20$ or 0.30 would further reduce the MSE for $\bar{x}$. Although not investigated in detail, it is known that a larger α would not materially increase the size of λ and γ which can be tolerated before the median should be used in preference to the mean.

In samples of size 5 use of the mean for treated samples results in most cases in a MSE *considerably smaller* than the MSE for the median. In cases of extreme contamination where the MSE for the median is smaller, it is only slightly smaller. The MSE for the mean or the median is very large for heavy contamination, however. Treatment is at the level $\alpha = 0{,}00$, 0.01, 0.05, or 0.10 which gives minimum MSE of $\bar{x}$. The use of the best treatment procedure still does not give us all that might be hoped for since the MSE is still large. The ratio of MSE for mean of treated data to MSE for mean of data with no contamination is an index of the extent

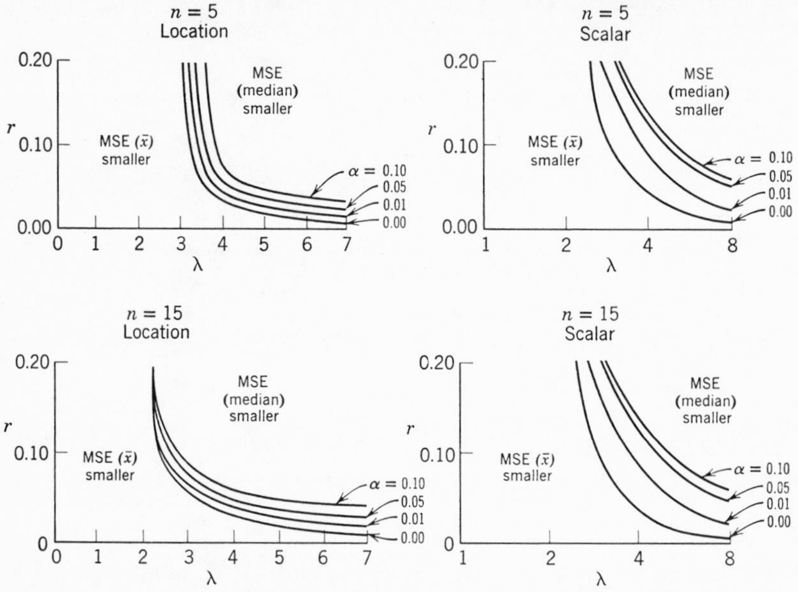

Fig. 10H.3 Contours indicating equality of MSE of median of untreated data and MSE of $\bar{x}$ of treated data.

of the contamination. We can also see from this index how much better the better estimate is. These ratios are given in Table C for samples of size 5. Reference 9 also gives tables for $n = 15$. For samples of size 15 the picture is changed since the MSE for the mean becomes very large in the region where the MSE for the median is less than the MSE for the mean.

From these ratios we can see that in samples of size 5, even with extreme contamination, the median is not a satisfactory substitute for $\bar{x}$ if the samples are treated for contamination. However, in samples of size 15 we should use the median if contamination beyond the $\alpha = 0.10$ curve (Fig. 10H.3) is expected.

The increase in MSE for $\bar{x}$ caused by removing occasional values which are not contaminators is very small in comparison to the reduction of MSE of $\bar{x}$ obtained by the removal of extreme contaminators.

TABLE C

$$\frac{\text{MSE }[\bar{x}, \text{treated data}, C_+(5, \gamma, \lambda)]}{\text{MSE }[\bar{x}, N(\mu, \sigma^2)]}$$

γ \ λ	0	2	3	5	7
0.01	1.00	1.04	1.08	1.2	1.3
0.05	1.00	1.3	1.5	1.8	2.2
0.10	1.00	1.6	2.2	3.4	5.1
0.20	1.00	2.4	4.0	8.5	15.0

$$\frac{\text{MSE }[\text{median}, C_+(5, \gamma, \lambda)]}{\text{MSE }[\bar{x}, N(\mu, \sigma^2)]}$$

γ \ λ	0	2	3	5	7
0.01	1.43	1.5	1.5	1.5	1.5
0.05	1.43	1.8	1.7	1.9	2.0
0.10	1.43	2.1	2.4	3.1	4.0
0.20	1.43	3.0	4.4	8.2	14.1

Use of a large value of α will discover more contaminators but, of course, will increase the MSE of $\bar{x}$ if samples do not contain outliers. This effect is, however, small. Use of $\alpha = 0.10$ in samples of size 5 containing no contamination will increase MSE of $\bar{x}$ from 0.200 to approximately 0.216. Therefore, unless the contamination is believed to be slight, a fairly large α should be used. In order to obtain minimum MSE for the estimate of μ, we can consider using one of the following procedures:

1. Use of $\bar{x}$ after treating for rejection with $\alpha = 0.01$.
2. Use of $\bar{x}$ after treating for rejection with $\alpha = 0.05$.
3. Use of $\bar{x}$ after treating for rejection with $\alpha = 0.10$.
4. Use of the median.

Reference 9 gives the procedure resulting in the least MSE among the four procedures considered for the various types of contamination and sample sizes. The resulting MSE is also given.

The MSE figures are not increased by more than 5% by the use of $\alpha = 0.10$ in place of $\alpha = 0.01$ or 0.05 (or by 10% over no treatment). This is a small effect compared to the 50% to 200% increase in MSE resulting if certain extreme contamination is not removed. This fact was taken into account in laying down general rules.

10H.11 Bias of s^2 and the Range

The effect of contamination on the estimate of variance was assessed by computing the amount of bias resulting. Let us define $B = E(s^2)/\sigma^2$.

TABLE D

APPROPRIATE α TO REMOVE BIAS IN s^2

γ \ λ	2	3	5	7
0.01	0.12	0.10	0.08	0.01
0.02	0.14	0.12	0.10	0.02
0.05	0.20	0.25		
0.10				
0.20				

Since removal of outliers will reduce the variance, it is possible to make $B = 1$ for any γ and λ by choosing α sufficiently large. Since investigation was carried out only for $\alpha = 0.01, 0.05, 0.10$ (and a few results for

TABLE E

BIAS IN s^2 FOR $C_+(5, \gamma, 5)$

α \ γ	0	0.10	0.20
0.00	1.00	3.52	6.0
0.01	0.99	1.90	5.3
0.05	0.95	1.52	4.4
0.10	0.91	1.26	4.0

$\alpha = 0.20$), it was not possible to state the appropriate α for heavy or extreme contamination. Table D is an example of the results. It was believed that the consideration of bias alone was sufficient in the case of estimating variance since in general the mean and MSE of the variance are closely related.

Here again it is much more serious to allow contamination to remain than to remove noncontaminators incorrectly, so in general we should lean toward a large α. Table E illustrates this effect. For example, if contamination is not present and we use $\alpha = 0.10$, we underestimate σ^2 by 9%; but if 10% contamination at 5σ is present, the use of the same rejection criterion will give us an overestimate of only 26% in place of 250% in samples of size 5.

In very small samples the *range* is often used to estimate the population standard deviation. Contamination will, of course, seriously affect the sample range, but the rejection criteria can effectively remove the bias in the range estimate of the population standard deviation for samples of size 5. Appropriate α which will result in an unbiased range estimate of σ in samples of size 5 are tabulated [9].

The bias of the range estimate of σ for one type of contamination is tabulated in Table F. As before, it is much more serious to leave contamination in than to remove a few observations from samples which contain no contamination.

TABLE F

BIAS OF THE RANGE ESTIMATE OF σ FOR $C_+(5, \gamma, 5)$

α \ γ	0	0.10	0.20
0.00	1.00	1.66	2.11
0.01	0.99	1.50	1.91
0.05	0.97	1.27	1.63
0.10	0.93	1.13	1.48

These results indicate that the range estimate of σ is less affected by contamination than s^2 even if no treatment is applied.

If very little is known about the contamination to be expected, about the best we can do is to "tag" observations and remove them from estimates of μ and σ.

If even a moderate amount of information about the type of contamination to be expected is available, a process can be prescribed that will minimize the effects of contamination on the estimates of mean and dispersion in small samples. The following rules result from the investigation of samples of size 5 and 15. Rules are presented for these two sample sizes with the expectation that rules for samples of approximately these sizes are approximately the same.

An attempt has been made to present simple rules for the estimation of both μ and σ. As a consequence the minimum MSE will not always be obtained. In most cases, however, the suggested procedure will yield a MSE which is not more than 5% larger than the minimum MSE. The rules will yield bias B between 0.90 and 1.10 for the indicated estimate of dispersion except in cases noted specifically in the rules.

Rules. Process data using r's as rejection criteria unless use of median is indicated. The appropriate α will be indicated in the rules below. Repeat application of criteria until no further observations are rejected.

Use the level of α indicated in the following statements.

$n = 5$, *Location contamination*

1. If $\gamma\lambda < 0.10$, use $\alpha = \gamma\lambda$, $\bar{x}$ for average, either s^2 or range for dispersion.
2. If $0.10 < \gamma\lambda < 0.45$, use $\alpha = 0.10$, $\bar{x}$ for average, range for dispersion.
3. If $\gamma\lambda > 0.45$, use median for average and use $\alpha = 0.10$ and range to estimate dispersion. The estimate of dispersion will be biased, giving an overestimation of σ of more than 10% ($B \simeq 1.1$ for $\gamma\lambda = 0.45$, $B \simeq 1.5$ for $\gamma\lambda = 1.00$).

$n = 5$, *Scalar contamination*

4. If $\gamma\lambda < 0.45$, use $\alpha = \frac{1}{2}\gamma\lambda$, $\bar{x}$ for average, s^2 for dispersion (for $\gamma\lambda > 0.30$ use range for dispersion, bias for both range and s^2 over 10%).
5. If $\gamma\lambda > 0.45$, use median for average, range for dispersion. The estimate of dispersion will be biased, giving an overestimate of σ of more than 40%.

$n = 15$, *Location contamination*

6. If $\gamma\lambda < 0.30$, use $\alpha = 0.10$, $\bar{x}$ for average, s^2 for dispersion. For $\gamma > 0.02$ the estimate of dispersion will have considerable bias ($B \simeq 1.2$ for $\gamma\lambda = 0.2$; $B \simeq 1.4$ for $\gamma\lambda = 0.3$).
7. If $\gamma\lambda > 0.30$, use median for average and use $\alpha = 0.10$ and s^2 for dispersion. s^2 is considerably biased ($B \simeq 2$ for $\gamma\lambda = 0.50$).

$n = 15$, *Scalar contamination*

8. If $\gamma\lambda < 1.00$, use $\alpha = 0.10$, $\bar{x}$ for average, s^2 for dispersion. For

$\gamma > 0.02$ (unless $\gamma\lambda < 0.15$) the estimate of dispersion will have considerable bias ($B \simeq 1.1$ for $\gamma\lambda = 0.2$; $B \simeq 1.5$ for $\gamma\lambda = 0.4$).

9. If $\gamma\lambda > 1.00$, use median for average and use $\alpha = 0.10$ and s^2 for dispersion. s^2 is considerably biased ($B \simeq 10$ for $\gamma\lambda = 1.6$).

Reference 10 simplifies these suggested rules further as follows.

Decide from past experience or from knowledge of the measuring apparatus whether the outliers are causing light, medium, or heavy effects on the samples. Table G gives examples to indicate what is meant by these rough categories. The column α indicates the percentiles of the r-distributions to be used in tagging outliers. The ratios are used repeatedly until

TABLE G

RULES FOR ESTIMATION IN THE PRESENCE OF OUTLIERS

			$n \leq 10$		$10 < n < 20$	
Degree	Examples	α	Mean	sd	Mean	sd
Light	Up to {10% obs. shifted 1σ; 5% obs. shifted 2σ; 1% obs. shifted 10σ}	0.05	$\bar{x}$	Range	$\bar{x}$	s
Medium	Up to {30% obs. shifted 1σ; 10% obs. shifted 3σ; 5% obs. shifted 9σ}	0.10	$\bar{x}$	Range	Median	s
Heavy	Over amounts for medium	0.20	Median	Range	Median	s

no additional observations can be tagged. The mean and standard deviations are then estimated from the remaining observations as recommended in the table, that is, the mean by $\bar{x}$ or the median and the standard deviation by the range or the sample standard deviation.

10H.12 Needed Research

It is obvious from the preceding discussion that much research remains to be done on the subject of rejection of observations. The problem has been of interest to many statisticians for many years as evidenced by the large number of papers referring to such problems. Except for B_1 (see reference 6), however, the performance of these many criteria has been investigated only for samples of size 5 and 15 and this by sampling methods. Also among the single sample tests proposed C'_1 was not investigated in

TABLE 10H.1

Percentage Points of the Extreme Standardized Deviate from Population Mean

$(x_{(n)} - \mu)/\sigma$ or $(\mu - x_{(1)})/\sigma$ for B_0

n	Lower percentage points						Upper percentage points					
	0·1	0·5	1·0	2·5	5·0	10·0	10·0	5·0	2·5	1·0	0·5	0·1
1	−3·090	−2·576	−2·326	−1·960	−1·645	−1·282	1·282	1·645	1·960	2·326	2·576	3·090
2	−1·858	−1·471	−1·282	−1·002	−0·760	−0·478	1·632	1·955	2·239	2·575	2·807	3·290
3	−1·282	−0·950	−0·788	−0·546	−0·336	−0·090	1·818	2·121	2·391	2·712	2·935	3·403
4	−0·924	−0·625	−0·478	−0·259	−0·068	0·157	1·943	2·234	2·494	2·806	3·023	3·481
5	−0·671	−0·395	−0·258	−0·055	0·124	0·334	2·036	2·319	2·572	2·877	3·090	3·540
6	−0·478	−0·218	−0·090	0·102	0·271	0·471	2·111	2·386	2·635	2·934	3·143	3·588
7	−0·325	−0·077	0·045	·229	·390	·582	2·172	2·442	2·687	2·981	3·188	3·628
8	−0·198	0·039	·157	·333	·489	·674	2·224	2·490	2·731	3·022	3·227	3·662
9	−0·090	·138	·252	·423	·574	·753	2·269	2·531	2·769	3·057	3·260	3·692
10	0·003	·224	·334	·500	·647	·822	2·309	2·568	2·803	3·089	3·290	3·719
11	0·084	0·300	0·407	0·568	0·711	0·882	2·344	2·601	2·834	3·117	3·317	3·743
12	·157	·367	·471	·629	·769	·936	2·376	2·630	2·862	3·143	3·341	3·765
13	·222	·427	·529	·684	·821	·985	2·406	2·657	2·887	3·166	3·363	3·785
14	·281	·482	·582	·733	·868	1·029	2·432	2·682	2·910	3·187	3·383	3·803
15	·334	·531	·630	·779	·911	1·070	2·457	2·705	2·932	3·207	3·402	3·820
16	0·384	0·577	0·674	0·821	0·951	1·107	2·480	2·726	2·952	3·226	3·420	3·836
17	·429	·620	·715	·859	·988	1·142	2·502	2·746	2·970	3·243	3·436	3·851
18	·471	·659	·753	·895	1·022	1·175	2·522	2·765	2·988	3·259	3·452	3·865
19	·511	·696	·788	·929	1·054	1·205	2·541	2·783	3·004	3·275	3·466	3·878
20	·547	·730	·822	·960	1·084	1·233	2·559	2·799	3·020	3·289	3·480	3·890
21	0·582	0·762	0·853	0·990	1·113	1·260	2·576	2·815	3·034	3·303	3·493	3·902
22	·614	·793	·882	1·018	1·139	1·285	2·592	2·830	3·049	3·316	3·506	3·914
23	·645	·821	·910	1·044	1·164	1·309	2·607	2·844	3·062	3·328	3·517	3·924
24	·674	·848	·936	1·069	1·188	1·332	2·621	2·857	3·075	3·340	3·529	3·934
25	·702	·874	·961	1·093	1·211	1·353	2·635	2·870	3·087	3·351	3·539	3·944
26	0·728	0·899	0·985	1·116	1·233	1·374	2·648	2·883	3·098	3·362	3·550	3·954
27	·753	·922	1·008	1·137	1·253	1·393	2·661	2·895	3·110	3·373	3·560	3·963
28	·777	·945	1·029	1·158	1·273	1·412	2·673	2·906	3·120	3·383	3·569	3·971
29	·800	·966	1·050	1·178	1·292	1·430	2·685	2·917	3·130	3·392	3·578	3·980
30	·822	·987	1·070	1·197	1·310	1·447	2·696	2·928	3·141	3·402	3·587	3·988

TABLE 10H.2

Percentage Points of the Extreme Standardized Deviate from Sample Mean

$(x_{(n)} - \bar{x})/\sigma$ or $(\bar{x} - x_{(1)})/\sigma$ for B_1

Size of sample n	Lower percentage points						Upper percentage points					
	0·1	0·5	1·0	2·5	5·0	10·0	10·0	5·0	2·5	1·0	0·5	0·1
3	0·03	0·06	0·09	0·14	0·20	0·29	1·50	1·74	1·95	2·22	2·40	2·78
4	0·09	0·16	0·20	0·27	0·35	0·45	1·70	1·94	2·16	2·43	2·62	3·01
5	0·16	0·25	0·30	0·38	0·47	0·58	1·83	2·08	2·30	2·57	2·76	3·17
6	0·23	0·33	0·38	0·48	0·56	0·68	1·94	2·18	2·41	2·68	2·87	3·28
7	0·30	0·40	0·46	0·56	0·65	0·76	2·02	2·27	2·49	2·76	2·95	3·36
8	0·36	0·47	0·53	0·62	0·72	0·84	2·09	2·33	2·56	2·83	3·02	3·43
9	0·41	0·53	0·59	0·69	0·78	0·90	2·15	2·39	2·61	2·88	3·07	3·48

These tables are reproduced from E. S. Pearson and H. O. Hartley, *Biometrika Tables for Statisticians*, Vol. 1, 1958, with permission of the Biometrika trustees.

TABLE 10H.3

PERCENTAGE POINTS OF THE EXTREME STANDARDIZED DEVIATE FROM SAMPLE MEAN

$(x_{(n)} - \bar{x})/\sigma$ or $(\bar{x} - x_{(1)})/\sigma$ for B_1

n	90%	95%	99%	99.5%
2	1.163	1.386	1.821	1.985
3	1.497	1.738	2.215	2.396
4	1.696	1.941	2.431	2.618
5	1.835	2.080	2.574	2.764
6	1.939	2.184	2.679	2.870
7	2.022	2.267	2.761	2.952
8	2.091	2.334	2.828	3.019
9	2.150	2.392	2.884	3.074
10	2.200	2.441	2.931	3.122
11	2.245	2.484	2.973	3.163
12	2.284	2.523	3.010	3.199
13	2.320	2.557	3.043	3.232
14	2.352	2.589	3.072	3.261
15	2.382	2.617	3.099	3.287
16	2.409	2.644	3.124	3.312
17	2.434	2.668	3.147	3.334
18	2.458	2.691	3.168	3.355
19	2.480	2.712	3.188	3.375
20	2.500	2.732	3.207	3.393
21	2.519	2.750	3.224	3.409
22	2.538	2.768	3.240	3.425
23	2.555	2.784	3.255	3.439
24	2.571	2.800	3.269	3.453
25	2.587	2.815	3.282	3.465

This table is reproduced from F. E. Grubbs, "Sample criterion for testing outlying observations," *Ann. Math. Statist.*, Vol. 21 (1950), pp. 27–28, with permission of the author and W. Kruskal, editor of *Annals of Mathematical Statistics*.

TABLE 10H.4

TABLE OF PERCENTAGE POINTS FOR $\dfrac{x_{(n)} - \bar{x}}{s} \left(\text{or } \dfrac{\bar{x} - x_{(1)}}{s} \right)$ for B'_1

n	1%	2.5%	5%	10%
3	1.414	1.414	1.412	1.406
4	1.723	1.710	1.689	1.645
5	1.955	1.917	1.869	1.791
6	2.130	2.067	1.996	1.894
7	2.265	2.182	2.093	1.974
8	2.374	2.273	2 172	2.041
9	2.464	2.349	2.237	2.097
10	2.540	2.414	2.294	2.146
11	2.606	2.470	2.343	2.190
12	2.663	2.519	2.387	2.229
13	2.714	2.562	2.426	2.264
14	2.759	2.602	2.461	2.297
15	2.800	2.638	2.493	2.326
16	2.837	2.670	2.523	2.354
17	2.871	2.701	2.551	2.380
18	2.903	2.728	2.577	2.404
19	2.932	2.754	2.600	2.426
20	2.959	2.778	2.623	2.447
21	2.984	2.801	2.644	2.467
22	3.008	2.823	2.664	2.486
23	3.030	2.843	2.683	2.504
24	3.051	2.862	2.701	2.520
25	3.071	2.880	2.717	2.537

$$x_{(1)} \le x_{(2)} \le x_{(3)} \ldots \le x_{(n)}$$

$$s^2 = \frac{1}{n} \sum_{i=1}^{n} (x_i - \bar{x})^2 \qquad \bar{x} = \frac{1}{n} \sum_{i=1}^{n} x_i$$

This table is reproduced from F. E. Grubbs, "Sample criterion for testing outlying observations," *Ann. Math. Statist.*, Vol. 21 (1950), pp. 27–58, with permission of the author and W. Kruskal, editor of *Annals of Mathematical Statistics*.

TABLE 10H.5

VALUES OF $P_1(\lambda)$, OR OF THE PROBABILITY THAT THE FIRST AND SECOND INDIVIDUALS IN A RANDOM SAMPLE OF n DIFFER BY MORE THAN λ TIMES THE STANDARD DEVIATION OF THE ORIGINAL POPULATION FOR B_2

	λ																								
n	·1	·2	·3	·4	·5	·6	·7	·8	·9	1·0	1·1	1·2	1·3	1·4	1·5	1·6	1·7	1·8	1·9	2·0	2·1	2·2	2·3	2·4	2·5
2	·944	·888	·832	·777	·724	·671	·621	·572	·524	·480	·437	·396	·358	·322	·289	·258	·229	·203	179	·157	·138	·120	·104	·090	·077
3	·917	·836	·760	·687	·618	·553	·493	·437	·386	·339	·296	·257	·222	·191	·163	·139	·118	·099	·083	·069	·057	·047	·039	·031	·025
10	·855	·727	·613	·513	·427	·353	·289	·235	·190	·152	·121	·096	·075	·059	·045	·035	·026	·020	·015	·011	·008	·007	·004	·003	·002
20	·827	·679	·553	·447	·359	·285	·226	·177	·138	·107	·082	·062	·047	·035	·026	·019	·014	·010	·007	·005	·004	·003	·002	·001	·001
30	·813	·656	·525	·417	·328	·257	·199	·153	·117	·089	·068	·050	·037	·027	·020	·014	·010	·007	·005	·004	·003	·002	·001	·001	·001
40	·803	·639	·505	·396	·308	·238	·182	·138	·104	·078	·058	·042	·031	·022	·016	·011	·008	·006	·004	·003	·002	·001	·001	·001	
50	·796	·628	·491	·382	·294	·225	·170	·128	·096	·071	·052	·038	·027	·019	·014	·010	·007	·005	·003	·002	·001	·001	·001		
60	·790	·619	·481	·371	·283	·215	·161	·120	·089	·065	·048	·034	·025	·017	·012	·009	·006	·004	·003	·002	·001	·001	·001		
70	·785	·611	·471	·361	·274	·206	·154	·114	·084	·061	·044	·032	·022	·016	·011	·008	·005	·004	·002	·002	·001	·001			
80	·780	·604	·464	·353	·267	·200	·148	·109	·080	·058	·041	·030	·021	·015	·010	·007	·005	·003	·002	·001	·001	·001			
90	·778	·600	·459	·348	·262	·195	·144	·106	·077	·055	·040	·028	·020	·014	·010	·007	·004	·003	·002	·001	·001	·001			
100	·775	·596	·454	·343	·257	·191	·141	·103	·075	·054	·038	·027	·019	·013	·009	·006	·004	·003	·002	·001	·001	·001			
200	·757	·567	·422	·311	·227	·165	·118	·084	·060	·042	·029	·020	·014	·009	·006	·004	·003	·002	·001	·001					
300	·746	·552	·405	·294	·212	·152	·107	·075	·052	·036	·025	·017	·011	·007	·005	·003	·002	·001	·001	·001					
400	·740	·543	·394	·284	·203	·144	·101	·070	·048	·033	·022	·015	·010	·007	·004	·003	·002	·001	·001						
500	·735	·536	·387	·277	·197	·138	·096	·067	·045	·031	·021	·014	·009	·006	·004	·002	·002	·001	·001						
600	·731	·530	·381	·271	·191	·134	·093	·064	·043	·029	·020	·013	·009	·005	·004	·002	·001	·001	·001						
700	·727	·525	·375	·266	·187	·130	·090	·061	·041	·028	·019	·012	·008	·005	·003	·002	·001	·001	·001						
800	·725	·521	·371	·262	·183	·127	·087	·059	·040	·027	·018	·012	·008	·005	·003	·002	·001	·001							
900	·722	·517	·367	·258	·180	·124	·085	·058	·039	·026	·017	·011	·007	·005	·003	·002	·001	·001							
1000	·720	·514	·364	·255	·177	·122	·083	·056	·038	·025	·016	·011	·007	·005	·003	002	·001	·001							

	λ																								
n	2·6	2·7	2·8	2·9	3·0	3·1	3·2	3·3	3·4	3·5	3·6	3·7	3·8	3·9	4·0	4·1	4·2	4·3	4·4	4·5	4·6	4·7	4·8	4·9	5·0
2	·066	·056	·048	·040	·034	·028	·024	·020	·016	·013	·011	·009	·007	·006	·005	·004	·003	·002	·002	·001	·001	·001	·001	·001	—
3	·021	·016	·013	·010	·008	·006	·005	·004	·003	·002	·002	·001	·001	·001	·001										
10	·002	·001	·001	·001																					
20	·001																								

This table is reproduced from J. O. Irwin, "On criterion for the rejection of outlying observations," *Biometrika*, Vol. 17 (1925), pp. 238–250, with permission of the author and E. S. Pearson, editor of *Biometrika*.

TABLE 10H.6

Upper Per Cent Points of the Studentized Extreme Deviate

$$\frac{x_{(n)} - \bar{x}}{s_\nu} \text{ OR } \frac{\bar{x} - x_{(1)}}{s_\nu}$$

ν_h \ n_j	3	4	5	6	7	8	9	10	12
					1% points				
10	2.78	3.10	3.32	3.48	3.62	3.73	3.82	3.90	4.04
11	2.72	3.02	3.24	3.39	3.52	3.63	3.72	3.79	3.93
12	2.67	2.96	3.17	3.32	3.45	3.55	3.64	3.71	3.84
13	2.63	2.92	3.12	3.27	3.38	3.48	3.57	3.64	3.76
14	2.60	2.88	3.07	3.22	3.33	3.43	3.51	3.58	3.70
15	2.57	2.84	3.03	3.17	3.29	3.38	3.46	3.53	3.65
16	2.54	2.81	3.00	3.14	3.25	3.34	3.42	3.49	3.60
17	2.52	2.79	2.97	3.11	3.22	3.31	3.38	3.45	3.56
18	2.50	2.77	2.95	3.08	3.19	3.28	3.35	3.42	3.53
19	2.49	2.75	2.93	3.06	3.16	3.25	3.33	3.39	3.50
20	2.47	2.73	2.91	3.04	3.14	3.23	3.30	3.37	3.47
24	2.42	2.68	2.84	2.97	3.07	3.16	3.23	3.29	3.38
30	2.38	2.62	2.79	2.91	3.01	3.08	3.15	3.21	3.30
40	2.34	2.57	2.73	2.85	2.94	3.02	3.08	3.13	3.22
60	2.29	2.52	2.68	2.79	2.88	2.95	3.01	2.06	3.15
120	2.25	2.48	2.62	2.73	2.82	2.89	2.95	3.00	3.08
∞	2.22	2.43	2.57	2.68	2.76	2.83	2.88	2.93	3.01
					5% points				
10	2.01	2.27	2.46	2.60	2.72	2.81	2.89	2.96	3.08
11	1.98	2.24	2.42	2.56	2.67	2.76	2.84	2.91	3.03
12	1.96	2.21	2.39	2.52	2.63	2.72	2.80	2.87	2.98
13	1.94	2.19	2.36	2.50	2.60	2.69	2.76	2.83	2.94
14	1.93	2.17	2.34	2.47	2.57	2.66	2.74	2.80	2.91
15	1.91	2.15	2.32	2.45	2.55	2.64	2.71	2.77	2.88
16	1.90	2.14	2.31	2.43	2.53	2.62	2.69	2.75	2.86
17	1.89	2.13	2.29	2.42	2.52	2.60	2.67	2.73	2.84
18	1.88	2.11	2.28	2.40	2.50	2.58	2.65	2.71	2.82
19	1.87	2.11	2.27	2.39	2.49	2.57	2.64	2.70	2.80
20	1.87	2.10	2.26	2.38	2.47	2.56	2.63	2.68	2.78
24	1.84	2.07	2.23	2.34	2.44	2.52	2.58	2.64	2.74
30	1.82	2.04	2.20	2.31	2.40	2.48	2.54	2.60	2.69
40	1.80	2.02	2.17	2.28	2.37	2.44	2.50	2.56	2.65
60	1.78	1.99	2.14	2.25	2.33	2.41	2.47	2.52	2.61
120	1.76	1.96	2.11	2.22	2.30	2.37	2.43	2.48	2.57
∞	1.74	1.94	2.08	2.18	2.27	2.33	2.39	2.44	2.52

The lower per cent points of Table 10H.6 are reproduced from E. S. Pearson and H. O. Hartley, *Biometrika Tables for Statisticians*, Vol. 1, p. 173 (1958), with permission of the Biometrika Trustees.

The upper per cent points of the same table are reproduced from H. A. David, "Revised upper percentage points of the extreme studentized deviate from the sample mean," *Biometrika*, Vol. 43 (1956), pp. 449–451, with permission of the author and E. S. Pearson, editor of *Biometrika*.

TABLE 10H.7

Percentage Points of the Distribution of the Range for C_1

Size of sample n	Lower percentage points						Upper percentage points					
	0·1	**0·5**	**1·0**	**2·5**	**5·0**	**10·0**	**10·0**	**5·0**	**2·5**	**1·0**	**0·5**	**0·1**
2	0·00	0·01	0·02	0·04	0·09	0·18	2·33	2·77	3·17	3·64	3·97	4·65
3	0·06	0·13	0·19	0·30	0·43	0·62	2·90	3·31	3·68	4·12	4·42	5·06
4	0·20	0·34	0·43	0·59	0·76	0·98	3·24	3·63	3·98	4·40	4·69	5·31
5	0·37	0·55	0·66	0·85	1·03	1·26	3·48	3·86	4·20	4·60	4·89	5·48
6	0·54	0·75	0·87	1·06	1·25	1·49	3·66	4·03	4·36	4·76	5·03	5·62
7	0·69	0·92	1·05	1·25	1·44	1·68	3·81	4·17	4·49	4·88	5·15	5·73
8	0·83	1·08	1·20	1·41	1·60	1·83	3·93	4·29	4·61	4·99	5·26	5·82
9	0·96	1·21	1·34	1·55	1·74	1·97	4·04	4·39	4·70	5·08	5·34	5·90
10	1·08	1·33	1·47	1·67	1·86	2·09	4·13	4·47	4·79	5·16	5·42	5·97
11	1·20	1·45	1·58	1·78	1·97	2·20	4·21	4·55	4·86	5·23	5·49	6·04
12	1·30	1·55	1·68	1·88	2·07	2·30	4·29	4·62	4·92	5·29	5·54	6·09
13	1·39	1·64	1·77	1·97	2·16	2·39	4·35	4·68	4·99	5·35	5·60	6·14
14	1·47	1·72	1·86	2·06	2·24	2·47	4·41	4·74	5·04	5·40	5·65	6·19
15	1·55	1·80	1·93	2·14	2·32	2·54	4·47	4·80	5·09	5·45	5·70	6·23
16	1·63	1·88	2·01	2·21	2·39	2·61	4·52	4·85	5·14	5·49	5·74	6·27
17	1·69	1·94	2·07	2·27	2·45	2·67	4·57	4·89	5·18	5·54	5·78	6·31
18	1·76	2·01	2·14	2·34	2·51	2·73	4·61	4·93	5·22	5·57	5·82	6·35
19	1·82	2·07	2·20	2·39	2·57	2·79	4·65	4·97	5·26	5·61	5·85	6·38
20	1·87	2·12	2·25	2·45	2·62	2·84	4·69	5·01	5·30	5·65	5·89	6·41

This table is reproduced from E. S. Pearson and H. O. Hartley, *Biometrika Tables for Statisticians*, Vol. 1, 1958, with permission of the Biometrika trustees.

TABLE 10H.8

PERCENTAGE POINTS OF THE DISTRIBUTION OF THE RATIO OF RANGE TO STANDARD DEVIATION, w/s, IN SAMPLES OF SIZE n FROM A NORMAL POPULATION FOR C_1

Size of Sample n	Lower Percentage Points 0.5	1.0	2.5	5.0	10.0	Upper Percentage Points 10.0	5.0	2.5	1.0	0.5	Size of Sample n
						1.997	1.999	2.000	2.000	2.000	**3**
						2.409	2.429	2.439	2.445	2.447	**4**
						2.712	2.753	2.782	2.803	2.813	**5**
						2.949	3.012	3.056	3.095	3.115	**6**
						3.143	3.222	3.282	3.338	3.369	**7**
						3.308	3.399	3.471	3.543	3.585	**8**
						3.449	3.552	3.634	3.720	3.772	**9**
10	2.47	2.51	2.59	2.67	2.77	3.57	3.685	3.777	3.875	3.935	**10**
11	2.53	2.58	2.66	2.74	2.84	3.68	3.80	3.903	4.012	4.079	**11**
12	2.59	2.65	2.73	2.80	2.91	3.78	3.91	4.01	4.134	4.208	**12**
13	2.65	2.70	2.78	2.86	2.97	3.87	4.00	4.11	4.244	4.325	**13**
14	2.70	2.75	2.83	2.91	3.02	3.95	4.09	4.21	4.34	4.431	**14**
15	2.75	2.80	2.88	2.96	3.07	4.02	4.17	4.29	4.43	4.53	**15**
16	2.80	2.85	2.93	3.01	3.13	4.09	4.24	4.37	4.51	4.62	**16**
17	2.84	2.90	2.98	3.06	3.17	4.15	4.31	4.44	4.59	4.69	**17**
18	2.88	2.94	3.02	3.10	3.21	4.21	4.38	4.51	4.66	4.77	**18**
19	2.92	2.98	3.06	3.14	3.25	4.27	4.43	4.57	4.73	4.84	**19**
20	2.95	3.01	3.10	3.18	3.29	4.32	4.49	4.63	4.79	4.91	**20**
30	3.22	3.27	3.37	3.46	3.58	4.70	4.89	5.06	5.25	5.39	**30**
40	3.41	3.46	3.57	3.66	3.79	4.96	5.15	5.34	5.54	5.69	**40**
50	3.57	3.61	3.72	3.82	3.94	5.15	5.35	5.54	5.77	5.91	**50**
60	3.69	3.74	3.85	3.95	4.07	5.29	5.50	5.70	5.93	6.09	**60**
80	3.88	3.93	4.05	4.15	4.27	5.51	5.73	5.93	6.18	6.35	**80**
100	4.02	4.09	4.20	4.31	4.44	5.68	5.90	6.11	6.36	6.54	**100**
150	4.30	4.36	4.47	4.59	4.72	5.96	6.18	6.39	6.64	6.84	**150**
200	4.50	4.56	4.67	4.78	4.90	6.15	6.38	6.59	6.85	7.03	**200**
500	5.06	5.13	5.25	5.37	5.49	6.72	6.94	7.15	7.42	7.60	**500**
1000	5.50	5.57	5.68	5.79	5.92	7.11	7.33	7.54	7.80	7.99	**1000**

This table is reproduced from H. A. David, H. O. Hartley, and E. S. Pearson, "The distribution of the ratio in a single sample of range to standard deviation," *Biometrika*, Vol. 41 (1954), pp. 482–493, with permission of the authors and E. S. Pearson, editor of *Biometrika*.

TABLE 10H.8*a*

BOUNDS OF THE DISTRIBUTION OF THE RATIO OF RANGE TO STANDARD DEVIATION, w/s, IN SAMPLES OF SIZE n FROM A NORMAL POPULATION FOR C_1

n	Percentage Points		n	Percentage Points		n	Percentage Points	
	Lower 0%	Upper 0%		Lower 0%	Upper 0%		Lower 0%	Upper 0%
			10	1.897	4.243	30	1.966	7.616
			11	1.915	4.472	40	1.975	8.832
			12	1.915	4.690	50	1.980	9.899
3	1.732	2.000	13	1.927	4.899	60	1.983	10.863
4	1.732	2.449	14	1.927	5.099	80	1.987	12.570
						100	1.990	14.071
5	1.826	2.828	15	1.936	5.292			
6	1.826	3.162	16	1.936	5.477	150	1.993	17.263
7	1.871	3.464	17	1.944	5.657	200	1.995	19.950
8	1.871	3.742	18	1.944	5.831	500	1.998	31.591
9	1.897	4.000	19	1.949	6.000	1000	1.999	44.699
			20	1.949	6.164			

This table is reproduced from George W. Thomson, "Bounds for the ratio of range to standard deviation," *Biometrika*, Vol. 42 (1955), pp. 268–270, with permission of the author and E. S. Pearson, editor of *Biometrika*.

TABLE 10H.9

TABLE OF PERCENTAGE POINTS FOR $\frac{S_n^2}{S^2}$ OR $\frac{S_1^2}{S^2}$ FOR D_1

n	1%	2.5%	5%	10%
3	.0001	.0007	.0027	.0109
4	.0100	.0248	.0494	.0975
5	.0442	.0808	.1270	.1984
6	.0928	.1453	.2032	.2826
7	.1447	.2066	.2696	.3503
8	.1948	.2616	.3261	.4050
9	.2411	.3101	.3742	.4502
10	.2831	.3526	.4154	.4881
11	.3211	.3901	.4511	.5204
12	.3554	.4232	.4822	.5483
13	.3864	.4528	.5097	.5727
14	.4145	.4792	.5340	.5942
15	.4401	.5030	.5559	.6134
16	.4634	.5246	.5755	.6306
17	.4848	.5442	.5933	.6461
18	.5044	.5621	.6095	.6601
19	.5225	.5785	.6243	.6730
20	.5393	.5937	.6379	.6848
21	.5548	.6076	.6504	.6958
22	.5692	.6206	.6621	.7058
23	.5827	.6327	.6728	.7151
24	.5953	.6439	.6829	.7238
25	.6071	.6544	.6923	.7319

$$S^2 = \sum_{i=1}^{n} (x_i - \bar{x})^2 \quad \text{where} \quad \bar{x} = \frac{1}{n} \sum_{i=1}^{n} x_i$$

$$S_n^2 = \sum_{i=1}^{n=1} (x_i - \bar{x}_n)^2 \quad \text{where} \quad \bar{x}_n = \frac{1}{n-1} \sum_{i=1}^{n-1} x_i$$

$$S_1^2 = \sum_{i=2}^{n} (x_i - \bar{x}_1)^2 \quad \text{where} \quad \bar{x}_1 = \frac{1}{n-1} \sum_{i=2}^{n} x_i$$

This table is reproduced from F. E. Grubbs, "Sample criterion for testing outlying observations," *Ann. Math. Statist.*, Vol. 21 (1950), pp. 27–58, with permission of the author and W. Kruskal, editor of the *Annals of Mathematical Statistics*.

TABLE 10H.10

TABLE OF PERCENTAGE POINTS FOR $\frac{S_{n-1,n}^2}{S^2}$ OR $\frac{S_{1,2}^2}{S^2}$ FOR D_2

n	1%	2.5%	5%	10%
4	.0000	.0002	.0008	.0031
5	.0035	.0090	.0183	.0376
6	.0186	.0349	.0565	.0921
7	.0440	.0708	.1020	.1479
8	.0750	.1101	.1478	.1994
9	.1082	.1492	.1909	.2454
10	.1415	.1865	.2305	.2863
11	.1736	.2212	.2666	.3226
12	.2044	.2536	.2996	.3552
13	.2333	.2836	.3295	.3843
14	.2605	.3112	.3568	.4106
15	.2859	.3367	.3818	.4345
16	.3098	.3603	.4048	.4562
17	.3321	.3822	.4259	.4761
18	.3530	.4025	.4455	.4944
19	.3725	.4214	.4636	.5113
20	.3909	.4391	.4804	.5269

$$S^2 = \sum_{i=1}^{n} (x_i - \bar{x})^2 \quad \text{where} \quad \bar{x} = \frac{1}{n} \sum_{i=1}^{n} x_i$$

$$S_{n-1,n}^2 = \sum_{i=1}^{n-2} (x_i - \bar{x}_{n-1,n})^2 \quad \text{where} \quad \bar{x}_{n-1,n} = \frac{1}{n-2} \sum_{i=1}^{n-2} x_i$$

$$S_{1,2}^2 = \sum_{i=3}^{n} (x_i - \bar{x}_{1,2})^2 \quad \text{where} \quad \bar{x}_{1,2} = \frac{1}{n-2} \sum_{i=3}^{n} x_i$$

This table is reproduced from F. E. Grubbs, "Sample criterion for testing outlying observations," *Ann. Math. Statist.*, Vol. 21 (1950), pp. 27–58, with permission of the author W. Kruskal, editor of the *Annals of Mathematical Statistics*.

TABLE 10H.11a

PERCENTAGE VALUES FOR r_{10}

$[\Pr(r_{10} > R) = \alpha]$

n \ α	.005	.01	.02	.05	.10	.20	.30	.40	.50	.60	.70	.80	.90	.95	α / n
3	.994	.988	.976	.941	.886	.781	.684	.591	.500	.409	.316	.219	.114	.059	3
4	.926	.889	.846	.765	.679	.560	.471	.394	.324	.257	.193	.130	.065	.033	4
5	.821	.780	.729	.642	.557	.451	.373	.308	.250	.196	.146	.097	.048	.023	5
6	.740	.698	.644	.560	.482	.386	.318	.261	.210	.164	.121	.079	.038	.018	6
7	.680	.637	.586	.507	.434	.344	.281	.230	.184	.143	.105	.068	.032	.016	7
8	.634	.590	.543	.468	.399	.314	.255	.208	.166	.128	.094	.060	.029	.014	8
9	.598	.555	.510	.437	.370	.290	.234	.191	.152	.118	.086	.055	.026	.013	9
10	.568	.527	.483	.412	.349	.273	.219	.178	.142	.110	.080	.051	.025	.012	10
11	.542	.502	.460	.392	.332	.259	.208	.168	.133	.103	.074	.048	.023	.011	11
12	.522	.482	.441	.376	.318	.247	.197	.160	.126	.097	.070	.045	.022	.011	12
13	.503	.465	.425	.361	.305	.237	.188	.153	.120	.092	.067	.043	.021	.010	13
14	.488	.450	.411	.349	.294	.228	.181	.147	.115	.088	.064	.041	.020	.010	14
15	.475	.438	.399	.338	.285	.220	.175	.141	.111	.085	.062	.040	.019	.010	15
16	.463	.426	.388	.329	.277	.213	.169	.136	.107	.082	.060	.039	.019	.009	16
17	.452	.416	.379	.320	.269	.207	.165	.132	.104	.080	.058	.038	.018	.009	17
18	.442	.407	.370	.313	.263	.202	.160	.128	.101	.078	.056	.036	.018	.009	18
19	.433	.398	.363	.306	.258	.197	.157	.125	.098	.076	.055	.036	.017	.008	19
20	.425	.391	.356	.300	.252	.193	.153	.122	.096	.074	.053	.035	.017	.008	20
21	.418	.384	.350	.295	.247	.189	.150	.119	.094	.072	.052	.034	.016	.008	21
22	.411	.378	.344	.290	.242	.185	.147	.117	.092	.071	.051	.033	.016	.008	22
23	.404	.372	.338	.285	.238	.182	.144	.115	.090	.069	.050	.033	.016	.008	23
24	.399	.367	.333	.281	.234	.179	.142	.113	.089	.068	.049	.032	.016	.008	24
25	.393	.362	.329	.277	.230	.176	.139	.111	.088	.067	.048	.032	.015	.008	25
26	.388	.357	.324	.273	.227	.173	.137	.109	.086	.066	.047	.031	.015	.007	26
27	.384	.353	.320	.269	.224	.171	.135	.108	.085	.065	.047	.031	.015	.007	27
28	.380	.349	.316	.266	.220	.168	.133	.106	.084	.064	.046	.030	.015	.007	28
29	.376	.345	.312	.263	.218	.166	.131	.105	.083	.063	.046	.030	.014	.007	29
30	.372	.341	.309	.260	.215	.164	.130	.103	.082	.062	.045	.029	.014	.007	30

This table is reproduced from W. J. Dixon, "Ratios involving extreme values," *Ann. Math. Statist.*, Vol. 22 (1951), pp. 68–78, with permission of W. Kruskal, editor of the *Annals of Mathematical Statistics*.

TABLE 10H.11*b*

PERCENTAGE VALUES FOR r_{11}

$[\Pr(r_{11} > R) = \alpha]$

n \ α	.005	.01	.02	.05	.10	.20	.30	.40	.50	.60	.70	.80	.90	.95	α / n
4	.995	.991	.981	.955	.910	.822	.737	.648	.554	.459	.362	.250	.131	.069	4
5	.937	.916	.876	.807	.728	.615	.524	.444	.369	.296	.224	.151	.078	.039	5
6	.839	.805	.763	.689	.609	.502	.420	.350	.288	.227	.169	.113	.056	.028	6
7	.782	.740	.689	.610	.530	.432	.359	.298	.241	.189	.140	.093	.045	.022	7
8	.725	.683	.631	.554	.479	.385	.318	.260	.210	.164	.121	.079	.037	.019	8
9	.677	.635	.587	.512	.441	.352	.288	.236	.189	.148	.107	.070	.033	.016	9
10	.639	.597	.551	.477	.409	.325	.265	.216	.173	.134	.098	.063	.030	.014	10
11	.606	.566	.521	.450	.385	.305	.248	.202	.161	.124	.090	.058	.028	.013	11
12	.580	.541	.498	.428	.367	.289	.234	.190	.150	.116	.084	.055	.026	.012	12
13	.558	.520	.477	.410	.350	.275	.222	.180	.142	.109	.079	.052	.025	.012	13
14	.539	.502	.460	.395	.336	.264	.212	.171	.135	.104	.075	.049	.024	.011	14
15	.522	.486	.445	.381	.323	.253	.203	.164	.129	.099	.072	.047	.023	.011	15
16	.508	.472	.432	.369	.313	.244	.196	.158	.124	.095	.069	.045	.022	.011	16
17	.495	.460	.420	.359	.303	.236	.190	.152	.119	.092	.067	.044	.021	.010	17
18	.484	.449	.410	.349	.295	.229	.184	.148	.116	.089	.065	.042	.020	.010	18
19	.473	.439	.400	.341	.288	.223	.179	.143	.112	.087	.063	.041	.020	.010	19
20	.464	.430	.392	.334	.282	.218	.174	.139	.110	.084	.061	.040	.019	.010	20
21	.455	.421	.384	.327	.276	.213	.170	.136	.107	.082	.059	.039	.019	.009	21
22	.446	.414	.377	.320	.270	.208	.166	.132	.104	.081	.058	.038	.018	.009	22
23	.439	.407	.371	.314	.265	.204	.163	.130	.102	.079	.056	.037	.018	.009	23
24	.432	.400	.365	.309	.260	.200	.160	.127	.100	.077	.055	.036	.018	.009	24
25	.426	.394	.359	.304	.255	.197	.156	.124	.098	.076	.054	.036	.017	.009	25
26	.420	.389	.354	.299	.250	.193	.154	.122	.096	.074	.053	.035	.017	.008	26
27	.414	.383	.349	.295	.246	.190	.151	.120	.095	.073	.052	.034	.017	.008	27
28	.409	.378	.344	.291	.243	.188	.149	.118	.093	.072	.051	.034	.016	.008	28
29	.404	.374	.340	.287	.239	.185	.146	.116	.092	.070	.051	.033	.016	.008	29
30	.399	.369	.336	.283	.236	.182	.144	.115	.090	.069	.050	.032	.016	.008	30

This table is reproduced from W. J. Dixon, "Ratios involving extreme values," *Ann. Math. Statist.*, Vol. 22 (1951), pp. 68–78, with permission of W. Kruskal, editor of the *Annals of Mathematical Statistics*.

TABLE 10H.11c

PERCENTAGE VALUES FOR r_{12}

$[\Pr(r_{12} > R) = \alpha]$

n \ α	.005	.01	.02	.05	.10	.20	.30	.40	.50	.60	.70	.80	.90	.95	α / n
5	.996	.992	.984	.960	.919	.838	.755	.669	.579	.483	.381	.268	.143	.074	5
6	.951	.925	.891	.824	.745	.635	.545	.465	.390	.316	.240	.165	.088	.049	6
7	.875	.836	.791	.712	.636	.528	.445	.374	.307	.245	.183	.123	.064	.031	7
8	.797	.760	.708	.632	.557	.456	.382	.317	.258	.203	.152	.101	.056	.025	8
9	.739	.701	.656	.580	.504	.409	.339	.270	.227	.177	.130	.086	.044	.021	9
10	.694	.655	.610	.537	.454	.373	.308	.258	.204	.158	.116	.075	.038	.019	10
11	.658	.619	.575	.502	.431	.345	.283	.232	.187	.145	.106	.069	.035	.017	11
12	.629	.590	.546	.473	.406	.324	.265	.217	.174	.135	.098	.063	.032	.016	12
13	.612	.554	.521	.451	.387	.307	.250	.204	.163	.126	.092	.059	.030	.015	13
14	.580	.542	.501	.432	.369	.292	.237	.193	.153	.118	.086	.055	.028	.014	14
15	.560	.523	.482	.416	.354	.280	.226	.184	.146	.112	.082	.053	.026	.013	15
16	.544	.508	.467	.401	.341	.269	.217	.177	.139	.107	.078	.050	.025	.013	16
17	.529	.493	.453	.388	.330	.259	.209	.170	.134	.103	.075	.048	.024	.012	17
18	.516	.480	.440	.377	.320	.251	.202	.163	.129	.099	.072	.047	.023	.012	18
19	.504	.469	.429	.367	.311	.243	.196	.157	.125	.096	.069	.045	.022	.011	19
20	.493	.458	.419	.358	.303	.237	.191	.153	.121	.093	.067	.044	.022	.011	20
21	.483	.449	.410	.349	.296	.231	.186	.148	.118	.090	.065	.042	.021	.010	21
22	.474	.440	.402	.342	.290	.225	.181	.145	.114	.088	.063	.041	.020	.010	22
23	.465	.432	.394	.336	.284	.220	.176	.141	.112	.086	.062	.040	.020	.010	23
24	.457	.423	.387	.330	.278	.216	.173	.138	.109	.084	.060	.039	.019	.010	24
25	.450	.417	.381	.324	.273	.212	.169	.135	.107	.082	.059	.038	.019	.009	25
26	.443	.411	.375	.319	.268	.208	.166	.132	.105	.080	.058	.037	.019	.009	26
27	.437	.405	.370	.314	.263	.204	.163	.130	.103	.079	.057	.037	.018	.009	27
28	.431	.399	.365	.309	.259	.201	.160	.128	.101	.077	.056	.036	.018	.009	28
29	.426	.394	.360	.305	.255	.197	.157	.126	.099	.076	.055	.035	.017	.009	29
30	.420	.389	.355	.301	.251	.194	.154	.124	.098	.075	.054	.035	.017	.009	30

This table is reproduced from W. J. Dixon, "Ratios involving extreme values," *Ann. Math. Statist.*, Vol. 22 (1951), pp. 68–78, with permission of W. Kruskal, editor of the *Annals of Mathematical Statistics*.

TABLE 10H.11*d*

Percentage Values for r_{20}

$[\Pr(r_{20} > R) = \alpha]$

n \ α	.005	.01	.02	.05	.10	.20	.30	.40	.50	.60	.70	.80	.90	.95	α / n
4	.996	.992	.987	.967	.935	.871	.807	.743	.676	.606	.529	.440	.321	.235	4
5	.950	.929	901	.845	.782	.694	.623	.560	.500	.440	.377	.306	.218	.155	5
6	.865	.836	.800	.736	.670	.585	.520	.463	.411	.358	.305	.245	.172	.126	6
7	.814	.778	.732	.661	.596	.516	.454	.402	.355	.306	.261	.208	.144	.099	7
8	.746	.710	.670	.607	.545	.468	.410	.361	.317	.274	.230	.184	.125	.085	8
9	.700	.667	.627	.565	.505	.432	.378	.331	.288	.250	.208	.166	.114	.077	9
10	.664	.632	.592	.531	.474	.404	.354	.307	.268	.231	.192	.153	.104	.070	10
11	.627	.603	.564	.504	.449	.381	.334	.290	.253	.217	.181	.143	.097	.065	11
12	.612	.579	.540	.481	.429	.362	.316	.274	.239	.205	.172	.136	.091	.060	12
13	.590	.557	.520	.461	.411	.345	.301	.261	.227	.195	.164	.129	.086	.057	13
14	.571	.538	.502	.445	.395	.332	.288	.250	.217	.187	.157	.123	.082	.054	14
15	.554	.522	.486	.430	.382	.320	.277	.241	.209	.179	.150	.118	.079	.052	15
16	.539	.508	.472	.418	.370	.310	.268	.233	.202	.173	.144	.113	.076	.050	16
17	.526	.495	.460	.406	.359	.301	.260	.226	.195	.167	.139	.109	.074	.049	17
18	.514	.484	.449	.397	.350	.293	.252	.219	.189	.162	.134	.105	.071	.048	18
19	.503	.473	.439	.379	.341	.286	.246	.213	.184	.157	.130	.101	.069	.047	19
20	.494	.464	.430	.372	.333	.279	.240	.208	.179	.152	.126	.098	.067	.046	20
21	.485	.455	.422	.365	.326	.273	.235	.203	.175	.148	.123	.096	.065	.045	21
22	.477	.447	.414	.358	.320	.267	.230	.199	.171	.145	.120	.094	.064	.044	22
23	.469	.440	.407	.352	.314	.262	.225	.195	.167	.142	.117	.092	.062	.043	23
24	.462	.434	.401	.347	.309	.258	.221	.192	.164	.139	.114	.090	.061	.042	24
25	.456	.428	.395	.343	.304	.254	.217	.189	.161	.136	.112	.089	.060	.041	25
26	.450	.422	.390	.338	.300	.250	.214	.186	.158	.134	.110	.087	.059	.041	26
27	.444	.417	.385	.334	.296	.246	.211	.183	.156	.132	.109	.086	.058	.040	27
28	.439	.412	.381	.330	.292	.243	.208	.180	.154	.130	.107	.085	.058	.040	28
29	.434	.407	.376	.326	.288	.239	.205	.177	.151	.128	.106	.083	.057	.039	29
30	.428	.402	.372	.322	.285	.236	.202	.175	.149	.126	.104	.082	.056	.039	30

This table is reproduced from W. J. Dixon, "Ratios involving extreme values," *Ann. Math. Statist.*, Vol. 22 (1951), pp. 68–78, with permission of W. Kruskal, editor of the *Annals of Mathematical Statistics*.

TABLE 10H.11e

Percentage Values for r_{21}

$[\Pr(r_{21} > R) = \alpha]$

n \ α	.005	.01	.02	.05	.10	.20	.30	.40	.50	60	.70	.80	.90	.95	α / n
5	.998	.995	.990	.976	.952	.902	.850	.795	.735	.669	.594	.501	.374	.273	5
6	.970	.951	.924	.872	.821	.745	.680	.621	.563	.504	.439	.364	.268	.195	6
7	.919	.885	.842	.780	.725	.637	.575	.517	.462	.408	.350	.285	.198	.138	7
8	.868	.829	.780	.710	.650	.570	.509	.454	.402	.352	.298	.240	.166	.117	8
9	.816	.776	.725	.657	.594	.516	.458	.407	.360	.313	.265	.212	.146	.103	9
10	.760	.726	.678	.612	.551	.474	.420	.374	.329	.286	.240	.189	.130	.089	10
11	.713	.679	.638	.576	.517	.442	.391	.348	.305	.265	.221	.173	.118	.080	11
12	.675	.642	.605	.546	.490	.419	.370	.326	.285	.247	.206	.161	.110	.074	12
13	.649	.615	.578	.521	.467	.399	.351	.308	.269	.232	.194	.152	.104	.070	13
14	.627	.593	.556	.501	.448	.381	.334	.293	.256	.219	.184	.144	.099	.066	14
15	.607	.574	.537	.483	.431	.366	.319	.280	.245	.208	.175	.138	.094	.062	15
16	.589	.557	.521	.467	.416	.353	.307	.269	.235	.199	.167	.132	.090	.059	16
17	.573	.542	.507	.453	.403	.341	.296	.259	.225	.192	.161	.127	.086	.057	17
18	.559	.529	.494	.440	.391	.331	.287	.250	.218	.186	.155	.122	.082	.054	18
19	.547	.517	.482	.428	.380	.322	.279	.243	.211	.180	.150	.117	.078	.052	19
20	.536	.506	.472	.419	.371	.314	.271	.236	.205	.174	.145	.113	.075	.050	20
21	.526	.496	.462	.410	.363	.306	.264	.229	.199	.170	.141	.110	.073	.049	21
22	.517	.487	.453	.402	.356	.299	.258	.223	.194	.165	.137	.107	.071	.048	22
23	.509	.479	.445	.395	.349	.293	.252	.218	.189	.161	.133	.105	.069	.046	23
24	.501	.471	.438	.388	.343	.287	.247	.214	.185	.158	.130	.103	.068	.045	24
25	.493	.464	.431	.382	.337	.282	.242	.210	.181	.154	.127	.100	.067	.043	25
26	.486	.457	.424	.376	.331	.277	.238	.206	.178	.151	.125	.098	.066	.042	26
27	.479	.450	.418	.370	.325	.273	.234	.203	.175	.149	.123	.096	.064	.041	27
28	.472	.444	.412	.365	.320	.269	.230	.200	.172	.146	.121	.094	.063	.041	28
29	.466	.438	.406	.360	.316	.265	.227	.197	.170	.144	.119	.092	.062	.040	29
30	.460	.433	.401	.355	.312	.261	.224	.194	.167	.142	.117	.091	.061	.040	30

This table is reproduced from W. J. Dixon, "Ratios involving extreme values," *Ann. Math. Statist.*, Vol. 22 (1951), pp. 68–78, with permission of W. Kruskal, editor of the *Annals of Mathematical Statistics*.

TABLE 10H.11*f*

PERCENTAGE VALUES FOR r_{22}

[$\Pr(r_{22} > R) = \alpha$]

n \ α	.005	.01	.02	.05	.10	.20	.30	.40	.50	.60	.70	.80	.90	.95	α / n
6	.998	.995	.992	.983	.965	.930	.880	.830	.780	.720	.640	.540	.410	.300	6
7	.970	.945	.919	.881	.850	.780	.730	.670	.610	.540	.470	.390	.270	.200	7
8	.922	.890	.857	.803	.745	.664	.602	.546	.490	.434	.375	.309	.218	.156	8
9	.873	.840	.800	.737	.676	.592	.530	.478	.425	.373	.320	.261	.186	.128	9
10	.826	.791	.749	.682	.620	.543	.483	.433	.384	.335	.285	.231	.150	.111	10
11	.781	.745	.703	.637	.578	.503	.446	.397	.351	.305	.258	.208	.142	.099	11
12	.740	.704	.661	.600	.543	.470	.416	.370	.325	.282	.238	.190	.130	.090	12
13	.705	.670	.628	.570	.515	.443	.391	.347	.304	.263	.222	.177	.122	.084	13
14	.674	.641	.602	.546	.492	.421	.370	.328	.287	.247	.208	.166	.115	.079	14
15	.647	.616	.579	.525	.472	.402	.353	.312	.273	.234	.196	.156	.109	.075	15
16	.624	.595	.559	.507	.454	.386	.338	.298	.261	.223	.186	.148	.104	.071	16
17	.605	.577	.542	.490	.438	.373	.325	.286	.250	.214	.178	.142	.099	.067	17
18	.589	.561	.527	.475	.424	.361	.314	.276	.241	.206	.171	.135	.094	.063	18
19	.575	.547	.514	.462	.412	.350	.304	.268	.233	.199	.165	.130	.090	.060	19
20	.562	.535	.502	.450	.401	.340	.295	.260	.226	.193	.160	.125	.086	.057	20
21	.551	.524	.491	.440	.391	.331	.287	.252	.220	.187	.155	.120	.082	.054	21
22	.541	.514	.481	.430	.382	.323	.280	.245	.213	.182	.150	.116	.078	.051	22
23	.532	.505	.472	.421	.374	.316	.274	.239	.207	.177	.146	.113	.075	.049	23
24	.524	.497	.484	.413	.367	.310	.268	.232	.201	.172	.142	.111	.074	.047	24
25	.516	.489	.457	.406	.360	.304	.262	.227	.196	.168	.138	.108	.073	.045	25
26	.508	.486	.450	.399	.354	.298	.257	.222	.192	.164	.135	.106	.072	.044	26
27	.501	.475	.443	.393	.348	.292	.252	.218	.189	.161	.132	.104	.071	.043	27
28	.495	.469	.437	.387	.342	.287	.247	.215	.186	.158	.130	.102	.069	.042	28
29	.489	.463	.431	.381	.337	.282	.243	.211	.183	.155	.128	.100	.068	.041	29
30	.483	.457	.425	.376	.332	.278	.239	.208	.180	.153	.126	.098	.067	.041	30

This table is reproduced from W. J. Dixon, "Ratios involving extreme values," *Ann. Math. Statist.*, Vol. 22 (1951), pp. 68–78, with permission of W. Kruskal, editor of the *Annals of Mathematical Statistics*.

TABLE 10H.12

Upper 5% Points of F_1, the Ratio of the Largest of k Independent Normal Ranges, Each of n Observations to the Total of These Ranges (for F_1)

No. of ranges k	No. of observations n in each range								
	2	3	4	5	6	7	8	9	10
2	0·962	0·862	0·803	0·764	0·736	0·717	0·702	0·691	0·682
3	·813	·667	·601	·563	·539	·521	·507	·498	·489
4	·681	·538	·479	·446	·425	·410	·398	·389	·382
5	·581	·451	·398	·369	·351	·338	·328	·320	·314
6	0·508	0·389	0·342	0·316	0·300	0·288	0·280	0·273	0·267
7	·451	·342	·300	·278	·263	·253	·245	·239	·234
8	·407	·305	·267	·248	·234	·225	·218	·213	·208
9	·369	·276	·241	·224	·211	·203	·197	·192	·188
10	·339	·253	·220	·204	·193	·185	·179	·174	·172

Upper 5% Points of $(k + 2)F_1$, Where F_1 Is the Ratio of the Largest of k Independent Normal Ranges, Each of n Observations, to the Total of These Ranges (for F_1)

No. of ranges k	No. of observations n in each range								
	2	3	4	5	6	7	8	9	10
10	4·06	3·04	2·65	2·44$_5$	2·30$_5$	2·21	2·14$_5$	2·09	2·05
12	4·06	3·03	2·63$_5$	2·42$_5$	2·29	2·20	2·13	2·07$_5$	2·04
15	4·06	3·02	2·62$_5$	2·41$_5$	2·28	2·18$_5$	2·12	2·06$_5$	2·02$_5$
20	4·13	3·03	2·62	2·41$_5$	2·28	2·18$_5$	2·11	2·05	2·01
50	4·26	3·11	2·67	2·44	2·29	2·19	2·11	2·06	2·01

This table is reproduced from C. I. Bliss, W. G. Cochran, and J. W. Tukey, "A rejection criterion based upon the range," *Biometrika*, Vol. 43 (1956), pp. 418–422, with permission of the authors and E. S. Pearson, editor of *Biometrika*.

TABLE 10H.13*a*

UPPER 5% LEVELS OF THE RATIO OF THE LARGEST TO THE SUM OF k INDEPENDENT ESTIMATES OF VARIANCE, EACH OF WHICH IS BASED ON n DEGREES OF FREEDOM (FOR F_2)

k \ n	1	2	3	4	5	6	7	8	9	10	16	36	144	∞
2	0.9985	0.9750	0.9392	0.9057	0.8772	0.8534	0.8332	0.8159	0.8010	0.7880	0.7341	0.6602	0.5813	0.5000
3	0.9669	0.8709	0.7977	0.7457	0.7071	0.6771	0.6530	0.6333	0.6167	0.6025	0.5466	0.4748	0.4031	0.3333
4	0.9065	0.7679	0.6841	0.6287	0.5895	0.5598	0.5365	0.5175	0.5017	0.4884	0.4366	0.3720	0.3093	0.2500
5	0.8412	0.6838	0.5981	0.5441	0.5065	0.4783	0.4564	0.4387	0.4241	0.4118	0.3645	0.3066	0.2513	0.2000
6	0.7808	0.6161	0.5321	0.4803	0.4447	0.4184	0.3980	0 3817	0.3682	0.3568	0.3135	0.2612	0.2119	0.1667
7	0.7271	0.5612	0.4800	0.4307	0.3974	0.3726	0.3535	0.3384	0.3259	0.3154	0.2756	0.2278	0.1833	0.1429
8	0.6798	0.5157	0.4377	0.3910	0.3595	0.3362	0.3185	0.3043	0.2926	0.2829	0.2462	0.2022	0.1616	0.1250
9	0.6385	0.4775	0.4027	0.3584	0.3286	0.3067	0.2901	0.2768	0.2659	0.2568	0.2226	0.1820	0.1446	0.1111
10	0.6020	0.4450	0.3733	0.3311	0.3029	0.2823	0.2666	0.2541	0.2439	0.2353	0.2032	0.1655	0.1308	0.1000
12	0.5410	0.3924	0.3264	0.2880	0.2624	0.2439	0.2299	0.2187	0.2098	0.2020	0.1737	0.1403	0.1100	0.0833
15	0.4709	0.3346	0.2758	0.2419	0.2195	0.2034	0.1911	0.1815	0.1736	0.1671	0.1429	0.1144	0.0889	0.0667
20	0.3894	0.2705	0.2205	0.1921	0.1735	0.1602	0.1501	0.1422	0.1357	0.1303	0.1108	0.0879	0.0675	0.0500
24	0.3434	0.2354	0.1907	0.1656	0.1493	0.1374	0.1286	0.1216	0.1160	0.1113	0.0942	0.0743	0.0567	0.0417
30	0.2929	0.1980	0.1593	0.1377	0.1237	0.1137	0.1061	0.1002	0.0958	0.0921	0.0771	0.0604	0.0457	0.0333
40	0.2370	0.1576	0.1259	0.1082	0.0968	0.0887	0.0827	0.0780	0.0745	0.0713	0.0595	0.0462	0.0347	0.0250
60	0.1737	0.1131	0.0895	0.0765	0.0682	0.0623	0.0583	0.0552	0.0520	0.0497	0.0411	0.0316	0.0234	0.0167
120	0.0998	0.0632	0.0495	0.0419	0.0371	0.0337	0.0312	0.0292	0.0279	0.0266	0.0218	0.0165	0.0120	0.0083
∞	0	0	0	0	0	0	0	0	0	0	0	0	0	0

This table is reproduced from C. Eisenhart, M. W. Hastay, and W. A. Wallis, *Selected Techniques in Statistical Analysis*, with permission of the publisher, McGraw-Hill Book Company.

TABLE 10H.13*b*

UPPER 1% LEVELS OF THE RATIO OF THE LARGEST TO THE SUM OF k INDEPENDENT ESTIMATES OF VARIANCE, EACH OF WHICH IS BASED ON n DEGREES OF FREEDOM (FOR F_2)

k \ n	1	2	3	4	5	6	7	8	9	10	16	36	144	∞
2	0.9999	0.9950	0.9794	0.9586	0.9373	0.9172	0.8988	0.8823	0.8674	0.8539	0.7949	0.7067	0.6062	0.5000
3	0.9933	0.9423	0.8831	0.8335	0.7933	0.7606	0.7335	0.7107	0.6912	0.6743	0.6059	0.5153	0.4230	0.3333
4	0.9676	0.8643	0.7814	0.7212	0.6761	0.6410	0.6129	0.5897	0.5702	0.5536	0.4884	0.4057	0.3251	0.2500
5	0.9279	0.7885	0.6957	0.6329	0.5875	0.5531	0.5259	0.5037	0.4854	0.4697	0.4094	0.3351	0.2644	0.2000
6	0.8828	0.7218	0.6258	0.5635	0.5195	0.4866	0.4608	0.4401	0.4229	0.4084	0.3529	0.2858	0.2229	0.1667
7	0.8376	0.6644	0.5685	0.5080	0.4659	0.4347	0.4105	0.3911	0.3751	0.3616	0.3105	0.2494	0.1929	0.1429
8	0.7945	0.6152	0.5209	0.4627	0.4226	0.3932	0.3704	0.3522	0.3373	0.3248	0.2779	0.2214	0.1700	0.1250
9	0.7544	0.5727	0.4810	0.4251	0.3870	0.3592	0.3378	0.3207	0.3067	0.2950	0.2514	0.1992	0.1521	0.1111
10	0.7175	0.5358	0.4469	0.3934	0.3572	0.3308	0.3106	0.2945	0.2813	0.2704	0.2297	0.1811	0.1376	0.1000
12	0.6528	0.4751	0.3919	0.3428	0.3099	0.2861	0.2680	0.2535	0.2419	0.2320	0.1961	0.1535	0.1157	0.0833
15	0.5747	0.4069	0.3317	0.2882	0.2593	0.2386	0.2228	0.2104	0.2002	0.1918	0.1612	0.1251	0.0934	0.0667
20	0.4799	0.3297	0.2654	0.2288	0.2048	0.1877	0.1748	0.1646	0.1567	0.1501	0.1248	0.0960	0.0709	0.0500
24	0.4247	0.2871	0.2295	0.1970	0.1759	0.1608	0.1495	0.1406	0.1338	0.1283	0.1060	0.0810	0.0595	0.0417
30	0.3632	0.2412	0.1913	0.1635	0.1454	0.1327	0.1232	0.1157	0.1100	0.1054	0.0867	0.0658	0.0480	0.0333
40	0.2940	0.1915	0.1508	0.1281	0.1135	0.1033	0.0957	0.0898	0.0853	0.0816	0.0668	0.0503	0.0363	0.0250
60	0.2151	0.1371	0.1069	0.0902	0.0796	0.0722	0.0668	0.0625	0.0594	0.0567	0.0461	0.0344	0.0245	0.0167
120	0.1225	0.0759	0.0585	0.0489	0.0429	0.0387	0.0357	0.0334	0.0316	0.0302	0.0242	0.0178	0.0125	0.0083
∞	0	0	0	0	0	0	0	0	0	0	0	0	0	0

This table is reproduced from C. Eisenhart, M. W. Hastay, and W. A. Wallis, *Selected Techniques in Statistical Analysis*, with permission of the publisher, McGraw-Hill Book Company.

reference 7. The k sample statistics F_1 and F_2 have not been given even this limited type of study. Needed are:

1. Definitions of power of tests for outliers.
2. Definition of alternatives to the null hypothesis.
3. Comparison of the many statistics proposed for sample sizes both small and large.

The basis for some of this research has already been set by investigations of the distribution of some of these criteria under assumptions other than normal. See, for example, reference 3.

REFERENCES

1. C. I. Bliss, W. G. Cochran, and J. W. Tukey, "A rejection criterion based upon the range," *Biometrika*, Vol. 43 (1956), pp. 418–422.
2. W. G. Cochran, "The distribution of the largest of a set of estimated variances as a fraction of their total," *Ann. Eugen.*, London, Vol. 11 (1941), pp. 47–52.
3. H. A. David, "The distribution of the range in certain non-normal populations," *Biometrika*, Vol. 41 (1954), pp. 463–468.
4. H. A. David, H. O. Hartley, and E. S. Pearson, "The distribution of the ratio, in a single normal sample, of range to standard deviations," *Biometrika*, Vol. 41 (1954), pp. 482–493.
5. H. A. David, "Revised upper percentage points of the extreme studentized deviate from the sample mean," *Biometrika*, Vol. 43 (1956), pp. 449–451.
6. H. A. David, "On the application to statistics of an elementary theorem in probability," *Biometrika*, Vol. 43 (1956), pp. 85–91.
7. W. J. Dixon, "Analysis of extreme values," *Ann. Math. Statist.*, Vol. 21 (1950), pp. 488–506.
8. W. J. Dixon, "Ratios involving extreme values," *Ann. Math. Statist.*, Vol. 22 (1951), pp. 68–78.
9. W. J. Dixon, "Processing data for outliers," *Biometrics*, Vol. 9 (1953), pp. 74–89.
10. W. J. Dixon and F. J. Massey, Jr., *Introduction to Statistical Analysis*, second edition, McGraw-Hill Book Co., New York, 1957.
11. C. Eisenhart, M. W. Hastay, and W. A. Wallis, *Selected Techniques of Statistical Analysis*, McGraw-Hill Book Co., New York, 1947.
12. F. E. Grubbs, "Sample criteria for testing outlying observations," *Ann. Math. Statist.*, Vol. 21 (1950), pp. 27–58.
13. J. O. Irwin, "On a criterion for the rejection of outlying observations," *Biometrika*, Vol. 17 (1925), pp. 238–250. $\Pr(B_2 > \lambda)$, $= 0.1(0.1)5.0$; $n = 2, 3, 10(10)100(100)$ 1000.
14. A. T. McKay, "The distribution of the difference between the extreme observation and the sample mean in samples of n from a normal universe," *Biometrika*, Vol. 27 (1935), pp. 466–471.
15. K. R. Nair, "The distribution of the extreme deviate from the sample mean and its studentized forms," *Biometrika*, Vol. 35 (1948), pp. 118–144.
16. D. Newman, "The distribution of ranges in samples from a normal population, expressed in terms of an independent estimate of the standard deviation," *Biometrika*, Vol. 31 (1940), pp. 20–30.

17. E. S. Pearson and H. O. Hartley, "The probability integral of the range in samples of n observations from the normal population," *Biometrika*, Vol. 32 (1942), pp. 301–310.
18. E. S. Pearson and H. O. Hartley, "Tables of the probability integral of the studentized range," *Biometrika*, Vol. 33 (1943), pp. 89–99.
19. E. S. Pearson and H. O. Hartley, *Biometrika Tables for Statisticians*, Vol. 1, Cambridge University Press, Cambridge, England, 1956.
20. E. S. Pearson and Chandra Sekar, "The efficiency of statistical tools and a criterion for the rejection of outlying observations," *Biometrika*, Vol. 28 (1936), pp. 308–320.
21. W. R. Thompson, "On a criterion for the rejection of observations and the distribution of the ratio of deviation to sample standard deviation," *Ann. Math. Statist.*, Vol. 6 (1935), pp. 214–219.
22. George W. Thomson, "Bounds for the ratio of range to standard deviation," *Biometrika*, Vol. 42 (1955), pp. 268–269.

CHAPTER 11

Exponential Distribution

ECONOMICS ★ LIBRARY ★ AND STATISTICS

B. G. GREENBERG and A. E. SARHAN

11A MOMENTS OF ORDER STATISTICS

The frequency distribution of an exponential distribution is

$$f(x) = \frac{1}{\sigma} e^{-(x-\theta)/\sigma}, \qquad \theta \leq x \leq \infty. \tag{11A.1}$$

The expected value of the standardized order statistic $u_{(r)}$ in samples from the exponential distribution is [1]

$$E(u_{(r)}) = \sum_{i=1}^{r} \frac{1}{n - i + 1}. \tag{11A.2}$$

The variances and covariances are [1]

$$V(u_{(r)}) = \underset{r<s}{\mathrm{Cov}}\,(u_{(r)}, u_{(s)}) = \sum_{i=1}^{r} \frac{1}{(n - 1 + i)^2}. \tag{11A.3}$$

Tables 11A.1 and 11A.2 are constructed to give the expected values (and their reciprocals) and the variances and covariances of the order statistics in samples of size ≤ 10 from the exponential distribution (11A.1) [2].

REFERENCES

1. A. E. Sarhan, "Estimation of the mean and standard deviation by order statistics," *Ann. Math. Statist.*, Vol. 25 (1954), pp. 317–328.
2. A. E. Sarhan and B. G. Greenberg, "Estimation problems in the exponential distribution using order statistics," *Proceedings of the Statistical Techniques in Missile Evaluation Symposium*, 1958, Blacksburg, Va., pp. 123–175.

TABLE 11A.1

EXPECTED VALUES OF THE rth ORDER STATISTICS $\left(\sum_{i=1}^{r} \frac{1}{n-1+1}\right)$ AND THEIR RECIPROCALS ($\beta_{r,n}$) IN FRACTIONS AND DECIMALS FROM THE EXPONENTIAL DISTRIBUTION (11.A.1) UP TO SAMPLES OF SIZE 10

r	n	2	3	4	5	6	7	8	9	10
1	E_1	$\frac{1}{2}$	$\frac{1}{3}$	$\frac{1}{4}$	$\frac{1}{5}$	$\frac{1}{6}$	$\frac{1}{7}$	$\frac{1}{8}$	$\frac{1}{9}$	$\frac{1}{10}$
		.5000 0000	.3333 3333	.2500 0000	.2000 0000	.1666 6667	.1428 5714	.1250 0000	.1111 1111	.1000 0000
	$\beta_{1,n}$	(2)	(3)	(4)	(5)	(6)	(7)	(8)	(9)	(10)
		(2.0000 0000)	(3.0000 0000)	(4.0000 0000)	(5.0000 0000)	(6.0000 0000)	(7.0000 0000)	(8.0000 0000)	(9.0000 0000)	(10.0000 0000)
2	E_2	$\frac{3}{2}$	$\frac{5}{6}$	$\frac{7}{12}$	$\frac{9}{20}$	$\frac{11}{30}$	$\frac{13}{42}$	$\frac{15}{56}$	$\frac{17}{72}$	$\frac{19}{90}$
		1.5000 0000	.8333 3333	.5833 3333	.4500 0000	.3666 6667	.3095 2381	.2678 5714	.2361 1111	.2111 1111
	$\beta_{2,n}$	$\left(\frac{2}{3}\right)$	$\left(\frac{6}{5}\right)$	$\left(\frac{12}{7}\right)$	$\left(\frac{20}{9}\right)$	$\left(\frac{30}{11}\right)$	$\left(\frac{42}{13}\right)$	$\left(\frac{56}{15}\right)$	$\left(\frac{72}{17}\right)$	$\left(\frac{90}{19}\right)$
		(.6666 6667)	(1.2000 0000)	(1.7142 8571)	(2.2222 2222)	(2.7272 7273)	(3.2307 6923)	(3.7333 3333)	(4.2352 9412)	(4.7368 4211)
3	E_3		$\frac{11}{6}$	$\frac{13}{12}$	$\frac{47}{60}$	$\frac{37}{60}$	$\frac{107}{210}$	$\frac{73}{168}$	$\frac{191}{504}$	$\frac{121}{360}$
			1.8333 3333	1.0833 3333	.7833 3333	.6166 6667	.5095 2381	.4345 2381	.3789 6825	.3361 1111
	$\beta_{3,n}$		$\left(\frac{6}{11}\right)$	$\left(\frac{12}{13}\right)$	$\left(\frac{60}{47}\right)$	$\left(\frac{60}{37}\right)$	$\left(\frac{210}{107}\right)$	$\left(\frac{168}{73}\right)$	$\left(\frac{504}{191}\right)$	$\left(\frac{360}{121}\right)$
			(.5454 5455)	(.9230 7692)	(1.2765 9574)	(1.6216 2162)	(1.9626 1682)	(2.3013 6986)	(2.6387 4346)	(2.9752 0661)
4	E_4			$\frac{25}{12}$	$\frac{77}{60}$	$\frac{19}{20}$	$\frac{319}{420}$	$\frac{533}{840}$	$\frac{275}{504}$	$\frac{1207}{2520}$
				2.0833 3333	1.2833 3333	.9500 0000	.7595 2381	.6345 2381	.5456 3492	.4789 6825
	$\beta_{4,n}$			$\left(\frac{12}{25}\right)$	$\left(\frac{60}{77}\right)$	$\left(\frac{20}{19}\right)$	$\left(\frac{420}{319}\right)$	$\left(\frac{840}{533}\right)$	$\left(\frac{504}{275}\right)$	$\left(\frac{2520}{1207}\right)$
				(.4800 0000)	(.7792 2078)	(1.0526 3158)	(1.3166 1442)	(1.5759 8499)	(1.8327 2727)	(2.0878 2104)

n							
5	E_5	$\frac{137}{60}$	$\frac{29}{20}$	$\frac{153}{140}$	$\frac{743}{840}$	$\frac{1879}{2520}$	$\frac{1627}{2520}$
		2.2833 3333	1.4500 0000	1.0928 5714	.8845 2381	.7456 3492	.6456 3492
	$\beta_{5,n}$	$\left(\frac{60}{137}\right)$	$\left(\frac{20}{29}\right)$	$\left(\frac{140}{153}\right)$	$\left(\frac{840}{743}\right)$	$\left(\frac{2520}{1879}\right)$	$\left(\frac{2520}{1627}\right)$
		(.4379 5620)	(.6896 5517)	(.9150 3268)	(1.1305 5182)	(1.3411 3890)	(1.5488 6294)
6	E_6		$\frac{49}{20}$	$\frac{223}{140}$	$\frac{341}{280}$	$\frac{2509}{2520}$	$\frac{2131}{2520}$
			2.4500 0000	1.5928 5714	1.2178 5714	.9956 3492	.8456 3492
	$\beta_{6,n}$		$\left(\frac{20}{49}\right)$	$\left(\frac{140}{223}\right)$	$\left(\frac{280}{341}\right)$	$\left(\frac{2520}{2509}\right)$	$\left(\frac{2520}{2131}\right)$
			(.4081 6327)	(.6278 0269)	(.8211 1437)	(1.0043 8422)	(1.1825 4341)
7	E_7			$\frac{363}{140}$	$\frac{481}{280}$	$\frac{3349}{2520}$	$\frac{2761}{2520}$
				2.5928 5714	1.7178 5714	1.3289 6825	1.0956 3492
	$\beta_{7,n}$			$\left(\frac{140}{363}\right)$	$\left(\frac{280}{481}\right)$	$\left(\frac{2520}{3349}\right)$	$\left(\frac{2520}{2761}\right)$
				(.3856 7493)	(.5821 2058)	(.7524 6342)	(.9127 1279)
8	E_8				$\frac{761}{280}$	$\frac{4609}{2520}$	$\frac{3601}{2520}$
					2.7178 5714	1.8289 6825	1.4289 6825
	$\beta_{8,n}$				$\left(\frac{280}{761}\right)$	$\left(\frac{2520}{4609}\right)$	$\left(\frac{2520}{3601}\right)$
					(.3679 3693)	(.5467 5635)	(.6998 0561)
9	E_9					$\frac{7129}{2520}$	$\frac{4861}{2520}$
						2.8289 6825	1.9289 6825
	$\beta_{9,n}$					$\left(\frac{2520}{7129}\right)$	$\left(\frac{2520}{4861}\right)$
						(.3534 8576)	(.5184 1185)
10	E_{10}						$\frac{7381}{2520}$
							2.9289 6825
	$\beta_{10,n}$						$\left(\frac{2520}{7381}\right)$
							(.3414 1715)

TABLE 11A.2

VARIANCES AND COVARIANCES OF THE rth ORDER STATISTICS FROM THE EXPONENTIAL DISTRIBUTION (11A.1) FOR SAMPLES OF SIZE $\leqq 10$

n	r \ s	1	2	3	4	5	6	7	8	9	10
2	1	$\frac{1}{4}$ (.2500 0000)	$\frac{1}{4}$ (.2500 0000)								
	2		$\frac{5}{4}$ (1.2500 0000)								
3	1	$\frac{1}{9}$ (.1111 1111)	$\frac{1}{9}$ (.1111 1111)	$\frac{1}{9}$ (.1111 1111)							
	2		$\frac{13}{36}$ (.3611 1111)	$\frac{13}{36}$ (.3611 1111)							
	3			$\frac{49}{36}$ (1.3611 1111)							
4	1	$\frac{1}{16}$ (.0625 0000)	$\frac{1}{16}$ (.0625 0000)	$\frac{1}{16}$ (.0625 0000)	$\frac{1}{16}$ (.0625 0000)						
	2		$\frac{25}{144}$ (.1736 1111)	$\frac{25}{144}$ (.1736 1111)	$\frac{25}{144}$ (.1736 1111)						
	3			$\frac{61}{144}$ (.4236 1111)	$\frac{61}{144}$ (.4236 1111)						
	4				$\frac{205}{144}$ (1.4236 1111)						

This Table is reproduced from A. E. Sarhan and B. G. Greenberg, "Estimation problems in the exponential distribution using order statistics," *Proceedings of the Statistical Techniques in Missile Evaluation Symposium*, 1958, Blacksburg, Va., pp. 123–173, with permission of the Commanding Officer, U.S. Army Research Office.

5							
	1	$\frac{1}{25}$ (.0400 0000)	$\frac{1}{25}$ (.0400 0000)	$\frac{1}{25}$ (.0400 0000)	$\frac{1}{25}$ (.0400 0000)	$\frac{1}{25}$ (.0400 0000)	
	2		$\frac{41}{400}$ (.1025 0000)	$\frac{41}{400}$ (.1025 0000)	$\frac{41}{400}$ (.1025 0000)	$\frac{41}{400}$ (.1025 0000)	
	3			$\frac{769}{3600}$ (.2136 1111)	$\frac{769}{3600}$ (.2136 1111)	$\frac{769}{3600}$ (.2136 1111)	
	4				$\frac{1669}{3600}$ (.4636 1111)	$\frac{1669}{3600}$ (.4636 1111)	
	5					$\frac{5269}{3600}$ (1.4636 1111)	
6							
	1	$\frac{1}{36}$ (.0277 7778)	$\frac{1}{36}$ (.0277 7778)	$\frac{1}{36}$ (.0277 7778)	$\frac{1}{36}$ (.0277 7778)	$\frac{1}{36}$ (.0277 7778)	$\frac{1}{36}$ (.0277 7778)
	2		$\frac{61}{900}$ (.0677 7778)	$\frac{61}{900}$ (.0677 7778)	$\frac{61}{900}$ (.0677 7778)	$\frac{61}{900}$ (.0677 7778)	$\frac{61}{900}$ (.0677 7778)
	3			$\frac{469}{3600}$ (.1302 7778)	$\frac{469}{3600}$ (.1302 7778)	$\frac{469}{3600}$ (.1302 7778)	$\frac{469}{3600}$ (.1302 7778)
	4				$\frac{869}{3600}$ (.2413 8889)	$\frac{869}{3600}$ (.2413 8889)	$\frac{869}{3600}$ (.2413 8889)
	5					$\frac{1769}{3600}$ (.4913 8889)	$\frac{1769}{3600}$ (.4913 8889)
	6						$\frac{5369}{3600}$ (1.4913 8889)

TABLE 11A.2 *Continued*

n	r \ s	1	2	3	4	5	6	7	8	9	10
7	1	$\frac{1}{49}$ (.0204 0816)	$\frac{1}{49}$ (.0204 0816)	$\frac{1}{49}$ (.0204 0816)	$\frac{1}{49}$ (.0204 0816)	$\frac{1}{49}$ (.0204 0816)	$\frac{1}{49}$ (.0204 0816)	$\frac{1}{49}$ (.0204 0816)			
	2		$\frac{85}{1764}$ (.0481 8594)	$\frac{85}{1764}$ (.0481 8594)	$\frac{85}{1764}$ (.0481 8594)	$\frac{85}{1764}$ (.0481 8594)	$\frac{85}{1764}$ (.0481 8594)	$\frac{85}{1764}$ (.0481 8594)			
	3			$\frac{3889}{44,100}$ (.0881 8594)	$\frac{3889}{44,100}$ (.0881 8594)	$\frac{3889}{44,100}$ (.0881 8594)	$\frac{3889}{44,100}$ (.0881 8594)	$\frac{3889}{44,100}$ (.0881 8594)			
	4				$\frac{26,581}{176,400}$ (.1506 8594)	$\frac{26,581}{176,400}$ (.1506 8594)	$\frac{26,581}{176,400}$ (.1506 8594)	$\frac{26,581}{176,400}$ (.1506 8594)			
	5					$\frac{46,181}{176,400}$ (.2617 9705)	$\frac{46,181}{176,400}$ (.2617 9705)	$\frac{46,181}{176,400}$ (.2617 9705)			
	6						$\frac{90,281}{176,400}$ (.5117 9705)	$\frac{90,281}{176,400}$ (.5117 9705)			
	7							$\frac{266,681}{176,400}$ (1.5117 9705)			
8	1	$\frac{1}{64}$ (.0156 2500)	$\frac{1}{64}$ (.0156 2500)	$\frac{1}{64}$ (.0156 2500)	$\frac{1}{64}$ (.0156 2500)	$\frac{1}{64}$ (.0156 2500)	$\frac{1}{64}$ (.0156 2500)	$\frac{1}{64}$ (.0156 2500)	$\frac{1}{64}$ (.0156 2500)		
	2		$\frac{113}{3136}$ (.0360 3316)	$\frac{113}{3136}$ (.0360 3316)	$\frac{113}{3136}$ (.0360 3316)	$\frac{113}{3136}$ (.0360 3316)	$\frac{113}{3136}$ (.0360 3316)	$\frac{113}{3136}$ (.0360 3316)	$\frac{113}{3136}$ (.0360 3316)		
	3			$\frac{1801}{28,224}$ (.0638 1094)	$\frac{1801}{28,224}$ (.0638 1094)	$\frac{1801}{28,224}$ (.0638 1094)	$\frac{1801}{28,224}$ (.0638 1094)	$\frac{1801}{28,224}$ (.0638 1094)	$\frac{1801}{28,244}$ (.0638 1094)		

	4				73,249/705,600 (.1038 1094)	73,249/705,600 (.1038 1094)	73,249/705,600 (.1038 1094)	73,249/705,600 (.1038 1094)	73,249/705,600 (.1038 1094)	
	5					117,349/705,600 (.1663 1094)	117,349/705,600 (.1663 1094)	117,349/705,600 (.1663 1094)	117,349/705,600 (.1663 1094)	
	6						195,749/705,600 (.2774 2205)	195,749/705,600 (.2774 2205)	195,749/705,600 (.2774 2205)	
	7							372,149/705,600 (.5274 2205)	372,149/705,600 (.5274 2205)	
	8								1,077,749/705,600 (1.5274 2205)	
9	1	1/81 (.0123 4568)	1/81 (.0123 4568)	1/81 (.0123 4568)	1/81 (.0123 4568)	1/81 (.0123 4568)	1/81 (.0123 4568)	1/81 (.0123 4568)	1/81 (.0123 4568)	1/81 (.0123 4568)
	2		145/5184 (.0279 7068)	145/5184 (.0279 7068)	145/5184 (.0279 7068)	145/5184 (.0279 7068)	145/5184 (.0279 7068)	145/5184 (.0279 7068)	145/5184 (.0279 7068)	145/5184 (.0279 7068)
	3			12,289/254,016 (.0483 7884)	12,289/254,016 (.0483 7884)	12,289/254,016 (.0483 7884)	12,289/254,016 (.0483 7884)	12,289/254,016 (.0483 7884)	12,289/254,016 (.0483 7884)	12,289/254,016 (.0483 7884)
	4				19,345/254,016 (.0761 5662)	19,345/254,016 (.0761 5662)	19,345/254,016 (.0761 5662)	19,345/254,016 (.0761 5662)	19,345/254,016 (.0761 5662)	19,345/254,016 (.0761 5662)
	5					737,641/6,350,400 (.1161 5662)	737,641/6.350,400 (.1161 5662)	737,641/6,350,400 (.1161 5662)	737,641/6.350,400 (.1161 5662)	737,641/6,350,400 (.1161 5662)
	6						1,134,541/6,350,400 (.1786 5662)	1,134,541/6,350,400 (.1786 5662)	1,134,541/6,350,400 (.1786 5662)	1,134,541/6,350,400 (.1786 5662)

TABLE 11A.2 *Continued*

n	r \ s	1	2	3	4	5	6	7	8	9	10
	7							$\frac{1,840,141}{6,350,400}$ (.2897 6773)	$\frac{1,840,141}{6,350,400}$ (.2897 6773)	$\frac{1,840,141}{6,350,400}$ (.2897 6773)	
	8								$\frac{3,427,741}{6,350,400}$ (.5397 6773)	$\frac{3,427,741}{6,350,400}$ (.5397 6773)	
	9									$\frac{9,778,141}{6,350,400}$ (1.5397 6773)	
10	1	$\frac{1}{100}$ (.0100 0000)	$\frac{1}{100}$ (.0100 0000)	$\frac{1}{100}$ (.0100 0000)	$\frac{1}{100}$ (.0100 0000)	$\frac{1}{100}$ (.0100 0000)	$\frac{1}{100}$ (.0100 0000)	$\frac{1}{100}$ (.0100 0000)	$\frac{1}{100}$ (.0100 0000)	$\frac{1}{100}$ (.0100 0000)	$\frac{1}{100}$ (.0100 0000)
	2		$\frac{181}{8100}$ (.0223 4568)	$\frac{181}{8100}$ (.0223 4568)	$\frac{181}{8100}$ (.0223 4568)	$\frac{181}{8100}$ (.0223 4568)	$\frac{181}{8100}$ (.0223 4568)	$\frac{181}{8100}$ (.0223 4568)	$\frac{181}{8100}$ (.0223 4568)	$\frac{181}{8100}$ (.0223 4568)	$\frac{181}{8100}$ (.0223 4568)
	3			$\frac{4921}{129,600}$ (.0379 7068)	$\frac{4921}{129,600}$ (.0379 7068)	$\frac{4921}{129,600}$ (.0379 7068)	$\frac{4921}{129,600}$ (.0379 7068)	$\frac{4921}{129,600}$ (.0379 7068)	$\frac{4921}{129,600}$ (.0379 7068)	$\frac{4921}{129,600}$ (.0379 7068)	$\frac{4921}{129,600}$ (.0379 7068)

4	$\frac{370,729}{6,350,400}$ (.0583 7884)	$\frac{370,729}{6,350,400}$ (.0583 7884)	$\frac{370,729}{6,350,400}$ (.0583 7884)	$\frac{370,729}{6,350,400}$ (.0583 7884)	$\frac{370,729}{6,350,400}$ (.0583 7884)	$\frac{370,729}{6,350,400}$ (.0583 7884)	$\frac{370,729}{6,350,400}$ (.0583 7884)
5		$\frac{547,129}{6,350,400}$ (.0861 5662)	$\frac{547,129}{6,350,400}$ (.0861 5662)	$\frac{547,129}{6,350,400}$ (.0861 5662)	$\frac{547,129}{6,350,400}$ (.0861 5662)	$\frac{547,129}{6,350,400}$ (.0861 5662)	$\frac{547,129}{6,350,400}$ (.0861 5662)
6			$\frac{801,145}{6,350,400}$ (.1261 5662)	$\frac{801,145}{6,350,400}$ (.1261 5662)	$\frac{801,145}{6,350,400}$ (.1261 5662)	$\frac{801,145}{6,350,400}$ (.1261 5662)	$\frac{801,145}{6,350,400}$ (.1261 5662)
7				$\frac{1,198,045}{6,350,400}$ (.1886 5662)	$\frac{1,198,045}{6,350,400}$ (.1886 5662)	$\frac{1,198,045}{6,350,400}$ (.1886 5662)	$\frac{1,198,045}{6,350,400}$ (.1886 5662)
8					$\frac{1,903,645}{6,350,400}$ (.2997 6773)	$\frac{1,903,645}{6,350,400}$ (.2997 6773)	$\frac{1,903,645}{6,350,400}$ (.2997 6773)
9						$\frac{3,491,245}{6,350,400}$ (.5497 6773)	$\frac{3,491,245}{6,350,400}$ (.5497 6773)
10							$\frac{9,841,645}{6,350,400}$ (1.5497 6773)

B. G. GREENBERG and A. E. SARHAN

11B BEST LINEAR UNBIASED ESTIMATES

11B.1 Estimates for θ and σ

Consider the general case where there is a sample of size n, with r_1 smallest and r_2 largest elements censored (i.e., $n - r_1 - r_2$ known middle elements). The best linear estimates of θ and σ of the exponential distribution (11A.1) are [3]

$$\theta^* = C\left\{\left[\frac{1}{C} + (n - r_1)\sum_{i=1}^{r_1+1}\frac{1}{n-i+1}\right]x_{(r_1+1)} - \left(r_2\sum_{i=1}^{r_1+1}\frac{1}{n-i+1}\right)x_{(n-r_2)} - \sum_{i=1}^{r_1+1}\frac{1}{n-i+1}\sum_{i=r_1+1}^{n-r_2}x_{(i)}\right\} \quad (11B.1.1)$$

and

$$\sigma^* = C\left[\sum_{i=r_1+1}^{n-r_2}x_{(i)} - (n - r_1)x_{(r_1+1)} + r_2x_{(n-r_2)}\right] \quad (11B.1.2)$$

where

$$C = \frac{1}{n - r_1 - r_2 - 1}.$$

Their variances are

$$V(\theta^*) = \left[C\left(\sum_{i=1}^{r_1+1}\frac{1}{n-i+1}\right)^2 + \sum_{i=1}^{r_1+1}\frac{1}{(n-i+1)^2}\right]\sigma^2. \quad (11B.1.3)$$

$$V(\sigma^*) = C\sigma^2 \quad (11B.1.4)$$

The estimate of the mean is

$$\mu^* = (\theta^* + \sigma^*) = C\left\{\frac{1}{C}x_{(r_1+1)} + \left[\left(\sum_{i=1}^{r_1+1}\frac{1}{n-i+1}\right) - 1\right](n - r_1)x_{(r_1+1)} - r_2\left[\left(\sum_{i=1}^{r_1+1}\frac{1}{n-i+1}\right) - 1\right]x_{(n-r_2)} - \left[\left(\sum_{i=1}^{r_1+1}\frac{1}{n-i+1}\right) - 1\right]\sum_{i=r_1+1}^{n-r_2}x_{(i)}\right\} \quad (11B.1.5)$$

with variance

$$V(\mu^*) = \sigma^2C\left[\left(\sum_{i=1}^{r_1+1}\frac{1}{n-i+1}\right)^2 + \frac{1}{C}\sum_{i=1}^{r_1+1}\frac{1}{(n-i+1)^2} - 2\sum_{i=1}^{r_1+1}\frac{1}{n-i+1} + 1\right] \quad (11B.1.6)$$

and with C standing for the same expression as before.

It is only a matter of substitution in these expressions to get the same results for special cases (r_1 or $r_2 = 0$) and $r_1 = r_2 = 0$, namely singly censored and complete samples.

For instance, when a complete sample is available, the results are

$$\theta^* = \frac{nx_{(1)} - \bar{x}}{n-1}, \tag{11B.1.7}$$

$$\sigma^* = \frac{n(\bar{x} - x_{(1)})}{n-1}, \tag{11B.1.8}$$

with variances

$$V(\theta^*) = \frac{1}{n(n-1)}, \tag{11B.1.9}$$

$$V(\sigma^*) = \frac{1}{n-1}. \tag{11B.1.10}$$

The estimate of the mean will be

$$\mu^* = \bar{x} \tag{11B.1.11}$$

with variance

$$V(\mu^*) = \frac{\sigma^2}{n}. \tag{11B.1.12}$$

The efficiencies of the general estimates obtained in (11B.1.1), (11B.1.2), and (11B.1.5) relative to the best linear estimates for a complete sample are

$$\text{R.E.}(\theta^*) = \frac{1}{n(n-1)} \bigg/ \left[C\left(\sum_{i=1}^{r_1+1} \frac{1}{n-i+1}\right)^2 + \sum_{i=1}^{r_1+1} \frac{1}{(n-i+1)^2}\right], \tag{11B.1.13}$$

$$\text{R.E.}(\sigma^*) = \frac{1}{n-1} \bigg/ C, \tag{11B.1.14}$$

$$\text{R.E.}(\mu^*) = \frac{1}{n} \bigg/ C\left[\left(\sum_{i=1}^{r_1+1} \frac{1}{n-i+1}\right)^2 + \frac{1}{C}\sum_{i=1}^{r_1+1} \frac{1}{(n-i+1)^2} - 2\sum_{i=1}^{r_1+1} \frac{1}{n-i+1} + 1\right]. \tag{11B.1.15}$$

Tables for the BLE of θ, σ and the mean, their variances, and relative efficiencies are given in reference 4 up to samples of size 10 and for all cases of censoring. Furthermore, reference 4 includes a discussion of certain characteristic features of these tables.

11B.2 General Best Linear Unbiased Estimates for the One-Parameter Exponential Distribution

Consider the one-parameter single-exponential distribution,

$$f(y) = \frac{1}{\sigma} e^{-x/\sigma}, \qquad 0 \le x \le \infty. \tag{11B.2.1}$$

If the observations on the smallest r_1 and largest r_2 are missing, the estimate is as follows,

$$\sigma^* = \frac{1}{K}\left\{\left[\sum_{i=1}^{r_1+1} \frac{1}{n-i+1} \Big/ \sum_{i=1}^{r_1+1} \frac{1}{(n-i+1)^2} - (n-r_1)\right] x_{(r_1+1)} + r_2 x_{(n-r_2)} + \sum_{i=r_1+1}^{n-r_2} x_{(i)}\right\} \tag{11B.2.2}$$

with variance

$$V(\sigma^*) = \frac{\sigma^2}{K} \tag{11B.2.3}$$

and

$$\text{R.E.}(\sigma^*) = \frac{K}{n} \tag{11B.2.4}$$

where

$$K = \left[\left(\sum_{i=1}^{r_1+1} \frac{1}{n-i+1}\right)^2 \Big/ \sum_{i=1}^{r_1+1} \frac{1}{(n-i+1)^2} + (n - r_1 - r_2 - 1)\right]. \tag{11B.2.5}$$

As before, special cases may be obtained by substituting r_1 or $r_2 = 0$, and $r_1 = r_2 = 0$.

For instance, consider the case where the largest r_2 items only are missing. In this event,

$$\sigma^* = \frac{\sum_{i=1}^{n-r_2} x_{(i)} + r_2 x_{(n-r_2)}}{n - r_2} \tag{11B.2.6}$$

with variance

$$V(\sigma^*) = \frac{\sigma^2}{n - r_2}. \tag{11B.2.7}$$

The estimate (11B.2.6) is exactly the same as the maximum-likelihood estimate.

11B.3 Estimation from a Multicensored Sample

Herd [2] considered the one-parameter exponential distribution for multicensored samples used in life-testing experiments. The most general case may be described as follows. A sample of size n is tested. When the first one fails at time t_1, a random sample of K_1 is withdrawn from the $n-1$ items still in test. The remaining items are observed until the second element fails at a time t_2, when K_2 elements are withdrawn. The process of withdrawing a random sample of K_i elements at time t_i when the ith failure occurs continues until the $(n-r'_2)$th failure occurs, after which the remainder of the items

$$K_{n-r'_2} = n - \sum_{i=1}^{n-r'_2-1} K_i - (n - r'_2)$$

are withdrawn.

The previous case of censoring is a special instance of this where $K_1 = K_2 = \ldots K_{r-1} = 0$.

Herd [2] obtained the best estimate of the parameter σ for the one-parameter exponential distribution from a multicensored sample from the right as

$$\sigma^* = \frac{1}{n - r'_2} \sum_{i=1}^{n-r'_2} (K_i + 1)x_{(i)} \tag{11B.3.1}$$

with variance

$$V(\sigma^*) = \frac{\sigma^2}{n - r'_2}. \tag{11B.3.2}$$

As a special case, if $K_i = 0$, this reduces to

$$\sigma^* = \frac{1}{n - r'_2}\left(\sum_{i=1}^{n-r'_2} x_{(i)} + r_2 x_{(r'_2)}\right). \tag{11B.3.4}$$

Example (Herd [5]). Eleven gyros were under test and, because of the number of different types, the test engineer decided to withdraw three setups at the time of the first failure. At the second and third failures he withdrew two setups, and the remaining set was allowed to go to failure as shown in Table A.

TABLE A

TIME TO FAILURE OF GYROSCOPES

Hours	Number of Failures	Number Withdrawn at Each Failure
34	1	3
113	1	2
169	1	2
237	1	0
Total	4	7

From (11B.3.1) we obtain

$$\sigma^* = \tfrac{1}{4}[(4\times 34) + (3\times 113) + (3\times 169) + (1\times 237)]$$
$$= 304.75 \text{ hours}$$

and
$$V(\sigma^*) = \frac{\sigma^2}{4}.$$

11B.4 Estimation of Percentile Statistics

In estimating the jth percentile, use is again made of the ordered arrangement to obtain the best linear estimates of the population parameters.

The jth percentile for a complete sample from the two-parameter single-exponential distribution is

$$\tilde{x}^*{}_j = \frac{n}{n-1}[1 + \lg(1-p)]x_{(1)} - \frac{1}{n-1}[1 + n\lg(1-p)]\bar{x} \quad (11B.4.1)$$

where lg denotes the natural logarithm, and where

$$p = \frac{j}{100}.$$

The variance is

$$V(\tilde{x}^*{}_j) = \frac{\sigma^2}{n(n-1)}\{1 + 2\lg(1-p) + n[\lg(1-p)]^2\}. \quad (11B.4.2)$$

As a special case, the estimate of the population median is

$$\tilde{x}^*{}_{50} = \theta^* + \sigma^* \lg 2 = \frac{1}{n-1}[0.3069nx_{(1)} - (1 - 0.6931n)\bar{x}] \quad (11B.4.3)$$

with variance

$$V(\tilde{x}^*{}_{50}) = \frac{\sigma^2}{n(n-1)}(0.4804n - 0.3862). \quad (11B.4.4)$$

Thus the variance of the estimate of the population median is smaller than the corresponding estimate of the population mean.

The semi-interquartile range (Q) can be estimated by

$$Q^* = \frac{\sigma^*}{2}\lg 3 = \frac{0.5493n}{n-1}(\bar{x} - x_{(1)}), \quad (11B.4.5)$$

and its variance is

$$V(Q^*) = \frac{0.3014}{n-1}\sigma^2. \quad (11B.4.6)$$

In particular, for the one-parameter single-exponential distribution, the jth percentile is

$$\tilde{x}^*_j = -\sigma^* \lg (1 - p) \tag{11B.4.7}$$

with variance

$$V(\tilde{x}^*_j) = \frac{\sigma^2}{n} [\lg (1 - p)]^2. \tag{11B.4.8}$$

Again, we have

$$\tilde{x}^*_{50} = \bar{x} \lg 2 = 0.6931\bar{x} \tag{11B.4.9}$$

with variance

$$V(\tilde{x}^*_{50}) = \frac{0.4804}{n} \sigma^2. \tag{11B.4.10}$$

Also,

$$Q^* = \frac{\sigma^*}{2} \lg 3 = 0.5493\bar{x} \tag{11B.4.11}$$

and

$$V(Q^*) = 0.3014 \frac{\sigma^*}{n}. \tag{11B.4.12}$$

11B.5 Estimates When Censoring Is from the Middle of the Distribution

The efficiency in estimating θ^* in the two-parameter exponential distribution shows that the first or smallest observation is very important [4]. When this observation is censored, the variance of the estimate is increased considerably. This emphasizes to the experimenter the importance of not missing the observation of the very first element if he wants to estimate θ. However, he might miss some of the subsequent observations without too serious an inflation of the precision in estimating θ.

Suppose there is a sample from a two-parameter exponential distribution with s smallest and the largest r elements known. That is, the middle $n-r-s$ elements are censored. Thus we have

$$x_{(1)} \leq \ldots \leq x_{(s)} \leq x_{(n-r+1)} \leq x_{(n-r+2)} \leq \ldots \leq x_{(n)}.$$

Here the best linear estimates in the two-parameter exponential distribution are given by the coefficients in the following matrix:

$$\begin{array}{lccccccccc}
\text{order:} & 1 & 2 & \ldots & s-1 & s & n-r+1 & n-r+2 & \ldots & n \\
\hline
\end{array}$$

$$\begin{bmatrix} \theta^* \\ \sigma^* \end{bmatrix} = \begin{bmatrix} 1 + \dfrac{n-1}{n\beta'} & \dfrac{-1}{n\beta'} & \cdots & \dfrac{-1}{n\beta'} & \dfrac{a'/a - (n - s + 1)}{n\beta'} & \dfrac{(r - 1) - a'/a}{n\beta'} & \dfrac{-1}{n\beta'} & \cdots & \dfrac{-1}{n\beta'} \\ \dfrac{1-n}{\beta'} & \dfrac{1}{\beta'} & \cdots & \dfrac{1}{\beta'} & \dfrac{(n - s + 1) - a'/a}{\beta'} & \dfrac{a'/a - (r - 1)}{\beta'} & \dfrac{1}{\beta'} & \cdots & \dfrac{1}{\beta'} \end{bmatrix} \tag{11B.5.1}$$

where

$$a = \sum_{i=s+1}^{n-r+1} \frac{1}{(n-i+1)^2}, \qquad a' = \sum_{i=s+1}^{n-r+1} \frac{1}{n-i+1}$$

and

$$\beta' = (s + r - 2) + \frac{a'^2}{a}. \tag{11B.5.2}$$

The variance of these estimates is given in the variance-covariance matrix as follows:

$$V\begin{bmatrix} \theta^* \\ \sigma^* \end{bmatrix} = \begin{bmatrix} \dfrac{\beta' + 1}{n^2\beta'} & -\dfrac{1}{n\beta'} \\ -\dfrac{1}{n\beta'} & \dfrac{1}{\beta'} \end{bmatrix}. \tag{11B.5.3}$$

The coefficients for the best linear estimate of the mean are, in order,

$$\mu^* = (\text{mean})^*$$

$$= \left\{\left[1 - \frac{(n-1)^2}{n\beta'}\right], \frac{n-1}{n\beta'}, \ldots, \frac{n-1}{n\beta'}, (n-1)\frac{(n-s+1) - (a'/a)}{n\beta'},\right.$$

$$\left.(n-1)\frac{(a'/a) - (n-s+1)}{n\beta'}, \frac{n-1}{n\beta'}, \ldots, \frac{n-1}{n\beta'}\right\}. \tag{11B.5.4}$$

The variance of the previous expression is

$$V(\mu^*) = V(\text{mean}^*) = \frac{\beta' + (n-1)^2}{n^2\beta'} = \frac{1}{n^2}\left[1 + \frac{(n-1)^2}{\beta'}\right]. \tag{11B.5.5}$$

In particular, for the one-parameter exponential distribution, the expressions (11B.5.1) and (11B.5.2) reduce to

$$\sigma^* = \frac{1}{\beta' + 1}\left\{1 \; 1 \ldots 1\left[(n - s + 1) - \frac{a'}{a}\right]\left[\frac{a'}{a} - (r - 1)\right]1 \ldots 1\right\} \tag{11B.5.6}$$

and

$$V(\sigma^*) = \frac{1}{\beta' + 1}.$$

If the smallest observation and the largest r elements are known (with $n-r-1$ censored middle elements), the best linear estimates of θ and σ

of the two-parameter exponential distribution will be

$$\theta^* = \frac{1}{K' \sum_{2}^{n-r+1} \frac{1}{n-i+1} + (r-1)} \times \left\{ \left[K' \sum_{1}^{n-r+1} \frac{1}{n-i+1} + (r-1) \right] x_{(1)} + \frac{1}{n}[(r-1) - K'] x_{(n-r+1)} - \frac{1}{n} x_{(n-r+2)} - \frac{1}{n} x_{(n-r+3)} - \cdots - \frac{1}{n} x_{(n)} \right\} \tag{11B.5.7}$$

where

$$K' = \sum_{2}^{n-r+1} \frac{1}{n-i+1} \Big/ \sum_{2}^{n-r+1} \frac{1}{(n-i+1)^2} \tag{11B.5.8}$$

and

$$\sigma^* = \frac{1}{K' \sum_{2}^{n-r+1} \frac{1}{n-i+1} + (r-1)} \times \{ -K' x_{(1)} + [K' - (r-1)] x_{(n-r+1)} + x_{(n-r+2)} + x_{(n-r+3)} + \cdots + x_{(n)} \}, \tag{11B.5.9}$$

and the estimate of the mean will be

$$\mu^* = (\text{mean}^*) = \frac{1}{K' \sum_{2}^{n-r+1} \frac{1}{n-i+1} + (r-1)} \times \left\{ \left[\left(\sum_{1}^{n-r+1} \frac{1}{n-i+1} - 1 \right) K' + (r-1) \right] x_{(1)} + \frac{n-1}{n} \times [K' - (r-1)] x_{(n-r+1)} + \frac{n-1}{n} x_{(n-r+2)} + \cdots + \frac{n-1}{n} x_{(n)} \right\}. \tag{11B.5.10}$$

Their variances will be

$$V(\theta^*) = \frac{K' \sum_{2}^{n-r+1} \frac{1}{n-i+1} + r}{n^2 \left[K' \sum_{2}^{n-r+1} \frac{1}{n-i+1} + (r-1) \right]} \sigma^2, \tag{11B.5.11}$$

$$V(\sigma^*) = \frac{1}{K' \sum_{2}^{n-r+1} \frac{1}{n-i+1} + (r-1)} \sigma^2, \tag{11B.5.12}$$

$$V(\mu^*) = V(\text{mean}^*) = \frac{1}{n^2} \left[\frac{(n-1)^2}{K' \sum_{2}^{n-r+1} \frac{1}{n-i+1} + (r-1)} + 1 \right]. \tag{11B.5.13}$$

The best linear estimate of σ for the one-parameter exponential distribution is

$$\sigma^* = \frac{1}{K' \sum_{2}^{n-r+1} \dfrac{1}{n-i+1} + r}$$
$$\times \{(n - K')x_{(1)} + [K' - (r-1)]x_{(n-r+1)}$$
$$+ x_{(n-r+2)} + x_{(n-r+3)} + \ldots + x_{(n)}\} \quad (11B.5.14)$$

with variance

$$V(\sigma^*) = \frac{1}{\beta' \sum_{2}^{n-r+1} \dfrac{1}{n-i+1} + r}\,\sigma^2. \quad (11B.5.15)$$

For example, suppose that $n = 10$, and $x_{(2)}$, $x_{(3)}$, and $x_{(4)}$ are missing so that the following are available in the sample from the two-parameter exponential distribution:

$$x_{(1)} < x_{(5)} < x_{(6)} < x_{(7)} < x_{(8)} < x_{(9)} < x_{(10)}$$

In this case, $r = 6, \quad n - r - 1 = 3$

$$\theta^* = 1.08042x_{(1)} - 0.02430x_{(5)} - 0.01122x_{(6)} - 0.01122x_{(7)}$$
$$-0.01122x_{(8)} - \ldots - 0.01122x_{(10)},$$

$$\sigma^* = -0.80418x_{(1)} + 0.24296x_{(5)} + 0.11224x_{(6)} + 0.11224x_{(7)}$$
$$+ \ldots + 0.11224x_{(10)},$$

$$\mu^* = (\text{mean}^*) = 0.27624x_{(1)} + 0.21867x_{(5)} + 0.10102x_{(6)} + 0.10102x_{(7)}$$
$$+ \ldots + 0.10102x_{(10)},$$

and

$$V(\theta^*) = 0.0111224\sigma^2,$$
$$V(\sigma^*) = 0.1122425\sigma^2,$$
$$V(\mu^*) = V(\text{mean}^*) = 0.1009165\sigma^2.$$

REFERENCES

1. B. Epstein and M. Sobel, "Life testing," *J. Amer. Statist. Ass.*, Vol. 48 (1953), pp. 486–502.
2. Ronald G. Herd, "Estimation of the parameters of a population from a multi-censored sample," doctoral thesis, Iowa State College, Ames, 1956.
3. A. E. Sarhan, "Estimation of the mean and standard deviation by order statistics, Part III," *Ann. Math. Statist.*, Vol. 26 (1955), pp. 576–592.
4. A. E. Sarhan and B. G. Greenberg, "Tables for the best linear estimates by order statistics of the parameters of single exponential distributions from singly and doubly censored samples," *J. Amer. Statist. Ass.*, Vol. 52 (1957), pp. 58–87.

BENJAMIN EPSTEIN

11C SIMPLE ESTIMATES OF THE PARAMETERS OF EXPONENTIAL DISTRIBUTIONS

11C.1 Introduction

Elsewhere in this monograph (11B) and in reference 5, Sarhan and Greenberg give best linear unbiased estimates for the parameters of one and two-parameter exponential distributions, when samples are censored in various ways. In this paper, we give another method of estimation. The technique for finding the estimates is based on statistical life test theory [3, 4] and is described in some detail in references 1 and 2.

In the two-parameter case, our estimates coincide with the best linear estimates given in reference 5 and (11B), no matter how the data are censored. In the one-parameter case, our estimates coincide with theirs when censoring is from the right.[1] If censoring is from the left or from both left and right,[1] our estimates do not coincide with theirs. That the estimates we give must coincide with those in reference 5 and Section 11B, when there is a two-parameter exponential distribution or when data are censored from the right in the one-parameter distribution, is an easy consequence of known results on the uniqueness of unbiased estimates of minimum variance based on sufficient statistics. In those cases for which our estimates do not coincide with those in reference 5 and Section 11B, we find that they are "almost best" in the sense that they are highly efficient. Distribution questions and the related problems of making confidence statements are solved readily by using results obtained in life test research.

11C.2 Some Results on Exponential Distributions

In the sequel we consider, as before, the one- and two-parameter distributions described respectively by the pdfs,[2]

$$f(x) = \frac{1}{\sigma} e^{-x/\sigma}, \qquad x > 0, \quad \sigma > 0 \tag{11C.2.1}$$

[1] We consider the observations arranged in increasing order, so that censoring from the right means omitting some largest observations, censoring from the left means omitting some smallest observations, and censoring from both left and right means omitting some smallest and some largest observations.

[2] The notation used in (11C.2.1) and (11C.2.2) designates θ and σ as the location and scale parameters of the exponential distributions. In life-testing research, θ is usually

and

$$f(x) = \frac{1}{\sigma} e^{-(x-\theta)/\sigma}, \qquad 0 \leq \theta \leq x < \infty, \quad \sigma > 0. \quad (11C.2.2)$$

Let a sample of size n be drawn from the pdf described by (11C.2.1), and let the observations become available in order, i.e., $x_{(1)} \leq x_{(2)} \leq \ldots \leq x_{(r)} \leq \ldots \leq x_{(n)}$, where by $x_{(i)}$ $(1 \leq i \leq n)$ is meant the ith smallest observation in a sample of n ordered observations. It was shown in reference 3 that if only the first r ordered observations are available (as happens in life testing), the maximum-likelihood estimate of σ given by

$$\hat{\sigma}_{r\,n} = \left[\sum_{i=1}^{r} x_{(i)} + (n-r)x_{(r)}\right] \Big/ r \qquad (11C.2.3)$$

is "best" in the sense that it is unbiased, minimum variance, efficient, and sufficient. Furthermore, it is shown in reference 3 that $2r\hat{\sigma}_{r,n}/\sigma$ is distributed as chi-square with $2r$ degrees of freedom [denoted as $\chi^2(2r)$]. This is proved readily by rewriting $\hat{\sigma}_{r,n}$ as

$$\hat{\sigma}_{r,n} = \sum_{i=1}^{r} \frac{Z_{(i)}}{r} \qquad (11C.2.4)$$

where the random variables $Z_{(i)}$ are defined as

$$Z_{(1)} = nY_{(1)} \quad \text{and} \quad Z_{(i)} = (n-i+1)Y_{(i)}, \qquad 2 \leq i \leq r \quad (11C.2.5)$$

and where the random variables $Y_{(i)}$ are defined as

$$Y_{(1)} = X_{(1)} \quad \text{and} \quad Y_{(i)} = X_{(i)} - X_{(i-1)}, \qquad 2 \leq i \leq r. \quad (11C.2.6)$$

The $Y_{(i)}$ are the waiting times between successive failures (the experiment is assumed to start at the time zero, so that $Y_{(1)}$ is the waiting time for the first failure) and are thus mutually independent, each $Y_{(i)}$ having the probability density function $\frac{n-i+1}{\sigma} e^{-(n-i+1)y/\sigma}$. Thus the $Z_{(i)}$ are mutually independent with common probability density function (11C.2.1). It then follows at once that $\frac{2r\hat{\sigma}_{r,n}}{\sigma} = 2\sum_{i=1}^{r} \frac{Z_{(i)}}{\sigma}$ is distributed as $\chi^2(2r)$.

Since the estimate (11C.2.3) is linear, unbiased, and of minimum variance, it coincides with the one given by Sarhan and Greenberg for the case in which the last $(n-r)$ observations are censored. In their notation we have a case with $r_1=0$ smallest missing observations and $r_2=n-r$ largest

---

used to represent mean life rather than the σ used herein. Similarly, the term guarantee period with the symbol A is used to designate what is referred to in this section as θ.

missing observations. The variance of $\hat{\sigma}$ is given by σ^2/r, and $100(1-\alpha)\%$ confidence intervals for σ are given by

$$\left[\frac{2r\hat{\sigma}_{r,n}}{\chi^2_{\alpha/2}(2r)}, \frac{2r\hat{\sigma}_{r,n}}{\chi^2_{1-\alpha/2}(2r)}\right]$$

where $\chi^2_{\alpha/2}(2r)$ and $\chi^2_{1-\alpha/2}(2r)$ are respectively the upper and lower $\alpha/2$ points of $\chi^2(2r)$.

11C.3 Simplified Estimates for the Mean of the One-Parameter Exponential Distribution

Formula (11C.2.3) gives the minimum variance unbiased estimate for σ when the data are censored from the right. We now show how to find simplified unbiased estimates for σ, when censoring is from the right, from the left, or from both left and right. These estimates are highly efficient when compared with the best linear estimates given in reference 5 and Section 11B.

Let us first give an alternative unbiased estimate for σ, when data are censored from the right, that is, only $x_{(1)} \leq x_{(2)} \leq \ldots \leq x_{(r)}$ are known. Since the "best" estimate $\hat{\sigma}_{r,n}$ weights the waiting time $x_{(r)}$ (measured from zero) $n-r+1$ times as much as it does the earlier failure times $x_{(i)}$, $1 \leq i \leq r-1$, we are led to try an unbiased estimate which involves only $x_{(r)}$. Since

$$E(x_{(r)}) = \sigma \sum_{j=1}^{r} \frac{1}{n-j+1}, \tag{11C.3.1}$$

an unbiased estimate of σ is given by

$$\sigma^{*\prime}_{r,n} = \beta_{r,n} x_{(r)} \tag{11C.3.2}$$

where

$$\beta_{r,n} = 1 \Big/ \sum_{j=1}^{r} \frac{1}{n-j+1}. \tag{11C.3.3}$$

In reference 1 it was shown that estimates $\sigma^{*\prime}_{r,n}$ are of very high efficiency (≥ 0.96) if $r/n \leq 0.5$ (≥ 0.90 if $r/n \leq \frac{2}{3}$), when compared with the "best" estimates $\hat{\sigma}_{r,n}$. Proofs of these facts and tables of $\beta_{r,n}$, variances of $\sigma^{*\prime}_{r,n}$, efficiencies of $\sigma^{*\prime}_{r,n}$ for $n = 1(1)20(5)30(10)100$ and $r = 1\,(1)\,n$ are given in reference 1. Although the exact distribution of $\sigma^{*\prime}$ can be found easily from the pdf of $x_{(r)}$, which is given by

$$f_{(r)}(x) = \frac{n!}{(r-1)!\,(n-r)!} \cdot \frac{(1-e^{-x/\sigma})^{r-1} e^{-(n-r+1)x/\sigma}}{\sigma}, \tag{11C.3.4}$$

it is adequate in most practical problems to treat $2r\sigma^{*\prime}/\sigma$ as $\chi^2(2r)$.

Suppose then that we have a sample which is censored from the left, that is, we assume that $x_{(a)} \leq x_{(a+1)} \leq \ldots \leq x_{(n)}$[3] are known. Then the preceding suggests the following unbiased estimate,

$$\sigma^{*\prime} = \frac{a\beta_{a,n}x_{(a)} + (n-a)(x_{(a+1)} - x_{(a)}) + \ldots + (x_{(n)} - x_{(n-1)})}{n} \tag{11C.3.5}$$

or

$$\sigma^{*\prime} = \left[(a\beta_{a,n} + a - n)x_{(a)} + \sum_{j=a+1}^{n} x_{(j)}\right] \Big/ n. \tag{11C.3.6}$$

The term $a\beta_{a,n}x_{(a)}$ in the numerator gives the contribution to the estimate arising from what happens in the time interval $[0, x_{(a)}]$ whereas the remaining $(n-a)$ terms in the numerator give the contributions arising from the intervals $[x_{(a)}, x_{(a+1)}]$, $[x_{(a+1)}, x_{(a+2)}], \ldots, [x_{(n-1)}, x_{(n)}]$. On the question of how $\sigma^{*\prime}$ is distributed, we can say that if $a/n \leq \frac{2}{3}$, then $2n\sigma^{*\prime}/\sigma$ is distributed almost like $\chi^2(2n)$. This follows from the fact that the $(n-a+1)$ terms in the numerator of (11C.3.5) are mutually independent, that $2a\beta_{a,n}x_{(a)}/\sigma$ is distributed approximately as $\chi^2(2a)$, and that

$$2(n-j+1)(x_{(j)} - x_{(j-1)})/\sigma$$

is for each j, with $a+1 \leq j \leq n$, distributed exactly as $\chi^2(2)$. The exact value of the variance of $\sigma^{*\prime}$ is given by

$$V(\sigma^{*\prime}) = [a^2K_{a,n} + (n-a)]\sigma^2/n^2 \tag{11C.3.7}$$

where

$$K_{a,n} = \sum_{j=1}^{a} \frac{1}{(n-j+1)^2} \Big/ \left(\sum_{j=1}^{a} \frac{1}{n-j+1}\right)^2.$$

The $K_{a,n}$ are tabulated in reference 1.

In a similar way, we can treat the doubly censored case where $x_{(a)} \leq x_{(a+1)} \leq \ldots \leq x_{(b)}$[4] with $1 \leq a \leq b \leq n$. As an unbiased estimate we now take

$$\sigma^{*\prime} = \frac{a\beta_{a,n}x_{(a)} + (n-a)(x_{(a+1)} - x_{(a)}) + \ldots + (n-b+1)(x_{(b)} - x_{(b-1)})}{b} \tag{11C.3.8}$$

or

$$\sigma^{*\prime} = \left[(a\beta_{a,n} + a - n)x_{(a)} + \sum_{j=a+1}^{b-1} x_{(j)} + (n-b+1)x_{(b)}\right] \Big/ b. \tag{11C.3.9}$$

[3] In the notation of reference 5 and Section 11B, this is the case where $r_1 = a - 1$ and $r_2 = 0$.

[4] In the notation of reference 5 and Section 11B, this is the case for which $r_1 = a - 1$ and $r_2 = n - b$.

Here $2b\sigma^{*\prime}/\sigma$ is distributed almost like $\chi^2(2b)$ and

$$V(\sigma^{*\prime}) = [a^2K_{a,n} + (b - a)]\sigma^2/b^2.$$

Numerical calculations show that the $\sigma^{*\prime}$ given by (11C.3.6) (censored from the left only) or by (11C.3.9) (censored from both the left and the right) have slightly higher variances than do the best estimates given in reference 5. However, the differences are very slight indeed. For example, if we have a situation where $a = 6$, $b = 10$, $n = 10$ (singly censored on the left), then $V(\sigma^{*\prime}) = 0.1035$, and the variance of the "best" linear unbiased estimate is given by 0.1034. Even for the extreme $a = 9$, $b = 10$, $n = 10$, $V(\sigma^{*\prime}) = 0.1297$, and the variance of the "best" linear unbiased estimate is given by 0.1287.

TABLE A

Number of Smallest Observations Censored	$V(\sigma^{*\prime})/\sigma^2$
1	0.10006
2	0.10025
3	0.10072
4	0.10158
5	0.10350
6	0.10703
7	0.11395
8	0.12972

Remark: It is interesting to point out that the variance of $\sigma^{*\prime}$ is increased much more by censoring from the right than by censoring from the left. The effect of censoring the largest r_2 observations is to change the variance from σ^2/n to $\sigma^2/(n - r_2)$. If the smallest r_1 observations are censored, the results are rather different. As computed from (11C.3.7), $V(\sigma^{*\prime})$ has the values listed in Table A when the sample size n equals 10. Thus, for example, although censoring the five largest observations increases the variance to $\sigma^2/5$, the censoring of the five smallest observations changes the variance only to $0.1035\sigma^2$.

11C.4 Simplified Estimates for the Parameters of the Two-Parameter Exponential Distribution

We now turn our attention to what happens when samples are drawn from the two-parameter exponential distribution described by (11C.2.2). We first treat a censored from the right situation where only $x_{(1)} \leq x_{(2)} \leq \ldots \leq x_{(r)}$ are known. It has been shown in reference 4 that the minimum-variance unbiased estimates for θ and σ are given by[5]

$$\theta^* = x_{(1)} - \frac{\sigma^*}{n} \qquad \text{and} \qquad \sigma^* = \sum_{i=1}^{r-1} \frac{(n-i)(x_{(i+1)} - x_{(i)})}{r-1}. \qquad (11C.4.1)$$

This simplifies to

$$\theta^* = \frac{(nr-1)x_{(1)} - x_{(2)} - x_{(3)} - \ldots - x_{(r-1)} - (n-r+1)x_{(r)}}{n(r-1)} \qquad (11C.4.2)$$

and

$$\sigma^* = \frac{-(n-1)x_{(1)} + x_{(2)} + x_{(3)} + \ldots + x_{(r-1)} + (n-r+1)x_{(r)}}{r-1}. \qquad (11C.4.3)$$

It is easily verified that

$$V(\sigma^*) = \frac{\sigma^2}{r-1} \qquad (11C.4.4)$$

and from the independence of $x_{(1)}$ and σ^* that

$$V(\theta^*) = V(x_{(1)}) + \frac{1}{n^2} V(\sigma^*) = \frac{\sigma^2}{n^2} + \frac{\sigma^2}{n^2(r-1)} = \frac{\sigma^2}{n^2}\left(\frac{r}{r-1}\right). \qquad (11C.4.5)$$

Since $2(r-1)\sigma^*/\sigma$ is distributed as $\chi^2(2r-2)$, a $100(1-\alpha)\%$ confidence interval on σ is given by

$$\left[\frac{2(r-1)\sigma^*}{\chi^2_{\alpha/2}(2r-2)}, \frac{2(r-1)\sigma^*}{\chi^2_{1-\alpha/2}(2r-2)}\right].$$

To find confidence intervals on θ we use the fact that the statistics $h = 2n(x_1 - \theta)/\sigma$ and $v = 2(r-1)\sigma^*/\sigma$ are independent and distributed respectively as $\chi^2(2)$ and $\chi^2(2r-2)$. Therefore the ratio $W = (2r-2)h/2v$ is distributed according to the F-distribution with degrees of freedom 2 and $2r-2$ respectively [denoted as $F(2, 2r-2)$].

From the F-table we can find, for selected values of γ and r, the w_γ such that $\Pr(0 \le W \le w_\gamma) = \gamma$. From the definition of W, a $100\gamma\%$ confidence interval on θ is given by $[x_{(1)} - w_\gamma\sigma^*/n, x_{(1)}]$. It has been shown in

[5] Maximum-likelihood estimates of $[\theta, \sigma]$ are $\left[x_{(1)}, \frac{(r-1)\sigma^*}{r}\right]$. The unique minimum-variance unbiased estimates of θ and σ are given by (11C.4.1). It should also be noted that the random variables $x_{(j)} - x_{(1)}$, $(2 \le j \le n)$, can be considered as $(n-1)$ ordered observations from the one-parameter exponential (11C.2.1). Thus the problem of estimating σ from (11C.2.2) is transformed into a problem of estimation from (11C.2.1).

reference 4 that this is the shortest $100\gamma\%$ confidence interval in the class of intervals used.

Remark: Tables of the F-distribution are useful in carrying out the computations just discussed. It may happen, however, that for the particular r and γ in question the value is not tabulated. It is then useful to have the following result proved in reference 4, namely that the random variable $Z = W/r - 1$ has the pdf $(r-1)/(1+z)^r$, with $z \geq 0$. From this it follows that $\Pr(0 \leq Z \leq z_\gamma) = \gamma$ is satisfied by taking

$$z_\gamma = \left(\frac{1}{1-\gamma}\right)^{1/r-1} - 1.$$

But since

$$Z = \frac{W}{r-1} = \frac{h}{v} = \frac{n(x_{(1)} - \theta)}{(r-1)\sigma^*}.$$

it follows that the desired $100\gamma\%$ confidence interval is given by $\left[x_{(1)} - \dfrac{z_\gamma \sigma^*(r-1)}{n}, x_{(1)}\right]$. Since $z_\gamma = w_\gamma/r - 1$, we have, of course, the same confidence interval as before. However, the simple formula for z_γ can be used for any r and any γ.

If observations on the pdf (11C.2.2) are censored from the left with $x_{(a)} \leq x_{(a+1)} \leq \ldots \leq x_{(n)}$ known, we can give the following minimum-variance unbiased estimates for θ and σ,

$$\theta^* = x_{(a)} - \sigma^* \sum_{j=1}^{a} \frac{1}{n-j+1} \tag{11C.4.6}$$

and

$$\sigma^* = \frac{(n-a)(x_{(a+1)} - x_{(a)}) + (n-a-1)(x_{(a+2)} - x_{(a+1)}) + \ldots + (x_{(n)} - x_{(n-1)})}{n-a}$$
$$= \frac{-(n-a)x_{(a)} + x_{(a+1)} + \ldots + x_{(n)}}{n-a}. \tag{11C.4.7}$$

From the form of (11C.4.7), $V(\sigma^*) = \dfrac{\sigma^2}{n-a}$ and from the independence of $x_{(a)}$ and σ^*,

$$V(\theta^*) = \sigma^2 \sum_{j=1}^{a} \frac{1}{(n-j+1)^2} + \frac{\sigma^2}{n-a}\left(\sum_{j=1}^{a} \frac{1}{n-j+1}\right)^2. \tag{11C.4.8}$$

Since $2(n-a)\sigma^*/\sigma$ is distributed as $\chi^2(2n-2a)$, a $100(1-\alpha)\%$ confidence interval on σ is given by

$$\left[\frac{2(n-a)\sigma^*}{\chi^2_{\alpha/2}(2n-2a)}, \frac{2(n-a)\sigma^*}{\chi^2_{1-\alpha/2}(2n-2a)}\right].$$

Approximate confidence intervals on θ are found by noting that $2a\beta_{a,n}(x_{(a)} - \theta)/\sigma$ is approximately distributed as $\chi^2(2a)$ and is independent of the random variable $2(n - a)\sigma^*/\sigma$ which is distributed as $\chi^2(2n - 2a)$. Therefore the ratio $W = \beta_{a,n}(x_{(a)} - \theta)/\sigma^*$ is distributed approximately as $F(2a, 2n - 2a)$. If w_γ is such that $\Pr(0 \le w \le w_\gamma) = \gamma$, a $100\gamma\%$ confidence interval for θ is given by $[x_{(a)} - \sigma^* w_\gamma/\beta_{a,n}, x_{(a)}]$.

In the doubly censored case where we have $x_{(a)} \le x_{(a+1)} \le \ldots \le x_{(b)}$, with $1 \le a \le b \le n$, we obtain the estimates

$$\theta^* = x_{(a)} - \sigma^* \sum_{j=1}^{a} \frac{1}{n - j + 1} \tag{11C.4.9}$$

and

$$\begin{aligned}\sigma^* &= \frac{(n - a)(x_{(a+1)} - x_{(a)}) + (n - a - 1)(x_{(a+2)} - x_{(a+1)}) + \ldots + (n - b + 1)(x_{(b)} - x_{(b-1)})}{b - a} \\ &= \frac{-(n - a)x_{(a)} + x_{(a+1)} + \ldots + x_{(b-1)} + (n - b + 1)x_{(b)}}{b - a}.\end{aligned} \tag{11C.4.10}$$

From the form of (11C.4.10), $V(\sigma^*) = \sigma^2/(b - a)$, and from the independence of $x_{(a)}$ and σ^*,

$$V(\theta^*) = \sigma^2 \sum_{j=1}^{a} \frac{1}{(n - j + 1)^2} + \frac{\sigma^2}{b - a}\left(\sum_{j=1}^{a} \frac{1}{n - j + 1}\right)^2. \tag{11C.4.11}$$

Since $2(b - a)\sigma^*/\sigma$ is distributed as $\chi^2(2b - 2a)$, a $100(1 - \alpha)\%$ confidence interval on σ is given by

$$\left[\frac{2(b - a)\sigma^*}{\chi^2_{\alpha/2}(2b - 2a)}, \frac{2(b - a)\sigma^*}{\chi^2_{1-\alpha/2}(2b - 2a)}\right].$$

Since $W = \beta_{a,n}(x_{(a)} - \theta)/\sigma^*$ is distributed approximately as $F(2a, 2b-2a)$, a $100\gamma\%$ confidence interval for θ is given by $[x_{(a)} - \sigma^* w_\gamma/\beta_{a,n}, x_{(a)}]$ where w_γ is such that $\Pr(0 \le W \le w_\gamma) = \gamma$.

Our estimates θ^* and σ^* coincide with those given by Sarhan and Greenberg, no matter how the sample is censored. It should be noted that in the case of the one-parameter exponential there was agreement only when observations were censored from the right.

Remark: The estimates given for σ for the one-parameter exponential and for σ and θ for the two-parameter exponential are so simple that we need to tabulate only $\sum_{j=1}^{a} \frac{1}{n - j + 1}$ and its reciprocal $\beta_{a,n}$. These values are tabulated for samples of up to 10 items in reference 2 and are given in

Table 11A.1. Another useful table for samples of up to 10 items, Table 11C.1, gives the constants $K_{r,n}$ for which $V(\beta_{r,n}X_{(r)}) = K_{r,n}\sigma^2$. More extensive tables are given in reference 1.

TABLE 11C.1

CONSTANTS $K_{r,n}$ FOR WHICH $V(\beta_{r,n}X_{(r)}) = K_{r,n}\sigma^2$

r \ n	2	3	4	5	6	7	8	9	10
1	1.0000	1.0000	1.0000	1.0000	1.0000	1.0000	1.0000	1.0000	1.0000
2	.5556	.5200	.5102	.5062	.5041	.5030	.5022	.5017	.5014
3		.4050	.3609	.3481	.3426	.3397	.3380	.3369	.3361
4			.3280	.2815	.2675	.2612	.2578	.2558	.2545
5				.2807	.2337	.2192	.2125	.2089	.2067
6					.2485	.2017	.1870	.1801	.1764
7						.2249	.1787	.1641	.1572
8							.2068	.1614	.1468
9								.1924	.1478
10									.1806

This table is reproduced from "Estimates of mean life based on the rth smallest value in a sample of size n drawn from an exponential population," by Benjamin Epstein, under research sponsored by the Office of Naval Research, Tech. Rep. 2, ONR Contract Nonr 451(100), NR–042–017. Reproduction in whole or part is permitted for any purpose of the United States Government.

11C.5 Some Related Results

We now give some related results which may be of interest. First we wish to point out that knowledge of $x_{(1)}$, the first failure time, is very important in the two-parameter problem. To make this statement explicit we wish to compare the estimation problem when only $x_{(a)} \le x_{(a+1)} \le \ldots \le x_{(n)}$ are known with that when $x_{(1)} \le x_{(a)} \le x_{(a+1)} \le \ldots \le x_{(n)}$ are known. When x_1 is also known, formulas for $\theta^{*\prime}$, and $\sigma^{*\prime}$ which are "nearly best" are

$$\theta^{*\prime} = x_{(1)} - \frac{\sigma^{*\prime}}{n} \tag{11C.5.1}$$

where

$$\begin{aligned}\sigma^{*\prime} &= [(a-1)\beta_{a-1,n-1}(x_{(a)} - x_{(1)}) + (n-a)(x_{(a+1)} - x_{(a)}) \\ &\quad + (n-a-1)(x_{(a+2)} - x_{(a+1)}) + \ldots + (x_{(n)} - x_{(n-1)})]/(n-1) \\ &= \{-(a-1)\beta_{a-1,n-1}x_{(1)} + [(a-1)\beta_{a-1,n-1} - (n-a)]x_{(a)} \\ &\quad + x_{(a+1)} + x_{(a+2)} + \ldots + x_{(n)}\}/(n-1).\end{aligned} \tag{11C.5.2}$$

It can be shown further that

$$V(\sigma^{*\prime}) \sim \frac{\sigma^2}{n-1} \qquad \text{if} \quad \frac{a}{n} \leq \frac{2}{3} \tag{11C.5.3}$$

and thus

$$V(\theta^{*\prime}) \sim \frac{\sigma^2}{n(n-1)}. \tag{11C.5.4}$$

To give some numerical results, consider $n = 10$ and $a = 5$. If $x_{(5)} \leq x_{(6)} \leq \ldots \leq x_{(10)}$ are known, then $V(\theta^{*\prime}) = 0.1695\sigma^2$ and $V(\sigma^{*\prime}) = 0.2\sigma^2$. If $x_{(1)} \leq x_{(5)} \leq x_{(6)} \leq x_{(7)} \leq x_{(8)} \leq x_{(9)} \leq x_{(10)}$ are known, calculations give $V(\theta^{*\prime}) = 0.0111\sigma^2$ and $V(\sigma^{*\prime}) = 0.1123\sigma^2$. Thus additional knowledge concerning the first failure time greatly reduces the variance of the estimates of θ and σ.

Another interesting question is to find estimates when the data contain gaps anywhere, that is, when observations may be missing not only at the beginning or end, but anywhere. We claim that the methods in Subsections 11C.3 and 11C.4 always yield good unbiased estimates. For simplicity consider just the one-parameter problem. Suppose, for example, in the case $n = 10$, we were given the following: $x_{(1)} \leq x_{(2)} \leq x_{(3)} \leq x_{(6)} \leq x_{(7)} \leq x_{(9)} \leq x_{(10)}$. We can write down the following unbiased estimate for σ:

$$\begin{aligned}\sigma^{*\prime} &= [10x_{(1)} + 9(x_{(2)} - x_{(1)}) + 8(x_{(3)} - x_{(2)}) + 3\beta_{3,7}(x_{(6)} - x_{(3)}) \\ &\quad + 4(x_{(7)} - x_{(6)}) + 2\beta_{2,3}(x_{(9)} - x_{(7)}) + (x_{(10)} - x_{(9)})]/10 \\ &= [x_{(1)} + x_{(2)} + 2.1122x_{(3)} + 1.8878x_{(6)} + 1.6000x_{(7)} \\ &\quad + 1.4000x_{(9)} + x_{(10)}]/10. \end{aligned} \tag{11C.5.5}$$

It is also easy to compute that $V(\sigma^{*\prime}) = 0.1014$. (Note that if *all* ten observations were known, the variance of $\sigma^{*\prime}$ would be equal to 0.1000. Thus very little is lost by not knowing $x_{(4)}$, $x_{(5)}$, and $x_{(8)}$.)

The structure of the estimate is interesting: $10x_{(1)}$ gives the contribution to the numerator of the right-hand side of (11C.5.5) in the time interval $[0, x_{(1)}]$; $9(x_{(2)} - x_{(1)})$ gives the contribution in $[x_{(1)}, x_{(2)}]$; $8(x_{(3)} - x_{(2)})$ in $[x_{(2)}, x_{(3)}]$; $3\beta_{3,7}(x_{(6)} - x_{(3)})$ in $[x_{(3)}, x_{(6)}]$; $4(x_{(7)} - x_{(6)})$ in $[x_{(6)}, x_{(7)}]$; $2\beta_{2,3}(x_{(9)} - x_{(7)})$ in $[x_{(7)}, x_{(9)}]$; and $(x_{(10)} - x_{(9)})$ in $[x_{(9)}, x_{(10)}]$. Essential use is made of the fact that the ordered statistics $(x_{(a+1)} - x_{(a)}) \leq (x_{(a+2)} - x_{(a)}) \leq \ldots \leq (x_{(n)} - x_{(a)})$ can be considered as $(n-a)$ ordered observations obtained when we draw a sample of size $(n-a)$ from the density function (11C.2.1).

In the general case we might be given only $x_{(r_1)} \leq x_{(r_2)} \leq \ldots \leq x_{(r_k)}$

where $1 \le r_1 \le r_2 \le \ldots \le r_k \le n$ and where $1 \le k \le n$. The unbiased estimate which we suggest is

$$\begin{aligned}\sigma^{*\prime} = [&r_1\beta_{r_1,n}x_{(r_1)} + (r_2 - r_1)\beta_{r_2-r_1,n-r_1}(x_{(r_2)} - x_{(r_1)}) \\ &+ (r_3 - r_2)\beta_{r_3-r_2,n-r_2}(x_{(r_3)} - x_{(r_2)}) \\ &+ \ldots + (r_k - r_{k-1})\beta_{r_k-r_{k-1},n-r_{k-1}}(x_{(r_k)} - x_{(r_{k-1})})]/r_k. \quad (11C.5.6)\end{aligned}$$

In this estimate the various terms in the numerator give the contributions of the time intervals $[0, x_{(r_1)}]$, $[x_{(r_1)}, x_{(r_2)}], \ldots, [x_{(r_{k-1})}, x_{(r_k)}]$. In most cases $V(\sigma^{*\prime}) \sim \dfrac{\sigma^2}{r_k}$ and $2r\sigma^{*\prime}/\sigma$ will be approximately distributed as $\chi^2(2r_k)$.

It is easy to extend these results to the two-parameter exponential.

REFERENCES

1. B. Epstein, "Estimates of mean life based on the rth smallest value in a sample of size n drawn from an exponential population," Wayne University Tech. Rep. 2, prepared under ONR Contract Nonr-451(00), NR-042-017, July 1952.
2. B. Epstein, "Simple estimators of the parameters of exponential distributions when samples are censored," *Ann. Inst. Statist. Math., Tokyo*, Vol. 8 (1956), pp. 15–26.
3. B. Epstein and M. Sobel, "Life testing," *J. Amer. Statist. Ass.*, Vol. 48 (1953) pp. 486–502.
4. B. Epstein and M. Sobel, "Some theorems relevant to life testing from an exponential population," *Ann. Math. Statist.*, Vol. 25 (1954), pp. 373–381.
5. A. E. Sarhan and B. G. Greenberg, "Tables for best linear unbiased estimates by order statistics of the parameters of single exponential distributions from singly and doubly censored samples," *J. Amer. Statist. Ass.*, Vol. 52 (1957), pp. 58–87.

JUNJIRO OGAWA

11D OPTIMUM SPACING AND GROUPING FOR THE EXPONENTIAL DISTRIBUTION

11D.1 Optimum Spacing

Suppose that we have the exponential distribution

$$g(x) = \begin{cases} \dfrac{1}{\sigma}\, e^{-x/\sigma}, & \text{if } x > 0 \\ 0, & \text{otherwise} \end{cases} \qquad (11D.1.1)$$

and that we are given an ordered sample of size n, where n is sufficiently large. In other words, the sample size n is large enough so that the conclusions drawn by making use of the limit distribution are valid with enough accuracy. For given k real numbers such that

$$0 < \lambda_1 < \lambda_2 < \ldots < \lambda_k < 1, \qquad (11D.1.2)$$

we select k sample λ_i-quantiles for $i = 1, 2, \ldots, k$, that is, k order statistics

$$x_{(n_1)}, x_{(n_2)}, \ldots, x_{(n_k)}$$

where

$$n_i = [n\lambda_i] + 1, \qquad i = 1, \ldots, k, \qquad (11D.1.3)$$

and the symbol $[n\lambda_i]$ stands for the greatest integer not exceeding $n\lambda_i$.

Furthermore, let the λ_i-quantile of the standardized exponential distribution, whose density is given by

$$f(x) = \begin{cases} e^{-x}, & \text{if } x > 0 \\ 0, & \text{otherwise} \end{cases} \qquad (11D.1.4)$$

be u_i, and that of (11D.1.1) be x_i; then it is clear that

$$x_i = u_i\sigma, \qquad i = 1, 2, \ldots, k. \qquad (11D.1.5)$$

The limiting joint distribution of the k sample quantiles $x_{(n_1)}, \ldots, x_{(n_k)}$ has the density function

$$h(x_{(n_1)}, x_{(n_2)}, \ldots, x_{(n_k)})$$
$$= C_{n,k} \exp\left\{-\frac{n}{2\sigma^2}\left[\sum_{i=1}^{k} \frac{\lambda_{i+1} - \lambda_{i-1}}{(\lambda_{i+1} - \lambda_i)(\lambda_i - \lambda_{i-1})} f_i^2(x_{(n_i)} - u_i\sigma)^2\right.\right.$$
$$\left.\left. - 2\sum_{i=2}^{k} \frac{f_i f_{i-1}}{\lambda_i - \lambda_{i-1}} (x_{(n_i)} - u_i\sigma)(x_{(n_{i-1})} - u_{i-1}\sigma)\right]\right\} \qquad (11D.1.6)$$

where

$$\begin{aligned} f_i &= e^{-u_i}, & i &= 1, 2 \ldots, k, \\ \lambda_i &= 1 - e^{-u_i}, & i &= 1, 2 \ldots, k. \end{aligned} \qquad (11D.1.7)$$

Hence we obtain

$$\log h = -\frac{k}{2}\log\sigma^2 - \frac{n}{2\sigma^2} S + \text{term which is independent of } \sigma \qquad (11D.1.8)$$

where

$$S = \sum_{i=1}^{k} \frac{\lambda_{i+1} - \lambda_{i-1}}{(\lambda_{i+1} - \lambda_i)(\lambda_i - \lambda_{i-1})} f_i^2(x_{(n_i)} - u_i\sigma)^2$$
$$- 2\sum_{i=2}^{k} \frac{f_i f_{i-1}}{\lambda_i - \lambda_{i-1}} (x_{(n_i)} - u_i\sigma)(x_{(n_{i-1})} - u_{i-1}\sigma). \qquad (11D.1.9)$$

Thus we obtain the amount of information of the systematic statistics with respect to the scale parameter σ, in this case

$$I_s(\sigma) = E\left(-\frac{\partial^2 \log h}{\partial \sigma^2}\right) = \frac{2k}{\sigma^2} + \frac{n}{\sigma^2} K_2 \qquad (11D.1.10)$$

where

$$K_2 = \sum_{i=1}^{k+1} \frac{(f_i u_i - f_{i-1} u_{i-1})^2}{\lambda_i - \lambda_{i-1}} = \sum_{i=1}^{k+1} \frac{(e^{-u_i} u_i - e^{-u_{i-1}} u_{i-1})^2}{e^{-u_{i-1}} - e^{-u_i}}. \qquad (11D.1.11)$$

Consequently we obtain the relative efficiency of the systematic statistics with respect to σ as

$$\eta(\sigma) = K_2. \qquad (11D.1.12)$$

The best linear unbiased estimator σ^* of σ is

$$\sigma^* = \frac{1}{K_2} Y \qquad (11D.1.13)$$

where

$$Y = \sum_{i=1}^{k+1} \frac{(e^{-u_i} u_i - e^{-u_{i-1}} u_{i-1})(e^{-u_i} x_{(n_i)} - e^{-u_{i-1}} x_{(n_{i-1})})}{e^{-u_{i-1}} - e^{-u_i}}, \qquad (11D.1.14)$$

and this can be written as

$$Y = \sum_{i=1}^{k} a_i x_{(n_i)} \qquad (11D.1.15)$$

where

$$a_i = e^{-u_i}\left(\frac{e^{-u_i} u_i - e^{-u_{i-1}} u_{i-1}}{e^{-u_{i-1}} - e^{-u_i}} - \frac{e^{-u_{i+1}} u_{i+1} - e^{-u_i} u_i}{e^{-u_i} - e^{-u_{i+1}}}\right). \qquad (11D.1.16)$$

The coefficients b_i for the optimum spacings are calculated in Table 11D.1, since from (11D.1.13) and (11D.1.15) we have

$$\sigma^* = \sum_{i=1}^{k} b_i x_{(n_i)} \qquad (11D.1.17)$$

where

$$b_i = \frac{a_i}{K_2}, \qquad i = 1, 2, \ldots, k. \qquad (11D.1.18)$$

The required optimum spacing is the set $(\lambda_1, \lambda_2, \ldots, \lambda_k)$, or equivalently the set of values $(u_1, u_2, \ldots, u_k)$ which gives the maximum value of the relative efficiency K_2. We can obtain the optimum spacings step by step as follows:

(i) The case where $k = 1$: in this case it is easily seen that

$$K_2 = \frac{u_1^2}{e^{u_1} - 1} \qquad (11D.1.19)$$

TABLE 11D.1

OPTIMUM SPACINGS, THE CORRESPONDING COEFFICIENTS, AND RELATIVE EFFICIENCIES FOR σ^* OF THE ONE-PARAMETER EXPONENTIAL DISTRIBUTION

k	1	2	3	4	5	6	7	8	9	10	11	12	13	14	15
u_1	1.5936	1.0177	.7541	.6003	.4994	.4274	.3741	.3323	.2988	.2719	.2494	.2303	.2137	.1994	.1875
λ_1	.7968	.6386	.5296	.4514	.3931	.3478	.3121	.2827	.2583	.2381	.2207	.2057	.1924	.1808	.1710
b_1	.6275	.5232	.4477	.3907	.3463	.3108	.2819	.2579	.2375	.2201	.2053	.1923	.1807	.1703	.1613
u_2		2.6113	1.7718	1.3544	1.0997	.9268	.8015	.7064	.6311	.5707	.5213	.4797	.4440	.4131	.3869
λ_2		.9266	.8300	.7419	.6670	.6042	.5513	.5066	.4680	.4349	.4063	.3810	.3585	.3384	.3208
b_2		.1790	.2266	.2361	.2320	.2228	.2119	.2009	.1905	.1804	.1711	.1627	.1551	.1479	.1412
u_3			3.3654	2.3721	1.8538	1.5271	1.3009	1.1338	1.0052	.9030	.8201	.7516	.6934	.6434	.6006
λ_3			.9655	.9067	.8434	.7828	.7277	.6782	.6340	.5946	.5596	.5284	.5001	.4745	.4515
b_3			.0775	.1195	.1402	.1492	.1519	.1511	.1483	.1446	.1402	.1356	.1312	.1268	.1224
u_4				3.9657	2.8715	2.2812	1.9012	1.6332	1.4326	1.2771	1.1524	1.0504	.9653	.8928	.8309
λ_4				.9810	.9434	.8978	.8506	.8047	.7613	.7212	.6841	.6502	.6191	.5905	.5643
b_4				.0409	.0709	.0902	.1017	.1082	.1116	.1127	.1124	.1111	.1093	.1073	.1051
u_5					4.4651	3.2989	2.6553	2.2335	1.9320	1.7045	1.5265	1.3827	1.2641	1.1647	1.0803
λ_5					.9885	.9631	.9297	.8928	.8551	.8181	.7827	.7491	.7175	.6880	.6605
b_5					.0243	.0456	.0615	.0725	.0799	.0847	.0875	.0891	.0896	.0895	.0889
u_6						4.8925	3.6730	2.9876	2.5323	2.2039	1.9539	1.7568	1.5964	1.4635	1.3522
λ_6						.9925	.9746	.9496	.9205	.8896	.8583	.8274	.7974	.7686	.7413
b_6						.0156	.0311	.0438	.0536	.0607	.0659	.0694	.0718	.0733	.0741
u_7							5.2666	4.0053	3.2864	2.8042	2.4533	2.1842	1.9705	1.7958	1.6510
λ_7							.9948	.9818	.9626	.9394	.9140	.8874	.8606	.8340	.8081
b_7							.0107	.0222	.0324	.0407	.0472	.0522	.0560	.0587	.0607

u_8								5.5989	4.3041	3.5583	3.0536	2.6836	2.3979	2.1699	1.9833
λ_8								.9963	.9865	.9715	.9528	.9317	.9091	.8858	.8624
b_8								.0076	.0164	.0246	.0316	.0374	.0421	.0458	.0486
u_9									5.8977	4.5760	3.8077	3.2839	2.8973	2.5973	2.3574
λ_9									.9973	.9897	.9778	.9625	.9448	.9255	.9053
b_9									.0056	.0124	.0191	.0250	.0301	.0344	.0380
u_{10}										6.1696	4.8254	4.0380	3.4976	3.0967	2.7848
λ_{10}										.9979	.9920	.9824	.9697	.9548	.9383
b_{10}										.0042	.0097	.0151	.0202	.0247	.0285
u_{11}											6.4190	5.0557	4.2517	3.6970	3.2842
λ_{11}											.9984	.9936	.9858	.9752	.9625
b_{11}											.0033	.0077	.0122	.0165	.0204
u_{12}												6.6493	5.2694	4.4511	3.8845
λ_{12}												.9987	.9949	.9883	.9794
b_{12}												.0026	.0062	.0100	.0137
u_{13}													6.8630	5.4688	4.6386
λ_{13}													.9990	.9958	.9903
b_{13}													.0021	.0051	.0083
u_{14}														7.0624	5.6563
λ_{14}														.9991	.9965
b_{14}														.0017	.0042
u_{15}															7.2499
λ_{15}															.9993
b_{15}															.0014
K_2	.6476	.8203	.8910	.9269	.9476	.9606	.9693	.9754	.9798	.9832	.9857	.9874	.9894	.9907	.9918

From A. E. Sarhan and B. G. Greenberg, "Estimation problems in exponential distribution using order statistics," *Proceedings of the Statistical Techniques in Missile Evaluation Symposium*, 1958, Blacksburg, Va., pp. 123–173, with permission of Commanding Officer, U.S. Army Research Office.

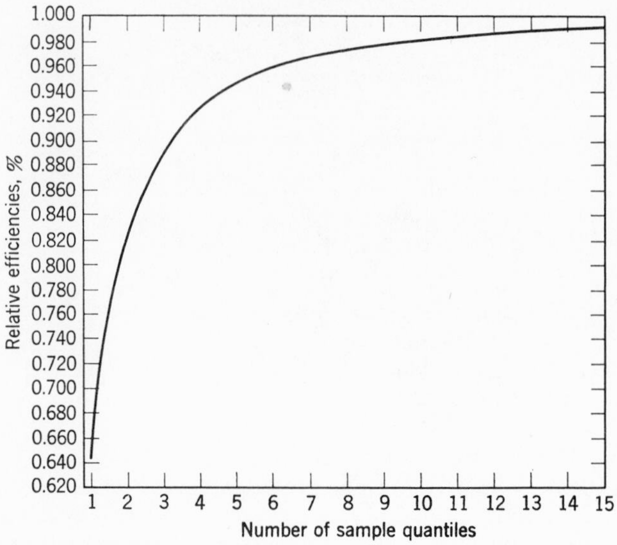

Fig. 11D.1 The curve of relative efficiencies against the number of selected sample quantiles to be used. Reproduced from A. E. Sarhan and B. G. Greenberg, "Estimation problems in the exponential distribution using order statistics," *Proceedings of Statistical Techniques in Missile Evaluation Symposium*, 1958, Blacksburg, Va., pp. 123–173, with permission of the Commanding Officer, U.S. Army Research Office.

which has only one maximum $K_2 = 0.6476$ at $u_1 = 1.5936$, and the corresponding probability is $\lambda_1 = 1 - e^{-1.5936} = 0.7968$.

(ii) The case where $k = 2$: put $u_2 = u_1 + x$; then we have

$$K_2 = e^{-u_1}\left(\frac{u_1^{\ 2}}{e^{u_1} - 1} + u_1^{\ 2} + \frac{x^2}{e^x - 1}\right), \qquad (11D.1.20)$$

and this function of x and u_1 is maximized at the point

$$u_1 = 1.0177, \qquad x = 1.5936,$$

that is,

$$u_1 = 1.0177, \qquad u_2 = 2.6113,$$

and the maximum value of K_2 is

$$K_2 = 0.8203.$$

(iii) The case where $k = 3$: put

$$n_2 = u_1 + x, \qquad u_3 = u_2 + y = u_1 + x + y;$$

then it follows after some calculations that

$$K_2 = e^{-u_1}\left[\frac{u_1^{\,2}}{e^{u_1} - 1} + u_1^{\,2} + e^{-x}\left(\frac{x^2}{e^x - 1} + x^2 + \frac{y^2}{e^y - 1}\right)\right]. \quad (11D.1.21)$$

It is easily seen that this function of x, y, and u_1 is maximized at the point

$$u_1 = 0.7541, \qquad x = 1.0177, \qquad y = 1.5936.$$

Hence we obtain the optimum spacing in this case as follows:

$$u_1 = 0.7541, \qquad u_2 = 1.7718, \qquad u_3 = 3.3654$$

and the corresponding maximum value of K_2 is

$$K_2 = 0.8910. \quad (11D.1.22)$$

In a similar way, the following results in Table 11D.1 have been calculated. In Table 11D.1, u_i stands for the λ_i-quantile of the standardized population. The bottom row of the table (representing the relative efficiencies K_2) has been graphed as Fig. 11D.1 to show the increasing rate of relative efficiencies against the number of sample quantiles which have been selected. It will be seen from Fig. 11D.1 that after $k = 10$ the gain in relative efficiency is not appreciable.

Example. As an illustration of the estimation procedure, we calculate the estimate of the standard deviation of the time intervals in days between explosions in mines, involving more than 10 men killed from 6 December 1875 to 29 May 1951. The data are from Maguire, Pearson, and Wynn [3]. It should be noted that this example may not be the best to point out the value of this method because the sample size ($n = 109$) is small enough that the labor necessary for the classical estimation is almost comparable to that necessary for our estimate. This example should be regarded as an illustration of the calculating procedure itself. There are cases, such as life testing of electric lamps and fatigue tests of certain material, in which the samples are naturally ordered in magnitude. Then the procedure here may be of great help in getting the estimate of σ quickly, especially for a large bulk of data.

Table A is reproduced overleaf with observations arranged in order of magnitude.

For $k = 10$, we can learn from Table 11D.1 that $n_1 = 26$, $n_2 = 48$, $n_3 = 65$, $n_4 = 79$, $n_5 = 90$, $n_6 = 97$, $n_7 = 103$, $n_8 = 106$, $n_9 = 108$, $n_{10} = 109$, and $K_2 = 0.9832$.

Thus we have

$$[\sigma^* = 242.1849].$$

If we compare the estimate with $\sigma = 241$, which was calculated using all the sample by the classical methods, we find a very good agreement.

Greenberg and Sarhan [1] used five spacings to estimate the average age at death for infants in the United States in 1955. The sample size was 106903. They also demonstrated the advantage of using optimum spacings in such cases.

TABLE A

TIME INTERVALS IN DAYS BETWEEN EXPLOSIONS IN MINES, INVOLVING MORE THAN TEN MEN KILLED FROM 6 DEC. 1875 TO 29 MAY 1951
(B. A. Maguire, E. S. Pearson, and A. H. A. Wynn)

Order	Observation	Order	Observation	Order	Observation
1	1	36	72	73	255
2	4	37	72	74	271
3	4	38	75	75	275
4	7	39	78		
5	11	40	78	76	275
				77	275
6	13	41	81	78	286
7	15	42	93	79	291
8	15	43	96	80	312
9	17	44	99		
10	18	45	108	81	312
				82	315
11	19	46	113	83	326
12	19	47	114	84	326
13	20	48	120	85	329
14	20	49	120		
15	22	50	123	86	330
				87	336
16	23	51	124	88	338
17	28	52	129	89	345
18	29	53	131	90	348
19	31	54	137		
20	32	55	145	91	354
				92	361
21	36	56	151	93	364
22	37	57	156	94	369
23	47	58	171	95	378
24	48	59	176		
25	49	60	182	96	390
				97	457
26	50	61	188	98	467
27	54	62	189	99	498
28	54	63	195	100	517
29	55	64	203		
30	58	65	208	101	566
				102	644
31	59	66	215	103	745
32	59	67	217	104	871
33	61	68	217	105	1205
34	61	69	217		
35	66	70	224	106	1312
				107	1357
		71	228	108	1613
		72	233	109	1630

11D.2 Estimation Using the Best Two Observations

The variance of the best linear unbiased estimate σ^* of σ based on $x_{(i)}$ and $x_{(j)}$, with $i < j$, from the two-parameter exponential distribution (11A.1) is

$$V(\sigma^*) = \frac{\dfrac{1}{(n-i)^2} + \dots + \dfrac{1}{(n-j+1)^2}}{\left(\dfrac{1}{n-i} + \dots + \dfrac{1}{n-j+1}\right)^2}. \tag{11D.2.1}$$

If we fix j, this variance of σ attains its minimum at $i = 1$ and, concerning the optimum selection of j, we have the following.

Result 1 [5]. The best linear unbiased estimate of the scale parameter σ of the exponential population given by (11D.1.1) based on two ordered observations $x_{(i)}$, $x_{(j)}$, with $i < j$, attains its maximum efficiency for the following spacings:

Sample size	2 . . . 6	7 . . . 10	11 . . . 15	16 . . . 20	21
i	1	1	1	1	1
j	n	$n-1$	$n-2$	$n-3$	$n-4$

Result 2 [5]. For the best linear unbiased estimate of the location parameter θ of the exponential population given by (11A.1) based on two ordered observations, the same results hold.

For the one-parameter exponential distribution given by (11D.1.1), the best linear unbiased estimate based on two ordered observations attains its maximum efficiency for the following spacings:

Sample size	2 . . . 4	5 . . . 7	8 . . . 11	12 . . . 15	16 . . . 18	19 . . . 21
i	$n-1$	$n-2$	$n-3$	$n-4$	$n-6$	$n-7$
j	n	n	n	n	$n-1$	$n-1$

11D.3 On Grouping for the One-Parameter Exponential

Strictly speaking, any measurements or observations should be regarded as grouped data, but here we are concerned with much coarser grouping.

Mathematically, the random variables in the grouped data are the frequencies obeying a multinomial probability distribution. Here naturally arises *a problem of optimum grouping*, that is, to find a partition of the sample space which is optimum in one sense or another. This problem was treated by Kulldorff [2] for the exponential distribution.

It should be pointed out that the asymptotic results for optimum grouping coincide with the optimum spacing of sample quantiles [3], as should be expected.

REFERENCES

1. B. G. Greenberg and A. E. Sarhan, "Application of order statistics to health data," *Amer. J. Publ. Health*, Vol. 48 (1958), pp. 1388–1394.
2. G. Kulldorff, "Maximum likelihood estimation for the exponential distribution when the sample is grouped," Dept. of Statistics, University of Lund, Sweden, 1958.
3. B. A. Maguire, E. S. Pearson, and A. H. A. Wynn, "The time intervals between industrial accidents," *Biometrika*, Vol. 39 (1952), pp. 168–180.
4. J. Ogawa, "A further contribution to the theory of systematic statistics," Institute of Statistics, University of North Carolina, Mimeograph Series 168, 1957.
5. Yoshimasa Ukita, "On the efficiency of order statistics," *J. Hokkaido College Sci. and Art.*, Vol. 6, No. 1 (1955), pp. 54–65.

JUNJIRO OGAWA

11E TESTS OF SIGNIFICANCE AND CONFIDENCE INTERVALS

To test the null hypothesis

$$H_0\colon\ \sigma = \sigma_0 \tag{11E.1}$$

starting with the frequency function given by (11D.1.1), we use the following procedure. If the null hypothesis H_0 is true, then

$$\frac{n}{\sigma_0^{\,2}}\left[\sum_{i=1}^{k} \frac{\lambda_{i+1} - \lambda_{i-1}}{(\lambda_{i+1} - \lambda_i)(\lambda_i - \lambda_{i-1})} f_i^2(x_{(n_i)} - u_i\sigma_0)^2 - 2\sum_{i=2}^{k} \frac{f_i f_{i-1}}{\lambda_i - \lambda_{i-1}}(x_{(n_i)} - u_i\sigma_0)(x_{(n_{i-1})} - u_{i-1}\sigma_0)\right] \tag{11E.2}$$

is distributed according to the χ^2-distribution with degrees of freedom k. This comes out as [1]

$$\frac{n}{\sigma_0^{\,2}}\left[\sum_{i=1}^{k+1} \frac{(f_i x_{(n_i)} - f_{i-1} x_{(n_{i-1})})^2}{\lambda_i - \lambda_{i-1}} + K_2(\sigma_0^{\,2} - 2\sigma_0\hat{\sigma})\right]. \tag{11E.3}$$

The minimum value S_0 of S under the variation of σ is given by

$$S_0 = \sum_{i=1}^{k+1} \frac{(f_i x_{(n_i)} - f_{i-1} x_{(n_{i-1})})^2}{\lambda_i - \lambda_{i-1}} - K_2\hat{\sigma}^2 \tag{11E.4}$$

and $(n/\sigma_0^{\,2})S_0$ is distributed according to the χ^2-distribution with degrees of freedom $k - 1$, provided H_0 is true. Hence

$$\frac{n}{\sigma^2} K_2(\hat{\sigma} - \sigma_0)^2 \tag{11E.5}$$

is independent of S_0 and is distributed according to the χ^2-distribution with 1 degree of freedom. Thus the statistic

$$t = \sqrt{k-1}\,\frac{\sqrt{K_2}(\hat{\sigma} - \sigma_0)}{\sqrt{S_0}} \tag{11E.6}$$

follows the Student t-distribution with degrees of freedom $k-1$ if the null hypothesis H_0 is true.

If the null hypothesis H_0 is not true, and an alternative hypothesis H: $\sigma = \sigma\ (\neq \sigma_0)$ is true, the distribution of t in (11E.6) follows the noncentral t-distribution with noncentrality parameter

$$\delta = \sqrt{K_2}\left(1 - \frac{\sigma_0}{\sigma}\right), \tag{11E.7}$$

and the power function of the t-test is an increasing function of the absolute value of δ. Hence it is reasonable for tests of significance to select sample quantiles, the spacing of which makes K_2 maximum, that is, optimum spacing for estimation purposes is also optimum for testing purposes. Thus we can also use Table 11D.1 for testing purposes.

Finally, it should be noted that the confidence interval of σ with confidence coefficient $100(1-\alpha)\%$ is given by

$$\hat{\sigma} - t_{k-1}(100\alpha)\sqrt{S_0/(k-1)K_2} < \sigma < \hat{\sigma} + t_{k-1}(100\alpha)\sqrt{S_0/(k-1)K_2}, \tag{11E.8}$$

where $t_{k-1}(100\alpha)$ stands for the $100\alpha\%$ point of the t-distribution with degrees of freedom $k-1$.

Example. We calculate the 95% confidence interval for σ in the example of Section 11D as an illustration of the procedure explained in this section. We consider case $k = 10$. Then we have

$$\begin{aligned} S_0 &= \sum_{i=1}^{11} \frac{(f_i x_{(n_i)} - f_{i-1} x_{(n_{i-1})})^2}{\lambda_i - \lambda_{i-1}} - K_2\hat{\sigma}^2 \\ &= \sum_{i=1}^{11} \frac{(f_i x_{(n_i)} - f_{i-1} x_{(n_{i-1})})^2}{\lambda_i - \lambda_{i-1}} - \frac{\left(\sum_1^{10} a_i x_{(n_i)}\right)^2}{K_2}, \end{aligned} \tag{11E.9}$$

and calculation will be executed as shown in Table 11E.1. The 95% confidence interval calculated in the table seems to be somewhat wide, perhaps because of the smallness of the sample size.

REFERENCE

1. J. Ogawa, "A further contribution to the theory of systematic statistics," Institute of Statistics, University of North Carolina, Mimeograph Series 168, 1957.

TABLE 11E.1
CALCULATING SCHEME FOR S_0

(1) i	(2) a_i	(3) λ_i	(4) $\lambda_i - \lambda_{i-1}$	(5) f_i	(6) $x_{(n_i)}$	(7) = (6) × (5) $f_i x_{(n_i)}$	(8) $f_i x_{(n_i)} - f_{i-1} x_{(n_{i-1})}$	(9) = (8)/(4) $\frac{f_i x_{(n_i)} - f_{i-1} x_{(n_{i-1})}}{\lambda_i - \lambda_{i-1}}$	(10) = (9) × (8) $\frac{(f_i x_{(n_i)} - f_{i-1} x_{(n_{i-1})})^2}{\lambda_i - \lambda_{i-1}}$	(11) = (2) × (6) $a_i x_{(n_i)}$
0	–	0.0000	–	1.00000	–	–	–	–	–	–
1	.21644	.2381	.2381	.76193	50	38.09650	38.09650	160.00210	6095.52000	10.82200
2	.17734	.4349	.1968	.56513	120	67.81560	29.71910	151.01169	4487.93143	21.28080
3	.14216	.5946	.1597	.40535	208	84.31280	16.49720	103.30119	1704.18039	29.56928
4	.11077	.7212	.1266	.27884	291	81.14244	−3.17036	−25.04234	79.39323	32.23407
5	.08327	.8181	.0969	.18186	348	63.28728	−17.85516	−184.26378	3290.05922	28.97796
6	.05964	.8896	.0715	.11037	457	50.43909	−12.84819	−179.69497	2308.75505	27.25548
7	.03997	.9394	.0498	.06056	745	45.11720	−5.32189	−106.86526	568.72516	29.77765
8	.02417	.9715	.0321	.02849	1312	37.37888	−7.73832	−241.06916	1865.47029	31.71104
9	.01224	.9897	.0182	.01030	1613	16.61390	−20.76498	−1140.93297	23691.45024	19.74312
10	.00417	.9979	.0082	.00209	1630	3.40670	−13.20720	−1610.63415	21271.96730	6.79710
11	–	1.0000	.0021	–	–	–	−3.40670	−1622.23810	5526.47852	–
Total									70889.93083	238.16850

$$S_0 = \sum_{i=1}^{11} \frac{(f_i x_{(n_i)} - f_{i-1} x_{(n_{i-1})})^2}{\lambda_i - \lambda_{i-1}} - \frac{\left(\sum_{i=1}^{10} a_i x_{(n_i)}\right)^2}{K_2} = 13196.44589$$

$$t_9(5) \cdot \sqrt{S_0/(k-1)K_2} = 2.262 \times \sqrt{\frac{13196.44589}{9 \times 0.98316}} = 87.35499$$

CHAPTER 12

Other Distributions

A. E. SARHAN and B. G. GREENBERG

12A RECTANGULAR DISTRIBUTION

12A.1 The Moments of Order Statistics

The frequency distribution of a rectangular distribution is

$$f(x) = \frac{1}{\theta_2}, \qquad \theta_1 - \tfrac{1}{2}\theta_2 \leq x \leq \theta_1 + \tfrac{1}{2}\theta_2, \tag{12A.1.1}$$

where θ_1 is the mean and θ_2 is the range.

The expected value of the standardized variable $u_{(r)}$ is [1]

$$E(u_{(r)}) = \frac{r}{n+1} \tag{12A.1.2}$$

and the covariance of $u_{(r)}$, $u_{(s)}$ is

$$\underset{r\leq s}{\operatorname{Cov}}\,(u_{(r)}, u_{(s)}) = \frac{r(n-s+1)}{(n+1)^2(n+2)}. \tag{12A.1.3}$$

12A.2 BLUE of θ_1 and θ_2

Suppose that a random sample of size n has been drawn from the rectangular distribution (12A.1.1) and that the smallest r_1 and largest r_2 elements are missing, that is, the observed values are

$$x_{(r_1+1)} \leq x_{(r_1+2)} \leq \ldots \leq x_{(n-r_2)}.$$

Using the expected values, variances, and covariances of order statistics given by (12A.1.2) and (12A.1.3) and applying the method of least squares, we obtain as in reference 2 the following:

$$\theta^*_1 = \frac{1}{2(n - r_1 - r_2 - 1)} [(n - 2r_2 - 1)x_{(r_1+1)} + (n - 2r_1 - 1)x_{(n-r_2)}] \tag{12A.2.1}$$

and

$$\theta^*_2 = \frac{n + 1}{n - r_1 - r_2 - 1} (x_{(n-r_2)} - x_{(r_2+1)}). \tag{12A.2.2}$$

From (12A.2.1), it is obvious that if $r_2 = \frac{1}{2}(n - 1)$, the smallest element will have zero weight. Then the mean of the rectangular population is estimated by its largest known observation. By symmetry, the same holds true for r_1 and subsequent use of only the smallest known observation.

The variances are

$$V(\theta^*_1) = \frac{(r_1 + 1)(n - 2r_2 - 1) + (r_2 + 1)(n - 2r_1 - 1)}{4(n + 2)(n + 1)(n - r_1 - r_2 - 1)} \theta_2^2, \tag{12A.2.3}$$

$$V(\theta^*_2) = \frac{r_1 + r_2 + 2}{(n + 2)(n - r_1 - r_2 - 1)} \theta_2^2. \tag{12A.2.4}$$

The efficiencies of θ^*_1 and θ^*_2 relative to the complete sample estimates are

$$\text{R.E.}(\theta^*_1) = \frac{2(n - r_1 - r_2 - 1)}{(r_1 + 1)(n - 2r_2 - 1) + (r_2 + 1)(n - 2r_1 - 1)} \tag{12A.2.5}$$

and

$$\text{R.E.}(\theta^*_2) = \frac{2(n - r_1 - r_2 - 1)}{(n - 1)(r_1 + r_2 + 2)}. \tag{12A.2.6}$$

Figures 12A.1 and 12A.2 show the relative efficiencies of θ^*_1 and θ^*_2 for different cases of censoring from a sample of size 10.

The symmetry of the graph in Fig. 12A.1 shows that the side from which censoring was done makes no difference but, given a fixed amount of censoring, the efficiency attains a maximum when there is equal censoring on each side. In Fig. 12A.2 the graph shows that, for a given amount of censoring, there is no change in the efficiency of estimating θ_2. In other words, in estimating the range of the rectangular distribution, it makes no difference from which end the values are censored.

If $r_1 = r_2 = 0$ (i.e., a complete sample), the estimates are [1]

$$\theta^*_1 = \tfrac{1}{2}(x_{(1)} + x_{(n)}) \tag{12A.2.7}$$

and

$$\theta^*_2 = \frac{n + 1}{n - 1} (x_{(n)} - x_{(1)}), \tag{12A.2.8}$$

that is, the estimate of the center of the distribution is a function of the sample range.

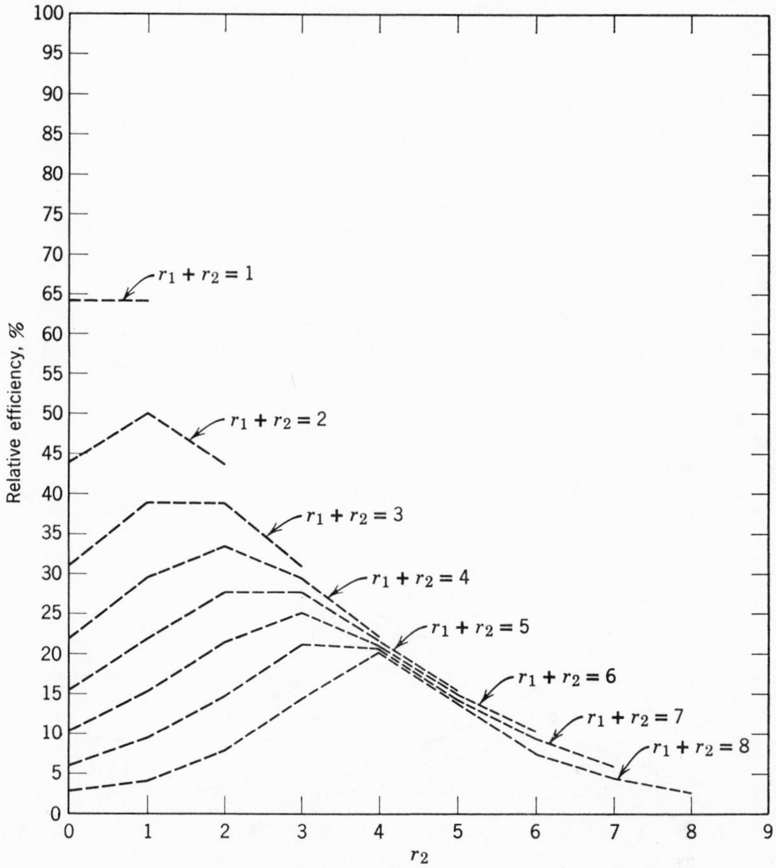

Fig. 12A.1 Relative efficiency of estimating θ_1 in rectangular distribution for given cases of censoring for a sample with 10 observations. Reproduced from A. E. Sarhan and B. G. Greenberg, "Estimation of location and scale parameters for the rectangular population from censored samples," *J. Roy. Stat. Soc.*, **B**, Vol. 21 (1959), pp. 356–363, with permission of the Royal Statistical Society.

The variances of the estimates are

$$V(\theta^*_1) = \frac{\theta_2^2}{2(n+1)(n+2)}, \tag{12A.2.9}$$

$$V(\theta^*_2) = \frac{2\theta_2^2}{(n+2)(n-1)}, \tag{12A.2.10}$$

and

$$\text{Cov}\,(\theta^*_1, \theta^*_2) = 0. \tag{12A.2.11}$$

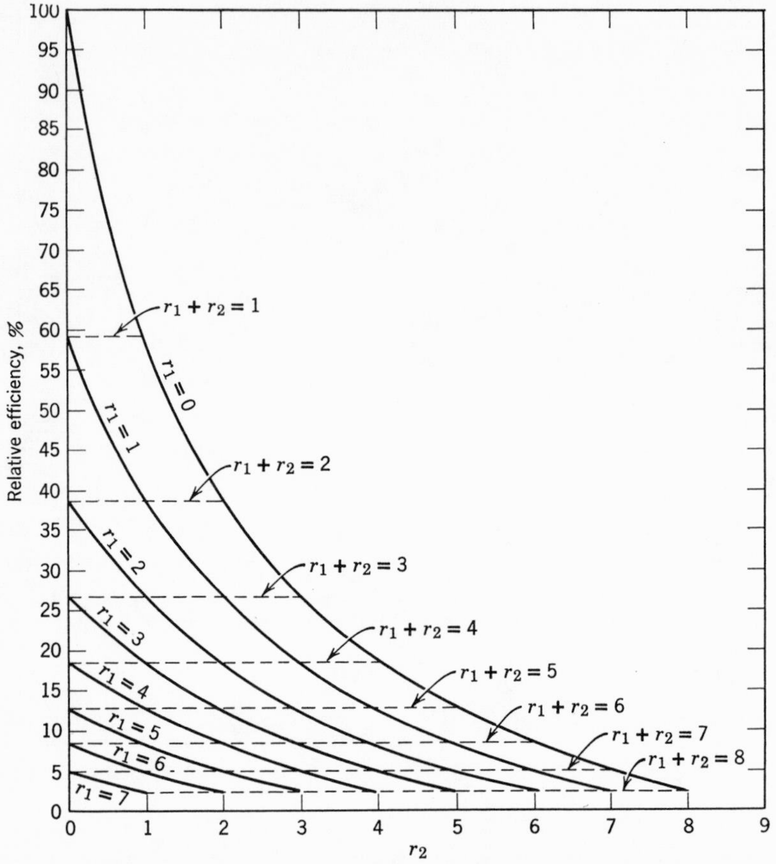

Fig. 12A.2 Relative efficiency of estimating θ_2 in rectangular distribution for given cases of censoring for a sample with 10 observations. Reproduced from A. E. Sarhan and B. G. Greenberg, "Estimation of location and scale parameters for the rectangular population from censored samples," *J. Roy. Stat. Soc.*, **B**, Vol. 21 (1959), pp. 356–363, with permission of the Royal Statistical Society.

It is to be noted that the extreme observations in this case are sufficient statistics. Since θ^*_1 and θ^*_2 are given in terms of the extreme observations, the estimates are the best among all other estimates and not only among linear unbiased estimates.

The estimates of a and b (the start and the end of the distribution) are

$$a^* = \theta^*_1 - \tfrac{1}{2}\theta^*_2 = x_{(r_1+1)} - \frac{r_1 + 1}{n - r_1 - r_2 - 1}\left[x_{(n-r_2)} - x_{(r_1+1)}\right] \tag{12A.2.12}$$

and

$$b^* = \theta^*_1 + \tfrac{1}{2}\theta^*_2 = x_{(n-r_2)} + \frac{r_2 + 1}{n - r_1 - r_2 - 1}\left[x_{(n-r_2)} - x_{(r_1+1)}\right], \qquad (12A.2.13)$$

with variances

$$V(a^*) = \frac{(r_1 + 1)(n - r_2)}{(n + 1)(n + 2)(n - r_1 - r_2 - 1)}\,\theta_2^2 \qquad (12A.2.14)$$

and

$$V(b^*) = \frac{(n - r_1)(r_2 + 1)}{(n + 1)(n + 2)(n - r_1 - r_2 - 1)}\,\theta_2^2. \qquad (12A.2.15)$$

The relative efficiencies of a^* and b^* are

$$\text{R.E.}(a^*) = \frac{n(n - r_1 - r_2 - 1)}{(n - 1)(r_1 + 1)(n - r_2)}, \qquad (12A.2.16)$$

$$\text{R.E.}(b^*) = \frac{n(n - r_1 - r_2 - 1)}{(n - 1)(r_2 + 1)(n - r_1)}. \qquad (12A.2.17)$$

Examination of the variance expressions of a^* and b^* (as well as their relative efficiencies) indicates an important relationship between each pair. In general,

$$V(a^*) = V(b^*)$$

by interchanging r_1 and r_2. This is understandable since a and b are both location parameters involving extremes of the distribution which are, in turn, related to r_1 and r_2.

Figures 12A.3 and 12A.4 are drawn to show the relative efficiencies of a^* and b^* for samples of size 10 for all possible cases of censoring. In Fig. 12A.3 the graph portrays the tremendous penalty we pay in estimating the start of the distribution by sacrificing the first observation or first two observations. In addition, it may be surprising to learn that the opposite end plays an important role in estimating a only when censoring is getting close to leaving two or three uncensored observations. Figure 12A.4 shows the same phenomenon for estimating b. The most important value therein is the last since the efficiency is always less than 50% when $r_2 > 1$.

If $r_1 = r_2 = 0$, then

$$a^* = x_{(1)} - \frac{1}{n - 1}(x_{(n)} - x_{(1)}) \qquad (12A.2.18)$$

and

$$b^* = x_{(n)} + \frac{1}{n - 1}(x_{(n)} - x_{(1)}) \qquad (12A.2.19)$$

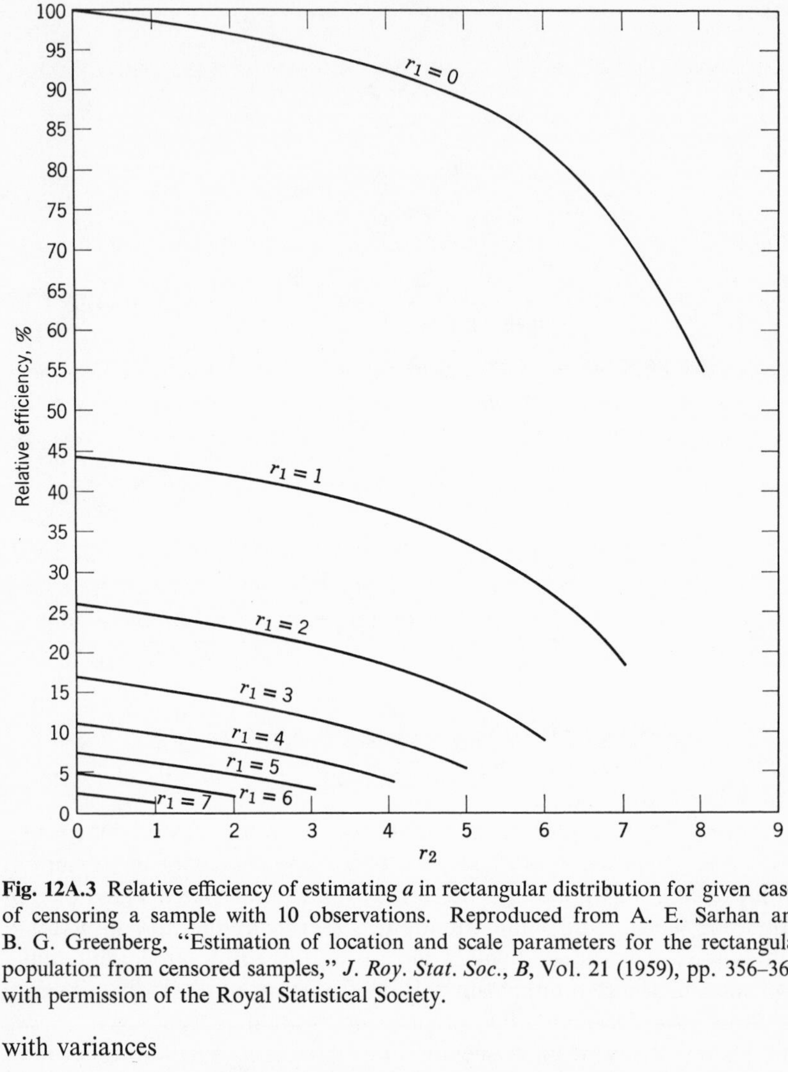

Fig. 12A.3 Relative efficiency of estimating a in rectangular distribution for given cases of censoring a sample with 10 observations. Reproduced from A. E. Sarhan and B. G. Greenberg, "Estimation of location and scale parameters for the rectangular population from censored samples," *J. Roy. Stat. Soc.*, *B*, Vol. 21 (1959), pp. 356–363, with permission of the Royal Statistical Society.

with variances

$$V(a^*) = V(b^*) = \frac{n}{(n^2 - 1)(n + 2)}\,\theta_2^{\,2}. \qquad (12A.2.20)$$

The covariance of a^* and b^* is

$$\text{Cov}\,(a^*, b^*) = -\,\frac{1}{(n^2 - 1)(n + 2)}\,\theta_2^{\,2}. \qquad (12A.2.21)$$

Now, consider a sample of size n from the rectangular distribution

$$f(x) = \frac{1}{\theta_2}\,, \qquad 0 \le x \le \theta_2, \qquad (12A.2.22)$$

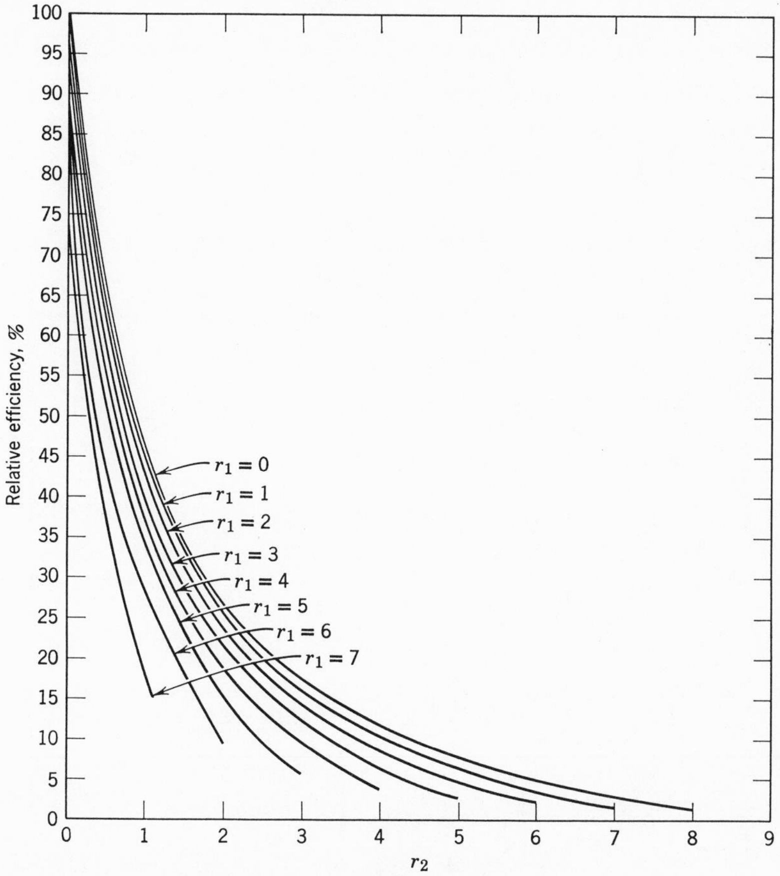

Fig. 12A.4 Relative efficiency of estimating b in rectangular distribution for given cases of censoring for a sample with 10 observations. Reproduced from A. E. Sarhan and B. G. Greenberg, "Estimation of parameters in censored samples from rectangular distribution," Tech. Rep. 6, OOR Project 1597, 1958, with permission of the Commanding Officer, U.S. Army Research Office.

with the smallest r_1 and largest r_2 observations missing. Then

$$\theta^*_2 = \frac{n+1}{n-r_2} x_{(n-r_2)} \tag{12A.2.23}$$

with variance

$$V(\theta^*_2) = \frac{r_2+1}{(n-r_2)(n+2)} \theta_2^2 \tag{12A.2.24}$$

and

$$\text{R.E.}(\theta^*_2) = \frac{n - r_2}{n(r_2 + 1)}. \tag{12A.2.25}$$

If $r_1 = r_2 = 0$, then

$$\theta^*_2 = \frac{n+1}{n} x_{(n)} \tag{12A.2.26}$$

and

$$V(\theta^*_2) = \frac{1}{n(n+2)} \theta_2^2. \tag{12A.2.27}$$

12A.3 Estimation of Percentiles

The jth percentile can be estimated by

$$\begin{aligned}\tilde{x}^*_j &= \theta^*_1 + (p - \tfrac{1}{2})\theta^*_2 \\ &= \frac{1}{n-1}\{n - p(n+1)x_{(1)} + [p(n+1) - 1]x_{(n)}\} \quad (12\text{A}.3.1),\end{aligned}$$

with variance

$$V(\tilde{x}^*_j) = \frac{n - 1 + 4(n+1)(p - \frac{1}{2})^2}{2(n+1)(n+2)(n-1)}. \tag{12A.3.2}$$

As a special case, we obtain

$$\tilde{x}^*_{50} = \tfrac{1}{2}[x_{(1)} + x_{(n)}] \tag{12A.3.3}$$

and

$$V(\tilde{x}^*_{50}) = \frac{\theta_2^2}{2(n+1)(n+2)}. \tag{12A.3.4}$$

If the rectangular distribution starts at the origin, we can obtain similar expressions.

REFERENCES

1. E. H. Lloyd, "Least squares estimation of location and scale parameters using order statistics," *Biometrika*, Vol. 39 (1952), pp. 88–95.
2. A. E. Sarhan and B. G. Greenberg, "Estimation of location and scale parameters for the rectangular population from censored samples," *J. Roy. Statist. Soc., B*, Vol. 21, No. 2 (1959), pp. 356–363.

A. E. SARHAN and B. G. GREENBERG

12B CERTAIN SYMMETRIC DISTRIBUTIONS

12B.1 The Moments of Order Statistics

The symmetric distributions considered here are as follows.

1. The U-shaped distribution [2]

$$f(x) = \frac{3(x - \theta_1)^2}{2\theta_2^{\,3}}, \qquad \theta_1 - \theta_2 \le x \le \theta_1 + \theta_2$$

where θ_1 is the mean and θ_2 is half the range ($\sigma = \sqrt{3/5}\theta_2$).

2. The parabolic distribution [2],

$$f(x) = \frac{6(x - \theta_1 + \frac{1}{2}\theta_2)(\theta_1 + \frac{1}{2}\theta_2 - x)}{\theta_2^{\,3}}, \qquad \theta_1 - \tfrac{1}{2}\theta_2 \le x \le \theta_1 + \tfrac{1}{2}\theta_2$$

where θ_1 is the mean and θ_2 is the range [$\sigma = (1/2\sqrt{5})\theta_2$].

3. The triangular distribution [1],

$$f(x) = \frac{4}{\theta_2^{\,2}}(\tfrac{1}{2}\theta_2 - |x - \theta_1|), \qquad |x - \theta_1| \le \tfrac{1}{2}\theta_2$$

where θ_1 is the mean and θ_2 is the range.

4. The double exponential distribution [1],

$$f(x) = \frac{1}{2\sigma}\, e^{-|x-\mu|/\sigma}.$$

The means, variances, and covariances of the order statistics up to samples of size 5 were calculated and those of symmetric distributions 3 and 4 are given in references 1 and 2.

12B.2 The Best Linear Unbiased Estimate

The coefficients α_{1i} and α_{2i} in the best linear estimate of the mean θ_1 and the standard deviation σ are calculated for the given distributions for samples up to size 5 and all possible cases of censoring.

These coefficients for which

$$\theta^*_1 = \sum_{i=r_1+1}^{n-r_2} \alpha_{1i} x_{(i)} \qquad \text{and} \qquad \sigma^* = \sum_{i=r_1+1}^{n-r_2} \alpha_{2i} x_{(i)}$$

TABLE 12B.1

COEFFICIENTS IN THE BEST LINEAR ESTIMATE OF THE MEAN AND STANDARD DEVIATION BASED ON THE ORDER STATISTIC $x_{(i)}$ FROM SINGLY AND DOUBLY CENSORED SAMPLES IN DIFFERENT POPULATIONS OF SIZE n, FOR THE MEAN $\theta^*_1 = \sum_{i=r_1+1}^{n-r_2} \alpha_{1i} x_{(i)}$, FOR THE STANDARD DEVIATION $\sigma^* = \sum_{i=r_1+1}^{n-r_2} \alpha_{2i} x_{(i)}$

$n\ r_1 r_2$	Population	α_{11}	α_{12}	α_{13}	α_{14}	α_{15}	α_{21}	α_{22}	α_{23}	α_{24}	α_{25}
5 0 0	U-shaped	.55848	−.04486	−.02724	−.04486	.55848	−.48903	.03185	0	−.03185	.48903
	Rectangular	.5000	0	0	0	.50000	−.43301	0	0	0	.43301
	Parabolic	.38629	.07954	.06835	.07954	.38629	−.41052	−.03926	0	.03926	.41052
	Triangular	.30608	.11885	.15014	.11885	.30608	−.39942	−.06372	0	.06372	.39942
	Normal	.20000	.20000	.20000	.20000	.20000	−.37238	−.13521	0	.13521	.37238
	D. expon.	.01664	.22130	.52413	.22130	.01664	−.32634	−.31697	0	.31697	.32634
5 0 1	U-shaped	.43872	−.04343	−.08306	.68777		−.59390	.03310	−.04888	.60968	
	Rectangular	.33333	0	0	.66667		−.57735	0	0	.57735	
	Parabolic	.23969	.07856	.08893	.59302		−.56652	−.04031	.02187	.58495	
	Triangular	.18406	.11224	.17776	.52594		−.55865	−.07234	.03604	.59496	
	Normal	.12516	.18305	.21472	.47708		−.51173	−.16678	.02740	.65111	
	D. expon.	.01141	.21631	.52432	.24796		−.43310	−.41912	.00378	.84845	
5 0 2	U-shaped	.03923	−.06537	1.02614			−.94803	.01365	.93438		
	Rectangular	0	0	1.00000			−.86603	0	.86603		
	Parabolic	−.03675	.07894	.95781			−.83901	−.03992	.87893		
	Triangular	−.04498	.10110	.94388			−.81775	−.08495	.90269		
	Normal	−.06377	.14983	.91395			−.76958	−.21212	.98170		
	D. expon.	−.06649	.16663	.89986			−.66555	−.62333	1.28888		
5 0 3	U-shaped	−1.50002	2.50002				−2.34961	2.34961			
	Rectangular	−1.00000	2.00000				−1.73205	1.73205			
	Parabolic	−.87097	1.87097				−1.60452	1.60452			
	Triangular	−.80131	1.80131				−1.54102	1.54102			
	Normal	−.74111	1.74111				−1.49713	1.49713			
	D. expon.	−.56411	1.56411				−1.39247	1.39247			
5 1 1	U-shaped		.55959	−.11917	.55959			−.78320	0	.78320	
	Rectangular		.50000	0	.50000			−.86603	0	.86603	
	Parabolic		.45091	.09817	.45091			−.92111	0	.92111	
	Triangular		.40518	.18964	.40518			−.96148	0	.96148	
	Normal		.38929	.22142	.38929			−1.01006	0	1.01006	
	D. expon.		.23779	.52442	.23779			−1.23422	0	1.23422	
5 1 2	U-shaped		0	1.00000				−1.56641	1.56641		
	Rectangular		0	1.00000				−1.73205	1.73205		
	Parabolic		0	1.00000				−1.84223	1.84223		
	Triangular		0	1.00000				−1.92296	1.92296		
	Normal		0	1.00000				−2.02012	2.02012		
	D. expon.		0	1.00000				−2.46845	2.46845		
4 0 0	U-shaped	.55307	−.05307	−.05307	.55307		−.52186	.02829	−.02829	.52186	
	Rectangular	.50000	0	0	.50000		−.48113	0	0	.48113	
	Parabolic	.40782	.09218	.09218	.40782		−.47042	−.03101	.03101	.47042	
	Triangular	.33789	.16211	.16211	.33789		−.47225	−.05414	.05414	.47225	
	Normal	.25000	.25000	.25000	.25000		−.45394	−.11018	.11018	.45394	
	D. expon.	.04730	.45270	.45270	.04730		−.43074	−.30037	.30037	.43074	
4 0 1	U-shaped	.33321	−.09237	.75916			−.72931	−.00879	.73810		
	Rectangular	.25000	0	.75000			−.72169	0	.72169		
	Parabolic	.18939	.10253	.70809			−.72238	−.01908	.74146		
	Triangular	.15237	.17011	.67753			−.72059	−.04232	.76291		
	Normal	.11607	.24084	.64310			−.69713	−.12682	.82395		
	D. expon.	.06627	.33333	.60040			−.73321	−.21290	.94611		
4 0 2	U-shaped	−.64291	1.64291				−1.67837	1.67837			
	Rectangular	−.50000	1.50000				−1.42338	1.42338			
	Parabolic	−.45506	1.45506				−1.39718	1.39718			
	Triangular	−.42914	1.42914				−1.37538	1.37538			
	Normal	−.40555	1.40555				−1.36544	1.36544			
	D. expon.	−.33005	1.33005				−1.35780	1.35780			
4 1 1	U-shaped		.50000	.50000				−1.30534	1.30534		
	Rectangular		.50000	.50000				−1.42338	1.42338		
	Parabolic		.50000	.50000				−1.53519	1.53519		
	Triangular		.50000	.50000				−1.60247	1.60247		
	Normal		.50000	.50000				−1.68344	1.68344		
	D. expon.		.50000	.50000				−2.05711	2.05711		

This table is reproduced from A. E. Sarhan, "Estimation of the mean and standard deviation by order statistics, Parts II and III," *Ann. Math. Statist.*, Vol. 26 (1955), pp. 505–511, 576–592, with permission of W. Kruskal, editor of the *Annals of Mathematical Statistics*.

TABLE 12B.1 *Continued*

$n\, r_1 r_2$ Population	α_{11}	α_{12}	α_{13}	α_{21}	α_{22}	α_{23}
3 0 0 U-shaped	.54000	−.08000	.54000	−.60246	0	.60246
Rectangular	.50000	0	.50000	−.57735	0	.57735
Parabolic	.44048	.11905	.44048	−.57973	0	.57973
Triangular	.39456	.21088	.39456	−.58321	0	.58321
Normal	.33333	.33333	.33333	−.59082	0	.59082
D. expon.	.14815	.70370	.14815	−.62222	0	.62222
3 0 1 U-shaped	.54000	.46000		−.41828	.41828	
Rectangular	.00000	1.00000		−1.15470	1.15470	
Parabolic	.00000	1.00000		−1.15944	1.15944	
Triangular	.00000	1.00000		−1.16642	1.16642	
Normal	.00000	1.00000		−1.18164	1.18164	
D. expon.	.00000	1.00000		−1.25636	1.25636	
2 0 0 U-shaped	.50000	.50000		−.90370	.90370	
Rectangular	.50000	.50000		−.86603	.86603	
Parabolic	.50000	.50000		−.86959	.86959	
Triangular	.50000	.50000		−.87482	.87482	
Normal	.50000	.50000		−.88623	.88623	
D. expon.	.50000	.50000		−.94281	.94281	

are given in Table 12B.1. The variances of these estimates and their relative efficiencies for the same distributions and same sample sizes with all possible cases of censoring are given in Table 12B.2. The values corresponding to the normal and rectangular distributions are given in the tables for comparative purposes.

The change of the coefficients in the estimates and some other interesting remarks are given in references 2 and 3. Some remarks are mentioned here.

1. *Pertinent Coefficients and Efficiencies in the BLE of the Mean for Symmetric Distributions.* (*a*) *For complete samples.* From Table 12B.1 we can see that the coefficients of the best linear estimate of the mean (for complete samples) vary as the parent distribution undergoes change. It is of interest to notice the sequence of this variation in which the middle elements are to be equally weighted, zero-weighted, and negatively weighted.

The full sequence of changing weights appears to be incomplete in its natural extension, and the complete sequence should read:

(1) negative weights in the middle and large positive weights at the tails,
(2) zero weights in the middle and equal weights at the tails,
(3) less weight in the middle than at the tails,
(4) equal weights throughout,
(5) more weight in the center and less weight in the tails, but all positive weights,
(6) all the weight in the middle observations and zero weight in the tails,
(7) more than unity weight in the middle observations and negative weights in the tails.

This is the sequence that might be anticipated. The results show that (1) is U-shaped; (2) is rectangular; (3) is triangular or parabolic; (4) is

TABLE 12B.2

VARIANCES AND EFFICIENCIES OF THE BEST LINEAR ESTIMATES OF THE MEAN (θ^*_1) AND STANDARD DEVIATION (σ^*) FROM COMPLETE AND CENSORED SAMPLES IN DIFFERENT POPULATIONS ($\sigma = 1$)

n	r_1	r_2	Population	Variance of θ^*_1	Efficiency	Variance of σ^*	Efficiency
5	0	0	U-shaped	.06755	100.00	.04702	100.00
			Rectangular	.14284	100.00	.07143	100.00
			Parabolic	.17901	100.00	.09255	100.00
			Triangular	.19341	100.00	.10796	100.00
			Normal	.20000	100.00	.13332	100.00
			D. Expon.	.15843	100.00	.22883	100.00
5	0	1	U-shaped	.22460	30.74	.16744	28.08
			Rectangular	.23810	59.99	.14286	50.00
			Parabolic	.23632	75.75	.15728	58.84
			Triangular	.23096	83.74	.17191	62.80
			Normal	.21772	91.86	.19476	68.45
			D. Expon.	.15861	99.88	.30093	76.04
5	0	2	U-shaped	.72094	9.37	.55747	8.43
			Rectangular	.42857	33.33	.28571	25.00
			Parabolic	.36027	49.60	.27788	33.00
			Triangular	.31845	60.75	.28388	38.03
			Normal	.28393	62.80	.31809	41.91
			D. Expon.	.17326	91.43	.46356	49.36
5	0	3	U-shaped	2.21138	3.27	1.79354	2.62
			Rectangular	1.00000	14.28	.71429	10.00
			Parabolic	.79206	22.60	.64148	14.43
			Triangular	.70024	27.62	.63303	17.05
			Normal	.61123	32.72	.69571	19.16
			D. Expon.	.42277	37.47	.97683	23.43
5	1	1	U-shaped	.32619	20.71	.35361	13.30
			Rectangular	.28571	49.99	.28571	25.00
			Parabolic	.26208	68.30	.30137	30.71
			Triangular	.24710	78.27	.32064	33.67
			Normal	.22579	88.58	.32969	40.44
			D. Expon.	.15871	99.82	.43868	52.16

Efficiency is measured relative to the variance of the best linear estimate in the complete sample.

This table is reproduced from A. E. Sarhan, "Estimation of the mean and standard deviation by order statistics, Parts II and III," *Ann. Math. Statist.*, Vol. 26 (1956), pp. 505–511 and 576–592, with permission of W. Kruskal, editor of the *Annals of Mathematical Statistics*.

TABLE 12B.2 *Continued*

n	r_1	r_2	Population	Variance of θ^*_1	Efficiency	Variance of σ^*	Efficiency
5	1	2	U-shaped	.72171	9.36	1.12848	4.17
			Rectangular	.42857	33.33	.71429	10.00
			Parabolic	.36111	49.57	.71463	12.96
			Triangular	.31981	60.48	.73004	14.79
			Normal	.28683	69.73	.74061	18.00
			D. Expon.	.17559	90.23	.89356	25.61
4	0	0	U-shaped	.12798	100.00	.09550	100.00
			Rectangular	.20000	100.00	.11111	100.00
			Parabolic	.23155	100.00	.13360	100.00
			Triangular	.24435	100.00	.15142	100.00
			Normal	.25000	100.00	.18005	100.00
			D. Expon.	.20777	100.00	.29265	100.00
4	0	1	U-shaped	.41192	31.07	.34829	27.42
			Rectangular	.35000	57.14	.25000	44.44
			Parabolic	.32613	71.00	.25944	51.49
			Triangular	.30903	79.07	.27371	55.32
			Normal	.28701	87.10	.30208	59.60
			D. Expon.	.21118	98.39	.45045	64.97
4	0	2	U-shaped	1.46227	8.75	1.34117	7.12
			Rectangular	.80000	25.00	.66667	16.67
			Parabolic	.65730	35.23	.62257	21.46
			Triangular	.58328	41.89	.61144	24.37
			Normal	.51299	48.73	.67303	26.75
			D. Expon.	.33358	62.29	.94581	30.94
4	1	1	U-shaped	.53432	23.95	.93468	10.22
			Rectangular	.40000	50.00	.66667	16.67
			Parabolic	.35473	65.27	.67556	19.78
			Triangular	.32786	74.53	.69482	21.79
			Normal	.29820	83.84	.70572	25.51
			D. Expon.	.21007	98.91	.85130	34.38
3	0	0	U-shaped	.25013	100.00	.21616	100.00
			Rectangular	.30000	100.00	.20000	100.00
			Parabolic	.32081	100.00	.22210	100.00
			Triangular	.32940	100.00	.24150	100.00
			Normal	.33333	100.00	.27548	100.00
			D. Expon.	.29475	100.00	.43210	100.00
3	0	1	U-shaped	.53400	46.84	.32040	14.69
			Rectangular	.60000	50.00	.60000	33.33
			Parabolic	.53247	60.25	.58873	37.73
			Triangular	.49286	66.83	.59864	40.34
			Normal	.44867	74.29	.63783	43.19
			D. Expon.	.31942	92.28	.87601	49.33

normal; (5) is double exponential; (6) is the case where the median gets all the weight, which is like a double exponential but not exactly. For (7) the authors do not know any example at this time, that is, a distribution for which it would be best to estimate the mean by giving the middle element a weight greater than one and the elements on the tails some negative weights. This distribution represents, however, a natural continuity in the sequence.

As shown in Table 12B.2, the variance of the BLE estimate of the mean is lowest for the U-shaped distribution for all sample sizes greater than 2. For samples of size 2, the BLE of the mean has a variance equal to one-half for all symmetric distributions.

(*b*) *For incomplete samples.* The efficiency of estimating the mean under all conditions of censoring in small samples appears, from Table 12B.2, to increase from the U-shaped distribution, through the rectangular, parabolic, triangular, and normal distributions, and finally to the double exponential distribution. This sequence is consistent in all instances of censoring studied in this table.

In small samples from all symmetric distributions, the efficiency of estimation is always greater when the censoring is in as symmetric a fashion as possible. Thus, if we censor 40% of the observations from a sample of 5, the case of $r_1 = r_2 = 1$ has more efficiency than the case of $r_1 = 0$ and $r_2 = 2$. The same relationship holds in comparing censoring of $r_1 = 1$ and $r_2 = 2$ versus $r_1 = 0$ and $r_2 = 3$.

2. *Pertinent Coefficients and Efficiencies in the BLE of the Standard Deviation for Symmetric Distributions.* (*a*) *Complete samples.* The coefficient for the middle observation in all samples containing an odd number of observations is zero for the BLE of the standard deviation of all symmetric distributions. The magnitude of the variances of the BLE is in the same sequence as that previously shown, except for the U-shaped distribution. For the U-shaped distribution the variance of the BLE is greater than that of the rectangular for samples of size 2 and 3. Starting at $n = 4$, however, and with increasing sample size we can see in Table 12B.2 that the variance of the U-shaped distribution becomes the smallest among the distributions studied.

(*b*) *Incomplete samples.* The censoring of terminal observations from symmetric distributions changes the efficiencies of estimating the standard deviation in differing ways. The U-shaped distribution suffers the greatest loss and becomes the least efficiently estimated. The sequence of efficiencies is unaltered, however, from that observed in estimating the mean. The efficiency for the BLE of the standard deviation is always lower than that for the BLE of the mean, and the discrepancy between the two increases with additional censoring.

REFERENCES

1. A. E. Sarhan, "Estimation of the mean and standard deviation by order statistics," *Ann. Math. Statist.*, Vol. 25 (1954), pp. 317–328.
2. A. E. Sarhan, "Estimation of the mean and standard deviation by order statistics, Part II," *Ann. Math. Statist.*, Vol. 26 (1955), pp. 505–511.
3. A. E. Sarhan, "Estimation of the mean and standard deviation by order statistics, Part III," *Ann. Math. Statist.*, Vol. 26 (1955), pp. 576–592.

JULIUS LIEBLEIN

12C EXTREME-VALUE DISTRIBUTION

12C.1 The Three Asymptotic Types

"Extreme-value distribution" is the term given to the *asymptotic* distribution[1] of the extreme member of a sample of size n, that is, the *maximum* order statistic $X_{(1)}$ or the minimum $X_{(n)}$. To every asymptotic distribution of largest values $F_{\max}(x)$ corresponds an asymptotic distribution of smallest values $F_{\min}(x)$ which is obtained from the relation

$$F_{\min}(x) = 1 - F_{\max}(-x), \qquad f_{\min}(x) = f_{\max}(-x) \tag{12C.1.1}$$

and involves appropriate changes in the parameters.[2] If we use "min" and "max" to denote the smallest- and largest-value case, respectively, the following relations may be shown to hold:

$$E_{\min}(x^k) = (-1)^k E_{\max}(x^k), \tag{12C.1.2}$$

$$E_{\min}(X^k_{(i)}) = (-1)^k E_{\max}(X^k_{(n-i+1)}), \tag{12C.1.3}$$

$$E_{\min}(X_{(i)}X_{(j)}) = E_{\max}(X_{(n-i+1)}X_{(n-j+1)}). \tag{12C.1.4}$$

Therefore it will be sufficient to discuss only one of these forms in any situation.

It was mentioned in Subsection 6.4 that if an asymptotic form exists, it must be one of the three following types, the formulas of which are repeated here for convenience.

[1] See Subsection 6.4.
[2] See Subsection 6.3.

1. The form in the first column of Table 6.1 is called type 1, or *exponential* type, and has been studied and applied very extensively by Gumbel [4, 5] and later given attention by Lieblein [8] and A. I. Johnson [6].

$$\Lambda(x) = e^{-e^{-x}}, \qquad -\infty < x < \infty.$$

2. The form in the second column of Table 6.1 is type II and has been termed "Tippett's" form by H. C. S. Thom [12]. It has also been considered by A. I. Johnson [6]. However, it should be attributed to Fréchet.[3]

$$\Phi_\alpha(x) = \begin{cases} 0, & \text{if } x \le 0, \\ e^{-x^{-\alpha}}, & \text{if } x > 0. \end{cases}$$

3. The form in the third column of Table 6.1 is type III, where for the smallest-value case this gives the "Weibull" form, which has been studied and applied extensively by Weibull [13, 14] and also considered by A. I. Johnson [6] and Lieblein and Zelen [10].

$$\Psi_{\alpha,\min}(x) = \begin{cases} 0, & \text{if } x \le 0, \\ 1 - e^{-x^{\alpha}} & \text{if } x > 0. \end{cases}$$

All distributions $F[(x - \theta_1)/\theta_2]$ with $\theta_2 > 0$ have the same general shape and are said to be of the same "type." The estimation problem is, of course, to estimate the parameter θ_1 and/or θ_2 by means of order statistics.

12C.2 Estimation through Order Statistics

Estimation of the parameters θ_1, θ_2 will be included in determining the more general parameter

$$\theta = \theta(a, b) = a\theta_1 + b\theta_2. \tag{12C.2.1}$$

This can serve for a wide variety of purposes. Thus, if we find the general estimator $\theta^*(a, b)$, the individual parameters are estimated by

$$\theta^*_1 = \theta^*(1, 0), \qquad \theta^*_2 = \theta^*(0, 1). \tag{12C.2.2}$$

Furthermore, the $100P$-percentage point θ_P is estimated by

$$\theta^*_P = \theta^*[1, y(P)] = \theta^*_1 + y(P)\,\theta^*_2 \tag{12C.2.3}$$

where, for type I,[4]

$$y(P) = \begin{cases} -\lg(-\lg P), & \text{for largest-value case} \\ \lg[-\lg(1 - P)], & \text{for smallest-value case} \end{cases} \tag{12C.2.4}$$

[3] See Subsection 6.4.

[4] For types II and III, the expressions for $y(P)$ may readily be obtained by solving $F_{\max}[y(P)] = P$ for $F(\ )$, the appropriate type. The corresponding results for smallest values then follow from (12C.1.1).

where lg stands for the natural logarithm. Thus, if $P = 0.50$, we have the median; if $P = 1/e \approx 0.36788$, we have the mode θ_1 of the distribution $F_{\max}[(x - \theta_1)/\theta_2]$. Similarly, $1 - P = 1/e$ estimates the mode for the smallest-value case. The parameter θ_2 is not the standard deviation of F but a fixed multiple of it:

$$\theta_2 = \frac{\sqrt{6}}{\pi}\,(\text{SD}).$$

Finally, the mean of the extreme-value distribution is estimated by

$$\theta^*(1, \gamma), \qquad \theta^*(1, -\gamma) \tag{12C.2.5}$$

for the largest- and smallest-value cases, respectively, where

$$\gamma = 0.5772156649\ldots$$

is Euler's constant. This is shown by writing (in the largest-value case)

$$y = \frac{x - \theta_1}{\theta_2}. \tag{12C.2.6}$$

The distribution of y is parameter-free and has the mean $E(y) = \gamma$, and therefore y has been called the "reduced variate" by Gumbel [4, p. 13]. It is perfectly analogous to the "standardized variable" for the normal distribution:

$$t = \frac{x - \mu}{\sigma}. \tag{12C.2.7}$$

Taking expected values in (12C.2.6) gives

$$E(x) = \theta_1 + \gamma\theta_2 = \theta(1, \gamma) \qquad \text{and} \qquad \sigma^2(x) = \frac{\pi^2}{6}\,\theta_2^{\,2}$$

verifying the statements given.

12C.2.1 *Moments of Extreme Order Statistics.* "Extremal" order statistics refers to the order statistics in a random sample of size n from an extreme-value distribution.

Explicit formulas for the kth moment of a single order statistic and the joint moment of any two of them have been given by Lieblein [7, 9]. In the type I case [7] the kth moment involves binomial coefficients and the first k derivatives of $\Gamma(t)$ at $t = 1$; the joint moment involves a function related to the dilogarithm treated in reference 15. For type II and type III [9], the kth moment (provided it exists) involves the gamma function, and the joint moment involves gamma and incomplete beta functions.

Such calculations rapidly become unwieldy with increasing n, and attention is called to a new type of approach by Gunnar Blom ([1] or see Section 4B), involving what he calls "nearly best linear estimates." He starts with the relation [1, (5.3.1)]

$$EX_{(i)} = F^{-1}\left(\frac{i}{n+1}\right) + R_i \tag{12C.2.1.1}$$

where $F[(x - \theta_1)/\theta_2]$ is the population for which parameter estimates are sought—in our case, an extreme-value distribution—and shows that the error term

$$|R_i| < \frac{M}{n} \to 0, \qquad n \to \infty \tag{12C.2.1.2}$$

where M does not depend on i or n. Then [1, (6.2.1)] he generalizes (12C.2.1.1) to

$$EX_{(i)} = F^{-1}(\pi_i) + R'_i \tag{12C.2.1.3}$$

where

$$\pi_i = \frac{i - \alpha_{in}}{n - \alpha_{in} - \beta_{in} + 1}, \qquad \alpha_{in} < i, \quad \beta_{in} < n - i + 1,$$

$$R'_i = O\left(\frac{1}{n}\right). \tag{12C.2.1.4}$$

He shows how to choose the α's and β's ("α,β-corrections") to give a better approximation to the mean $EX_{(i)}$ than the more classical (12C.2.1.1). An analogous result is given [1, (6.3.1)] for the covariances of the order statistics:

$$\operatorname{Cov}(X_{(i)}, X_{(j)}) = \frac{\pi_i(1 - \pi_j)}{n+2} G'(\pi_i)G'(\pi_j) + R'_{ij}, \qquad i \leq j \tag{12C.2.1.5}$$

$$\pi_\nu = \frac{\nu - \alpha_{ij}}{n+1}, \qquad \nu = i, j$$

$$n' = n - \alpha_{ij} - \beta_{ij}, \qquad \alpha_{ij} < i, \qquad \beta_{ij} < n - i + 1$$

$$R'_{ij} = O\left(\frac{1}{n^2}\right).$$

With the aid of these tools suitably developed and generalized, he infers the conclusion [1, p. 130] that "*the exact least-squares method for finding best estimates can, in many cases encountered in practical applications, be replaced by the approximate method without any appreciable loss of efficiency*" (emphasis his).

12C.2.2 *The General Censored Case. Type I Distribution.* In the general case of a doubly censored sample, we have the observed values not, in general, for all the n order statistics but only for those left when the first r_1 and last r_2 (say) are unavailable:

$$X_{(r_1+1)} \leq X_{(r_1+2)} \leq \ldots \leq X_{(n-r_2)}, \qquad 0 < r_1 < n - r_2, \quad 0 < r_2 < n. \tag{12C.2.2.1}$$

Cases $r_1 = 0$ and/or $r_2 = 0$ give singly censored or uncensored cases.

An estimator for the general parameter θ is formed linearly,

$$\theta^* = \sum_{i=r_1+1}^{n-r_2} \omega_i(n, r_1, r_2)x_{(i)}, \tag{12C.2.2.2}$$

with the unknown weights to be determined so as to yield a minimum-variance unbiased estimator, according to the general least-squares procedure discussed in Chapter 3. Corresponding to (12C.2.1), the weights ω_i take the form

$$\omega_i(n, r_1, r_2) = aa_i(n, r_1, r_2) + bb_i(n, r_1, r_2), \qquad i = r_1 + 1, \ldots, n - r_2. \tag{12C.2.2.3}$$

The table of weights for the estimator θ^*, when $n = 2, 3, 4, 5, 6$ with $r_1 = 0$ and $k(= n - r_2)$ varying from 2 to 6, is reproduced from reference 10 and is shown in Table 12C.1. Here the constants a, b, although fixed, may remain unspecified throughout the calculation, giving a completely general solution. The values of a_i, b_i have been given:

in the uncensored case, $r_1 = r_2 = 0$, for $n = 1$ to 6 in Lieblein [8], in the singly censored case for smallest values, $r_1 = 0$, $r_2 = 0$ to $n - 2$, and $n = 2$ to 6, in Lieblein and Zelen [10]. This is shown in Table 12C.2.

The method can be extended beyond samples of six by breaking up larger samples into independent subgroups of six and averaging the estimates from the various subgroups, much as is done in using the average range.

An alternative order statistics method which avoids such subgroups—which some may consider an arbitrary feature—may be based on the "nearly best linear estimates" approach of Gunnar Blom described in Subsection 12C.2.1, which is applicable to censored samples as well.

A method analogous to fitting the straight line (12C.2.6) by least squares has been given by Gumbel [4]. Here, x is the observation, and y, the reduced variate, is the function [cf. $y(P)$ in (12C.2.4)]:

$$y = y(\Phi) = -\lg(-\lg \Phi)$$

where $\Phi = i/(n + 1)$ with i the rank of x in ascending order. The function $y(\Phi)$ is extensively tabulated [11, Table 2], or given in a graphical scale (see reference 4 for discussion of probability papers). Although the method was developed by Gumbel for complete samples, it can be extended to the censored case as indicated in Subsection 12C.2.4.

It may be pointed out that only classical asymptotic methods have been available for determining variances and efficiencies for the estimates from this method. However, the aforementioned method of Blom can be expected to give better approximations for the expected values and covariances and therefore for the efficiencies.

12C.2.3 *Treatment of Types II and III. Uncensored Samples.* The procedures given were described specifically for the type I distribution. They may be used in certain cases directly for types II and III, however, if the observations are replaced by their logarithms. For the transformation

$$y = \log x \tag{12C.2.3.1}$$

converts:

$$\text{type II, } \Phi_{\alpha,\max}(x) \quad \text{into} \quad e^{-e^{-\alpha y}}, \qquad -\infty < y < \infty, \quad 0 < \alpha < \infty$$

which is type I, $\Phi_{\max}$; also, the Weibull form,

$$\text{type III, } \Psi_{\alpha,\min}(x) = \begin{cases} 0, & x \leq 0 \\ 1 - e^{-x^{\alpha}}, & x > 0, \quad 0 < \alpha < \infty \end{cases}$$

is converted into $1 - e^{-e^{\alpha y}}$, or type I, $\Phi_{\min}$. Applications of this technique are discussed thoroughly in Lieblein and Zelen [10].

It should be noted that this logarithmic transformation is not general and does not allow for parameters in the general forms of types II and III, $\Phi_{\alpha}[(x - \theta_1)/\theta_2]$, $\Psi_{\alpha}[(x - \theta_1)/\theta_2]$. If θ_1 and θ_2, or even θ_1 alone, are absent, this transformation makes it possible to estimate the "shape" parameter α, and even θ_2, if the method is modified slightly. For example, with θ_2 alone present, type II becomes

$$\Phi_{\alpha,\max}\left(\frac{x}{\theta_2}\right) = \exp\left[-\left(\frac{x}{\theta_2}\right)^{-\alpha}\right] = \exp\left[-e^{-\alpha(y-\theta'_2)}\right], \qquad -\infty < y < \infty \tag{12C.2.3.2}$$

where

$$\theta'_2 = \lg \theta_2, \qquad y = \lg x. \tag{12C.2.3.3}$$

The extremal parameters α and θ'_2 can be evaluated by the straightforward procedure for type I, and then θ_2 can be obtained from (12C.2.3.3).

Further discussion will be in terms of type II. The modifications for type III will be apparent.

If, however, both θ_1 and θ_2 are present, whether or not α is known, a more empirical method is necessary. The simple transformation (12C.2.3.1) is replaced by

$$\left(\frac{x-\theta_1}{\theta_2}\right)^{-\alpha} = e^{-y}, \qquad (12C.2.3.4)$$

that is,

$$x = \theta_1 + \theta_2 e^{(1/\alpha)y} \qquad (12C.2.3.5)$$

(cf. Table 6.2 and Gumbel [5, p. 163, eq. 5]). Here x is the observed value; y is analogous to the reduced variate for type I, since (12C.2.3.5) converts

$$\Phi_{\alpha,\max}[(x-\theta_1)/\theta_2]$$

into

$$e^{-e^{-y}}.$$

Thus one approach for the general three-parameter case is as follows.[5] Order the observations in increasing size for the largest-value distribution, in decreasing size for the smallest-value case. Plot each observation x_i and its rank, $P_i = i/(n+1)$, on the usual extreme-value probability paper for type I. The corresponding reduced variate

$$y_i = \lg(-\lg P_i)$$

is given on a scale parallel to P_i [$\Phi(x)$ is used in place of P_i on the chart; see reference 4 for a specimen]. If the distribution is of type II, the points (x, y) will lie on a curve of the form (12C.2.3.5).[6] The three parameters in this curve may be evaluated empirically, for example, by a method used by Davis [2, p. 5 (type 5)], thus completing the estimation problem.

12C.2.4 *Alternative Method for Censored Samples.* The least-squares method of Gumbel for complete samples mentioned in Subsection 12C.2.2 can be extended to the censored case as well, as suggested by Godfrey [3]. The method depends on fitting a straight line (12C.2.6) for type I or the more general curve (12C.2.3.5) for types II and III by analytical or graphical means. The methods are essentially the same as in the censored case. For censoring merely loses some of the points (x, y) at the beginning and/or end of the line or curve, but the middle body of it is known, that is, all the points (x_i, y_i), $r_i + 1 \leq i \leq n - r_2$. This is so because y_i depends only on the rank, and rank is known for every actual observation. For example, if out of 50 failure test values the first 10 are lost, and 7 specimens still have not failed when the test is stopped, we have $50 - 10 - 7 = 33$ actual observations, with ranks running from 11 to 43.

[5] See Subsection 6.5.

[6] It has been pointed out by Gumbel that for suitably large α, types II and III approximate type I suitably scaled, and the curve becomes the straight line we should expect.

TABLE 12C.1

WEIGHTS w_i FOR THE ORDER STATISTICS ESTIMATOR $T_{n,k}$ FOR THE PARAMETER $t_F = u + \beta y_F$ OF THE EXTREME-VALUE DISTRIBUTION (SMALLEST VALUES) FROM A CENSORED SAMPLE OF $n = 2$ to 6, WHERE ONLY THE k SMALLEST VALUES ARE KNOWN

$$T_{n,k} = w_1x_1 + w_2x_2 + \ldots + w_kx_k w_j = a_j + b_jy_F$$
$$x_1 \leq x_2 \leq \ldots \leq x_k, k = 2 \text{ to } n$$

n	i	Means* $E_S(y_i')$ $= -E_L(y_i)$	Variances and covariances,* $\sigma'_{ij} = \sigma'_{ji} = \sigma_{ij} = \sigma_{ji}$					
			$j=1$	$j=2$	$j=3$	$j=4$	$j=5$	$j=6$
2	1	0. 11593 152	0. 68402 804	0. 48045 301				
	2	−1. 27036 285		1. 64493 407				
3	1	0. 40361 359	. 44849 796	0. 30137 144	0. 24375 810			
	2	−. 45943 263		. 65852 235	. 54629 438			
	3	−1. 67582 795			1. 64493 407			
4	1	0. 57351 263	. 34402 417	. 22455 344	0. 17903 454	0. 15388 918		
	2	−. 10608 352		. 41553 113	. 33720 966	. 29271 188		
	3	−. 81278 175			. 65180 236	. 57432 356		
	4	−1. 96351 003				1. 64493 407		
5	1	0. 69016 715	. 28486 447	. 18202 536	. 14358 737	0. 12257 865	0. 10901 329	
	2	. 10689 454		. 30849 748	. 24676 731	. 21226 644	. 18967 383	
	3	−. 42555 061			. 40598 292	. 35267 072	. 31716 095	
	4	−1. 07093 582				. 64907 319	. 58991 519	
	5	−2. 18665 358					1. 64493 407	
6	1	0. 77729 368	. 24658 20	. 15496 74	. 12121 61	. 10291 64	0. 09116 19	0. 08285 42
	2	. 25453 448		. 24854 56	. 19670 62	. 16806 28	. 14945 32	. 13619 10
	3	−. 18838 534			. 29761 59	. 25616 60	. 22887 90	. 20925 46
	4	−. 66271 588				. 40185 52	. 36145 55	. 33204 51
	5	−1. 27504 579					. 64769 96	. 59985 67
	6	−2. 36897 513						1. 64493 41

*The means are for smallest values (denoted by subscript S); for largest values, change all signs and reverse order of y's. The σ_{ij} are the same for both.

This table is reproduced from J. Lieblein and M. Zelen, "Statistical investigation of the fatigue life of deep-groove ball bearings," *J. Res., Nat. Bur. Stand.*, Vol. 57, No. 5 (1956), pp. 273–316.

TABLE 12C.2

MEANS, VARIANCES, AND COVARIANCES OF ORDER STATISTICS y_i IN SAMPLES OF n FROM THE REDUCED EXTREME-VALUE DISTRIBUTION $G(y) = \exp(-\epsilon^{-y})$, $n = 2$ to 6

For distribution of largest values, $y_1 \leq y_2 \leq \ldots \leq y_n$
For distribution of smallest values $y'_1 \geq y'_2 \geq \ldots \geq y'_n$

n	k		x_1	x_2	x_3	x_4	x_5	x_6
2	2	a_i	0. 0836269	0. 9163731				
		b_i	—. 7213475	. 7213475				
3	2	a_i	—. 3777001	1. 3777001				
		b_i	—. 8221012	0. 8221012				
	3	a_i	. 0879664	. 2557135	0. 6563201			
		b_i	—. 3747251	—. 2558160	. 6305411			
4	2	a_i	—. 7063194	1. 7063194				
		b_i	—. 8690149	0. 8690149				
	3	a_i	—. 0801057	. 0604316	1. 0196741			
		b_i	—. 4143997	—. 3258576	0. 7402573			
	4	a_i	. 0713800	. 1536799	. 2639426	0. 5109975		
		b_i	—. 2487965	—. 2239192	—. 0859035	. 5586192		
5	2	a_i	—. 9598627	1. 9598627				
		b_i	—. 8962840	0. 8962840				
	3	a_i	—. 2101141	—. 0860231	1. 2961372			
		b_i	—. 4343419	—. 3642463	0. 7985882			
	4	a_i	—. 0153832	. 0519642	. 1520750	. 8113440		
		b_i	—. 2730342	—. 2499429	—. 1491094	. 6720865		
	5	a_i	. 0583502	. 1088236	. 1676091	. 2462831	0. 4189341	
		b_i	—. 1844826	—. 1816564	—. 1304534	—. 0065354	. 5031278	
6	2	a_i	—1. 1655650	2. 1655650				
		b_i	—0. 9141358	0. 9141358				
	3	a_i	—. 3153968	—. 2034315	1. 5188283			
		b_i	—. 4466018	—. 3886492	0. 8352510			
	4	a_i	—. 0865378	—. 0280534	. 0649390	1. 0496521		
		b_i	—. 2858647	—. 2654739	—. 1858756	0. 7372142		
	5	a_i	. 0057311	. 0465729	. 1002523	. 1722784	. 6751653	
		b_i	—. 2015431	—. 1972753	—. 1536040	—. 0645894	. 6170118	
	6	a_i	. 0488669	. 0835221	. 1210527	. 1656192	. 2254909	0. 3554481
		b_i	—. 1458072	—. 1495332	—. 1267277	—. 0731937	. 0359868	. 4592751

[a] The means are for smallest values (denoted by subscript S); for largest values, change all signs and reverse order of y's. The σ_{ij} are the same for both.

This table is reproduced from J. Lieblein and M. Zelen, "Statistical investigation of the fatigue life of deep-groove ball bearings," *J. Res., Nat. Bur. Stand.*, Vol. 57, No. 5 (1956), pp. 273–316.

REFERENCES

1. Gunnar Blom, *Statistical Estimates and Transformed Beta Variables*, Almqvist and Wicksells, Uppsala, Sweden, 1958, John Wiley and Sons, New York, 1958.
2. D. S. Davis, *Empirical Equations and Nomography*, first edition, McGraw-Hill Book Co., New York, 1943.
3. M. L. Godfrey, "Theory of extreme values applied in tests," *Industrial Laboratories*, August 1958.
4. E. J. Gumbel, "Statistical theory of extreme values and some practical applications," *Appl. Math. Ser.*, 33, U.S. Dept. Commerce, Washington, D.C., 1954.

5. E. J. Gumbel, *Extremes, A Statistical Study*, John Wiley and Sons, New York, 1958.
6. A. I. Johnson, "Strength, safety, and economical dimensions of structures," *Bulletin of the Division of Building Statics and Structural Engineering*, No. 12 (1953), Royal Institute of Technology, Stockholm.
7. J. Lieblein, "On the exact evaluation of the variances and covariances of order statistics in samples from the extreme-value distribution," *Ann. Math. Statist.*, Vol. 24 (1953), pp. 282–287.
8. J. Lieblein, "A new method of analysing extreme-value data," NACA TN 3053, 1954.
9. J. Lieblein, "On moments of order statistics from the Weibull distribution," *Ann. Math. Statist.*, Vol. 26 (1955), pp. 330–333.
10. J. Lieblein and M. Zelen, "Statistical analysis of the fatigue life of deep groove ball bearings," *J. Res. Nat. Bur. Stand.*, Vol. 57 (Nov. 1956), RP 2719, pp. 273–316.
11. National Bureau of Standards, "Probability tables for the analysis of extreme-value data," Appl. Math. Ser., 22, U.S. Dept. Commerce, Washington, D.C. (1953).
12. H. C. S. Thom, "Frequency of maximum Wind Speeds," *Proc. Amer. Soc. Civil Engineers*, Vol. 80 (1954); separate, No. 539.
13. W. Weibull, "The phenomenon of rupture in solids," *Ing. Vetenskaps. Akad.*, Handl. 153 (1939).
14. W. Weibull, "A statistical representation of fatigue failure in solids," *Trans. Roy. Inst. Tech.*, Stockholm, No. 27, (1949).
15. L. Lewin, *Dilogarithm and Associated Functions*, MacDonald, London, 1958.

E. J. GUMBEL

12C.3 "Statistical Estimation of the Endurance Limit," An Application of Extreme-Value Theory[1,2]

12C.3.1 *Introduction.* The asymptotic theory of extreme values explained in Subsections 2.2 and 12C.1 and 2 has been used for analysis of oldest ages, the prediction of floods and droughts, in climatology, geology, aeronautics, and in the analysis of fatigue failure and breaking strength of materials (see reference [11]).

This section belongs to the latter category. It aims at a physical definition and a statistical procedure for the estimation of the endurance limit which is believed to be adequate to the underlying experimental design. The method is based on a specific interpretation of the existing

[1] Work done in part under a grant from the National Science Foundation.
[2] The author is greatly obliged to Professors S. B. Littauer and A. M. Freudenthal, Departments of Industrial and Civil Engineering, Columbia University, for their friendly help and constructive criticism.

data. It is linked to previous work on fatigue by the use of the probabilities of survival and by a common statistical theory, namely the asymptotic theory of smallest values. The endurance limit will be estimated as a parameter in this distribution.

In the usual fatigue tests, a number of specimens are submitted to a fixed stress S (load per unit of surface) during an increasing number of cycles N. In many observations all specimens tested break after a certain number of cycles. However, engineers often report specimens that survive millions of cycles. There are two interpretations: in the first, the phenomenon is considered the result of truncation at a certain number of cycles when the experiment is stopped. Then the mathematical treatment is similar to the treatment of truncated distributions. In the second, the phenomenon is considered to represent a physical reality which requires a specific approach. In the following, this line of thought is developed.

Data on fatigue failures lead to estimations of the probabilities of survival of a given number of cycles under a fixed stress. The probability of survival $l(x)$ of a nonnegative variate x is defined by $l(x) = 1 - F(x)$ where $F(x)$ stands for the usual probability function. The *minimum life* is defined as the greatest number of cycles for which the probability of survival for a given stress is unity. It is either zero or positive. The *true endurance limit* is defined as the greatest stress for which the probability of surviving an indefinite number of cycles is unity. Again it may be zero or positive. The validity of an estimation of the minimum life can be checked, because no specimen should break before this number of cycles under the given stress. But the estimate of the true endurance limit cannot be checked, since we cannot let the testing machine run for an indefinite number of cycles. For this reason, it has been customary to replace infinity by 10^7 cycles and to define the *endurance limit* as the largest stress for which the probability of surviving 10^7 cycles at this stress is unity. Since the verification of any theory must be based on observations, we have to accept this restriction, although it seems desirable that experiments be carried through to a higher number of cycles. Thus the estimation of the endurance limit based on 10^7 cycles is used as estimation of the true endurance limit, valid for an indefinite number of cycles.

Instead of the endurance limit, some authors [2, 4, 5] study the median fatigue stress, namely, that stress at which one-half the specimens tested for 10^7 cycles fail and the other half survive. This notion implies the interpretation of the stress as a statistical variate. It is also basic for our method. The median can be easily estimated, and the result is essentially independent of the distribution theory used. In contrast, estimates of the endurance limit depend strongly on the probabilistic interpretation of the data. The knowledge of the median fatigue stress is interesting for the comparison of different metals, alloys, heat treatments, and testing procedures. But it does not contribute to the safety of structures. In contrast, the knowledge of the true endurance limit would be very helpful for this purpose.

The tool for our estimation is the probability of permanent survival,[2] which is a function of the fatigue stress. This probability will be estimated from the numbers of specimen that failed and the numbers that survived a certain stress. Then it will be analyzed with the help of the third asymptotic distribution of smallest values, often called Weibull's distribution. This will lead to an estimation of the endurance limit. Numerical examples will show how the procedure can be carried through, but also that the amount of information now available is barely sufficient to warrant numerical results. Therefore, a testing program is given at the end, which, if carried through, will allow realization of the estimation.

12C.3.2 *The Probability of Permanent Survival and Its Estimation.* There are three representations of fatigue corresponding to two testing procedures.

1. A number of specimens n_S is submitted to a constant stress during an increasing number of cycles N up to failure. The numbers N are recorded, but the experiment is stopped at a high number, say $N = 10^7$ or $N = 10^8$. Either all specimens tested fail or all survive, or a certain proportion survive. This experiment is repeated for r different stresses. The corresponding theoretical concept is the probability of survival $l(N \mid S) = l_S(N)$ as a function of the variate N, for a constant value of S.

The survivorship function $l_S(N)$ has two important properties. (*a*) For constant values of S the probability $l_S(N)$ decreases if N increases. This follows immediately from the definition. (*b*) For constant values of N the probability $l_S(N)$ increases as S decreases. This follows from the physical aspect. Both properties are basic for the three representations and the estimations of the probabilities of survival.

2. A number of specimens n_S is submitted to a fixed stress S, and the experiment stops at N cycles. Each specimen either fails or survives. Thus there may be a proportion of survivors for this stress. The experiment is repeated for the same number of cycles under lower and higher stresses.

It is desirable that the domain of variation of the stress reach from the low stress where all specimens survive up to the high stress where all specimens may fail for the same number of cycles. The theoretical concept which corresponds to the proportion of survivals is the probability of survival $l(S \mid N) = l_N(S)$ as a function of S for constant numbers of cycles N. As soon as we interpret the percentage of survivals as a probability

[2] The author is obliged to Professors S. B. Littauer and A. M. Freudenthal, Columbia University, for their help and constructive criticism.

function, we are bound to consider the stress as the statistical variate to which this probability corresponds—although the stress is constant within each experiment.

Usually statistical observations show how often a certain value of the variate has occurred. From such data we construct the number of cases when a certain value is exceeded. In our problem the variate, the stresses, is given as a fixed value, and we observe for each stress the percentage of survivors. The specimens that survive a certain stress will fail under a larger stress, and those that fracture may fail under a smaller stress; but the influence of prestressing will not be considered here.

3. To a constant value of the probability of survival l corresponds a series consisting of numbers N_l for different values of S or S_l for different values of N. If N is plotted on the abscissa and S on the ordinate, an $(S,N)_l$ curve is obtained where S decreases for increasing values of N. Therefore, we may consider S_l as a function of N or N_l as a function of S. For decreasing values of the probability l the curves are shifted to the left, and no two such theoretical curves can ever intersect for homogeneous specimens and testing procedures. The $(S,N)_l$ diagram may be obtained from the $l_S(N)$ curves for different S, and in its turn leads to the $l_N(S)$ curves for different N.

The three representations are linked; each one must be compatible with the two others. Hence it is unacceptable to use an empirical relation for one of these functions if this expression contradicts the theoretical properties of the other two functions. Since there is no reason to doubt the continuity of the survivorship functions, any conclusion drawn from an alleged discontinuity of the $(S,N)_l$ diagram must be wrong. The three representations have an important common property. No two curves can ever intersect for homogeneous specimens, materials, and testing procedures. If intersections are observed they are due to errors of observation or (and) lack of homogeneity.

The terminology to be used in the following can best be explained by the study of a schematic $(S,N)_l$ diagram shown in Fig 12C.3.1. A doubly logarithmic scale is used here, because, as shown in a previous publication [7], this scale leads to straight lines in the special case for which the minimum life $N_{0,S}$ vanishes or is independent of S. If we draw straight lines parallel to the abscissa, we obtain survivorship functions in terms of N for constant values of S. If we draw straight lines parallel to the ordinate, we obtain survivorship functions in terms of S for constant values of N. Thus the existence of the $l_S(N)$ functions implies the existence of the $l_N(S)$ functions. Anybody willing to deny the existence of one function has to deny the existence of the other one too.

Each curve in Fig. 12C.3.1 corresponds to a fixed probability of survival. For reasons that will be shown later, the probability chosen for the curve designated by (2) is $l = 1/e = 0.36788$. The corresponding values of N as a function of S are written V_S and called *characteristic numbers of cycles* at failure. Inversely, the values of S as a function of N on this curve are written S_V and called *characteristic stresses*. The curve (3) corresponds to a small probability of survival, say $l = 10^{-5}$. For all combinations of S and N lying above this curve, failure is practically certain. The curve (1) shows the minimum lives. The corresponding

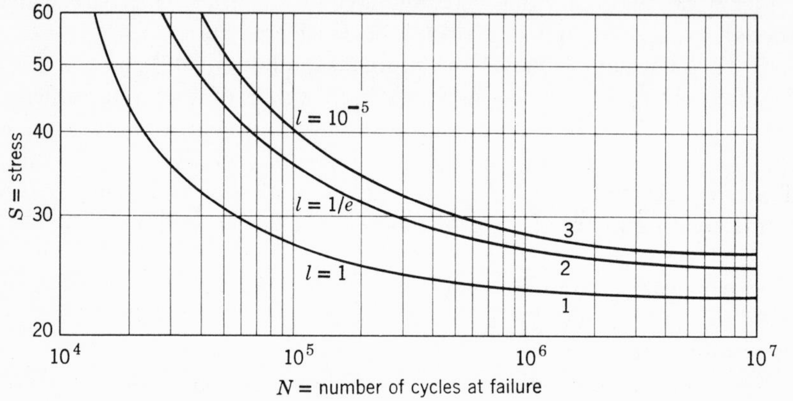

Fig. 12C.3.1 Schematic $(S, N)_l$ diagram.

stresses $S_{0,N}$ as functions of N are called *endurances*. Survival is certain for all combinations of S and N below curve (1). The stress

$$\lim_{N=\infty} S_{0,N} = S_0 \geq 0 \tag{12C.3.2.1}$$

is the true *endurance limit*.

Of course, the curves (1) and (3) cannot be actually observed but can only be extrapolated on the basis of a specific distribution theory.

If an analytic expression for $S_{0,N}$ could be derived from physical considerations, its extrapolation for $N = \infty$ would lead to knowledge of the true endurance limit. Since no such expression is known, S_0 has to be estimated by extrapolation from the probability of survival $l_N(S)$ valid for large values of N. For this purpose, we need a specific distribution, which will be introduced in a subsequent paragraph.

The $(S,N)_l$ curves in Fig. 12C.3.1 become parallel to the N-axis as N approaches 10^7. The stresses corresponding to these numbers of cycles will be called *fatigue stresses*. They are those stresses used in the testing of specimens up to 10^7 cycles. The fatigue stress corresponding to the probability curve of survival of 10^7 cycles will be used as an estimation of the true endurance limit.

The survivorship function $l_S(N)$ *in terms of the number of cycles* fulfills the boundary condition

$$l_S(N_{0,S}) = 1 \tag{12C.3.2.2}$$

where $N_{0,S} \geq 0$ is the minimum life. An axiomatic interpretation of this function was given by L. G. Johnson [12].

The second boundary condition for this survivorship function, namely

$$\lim_{N=\infty} l_S(N) = 0, \tag{12C.3.2.3}$$

holds for certain soft metals such as pure nickel, copper, and aluminum. To take account of the fact that for other metals and for small stresses there are specimens which survive 10^7 or more cycles, we have to introduce a boundary condition *in terms of stress*, namely

$$l_\infty(S) \geq 0, \tag{12C.3.2.4}$$

where $l_\infty(S)$ is called the *probability of permanent survival* for the stress S. For sufficiently large stresses, all pieces break after a finite number of cycles and $l_\infty(S)$ becomes zero. With decreasing values of S this probability in creases and reaches unity at the true endurance limit S_0. Since this extrapolation may lead to a value $S_0 = 0$, and since the minimum lives may be zero, the existence of nonvanishing minimum lives does not imply the existence of a nonvanishing true endurance limit, and vice versa.

The question now is how to estimate the probabilities $l_S(N)$ and $l_\infty(S)$. Let n_S specimens be tested under a fixed stress S and assume they all break. Let $N_1 \leq N_2 \leq \ldots \leq N_m \leq \ldots \leq N_n$ be the observed numbers of cycles at fracture. Then the probability $l_S(N)$ of surviving N_m cycles is estimated as the rate

$$\hat{l}_S(N_m) = 1 - \frac{m}{(n_S + 1)}, \tag{12C.3.2.5}$$

which is largest, but less than unity, for the smallest cycle N_1 and is smallest, but greater than zero, for the largest cycle N_n. This "plotting position" is distribution-free and is especially designed for use on probability paper. The reasons for this choice are explained in reference 9. The characteristic number of cycles at failure V_S can be estimated from (12C.3.2.5) as the value N'_m corresponding to $\hat{l}_S(N'_m) = 0.36788$.

The plotting position will also be used to estimate the probability of permanent survival $l_\infty(S)$. Assume that only n'_S specimens fail and that

$n_S - n'_S$ specimens survive $N = 10^7$ cycles. Then the usual estimate for the probability of permanent survival is

$$\hat{l}_\infty(S) = 1 - \frac{n'_S}{n_S} = \frac{n_S - n'_S}{n_S}. \tag{12C.3.2.6}$$

In contrast to this procedure, we use the estimate

$$\hat{l}_\infty(S) = 1 - \frac{n'_S + 1}{n_S + 1} = \frac{n_S - n'_S}{n_S + 1}. \tag{12C.3.2.7}$$

Both rates are zero for $n'_S = n_S$, that is, when all specimens break. However, the first estimate is equal to unity if $n'_S = 0$, that is, when no specimens break, whereas the second estimate leads to $1 - 1/(n_S + 1)$, an expression which converges to unity for n_S increasing.

It is easy to show that the estimate (12C.3.2.7) is consistent with (12C.3.2.5). According to this formula, the frequency of survival diminishes from one observed number of cycles to the next one by $1/(n_S + 1)$. Let the largest number of cycles at failure be $N_{n'_S}$. Since n'_S specimens break, the corresponding probability of survival is estimated from (12C.3.2.5) as

$$\hat{l}_S(N_{n'_S}) = 1 - \frac{n'_S}{n_S + 1}. \tag{12C.3.2.8}$$

The estimated probability of survival for the next specimen which does not break is the estimate of permanent survival, which leads by subtracting $1/(n_S + 1)$ from the preceding expression to

$$\hat{l}_\infty(S) = 1 - \frac{n'_S + 1}{n_S + 1}$$

as claimed in (12C.3.2.7). Another proof for this formula is given in reference 7.

The estimate (12C.3.2.7) is slightly smaller than (12C.3.2.6), and the difference between both increases with increasing probability, that is, with decreasing values of the stress. Therefore, the use of (12C.3.2.7) will lead to a smaller estimate for the median stress than the usual one.

There is a logical difference between the estimates $l_\infty(S)$ and $l_S(N)$. In the latter formula each observed number of cycles at failure corresponds to one or several broken specimens. In the graphs the observed numbers of cycles $N_m (m = 1,2, \ldots, n)$ are from (12C.3.2.5) equally spaced on the probability scale. In the first formula, however, only the percentage of fractures is used for each stress level. Therefore these estimates have no direct relation to the total number of fractures.

The error of estimation $\sigma[\hat{l}_\infty(S)]$ given in reference 8 is

$$\sigma[\hat{l}_\infty(S)]\sqrt{n+2} = \sqrt{\hat{l}_\infty(S)[1 - \hat{l}_\infty(S)]}. \qquad (12C.3.2.9)$$

The right side is equal to one-half for the median fatigue stress and diminishes if we pass on to larger and smaller probabilities of permanent survival, that is, to smaller and larger stresses. Therefore, it is a safe procedure to use the same number of specimens n_S for all stresses. Then the large probabilities of permanent survival corresponding to the small stresses, in which we are particularly interested in our endeavor to estimate the endurance limit, have a smaller error of estimation.

Formula 12C.3.2.9 does not solve the question of what experimental errors can be tolerated. As an answer, we use the following *postulate*. The experimental errors are too large if a rate of permanent survival increases with increasing stress, that is, moves in the wrong direction. Of course, this statement cannot be proved, but it turns out to be a good working hypothesis. The question what should be done if the postulate is not fulfilled will be answered in connection with the study of observations in Subsection 12C.3.4.

If the probabilities of permanent survival are estimated for given values of the fatigue stresses S, or if S is given in terms of these probabilities, a procedure proposed by Weibull [16], extrapolation toward small probabilities leads to a large stress where the probability of survival is so small that all pieces tested should break. This can be checked from the observations. An estimate of the median fatigue stress is obtained by interpolation as the value corresponding to the probability one-half. Finally, extrapolation toward a probability equal to unity leads to the estimation $\hat{S}_0$ of the endurance limit.

Up to now it was assumed that the $(S, N)_l$ curves in Fig. 12C.3.1 are and remain parallel to the N-axis after 10^7 cycles. An alternative assumption is that the curves converge with increasing N to a single curve, namely, the $N_{0,S}$ curve, which is and remains parallel to the abscissa from $N = 10^7$ onward. In this case, the indices ∞ in the preceding and following formulas have to be replaced by 10^7, but the essence of the theory and methods remains the same, since it is reasonable to assume that the value S_0 obtained by extrapolating $l_N(S)$ for $N = 10^7$ to unity will be the same as that value obtained by extrapolating the $S_{0,N}$ curve to infinity.

12C.3.3 *Estimation of the Endurance Limit.* For the extrapolation of the $l_\infty(S)$ curve toward unity we need analytic expressions for the probability of permanent survival.

The prevailing statistical analysis is as follows. First, the existence of a nonvanishing true endurance limit is either expressly or tacitly accepted as a well-known "empirical fact;" second, the normal or the logarithmic normal probability function is introduced to estimate the median fatigue stress.[3]

The consequences of the normal assumption are as follows. Let $\breve{S}$ be the median fatigue stress and let S_1 and S_2 be two fatigue such stresses that

$$\breve{S} - S_1 = S_2 - \breve{S}.$$

To the interval $S_1 \pm \Delta S$ corresponds then the same probability of failure as that to the interval $S_2 \pm \Delta S$. In reality, a decrease in the stress cannot have the same effect as an increase by the same amount. Therefore, this model cannot be used to estimate the median fatigue stress. In addition, the endurance limit cannot be defined for this distribution.

Other authors use the logarithmic normal distribution where the stresses are replaced by their logarithms. With a relative increase or decrease of the stresses, the probability of survival tends then in the same way toward zero or unity. In reality, a small relative increase of the stress may lead to failure of all specimens, whereas a corresponding small decrease may have no large-scale influence.

To find an adequate probability function, we start from the fact that each cycle sustained under a given stress constitutes an observation on failure or survival. The number of *these* observations is very large, $N = 10^7$ or 10^8. Therefore, the probability of permanent survival as a function of the stresses has an asymptotic character, valid for large numbers of observations.

The stress at failure considered as a variate measures the strength of the specimen. Now each specimen contains impurities which weaken the body, and the piece with the largest crack will have the smallest strength. Therefore, the stress at failure is a smallest value. Both arguments point in the direction of the asymptotic probability of the smallest value of a nonnegative variate.

A third argument is as follows. If we consider smaller or larger specimens, the probability of failure as a function of the stress should remain the same except for changes in the parameters. This stability—the size effect in physical terminology—holds for this probability function.

[3] The normal distribution of the stresses has been proposed by F. Bastenaire in his thesis, "Etude statistique et physique de la dispersion des resistances et des endurances à la fatigue" (Paris, 1960), and in his paper "Etude de la rupture par fatigue par les methodes statistiques," *Bull. Inst. Int. Statist.*, 33e Session (Paris, 1961). A systematic comparison of the results of different distributions used for estimating the endurance limit is given in the thesis of D. Dorf, "Vergleich verschiedener statistischer Transformationsverfahren auf ihre Anwendbarkeit zur Ermittlung der Dauerschwingfestigkeit" (Berlin, 1961), which appeared after this article was finished.

Other physical reasons for the use of this theory are given in an earlier publication [7].

If we accept it, the probability of permanent survival as a function of the stress is

$$l_\infty(S) = \exp\left[-\left(\frac{S - S_0}{S_V - S_0}\right)^\beta\right], \qquad l_\infty(S_0) = 1 \quad (12C.3.3.1)$$

where S_V, henceforth called the *characteristic fatigue stress*, is such that

$$l_\infty(S_V) = \frac{1}{e}. \qquad (12C.3.3.1a)$$

Formula 12C.3.3.1 was first used by Weibull [16] on a purely heuristic basis. It has been analyzed [6, 10] in connection with a probability paper which facilitates its use. Tables of a probability function which is linked to (12C.3.3.1) were published by the National Bureau of Standards [15].

The endurance limit S_0 is reached by extrapolation of (12C.3.3.1) to unity. This means that its estimation is reduced to the problem of estimating a parameter in the probability function (12C.3.3.1).

The endurance limit S_0 and the characteristic fatigue stress S_V are parameters of location. Therefore, it is natural to use S_V as a representative of a given series of observations instead of the median or mean fatigue stress which depends on the value of the other parameter β. This parameter has no dimension. The case $\beta = 1$ leads to the exponential distribution; the case $\beta = 2$ is called Rayleigh's distribution. With increasing values of $1/\beta$, the probability of survival decreases and the distribution spreads.

The analysis of the probability function (12C.3.3.1) is facilitated by the transformation

$$\left(\frac{S - S_0}{S_V - S_0} = e^y\right)^\beta$$

which links the third asymptotic distribution of smallest values to the first one [11, p. 288] and (12C.3.2.3). It follows from (12C.3.3.1) that

$$y = \lg\left[-\lg l_\infty(S)\right] \qquad (12C.3.3.2)$$

and

$$y = \beta[\lg(S - S_0) - \lg(S_V - S_0)], \qquad (12C.3.3.2a)$$

where lg stands for the natural logarithm. Since the expectation Ey and the standard deviation σ_y of the reduced variable y are [11, p. 173]

$$Ey = -\gamma, \qquad \sigma_y = \frac{\pi}{\sqrt{6}}$$

respectively, it follows that the expectation E and standard deviation σ of $\lg(S - S_0)$ are

$$E \lg(S - S_0) = \lg(S_V - S_0) - \frac{\gamma}{\beta},$$

$$\sigma[\lg(S - S_0)] = \frac{1}{\beta}\frac{\pi}{\sqrt{6}},$$

whence

$$\frac{1}{\beta} = \frac{\sqrt{6}\sigma[\lg(S - S_0)]}{\pi}. \qquad (12C.3.3.3)$$

The value of β depends on the units in which the stresses are measured. The formula (12C.3.3.3) indicates that the estimation of β depends on the estimation of S_0.

It has been shown previously [10] that for this type of distribution

$$\sigma[\lg(S - S_0)] > \sigma[\lg S], \qquad \text{if } S_0 > 0.$$

If we write $1/\beta_1$ for the case $S_0 = 0$, it follows that

$$1/\beta > 1/\beta_1. \qquad (12C.3.3.3a)$$

Consequently, we have to expect that the estimation of $1/\beta_1$ made under the assumption $S_0 = 0$ will lead to a smaller value than the estimation of $1/\beta$ made under the assumption $S_0 > 0$.

Formula 12C.3.3.3 cannot be used for the estimation of β, since S_0 is unknown. The estimations, obtained by another method to be shown later, lead to values $\beta > 1$.

If the characteristic fatigue stress S_V lies within the range of the stress used, that is, if two stresses $S_1 < S_2$ exist for which the rates of permanent survival are slightly above and below $l_\infty(S_V) = 0.36788$, the characteristic fatigue stress may be estimated from (12C.3.3.1*a*) and (12C.3.3.2*a*) as the stress corresponding to $y = 0$. This estimation is obtained by linear interpolation between the logarithms of the two stresses S_1 and S_2 according to the corresponding values of $y_1 > 0$, $y_2 < 0$. If only a few stresses have been used in the experimentation, however, it seems better to use all observations for the estimation of each parameter.

The estimation of the parameters in extremal distribution is a thorny problem (see references 6, 9, 10, 13, and 14, the literature quoted in reference 13, and Section 12C). Neither the maximum likelihood nor the minimum χ^2 method nor the use of order statistics leads to simple solutions. The method of moments used [6] for a similar problem requires the calculation of the skewness which is affected by a high error of estimation. Since in the present problem the number of observations is very small, this method was not chosen. Instead, the classical least-squares method is applied since it is known that it leads to unbiased, consistent, and efficient estimates.

For r stresses S_i used in the experimentation equation (12C.3.3.2a) leads to the r equations

$$y_i = \beta \lg (S_i - S_0) - \beta \lg (S_V - S_0), \qquad i = 1, 2, \ldots, r. \qquad (12C.3.3.4)$$

The values y_i are obtained from the Bureau of Standards' tables [15] after replacing the probabilities $l_\infty(S)$ in (12C.3.3.2) by their estimates (12C.3.2.8).

In the particular case that the true endurance limit vanishes, $S_0 = 0$, equation 12C.3.3.4 simplifies to

$$y_i = \beta \lg S_i - \beta \lg S_V. \qquad (12C.3.3.4a)$$

This relation, which is linear in y_i and $\lg S_i$, can be used on the logarithmic extremal probability paper [6, 9, 11]. In this scheme $\log S$ (where log stands for the decimal logarithm) is traced in linear scale on the abscissa. On the ordinate we trace y, also in linear scale, and write $l_\infty(S)$ on a parallel scale at the corresponding place obtained from (12C.3.3.2) with the help of the Bureau of Standards table [15].

If the reduced values y_i traced against the logarithms of the stresses are sufficiently near the straight line (12C.3.3.4a), the true endurance limit may be, but need not be assumed to be, zero. If $S_0 > 0$, then (12C.3.3.4) does not represent a straight line. Instead, the $l_\infty(S)$ curve is bent to the right for values of S approximating S_0 and finally converges to a parallel to the ordinate. Conversely, if the rates $\hat{l}_\infty(S)$ traced against $\log S$ form such a curve, this is to be taken as an indication of the existence of a nonvanishing endurance limit. Thus the behavior of the curve representing the probability of permanent survival at the low stresses is decisive for the acceptance or rejection of the hypothesis that the true endurance limit vanishes. The method would fail if the estimated probabilities of permanent survival traced on extremal paper against the logarithms of the stresses were definitely bent to the left—a phenomenon which so far has not been observed for homogeneous materials.

Consider first that the estimated probabilities of permanent survival lie approximately on a straight line which allows the estimate $\hat{S}_0 = 0$. The study of this case is necessary since we want to compare it to the consequences implied in the estimation $\hat{S}_0 > 0$. Equation 12C.3.3.1 becomes

$$l_\infty(S) = \exp [-(S/S_V)^{\beta_1}]. \qquad (12C.3.3.1b)$$

We write here β_1 instead of β since the two scale parameters influence the probabilities (12C.3.3.1) and (12C.3.3.1*b*) in different ways. The two parameters S_V and β_1 are estimated from the equations

$$y_i = \beta'_1 \log S_i - k_1, \qquad i = 1, 2, \ldots, r, \qquad (12C.3.3.4b)$$

where

$$\beta'_1 = 2.30259\beta_1, \qquad k_1 = \beta'_1 \log S_V. \qquad (12C.3.3.5)$$

If we assume the S_i as fixed and minimize the errors in y_i, the method of least squares leads to the two normal equations

$$\sum y_i = \beta'_1 \sum \log S_i - rk_1 \qquad (12C.3.3.6)$$
$$\sum y_i \log S_i = \beta'_1 \sum (\log S_i)^2 - k_1 \sum \log S_i$$

where the sums extend from 1 to r and have to be weighted according to the number n_S of specimens tested under the different stresses. Let $1/\hat{\beta}'_1$ and $\hat{k}_1$ be the solutions. Then the characteristic fatigue stress is estimated from (12C.3.3.5) as

$$\log \hat{S}_V = \hat{k}_1/\hat{\beta}'_1. \qquad (12C.3.3.7)$$

A check on the calculations is furnished by the comparison of this value to the independent estimate of S_V outlined after (12C.3.3.3*a*). The theoretical stresses obtained from

$$\log \hat{S} = \log \hat{S}_V + y/\hat{\beta}'_1 \qquad (12C.3.3.8)$$

may be traced on the logarithmic extremal probability paper, together with the observations. This provides a graphical comparison between the theory and the observations. The value $\check{y}$ corresponding to the median fatigue stress is obtained from (12C.3.3.2) with the help of the Bureau of Standards tables [15] as $\check{y} = -0.36651$. The introduction of this value into (12C.3.3.8) leads to the estimate of the median fatigue stress.

Consider now the case $S_0 > 0$. Since the function including the unknown parameter S_0 in (12C.3.3.4) is logarithmic, it has to be estimated by approximation and, if necessary, iterations. We choose a certain small stress E, which is smaller than the smallest observed stress, and put

$$S_0 = E - \epsilon \qquad (12C.3.3.9)$$

where ϵ is a positive or negative small stress to be estimated. The choice of E is facilitated by tracing the differences $S_i - E$ on logarithmic extremal probability paper and choosing E in such a way that an approximately straight line is obtained. In addition, we put as previously

$$\beta' = 2.30259\beta, \qquad k = \beta' \log (S_V - S_0), \qquad \text{and} \quad \delta = \beta\epsilon. \qquad (12C.3.3.10)$$

The equations (12C.3.3.4) become in first approximation after expansion of the natural logarithm and introduction of the decimal logarithms

$$y_i = \beta' c_i + \delta h_i - k, \qquad i = 1, 2, \ldots, r \qquad (12C.3.3.11)$$

where

$$c_i = \log (S_i - E), \qquad h_i = 1/(S_i - E) > 0 \qquad (12C.3.3.12)$$

are known numerical values. The parameter δ has the dimension of a stress, whereas the factors h_i have the dimension of the reciprocal of a stress. The quotient

$$\epsilon = \delta/\beta \qquad (12C.3.3.13)$$

is from (12C.3.3.9) and (12C.3.3.10), the correction for the first estimation E of the true endurance limit.

Since the equations (12C.3.3.11) are linear in the three parameters β', δ, and k, the method of least squares leads as previously to normal equations which are now

$$\begin{aligned} \sum y_i &= \beta' \sum c_i + \delta \sum h_i - rk, \\ \sum y_i c_i &= \beta' \sum c_i^2 + \delta \sum h_i c_i - k \sum c_i, \\ \sum y_i h_i &= \beta' \sum c_i h_i + \delta \sum h_i^2 - k \sum h_i. \end{aligned} \qquad (12C.3.3.14)$$

The sums taken from 1 to r have to be weighted according to the numbers n_S of specimens. Elimination of k reduces the system (12C.3.3.14) to two equations which lead to the estimates $\hat{\beta}'$ and $\hat{\delta}$. Then $1/\beta$ is estimated from (12C.3.3.10), and the true endurance limit is estimated from (12C3.3.9.) as

$$\hat{S}_0 = E - \hat{\delta}/\hat{\beta}. \qquad (12C.3.3.15)$$

Of course the estimate (12C.3.3.15) of the endurance limit has a standard error which will decrease with an increasing number of stresses used and with the number of specimens tested at each stress level.

For the comparison of the observed and theoretical survivorship function in terms of stress, we need the characteristic fatigue stress, which requires the knowledge of k/β. The estimate $\hat{k}/\hat{\beta}$ is obtained from the first equation (12C.3.3.14) as

$$\hat{k}/\hat{\beta} = 2.30259\bar{c} + \hat{\delta}\bar{h}/\hat{\beta} - \bar{y}/\hat{\beta} \qquad (12C.3.3.16)$$

where the bars indicate sample means. Then the characteristic fatigue stress is estimated from (12C.3.3.10) as

$$\hat{S}_V = \hat{S}_0 + e^{\hat{k}/\hat{\beta}}. \qquad (12C.3.3.17)$$

This may be checked against the independent estimate mentioned earlier. Finally, the theoretical values $\hat{S}$ as functions of the reduced variate y are obtained from (12C.3.3.2a) as

$$\log(\hat{S} - \hat{S}_0) = \log(S_V - \hat{S}_0) + y/\hat{\beta}' \qquad (12C.3.3.18)$$

or

$$\hat{S} = \hat{S}_0 + (\hat{S}_V - \hat{S}_0)e^{y/\hat{\beta}}. \qquad (12C.3.3.18a)$$

The median fatigue stress is estimated by introducing $\breve{y} = -0.36651$ in (12C.3.3.18).

The theoretical stresses obtained from (12C.3.3.18a) are compared to the observations by tracing both series on extremal probability paper. If the fit is deemed insufficient because the scatter is too large, the procedure has to be repeated by choosing the estimate $\hat{S}_0$ as a new starting value E.

A numerical test is obtained from the sum of the weighted squared deviations between the observed and theoretical values of S_i:

$$D^2 = (\hat{S}_i - S_i)^2 w_i \qquad (12C.3.3.19)$$

where w_i stands for the weight of the stress S_i. This value will be calculated for the two-parameter and the three-parameter curves, and the hypothesis leading to a larger value of D^2 will be rejected. However, the two theories $S_0 = 0$ and $S_0 > 0$ are not strictly comparable, because the parameters, two in the first case and three in the second, are estimated by the same principle but different procedures. In the second case we may need successive approximations. Therefore the errors of estimation differ.

In general, a curve with three parameters will give a better fit than a curve based on two parameters. Inversely, if the linear function gives a better fit than the three-parameter curve, the estimation of zero for the true endurance limit is to be preferred. In making this choice, we assume that the better fit to the observed data also yields a better extrapolation. This assumption may not always hold. If the estimation of zero for the endurance limit cannot be accepted on the basis of physical considerations, the calculation only proves that the experiments were stopped too soon and have to be repeated for lower stresses, higher numbers of cycles, and/or for a larger number of specimens.

12C.3.4 *Numerical Examples.* The methods outlined in the preceding paragraphs will now be used for the few sets of observations on permanent survival which are adequate for statistical interpretation. As an example of the experimental difficulties, consider the observations (Table A) recorded by Cummings, Stulen, and Schulte [3] for $n_S = 10$ notched specimens of SAE 4340 steel of nominal 260-k.s.i. hardness tested for 10^7 cycles by 10 machines claimed to be homogeneous.

TABLE A

RATES OF PERMANENT SURVIVAL—CUMMINGS, STULEN, AND SCHULTE

Stress S in 1000 p.s.i.	Survivors $n_S - n'_S$	Estimation $\hat{l}_\infty(S)$
31	10	0.909
36	9	0.818
41	9	0.818
43.5	9	0.818
46	7	0.633
48.5	10	0.909
51	3	0.273
53.5	4	0.364
56	1	0.091
58.5	1	0.091

The rates in column 3 are obtained from (12C.3.2.7). Instead of decreasing with increasing stress, some rates remain constant, others increase. This proves that either the machines or the specimens were not homogeneous or the stress levels were not sufficiently separated. The machines were insensitive to the differences of the stresses. Finally, the sample size is too small. Clearly, these data cannot be used for the estimation of permanent survival. In such cases, where the rates of survival for different stresses are equal or even move in the wrong direction, further observations under the same stress levels may lead to a clear distinction, provided the stress levels are sufficiently separated. But whether this is so will be known only by the outcome of the experiment.

Other experimental results are shown in Table B.

The first three lines are taken from Bender's observations [1], where the amplitudes of vibration were considered as proportional to S. The two following series were observed by Cazaud [2] for conical and toroidal steel specimens respectively and for $N = 10^8$. The stresses are measured in kg/mm^2. In the fourth series for SAE 1050 steel, due to Epremian and Mehl [5], and in the fifth series for SAE 1050 spheroidized eutectoid steel, observed by Dieter, Mehl, and Horne [4], the stresses are given in 1000 p.s.i. The estimations in column 4 are obtained from (12C.3.2.7), and the reduced variates, column 5, are obtained from (12C.3.3.2) with the help of the Bureau of Standards table [15].

The five series of permanent survival rates $\hat{l}_\infty(S)$ of Table B in terms of stress for constant numbers of cycles are traced against log S on extremal probability paper[4] in Figs. 12C.3.2 (Cazaud I and II),

[4] The word frequency in the graphs has the same meaning as rate in the text.

TABLE B

RATES OF PERMANENT SURVIVAL

	1 Stress, S	2 Sample Size, n_S	3 Survivors, $n_S - n'_S$	4 Estimation, $\hat{l}_\infty(S)$	5 Reduced Variate, y
Bender					
	100	122	90	0.73171	−1.16356
	110	122	40	0.32520	+0.11628
	120	122	6	0.04878	+1.10540
Cazaud I					
	20.5	22	21	0.91304	−2.39716
	21.5	20	12	0.57143	−0.58050
	22.5	21	2	0.09091	+0.87464
Cazaud II					
	20.1	19	18	0.90000	−2.25037
	21.1	21	11	0.50000	−0.36651
	22.1	20	5	0.23810	+0.36121
Epremian and Mehl					
	40.0	17	13	0.72222	−1.12264
	40.5	21	13	0.59090	−0.64223
	41.0	21	7	0.31818	+0.13553
	41.5	20	7	0.33333	+0.09405
	42.0	18	2	0.10526	+0.81152
	42.5	21	1	0.04545	+1.12854
Dieter, Mehl, Horne					
	40.0	20	15	0.71429	−1.08930
	41.5	20	10	0.47619	−0.29850
	43.0	20	3	0.14286	+0.66572
	45.0	20	1	0.04762	+1.11334

TABLE C

MODIFIED RATES OF PERMANENT SURVIVAL (EPREMIAN AND MEHL)

Stress Level S in 1000 p.s.i.	 Log S	Sample Size, n_S	Survivors, $n_S - n'_S$	Estimate, $\hat{l}_\infty(S)$	Reduced Variate, y
40.0	1.60206	17	13	0.72222	−1.12264
40.5	1.60746	21	13	0.59090	−0.64223
41.25	1.61542	41	14	0.33333	+0.09405
42.0	1.62325	18	2	0.10526	+0.81152
42.5	1.62839	21	1	0.04545	+1.12854

12C.3.3 (Bender), 12C.3.4 (Epremian and Mehl), and 12C.3.6 (Dieter, Mehl, and Horne). In Fig. 12C.3.5 the data of Epremian and Mehl are drawn in linear scales.

In Epremian and Mehl's observations, the estimated rate of permanent survival for the stress 41.5 exceeds that of the stress 41.0. From a purely statistical standpoint, such a phenomenon can easily happen. The number of specimens tested is small, 21 and 20 respectively. The use of (12C.3.2.9) shows that the difference 0.01515 is far below the standard error of this difference. In order to use these observations, we bring the two critical groups for $S = 41$ and 41.5 into one group, to which is attributed a mean stress 41.25. This is done in Table C.

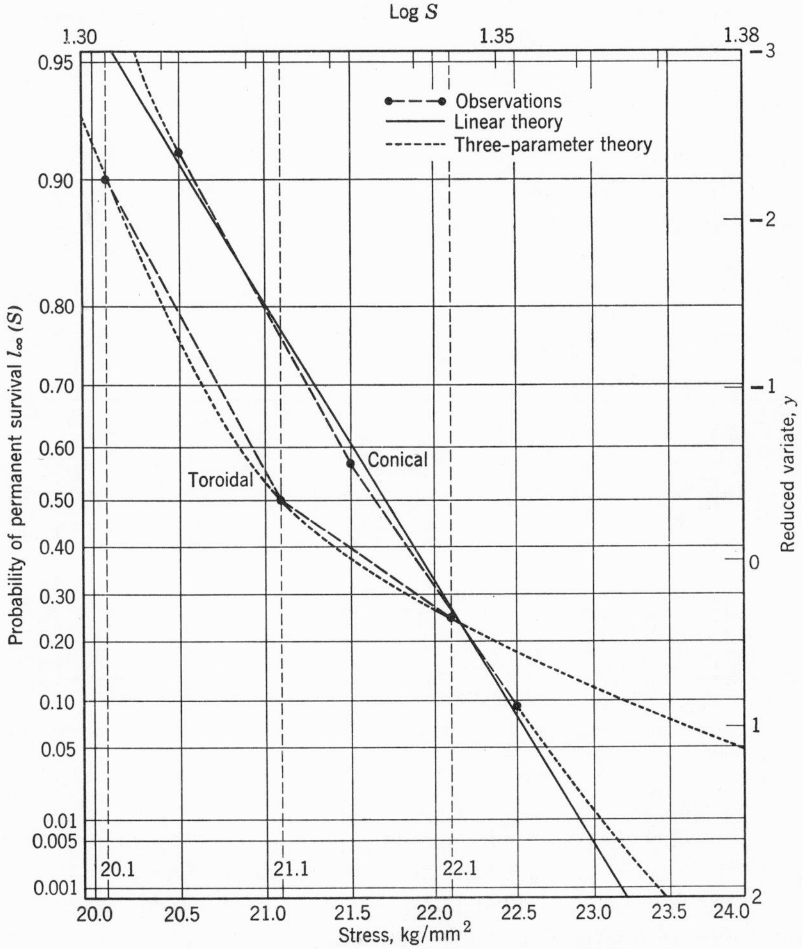

Fig. 12C.3.2 Frequencies of permanent survival (Cazaud).

We could as well, however, lump the observations corresponding to the stresses 41.5 and 42 into one class of $20 + 18 = 38$ specimens, out of which $7 + 2 = 9$ survived. The result would be an estimation $\hat{l}_{\infty}(S) = 0.23077$ for the stress 41.75. The two modifications are traced in Fig.

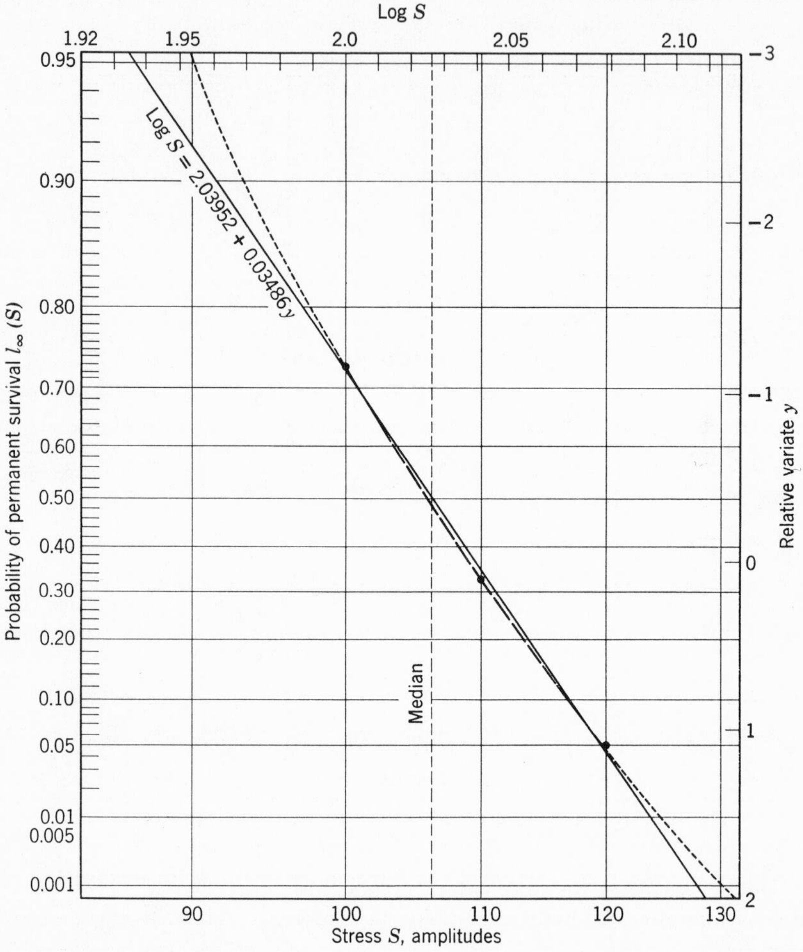

Fig. 12C.3.3 Frequencies of permanent survival (Bender).

12C.3.7. Since the result of the second modification is less regular than the first one, it was not used for the calculation of the parameters.

In principle, such combinations should be discouraged because the estimation of the endurance limit may depend on the way in which they are carried through. It is done here only in order to show the results.

The estimated values of the three (or two) parameters for the six series and the two interpretations calculated with the collaboration of Mr. Taro Yamane (New York University) are given in Table D. For Cazaud's second series, Fig. 12C.3.2, the linear approximation seems unacceptable. Therefore this series was fitted by the three-parameter theory only.

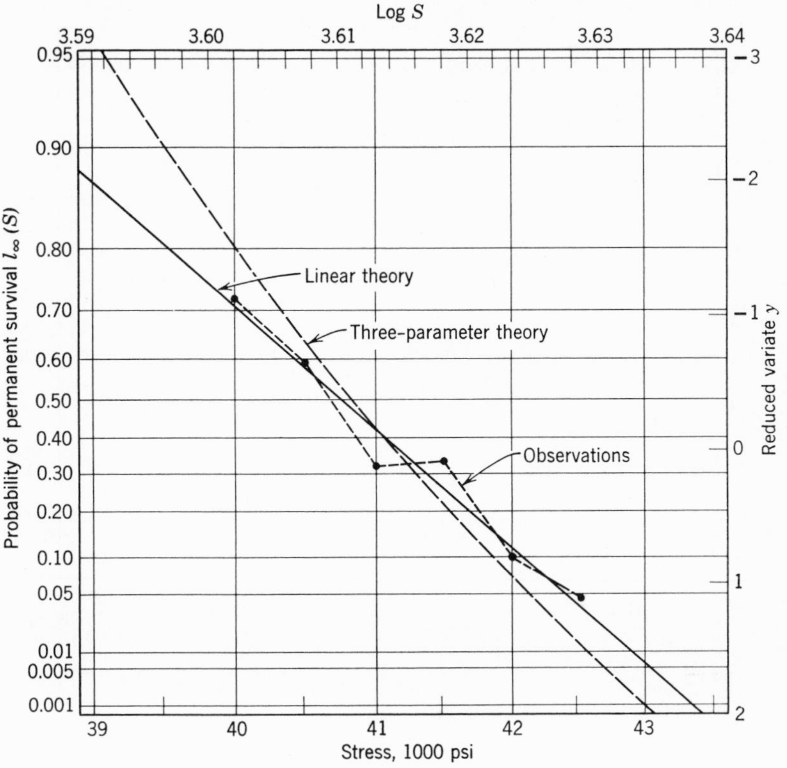

Fig. 12C.3.4 Frequencies of permanent survival (Epremian and Mehl).

Within each series the two theories lead to practically the same estimations for the characteristic fatigue stress S_V. The $1/\hat{\beta}$ in the three-parameter interpretation exceed the $1/\hat{\beta}_1$ in the two-parameter interpretation, as they should. The estimate of the endurance limit for the modified observations of Epremian and Mehl is practically the same as that for the original observations.

The estimated stresses obtained from the parameters are given in Table E, column 2 and column 3.

The median fatigue stresses, Table E, columns 5 and 6, are practically independent of the estimation procedure, as claimed before. The theoretical survivorship functions resulting from Table E, column 2 and column 3, are traced in Figs. 12C.3.2 to 7. In all cases, the linear theory leads to a good fit. The question is, however, whether the three-parameter theory, which implies the existence of a nonvanishing endurance limit, does not lead to a better fit. The curves do not lead to a decision

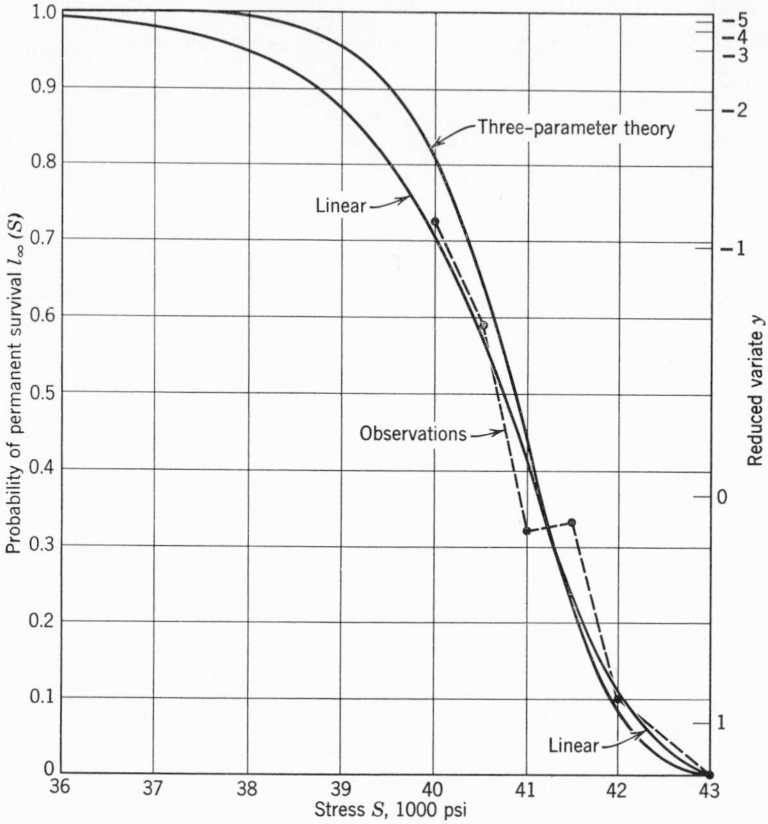

Fig. 12C.3.5 Three-parameter frequencies of permanent survival (Epremian and Mehl).

about which theory should be preferred, except for Epremian and Mehl's original observations about where the linear theory seems preferable. The sums of the squared deviations between theory and observation given in Table E, columns 7 and 8, however, clearly give preference to the second hypothesis that the endurance limit does not vanish. This holds also for Epremian and Mehl's modified observations about where the estimation $\hat{S}_0 = 35.47$ p.s.i. should be accepted.

12C.3.5 *Conclusions.* The knowledge of the median fatigue stress is of

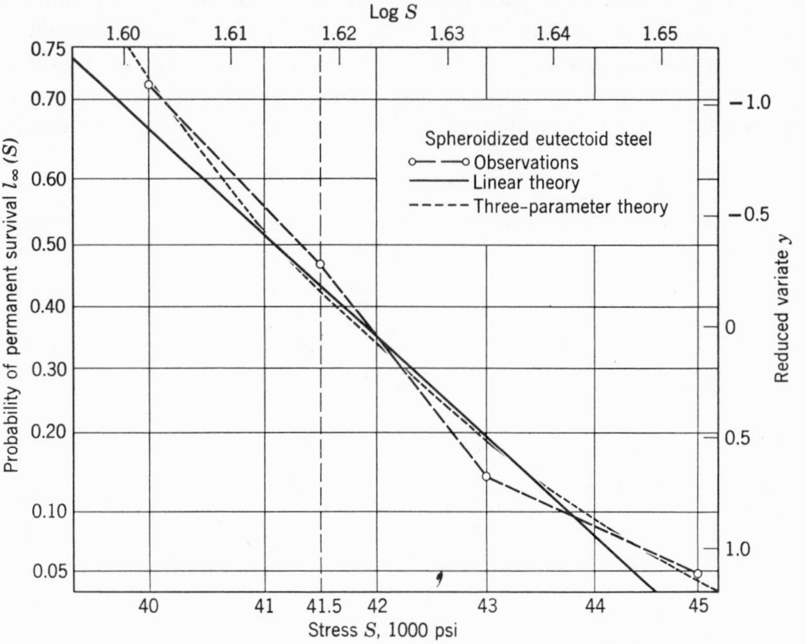

Fig. 12C.3.6 Frequency of permanent survival (Dieter, Mehl, and Horne).

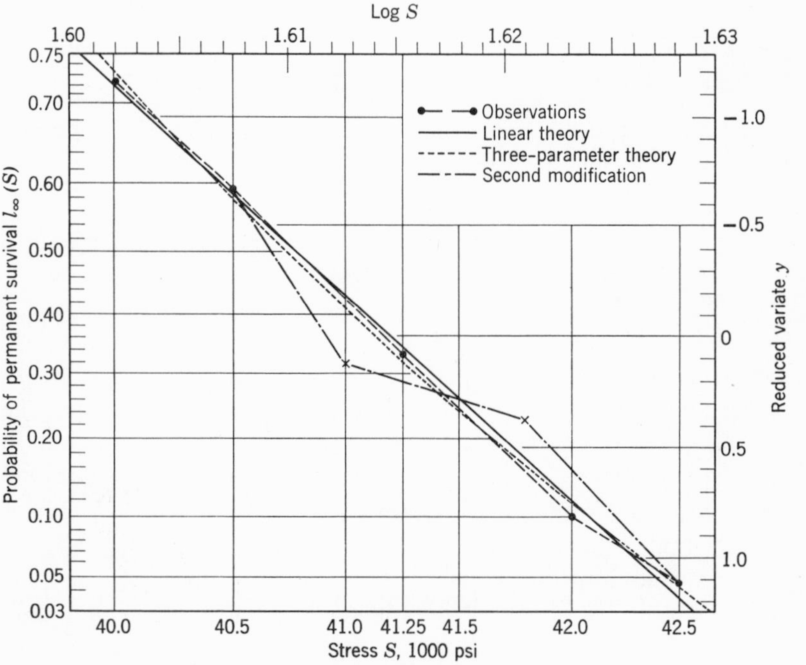

Fig. 12C.3.7 Epremian and Mehl's modified observations.

no practical interest for the safe design of structures. For this purpose we need an estimation of the true endurance limit, which may be obtained from the probability of permanent survival. A method is developed to estimate this probability from the number of pieces broken in a sample of given size. The third asymptotic probability of smallest values, first used by Weibull

TABLE D

ESTIMATION OF THE PARAMETERS

Author	$1/\hat{\beta}_1$ = Linear $1/\hat{\beta}$ = 3-Param.	Scale Parameter	Characteristic Fatigue Stress, $\hat{S}_V$	Endurance Limit, $\hat{S}_0$	Number of Fig. 12C.3.
Bender	linear	0.08027	109.53	0	3
	3-param.	0.22808	108.68	70.50	
	unit	no dim.	ampl. of vib.	ampl. of vib.	
Cazaud I	linear	0.02844	21.92	0	2
	3-param.	0.13640	21.88	16.94	
	unit	no dim.	kg/mm²	kg/mm²	
Cazaud II	linear	—	—	—	2
	3-param.	0.81101	21.53	19.86	
	unit	no dim.	kg/mm²	kg/mm²	
Epremian and Mehl	linear	0.02723	41.17	0	4
	3-param.	0.13794	41.14	35.04	5
	unit	no dim.	p.s.i.	p.s.i.	
Epremian and Mehl (modified)	linear	0.01146	41.18	0	7
	3-param.	0.19083	41.13	35.47	
	unit	no dim.	p.s.i.	p.s.i.	
Dieter, Mehl, and Horne	linear	0.05192	42.12	0	6
	3-param.	0.43341	41.84	37.06	
	unit	no dim.	p.s.i.	p.s.i.	

[16], leads to an estimation of the true endurance limit as one of the parameters.

Unfortunately, most existing observations use only three or four stress levels. Since three values may easily be situated close to a straight line, the estimation of the true endurance limit may be zero, although in reality it does not vanish. Inversely, we may "discover" a positive endurance limit which does not exist. Such are the consequences of the use of only three stress levels. On the other hand, when more stress levels but too few specimens are used, the estimated rates of permanent survival may move in the wrong direction, and such observations are barely suitable for statistical analysis. The practical application of our methods is thus

TABLE E

THEORETICAL STRESSES

1	2	3	4
Author	Linear Theory, $\log \hat{S} = \log \hat{S}_V + y/\hat{\beta}_1$	3-Parameter Theory, $\hat{S} = \hat{S}_0 + (\hat{S}_V - \hat{S}_0)\exp(y/\hat{\beta})$	Preliminary Estimation E
Bender	$2.03953 + 0.03486y$	$70.50 + 38.47\exp(0.2281y)$	70.65
Cazaud I	$1.34078 + 0.01235y$	$16.94 + 4.93\exp(0.1364y)$	16.95
Cazaud II	– –	$19.86 + 1.67\exp(0.8110y)$	19.95
Epremian and Mehl	$1.61453 + 0.01183y$	$35.04 + 6.10\exp(0.1379y)$	37.00
Epremian and Mehl Mod.	$1.61470 + 0.01146y$	$35.47 + 5.66\exp(0.1908y)$	37.00
Dieter, Mehl and Horne	$1.62449 + 0.02255y$	$37.06 + 4.77\exp(0.4334y)$	37.00

1	5	6	7	8
	Med. Fatigue Stress		$\Delta^2 = \Sigma(\hat{S}_i - S_i)^2$	
Author	Linear	3-Param.	Linear	3-Param.
Bender	106.41	105.88	0.152	–
Cazaud I	21.69	21.63	1.7×10^{-3}	–
Cazaud II	–	21.10	–	0.001
Epremian and Mehl	40.76	40.84	0.171	0.358
Epremian and Mehl Mod.	40.79	40.75	0.0125	0.008
Dieter, Mehl, and Horne	41.33	41.13	0.540	0.258

seriously hampered by the scarcity of the available data, especially at low stresses where the probabilities of permanent survival are high.

We are fully aware of the trivial fact that a three-parameter formula applied to a few observations which do not lie exactly on a straight line will usually give a good fit. We do not attribute much importance to conclusions drawn from three to six observations. The numerical examples given are meant only as illustrations and not as proofs for the existence or the values of nonvanishing endurance limits. Still, our analysis may be taken as an indication that nonvanishing true endurance limits exist and may be estimated by the use of the three-parameter model.

We seriously doubt the validity of the usual estimations of the endurance limit given in the literature. For a statistical estimation forty-nine specimens should be used for at least six stress levels in such a way that the proportions of permanent survival defined for 10^7 or, preferably, 10^8 cycles should be in the order of magnitude 0.02, 0.20, 0.50, 0.80, 0.90, 0.98. If the estimated rates of permanent survival are equal for two stresses or move in the wrong direction, further specimens should be tested until the anomaly disappears.

Only such observations can tell whether our analysis of the stresses as smallest values is adequate. But even then the estimation of the endurance limit may differ from the true value valid for $N = \infty$ for which we are aiming, perhaps in vain.

REFERENCES

1. A. Bender and A. Hamm, "The application of probability paper to life or fatigue testing," Rep. Delco-Remy, Anderson, Indiana.
2. R. Cazaud, "Contributions à l'étude statistique de la dispersion dans les essais de flexion rotative," *Rev. Metallurgie*, Paris (1954), p. 291.
3. H. N. Cummings, F. B. Stulen, and W. C. Schulte, "Investigations of metals fatigue problems applicable to propellor design," WADC Tech. Rep. 54-531, Wright Air Development Center, May 1955.
4. G. E. Dieter, R. F. Mehl, and G. T. Horne, "The statistical fatigue properties of laminar and spheroidal eutectoid steel," *Trans. Amer. Soc. for Metals*, Vol. 47, preprint 25 (1954).
5. E. Epremian and R. F. Mehl, "The statistical behavior of fatigue properties and the influence of metallurgical factors," Symposium on Fatigue with Emphasis on Statistical Approach, II, American Society for Testing Materials, Philadelphia, 1953.
6. A. M. Freudenthal and E. J. Gumbel, "Minimum life in fatigue," *J. Amer. Statist. Ass.*, Vol. 49, No. 267 (1954), pp. 575–597.
7. A. M. Freudenthal and E. J. Gumbel, "Physical and statistical aspects of fatigue," *Advanc. Appl. Mech.*, Vol. 4 (1956), pp. 117–158.
8. E. J. Gumbel, "Simple tests for given hypotheses," *Biometrika*, Vol. 32 (1942), pp. 317–332.
9. E. J. Gumbel, "Statistical theory of extreme values and some practical applications," Appl. Math. Ser. 33, U.S. Dept. Commerce, Washington, D.C., 1954.
10. E. J. Gumbel, "Etude statistique de la fatigue des materiaux," *Rev. statist. appl.*, Paris, Vol. 5, No. 4 (1957), pp. 51–86.
11. E. J. Gumbel, *Statistics of Extremes*, Columbia University Press, New York, 1959.
12. L. G. Johnson, "An axiomatic derivation of a general *S–N* equation," *Industr. Math.*, Vol. 4 (1953), pp. 1–8, Detroit, 1954.
13. B. F. Kimball, "Practical applications of the theory of extreme values," *J. Amer. Statist. Ass.*, Vol. 50 (1955), pp. 517–528.

14. J. Lieblein and M. Zelen, "Statistical analysis of the fatigue lives of deep-groove ball bearings," *J. Res. Nat. Bur. Stand.*, Vol. 57, No. 5 (Nov. 1956), RP 2719, pp. 273–316.
15. National Bureau of Standards, "Probability tables for the analysis of extreme-value data," Appl. Math. Ser. 22, U.S. Dept. Commerce, Washington, D.C., 1953.
16. W. Weibull, "A statistical representation of fatigue failures in solids," *Trans. Roy. Inst. Tech.*, Stockholm, No. 27 (1949).

SHANTI S. GUPTA

12D GAMMA DISTRIBUTION

12D.1 Moments of the kth Order Statistic

Suppose that we have n independent random variables $x_1, x_2 \ldots, x_n$ each distributed according to the gamma probability density function (pdf)

$$g_r(x) = e^{-x} \frac{x^{r-1}}{\Gamma(r)}, \qquad 0 \le x < \infty \tag{12D.1.1}$$

where r is assumed to be a positive integer. The distribution (12D.1.1) arises, for instance, as the convolution of r independent and identical chance variables with the exponential density function e^{-x}. Let $G_r(x)$ be the cumulative distribution function of x; then it is easy to see that $G_r(x)$ can be written as a partial sum of probabilities in a Poisson distribution as follows:

$$G_r(x) = \sum_{j=r}^{\infty} \frac{e^{-x} x^j}{j!}. \tag{12D.1.2}$$

Let $x_{(k)}$ denote the kth smallest x when the x_i are arranged in the increasing order, namely

$$x_{(1)} \le x_{(2)} \le \ldots \le x_{(k)} \le \ldots \le x_{(n)}, \tag{12D.1.3}$$

and let $y = x_{(k)}$; then the ith moment about the origin, $\mu'_i(k, n)$ of the kth order statistic from a sample of size n from the gamma pdf $g_r(x)$ is given by

$$\mu'_i(k, n) = \frac{n!}{(k-1)!\,(n-k)!} \times \int_0^\infty \left(1 - \sum_{j=0}^{r-1} \frac{e^{-y}(y)^j}{j!}\right)^{k-1} \left(\sum_{j=0}^{r-1} \frac{e^{-y}(y)^j}{j!}\right)^{n-k} \frac{e^{-y} y^{r+i-1}}{\Gamma(r)}\, dy \tag{12D.1.4}$$

which reduces to (details omitted)

$$\mu'_i(k, n) = \frac{n!}{(k-1)!\,(n-k)!\,\Gamma(r)} \sum_{p=0}^{k-1} (-1)^p \binom{k-1}{p}$$
$$\times \sum_{m=0}^{(r-1)(n-k+p)} a_m(r, n-k+p) \frac{\Gamma(r+i+m)}{(n-k+p+1)^{r+i+m}} \qquad (12D.1.5)$$

where $a_m(r, p)$ is the coefficient of t^m in the expansion of $\left(\sum_{j=0}^{r-1} \frac{t^j}{j!}\right)^p$. For $k = 1$, we have from (12D.1.5)

$$\mu'_i(1, n) = \frac{n}{\Gamma(r)} \sum_{m=0}^{(r-1)(n-1)} a_m(r, n-1) \frac{\Gamma(r+i+m)}{n^{r+i+m}}. \qquad (12D.1.6)$$

The ith moment of the kth order statistic can be expressed in terms of the ith moments of first (smallest) order statistic as follows:

$$\mu'_i(k, n) = \frac{n!}{(k-1)!\,(n-k)!} \sum_{p=0}^{k-1} (-1)^p \binom{k-1}{p} \frac{\mu'_i(1, n-k+p+1)}{n-k+p+1}.$$
$$(12D.1.7)$$

Also, the coefficients $a_m(r, p)$ satisfy the following basic recursion relation:

$$a_m(r, p) = a_m(r, p-1) + a_{m-1}(r, p-1) + \frac{1}{2!} a_{m-2}(r, p-1)$$
$$+ \cdots + \frac{1}{(r-1)!} a_{m-r+1}(r, p-1). \qquad (12D.1.8)$$

Since for $p = 1$ these coefficients are $1, 1, \frac{1}{2!}, \ldots, \frac{1}{(r-1)!}$, we can compute them for any value of p by repeated applications of (12D.1.8). If we define

$$\nu'_i(k, n) = \int_0^\infty x^i G_r^{k-1}(x)[1 - G_r(x)]^{n-k} g_r(x)\, dx$$
$$= \frac{(k-1)!\,(n-k)!\,\Gamma(r)}{n!} \mu'_i(k, n). \qquad (12D.1.9)$$

then $\nu'_i(k, n)$ satisfy the following recursion formulas:

$$\nu'_i(k, n) = \sum_{\alpha=0}^{n-k} (-1)^\alpha \binom{n-k}{\alpha} \nu'_i(k+\alpha, k+\alpha). \qquad (12D.1.10)$$

A slightly more generalized form of (12D.1.10) is the following one:

$$\nu'_i(k, n) = \sum_{p=0}^{\beta} (-1)^p \binom{\beta}{p} \nu'_i(k+p, n-\beta+p). \qquad (12D.1.11)$$

where β is any positive integer less than or equal to $n - k$. Also, the relation (12D.1.7) can be written as

$$\nu'_i(k, n) = \sum_{p=0}^{k-1}(-1)^p\binom{k-1}{p}\nu'_i(1, n-k+p+1). \quad (12D.1.12)$$

From (12D.1.11), we have, by putting $\beta = 1$,

$$\nu'_i(k, n-1) = \nu'_i(k, n) + \nu'_i(k+1, n), \qquad k \leq n-1. \quad (12D.1.13)$$

These relations were used to compute the values of $\mu'_i(k, n)$ with $i = 1, 2, 3, 4$. Table 12D.1 gives these moments for selected values of k, n, and r. For the covariance let $\xi = x_{[l]}$ and $\eta = x_{[m]}$ be the lth and mth ($m > l$) order statistics from the gamma distribution (12D.1.1), Then we have

$$E(\xi\eta) = C\int_0^\infty\int_\xi^\infty \xi\eta G_r^{l-1}(\xi)[G_r(\eta) - G_r(\xi)]^{m-l-1} \times [1 - G_r(\eta)]^{n-m} g_r(\xi)g_r(\eta)\, d\xi\, d\eta \quad (12D.1.14)$$

where $C = \dfrac{n!}{(l-1)!\ (m-l-1)!\ (n-m)!}$. The expression on the right side of (12D.1.14) can be written as

$$E(\xi\eta) = C\sum_{\alpha,\beta}(-1)^{\alpha+\beta}\binom{l-1}{\alpha}\binom{m-l-1}{\beta}\int_0^\infty e^{-qu}\left(\sum_{j=0}^{r-1}\frac{u^j}{j!}\right)^{q-1}\frac{u^r}{\Gamma(r)}\,du \times \int_u^\infty e^{-sv}\left(\sum_{j=0}^{r-1}\frac{v^j}{j!}\right)^{s-1}\frac{v^r}{\Gamma(r)}\,dv \quad (12D.1.15)$$

where $q = \alpha + m - l - \beta$ and $s = n - m + \beta + 1$ and the first summation on the right side is over the positive integers α, β, with $0 \leq \alpha \leq l - 1$, $0 \leq \beta \leq m - l - 1$. As before, let $a_t(r, p)$ denote the coefficient of u^t in the expansion for $\left(\sum_{j=0}^{r-1}\dfrac{u^j}{j!}\right)^p$. Then (12D.1.15) simplifies to

$$E(\xi\eta) = \frac{C}{[\Gamma(r)]^2}\sum_{\alpha,\beta}(-1)^{\alpha+\beta}\binom{l-1}{\alpha}\binom{m-l-1}{\beta}\sum_{t=0}^{(r-1)(s-1)}\frac{a_t(r, s-1)\Gamma(t+r+1)}{s^{t+r+1}} \times \left[\sum_{j=0}^{t+r}\left(\frac{s^j}{j!}\right)\sum_{p=0}^{(r-1)(q-1)}\frac{\Gamma(j+r+p+1)a_p(r, q-1)}{(s+q)^{j+r+p+1}}\right]. \quad (12D.1.16)$$

or

$$E(\xi\eta) = \frac{C}{[\Gamma(r)]^2}\sum_{\alpha,\beta,t,j,p}(-1)^{\alpha+\beta}\binom{l-1}{\alpha}\binom{m-l-1}{\beta} \times \frac{a_t(r,s-1)a_p(r,q-1)\Gamma(t+r+1)\Gamma(j+r+p+1)}{j!\,s^{t+r-j+1}(s+q)^{j+r+p+1}}. \quad (12D.1.17)$$

From (12D.1.17) we can obtain the covariance (ξ, η) by subtracting from $E(\xi\eta)$ the product $E(\xi)E(\eta)$ which we get from the results obtained before.

12D.2 Best Linear Unbiased Estimates

Let us consider the density in the form

$$g_r(x, \lambda) = \lambda^{r-1}e^{-\lambda x}\frac{x^{r-1}}{\Gamma(r)}, \qquad 0 \leq x < \infty, \quad 0 < \lambda \quad (12D.2.1)$$

where λ is assumed to be unknown. Then we may be interested in estimating λ. The best linear unbiased estimate of λ when all the observations are available is well known. However, for censored samples the best linear unbiased estimates for the cases of $r = 2, 3$ will be computed later using the method of the least squares as described by Lloyd in Chapter 3. For $r = 1$, that is, for the case of the exponential distribution, these have been obtained in reference 8.

12D.3 Some Remarks about the Distribution of the *k*th Order Statistic

The Mode of the kth Order Statistic. The modal value t of the kth order statistic from a sample of size n from the gamma distribution with parameter r is given by

$$\frac{\partial}{\partial t}\{e^{-nt}t^{r-1}\psi^{n-k}(r, t)[e^t - \psi(r, t)]^{k-1}\} = 0 \qquad (12D.3.1)$$

where

$$\psi(r, t) = \sum_{j=0}^{r-1}\frac{t^j}{j!}, \qquad r \geq 1$$

$$= 0, \quad \text{otherwise.} \qquad (12D.3.2)$$

The function $\psi(r, t)$ satisfies the following difference-differential equation

$$\frac{\partial\psi(r, t)}{\partial t} = \psi'(r, t) = \psi(r-1, t). \qquad (12D.3.3)$$

Using equation (12D.3.3) in (12D.3.1) we obtain after some simplification

$$(-nt + r - 1)\psi(r, t)[e^t - \psi(r, t)] + (n - k)t\psi(r - 1, t)[e^t - \psi(r, t)]$$
$$+ (k - 1)t\psi(r, t)[e^t - \psi(r - 1, t)] = 0, \quad (12D.3.4)$$

or

$$(r - t - 1)\left(\sum_{j=0}^{r-1}\frac{t^j}{j!}\right)\left(e^t - \sum_{j=0}^{r-1}\frac{t^j}{j!}\right) = \frac{t^r}{(r - 1)!}\left[(n - k)e^t - (n - 1)\sum_{j=0}^{r-1}\frac{t^j}{j!}\right],$$
$$(12D.3.5)$$

Equation (12D.3.5) can be used to solve for t by an iterative procedure.

The cases $k = 1$ and $k = n$ are of particular interest and for these we obtain

$$\sum_{j=0}^{r-1} \frac{e^{-t}t^j}{j!} = \frac{n-1}{(r-1)!} \frac{e^{-t}t^r}{r-t-1} \qquad (12D.3.6)$$

$$\sum_{j=0}^{r-1} \frac{e^{-t}t^j}{j!} = \frac{n-1}{(r-1)!} \frac{e^{-t}t^r}{r-t-1} + 1 \qquad (12D.3.7)$$

which give the modal values of the smallest and the largest order statistics, respectively. It should be noted that the present forms (12D.3.6) and (12D.3.7) are helpful in that the value of the left-side expression can be obtained from a table of cumulative Poisson distribution.

It is easy to show that there are unique solutions for (12D.3.6) and (12D.3.7) in the open intervals $0 < t < r - 1$ and $r - 1 < t < \infty$, respectively, provided $n \geq 2$. For $n = 1$, $t = r - 1$, since in this case the mode is the same as that of a gamma distribution. Moreover, t increases monotonically with n for the largest order statistic and decreases monotonically with n for the smallest order statistic.

Another particular case of interest is $r = 1$, since for this the gamma distribution reduces to the exponential distribution. For this case equation (12D.3.5) reduces to the simple and explicit form

$$t = \lg n - \lg (n - k + 1) \qquad (12D.3.8)$$

where lg stands for the natural logarithm.

Equations (12D.3.6) and (12D.3.7) were solved by iterative methods on IBM 650 for selected values of n and r. The results of these computations are given in Table 12D.2.

Cumulative Distribution Function of the Order Statistics. The cumulative distribution function $F_r(y; k, n)$ of the kth order statistic $y = x_{(k)}$ from the gamma distribution is

$$\begin{aligned} F_r(y; k, n) &= \frac{n!}{(k-1)!\,(n-k)!} \int_0^y G_r^{k-1}(x)[1 - G_r(x)]^{n-k} g_r(x)\, dx \\ &= \frac{n!}{(k-1)!\,(n-k)!} \int_0^{G_r(y)} u^{k-1}(1-u)^{n-k}\, du \\ &= I_{G_r(y)}(k, n-k+1), \end{aligned} \qquad (12D.3.9)$$

where $I_{G_r(y)}(k, n - k + 1)$ is the ratio of the incomplete beta function to the complete beta function and is tabulated in reference 6. For a given value of y we can compute the cdf $F_r(y; k, n)$ by first consulting a table of the cumulative distribution of the Poisson or gamma distribution to get

$G_r(y)$ and then consulting the table of the cumulative of the beta distribution. Again,

$$F_r(y; k, n) = \frac{n!}{(k-1)!(n-k)!} \sum_{\alpha=0}^{n-k} \frac{(-1)^\alpha}{\alpha + k} \binom{n-k}{\alpha} \left(\sum_{j=r}^{\infty} \frac{e^{-y} y^j}{j!} \right)^{\alpha+k} \quad (12D.3.10)$$

$$F_r(y; k, n) = \frac{n!}{(k-1)!(n-k)!} \left[\sum_{j=k}^{n} F_r(y; j, j) \binom{n-k}{j-k} \frac{(-1)^{j-k}}{j} \right]. \quad (12D.3.11)$$

The function $F_r(y;\ j, j)$ is the cdf of the largest of $x_i (i = 1, 2, \ldots, j)$ and, using K. Pearson's notation [7] for the incomplete gamma function, can be written as

$$F_r(y;\ j, j) = G_r^j(y) = I^j\left(\frac{y}{\sqrt{r}}, r - 1\right) = \left(\sum_{j=r}^{\infty} \frac{e^{-y} y^j}{j!} \right)^j. \quad (12D.3.12)$$

In addition, for $k = 1$ and $k = n$, that is, for the distribution of the smallest and the largest, respectively, we obtain the following simple forms:

$$F_r(y;\ 1, n) = 1 - (1 - G_r(y))^n = 1 - e^{-ny} \left(\sum_{j=0}^{r-1} \frac{y^j}{j!} \right)^n. \quad (12D.3.13)$$

$$F_r(y;\ n, n) = G^n(y) = e^{-ny} \left(\sum_{j=r}^{\infty} \frac{y^j}{j!} \right)^n. \quad (12D.3.14)$$

The cdf of the median, that is, of $x_{(m+1)}$ when $n = 2m + 1$, is

$$F_r(y;\ m + 1, 2m + 1) = \frac{(2m+1)!}{(m!)^2} \sum_{\alpha=0}^{m} \frac{(-1)^\alpha}{\alpha + m + 1} \binom{m}{\alpha} \left(\sum_{j=r}^{\infty} \frac{e^{-y} y^j}{j!} \right)^{\alpha+m+1}. \quad (12D.3.15)$$

Probabilities in (12D.3.10) . . . (12D.3.15) can be obtained with the help of a table of cumulative Poisson distribution [4] and also with the help of a table of the incomplete gamma function [7].

The Percentage Points of the kth Order Statistic. If $I_\alpha(k, n - k + 1)$ denotes the alpha percentage point of the beta distribution, then y_α, the alpha percentage point of the kth order statistic, is the solution of

$$G_r(y_\alpha) = I_\alpha(k, n - k + 1). \quad (12D.3.16)$$

Equation (12D.3.16) can be written as

$$-y_\alpha + \lg \left[\sum_{j=0}^{r-1} \frac{(y_\alpha)^j}{j!} \right] = \lg\left[1 - I_\alpha(k, n - k + 1)\right] \quad (12D.3.17)$$

where lg stands for the natural logarithm as before. This equation was used to find y_α by an iterative procedure. The values of $I_\alpha(k, n - k + 1)$ were obtained from reference 5. For those values of k and $n - k + 1$ for which $I_\alpha(k, n - k + 1)$ was not available, inverse interpolation was performed in the tables of the incomplete beta function [6]. The latter is not necessary for $k = 1$ and $k = n$ since for these cases we have, respectively,

$$G_r(y_\alpha) = 1 - (1 - \alpha)^{1/n} \qquad (12D.3.18)$$

and

$$G_r(y_\alpha) = (\alpha)^{1/n}. \qquad (12D.3.19)$$

Values of the alpha percentage points of the kth smallest order statistics for samples of size n $(1 \le k \le n)$, $n = 1(1)10$ and for selected values of α are given in Tables 12D.3*a*, *b*, *c*, *d* and *e*.

12D.4 Applications to Life Testing, Reliability, and Other Problems and Some Further Remarks

Time to rth Failure. The time to rth failure from an exponential distribution $f(x) = \lambda e^{-\lambda x}$ (with replacement) follows the gamma distribution. Thus the results of this paper will be useful in finding the probability that the smallest (or any other ordered value) of the times to the rth failures in n life-test experiments will be at least as large as a given value. In addition, the expected values and other moments of the ordered times to kth failure may be of interest, and these can be looked up in Table 12D.1.

Illustration 1. Life tests (with replacements) are to be carried on $m = 10$ units, each of the same type in $n = 3$ test sets. We would like to know the probability that in none of the three sets four failures will take place in less than $c = \frac{1}{5}$ times the average life time. The required probability is $P = 1 - F_4(2; 1, 3)$, which we can find from a table of the Poisson distribution (the parameter of the Poisson distribution being $mc = 2$) as indicated in formula (12D.3.13). Thus, $P = (0.857123)^3 = 0.6297$. Also from Table 12D.3, we can put one-sided or two-sided confidence limits on the smallest (or any other) time to rth failure in terms of the average life or vice versa. For the present example $r = 4$, and from Table 12D.3*d* we find that the 90% lower confidence limit on $x_{(1)}$, the smallest time to the fourth failure, is 1.2085 times the average life θ. Again the 90% lower confidence limit on θ based on $x_{(1)}$, say, is $(10/3.8458)\, x_{(1)} = 2.6002 x_{(1)}$.

Again by using Table 12D.1 ($r = 4$) we find

expected value of the smallest time to the fourth failure = 0.2449 av. life
expected value of the median time to the fourth failure = 0.3820 av. life
expected value of the largest time to the fourth failure = 0.5731 av. life.

If we have n systems and the rth failure of a unit in any of these means that the system becomes unsatisfactory or unreliable (replacements are made until the $(r-1)$th failure), then the probability that 0, 1, 2, . . . , n of the systems arrive at an unsatisfactory state before a certain time can be obtained from the formulas of Subsection 12D.3 and also individual and joint confidence limits can be placed on the reliability of these systems.

Total Life. If $t_1, t_2, \ldots, t_r$ are the times to 1st, 2nd, ..., rth failures in n units on test (without replacement) that follow the exponential law $f(t) = \lambda e^{-\lambda t}$, the total life T defined by

$$T = t_1 + t_2 + \ldots + t_r + (n - r)t_r \tag{12D.4.1}$$

has the gamma density function

$$g(T) = \lambda^r e^{-\lambda T} \frac{T^{r-1}}{\Gamma(r)}, \qquad T \geq 0 \tag{12D.4.2}$$

so that results of this subsection will be applicable in comparing two or more populations using total life as the criterion.

The distributions of the statistic T when t's come from exponential and uniform distribution are derived in references 1 and 3, respectively.

Illustration 2. The most probable value of the largest order statistic is of importance in the study of breakdown voltages of paper capacitors of several layers. It is assumed that the size of the conducting particles (impurities) follows an exponential distribution and that the particles of one layer are lined up against those of the next layer. Under this assumption the total length of the r conducting particles follows a gamma distribution. We are then interested in the mode of the largest of a sample of n from a gamma distribution.

Let $n = 10$ be the number of particles per square unit area on each of the $r=3$ layers. Then from Table 12D.2 we find that the modal value of the largest length of the conducting particle is equal to $5.448/\lambda$ where λ is the parameter of the exponential distribution $\lambda e^{-\lambda x}$.

Relation to Order Statistics from the χ^2-Distribution. The random variable $\frac{1}{2}\chi_{2\nu}^2$ with 2ν degrees of freedom has the gamma density function (12D.1.1) with parameters $r = \nu$. If y and y' denote the kth order statistic of a sample of size n from the standardized gamma distribution with parameter r and χ_{2r}^2 (with $2r$ degrees of freedom), respectively, we have

$$P(y' \leq c) = P\left(y \leq \frac{c}{2}\right) \tag{12D.4.3}$$

$$y'_\alpha = 2y_\alpha \tag{12D.4.4}$$

where y'_α and y_α refer to the alpha percentage points of y' and y respectively. In addition

$$E(y')^i = 2^i E y^i. \tag{12D.4.5}$$

Application to Distribution of Ordered Sample Variances from Normal Populations. If s_ν^2 is the sample variance based on ν degrees of freedom from a normal distribution with variance σ^2, then $\nu s_\nu^2/\sigma^2$ is distributed like a χ_ν^2 with ν degrees of freedom. This enables us to obtain the moments and distribution of the ordered sample variances for $\nu = 2r$ degrees of freedom from the results and tables of this section.

For further applications and details of derivation see reference 2.

TABLE 12D.1

Moments about the Origin $\mu'_i(k, n)$ and the Central Moments $\mu_i(k, n)$ of the kth Order Statistic of a Sample of Size n from a Standardized Gamma Distribution with Parameter r

$r = 1$

n	k	$\mu'_1(k, n)$	$\mu'_2(k, n)$	$\mu'_3(k, n)$	$\mu'_4(k, n)$	$\mu_2(k, n)$	$\mu_3(k, n)$	$\mu_4(k, n)$
1	1	1.000	2.000	6.000	24.00	1.000	2.000	9.000
2	1	.5000	.5000	.7500	1.500	.2500	.2500	.5625
	2	1.500	3.500	11.25	46.50	1.250	2.250	11.06
3	1	.3333	.2222	.2222	.2963	.1111	.07407	.1111
	2	.8333	1.056	1.806	3.907	.3611	.3241	.8403
	3	1.833	4.722	15.97	67.80	1.361	2.324	1.201
4	1	.2500	.1250	.09375	.09375	.06250	.03125	.03516
	2	.5833	.5139	.6076	.9039	.1736	.1053	.1879
	3	1.083	1.597	3.003	6.911	.4236	.3553	1.011
	4	2.083	5.764	20.30	88.09	1.424	2.355	12.55
5	1	.2000	.08000	.04780	.03840	.04000	.01600	.01440
	2	.4500	.3050	.2768	.3152	.1025	.04725	.06456
	3	.7833	.8272	1.104	1.787	.2136	.1213	.2440
	4	1.283	2.111	4.270	10.33	.4636	.3713	1.127
	5	2.283	6.677	24.30	107.5	1.464	2.371	12.91
6	1	.1667	.05556	.02778	.01852	.02778	.009259	.006944
	2	.3667	.2022	.1491	.1378	.06778	.02526	.02801
	3	.6167	.5106	.5320	.6698	.1303	.05651	.08858
	4	.9500	1.144	1.676	2.904	.2414	.1306	.2865
	5	1.450	2.594	5.567	14.04	.4914	.3806	1.211
	6	2.450	7.494	28.05	126.2	1.491	2.381	13.16
7	1	.1429	.04082	.01749	.009996	.02041	.005831	.003748
	2	.3095	.1440	.08949	.06965	.04819	.01509	.01409
	3	.5095	.3478	.2982	.3082	.08819	.03109	.04006
	4	.7595	.7276	.8438	1.152	.1507	.06234	.1083
	5	1.093	1.456	2.300	4.219	.2619	.1364	.3199
	6	1.593	3.049	6.873	17.97	.5118	.3864	1.275
	7	2.593	8.235	31.58	144.3	1.512	2.386	13.35
8	1	.1250	.03125	.01172	.005859	.01562	.003906	.002197
	2	.2679	.1078	.05791	.03895	.03603	.009737	.007859
	3	.4345	.2526	.1842	.1618	.06381	.01900	.02081
	4	.6345	.5064	.4881	.5522	.1038	.03500	.05052
	5	.8845	.9487	1.200	1.752	.1663	.06625	.1246
	6	1.218	1.761	2.960	5.699	.2774	.1403	.3466
	7	1.718	3.478	8.178	22.05	.5274	.3903	1.325
	8	2.718	8.914	34.92	161.7	1.527	2.390	13.49
9	1	.1111	.02469	.008230	.003658	.01235	.002743	.001372
	2	.2361	.08372	.03963	.02347	.02797	.006650	.004726
	3	.3790	.1920	.1219	.09313	.04838	.01248	.01190
	4	.5456	.3739	.3088	.2990	.07616	.02174	.02691
	5	.7456	.6721	.7121	.8687	.1162	.03774	.05959
	6	.9956	1.170	1.590	2.458	.1787	.06899	.1383
	7	1.329	2.056	3.646	7.319	.2898	.1431	.3685
	8	1.829	3.885	8.473	26.26	.5398	.3931	1.366
	9	2.829	9.543	38.10	178.7	1.540	2.393	13.60
10	1	.1000	.02000	.006000	.002400	.01000	.002000	.0009000
	2	.2111	.06691	.02830	.01498	.02235	.004743	.003012
	3	.3361	.1509	.08491	.05743	.03797	.008650	.007305
	4	.4790	.2878	.2082	.1764	.05838	.01448	.01570
	5	.6456	.5030	.4597	.4829	.08616	.02374	.03238
	6	.8456	.8413	.9645	1.255	.1262	.03974	.06746
	7	1.096	1.389	2.006	3.261	.1887	.07100	.1499
	8	1.429	2.342	4.348	9.058	.2998	.1450	.3868
	9	1.929	4.271	10.75	30.57	.5498	.3951	1.399
	10	2.929	10.13	41.14	195.1	1.550	2.395	13.70
11	1	.09091	.01653	.004508	.001639	.008264	.001503	.0006147
12	1	.08333	.01389	.003472	.001157	.006944	.001157	.0004340
13	1	.07692	.01183	.002731	.0008403	.005917	.0009103	.0003151
14	1	.07143	.01020	.002187	.0006247	.005102	.0007289	.0002343
15	1	.06667	.008889	.001778	.0004741	.004444	.0005926	.0001778

Note: μ'_1 and μ'_2 are also given in Tables 11A.1 and 11A.2.

This table is reproduced from S. S. Gupta, "Order statistics from the gamma distribution," *Technometrics*, Vol. 2 (1960), pp. 243–262, with permission of J. S. Hunter, editor of *Technometrics*.

$r = 2$

n	k	$\mu'_1(k, n)$	$\mu'_2(k, n)$	$\mu'_3(k, n)$	$\mu'_4(k, n)$	$\mu_2(k, n)$	$\mu_3(k, n)$	$\mu_4(k, n)$
1	1	2.000	6.000	24.00	120.0	2.000	4.000	24.00
2	1	1.250	2.250	5.250	15.00	.6875	.7188	2.520
	2	2.750	9.750	42.75	225.0	2.188	3.906	25.58
3	1	.9630	1.309	2.272	4.774	.3813	.2770	.7251
	2	1.824	4.133	11.21	35.45	.8055	.7299	2.976
	3	3.213	12.56	58.52	319.8	2.236	3.806	25.83
4	1	.8047	.9023	1.280	2.183	.2548	.1441	.3096
	2	1.438	2.528	5.246	12.55	.4603	.2879	.9082
	3	2.210	5.738	17.17	58.36	.8522	.7178	3.161
	4	3.547	14.83	72.31	406.9	2.250	3.733	25.78
5	1	.7021	.6808	.8297	1.208	.1879	.08789	.1629
	2	1.215	1.788	3.082	6.079	.3119	.1513	.4006
	3	1.772	3.636	8.490	.2225	.4970	.2866	1.001
	4	2.503	7.139	22.95	82.43	.8753	.7047	3.248
	5	3.808	16.76	84.64	488.0	2.253	3.678	25.66
6	1	.6291	.5430	.5861	.7527	.1473	.05917	.09753
	2	1.067	1.370	2.048	3.487	.2315	.09264	.2148
	3	1.512	2.626	5.151	11.26	.3408	.1520	.4525
	4	2.032	4.647	11.83	33.23	.5177	.2831	1.055
	5	2.738	8.385	28.51	107.0	.8880	.6932	3.292
	6	4.022	18.43	95.87	564.2	2.251	3.635	25.51
7	1	.5740	.4497	.4387	.5077	.1202	.04258	.06368
	2	.9597	1.103	1.470	2.223	.1819	.06235	.1300
	3	1.335	2.037	3.493	6.647	.2549	.09358	.2467
	4	1.747	3.410	7.361	17.42	.3584	.1510	.4858
	5	2.246	5.574	1.518	45.09	.5306	.2793	1.088
	6	2.935	9.509	33.85	131.8	.8952	.6834	3.313
	7	4.204	19.92	106.2	636.3	2.247	3.601	25.36
8	1	.5306	.3827	.3425	.3626	.1011	.03215	.04427
	2	.8778	.9192	1.113	1.524	.1487	.04476	.08543
	3	1.205	1.654	2.542	4.321	.2012	.06320	.1509
	4	1.551	2.675	5.078	10.52	.2697	.09341	.2683
	5	1.943	4.146	9.645	24.31	.3700	.1496	.5083
	6	2.427	6.431	18.50	57.56	.5391	.2756	1.110
	7	3.104	10.54	38.96	156.6	.8994	.6752	3.322
	8	4.361	21.26	115.8	704.8	2.242	3.572	25.21
9	1	.4954	.3323	.2759	.2703	.08691	.02517	.03225
	2	.8127	.7855	.8752	1.101	.1250	.03367	.05959
	3	1.106	1.387	1.943	3.004	.1689	.04545	.09995
	4	1.405	2.189	3.741	6.957	.2139	.06334	.1658
	5	1.733	3.282	6.749	14.98	.2801	.09275	.2841
	6	2.112	4.838	11.96	31.78	.3780	.1482	.5237
	7	2.585	7.228	21.77	70.45	.5449	.2721	1.126
	8	3.252	11.48	43.87	181.2	.9017	.6683	3.322
	9	4.499	22.48	124.8	770.3	2.237	3.547	25.08
10	1	.4660	.2932	.2278	.2084	.07603	.02027	.02438
	2	.7595	.6842	.7090	.8276	.1074	.02625	.04349
	3	1.026	1.191	1.540	2.193	.1389	.03422	.07009
	4	1.292	1.845	2.885	4.896	.1759	.04563	.1106
	5	1.575	2.704	5.024	10.05	.2229	.06324	.1766
	6	1.890	3.860	8.474	19.92	.2877	.09166	.2965
	7	2.260	5.490	14.29	39.69	.3836	.1473	.5334
	8	2.725	7.973	24.98	83.63	.5492	.2685	1.138
	9	3.384	12.36	48.60	205.5	.9028	.6628	3.317
	10	4.623	23.60	133.3	833.0	2.231	3.526	24.95
11	1	.4411	.2620	.1918	.1650	.06743	.01669	.01897
12	1	.4197	.2366	.1641	.1336	.06049	.01400	.01512
13	1	.4010	.2155	.1423	.1101	.05477	.01193	.01229
14	1	.3844	.1978	.1248	.09215	.04999	.01029	.01016
15	1	.3697	.1826	.1105	.07816	.04594	.008981	.008518

$r = 3$

n	k	$\mu'_1(k, n)$	$\mu'_2(k, n)$	$\mu'_3(k, n)$	$\mu'_4(k, n)$	$\mu_2(k, n)$	$\mu_3(k, n)$	$\mu_4(k, n)$
1	1	3.000	12.00	60.00	360.0	3.000	6.000	45.00
2	1	2.063	5.438	17.34	64.69	1.184	1.247	6.098
	2	3.938	18.56	102.7	655.3	3.059	5.480	44.11
3	1	1.683	3.550	8.916	25.84	.7172	.5270	2.080
	2	2.821	9.212	34.20	142.4	1.253	1.139	6.338
	3	4.496	23.24	136.9	911.8	3.027	5.202	42.71
4	1	1.466	2.661	5.695	13.95	.5117	.2935	1.010
	2	2.334	6.217	18.58	61.53	.7680	.4812	2.227
	3	3.308	12.21	49.82	223.2	1.264	1.072	6.298
	4	4.891	26.91	165.9	1141	2.988	5.028	41.52
5	1	1.321	2.143	4.072	8.801	.3976	.1890	.5897
	2	2.045	4.731	12.19	34.54	.5489	.2665	1.094
	3	2.768	8.447	28.17	102.0	.7829	.4533	2.258
	4	3.668	14.71	64.25	304.0	1.261	1.026	6.201
	5	5.197	29.96	191.3	1351	2.952	4.906	40.55
6	1	1.216	1.804	3.118	6.105	.3254	.1331	.3851
	2	1.848	3.840	8.840	22.28	.4255	.1702	.6404
	3	2.439	6.513	18.88	59.07	.5624	.2513	1.123
	4	3.097	10.38	37.46	145.0	.7871	.4336	2.254
	5	3.953	16.88	77.64	383.6	1.253	.9933	6.094
	6	5.446	32.58	214.1	1544	2.920	4.814	39.74
7	1	1.135	1.564	2.500	4.513	.2758	.09951	.2711
	2	1.703	3.245	6.825	15.66	.3469	.1186	.4175
	3	2.212	5.328	13.88	38.82	.4369	.1604	.6617
	4	2.743	8.094	25.56	86.06	.5681	.2406	1.132
	5	3.363	12.09	46.38	189.1	.7869	.4186	2.238
	6	4.189	18.80	90.14	461.4	1.245	.9681	5.990
	7	5.656	34.88	234.7	1724	2.892	4.741	39.06
8	1	1.070	1.384	2.072	3.490	.2397	.07770	.2013
	2	1.590	2.819	5.499	11.67	.2927	.08780	.2928
	3	2.042	4.524	10.80	27.63	.3564	.1117	.4327
	4	2.495	6.667	19.00	57.48	.4427	.1535	.6719
	5	2.992	9.520	32.13	114.6	.5701	.2327	1.130
	6	3.585	13.64	54.93	233.8	.7849	.4061	2.219
	7	4.391	20.52	101.9	537.2	1.236	.9484	5.890
	8	5.836	36.93	253.7	1894	2.867	4.682	38.48
9	1	1.016	1.245	1.759	2.792	.2122	.06267	.1556
	2	1.498	2.498	4.570	9.074	.2531	.06785	.2163
	3	1.908	3.942	8.752	20.76	.3005	.08249	.3039
	4	2.308	5.688	14.90	41.36	.3615	.1073	.4403
	5	2.729	7.891	24.11	77.64	.4457	.1477	.6782
	6	3.202	10.82	38.53	144.2	.5700	.2275	1.119
	7	3.777	15.05	63.13	278.6	.7822	.3945	2.205
	8	4.566	22.08	113.0	611.1	1.227	.9335	5.791
	9	5.995	38.79	271.3	2054	2.846	4.631	37.98
10	1	.9711	1.134	1.523	2.293	.1905	.05184	.1240
	2	1.423	2.248	3.887	7.284	.2230	.05417	.1662
	3	1.800	3.501	7.300	16.23	.2596	.06360	.2244
	4	2.160	4.972	12.14	31.32	.3052	.07901	.3105
	5	2.529	6.762	19.05	56.41	.3643	.1043	.4427
	6	2.928	9.021	29.18	98.87	.4478	.1411	.6876
	7	3.385	12.02	44.77	174.5	.5681	.2268	1.091
	8	3.945	16.34	71.00	323.2	.7798	.3804	2.213
	9	4.722	23.51	123.4	683.0	1.218	.9237	5.683
	10	6.137	40.48	287.7	2207	2.826	4.587	37.55
11	1	.9323	1.042	1.338	1.923	.1731	.04375	.1013
12	1	.8985	.9660	1.191	1.640	.1587	.03753	.08444
13	1	.8687	.9013	1.070	1.419	.1467	.03264	.07155
14	1	.8422	.8457	.9707	1.242	.1364	.02872	.06147
15	1	.8183	.7972	.8868	1.098	.1276	.02551	.05344

$r = 4$

n	k	$\mu'_1(k, n)$	$\mu'_2(k, n)$	$\mu'_3(k, n)$	$\mu'_4(k, n)$	$\mu_2(k, n)$	$\mu_3(k, n)$	$\mu_4(k, n)$
1	1	4.000	20.00	120.0	840.0	4.000	8.000	72.00
2	1	2.906	10.16	41.25	190.3	1.710	1.794	11.46
	2	5.094	29.84	198.8	1490	3.897	7.028	6.653
3	1	2.449	7.088	23.49	87.26	1.088	.7918	4.329
	2	3.820	16.29	76.78	396.4	1.701	1.548	10.92
	3	5.731	36.62	259.7	2036	3.779	6.5774	62.58
4	1	2.183	5.569	16.12	51.92	.8047	.4537	2.266
	2	3.250	11.65	45.58	193.3	1.085	.6768	4.177
	3	4.390	20.94	10.80	59.96	1.667	1.424	10.39
	4	6.178	41.85	310.3	2515	3.684	6.300	59.73
5	1	2.002	4.651	12.18	35.32	.6430	.2983	1.404
	2	2.905	9.239	31.87	118.3	.7989	.3837	2.185
	3	3.767	15.26	66.15	305.7	1.069	.6202	4.014
	4	4.806	24.73	135.9	795.5	1.634	1.346	9.943
	5	6.521	46.13	353.9	2945	3.608	6.112	57.58
6	1	1.869	4.032	9.761	26.05	.5386	.2134	.9630
	2	2.667	7.748	24.30	81.68	.6342	.2493	1.345
	3	3.381	12.22	47.00	191.6	.7886	.3512	2.111
	4	4.152	18.29	85.29	419.8	1.053	.5838	3.872
	5	5.132	27.94	161.2	983.3	1.604	1.291	9.577
	6	6.798	49.76	392.5	3338	3.546	5.972	55.89
7	1	1.765	3.582	8.130	20.27	.4655	.1616	.7069
	2	2.490	6.726	19.55	60.71	.5274	.1762	.9147
	3	3.111	10.30	36.17	134.1	.6258	.2278	1.301
	4	3.742	14.78	61.44	268.3	.7782	.3304	2.045
	5	4.460	20.93	103.2	533.3	1.037	.5572	.3751
	6	5.401	30.75	184.4	1163	1.578	1.251	9.269
	7	7.031	52.93	427.2	3700	3.495	5.862	54.50
8	1	1.682	3.240	6.961	16.39	.4114	.1275	.5445
	2	2.351	5.978	16.31	47.45	.4526	.1319	.6650
	3	2.907	8.971	29.26	100.5	.5196	.1608	.8838
	4	3.450	12.52	47.68	190.1	.6184	.2138	1.266
	5	4.033	17.03	75.20	346.6	.7681	.3161	1.984
	6	4.717	23.27	120.0	645.4	1.023	.5356	3.654
	7	5.629	33.24	205.8	1336	1.555	1.220	8.997
	8	7.231	55.74	458.8	4038	3.451	5.772	53.35
9	1	1.612	2.970	6.084	13.63	.3697	.1037	.4347
	2	2.238	5.405	13.98	38.44	.3972	.1028	.5071
	3	2.746	7.986	24.50	78.97	.4451	.1199	.6414
	4	3.229	10.94	38.79	143.6	.5134	.1517	.8584
	5	3.727	14.50	58.81	248.2	.6119	.2021	1.242
	6	4.278	19.06	88.32	425.3	.7580	.3086	1.913
	7	4.936	25.38	135.8	755.4	1.011	.5142	3.591
	8	5.827	35.49	225.8	1502	1.534	1.199	8.737
	9	7.407	58.28	487.9	4355	3.413	5.695	52.38
10	1	1.552	2.750	5.403	11.59	.3366	.08639	.3568
	2	2.143	4.949	12.21	32.00	.3547	.08269	.4009
	3	2.615	7.227	21.03	64.20	.3898	.09341	.4872
	4	3.053	9.759	32.59	113.4	.4399	.1121	.6262
	5	3.493	12.71	48.08	188.9	.5072	.1474	.8281
	6	3.961	16.29	69.53	307.4	.6074	.1863	1.249
	7	4.489	20.90	100.9	503.9	.7467	.3133	1.797
	8	5.128	27.30	150.7	863.1	1.002	.4851	3.611
	9	6.001	37.53	244.6	1662	1.515	1.186	8.478
	10	7.563	60.58	514.9	4654	3.380	5.627	51.56
11	1	1.502	2.567	4.860	10.03	.3095	.07335	.2993
12	1	1.458	2.412	4.416	8.800	.2870	.06325	.2555
13	1	1.418	2.279	4.048	7.813	.2680	.05525	.2214
14	1	1.383	2.164	3.736	7.007	.2517	.04879	.1942
15	1	1.351	2.062	3.470	6.336	.2376	.04349	.1721

$r = 5$

n	k	$\mu'_1(k, n)$	$\mu'_2(k, n)$	$\mu'_3(k, n)$	$\mu'_4(k, n)$	$\mu_2(k, n)$	$\mu_3(k, n)$	$\mu_4(k, n)$
1	1	5.000	30.00	210.0	1680	5.000	10.00	105.0
2	1	3.770	16.46	81.42	448.3	2.255	2.347	18.71
	2	6.230	43.54	338.6	2992	4.716	8.569	92.75
3	1	3.245	12.01	49.65	225.8	1.482	1.058	7.579
	2	4.819	25.37	145.0	893.3	2.149	1.957	16.73
	3	6.936	52.62	435.4	3921	4.506	7.940	85.33
4	1	2.934	9.731	35.75	143.4	1.121	.6133	4.172
	2	4.176	18.85	91.36	472.9	1.408	.8720	6.779
	3	5.462	31.90	198.5	1314	2.065	1.776	15.40
	4	7.428	59.52	514.4	4790	4.354	7.568	80.34
5	1	2.722	8.321	28.02	102.5	.9120	.4058	2.688
	2	3.783	15.37	66.65	306.9	1.057	.5001	3.699
	3	4.766	24.07	128.4	721.9	1.356	.7872	6.271
	4	5.926	37.12	245.3	1708	1.998	1.666	14.45
	5	7.803	65.12	581.6	5560	4.238	7.315	76.70
6	1	2.564	7.351	23.12	78.71	.7750	.2913	1.905
	2	3.510	13.17	52.53	221.7	.8519	.3273	2.355
	3	4.331	19.77	94.89	477.5	1.017	.4509	3.423
	4	5.201	28.36	161.9	966.4	1.316	.7339	5.905
	5	6.289	41.49	287.0	2079	1.945	1.591	13.71
	6	8.106	69.85	640.5	6257	4.456	7.127	73.89
7	1	2.441	6.636	19.73	63.33	.6781	.2208	1.437
	2	3.304	11.64	43.43	170.9	.7175	.2325	1.646
	3	4.023	17.01	75.30	348.5	.8188	.2946	2.176
	4	4.741	23.46	121.0	649.5	.9883	.4207	3.223
	5	5.546	32.04	192.6	1204	1.283	.6952	5.628
	6	6.586	45.27	32.47	2429	1.901	1.536	13.11
	7	8.539	73.95	693.2	6895	4.071	6.979	71.64
8	1	2.341	6.085	17.25	52.70	.6057	.1741	1.133
	2	3.142	10.50	37.07	137.8	.6224	.1744	1.225
	3	3.790	15.05	62.48	270.4	.6878	.2095	1.513
	4	4.412	20.26	96.67	478.6	.7958	.2734	2.059
	5	5.069	26.66	145.4	820.4	.9646	.4014	3.054
	6	5.832	35.27	221.0	1434	1.257	.6621	5.435
	7	6.837	48.60	359.3	2761	1.864	1.496	12.59
	8	8.577	77.57	740.9	7485	4.008	6.858	69.80
9	1	2.257	5.644	15.36	44.95	.5494	.1414	.9237
	2	3.010	9.613	32.39	114.7	.5515	.1363	.9533
	3	3.605	13.59	53.45	218.7	.5952	.1562	1.126
	4	4.160	17.98	80.55	373.6	.6675	.1975	1.413
	5	4.726	23.11	116.8	609.8	.7787	.2521	2.008
	6	5.344	29.51	168.2	988.8	.9431	.3980	2.834
	7	6.076	38.15	247.4	1657	1.235	.6250	5.358
	8	7.054	51.59	391.2	3076	1.831	1.471	12.09
	9	8.767	80.82	784.6	8036	3.954	6.753	68.28
10	1	2.186	5.282	13.87	39.08	.5044	.1175	.7723
	2	2.899	8.903	28.80	97.76	.4966	.1096	.7678
	3	3.453	12.45	46.75	182.4	.5257	.1228	.8671
	4	3.959	16.26	69.08	303.5	.5781	.1425	1.078
	5	4.462	20.56	97.74	478.9	.6500	.2000	1.269
	6	4.989	25.66	13.59	740.8	.7684	.2094	2.147
	7	5.581	32.07	189.7	1154	.9197	.4310	2.389
	8	6.288	40.76	272.2	1872	1.220	.5602	5.597
	9	7.246	54.30	421.0	3377	1.800	1.470	11.48
	10	8.936	83.76	825.0	8554	3.907	6.658	67.03
11	1	2.124	4.978	12.66	34.50	.4674	.09943	.6588
12	1	2.069	4.719	11.66	30.83	.4364	.08542	.5712
13	1	2.021	4.494	10.82	27.83	.4101	.07431	.5019
14	1	1.978	4.298	10.10	25.35	.3874	.06532	.4460
15	1	1.938	4.124	9.477	23.25	.3676	.05794	.4001

TABLE 12D.2

MODAL VALUES OF THE SMALLEST (TOP NUMBER) AND THE LARGEST (BOTTOM NUMBER) OF A SAMPLE OF SIZE n FROM THE STANDARDIZED GAMMA DISTRIBUTION WITH PARAMETER r

n \ r	1	2	3	4	5	6	7	8	9	10
1	.0000	1.0000	2.0000	3.0000	4.0000	5.0000	6.0000	7.0000	8.0000	9.0000
	.0000	1.0000	2.0000	3.0000	4.0000	5.0000	6.0000	7.0000	8.0000	9.0000
2	.0000	.7070	2.0000	2.3724	3.2442	4.1300	5.0260	5.9298	6.8399	7.7552
	.6932	1.9375	3.1143	4.2594	5.3855	6.4983	7.6014	8.6970	9.7863	10.8706
3	.0000	.5773	1.3007	2.0774	2.8849	3.7131	4.5564	5.4115	6.2760	7.1482
	1.0986	2.4647	3.7301	4.9486	6.1384	7.3085	8.4640	9.6081	10.7429	11.8701
4	.0000	.5000	1.1654	1.8942	2.6599	3.4506	4.2596	5.0838	5.9174	6.7615
	1.3863	2.8310	4.1542	5.4204	6.6520	7.8595	9.0493	10.2252	11.3899	12.5452
5	.0000	.4472	1.0710	1.7650	2.5003	3.2636	4.0474	4.8473	5.6601	6.4835
	1.6094	3.1113	4.4767	5.7779	7.0400	8.2750	9.4900	10.6892	11.8758	13.0518
6	.0000	.4083	1.0000	1.6671	2.3787	3.1205	3.8848	4.6664	5.4621	6.2694
	1.7918	3.3382	4.7365	6.0650	7.3510	8.6075	9.8422	11.0597	12.2635	13.4557
7	.0000	.3780	.9440	1.5892	2.2815	3.0059	3.7542	4.5209	5.3026	6.0967
	1.9459	3.5285	4.9536	6.3045	7.6100	8.8841	10.1349	11.3674	12.5852	13.7906
8	.0000	.3535	.8982	1.5251	2.2012	2.9110	3.6458	4.4001	5.1700	5.9529
	2.0794	3.6923	5.1400	6.5096	7.8316	9.1205	10.3849	11.6300	12.8596	14.0763
9	.0000	.3333	.8597	1.4710	2.1333	2.8306	3.5538	4.2972	5.0570	5.8304
	2.1972	3.8361	5.3032	6.6889	8.0250	9.3267	10.6028	11.8588	13.0986	14.3249
10	.0000	.3162	.8269	1.4245	2.0747	2.7610	3.4741	4.2081	4.9590	5.7240
	2.3026	3.9642	5.4482	6.8481	8.1966	9.5094	10.7958	12.0613	13.3100	14.5448
15	.0000	.2582	.7125	1.2607	1.8668	2.5129	3.1889	3.8883	4.6066	5.3408
	2.7081	4.4525	5.9986	7.4504	8.8445	10.1984	11.5224	12.8230	14.1047	15.3705
20	.0000	.2236	.6416	1.1576	1.7345	2.3539	3.0053	3.6816	4.3782	5.0918
	2.9957	4.7950	6.3824	7.8689	9.2933	10.6747	12.0240	13.3481	14.6518	15.9385
25	.0000	.2000	.5919	1.0841	1.6395	2.2393	2.8724	3.5316	4.2121	4.9103
	3.4012	5.0587	6.6766	8.1889	9.6360	11.0378	12.4059	13.7476	15.0677	16.3700
50	.0000	.1414	.4618	.8874	1.3818	1.9251	2.5056	3.1155	3.7494	4.4033
	3.9120	5.8678	7.5740	9.1606	10.6733	12.1346	13.5573	14.9497	16.3177	17.6652
100	.0000	.1000	.3615	.7297	1.1703	1.6635	2.1969	2.7624	3.3542	3.9681
	4.6052	6.6643	8.4501	10.1040	11.6763	13.1915	14.6639	16.1027	17.5143	18.9031

This table is reproduced from S. S. Gupta, "Order statistics from the gamma distribution," *Technometrics*, Vol. 2 (1960), pp. 243–262, with permission of J. S. Hunter, editor of *Technometrics*.

TABLE 12D.3

THE ALPHA PERCENTAGE POINTS OF THE kTH SMALLEST ORDER STATISTIC OF A SAMPLE OF SIZE n [$1 \le k \le n, n = 1(1)10$ AND SELECTED VALUES OF α] FROM A STANDARDIZED GAMMA DISTRIBUTION WITH PARAMETER r

$r = 1$

n	k \ α	.01	.05	.10	.25	.50	.75	.90	.95	.99
1	1	.01005	.05129	.10536	.28768	.69315	1.38629	2.30259	2.99573	4.60517
2	1	.00503	.02565	.05268	.14384	.34657	.69315	1.15129	1.49785	2.30259
	2	.10536	.25310	.38013	.69315	1.22796	2.01014	2.96973	3.67612	5.29580
3	1	.00335	.01710	.03512	.09589	.23105	.46210	.76753	.99859	1.53507
	2	.06071	.14543	.21791	.39504	.69315	1.11978	1.63066	1.99989	2.83186
	3	.24263	.45950	.62392	.99414	1.57842	2.39207	3.36648	4.07737	5.70044
4	1	.00251	.01282	.02634	.07192	.17328	.34657	.57565	.74893	1.15129
	2	.04291	.10271	.15380	.27842	.48732	.78456	1.13800	1.39191	1.95992
	3	.15184	.28582	.38634	.60939	.95262	1.41461	1.94799	2.32677	3.17011
	4	.38013	.64031	.82631	1.22796	1.83822	2.66794	3.64981	4.36293	5.98771
5	1	.00201	.01026	.02107	.05754	.13863	.27726	.46051	.59915	.94209
	2	.03323	.07952	.11905	.21537	.37660	.60547	.87681	1.07122	1.50476
	3	.11165	.20981	.28321	.44541	.69315	1.02321	1.39983	1.66463	2.24772
	4	.25112	.41945	.53804	.78926	1.15897	1.64114	2.18712	2.57125	3.42093
	5	.50768	.79691	.99685	1.41824	2.04446	2.88396	3.87031	4.58478	6.21062
1	1	.00168	.00855	.01756	.04795	.11552	.23105	.36920	.49929	.76753
	2	.02713	.06491	.09717	.17574	.30714	.49344	.71400	.87180	1.22312
	3	.08854	.16624	.22428	.35228	.54716	.80564	1.09904	1.30438	1.75406
	4	.19004	.31655	.40525	.59204	.86415	1.21429	1.60490	1.87627	2.46829
	5	.34858	.54163	.67272	.94294	1.33010	1.82536	2.37952	2.76700	3.62073
	6	.62392	.93384	1.14347	1.57842	2.21549	3.06153	4.05088	4.76623	6.39272
7	1	.00144	.00733	.01505	.04110	.09902	.19804	.32893	.42796	.65788
	2	.02293	.05485	.08210	.14847	.25999	.41659	.60250	.73543	1.03103
	3	.07344	.13784	.18590	.29178	.45275	.66573	.90679	1.07511	1.44257
	4	.15347	.25531	.32656	.47618	.69315	.97061	1.27798	1.49023	1.95003
	5	.26961	.41743	.51721	.72134	1.01027	1.37409	1.77408	2.04981	2.64784
	6	.44105	.65258	.79283	1.07672	1.47626	1.98072	2.54055	2.93041	3.78693
	7	.72971	1.05509	1.27186	1.71669	2.36149	3.21230	4.20378	4.91977	6.54659
8	1	.00126	.00641	.01317	.03596	.08664	.17328	.28783	.37446	.57565
	2	.01985	.04708	.07109	.12855	.22456	.36054	.52130	.63616	.89145
	3	.06277	.11778	.15882	.24921	.38643	.56777	.77267	.91552	1.22680
	4	.12891	.21431	.27399	.39911	.58010	.81078	1.06531	1.24050	1.66495
	5	.22090	.34142	.42254	.58790	.82062	1.11145	1.42853	1.64558	2.11238
	6	.34705	.51134	.61949	.83653	1.13781	1.51149	1.91834	2.19723	2.79951
	7	.52773	.75358	.90079	1.19501	1.60380	2.11503	2.67917	3.07110	3.92410
	8	.82631	1.16366	1.38585	1.83822	2.48891	3.34308	4.33638	5.05283	6.67943
9	1	.00112	.00570	.01171	.03196	.07702	.15404	.25585	.33286	.51169
	2	.01744	.04187	.06269	.11334	.19799	.31783	.45944	.56061	.78533
	3	.05485	.10285	.13868	.21750	.33580	.49518	.67350	.79771	1.06802
	4	.11122	.18482	.23623	.34389	.49936	.69714	.91484	1.06438	1.38617
	5	.18750	.28951	.35806	.49751	.69315	.93660	1.20074	1.38083	1.76627
	6	.28772	.42303	.51179	.68918	.93374	1.23447	1.55874	1.77934	2.25132
	7	.42112	.59849	.71319	.94022	1.25092	1.63234	2.04414	2.32550	2.93043
	8	.60875	.84597	.99869	1.30096	1.71691	2.23348	2.80081	3.19402	4.05745
	9	.91499	1.26185	1.48837	1.94659	2.60194	3.45907	4.45348	5.17026	6.80331
10	1	.00101	.00513	.01054	.02877	.06931	.13863	.23026	.29958	.46051
	2	.01524	.03700	.05604	.10136	.17705	.28418	.41075	.50114	.70189
	3	.05104	.09123	.12737	.19303	.29918	.43919	.59711	.70704	.94608
	4	.09806	.16255	.21042	.30225	.43866	.61194	.80236	.93298	1.21362
	5	.16304	.25159	.31105	.43183	.60091	.81078	1.03784	1.19224	1.52170
	6	.24634	.36174	.43730	.58790	.79476	1.04788	1.31931	1.50310	1.89419
	7	.35257	.49985	.59470	.78154	1.03536	1.34382	1.66201	1.89693	2.37082
	8	.49145	.67944	.79940	1.03440	1.35259	1.73987	2.12370	2.43963	3.00051
	9	.68448	.93100	1.08812	1.39687	1.81856	2.33935	2.90958	3.31536	4.19147
	10	.99685	1.35143	1.58148	2.04446	2.70351	3.56285	4.55819	5.27534	6.90327

For given $n, k, (1 \le k \le n)$ and α the entries in this table are the values of y for which $\frac{n!}{(k-1)!\,(n-k)!}\int_0^y G_r^{k-1}(z)\,[1 - G_r(z)]^{n-k} g_r(z)\,dz = \alpha$, where $g_r(z)$ and $G_r(z)$ refer to the pdf and cdf of the standardized gamma chance variable, respectively.

This table is reproduced from S. S. Gupta, "Order statistics from the gamma distribution," *Technometrics*, Vol. 2 (1960), pp. 243–262, with permission of J. S. Hunter, editor of *Technometrics*.

$r = 2$

n	k \ α	.01	.05	.10	.25	.50	.75	.90	.95	.99
1	1	.14855	.35536	.53181	.96128	1.67835	2.69263	3.88972	4.74386	6.63835
2	1	.10363	.24389	.36062	.63623	1.07795	1.67835	2.36459	2.84449	3.88972
	2	.53181	.88931	1.14176	1.67835	2.47297	3.51827	4.71237	5.55659	7.42727
3	1	.08410	.19649	.28894	.50407	.84178	1.29116	1.79556	2.14412	2.89469
	2	.39005	.64032	.81276	1.16958	1.67835	2.31964	3.02259	3.50510	4.54471
	3	.86692	1.28654	1.56644	2.13760	2.95286	4.00189	5.18930	6.02715	7.88478
4	1	.07257	.16880	.24741	.42865	.70946	1.07795	1.48654	1.76653	2.36459
	2	.32221	.52414	.66156	.94228	1.33558	1.82201	2.34566	2.70033	3.45364
	3	.65661	.95747	1.15338	1.54257	2.07637	2.73139	3.43825	3.92009	4.95421
	4	1.14176	1.59320	1.88628	2.47297	3.29588	4.34390	5.52554	6.35883	8.20776
5	1	.06475	.15016	.21957	.37862	.62276	.93989	1.28834	1.52564	2.06075
	2	.28040	.45348	.57036	.80709	1.13513	1.53609	1.96301	2.24982	2.85383
	3	.54972	.79458	.95214	1.26139	1.67835	2.18013	2.71117	3.06772	3.82062
	4	.88510	1.21445	1.42308	1.82929	2.37552	3.03652	3.74400	4.22463	5.25418
	5	1.37099	1.84110	2.14157	2.73635	3.56228	4.60819	5.78502	6.61488	8.45742
6	1	.05900	.13652	.19929	.34243	.56058	.84178	1.12116	1.35645	1.79556
	2	.25135	.40482	.50785	.71536	1.00057	1.34627	1.71151	1.95544	2.46617
	3	.48178	.69238	.82691	1.08894	1.43858	1.85456	2.28990	2.57965	3.18574
	4	.74919	1.01930	1.18844	1.51385	1.94388	2.45375	2.98825	3.34539	4.09692
	5	1.08182	1.42918	1.64562	2.06202	2.61527	3.27910	3.98619	4.46545	5.49118
	6	1.56644	2.04849	2.35347	2.95286	3.77991	4.82342	5.99626	6.82334	8.66079
7	1	.05455	.12599	.18368	.31474	.51334	.76774	1.04369	1.22992	1.62170
	2	.22968	.36875	.46171	.64807	.90389	1.20924	1.53119	1.74533	2.19153
	3	.43368	.62069	.73949	.96963	1.27451	1.63437	2.00809	2.25544	2.76951
	4	.66071	.89399	1.03904	1.31604	1.67835	2.10298	2.54293	2.83419	3.44088
	5	.92403	1.21077	1.38743	1.72312	2.16123	2.67588	3.21202	3.56913	4.31915
	6	1.25356	1.61313	1.83481	2.25777	2.81528	3.48044	4.18664	4.66466	5.68712
	7	1.73632	2.22649	2.53440	3.13655	3.96362	5.00487	6.17428	6.99910	8.83226
8	1	.05096	.11755	.17119	.29267	.47594	.70946	.96158	1.13110	1.48654
	2	.21268	.33902	.42587	.59612	.82752	1.10472	1.39445	1.58645	1.98508
	3	.39734	.56685	.67409	.88102	1.15354	1.47333	1.80355	2.02116	2.47134
	4	.59711	.80470	.93313	1.17710	1.49399	1.86247	2.24128	2.49056	3.06814
	5	.81941	1.06800	1.22009	1.50699	1.87756	2.30771	2.75040	3.04243	3.64904
	6	1.07888	1.37731	1.55917	1.90190	2.34540	2.86292	3.39993	3.75681	4.50520
	7	1.40549	1.77379	1.99910	2.42657	2.98679	3.65241	4.35771	4.83497	5.84806
	8	1.88628	2.38218	2.69203	3.29588	4.12257	5.16138	6.32810	7.15097	8.98001
9	1	.04801	.11060	.16091	.27459	.44541	.66215	.89514	1.05137	1.37792
	2	.19859	.31794	.39704	.55449	.76762	1.02183	1.28643	1.46130	1.82320
	3	.36875	.52454	.62288	.81185	1.05710	1.34930	1.64688	1.84233	2.24519
	4	.54853	.73696	.85308	1.07277	1.35656	1.68471	2.02015	2.23994	2.69247
	5	.74325	.96501	1.10000	1.35336	1.67835	2.05258	2.43466	2.68514	3.20177
	6	.96136	1.22097	1.37809	1.67200	2.04834	2.48210	2.92649	3.21891	3.82517
	7	1.21750	1.52456	1.71021	2.05798	2.50516	3.02482	3.56187	3.91850	4.66468
	8	1.54151	1.91628	2.14428	2.57490	3.13685	3.80265	4.50679	4.98293	6.00392
	9	2.02037	2.52043	2.83167	3.43644	4.26255	5.29955	6.46350	7.28466	9.11758
10	1	.04551	.10473	.15227	.25942	.41990	.62276	.84005	.98540	1.28834
	2	.18489	.29722	.37314	.52020	.71851	.95412	1.19855	1.35965	1.69227
	3	.35440	.49002	.59296	.75616	.98460	1.25021	1.52227	1.70047	2.06667
	4	.51050	.68332	.79596	.99078	1.24926	1.54676	1.84950	2.04720	2.45281
	5	.68451	.88611	1.00837	1.23694	1.52857	1.86247	2.20144	2.42266	2.87668
	6	.87488	1.10702	1.24681	1.50699	1.83778	2.21603	2.60034	2.85158	3.36864
	7	1.08949	1.35742	1.51827	1.81733	2.19783	2.63421	3.06423	3.37220	3.97531
	8	1.34279	1.65642	1.84494	2.19643	2.64630	3.16708	3.66346	4.06124	4.74965
	9	1.66450	2.04425	2.27419	2.70713	3.27022	3.93588	4.63935	5.12827	6.15998
	10	2.14157	2.64470	2.95696	3.56228	4.38761	5.42268	6.58427	7.40406	9.22844

$r = 3$

n	k \ α	.01	.05	.10	.25	.50	.75	.90	.95	.99
1	1	.43605	.81769	1.10207	1.72730	2.67406	3.92040	5.32232	6.29579	8.40595
2	1	.33817	.62178	.82656	1.26086	1.88744	2.67406	3.52510	4.10147	5.32232
	2	1.10207	1.62688	1.97379	2.67406	3.65638	4.89287	6.26019	7.20790	9.27067
3	1	.29218	.53226	.70303	1.05886	1.55977	2.17301	2.82228	3.25570	4.16107
	2	.87562	1.26697	1.51846	2.01118	2.67406	3.47044	4.31244	4.87757	6.07034
	3	1.59535	2.16691	2.53118	3.24769	4.23001	5.45120	6.79717	7.73102	9.76927
4	1	.26364	.47752	.62823	.93880	1.36916	1.88744	2.42827	2.78570	3.52510
	2	.76114	1.09016	1.29858	1.70092	2.23154	2.85554	3.50209	3.92961	4.81770
	3	1.29122	1.72202	1.98942	2.50052	3.17223	3.96672	4.79978	5.35725	6.53302
	4	1.97379	2.56548	2.93609	3.65638	4.63359	5.84213	7.17326	8.09787	10.12013
5	1	.24355	.43938	.57644	.85667	1.24067	1.69759	2.16929	2.47873	3.15294
	2	.68787	.97878	1.16134	1.51037	1.96485	2.49218	3.03177	3.38527	4.11256
	3	1.12972	1.49245	1.71462	2.13363	2.67406	3.29993	3.94257	4.36567	5.24275
	4	1.62095	2.07121	2.34596	2.86468	3.53836	4.32888	5.15434	5.70614	6.86989
	5	2.27797	2.87951	3.25257	3.97264	4.94398	6.14229	7.46226	8.38012	10.39075
6	1	.22834	.41070	.53769	.79577	1.14639	1.55977	1.94600	2.25892	2.82228
	2	.63546	.89996	1.06478	1.37779	1.78157	2.24558	2.71614	3.02236	3.64816
	3	1.02380	1.34410	1.53863	1.90237	2.36610	2.89639	3.43420	3.78493	4.50452
	4	1.42702	1.80732	2.03646	2.46354	3.00796	3.63315	4.27187	4.69146	5.56013
	5	1.89270	2.35389	2.63243	3.15450	3.82771	4.61396	5.43319	5.98038	7.13492
	6	2.53118	3.13778	3.51158	4.23001	5.19580	6.38562	7.69678	8.60932	10.61084
7	1	.21627	.38805	.50719	.74820	1.07335	1.45385	1.84074	2.09182	2.60191
	2	.59542	.84020	.99193	1.27852	1.64732	2.06426	2.48588	2.75893	3.31391
	3	.94693	1.23757	1.41295	1.73887	2.15100	2.61808	3.08775	3.39213	4.01221
	4	1.29732	1.63345	1.83437	2.20583	2.67406	3.20505	3.74076	4.08922	4.80284
	5	1.67549	2.06629	2.29947	2.73084	3.27674	3.90036	4.53536	4.95192	5.81394
	6	2.12324	2.59097	2.87161	3.39498	4.06672	4.84889	5.66274	6.20623	7.35334
	7	2.74755	3.35673	3.73049	4.44672	5.40727	6.59003	7.89393	8.80219	10.79615
8	1	.20635	.36953	.48234	.70961	1.01454	1.36916	1.72771	1.95942	2.42827
	2	.56337	.78998	.93428	1.20052	1.53950	1.92377	2.30864	2.55683	3.05919
	3	.88766	1.15598	1.31713	1.61521	1.98964	2.41118	2.83234	3.10394	3.65441
	4	1.20201	1.50695	1.68818	2.02127	2.43790	2.90629	3.37483	3.67762	4.36617
	5	1.52795	1.87391	2.07872	2.45468	2.92518	3.45591	3.98940	4.33585	5.04455
	6	1.88870	2.28624	2.52185	2.95560	3.50177	4.12336	4.75512	5.16914	6.02552
	7	2.32303	2.79486	3.07660	3.60026	4.27014	5.04845	5.85785	6.39866	7.53231
	8	2.93609	3.54646	3.91968	4.63359	5.58949	6.76585	8.06394	8.96857	10.95566
9	1	.19801	.35400	.46152	.67748	.96583	1.29945	1.63506	1.85122	2.28703
	2	.53633	.75376	.88717	1.13704	1.45368	1.81079	2.16676	2.39560	2.85703
	3	.84019	1.09078	1.24086	1.51716	1.85905	2.24955	2.63403	2.88105	3.37961
	4	1.12787	1.40928	1.57577	1.88040	2.25907	2.68214	3.10270	3.37319	3.92021
	5	1.41842	1.73246	1.91737	2.25487	2.67406	3.14284	3.61006	3.91143	4.52334
	6	1.72741	2.07990	2.28726	2.66600	3.13759	3.66741	4.19878	4.54345	5.24799
	7	2.07528	2.47734	2.71450	3.14951	3.69524	4.31507	4.94350	5.35542	6.20626
	8	2.49915	2.97356	3.25590	3.77922	4.44707	5.22203	6.02732	6.56535	7.70527
	9	3.10297	3.71365	4.08622	4.79767	5.74941	6.92069	8.21335	9.11485	11.10404
10	1	.19083	.34070	.44376	.65014	.92459	1.24067	1.55731	1.76066	2.16929
	2	.50957	.71763	.84753	1.08404	1.38239	1.71737	2.04998	2.26313	2.69174
	3	.81608	1.03680	1.19573	1.43712	1.75956	2.11879	2.47439	2.70214	3.16026
	4	1.06891	1.33076	1.49444	1.76808	2.11753	2.50590	2.89005	3.13619	3.63201
	5	1.33252	1.62238	1.79231	2.10115	2.48250	2.90629	3.32606	3.59552	4.13970
	6	1.60657	1.92688	2.11427	2.45468	2.87534	3.34393	3.80978	4.10989	4.71862
	7	1.90311	2.26020	2.46923	2.84966	3.32164	3.85043	4.36157	4.72277	5.42069
	8	2.24101	2.64618	2.88432	3.31993	3.86493	4.48261	5.06123	5.51926	6.30233
	9	2.65646	3.13254	3.41503	3.93773	4.60356	5.37540	6.17758	6.72869	7.87811
	10	3.25257	3.86302	4.23485	4.94398	5.89189	7.05841	8.34641	9.24532	11.22351

$r = 4$

n	k \ α	.01	.05	.10	.25	.50	.75	.90	.95	.99
1	1	.82325	1.36632	1.74477	2.53532	3.67206	5.10943	6.68078	7.75366	10.04512
2	1	.67269	1.09427	1.37838	1.95001	2.73162	3.67206	4.65871	5.31458	6.68078
	2	1.74477	2.41115	2.83667	3.67206	4.80885	6.20322	7.71463	8.74903	10.97414
3	1	.59931	.96562	1.20850	1.68825	2.32766	3.07712	3.84580	4.34905	5.38194
	2	1.44477	1.95784	2.27604	2.88199	3.67206	4.59606	5.55268	6.18615	7.50625
	3	2.37197	3.06979	3.50367	4.33981	5.45977	6.82355	8.30184	9.31638	11.50771
4	1	.55271	.88522	1.10343	1.52947	2.08803	2.73162	3.38180	3.80301	4.65871
	2	1.28893	1.72923	1.99825	2.50279	3.14730	3.88467	4.63235	5.11988	6.11932
	3	1.98885	2.52881	2.85562	3.46742	4.25264	5.16198	6.09930	6.71950	8.01337
	4	2.83667	3.54418	3.97861	4.80885	5.91341	7.25519	8.71138	9.71291	11.88236
5	1	.51934	.82826	1.02952	1.41919	1.92412	2.49867	3.07265	3.44163	4.23033
	2	1.18735	1.58265	1.82182	2.26592	2.82581	3.45755	4.08988	4.49826	5.32712
	3	1.78078	2.24346	2.51969	3.02978	3.67206	4.40004	5.13458	5.61262	6.59251
	4	2.40379	2.95457	3.28393	3.89534	4.67390	5.57120	6.49434	7.10527	8.38113
	5	3.20283	3.91264	4.34544	5.16869	6.26022	7.58527	9.02519	10.01729	12.17089
6	1	.49373	.78489	.97351	1.33642	1.80244	2.32766	2.80291	3.18007	3.84580
	2	1.11367	1.47750	1.69602	2.09896	2.60208	3.16410	3.72148	4.07895	4.79947
	3	1.64215	2.05621	2.30126	2.74982	3.30792	3.93233	4.55447	4.95542	5.76868
	4	2.16119	2.63366	2.91258	3.42362	4.06222	4.78232	5.50699	5.97820	6.94403
	5	2.73803	3.29338	3.62309	4.23214	5.00411	5.89141	6.80361	7.40736	8.66968
	6	3.50367	4.21279	4.64323	5.45977	6.54039	7.85207	9.27931	10.26406	12.40528
7	1	.47316	.75026	.92898	1.27111	1.70724	2.19497	2.67457	2.97943	3.58715
	2	1.05672	1.39689	1.60007	1.97262	2.43650	2.94617	3.45009	3.77166	4.41615
	3	1.54032	1.92013	2.14342	2.54957	3.05068	3.60620	4.15484	4.50615	5.21354
	4	1.99664	2.41930	2.66679	3.11650	3.67206	4.29058	4.90511	5.30072	6.10272
	5	2.47136	2.94863	3.22850	3.73873	4.37331	5.08667	5.80328	6.26907	7.22414
	6	3.01728	3.57424	3.90343	4.50941	5.27526	6.15414	7.05738	7.65544	8.90700
	7	3.75832	4.46544	4.89340	5.70376	6.77492	8.07569	9.49260	10.47143	12.60245
8	1	.45611	.72168	.89235	1.21766	1.62996	2.08803	2.53583	2.81921	3.38180
	2	1.01070	1.32850	1.52344	1.87246	2.30235	2.77588	3.23945	3.53397	4.12171
	3	1.46097	1.81487	2.02190	2.39666	2.85589	3.36151	3.85757	4.17360	4.80660
	4	1.87438	2.26164	2.48705	2.89420	3.39322	3.94388	4.48626	4.83310	5.61318
	5	2.28791	2.71510	2.96363	3.41312	3.96590	4.57938	5.18770	5.57906	6.37223
	6	2.73315	3.21272	3.49265	4.00133	4.63198	5.33933	6.04940	6.51078	7.45699
	7	3.25662	3.81373	4.14190	4.74474	5.50503	6.37657	7.27251	7.86634	9.10114
	8	3.97861	4.68317	5.10861	5.91341	6.97648	8.26767	9.67627	10.65012	12.77203
9	1	.44163	.69751	.86142	1.17282	1.56546	1.99935	2.42130	2.68739	3.21366
	2	.97155	1.27877	1.46032	1.79030	2.19477	2.63791	3.06961	3.34299	3.88641
	3	1.39688	1.73004	1.92436	2.27442	2.69696	3.16885	3.62498	3.91445	4.49175
	4	1.77838	2.13880	2.34761	2.72302	3.18025	3.68155	4.17215	4.48437	5.10920
	5	2.15033	2.54168	2.76808	3.17522	3.67206	4.21865	4.75593	5.09925	5.78980
	6	2.53546	2.96506	3.21393	3.66258	4.21257	4.82144	5.42452	5.81236	6.59833
	7	2.95948	3.43997	3.71955	4.22636	4.85320	5.55565	6.25968	6.71748	7.65547
	8	3.46580	4.02223	4.34928	4.94892	5.70415	6.56952	7.45897	8.04871	9.28851
	9	4.17248	4.87421	5.29733	6.09695	7.15300	8.43650	9.83751	10.80708	12.92968
10	1	.42908	.67667	.83485	1.13440	1.51050	1.92412	2.32459	2.57639	3.07265
	2	.93247	1.22880	1.40683	1.72123	2.10479	2.52309	2.92893	3.18509	3.69283
	3	1.36412	1.65927	1.86628	2.17392	2.57502	3.01193	3.43648	3.70505	4.23879
	4	1.70143	2.03925	2.24595	2.58551	3.01041	3.47378	3.92494	4.21094	4.78102
	5	2.04149	2.40556	2.61525	2.99068	3.44609	3.94388	4.43014	4.73932	5.35780
	6	2.38592	2.77966	3.00648	3.41312	3.90779	4.45071	4.98371	5.32410	6.00858
	7	2.75072	3.18159	3.43037	3.87780	4.42504	5.02994	5.60800	6.01322	6.78978
	8	3.15863	3.63927	3.91862	4.42308	5.04642	5.74407	6.39080	6.89885	7.76082
	9	3.65137	4.20672	4.53245	5.12910	5.87976	6.73962	7.62401	8.22713	9.47549
	10	4.34544	5.04424	5.46524	6.26022	7.30999	8.58646	9.98097	10.94696	13.05655

$r = 5$

n	k \ α	.01	.05	.10	.25	.50	.75	.90	.95	.99
1	1	1.27911	1.97015	2.43259	3.36860	4.67091	6.27443	7.99359	9.15352	11.60463
2	1	1.07859	1.62909	1.98508	2.67891	3.59649	4.67091	5.77549	6.50055	7.99359
	2	2.43259	3.22364	3.71785	4.67091	5.94204	7.47399	9.11148	10.22207	12.59055
3	1	.97876	1.46445	1.77335	2.36426	3.12580	3.99425	4.86685	5.43081	6.57468
	2	2.06703	2.68826	3.06515	3.77010	4.67091	5.70588	6.76231	7.45537	8.88685
	3	3.17778	3.98586	4.48034	5.42049	6.66025	8.14850	9.74280	10.82837	13.15516
4	1	.91450	1.36023	1.64072	2.17098	2.84312	3.59649	4.34196	4.81865	5.77549
	2	1.87399	2.41383	2.73643	3.33069	4.07458	4.91059	5.74622	6.28596	7.38247
	3	2.72523	3.36102	3.73971	4.43921	5.32315	6.33241	7.36062	8.03562	9.43296
	4	3.71785	4.52624	5.01617	5.94204	7.15753	8.61577	10.18176	11.25109	13.55094
5	1	.86804	1.28570	1.54654	2.03550	2.64799	3.32589	3.98913	4.40993	5.29822
	2	1.74676	2.23594	2.52539	3.05324	3.70533	4.42801	5.14100	5.59710	6.51436
	3	2.47601	3.02680	3.35038	3.93999	4.67091	5.48769	6.30219	6.82809	7.89772
	4	3.21503	3.85361	4.23056	4.92259	5.79236	6.78264	7.79100	8.45366	9.82788
	5	4.13804	4.94205	5.42678	6.33981	7.53612	8.97208	10.51742	11.57503	13.85539
6	1	.83210	1.22850	1.47463	1.93307	2.50208	3.12580	3.67890	4.11204	4.86685
	2	1.65370	2.10727	2.37366	2.85607	3.44627	4.09379	4.72671	5.12875	5.93165
	3	2.30835	2.80536	3.09480	3.61755	4.25788	4.96419	5.65964	6.10429	6.99914
	4	2.92973	3.48295	3.80532	4.38949	5.10999	5.91264	6.71211	7.22836	8.27909
	5	3.60391	4.24133	4.61555	5.30023	6.15811	7.13347	8.12688	8.78014	10.13712
	6	4.48034	5.27860	5.75830	6.66025	7.84107	9.25946	10.78882	11.83733	14.10250
7	1	.80304	1.18255	1.41710	1.85175	2.38725	2.96963	3.53042	3.88219	4.57489
	2	1.58129	2.00797	2.25717	2.70589	3.25329	3.84396	4.41954	4.78332	5.50564
	3	2.18425	2.64323	2.90872	3.38519	3.96395	4.59645	5.21375	5.60588	6.38926
	4	2.73451	3.23318	3.52139	4.03935	4.67091	5.36554	6.04863	6.48530	7.36436
	5	3.29402	3.84679	4.16735	4.74617	5.45787	6.24931	7.03703	7.54577	8.58221
	6	3.92565	4.56029	4.93169	5.60952	6.45726	7.42046	8.40183	9.04772	10.39107
	7	4.76827	5.56056	6.03567	6.92802	8.09575	9.49995	11.01634	12.05753	14.31023
8	1	.77880	1.14442	1.36952	1.78484	2.29353	2.84312	3.36920	3.69772	4.34196
	2	1.52242	1.92323	2.16361	2.58616	3.09608	3.64767	4.17983	4.51468	5.17667
	3	2.08696	2.51704	2.76458	3.20669	3.74002	4.31889	4.88009	5.23476	5.93955
	4	2.58846	3.04820	3.31233	3.78416	4.35494	4.97716	5.58374	5.96891	6.82870
	5	3.07911	3.57737	3.86403	4.37756	5.00190	5.68735	6.36077	6.79126	7.65813
	6	3.59827	4.14933	4.46783	5.04168	5.74580	6.52780	7.30614	7.80888	8.83370
	7	4.19942	4.83073	5.19927	5.87096	6.70998	7.66286	8.63449	9.27483	10.59858
	8	5.01617	5.80265	6.27353	7.15753	8.31423	9.70614	11.21207	12.24712	14.48879
9	1	.75811	1.11201	1.32917	1.72846	2.21497	2.73775	3.23551	3.54527	4.15040
	2	1.47210	1.86132	2.08616	2.48789	2.96939	3.48789	3.98565	4.29782	4.91255
	3	2.00796	2.41481	2.64828	3.06324	3.55635	4.09922	4.61769	4.94408	5.58985
	4	2.47312	2.90325	3.14921	3.58654	4.11224	4.68163	5.23314	5.58164	6.27418
	5	2.91689	3.37601	3.63866	4.10650	4.67091	5.28515	5.88338	6.26319	7.02227
	6	3.36876	3.86567	4.15071	4.66020	5.27835	5.95599	6.62151	7.04697	7.90404
	7	3.85926	4.40805	4.72454	5.29378	5.99117	6.76556	7.53554	8.03342	9.04775
	8	4.43738	5.06513	5.43106	6.09710	6.92844	7.87273	8.83584	9.47096	10.79864
	9	5.23350	6.01443	6.48157	7.35805	8.50529	9.88726	11.38376	12.41354	14.65471
10	1	.74013	1.08395	1.29435	1.67996	2.14775	2.65799	3.12219	3.41640	3.98913
	2	1.42162	1.79881	2.02025	2.40415	2.86298	3.35435	3.82413	4.11778	4.69437
	3	1.96742	2.32913	2.57875	2.94477	3.41481	3.91950	4.40409	4.70816	5.30767
	4	2.38022	2.78521	3.02974	3.42700	3.91776	4.44643	4.95587	5.27654	5.91119
	5	2.78787	3.21710	3.46157	3.89511	4.41500	4.97716	5.52123	5.86495	6.54813
	6	3.19411	3.65204	3.91325	4.37756	4.93659	5.54415	6.13557	6.51104	7.26155
	7	3.61859	4.11378	4.39715	4.90286	5.51555	6.18666	6.82302	7.26662	8.11187
	8	4.08754	4.63385	4.94836	5.51336	6.20487	6.97219	7.67835	8.23014	9.16123
	9	4.64752	5.27181	5.63515	6.29613	7.12073	8.05745	9.01383	9.66262	10.99810
	10	5.42678	6.20246	6.66626	7.53612	8.67498	10.04798	11.53640	12.56177	14.78816

REFERENCES

1. B. Epstein and M. Sobel, "Some theorems relevant to life testing from an exponential distribution," *Ann. Math. Statist.*, Vol. 25 (1954), pp. 373–381.
2. S. S. Gupta, "Order statistics from the gamma distribution," *Technometrics*, Vol. 2 (1960), pp. 243–262.
3. S. S. Gupta and M. Sobel, "On the distribution of a statistic based on ordered uniform chance variables," *Ann. Math. Statist.*, Vol. 29 (1958), pp. 274–281.
4. E. C. Molina, *Poisson's Exponential Binomial Limit*, Van Nostrand Co., Princeton, N.J., 1942.
5. E. S. Pearson, and H. O. Hartley, *Biometrika Tables for Statisticians*, Vol. 1, Cambridge University Press, Cambridge, England, 1954.
6. K. Pearson, *Tables of the Incomplete Beta Function*, Cambridge University Press, Cambridge, England, 1948.
7. K. Pearson, *Tables of the Incomplete Gamma Function*, Cambridge University Press, Cambridge, England, 1957.
8. A. E. Sarhan, "Estimation of the mean and standard deviation by order statistics, Part III," *Ann. Math. Statist.*, Vol. 26 (1955), pp. 576–592.

E. H. LLOYD

12E RIGHT-TRIANGULAR DISTRIBUTION

12E.1 Moments of Order Statistics in Samples from a Right-Triangular Distribution

The density function for the right-triangular distribution may be written as [1]

$$f(x) = \frac{(x - \theta_1)/\sigma + 2\sqrt{2}}{9\sigma}, \tag{12E.1.1}$$

$$\theta_1 - 2\sqrt{2}\sigma \le x \le \theta_1 + \sqrt{2}\sigma.$$

The expected values, variances, and covariances of the standardized order statistics $u_{(r)}$ in samples from the right-triangular distribution are [1]

$$E(u_{(r)}) = \frac{6n^{n-r+1}2^{n-r+1}/(2n + 1)^{n-r+1} - 4}{\sqrt{2}} \tag{12E.1.2}$$

and

$$v_{rr} = V(u_{(r)}) = 18\left\{r/(n+1) - \left[\frac{n^{n-r+1}2^{n-r+1}}{(2n+1)^{n-r+1}}\right]^2\right\}, \quad (12E.1.3)$$

$$\underset{r<s}{\operatorname{Cov}}\,(u_{(r)}, u_{(s)}) = \frac{(s-1)^{s-r}2^{s-r}v_{ss}}{(2s-1)^{s-r}}.$$

Tables 1 and 2 in reference 1 give the expected values and variances and covariances of the order statistics for samples up to size 10.

12E.2 The Best Linear Estimates of the Parameters of the Right-Triangular Distribution

The best linear estimates of the parameters θ_1 and σ of the right-triangular distribution from samples of size n are [1]

$$\theta^*_1 = \frac{n-1}{3}\left(\sum_{i=1}^{n}\frac{x_{(i)}}{i} + 2x_{(1)} + \frac{2n+1}{n-1}x_{(n)}\sum_{i=2}^{n}\frac{1}{i}\right)\Big/\left(n\sum_{i=1}^{n}\frac{1}{i} - 1\right) \quad (12E.2.1)$$

$$\sigma^* = \frac{2n-1}{6\sqrt{2}}\left[\left(\sum_{i=1}^{n}\frac{1}{i} + 2\right)x_{(n)} - 2x_{(1)} - \sum_{i=1}^{n}\frac{x_{(i)}}{i}\right]\Big/\left(n\sum_{i=1}^{n}\frac{1}{i} - 1\right), \quad (12E.2.2)$$

and

$$V(\theta^*_1) = \frac{2\sigma^2}{n+1}\left[\sum_{i=1}^{n}\frac{1}{i} + n - 2\right]\Big/\left(n\sum_{i=1}^{n}\frac{1}{i} - 1\right) \quad (12E.2.3)$$

$$V(\sigma^*) = \frac{\sigma^2}{4(n+1)}\left[\sum_{i=1}^{n}\frac{1}{i} + 4(n+1)\right]\Big/\left(n\sum_{i=1}^{n}\frac{1}{i} - 1\right) \quad (12E.2.4)$$

$$\operatorname{Cov}(\theta^*_1, \sigma^*) = \frac{\sigma^2}{\sqrt{2}(n+1)}\left(2n - 1 - \sum_{i=1}^{n}\frac{1}{i}\right)\Big/\left(n\sum_{i=1}^{n}\frac{1}{i} - 1\right). \quad (12E.2.5)$$

Tables 12E.1 and 12E.2 give the values of α_{1i} and α_{2i} up to samples of size 10 such that

$$\theta^*_1 = \sum_{i=1}^{n}\alpha_{1i}x_{(i)},$$

$$\sigma^* = \sum_{i=1}^{n}\alpha_{2i}x_{(i)}.$$

Table 12E.3 gives the values of $V(\theta^*_1)$, $V(\sigma^*)$, and $\operatorname{Cov}(\theta^*, \sigma^*)$ in terms of σ^2.

In the case of this distribution it is perhaps more natural to use the extremities λ_1 and λ_2 as parameters. Converting Downton's values, these become

$$\lambda^*_1 = \frac{1}{3n}[2 - 3h(2n - 1)]x_{(n)} + h\left(1 - \frac{2}{3n}\right)\theta \qquad (12E.2.6)$$

$$\lambda^*_2 = \left(1 + \frac{1 + 3h}{6n}\right)x_{(n)} - \frac{h}{6n}b \qquad (12E.2.7)$$

where

$$\theta = 2x_{(1)} + \sum \frac{x_{(r)}}{r}, \qquad \frac{1}{h} = \sum \frac{1}{r} - 1$$

These formulas are necessarily less simple than the corresponding estimates of the rectangular distribution, but it is of interest to note that in the right-triangular case the estimate of λ_2, the right-hand end point (i.e., the one where the discontinuity occurs), is

$$\lambda^*_2 = x_{(n)} + O(n^{-1}).$$

Exactly as in the rectangular distribution, *the estimate is determined mainly by the extreme observations* and is relatively insensitive to the others. The estimate of the other end point λ_1, where the distribution has a corner but not a discontinuity, is, as we would expect, not so clearly dominated by any particular observation.

TABLE 12E.1

COEFFICIENTS FOR ESTIMATING θ^*_1 (α_{1i}) IN A RIGHT-TRIANGULAR DISTRIBUTION

$n = 2$	.5000	.5000								
3	.4444	.0741	.4815							
4	.4091	.0682	.0455	.4773						
5	.3840	.0640	.0427	.0320	.4773					
6	.3650	.0608	.0406	.0304	.0243	.4789				
7	.3449	.0583	.0389	.0292	.0233	.0194	.4810			
8	.3375	.0562	.0375	.0281	.0225	.0187	.0161	.4834		
9	.3271	.0545	.0363	.0273	.0218	.0182	.0156	.0136	.4857	
10	.3181	.0530	.0353	.0265	.0212	.0177	.0151	.0133	.0118	.4879

TABLE 12E.2

COEFFICIENTS FOR ESTIMATING σ^* (α_{2i}) IN A RIGHT-TRIANGULAR DISTRIBUTION

$n = 2$	−.8839	+.8839								
3	−.5500	−.0917	+.6416							
4	−.4339	−.0723	−.0482	+.5544						
5	−.3734	−.0622	−.0415	−.0311	+.5082					
6	−.3355	−.0559	−.0373	−.0280	−.0224	+.4790				
7	−.3030	−.0505	−.0337	−.0253	−.0202	−.0168	+.4495			
8	−.2898	−.0483	−.0322	−.0241	−.0193	−.0161	−.0138	+.4436		
9	−.2746	−.0458	−.0305	−.0229	−.0183	−.0153	−.0131	−.0114	+.4319	
10	−.2624	−.0437	−.0292	−.0219	−.0175	−.0146	−.0125	−.0109	−.0097	+.4225

TABLE 12E.3

VARIANCE AND COVARIANCE OF ESTIMATES (θ^*_1 AND σ^*) IN A RIGHT-TRIANGULAR DISTRIBUTION

n	$V(\theta^*_1)$	$V(\sigma^*)$	Cov (θ^*_1, σ^*)
2	0.5000	0.5625	0.1768
3	0.3148	0.2477	0.1244
4	0.2227	0.1506	0.09482
5	0.1691	0.1051	0.07599
6	0.1345	0.07938	0.06304
7	0.1107	0.06303	0.05364
8	0.09340	0.04946	0.04652
9	0.08037	0.04205	0.04097
10	0.07024	0.03641	0.03652

These tables are reproduced from F. Downton, "Least squares estimates using ordered observations," *Ann. Math. Statist.*, Vol. 25 (1954), pp. 303–316, with permission of the author and W. Kruskal, editor of the *Annals of Mathematical Statistics*.

REFERENCE

1. F. Downton, "Least-squares estimates using ordered observations," *Ann. Math. Statist.*, Vol. 25 (1954), pp. 303–316.

References

S. H. Abdel-Aty, "Ordered variables in discontinuous distributions," *Statist. Neerlandica*, Vol. 8 (1954), pp. 61–82.

A. C. Aitken, "On least squares and linear combinations of observations," *Proc. Roy. Soc. Edin.*, Vol. 55 (1935), pp. 42–48.

G. N. Alexander, "Return period relationships," *J. Geophysical Res.*, Vol. 64, No. 6 (1959), pp. 675–682.

R. E. Bechhofer, "A single-sample multiple decision procedure for ranking means of normal populations with known variances," *Ann. Math. Statist.*, Vol. 25 (1954), pp. 16–39.

M. H. Belz and R. Hooke, "Approximate distribution of the range in the neighborhood of low percentage points," *J. Amer. Statist. Ass.*, Vol. 49 (1954), pp. 620–636.

A. Bender and A. Hamm, "The application of probability paper to life or fatigue testing," Rep. Delco-Remy, Anderson, Indiana.

C. A. Bennett, "Asymptotic properties of ideal linear estimators," unpublished dissertation, University of Michigan, Ann Arbor, 1952.

M. J. Bernier, "Sur l'application des diverses lois limités des valeurs extrêmes au problème des débits de crues," *Rev. statist. appl.*, Paris, No. 5 (1957), pp. 91–101.

M. J. Bernier, "Comparison des lois de Gumbel et de Fréchet sur l'estimation des débits maxima," *La Houille Blanche*, Vol. 14 (1959), pp. 47–56.

C. I. Bliss, W. G. Cochran, and J. W. Tukey, "A rejection criterion based upon the range," *Biometrika*, Vol. 43 (1956), pp. 418–422.

G. Blom, "On linear estimates with nearly minimum variance," *Ark. Mat.*, Band 3 Nr. 31 (1956), p. 365.

G. Blom, *Statistical Estimates and Transformed Beta Variables*, Almqvist and Wiksell, Uppsala, Sweden, 1958, John Wiley and Sons, New York, 1958.

G. E. P. Box, "Non-normality and tests on variances," *Biometrika*, Vol. 40 (1953), pp. 318–335.

British Association for the Advancement of Science, *Mathematical Tables*, Vol. 6, Part I, Cambridge University Press, Cambridge, England, 1937.

I. W. Burr, "Calculation of exact sampling distribution of ranges from a discrete population," *Ann. Math. Statist.*, Vol. 26 (1955), pp. 530–532.

J. H. Cadwell, "Approximating to the distributions of measures of dispersion by a power of χ^2," *Biometrika*, Vol. 40 (1953), pp. 336–346.

J. H. Cadwell, "The distribution of quasi-ranges in samples from a normal population," *Ann. Math. Statist.*, Vol. 24 (1953), pp. 603–613.

P. G. Carlson, "A recurrence formula for the mean range for odd sample sizes," *Skand. Aktuartidskr.*, Vol. 41 (1958), pp. 47–54.

P. G. Carlson, "Tests of hypothesis on the exponential lower limit," *Skand. Aktuartidskr.*, Vol. 41 (1958), pp. 47–54.

R. Cazaud, "Contributions à l'etude statistique de la dispersion dans les essais de flexion rotative," *Rev. Metallurgie*, Paris (1954), p. 291.

H. Chernoff and G. J. Lieberman, "Use of normal probability paper," *J. Amer. Statist. Ass.*, Vol. 49 (1954), pp. 778–785.

H. Chernoff and G. J. Lieberman, "The use of generalized probability paper for continuous distributions," *Ann. Math. Statist.*, Vol. 27 (1956), pp. 806–818.

J. T. Chu, "The inefficiency of the sample median for many familiar symmetric distributions," *Biometrika*, Vol. 42 (1955), pp. 520–521.

J. T. Chu, "On the distribution of the sample median," *Ann. Math. Statist.*, Vol. 26 (1955), pp. 112–116.

W. G. Cochran, "The distribution of the largest of a set of estimated variances as a fraction of their total," *Ann. Eugen., London*, Vol. 11 (1941), pp. 47–52.

R. H. Cole, "Relations between moments of order statistics," *Ann. Math. Statist.*, Vol. 22 (1951), pp. 308–310.

D. R. Cox, "A note on the asymptotic distribution of range," *Amer. Math. Statist.*, Vol. 35 (1948), pp. 310–315.

D. R. Cox, "The use of the range in sequential analysis," *J. R. Statist. Soc., B*, Vol. 11 (1949), pp. 101–114.

D. R. Cox, "The mean and coefficient of variation of range in small samples from non-normal populations," *Biometrika*, Vol. 41 (1954), pp. 469–481.

D. R. Cox, "Note on grouping." *J. Amer. Statist. Ass.*, Vol. 52 (1957), pp. 543–547.

H. S. M. Coxeter, "The functions of Schläfli and Lobachewski," *Quart. J. Math.*, Vol. 6 (1935), pp. 13–29.

H. S. M. Coxeter, *Regular Polytopes*, Methuen and Co. Ltd., London, 1948.

H. Cramér, "A contribution to the theory of statistical estimation," *Skand. Aktuartidskr.*, Vol. 29 (1946), pp. 85–94.

H. Cramér, *Mathematical Methods of Statistics*, Princeton, 1946.

H. N. Cummings, F. B. Stulen, and W. C. Schulte, "Investigations of metals fatigue problems applicable to propellor design," WADC Tech. Rep. 54–531, Wright Air Development Center, May 1955.

J. F. Daly, "On the use of the sample range in an analogue of Student's t-test," *Ann. Math. Statist.*, Vol. 17 (1946), pp. 71–74.

J. H. Darwin, "The difference between consecutive members of a series of random variables arranged in order of size," *Biometrika*, Vol. 44 (1957), pp. 211–218.

F. N. David and N. L. Johnson, "Statistical treatment of censored data, Part I, Fundamental formulae," *Biometrika*, Vol. 41 (1954), pp. 228–240.

F. N. David and N. L. Johnson, "A test for skewness with ordered variables," *Ann. Eugen., London*, Vol. 18 (1954), pp. 351–353.

F. N. David and N. L. Johnson, "Some tests of significance with ordered variables," *J. R. Statist. Soc., B*, Vol. 18 (1956), pp. 1–20.

H. A. David, "Further applications of range to the analysis of variance," *Biometrika*, Vol. 38 (1951), pp. 393–409.

H. A. David, "Upper 5 and 1% points of the maximum F-ratio," *Biometrika*, Vol. 39 (1952), pp. 442–424.

H. A. David, "The power function of some tests based on range," *Biometrika*, Vol. 40 (1953), pp. 347–353.

H. A. David, "The distribution of range in certain non-normal populations," *Biometrika*, Vol. 41 (1954), pp. 463–468.

H. A. David, "On the application to statistics of an elementary theorem in probability," *Biometrika*, Vol. 43 (1956), pp. 85–91.

H. A. David, "The ranking of variances in normal populations," *J. Amer. Statist. Ass.*, Vol. 51 (1956), pp. 621–626.

H. A. David, "Revised upper percentage points of the extreme studentized deviate from the sample mean," *Biometrika*, Vol. 43 (1956), pp. 449–451.

H. A. David, H. O. Hartley, and E. S. Pearson, "The distribution of the ratio, in a single normal sample, of range to standard deviation," *Biometrika*, Vol. 41 (1954), pp. 482–493.

O. L. Davies and E. S. Pearson, "Methods of estimating from samples the population standard deviation," *J. R. Statist. Soc.*, Suppl., Vol. 1 (1934), pp. 76–93.

D. S. Davis, *Empirical Equations and Nomography*, first edition, McGraw-Hill Book Co., New York, 1943.

G. E. Dieter, R. F. Mehl, and G. T. Horne, "The statistical fatigue properties of laminar and spheroidal eutectoid steel," *Trans. Amer. Soc. Metals*, Vol. 47, preprint 25 (1954).

W. J. Dixon, "Analysis of extreme values," *Ann. Math. Statist.*, Vol. 21 (1950), pp. 488–506.

W. J. Dixon, "Ratios involving extreme values," *Ann. Math. Statist.*, Vol. 22 (1951), pp. 68–78.

W. J. Dixon, "Processing data for outliers," *Biometrics*, Vol. 9 (1953), pp. 74–89.

W. J. Dixon, "Estimates of the mean and standard deviation of a normal population," *Ann. Math. Statist.*, Vol. 28 (1957), pp. 806–809.

W. J. Dixon and F. J. Massey, Jr., *Introduction to Statistical Analysis*, second edition, McGraw-Hill Book Co., New York, 1957.

R. Doornbos, "Significance of the smallest of a set of estimated normal variances," *Statist. Neerlandica*, Vol. 10 (1956), pp. 117–126.

R. Doornbos and H. J. Prins, "Slippage tests for a set of gamma-variates," *Indag. Math.*, Vol. 18 (1956), pp. 329–337.

R. Doornbos and H. J. Prins, "On slippage tests," *Indag. Math.*, Vol. 20 (1958), I, pp. 38–46; II, pp. 47–55.

F. Downton, "A note on ordered least squares estimation," *Biometrika*, Vol. 40 (1953), pp. 457–458.

F. Downton, "Least-squares estimates using ordered observations," *Ann. Math. Statist.*, Vol. 25 (1954), pp. 303–316.

J. J. Dronkers, "Approximate formulae for the statistical distribution of extreme values," *Biometrika*, Vol. 45 (1958), pp. 447–470.

Daniel Dugué, *Traité de statistique théorique et appliquée*, Masson et Cie, Paris, 1958.

A. J. Duncan, "Design and operation of a double-limit variables sampling plan," *J. Amer. Statist. Ass.*, Vol. 53 (1958), pp. 543–550.

D. B. Duncan, "Multiple range and multiple *F* tests," *Biometrics*, Vol. 11 (1955), pp. 1–42.

D. B. Duncan, "Multiple range tests for correlated and heteroscedastic means," *Biometrics*, Vol. 13 (1957), pp. 164–176.

C. W. Dunnett, "A multiple comparison procedure for comparing several treatments with a control," *J. Amer. Statist. Ass.*, Vol. 50 (1955), pp. 1096–1121.

C. Eisenhart, M. W. Hastay, and W. A. Wallis, *Selected Techniques of Statistical Analysis*, McGraw-Hill Book Co., New York, 1947.

E. Epremian and R. F. Mehl, "The statistical behavior of fatigue properties and the influence of metallurgical factors," Symposium on Fatigue with Emphasis on Statistical Approach, II, American Society for Testing Materials, Philadelphia, 1953.

B. Epstein, "Estimates of mean life based on the rth smallest value in a sample of size n drawn from an exponential population," Wayne University Tech. Rep. 2, prepared under ONR Contract, Nonr-451(00), NR-042-017, July 1952.

B. Epstein, "Sample estimates of the parameters of exponential distributions when samples are censored," *Ann. Inst. Statist. Math., Tokyo*, Vol. 8 (1956), pp. 15–26.

B. Epstein and M. Sobel, "Life testing," *J. Amer. Statist. Ass.*, Vol. 48 (1953), pp. 486–502.

B. Epstein and M. Sobel, "Some theorems relevant to life testing from an exponential distribution," *Ann. Math. Statist.*, Vol. 25 (1954), pp. 373–381.

D. J. G. Farlie, "The performance of some correlation coefficients for a general bivariate distribution," *Biometrika*, Vol. 47 (1960), pp. 307–333.

W. T. Federer, *Experimental Design*, Macmillan, New York, 1955.

B. V. Finkelstein, "On the limiting distributions of the extreme terms of a variational series of a two-dimensional random quantity," *Dokl. Akad. Nauk.*, SSSR (N.S.), Vol. 91 (1953), p. 209 (Russian).

D. J. Finney, "The joint distribution of variance ratios based on a common error mean square," *Ann. Eugen., London*, Vol. 11 (1941), pp. 136–140.

R. A. Fisher, "On the mathematical foundations of theoretical statistics," *Phil. Trans. A.*, Vol. 222 (1921), pp. 309–368.

R. A. Fisher, "Tests of significance in harmonic analysis," *Proc. Roy. Soc., A.*, Vol. 125 (1929), pp. 54–59.

R. A. Fisher, "On the similarity of the distributions found for the test of significance in harmonic analysis, and in Steven's problem in geometrical probability," *Ann. Eugen., London*, Vol. 10 (1940), pp. 14–17.

R. A. Fisher, *Contributions to Mathematical Statistics*, John Wiley and Sons, New York, 1950.

R. A. Fisher and L. H. C. Tippett, "Limiting forms of the frequency distribution of the largest or smallest member of a sample," *Proc. Camb. Phil. Soc.*, Vol. 24 (1928), pp. 180–190.

R. A. Fisher and F. Yates, *Statistical Tables for Biological, Agricultural, and Medical Research*, Oliver and Boyd Ltd., London, 1949.

L. Fox and J. G. Hayes, "More practical methods for the inversion of matrices," *J. R. Statist. Soc., B.*, Vol. 13 (1951), pp. 83–91.

D. A. S. Fraser, "Sequentially determined statistically equivalent blocks," *Ann. Math. Statist.*, Vol. 22 (1951), pp. 372–381.

M. Frechét, "Sur la loi de probabilité de l'écart maximum," *Ann. de la Soc. Polonoise de Math.*, Cracow, Vol. 6 (1927), pp. 93–116.

M. Fréchet, "Sur les tableaux de corrélation dont les magres sont données," *Ann. Univ. Lyon., A.*, Vol. 14 (1951), pp. 53–77.

A. M. Freudenthal and E. J. Gumbel, "Minimum life in fatigue," *J. Amer. Statist. Ass.*, Vol. 49, No. 267 (1954), pp. 575–597.

A. M. Freudenthal and E. J. Gumbel, "Physical and statistical aspects of fatigue," *Advanc. Appl. Mech.*, Vol. 4 (1956), pp. 117–158.

A. M. Freudenthal and E. J. Gumbel, "Distribution functions for the prediction of fatigue life and fatigue strength," International Conference on Fatigue of Metals, London, 1957.

Jean Geffroy, "Sur la notion d'indépendence limite de deus variables aléatoires, application à l'etendu et au milieu d'un échantillon," *C. R. Acad. Sci., Paris*, Vol. 245 (1957), pp. 1291–1293.

Jean Geffroy, "Contributions a la théorie des valeurs extrêmes," *Publ. Inst. Statist., Paris*, Vol. 7 (1958), pp. 37–121; Vol. 8 (1959), pp. 123–184.

Jean Geffroy, "Etude de la stabilité presque certain des valeurs extrême d'un echantillon et de la convergence presque certain de son milieu," *C. R. Acad. Sci., Paris*, Vol. 246 (1958), pp. 1154–1156.

Jean Geffroy, "Stabilité presque complete des valeurs extrêmes d'un échantillon et convergence presque complete du milieu vers une limite certaine," *C. R. Acad. Sci., Paris*, Vol. 246 (1958), pp. 224–226.

Gesammelle Mathematische Abhandlugen, Vol. 1. (Lehre von der Sphärischen Kontinuen, pp. 227–298), Verlag Birkhäuser Basel.

F. N. Gjeddebaeck, "Contributions to the study of grouped observations, application of the method of maximum likelihood in case of normally distributed observations," *Skand. Aktuartidskr.*, Vol. 32 (1949), pp. 135–159.

B. Gnedenko, "Sur la distribution limite du terme maximum d'une serie aléatoire," *Ann. Math.*, Vol. 44 (1943), pp. 423–453.

M. L. Godfrey, "Theory of extreme values applied in tests," Industrial Laboratories, August 1958.

H. J. Godwin, "On the estimation of dispersion by linear systematic statistics," *Biometrika*, Vol. 36 (1949), pp. 92–100.

H. J. Godwin, "Some low moments of order statistics," *Ann. Math. Statist.*, Vol. 20 (1949), pp. 279–285.

B. G. Greenberg and A. E. Sarhan, "Application of order statistics to health data," *Amer. J. Publ. Health*, Vol. 48 (1958), pp. 1388–1394.

F. E. Grubbs, "Sample criteria for testing outlying observations," *Ann. Math. Statist.*, Vol. 21 (1950), pp. 27–58.

F. E. Grubbs and C. L. Weaver, "The best unbiased estimate of population standard deviation based on group ranges," *J. Amer. Statist. Ass.*, Vol. 42 (1947), pp. 224–241.

E. J. Gumbel, "Simple tests for given hypotheses," *Biometrika*, Vol. 32 (1942), pp. 317–332.

E. J. Gumbel, "Probability tables for the range," *Biometrika*, Vol. 36 (1949), pp. 142–148.

E. J. Gumbel, "The maxima of the mean largest value and of the range," *Ann. Math. Statist.*, Vol. 25 (1954), pp. 76–84.

E. J. Gumbel, "Statistical theory of extreme values and some practical applications," Appl. Math. Ser. 33, U.S. Dept. Commerce, Washington, D.C., 1954.

E. J. Gumbel, "Etude statistique de la fatigue des materiaux," *Rev. statist. appl.*, Paris, Vol. 5, No. 4 (1957), pp. 51–86.

E. J. Gumbel, "Distributions a plusieurs variables dont les marges sont données with remarks by M. Fréchet," *C. R. Acad. Sci., Paris*, Vol. 246 (1958), pp. 2717–2720.

E. J. Gumbel, *Extremes, A Statistical Study*, John Wiley and Sons, New York, 1958.

E. J. Gumbel, "Fonctions de probabilités a deux variables extrémales indépendantes," *C. R. Acad. Sci., Paris*, Vol. 246 (1958), pp. 49–50.

E. J. Gumbel, "Statistical theory of floods and droughts," *J. Inst. Water Engineers*, London, Vol. 12 (1958), pp. 157–184.

E. J. Gumbel, *Statistics of Extremes*, Columbia University Press, New York, 1958.

E. J. Gumbel, "The *m*th range," *J. Math.*, Paris, Tome 39, Fasc. 3 (1959), pp. 253–265.

E. J. Gumbel, "Théorie statistiqué des débits d'étiage," *La Houille Blanche*, Vol. 14 (1959), pp. 57–65.

E. J. Gumbel, "Bivariate exponential distributions," *J. Amer. Statist. Ass.*, Vol. 55 (1960), pp. 698–707.

E. J. Gumbel, "Bivariate logistic distributions," *J. Amer. Statist. Ass.*, Vol. 56 (1961), pp. 335–349.

E. J. Gumbel, "Distributions des valeurs extrêmes en plusieurs dimensions," *Publ. Inst. Statist., Paris*, Vol. 9 (1960), pp. 171–173.

E. J. Gumbel, A. D. Benham, and D. H. Thomson, "Communications on the statistical theory of floods and droughts," *J. Inst. Water Engineers*, London, Vol 13 (1959), pp. 71–102.

E. J. Gumbel and L. H. Herbach, "The exact distribution of the extremal quotient," *Ann. Math. Statist.*, Vol. 22 (1951), pp. 418–426.

E. J. Gumbel and R. D. Keeney, "The extremal quotient," *Ann. Math. Statist.*, Vol. 21 (1950), pp. 523–538.

A. K. Gupta, "Estimation of the mean and standard deviation of a normal population from a censored sample," *Biometrika*, Vol. 39 (1952), pp. 260–273.

S. S. Gupta, "On a decision rule for a problem in ranking means," Institute of Statistics, University of North Carolina, Mimeograph Ser. 150, May 1956.

S. S. Gupta, "Order statistics from gamma distribution," *Technometrics*, Vol. 2 (1960), pp. 243–262.

S. S. Gupta and M. Sobel, "On a statistic which arises in selection and ranking problems," *Ann. Math. Statist.*, Vol. 28 (1957), pp. 957–967.

S. S. Gupta and M. Sobel, "On selecting a subset which contains all populations better than a standard," *Ann. Math. Statist.*, Vol. 29 (1958), pp. 235–244.

S. S. Gupta and M. Sobel, "On the distribution of a statistic based on ordered uniform chance variables," *Ann. Math. Statist.*, Vol. 29 (1958), pp. 274–281.

A. Hald, *Statistical Theory with Engineering Applications*, John Wiley and Sons, New York, 1952.

M. Halperin, S. W. Greenhouse, J. Cornfield, and J. Zalokar, "Tables of percentage points for the studentized maximum absolute deviate in normal samples," *J. Amer. Statist. Ass.*, Vol. 50 (1955), pp. 185–195.

B. I. Harley and E. S. Pearson, "The distribution of range in normal samples with $n = 200$," *Biometrika*, Vol. 44 (1957), pp. 257–260.

H. L. Harter and D. S. Clemm, "The probability integrals of the range and of the studentized range: probability integral, percentage points, and moments of the range," WADC Tech. Rep. 58–484, Vol. 11, 1959.

H. L. Harter, D. S. Clemm, and E. H. Guthrie, "The probability integrals of the range and of the studentized range: probability integral and percentage points of the studentized range; critical values for Duncan's new multiple range test," WADC Tech. Rep. 58–484, Vol. 2, 1959.

H. O. Hartley, "Studentization and large-sample theory," *J. R. Statist. Soc.*, Suppl., Vol. 5 (1938), pp. 80–88.

H. O. Hartley, "The range in random samples," *Biometrika*, Vol. 32 (1942), pp. 334–348.

H. O. Hartley, "Studentization," *Biometrika*, Vol. 33 (1944), pp. 173–180.

H. O. Hartley, "The maximum *F*-ratio as a short-cut test for heterogeneity of variance," *Biometrika*, Vol. 37 (1950), pp. 308–312.

H. O. Hartley, "The use of range in analysis of variance," *Biometrika*, Vol. 37 (1950), pp. 271–280.

H. O. Hartley, "Some recent developments in analysis of variance," *Comm. Pure and Appl. Math.*, Vol. 8 (1955), pp. 47–72.

H. O. Hartley and H. A. David, "Universal bounds for mean range and extreme observation," *Ann. Math. Statist.*, Vol. 25 (1954), pp. 85–99.

C. Hastings, Jr., F. Mosteller, J. W. Tukey, and C. P. Winsor, "Low moments for small samples: a comparative study of order statistics," *Ann. Math. Statist.*, Vol. 18 (1947), pp. 413–426.

W. C. Healy, "Two-sample procedures in simultaneous estimation," *Ann. Math. Statist.*, Vol. 27 (1956), pp. 687–702.

H. W. Henry, "Evaluation of statistics of extremes for analysis of injury experience of industrial personnel," master's thesis, University of Tennessee, Knoxville, 1959.

R. G. Herd, "Estimation of the parameters of a population from a multi-censored sample," doctoral thesis, Iowa State College, Ames, 1956.

D. M. Hershfield and M. A. Kohler, "An empirical appraisal of the Gumbel extreme-value procedure," *J. Geographical Res.*, Vol. 64 (1959), p. 1106.

I. Higuchi, "On the solutions of certain simultaneous equations in the theory of systematic statistics," *Ann. Inst. Statist. Math., Tokyo*, Vol. 5, No. 2 (1956), pp. 77–90.

W. Hoeffding, "The extrema of the expected value of a function of independent random variables," *Ann. Math. Statist.*, Vol. 26 (1955), pp. 268–275.

T. Hojo, "Distribution of the median, quartiles and interquartile distance in samples from a normal population," *Biometrika*, Vol. 23 (1931), pp. 315–360.

E. R. E. Hoppe, "Berechnung einiger viehrdenigen Winkel," *Arch. Math. Phys.*, Vol. 67 (1882), pp. 269–290.

H. Hyrenius, "On the use of ranges, cross-ranges and extremes in comparing small samples," *J. Amer. Statist. Ass.*, Vol. 48 (1953), pp. 534–545.

J. O. Irwin, "On a criterion for the rejection of outlying observations," *Biometrika*, Vol. 17 (1925), pp. 238–250.

J. E. Jackson and E. L. Ross, "Extended tables for use with the "G" test for means," *J. Amer. Statist. Ass.*, Vol. 50 (1955), pp. 416–433.

A. I. Johnson, "Strength safety, and economical dimensions of structures," *Bulletin of the Divison of Building Statics and Structural Engineering*, No. 12 (1953), Royal Institute of Technology, Stockholm.

L. G. Johnson, "An axiomatic derivation of a general *S-N* equation," *Industr. Math.*, Vol. 4 (1953), pp. 1–8, Detroit, 1954.

A. E. Jones, "A useful method for the routine estimation of dispersion from large samples," *Biometrika*, Vol. 33 (1946), pp. 274–282.

H. L. Jones, "Exact lower moments of order statistics in small samples from a normal population," *Biometrika*, Vol. 19 (1948), pp. 270–273.

J. Jung, "On linear estimates defined by a continuous weight function," *Ark. mat.*, Band 3 Nr. 15 (1955), pp. 199–209.

M. Keuls, "The use of the studentized range in connection with an analysis of variance," *Euphytica*, Vol. 1 (1952), pp. 112–122.

B. F. Kimball, "Practical applications of the theory of extreme values," *J. Amer. Statist. Ass.*, Vol. 50 (1955), pp. 517–528.

B. F. Kimball, "On the choice of plotting positions on probability paper," *J. Amer. Statist. Ass.*, Vol. 55 (1960), pp. 546–560.

E. P. King, "Estimating the standard deviation of a normal population," *Industr. Qual. Contr.*, Vol. 10, No. 2 (1953), pp. 1–4.

R. M. Kozelka, "Approximate upper percentage points for extreme values in multinomial sampling," *Ann. Math. Statist.*, Vol. 27 (1956), pp. 507–512.

C. Y. Kramer, "Extension of multiple range tests to group means with unequal number of replications," *Biometrics*, Vol. 12 (1956), pp. 307–310.

C. Y. Kramer, "Extension of multiple range tests to group correlated adjusted means," *Biometrics*, Vol. 13 (1957), pp. 13–18.

A. Kudô, "On the testing of outlying observations," *Sankhyā*, Vol. 17 (1956), pp. 67–76.

A. Kudô, "On the distribution of the maximum value of an equally correlated sample from a normal population," *Sankhyā*, Vol. 20 (1958), pp. 309–316.

G. Kulldorff, "Maximum likelihood estimation for the exponential distribution when the sample is grouped," Dept. of Statistics, University of Lund, Sweden, 1958.

E. L. Lehmann, "A theory of some multiple decision problems," *Ann. Math. Statist.*, Vol. 28 (1957), I, pp. 1–25; II, pp. 547–572.

J. Lieblein, "Properties of certain statistics involving the closest pair in a sample of three observations," *J. Res. Nat. Bur. Stand.*, Vol. 48, No. 3 (March 1952), pp. 255–268.

J. Lieblein, "On the exact evaluation of the variances and covariances of order statistics in samples from the extreme-value distribution," *Ann. Math. Statist.*, Vol. 24 (1953), pp. 282–287.

J. Lieblein, "A new method of analyzing extreme-value data," NACA TN 3053, 1954.

J. Lieblein, "On moments of order statistics from the Weibull distribution," *Ann. Math. Statist.*, Vol. 26 (1955), pp. 330–333.

J. Lieblein and M. Zelen, "Statistical analysis of the fatigue-life of deep-groove ball bearings," *J. Res. Nat. Bur. Stand.*, Vol. 57 (Nov. 1956), RP 2719, pp. 273–316.

R. F. Link, "The sampling distribution of the ratio of two ranges from independent samples," *Ann. Math. Statist.*, Vol. 21 (1950), pp. 112–116.

E. H. Lloyd, "Least-squares estimation of location and scale parameters using order statistics," *Biometrika*, Vol. 39 (1952), pp. 88–95.

E. Lord, "The use of range in place of standard deviation in the *t*-test," *Biometrika*, Vol. 34 (1947), pp. 41–67.

E. Lord, "Power of the modified *t*-test (*u*-test) based on range," *Biometrika*, Vol. 37 (1950), pp. 64–77.

J. Machek, "On a two-sample procedure for testing Student's hypothesis using mean range," *Aplik. Mat.*, Vol. 4 (1959).

B. A. Maguire, E. S. Pearson, and A. H. A. Wynn, "The time intervals between industrial accidents," *Biometrika*, Vol. 39 (1957), pp. 168–180.

N. Mantel, "Rapid estimation of standard errors of means for small samples," *Amer. Statist.*, Vol. 5, No. 14 (1951), pp. 26–27.

M. Masuyama, "The use of sample range in estimating the standard deviation or the variance of any population," *Sankhyā*, Vol. 18 (1957), pp. 159–162.

A. T. McKay, "The distribution of the difference between the extreme observation and the sample mean in samples of *n* from a normal universe," *Biometrika*, Vol. 27 (1935), pp. 466–471.

R. Von Mises, "La distribution de la plus grande de *n* valeurs," *Rev. Math. de l'Union Interbalkanique*, Athens, No. 1 (1936), pp. 1–20.

S. K. Mitra, "Tables for tolerance limits for a normal population based on sample mean and range or mean range," *J. Amer. Statist. Ass.*, Vol. 52 (1957), pp. 88–94.

E. C. Molina, *Poisson's Exponential Binomial Limit*, Van Nostrand Co., Princeton, N.J., 1942.

P. G. Moore, "Normality in quality control charts," *Appl. Statist.*, Vol. 6 (1957), pp. 171–179.

P. G. Moore, "The two-sample *t*-test based on range," *Biometrika*, Vol. 44 (1957), pp. 482–489.

P. G. Moore, "The ranges and correlated samples," *Trab. Estadist.*, Vol. 9 (1958), pp. 3–12.

S. Moriguti, "Extremal properties of extreme value distributions," *Ann. Math. Statist.*, Vol. 22 (1951), pp. 523–536.

S. Moriguti, "A modification of Schwarz's inequality with application to distributions," *Ann. Math. Statist.*, Vol. 24 (1953), pp. 107–113.

S. Moriguti, "Bounds for second moments of the sample range," *Rep. Statist. Appl. Res.*, JUSE, Vol. 3, No. 3 (1954), pp. 57–64.

L. E. Moses, "Some theoretical aspects of the lot plot sampling inspection plan," *J. Amer. Statist. Ass.*, Vol. 51 (1956), pp. 84–107.

J. Moshman, "Testing a straggler mean in a two-way classification using the range," *Ann. Math. Statist.*, Vol. 23 (1952), pp. 126–132.

F. Mosteller, "On some useful 'inefficient' statistics," *Ann. Math. Statist.*, Vol. 17 (1946), pp. 377–407.

V. N. Murty, "The distribution of the quotient of maximum values in samples from a rectangular distribution," *J. Amer. Statist. Ass.*, Vol. 50 (1955), pp. 1136–1141.

K. R. Nair, "The distribution of the extreme deviate from the sample mean and its studentized form," *Biometrika*, Vol. 35 (1948), pp. 118–144.

K. R. Nair, "The studentized form of the extreme mean square test in the analysis of variance," *Biometrika*, Vol. 35 (1948), pp. 16–31.

K. R. Nair, "Efficiencies of certain linear systematic statistics for estimating dispersion from normal samples," *Biometrika*, Vol. 37 (1950), pp. 182–183.

National Bureau of Standards, "Tables of the binomial probability distribution," Appl. Math. Ser. 6, U.S. Dept. Commerce, Washington, D.C., 1950.

National Bureau of Standards, "Probability tables for the analysis of extreme-value data," Appl. Math. Ser. 22, U.S. Dept. Commerce, Washington, D.C., 1953.

D. Newman, "Range in samples from a normal population," *Biometrika*, Vol. 31 (1939), pp. 20–30.

D. Newman, "The distribution of ranges in samples from a normal population, expressed in terms of an independent estimate of the standard deviation," *Biometrika*, Vol. 31 (1940), pp. 20–30.

G. E. Noether, "Use of the range instead of the standard deviation," *J. Amer. Statist. Ass.*, Vol. 50 (1955), pp. 1040–1055.

J. Ogawa, "Contributions to the theory of systematic statistics, I," *Osaka Math. J.*, Vol. 3, No. 2 (1951), pp. 175–213.

J. Ogawa, "Contribution to the theory of systematic statistics, II, Large sample theoretical treatments of some problems arising from dosage and time-mortality curves," *Osaka Math. J.*, Vol. 4 (1952), pp. 41–61.

J. Ogawa, "A further contribution to the theory of systematic statistics," Institute of Statistics, University of North Carolina, Mimeograph Ser. 168, 1957.

B. Ostle and G. P. Steck, "Correlation between sample means and sample ranges," *J. Amer. Statist. Ass.*, Vol. 54 (1959), pp. 465–471.

P. B. Patnaik, "The use of mean range as an estimator of variance in statistical tests," *Biometrika*, Vol. 37 (1950), pp. 78–87.

E. Paulson, "An optimum solution to the k-sample slippage problem for the normal distribution," *Ann. Math. Statist.*, Vol. 23 (1952), pp. 610–616.

E. Paulson, "On the comparison of several experimental categories with a control," *Ann. Math. Statist.*, Vol. 23 (1957), pp. 239–246.

E. S. Pearson, "A further note on the distribution of range in samples taken from a normal population," *Biometrika*, Vol. 18 (1926), pp. 173–194.

E. S. Pearson, "The percentage limits for the distribution of range in samples from a normal population," *Biometrika*, Vol. 24 (1932), pp. 404–417.

E. S. Pearson, "Some notes on the use of range," *Biometrika*, Vol. 37 (1950), pp. 88–92.

E. S. Pearson, "Comparison of two approximations to the distribution of the range in small samples from normal populations," *Biometrika*, Vol. 39 (1952), pp. 130–136.

E. S. Pearson and N. K. Adyanthaya, "Distribution of frequency constants from symmetrical populations," *Biometrika*, Vol. 20A (1928), pp. 356–360.

E. S. Pearson and J. Haines, "The use of range in place of standard deviation in small samples," *J. R. Statist. Soc.*, Suppl., Vol. 2 (1935), pp. 83–98.

E. S. Pearson and H. O. Hartley, "The probability integral of the range in samples of *n* observations from the normal population," *Biometrika*, Vol. 32 (1942), pp. 301–310.

E. S. Pearson and H. O. Hartley, "Tables of the probability integral of the studentized range," *Biometrika*, Vol. 33 (1943), pp. 89–99.

E. S. Pearson and H. O. Hartley, "Moment constants for the distribution of range," *Biometrika*, Vol. 38 (1951), pp. 463–464.

E. S. Pearson and H. O. Hartley, *Biometrika Tables for Statisticians*, Vol. 1, Cambridge University Press, Cambridge, England, 1956.

E. S. Pearson and Chandra Sekar, "The efficiency of statistical tools and a criterion for the rejection of outlying observation," *Biometrika*, Vol. 28 (1936), pp. 308–320.

K. Pearson, *Tables for Statisticians and Biometricians*, Vol. 11, third edition, London, 1931.

K. Pearson, *Tables of the Incomplete Beta Function*, Cambridge University Press, Cambridge, England, 1948.

K. Pearson, *Tables of the Incomplete Gamma Function*, Cambridge University Press, Cambridge, England, 1957.

K. C. S. Pillai, "On the distribution of mid-range and semi-range in samples from a normal population," *Ann. Math. Statist.*, Vol. 21 (1950), pp. 100–105.

K. C. S. Pillai, "Some notes on ordered samples from a normal population," *Sankhyā*, Vol. 11 (1951), pp. 23–28.

K. C. S. Pillai, "On the distribution of 'studentized' range," *Biometrika*, Vol. 39 (1952), pp. 194–195.

K. C. S. Pillai and K. V. Ramachandran, "On the distribution of the ratio of the *i*th observation in an ordered sample from a normal population to an independent estimate of the standard deviation," *Ann. Math. Statist.*, Vol. 25 (1954), pp. 565–572.

R. L. Plackett, "Limits of the ratio of mean range to standard deviation," *Biometrika*, Vol. 34 (1947), pp. 120–122.

R. L. Plackett, "A reduction formula for normal multivariate integrals," *Biometrika*, Vol. 41 (1954), pp. 351–360.

R. L. Plackett, "Linear estimation from censored data," *Ann. Math. Statist.*, Vol. 29 (1958), pp. 131–142.

L. Rade, "A note on a modified *t*-test," *Skand. Aktuartidskr.*, Vol. 37 (1954), pp. 65–70.

M. S. Raff, "On approximating the point binomial," *J. Amer. Statist. Ass.*, Vol. 51 (1956), pp. 293–303.

K. V. Ramachandran, "Contributions to simultaneous confidence interval estimation," *Biometrics*, Vol. 12 (1956), pp. 51–56.

K. V. Ramachandran and C. G. Khatri, "On a decision procedure based on the Tukey statistic," *Ann. Math. Statist.*, Vol. 28 (1957), pp. 802–806.

RAND Corporation, *A Million Random Digits with 100,000 Normal Deviates*, Free Press, Glencoe, Ill., 1955.

C. R. Rao, "Minimum variance and the estimation of several parameters," *Proc. Camb. Phil. Soc.*, Vol. 43 (1947), pp. 280–288.

G. J. Resnikoff, "The distribution of the average-range for subgroups of five," Tech.

Rep. 15, Applied Mathematics and Statistical Laboratories, Stanford University, California, 1954, pp. 1–17.

G. J. Resnikoff, "Two-sided tolerance limits for normal distributions using the range," Tech. Rep. 33, Applied Mathematics and Statistical Laboratories, Stanford University, California, 1957, pp. 1–18.

H. W. Richmond, "The volume of a tetrahedron in elliptic space," *Quart. J. Pure Appl. Math.*, Vol. 34 (1903), pp. 175–177.

P. R. Rider, "The distribution of the quotient of ranges in samples from a rectangular population," *J. Amer. Statist. Ass.*, Vol. 46 (1951), pp. 502–507.

P. R. Rider, "The distribution of the range in samples from a discrete rectangular population," *J. Amer. Statist. Ass.*, Vol. 46 (1951), pp. 375–378.

P. R. Rider, "The midrange of a sample as an estimator of the population midrange," *J. Amer. Statist. Ass.*, Vol. 52 (1957), pp. 537–542.

P. R. Rider, "Generalized Gauchy distribution," *Ann. Inst. Statist. Math., Tokyo*, Vol. 9, No. 3 (1958), pp. 215–223.

P. R. Rider, "Quasi-ranges of samples from an exponential population," *Ann. Math. Statist.*, Vol. 30 (1959), pp. 252–254.

H. Robbins, "On distribution-free tolerance limits in random sampling," *Ann. Math. Statist.*, Vol. 15 (1944), pp. 214–216.

Barkley Rosser, "Numerical computation of low moments of order statistics from a normal population," Nat. Bur. Stand. Rep., 1951.

S. N. Roy and R. C. Bose, "Simultaneous confidence interval estimation," *Ann. Math. Statist.*, Vol. 24 (1953), pp. 513–536.

H. Ruben, "On the moments of order statistics in samples from normal population," *Biometrika*, Vol. 41 (1954), pp. 200–227.

H. Ruben, "On the moments of the range and product moments of extreme order statistics in normal samples," *Biometrika*, Vol. 43 (1956), pp. 458–460.

H. Ruben, "On the sum of squares of normal scores," *Biometrika*, Vol. 43, (1956), pp. 456–458.

S. Rushton, "On sequential tests of the equality of variances of two normal populations with known means," *Sankhyā*, Vol. 12 (1952), pp. 63–78.

A. E. Sarhan, "Estimation of the mean and standard deviation by order statistics," *Ann. Math. Statist.*, Vol. 25 (1954), pp. 317–328.

A. E. Sarhan, "Estimation of the mean and standard deviation by order statistics, Part II," *Ann. Math. Statist.*, Vol. 26 (1955), pp. 505–511.

A. E. Sarhan, "Estimation of the mean and standard deviation by order statistics, Part III," *Ann. Math. Statist.*, Vol. 26 (1955), pp. 576–592.

A. E. Sarhan and B. G. Greenberg, "Estimation of location and scale parameters by order statistics from singly and doubly censored samples, Part I, The normal distribution up to samples of size 10," *Ann. Math. Statist.*, Vol. 27 (1956), pp. 427–451.

A. E. Sarhan and B. G. Greenberg, "Tables for the best linear estimates by order statistics of the parameters of single exponential distributions from singly and doubly censored samples," *J. Amer. Statist. Ass.*, Vol. 52 (1957), pp. 58–87.

A. E. Sarhan and B. G. Greenberg, "Estimation of location and scale parameters by order statistics from singly and doubly censored samples, Part II," *Ann. Math. Statist.*, Vol. 29 (1958), pp. 79–105.

A. E. Sarhan and B. G. Greenberg, "Estimation of location and scale parameters by order statistics from singly and doubly censored samples, Part III," Tech. Rep. 4, OOR Project 1597, 1958.

A. E. Sarhan and B. G. Greenberg, "Estimation problems in the exponential distribution using order statistics," *Proceedings of the Statistical Techniques in Missile Evaluation Symposium*, 1958, Blacksburg, Va., pp. 123–175.

A. E. Sarhan and B. G. Greenberg, "Estimation of location and scale parameters for the rectangular population from censored samples," *J. R. Statist. Soc., B*, Vol. 21, No. 2 (1959), pp. 356–363.

J. G. Saw, "Estimation of the normal population parameters given a singly censored sample," *Biometrika*, Vol. 46 (1959), pp. 150–159.

H. Scheffé, "Operating characteristics of average and range charts," *Industr. Qual. Contr.*, Vol. 6, No. 6 (1949), pp. 13–18.

H. Scheffé, "A method for judging all contrasts in the analysis of variance," *Biometrika*, Vol. 40 (1953), pp. 87–104.

L. Schläfi, "On the multiple integral $\int^n dx\, dy \ldots dz$ whose limits are $p_1 = a_1x + b_1y \ldots + h_1z > 0$, $p_2 > 0, \ldots, p_n > 0$, and $x^2 + y^2 + \ldots + z^2 < 1$," *Quart. J. Pure Appl. Math.*, Vol. 2 (1858), pp. 269–301; Vol. 3 (1858), pp. 54–68, 97–108.

K. C. Seal, "On a class of decision procedures for ranking means of normal populations," *Ann. Math. Statist.*, Vol. 26 (1955), pp. 387–398.

K. C. Seal, "On ranking parameters of scale in Type III populations," *J. Amer. Statist. Ass.*, Vol. 53 (1958), pp. 164–175.

L. A. Seder and D. Cowan, "The span plan method process capability analysis," A.S.Q.C. Gen. Publ., 3, 1956, pp. 1–59.

G. R. Seth, "On the distribution of the two closest among a set of three observations," *Ann. Math. Statist.*, Vol. 21 (1950), pp. 298–301.

W. F. Sheppard, *The Probability Integral, British Associated Mathematical Tables*, Cambridge University Press, Cambridge, England, 1939.

S. Shimada, "Power of *R*-chart," *Rep. Statist. Appl. Res.*, JUSE, Vol. 3, No. 3 (1954), pp. 14–18.

M. Sibuya, "Bivariate extreme statistics I," *Ann. Inst. Statist. Math., Tokyo*, Vol. 11 (1960), pp. 195–210.

M. Siotani, "An estimate of standard deviation of normal population based on the difference between means of two groups divided by sample mean," *Ann. Inst. Statist. Math., Tokyo*, Vol. 6 (1954), pp. 153–160.

M. Siotani, "On the distribution of the sum of the positive or negative deviations from the mean in the sample drawn from the normal population," *Proc. Inst. Statist. Math.*, Tokyo, Vol. 2 (1954), pp. 63–74 (Japanese).

M. Siotani, "Order statistics for discrete case with a numerical application to the binomial distribution," *Ann. Inst. Statist. Math., Tokyo*, Vol. 8 (1956), pp. 95–104.

M. Siotani, "The extreme value of the generalized distances of the individual points in the multivariate normal sample," *Ann. Inst. Statist. Math., Tokyo*, Vol. 10 (1959), pp. 183–200.

D. M. Y. Sommerville, *An Introduction to the Geometry of N Dimensions*, Methuen and Co. Ltd., London, 1929.

D. Teichroew, "Tables of expected values of order statistics and products of order statistics for samples of size 20 and less from the normal distribution," *Ann. Math. Statist.*, Vol. 27 (1956), pp. 410–426.

T. J. Terpstra, "A confidence interval for the probability that a normally distributed variable exceeds a given value, based on the mean and the mean range of a number of samples," *App. Sci. Res.*, Section A, Vol. 3 (1953), pp. 297–307.

H. C. S. Thom, "Frequency of maximum wind speeds," *Proc. Amer. Soc. Civil Engineers*, Vol. 80 (1954), separate, No. 539.

W. R. Thompson, "On a criterion for the rejection of observations and the distribution of the ratio of deviation to sample standard deviation," *Ann. Math. Statist.*, Vol. 6 (1935), pp. 214–219.

G. W. Thomson, "Scale factor and degrees of freedom for small sample sizes for χ-approximation to the range," *Biometrika*, Vol. 40 (1953), pp. 449–450.

G. W. Thomson, "Bounds for the ratio of range to standard deviation," *Biometrika*, Vol. 42 (1955), pp. 268–269.

J. Tiago de Oliveira, "Extremal distributions," *Faculdade de Ciencias de Lisboa*, No. 39 (1959).

L. H. C. Tippett, "On the extreme individuals and the range of samples taken from a normal population," *Biometrika*, Vol. 17 (1925), pp. 364–387.

D. R. Truax, "An optimum slippage test for the variances of k normal distributions," *Ann. Math. Statist.*, Vol. 24 (1953), pp. 669–674.

J. W. Tukey, "Non-parametric estimation, II, Statistically equivalent blocks and tolerance regions—the continuous case," *Ann. Math. Statist.*, Vol. 18 (1947), pp. 529–539.

J. W. Tukey, "Non-parametric estimation, III, Statistically equivalent blocks and multivariate tolerance regions—the discontinuous case," *Ann. Math. Statist.*, Vol. 19 (1948), pp. 30–39.

J. W. Tukey, "Comparing individual means in the analysis of variance," *Biometrics*, Vol. 5 (1949), pp. 99–114.

J. W. Tukey, "The simplest signed-rank tests," Memorandum Rep. 17, Statistical Research Group, Princeton University, Princeton, N.J., 1949 (duplicated).

J. W. Tukey, "Quick and dirty methods in statistics, Part II, Simple analyses for standard designs," *Proceedings of the Fifth Annual Convention, American Society for Quality Control*, 1951, pp. 189–197.

J. W. Tukey, "The problem of multiple comparisons," unpublished memorandum, Princeton University, Princeton, N.J., 1953, 396 pp.

J. W. Tukey, "Some selected and easy methods of statistical analysis," *Trans. N.Y. Acad. Sci.*, Ser. II, Vol. 16 (1953), pp. 88–97.

J. W. Tukey, "Interpolations and approximations related to the normal range," *Biometrika*, Vol. 42 (1955), pp. 480–485.

Y. Ukita, "On the efficiency of order statistics," *J. Hokkaido College Sci. and Art*, Vol. 6, No. 1 (1955), pp. 54–65.

H. R. Van Der Vaart, "The content of certain spherical polyhedra for any number of dimensions," *Experentia*, Vol. 9 (1953), pp. 88–89.

H. R. Van Der Vaart, "The content of some classes of non-Euclidean polyhedra for any number of dimensions with several applications," *Proc. Kon. Ned. Akad. Wetensch. A.*, Amsterdam, Vol. 58 (1955), pp. 199–221.

C. J. Velz, *Drought Flow of Michigan Streams*, School of Public Health, University of Michigan, 1960.

J. Walker, "*Optimum decomposition of sample space*," doctoral thesis, University of North Carolina, Chapel Hill, 1957.

J. E. Walsh, "Some significance tests for the median which are valid under very general conditions," unpublished doctoral dissertation, Princeton University, Princeton, N.J., 1947.

J. E. Walsh, "Some significance tests for the median which are valid under very general conditions," *Ann. Math. Statist.*, Vol. 20 (1949), pp. 64–81.

J. E. Walsh, "On the range-midrange test and some tests with bounded significance levels," *Ann. Math. Statist.*, Vol. 12 (1952), pp. 257–267.

G. A. Watterson, "Linear estimation in censored samples from multivariate normal populations," *Ann. Math. Statist.*, Vol. 30 (1959), pp. 814–824.

Weather Bureau, "Rainfall intensity frequency regime," Tech. Paper 29, Washington, D.C., 1958.

W. Weibull, "The phenomenon of systems in solids," *Ing. Vetenskaps. Akad., Handl.*, No. 153 (1939).

W. Weibull, "A statistical representation of fatigue failures in solids," *Trans. Roy. Inst. Tech.*, Stockholm, No. 27 (1949).

W. Weibull, "Statistical evaluation of data from fatigue and creep-rupture tests, Fundamental concepts and general methods," WADC Tech. Rep. 59-400, Part I, Wright Air Development Center, 1959.

L. Weiss, "The limiting joint distribution of the largest and smallest sample spacings," *Ann. Math. Statist.*, Vol. 30 (1959), pp. 590–593.

F. Wilcoxon, "Individual comparisons of grouped data by ranking methods," *Biometrics Bull.*, Vol. 1 (1945), pp. 80–83.

F. Wilcoxon, *Some Rapid Approximate Statistical Procedures*, American Cyanamid Co., Stamford Research Laboratories, 1949.

S. S. Wilks, "On the determination of sample sizes for setting tolerance limits," *Ann. Math. Statist.*, Vol. 12 (1941), pp. 91–96.

S. S. Wilks, "Order statistics," *Bull. Amer. Math. Soc.*, Vol. 54 (1948), pp. 6–50.

S. S. Wilks, *Mathematical Statistics*, Princeton University Press, Princeton, N.J., 1950.

C. B. Winsten, "Inequalities in terms of mean range," *Biometrika*, Vol. 33 (1946), pp. 283–295.

E. K. Yost, "Joint estimation of mean and standard deviation of percentiles," Unpublished master's thesis, University of Oregon, Eugene Oregon, 1948.

Index

Greek letters are indexed under their Roman equivalents, for example χ^2 under chi-squared.

ECONOMICS ★ LIBRARY ★ AND STATISTICS